2013–2014
Oregon Blue Book

Compiled and
published by

Kate Brown
Secretary of State

Julie Yamaka, Managing Editor
Phil Wiebe, Copy Editor
Gary Halvorson, Photo and Web Editor

Archives Division
Office of the Secretary of State
Salem, Oregon 97310

Acknowledgements and special thanks to the following people:

Office of the Secretary of State:
Archives Division, Mary Beth Herkert, State Archivist
Fact gathering and verification: Linda Bjornstad, Andrew Needham, Edalene Roseberry and Austin Schulz
Proofreader: Kay Kinsley
Publications Unit: Steve Mabry, marketing; Colleen Needham, section formatting
Section review: Connor Edmonds and Layne Sawyer, Managers

Elections Division: Brenda Bayes, Manager; Tami Dettwyler
Business Services Division: Jeff Morgan, Director; Sheila Castelanos, Jennifer Friesen

Department of Administrative Services, Geospatial Enterprise Office

Oregon Employment Department: Dave Yamaka, graphics

Office of the State Court Administrator: Kim Blanding

www.bluebook.state.or.us

Orders:
Office of the Secretary of State
Oregon Blue Book
255 Capitol St. NE, Suite 180
Salem, OR 97310
503-986-2204

ISBN 978-0-9669719-8-9
ISSN 0196-4577
Library of Congress Catalog Card No. sn 79-19170
Printed by Sheridan Books, Inc. in Ann Arbor, MI

Table of Contents

Kate Brown
SECRETARY OF STATE

STATE OF OREGON
SECRETARY OF STATE
136 STATE CAPITOL
SALEM, OREGON 97310-0722

January 2013

Dear Fellow Oregonians:

Welcome to the 2013-2014 edition of the *Oregon Blue Book*. As always, the stunning *Blue Book* is the most complete source available for information regarding Oregon's history, economy, government and culture. Every edition promises new and interesting information.

This year's color insert celebrates 100 years of open Oregon beaches. In 1913, the legislature declared the entire length of the ocean shore from Washington to California as state highway. Oregon Governor Oswald West led the effort after the Oregon State Land Board sold about 23 miles of tideland, closing the beach to public. Governor West made the argument for public ownership based on the need for transportation.

We also celebrate 100 years since the birth of Governor Tom McCall. He was responsible for the second beach bill that was passed and signed in 1967, keeping Oregon's beaches open and public. To this day, Oregonians enjoy "free and uninterrupted use of the beaches." State and federal courts continue to uphold Oregon's right to regulate development of these lands and preserve public access.

Also in this edition you will notice new legislative maps. The Oregon Legislature completed re-districting in 2011. More new and interesting information includes Jory soil, Oregon's newly-designated official state soil, named for the Jory pioneer family of South Salem.

You can find a continuously updated version of the *Oregon Blue Book* online at www.bluebook.state.or.us. Whether online or in print, please enjoy learning more about why Oregon is such a great place in which to live, work and play.

Best,

Kate Brown
Secretary of State

P.S. You can also use the *Oregon Blue Book* Web site to help us keep it updated and make it better and easier to use.

Dedication

The *2013–2014 Oregon Blue Book* is dedicated to the many Oregonians who successfully led the battle to pass the nation's most progressive land use law in 1973. We now celebrate the 40th Anniversary of the signing of Oregon Senate Bill 100 and recognize three Oregonians who made it their mission to protect our state's beauty:

- To Governor Tom McCall, whose foresight and leadership helped establish the land use system that protects so much of what we love about Oregon.

- To Senator Ted Hallock, a determined visionary, who locked legislators in a hearing room for 24 hours until an agreement was reached on Senate Bill 100.

- To Senator Hector Macpherson, a dairy farmer turned legislator, who spent his life protecting farmland and who created this land use policy with a purpose to serve the health, safety and welfare of the people of this great state. Macpherson admits that not everyone agrees that preserving farmland was more important than development.

For their leadership and commitment to Oregon's productivity, beauty and livability, we salute these Oregonians and dedicate this book — this celebration of our state — to them.

John Kitzhaber
GOVERNOR

January 2013

Fellow Oregonians:

The *Oregon Blue Book* provides a vital snapshot of all our state has to offer. With comprehensive information on Oregon history, economy, and governance — plus an introduction to our arts, culture, and environment — this book shows why Oregon is a great place to live and to work.

As I work with people across the state to preserve our state's rich quality of life, I am continually inspired by Oregonians' deep commitment to one another. Of all of Oregon's abundant natural assets, our most important is our citizens, who time and time again have had the courage and discipline necessary to weather challenging times while emerging more successful and more united.

The *Oregon Blue Book* provides a glimpse of our shared history of building a better and stronger state, and we are writing the next chapter now, driven by our common vision of the future — one with ample opportunity for every Oregonian in every community in the state and one in which we remain committed to future generations of Oregonians whose prosperity depends on the decisions we make now.

To every Oregonian, thank you for believing in our state. Thank you for believing in and supporting one another, and thank you for coming together to shape Oregon's future.

Sincerely,

John Kitzhaber
Governor

Almanac

Two kayakers paddle on Sparks Lake in view of the South Sister in the Cascade Mountains—Oregon State Archives Scenic Photograph desDB3287

Facts, like maps, help us envision a complete picture of Oregon. This section includes an almanac with interesting statistics and general information about Oregon, a list of Oregon Olympic Games medal winners, "Oregon, My Oregon" — our state song, and a map of Oregon showing counties and major roads.

Almanac

For entries with an asterisk (*) see related photo in the color insert pages.

Abbreviation, Oregon: OR (postal)

Airports: 97 public, 317 private

Alternative Energy Projects, Largest

Wind Projects

Biglow Canyon Wind Farm, Sherman County, 2006: 217 turbines generating 450 megawatts peak capacity

Klondike III Wind Project, Sherman County, 2006: 176 turbines generating 300 megawatts peak capacity

Leaning Juniper II Wind Power Project, Gilliam County, 2007: generating 201 megawatts peak capacity

Shepherds Flat North Wind Farm, Gilliam County, 2009: generating 265 megawatts peak capacity

Stateline Wind Project, Umatilla County, 2001: generating 222 megawatts peak capacity

Gas Projects

Columbia Ethanol Project, Morrow County, 2007: 35 million gallons per year production capacity

Hermiston Generating Project, Umatilla County, 1994: 469 megawatt natural gas combined cycle combustion turbine

Hermiston Power Project, Umatilla County, 1996: 546 megawatt natural gas combined cycle combustion turbine

Klamath Cogeneration Project, Klamath County, 1997: 475 megawatt natural gas combined cycle combustion turbine

Port Westward Generating Project, Columbia County, 2002: 650 megawatt natural gas combined cycle combustion turbine

Geothermal Projects

Klamath Falls Geothermal District Heating System, City of Klamath Falls, 1981: geothermal heat provided to downtown-area buildings

Solar Projects

King Estate solar, Lane County, 2011: 973.8 kilowatts

Oregon solar projects, 2011: 4,574 kilowatts

Portland Habilitation Center Project, Multnomah County, 2008: 858 kilowatts

ProLogis (seven-warehouse rooftop project) Multnomah and Clackamas Counties, 2010: 2,400 kilowatts

Yamhill Solar Project, Yamhill County, 2011: 1,190 kilowatts

Altitudes

Highest: Mt. Hood (11,239')

Lowest: Pacific Ocean (sea level)

Amusement Park, Oldest

Oaks Amusement Park, Portland: Opening on May 30, 1905, it is one of the oldest continuously operated amusement parks in the United States.

Animal, State*

The American Beaver *(Castor canadensis)* was named the Oregon state animal by the 1969 Legislature. Prized for its fur, the beaver was overtrapped by early settlers and eliminated from much of its original range. Through proper management and partial protection, the beaver has been reestablished in watercourses throughout the state and remains an important economic asset. The beaver has been referred to as "nature's engineer," and its dam-building activities are important to natural water flow and erosion control. Oregon is known as the "Beaver State." The beaver is mascot for Oregon State University, which calls its athletic teams the Beavers.

Apportionment, U.S. House of Representatives (number of U.S. Representatives from Oregon)

1860–1880.......... 1
1890–1900.......... 2
1910–1930.......... 3
1940–1970.......... 4
1980–2012.......... 5

Awards (Nobel, Pulitzer)

1934: Medford *Mail Tribune,* Pulitzer, Journalism

1939: Ronald Callvert, *The Oregonian,* Pulitzer, Editorial Writing

1954: Linus Pauling, Nobel, Chemistry

1956: Walter H. Brattain, Nobel, Physics

1957: Wallace Turner and William Lambert, *The Oregonian,* Pulitzer, Reporting (No Edition Time)

1962: Linus Pauling, Nobel, Peace

1999: Richard Read, *The Oregonian,* Pulitzer, Explanatory Writing

2001: Carl Weiman, Nobel, Physics

2001: *The Oregonian,* Pulitzer, Public Service

2001: Tom Hallman, Jr., *The Oregonian,* Pulitzer, Feature Writing

2005: Nigel Jaquiss, *Willamette Week,* Pulitzer, Investigative Reporting

2006: Rick Attig and Doug Bates, *The Oregonian,* Pulitzer, Editorial Writing

2007: *The Oregonian,* Pulitzer, Breaking News Reporting

2010: Dale T. Mortensen, Nobel, Economics

Beverage, State

Milk was designated Oregon's state beverage in 1997. The Legislature recognized that milk production and the manufacture of dairy products are major contributors to the economic well-being of Oregon agriculture.

Bird, State*

The Western Meadowlark *(Sturnella neglecta)* was chosen the Oregon state bird in 1927 by Oregon's school children in a poll sponsored by the Oregon Audubon Society. Native throughout western North America, the bird has brown plumage with buff and black markings. Its underside is bright yellow with a black V-shape on the breast. The outer tail feathers are mainly white and are easily visible when it flies. The Western Meadowlark is known for its distinctive, flute-like song.

Births: 45,479 (2011)

Borders and Boundaries

Washington on the north;

California on the south: established by a treaty between Spain and the United States in 1819;

Idaho on the east;

Pacific Ocean on the west;

Nevada on the southeast.

Bridges

Highest: Thomas Creek Bridge (north of Brookings), 345'

Longest: Megler Bridge (Astoria), 21,474'

Covered bridges: 50 throughout the state

Buildings, Tallest (Portland)

1. Wells Fargo Tower (1972), 546', 41 floors
2. U.S. Bancorp Tower (1983), 536', 42 floors
3. KOIN Tower (1984), 509', 35 floors

Campsites, Overnight Use

During 2011, a total of 177,906 reservations were made for overnight campsites in Oregon State Parks. Oregon residents made 118,021 of these reservations (66.3%), while non-residents made the remaining 59,885 (33.7%).

Cities, Total Incorporated: 242

Largest Populations (2011)

1. Portland (585,845)
2. Eugene (157,010)
3. Salem (155,710)
4. Gresham (105,795)
5. Hillsboro (92,350)
6. Beaverton (90,835)

Counties, Total: 36

Largest Area, Square Miles

1. Harney (10,228)
2. Malheur (9,928)
3. Lake (8,359)
4. Klamath (6,135)
5. Douglas (5,071)

Smallest Area, Square Miles

1. Multnomah (465)
2. Hood River (533)
3. Benton (679)
4. Columbia (687)
5. Yamhill (718)

Largest Populations (2011)

1. Multnomah (741,925)
2. Washington (536,370)
3. Clackamas (378,480)
4. Lane (353,155)
5. Marion (318,150)

Crustacean, State

The 2009 Legislature designated the Dungeness Crab *(Metacarcinus magister)* as the official state crustacean. The action followed petitioning by the 4th grade class of Sunset Primary School in West Linn. Common to the Pacific coastline from the Alaskan Aleutian Islands to Santa Cruz, California, Dungeness Crab is considered the most commercially important crab in the Pacific Northwest.

Dance, State

In 1977, the Legislature declared the Square Dance to be the Oregon state dance. The dance is a combination of various steps and figures danced with four couples grouped in a square. The pioneer origins of the dance and the characteristic dress are deemed to reflect Oregon's heritage. The lively spirit of the dance exemplifies the friendly, free nature and enthusiasm that are a part of the Oregon character.

Deaths: 32,747 (2011)

Divorces: 14,470 (2011)

Electoral Votes for U.S. President: 7

Fair, Oregon State: Early History

1858: The State Fair was unofficially started by a group of farmers known as the Oregon Fruitgrowers Association.

1861: The first official Oregon State Fair was held along the Clackamas River in the Gladstone/Oregon City area.

1862: The second State Fair took place in Salem, at the same location where it is held today.

1871: Women's suffrage activists Susan B. Anthony and Abigail S. Duniway camped at the State Fairgrounds during an extended visit to Oregon.

Father of Oregon*

The 1957 Legislature bestowed upon Dr. John McLoughlin the honorary title of "Father of Oregon" in recognition of his great contributions to the early development of the Oregon Country. Originally Dr. McLoughlin came to the Northwest region in 1824, as a representative of the Hudson's Bay Company.

Fish, State*

The Chinook Salmon *(Oncorhynchus tshawytscha)*, also known as the spring, king or tyee salmon, is the largest of the Pacific salmons and the most highly prized for the fresh fish trade. Declared the Oregon state fish by the 1961 Legislature, the Chinook Salmon is found from southern California to the Canadian Arctic. Record-sized catches of 53 inches and 126 pounds have been reported.

Flag, State*

The Oregon state flag, adopted in 1925, is navy blue with gold lettering and symbols. Blue and gold are the state colors. On the flag's face the legend "STATE OF OREGON" is written above a shield, which is surrounded by 33 stars. Below the shield, which is part of the state seal, is written "1859," the year of Oregon's admission to The Union as the 33rd state. The flag's reverse side depicts a beaver. Oregon has the distinction of being the only state in The Union whose flag has a different pattern on the reverse side. The dress or parade flag has a gold fringe, and the utility flag has a plain border.

Flower, State*

The Legislature designated the Oregon Grape *(Mahonia aquifolium)* as the Oregon state flower by resolution in 1899. A low-growing plant, the Oregon Grape is native to much of the Pacific Coast and is found sparsely east of the Cascades. Its year-round foliage of pinnated, waxy green leaves resembles holly. The plant bears clusters of small yellow flowers in early summer and a dark blue berry that ripens late in the fall. The fruit can be used in cooking.

Fossil, State*

The Legislature designated the Metasequoia, or Dawn Redwood *(Metasequoia glyptostroboides)*, as the Oregon state fossil by resolution in 2005. The Metasequoia flourished in the Miocene Epoch of 25 to 5 million years ago and left its record embedded in rocks across the Oregon landscape. While long extinct in Oregon, paleontologists discovered living 100-foot Metasequoia trees in a remote area of China over 50 years ago and brought specimens back to the United States for propagation, thus ensuring that live Metasequoia trees can be found today.

Fruit, State*

The Legislature designated the pear *(Pyrus communis)* as the Oregon state fruit by resolution in 2005. Oregon produces a variety of pears including Comice, Anjou, Bosc and Bartlett. The pear ranks as the top-selling tree fruit crop in the state and grows particularly well in the Rogue River Valley and along the Columbia River near Mt. Hood.

Gemstone, State*

The 1987 Legislature designated the Oregon sunstone as the Oregon state gemstone. Uncommon in its composition, clarity and colors, it is a large, brightly colored transparent gem in the feldspar family. The Oregon sunstone attracts collectors and miners and has been identified as a boon to tourism and economic development in southeastern Oregon counties.

Geographic Center

The geographic center of Oregon lies in Crook County 25, miles south-southeast of Prineville.

Gorge, Deepest

Hell's Canyon, Wallowa County: Up to 7,913' in depth along the Snake River, it is the deepest gorge in North America.

Highways, Notable

Historic Columbia River Highway: The 74-mile stretch of the Columbia River Highway from Troutdale to The Dalles was built from 1913 to 1922. For many years, it was designated U.S. 30. Beginning in the 1950s, Interstate 84 replaced the historic highway as the main route through the Columbia Gorge. The historic highway became a National Scenic Byway All-American Road in 1999. In 2000, the U.S. Secretary of the Interior designated it a National Historic Landmark, which recognized the highway as a significant national heritage resource. The route became the first highway in the country to be given either of these national designations.

Interstate 205: The East Portland Freeway (Interstate 205), which runs in Oregon from a junction with Interstate 5 in Wilsonville north to the Glenn Jackson Bridge over the Columbia River, was built from the mid-1970s through the mid-1980s. It provided an eastside bypass around greater Portland, Oregon and Vancouver, Washington. In November 2000, the portion in Oregon was designated the "Veterans Memorial Highway."

Oregon 99: Originally known as the Pacific Highway, Oregon 99 runs from the Oregon/California border north to Junction City, Oregon, where it splits into Oregon 99E and Oregon 99W. The Pacific Highway, once designated U.S. 99, U.S. 99E, and U.S. 99W, was the main north-south highway in Oregon from the 1920s until Interstate 5 replaced it in1964.

U.S. 97: The 2009 Legislature designated The Dalles–California Highway U.S. 97 the "World War II Veterans Historic Highway." U.S. 97 runs north-south in central Oregon past World War II training sites in Rufus, Madras, Redmond, Prineville, Bend, Sunriver and Klamath Falls. Sunriver Resort sits on the former site of Camp Abbot, a World War II combat engineers training center.

U.S. 101: Completed in the 1930s, the Oregon Coast Highway (U.S. 101) runs the entire length of Oregon's Pacific Coast from Astoria on the Columbia River to the Oregon/California border. The highway was designated an Oregon Scenic Byway in 1991 and a National Scenic Byway All-American Road in 2002.

Historian Laureate

For his years as keeper of Oregon's memory and heritage, the 1989 Legislature named Thomas Vaughan as historian laureate of Oregon. His dedicated leadership and distinguished record of professional study and publication have brought worldwide recognition to the Oregon Historical Society and contributed greatly to historical interest and knowledge.

Hot Springs

Notable hot springs: Alvord, Austin, Bagby, Belknap, Bigelow, Blue Mountain, Breitenbush, Couger (Terwilliger), Crane, East Lake, Echo Rock, Hart Mt. (Antelope), Hot Lake, Hunter's, Juntura, Kah-Nee-Ta, Kropp, Lehman, Luce, McCredie, Olene Gap, Paulina Lake, Snively, Summer Lake, Umpqua, Wall Creek, Weberg, Whitehorse

Hydroelectric Projects and Dams, Largest

Owyhee Dam: Owyhee River, 1932
Bonneville Dam: Columbia River, 1938
McNary Dam: Columbia River, 1954
The Dalles Dam: Columbia River, 1957
John Day Dam: Columbia River, 1971

Insect, State*

In 1979, the Legislature designated the Oregon Swallowtail *(Papilio oregonius)* as the Oregon state insect. A true native of the Northwest, the Oregon Swallowtail is at home in the lower sagebrush canyons of the Columbia River and its tributaries, including the Snake River drainage. This strikingly beautiful butterfly has a wingspan of 2-1/2 to 3 inches and is bright yellow and black with a reddish-orange hindspot.

Jails/Correctional Institutions and Facilities

189 secure facilities, including adult jails, lock-ups and correctional facilities, court holding facilities, juvenile detention centers and correctional facilities, and mental health centers;

175 non-secure facilities, including law enforcement centers and residential centers;

14 institutions operated by the Department of Corrections, including release, work centers and camps;

One federal penal institution.

Judicial Districts: 27

Lakes

Deepest: Crater Lake, 1,943' (deepest in the United States)

Largest:

Upper Klamath Lake, 58,922 surface acres
Malheur Lake, 49,000 surface acres

Note: Size may vary depending on seasons and precipitation. At times, Malheur Lake may have a larger surface area than Upper Klamath Lake.

Number: Approximately 1,780 lakes in Oregon

Legal Holidays and Days of Special Observance

New Year's Day
1/1/13, 1/1/14, 1/1/15

Martin Luther King, Jr.'s Birthday (observed)
1/21/13, 1/20/14, 1/19/15

President's Day
2/18/13, 2/17/14, 2/16/15

Memorial Day
5/27/13, 5/26/14, 5/25/15

Independence Day
7/4/13, 7/4/14, 7/3/15

Labor Day
9/2/13, 9/1/14, 9/7/15

Veterans Day
11/11/13, 11/11/14, 11/11/15

Thanksgiving Day
11/28/13, 11/27/14, 11/26/15

Christmas Day
12/25/13, 12/25/14, 12/25/15

Additionally, other days may be legal holidays in Oregon. These are every day appointed by the governor as a holiday and every day appointed by the president of the United States as a day of mourning, rejoicing or other special observance when the governor also appoints that day as a holiday.

Whenever a holiday falls on a Sunday, the following Monday shall be observed as the holiday. Whenever a holiday falls on a Saturday, the preceding Friday shall be observed as the holiday.

At various intervals throughout the year, the governor may also proclaim days or weeks to give special recognition and attention to individuals or groups and to promote issues and causes.

Lighthouses

Cape Arago Lighthouse, Coos Bay
Cape Blanco Lighthouse, Port Orford
Cape Meares Lighthouse, Tillamook
Cleft of the Rock Lighthouse, Yachats (privately-owned, not open to the public)
Coquille River Lighthouse, Bandon
Heceta Head Lighthouse, Florence
Port of Brookings Lighthouse, Brookings (privately-owned, not open to the public)
Tillamook Rock Lighthouse, Cannon Beach
Umpqua River Lighthouse, Reedsport
Yaquina Bay Lighthouse, Newport
Yaquina Head Lighthouse, Newport

Marriages: 25,519 (2011)

Mileage Distances (in Oregon), Highways and Interstates

I-5: 308 miles
I-84: 375 miles
U.S. 20: 450 miles
U.S. 26: 471 miles
U.S. 97: 296 miles
U.S. 101: 353 miles
U.S. 395: 384 miles

Mileage Distances, Road (from Portland)

Albuquerque, New Mexico	1,363
Atlanta, Georgia	2,596
Boise, Idaho	431
Chicago, Illinois	2,118

Denver, Colorado	1,240
Fargo, North Dakota	1,451
Houston, Texas	2,201
Los Angeles, California	962
Miami, Florida	3,236
New York, New York	2,893
Omaha, Nebraska	1,656
Phoenix, Arizona	1,312
St. Louis, Missouri	2,045
Salt Lake City, Utah	766
San Francisco, California	633
Seattle, Washington	174

Mother of Oregon*

Honored by the 1987 Legislature as "Mother of Oregon," Tabitha Moffatt Brown "represents the distinctive pioneer heritage and the charitable and compassionate nature of Oregon's people." At 66 years of age, she financed her own wagon for the trip from Missouri to Oregon. The boarding school for orphans that she established later became known as Tualatin Academy and eventually was chartered as Pacific University.

Motto, State

"She Flies With Her Own Wings" was adopted by the 1987 Legislature as the Oregon state motto. The phrase originated with Judge Jessie Quinn Thornton and was pictured on the territorial seal in Latin: *Alis Volat Propriis*. The new motto replaces "The Union," which was adopted in 1957.

Mountains, Major

Blue Mountains: This northeastern Oregon mountain chain is part of the Columbia Plateau, which also extends into southeastern Washington. Lava flows cover much of the surface, and the upper, wooded slopes have been used for lumbering. Recreation and livestock grazing are the mountains principal economic uses. The highest elevation is Rock Creek Butte (9,105'), located on the Elkhorn Ridge a few miles west of Baker City.

Cascade Range: This lofty mountain range extends the entire north-south length of Oregon east of the Willamette Valley. It lies about 100 to 150 miles inland from the coastline and forms an important climatic divide, with the western slopes receiving abundant precipitation but the eastern slopes very little. The western slopes are heavily wooded, with the eastern section mainly covered by grass and scrub plants. Many lakes and several large rivers are in the mountains, the latter harnessed for hydroelectric power. The range is used frequently for outdoor recreation, including camping, hiking and skiing. The highest elevations are Mt. Hood (11,239'), located in Clackamas and Hood River Counties, and Mt. Jefferson (10,495'), located in Jefferson, Linn and Marion Counties.

Coast Range: The Coast Range runs the length of the state along the western coastline, from the Columbia River in the north to the Rogue River in the south. These mountains contain dense softwood forests which, historically, made lumbering an important economic activity. Their eastern slopes mark the western edge of the Willamette Valley. The highest elevation north of Coquille is Mary's Peak (4,097'), located in Benton County. The highest elevation south of Coquille is Mt. Bolivar (4,319') in Coos and Curry Counties.

Klamath Mountains: The Klamath Mountains in southwestern Oregon are sometimes included as part of the Coast Range. These mountains include numerous national forest and wildlife preserves and contain scenic portions of the Klamath River. The highest elevation is Mt. Ashland (7,532'), located in Jackson County.

Steens Mountain: This is a massive, 30-mile-long mountain in the Alvord Valley featuring valleys and U-shaped gorges that were cut by glaciers one million years ago. It is located in Harney County in southeastern Oregon and is 9,773' in elevation.

Mushroom, State*

The 1999 Legislature recognized the Pacific golden chanterelle *(Cantharellus formosus)* as the Oregon state mushroom. This mushroom is a wild, edible fungus of high culinary value that is unique to the Pacific Northwest. More than 500,000 pounds of Pacific golden chanterelles are harvested annually in Oregon, representing a large portion of the commercial mushroom business.

Musician Laureate

In 2002, Governor John Kitzhaber named composer and recording artist Mason Williams as Oregon's musician laureate. Williams is best known for his instrumental "Classical Gas" which earned him three Grammy Awards in 1968. In addition to his musical talents, Williams is also a comedy writer who has written for *The Smothers Brothers Comedy Hour* and *Saturday Night Live* and for personalities including Steve Martin, Dinah Shore and Andy Williams. In recognition of his outstanding contributions to the arts, Williams received the annual Oregon Governor's Art Award in 1990 and the University of Oregon's Distinguished Service Award in 1999.

Name of Oregon

The first written record of the name "Oregon" comes to us from a 1765 proposal for a journey written by Major Robert Rogers, an English army officer. It reads, "The rout . . . is from the Great Lakes towards the Head of the Mississippi, and from thence to the River called by the Indians Ouragon. . . ." His proposal rejected, Rogers reapplied in 1772, using the spelling "Ourigan." The first printed use of the current spelling appeared in Captain Jonathan Carver's 1778 book, *Travels Through the Interior Parts of North America 1766, 1767 and 1768*. He listed the four great rivers of the continent including "the River

Oregon, or the River of the West, that falls into the Pacific Ocean at the Straits of Annian."

While no definitive pronounciation of "Oregon" is given in *Oregon Geographic Names,* the most common pronunciation by long-time Oregonians is "OR-ee-gun."

National Cemeteries

Willamette, Portland
Eagle Point, Eagle Point
Roseburg, Roseburg

National Fish Hatcheries

Eagle Creek, Estacada
Warm Springs, Warm Springs

National Forests

Deschutes, Fremont-Winema, Malheur, Mt. Hood, Ochoco, Rogue River-Siskiyou, Siuslaw, Umatilla, Umpqua, Wallowa-Whitman, Willamette

National Grassland

Crooked River, near Madras

National Historic Site

Fort Vancouver (Oregon, Washington)

National Monuments

Cascade-Siskiyou, near Ashland

John Day Fossil Beds, located in three units near Kimberly, Mitchell and Fossil

Newberry National Volcanic Monument, near Bend

Oregon Caves, near Cave Junction

National Parks

Crater Lake

Lewis and Clark National Historical Park

Nez Perce National Historical Park (Oregon, Idaho, Montana, Washington)

National Recreation Areas

Hell's Canyon National Recreation Area (Oregon, Idaho)

Oregon Dunes National Recreation Area

National Scenic Area

Columbia River Gorge

National Trails

California National Historic Trail

Lewis and Clark National Historic Trail

Oregon National Historic Trail: Its length is 2,170 miles from Independence, Missouri to the Willamette Valley, Oregon. It passes through Missouri, Kansas, Nebraska, Wyoming, Idaho and Oregon.

National Wildlife Refuges

Ankeny, near Jefferson
Bandon Marsh, near Bandon
Baskett Slough, near Dallas
Bear Valley, near Klamath Falls
Cape Meares, near Tillamook
Cold Springs, near Hermiston
Hart Mountain National Antelope Refuge, near Lakeview
Klamath Marsh, near Klamath Falls
Malheur, near Burns
McKay Creek, near Pendleton
Nestucca Bay, near Pacific City
Oregon Islands, off southern Oregon coast
Siletz Bay, near Lincoln City
Three Arch Rocks, off coast near Oceanside
Tualatin River, near Sherwood
Upper Klamath, near Klamath Falls
William L. Finley, near Corvallis

Native American and Tribal Peoples

Estimated population in Oregon, including tribal members, members of tribes without federal recognition, and those who self-identify as American Indian or Alaskan Native: 109,223 (2010 Census)

Nine federally-recognized tribes with reservation lands in Oregon:

Burns Paiute Tribe (349 members)

Confederated Tribes of Coos, Lower Umpqua and Siuslaw (953 members)

Confederated Tribes of the Grand Ronde Community (5,200 members)

Confederated Tribes of Siletz (4,677 members)

Confederated Tribes of the Umatilla Indian Reservation (2,893 members)

Confederated Tribes of Warm Springs Reservation (4,306 members)

Coquille Indian Tribe (963 members)

Cow Creek Band of Umpqua Tribe (1,536 members)

Klamath Tribes (3,700 members)

One federally-recognized tribal community: Celilo Village, located east of The Dalles

One federally-recognized tribal government in Nevada and Oregon: Fort McDermitt Paiute-Shoshone Tribe

Nut, State*

The hazelnut, or filbert *(Corylus avellana)* was named the state nut by the 1989 Legislature. Oregon grows 99 percent of the entire U.S. commercial crop. The Oregon hazelnut, unlike wild varieties, grows on single-trunked trees up to 30 or 40 feet tall. Adding a unique texture and flavor to recipes and products, hazelnuts are preferred by chefs, bakers, confectioners, food manufacturers and homemakers worldwide.

Parks, State: 263 (2012)

Physical Dimensions

United States Rank in Total Area = 10
Land Area = 95,179 square miles
Water Area = 1,926 square miles
Total = 97,105 square miles
Coastline = 370 miles

Poet Laureate*

Paulann Peterson of Portland was named Oregon's poet laureate by Gov. Ted Kulongoski in

2010. The position was created in 1923. Lawson Inada was Oregon's previous poet laureate, serving from 2006 to 2010. Peterson was born and raised in Oregon, spending half of her adult life in Klamath Falls. A graduate of Southern Oregon University, she has taught English at Mazama and West Linn High Schools. Her books of poetry are *The Wild Awake, Blood-Silk, A Bride of Narrow Escape,* and *Kindle*. She has received several awards including Stanford University's Wallace Stegner Fellowship.

Population

1850 = 12,093	1950 = 1,521,341
1860 = 52,465	1960 = 1,768,687
1870 = 90,923	1970 = 2,091,533
1880 = 174,768	1980 = 2,633,321
1890 = 317,704	1990 = 2,842,321
1900 = 413,536	2000 = 3,421,399
1910 = 672,765	2004 = 3,582,600
1920 = 783,389	2007 = 3,747,455
1930 = 953,786	2010 = 3,831,074
1940 = 1,089,684	2011 = 3,871,859

Oregon is ranked 41st in population density with 39.9 inhabitants per square mile.

Precipitation

Record 24-hour maximum rainfall: 14.3" on November 6, 2006 at Lees Camp in the Tillamook County Coast Range

Average yearly precipitation at Salem: 39.67"

Record 24-hour snowfall: 39" on January 9, 1980 at Bonneville Dam

Record annual snowfall: 903" in 1950 at Crater Lake

Reservoir, Longest: Lake Owyhee, 52 miles

Rivers, Longest

Partially in the State of Oregon:
Columbia River, 1,232 miles
Snake River, 1,038 miles

Entirely in the State of Oregon:
John Day River, 281 miles
Willamette River, 187 miles

Rock, State*

The Thunder-egg (geode) was named the Oregon state rock by the 1965 Legislature after rockhounds throughout Oregon voted it first choice. Thunder-eggs range in diameter from less than one inch to over four feet. Nondescript on the outside, they reveal exquisite designs in a wide range of colors when cut and polished. They are found chiefly in Crook, Jefferson, Malheur, Wasco and Wheeler Counties.

Schools, Public

Education Service Districts	19
Schools	1,270
School Districts	197
Student population (2011–12)	560,950

Seal, State*

The state seal consists of an escutcheon, or shield, supported by 33 stars and divided by an ordinary, or ribbon, with the inscription "The Union." Above the ordinary are the mountains and forests of Oregon, an elk with branching antlers, a covered wagon and ox team, the Pacific Ocean with setting sun, a departing British man-of-war ship signifying the departure of British influence in the region and an arriving American merchant ship signifying the rise of American power. Below the ordinary is a quartering with a sheaf of wheat, plow and pickax, which represent Oregon's mining and agricultural resources. The crest is the American Eagle. Around the perimeter of the seal is the legend "State of Oregon 1859." On September 17, 1857, the Constitutional Convention adopted a resolution that authorized the U.S. president to appoint a committee of three—Benjamin F. Burch, L. F. Grover and James K. Kelly—to report on a proper device for the seal of the state of Oregon. Harvey Gordon created a draft, to which the committee recommended certain additions that are all incorporated in the state seal.

Seashell, State*

In 1848, a conchologist (shell expert) named Redfield named the *Fusitriton oregonensis* after the Oregon Territory. Commonly called the Oregon hairy triton, the shell is one of the largest found in the state, reaching lengths up to five inches. The shells are found from Alaska to California and wash up on the Oregon coast at high tide. The Legislature named the state shell in 1991.

Shoes, Oldest

Nine-thousand-year-old sandals made of sagebrush and bark were found at Fort Rock Cave in central Oregon in 1938 by archaeologist Luther Cressman.

Skiing

Downhill: Anthony Lakes, near Union; Mt. Ashland, near Ashland; Mt. Bachelor, near Bend; Mt. Bailey snowcat skiing, near Diamond Lake; Cooper Spur, at Mt. Hood; Ferguson Ridge, near Joseph; Hoodoo, near Sisters; Mt. Hood Meadows, at Mt. Hood; SkiBowl, at Mt. Hood; Spout Springs, near Elgin; Summit, at Government Camp; Timberline, at Mt. Hood; Warner Canyon, near Lakeview; Willamette Pass, near Oakridge

Cross Country: National Forests: Deschutes, Fremont-Winema, Malheur, Mt. Hood, Ochoco, Rogue River-Siskiyou, Umatilla, Umpqua, Wallowa-Whitman, Willamette. Also, Crater Lake National Park and Hell's Canyon National Recreation Area.

Soil, State

The Legislature designated Jory soil as the Oregon state soil by concurrent resolution in 2011. The Jory soil is distinguished by its brick-red, clayish nature as it has developed on old volcanic rocks through thousands of years of weathering. It is estimated to exist on more than 300,000 acres of western Oregon hillsides and is named after Jory Hill in Marion County.

Jory soil is very productive and generally supports forest vegetation such as Douglas fir and Oregon white oak. Many areas with the soil have been cleared and are now used for agriculture. Jory soil, coupled with the Willamette Valley climate, provides an ideal setting for various crops, including wine grapes, wheat, Christmas trees, berries, hazelnuts and grass seed.

Song, State

J. A. Buchanan of Astoria and Henry B. Murtagh of Portland wrote "Oregon, My Oregon," in 1920. With this song, Buchanan and Murtagh won a statewide competition sponsored by the Society of Oregon Composers, gaining statewide recognition. The song became the Oregon state song in 1927. (See music score on page 11.)

Standard of Time

The standard time zones were established by Congress in 1918. Oregon lies within the Pacific Standard Time zone with the exception of most of Malheur County along the Idaho border, which is on Mountain Standard Time.

Due to the *Energy Policy Act of 2005,* Pacific Daylight Saving Time began earlier and ended later starting in 2007.

Clocks "spring forward" one hour at 2:00 a.m. on the second Sunday of March: 3/10/13, 3/9/14, 3/8/15.

Clocks "fall back" one hour at 2:00 a.m. on the first Sunday of November: 11/3/13, 11/2/14, 11/1/15.

Temperatures, Records and Averages

Highest: 119°F on July 29, 1898 in Pendleton and on August 10, 1898 in Prineville

Lowest: -54°F on February 9, 1933 in Ukiah (50 miles south of Pendleton) and on February 10, 1933 in Seneca (105 miles southwest of Baker City)

Average January/July Temperatures:

Burns	January 24.8°F/July 66.6°F
Grants Pass	January 40.9°F/July 71.8°F
Newport	January 45.9°F/July 58.3°F
Redmond	January 32.7°F/July 65.9°F
Salem	January 41.2°F/July 67.6°F

Tree, State*

The Douglas Fir *(Pseudotsuga menziesii),* named for David Douglas, a 19th century Scottish botanist, was designated the Oregon state tree in 1939. Great strength, stiffness and moderate weight make it an invaluable timber product said to be stronger than concrete. Averaging up to 200' in height and six feet in diameter, heights of 325' and diameters of 15' can also be found.

Trees, Large

Tree species in Oregon listed on the National Register of Big Trees.

Baker Cypress *(Cupressus bakeri):* 98' tall, 107" circumference, Rogue River National Forest

Bigleaf Maple *(Acer macrophyllum):* 103' tall, 528" circumference, Clatsop County

Big Sagebrush *(Artemisia tridentata):* 15' tall, 30" circumference, Jefferson County

Black Walnut *(Juglans nigra):* 145' tall, 312" circumference, Multnomah County

Brewer Spruce *(Picea breweriana):* 120' tall, 237" circumference, Josephine County

Cascara Buckthorn *(Rhamnus purshiana):* 39' tall, 104" circumference, Curry County

Giant Chinkapin *(Chrysolepis chrysophylla):* 106' tall, 182" circumference, Douglas County

Hooker Willow *(Salix hookeriana):* 50' tall, 65" circumference, Tillamook County

Knobcone Pine *(Pinus attenuate):* 117' tall, 118" circumference, Josephine County

Oregon Ash *(Fraxinus latifolia):* 81' tall, 285" circumference, Portland

Oregon White Oak *(Quercus garryana):* 93' tall, 276" circumference, Douglas County

Pacific Dogwood *(Cornus nuttallii):* 61' tall, 150" circumference, Multnomah County

Pacific Rhododendron *(Rhododendron macrophyllum):* 24' tall, 37" circumference, Lane County

Port Orford Cedar *(Chamaecyparis lawsoniana):* 242' tall, 522" circumference, Siskiyou National Forest

Tanoak *(Lithocarpus densiflorus):* 135' tall, 303" circumference, Curry County

Water Birch *(Betula occidentalis):* 53' tall, 113" circumference, Wallowa County

Western Dogwood *(Cornus sericea ssp. occidentalis):* 25' tall, 32" circumference, Polk County

White Alder *(Alnus rhombifolia):* 92' tall, 149" circumference, Polk County

Waterfall, Highest

Multnomah Falls, 620'

Olympic Games Medalists from Oregon (1906–2012)

1906		
Kerrigan, H.W. (Bert)	High Jump	Bronze
1908		
Gilbert, Alfred C.	Pole Vault	Gold
Kelly, Dan	Broad Jump	Silver
Smithson, Forrest	Hurdles	Gold
1912		
Hawkins, Martin	Hurdles	Bronze
1920		
Balbach, Louis J.	Diving	Bronze
Kuehn, Louis (Hap)	Diving	Gold
Ross, Norman	Swimming	Gold (3)

Sanborn-Payne, Thelma	Diving	Bronze
Sears, Robert	Fencing	Bronze
1924		
Newton, Chester	Wrestling	Silver
Reed, Robin	Wrestling	Gold
1928		
Hamm, Edward B.	Broad Jump	Gold
1932		
Graham, Norris	Rowing	Gold
Hill, Ralph	5000m	Silver
LaBorde, Henri J.	Discus	Silver**1936**
Robinson, Mack	200m	Silver
1948		
Beck, Lewis W. Jr.	Basketball	Gold
Brown, David P.	Rowing	Gold
Gordien, Fortune	Discus	Bronze
Helser (de Morelos), Brenda	Swimming	Gold
Zimmerman-Edwards, Suzanne	Swimming	Silver
1952		
Proctor, Hank	Rowing	Gold
Smith, William T.	Wrestling	Gold
1956		
Fifer, James	Rowing	Gold
Gordien, Fortune	Discus	Silver
1960		
Davis, Otis	400m	Gold (2)
Dischinger, Terry G.	Basketball	Gold
Imhoff, Darrall	Basketball	Gold
Wood, Carolyn	Swimming	Gold
1964		
Carr, Ken	Basketball	Gold
Counts, Mel G.	Basketball	Gold
Dellinger, William S.	Track and Field	Bronze
Freeman, Kevin	Equestrian	Silver
Saubert, Jean M.	Skiing	Silver/Bronze
Schollander, Don	Swimming	Gold (4)
1968		
Fosbury, Richard D.	High Jump	Gold
Freeman, Kevin	Equestrian	Silver
Garrigus, Thomas I.	Trapshooting	Silver
Johnson Bailes, Margaret	4x100	Gold
Sanders, Richard J.	Wrestling	Silver
Schollander, Don	Swimming	Gold/Silver
1972		
Freeman, Kevin	Equestrian	Silver
Peyton McDonald, Kim	Swimming	Gold
Sanders, Richard J.	Wrestling	Silver
1976		
Peyton McDonald, Kim	Swimming	Gold
Wilkins, Mac M.	Discus	Gold

1984		
Burke, Douglas L.	Water Polo	Silver
Herland, Douglas J.	Rowing	Bronze
Huntley (Ruete), Joni	High Jump	Bronze
Johnson, William D.	Skiing	Gold
King (Brown), Judith	400m Hurdles	Silver
Menken-Schaudt, Carol	Basketball	Gold
Schultz, Mark P.	Wrestling	Gold
Wilkins, Mac M.	Discus	Silver
1988		
Brown, Cynthia L.	Basketball	Gold
Lang, Brent	Swimming	Gold
1992		
Johnson, Dave	Decathlon	Bronze
Jorgenson, Dan	Swimming	Bronze
1994		
Street, Picabo	Skiing	Silver
1996		
Deal, Lance	Hammer	Silver
MacMillan, Shannon	Soccer	Gold
Milbrett, Tiffany	Soccer	Gold
O'Brien, Dan	Decathlon	Gold
Schneider, Marcus	Rowing	Bronze
Steding, Katy	Basketball	Gold
1998		
Street, Picabo	Skiing	Gold
2000		
French, Michelle	Soccer	Silver
Kinkade, Mike	Baseball	Gold
Lindland, Matt	Wrestling	Silver
MacMillan, Shannon	Soccer	Silver
Milbrett, Tiffany	Soccer	Silver
Thompson, Chris	Swimming	Bronze
2002		
Steele, Dan	Bobsled	Bronze
Klug, Chris	Snow Board	Bronze
2004		
Hansen, Joey	Rowing	Gold
Johnson, Kate	Rowing	Silver
Zagunis, Mariel	Fencing	Gold
2008		
Cox, Stephanie Lopez	Soccer	Gold
Inman, Josh	Rowing	Bronze
Ward, Rebecca	Fencing	Bronze (2)
Windes, Elsie	Water Polo	Silver
Zagunis, Mariel	Fencing	Gold/Bronze
2012		
Eaton, Ashton	Decathlon	Gold
Rupp, Galen	10,000m	Silver

Olympic Games medal information courtesy of Jack Elder, Olympian, Luge 1972.

State Song

Words
J.A. Buchanan

Music
Henry B. Murtagh

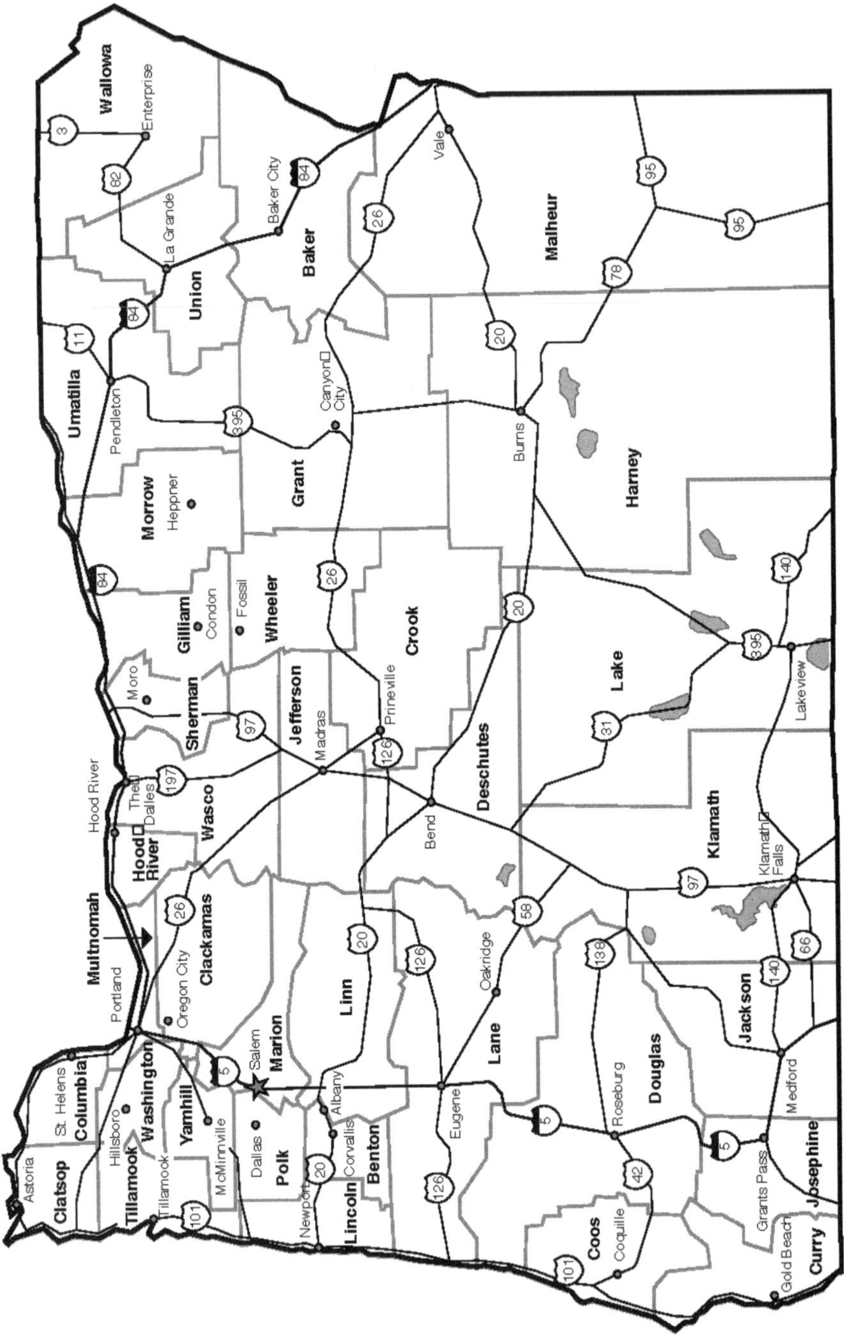
Wallowa
Enterprise
Union
La Grande
Baker
Baker City
Malheur
Vale
Umatilla
Pendleton
Morrow
Heppner
Grant
Canyon City
Harney
Burns
Gilliam
Condon
Wheeler
Fossil
Crook
Prineville
Sherman
Moro
Jefferson
Madras
Lake
Lakeview
Wasco
The Dalles
Hood River
Hood River
Deschutes
Bend
Klamath
Klamath Falls
Multnomah
Portland
Clackamas
Oregon City
Marion
Salem
Linn
Albany
Lane
Eugene
Oakridge
Douglas
Roseburg
Jackson
Medford
Josephine
Grants Pass
Curry
Gold Beach
Coos
Coquille
Benton
Corvallis
Lincoln
Newport
Polk
Dallas
Yamhill
McMinnville
Washington
Hillsboro
Tillamook
Tillamook
Columbia
St. Helens
Clatsop
Astoria
3
82
84
26
95
78
20
11
395
97
197
126
31
140
58
138
66
5
42
101

Executive

Tugboats docked at Coos Bay—Oregon State Archives Scenic Photograph cooDA0014

Oregonians elect five officials for statewide office to manage our executive branch of government: governor, secretary of state, treasurer, attorney general, and commissioner of labor and industries. This section introduces these officials, describes their responsibilities, and lists the administrative agencies and the services they provide.

JOHN KITZHABER *was born in Colfax, Washington on March 5, 1947, and moved to Oregon with his family at age 11. After earning his bachelor's degree at Dartmouth College, Kitzhaber returned to Oregon to study medicine at the University of Oregon Medical School (now Oregon Health and Science University).*

Kitzhaber practiced emergency room medicine in Roseburg from 1974 to 1988, where he developed a deep interest in health care public policy. This interest, together with a concern for the livelihoods of rural Oregonians, compelled him to seek public service.

As a legislator, including eight years as Senate President, Kitzhaber brought lawmakers and interest groups together to enact a number of groundbreaking laws, such as the Oregon Health Plan. In 1994 and 1998, Oregonians elected Kitzhaber governor. While leading state government, he presided over eight years of significant economic growth. He won acclaim for his pioneering work on the Oregon Plan for Salmon and Watersheds, a collaborative effort that brought together government and private landowners to protect clean water and native salmon runs.

After two terms as governor, Kitzhaber continued working to improve access to cost-effective health care, becoming one of the nation's most respected voices on health care reform.

In 2010, he won election to an unprecedented third term as governor. Now over two years into this term, Governor Kitzhaber has presided over transformative changes to the state's delivery of health care and education services. His efforts have focused on streamlining government, improving accountability and demanding better results to ensure that an enduring prosperity reaches Oregonians in every corner of the state.

Governor John Kitzhaber

State Capitol Building, 900 Court St. NE, Suite 254, Salem 97301-4047; 503-378-3111

Governor John Kitzhaber, Salem; Democrat; elected 2010; term expires January 2015.

The governor is elected to a four-year term and is limited to two consecutive terms in office during any 12-year period. The governor must be a U.S. citizen, at least 30 years old and an Oregon resident for three years before taking office.

The governor provides leadership, planning and coordination for the executive branch of state government. He appoints many department and agency heads within the executive branch and appoints members to nearly 300 policymaking, regulatory and advisory boards and commissions.

The governor proposes a two-year budget to the Legislature, recommends a legislative program to each regular session and may also call special sessions. He reviews all bills passed by the Legislature and may veto measures he believes are not in the public interest.

The governor chairs both the State Land Board, which manages state-owned lands, and the Progress Board, which sets strategic goals for Oregon. The governor acts as Superintendent of Public Instruction, directs state government's coordination with local and federal governments and is commander-in-chief of the state's military forces.

The governor appoints judges to fill vacancies in judicial office, has extradition authority and may grant reprieves, commutations and pardons of criminal sentences.

If the office of governor becomes vacant, the office passes, in order, to the secretary of state, state treasurer, president of the Senate and speaker of the House of Representatives. There is no lieutenant governor in Oregon.

For additional information, see page 19.

Executive

***KATE BROWN** was born in Torrejón de Ardoz, Spain, on June 21, 1960. After spending most of her childhood in Minnesota, Brown earned a B.A. degree in Environmental Conservation with a Certificate in Women's Studies from the University of Colorado at Boulder. She earned her law degree and Certificate in Environmental Law from the Northwestern School of Law at Lewis & Clark College in Portland.*

Brown has taught at Portland State University and practiced family and juvenile law. She was appointed to the Oregon House of Representatives in 1991. In 1996, after serving two more House terms, she won election to the Oregon Senate. Two years later she was elected Senate Democratic Leader and, in 2004, became the first woman to serve as Oregon's Senate Majority Leader.

In her legislative career, Brown made Oregon's government more accessible by holding legislative committee hearings around the state. She also ensured funding for a comprehensive review for Oregon's ethics laws, spearheaded legislation creating ORESTAR, a searchable online database of campaign contributions and expenditures, and reformed Oregon's initiative process to reduce fraud and protect the citizen's right to petition.

In 2008, Brown was elected Oregon's 24th Secretary of State, and in 2012 she was reelected. As Oregon's chief auditor, her team has conducted more than 246 audits and reviews of state and local agencies, cutting waste and identifying ways to save taxpayer dollars and deliver services more effectively. In the Corporation Division, she worked collaboratively with private businesses and other state agencies to create an online business portal where business owners and entrepreneurs can access state resources to help grow their businesses and create jobs. As chief elections officer, Brown implemented Oregon's online voter registration system and the state led the nation in providing tablet technology for voters with disabilities to mark their ballots.

Secretary Brown lives in Portland with her husband Dan.

Secretary of State Kate Brown

136 State Capitol Building., 900 Court St. NE, Salem 97310-0722; 503-986-1523

Kate Brown, Portland; Democrat; elected 2008; reelected 2012; term expires January 2017. The secretary of state is one of three constitutional officers and a statewide elected official. The secretary serves a four-year term and, if reelected, can hold office for two terms.

As auditor of public accounts, the secretary examines and audits accounts of all publicly funded boards, commissions and agencies.

As chief elections officer, she interprets and applies state election laws, compiles and publishes the *Voter's Pamphlet* and supervises all elections, local and statewide.

As the chief records officer of the state, the secretary houses and provides access to the permanently valuable records of state government through the Archives Division and provides storage for inactive state agency records through the State Records Center. The division also provides records management advice to state agencies and political subdivisions, and files, codifies and publishes state agency administrative rules.

Through the Corporation Division, the secretary keeps public records of businesses authorized to transact business in Oregon, nonprofit corporations, and trade and service marks. Other public business records include notices of security interests in moveable and personal property, statutory liens and warrants.

As a member of the State Land Board, the secretary shares responsibility with the governor and state treasurer in supervising the management of state-owned lands.

The secretary of state is the custodian of the Seal of the State of Oregon and regulates Oregon notaries public.

The secretary of state also publishes the *Oregon Blue Book*.

If the office of governor becomes vacant, the office passes to the secretary of state. There is no lieutenant governor in Oregon.

For additional information, see page 21.

TED WHEELER *is Oregon's 28th State Treasurer. A sixth-generation Oregonian, he cares deeply about the state's financial health. He is committed to protecting the state's current strong credit ratings, to ensuring that public investments remain both prudent and profitable, and to conservatively managing Oregon's debt.*

A former manager and director at a local investment firm and chairman and chief executive officer of Multnomah County, Wheeler was appointed as treasurer in March 2010, elected in November 2010, and reelected in 2012.

He has directed efforts to help make the State Treasury a more efficient operation, a more responsible investor and more relevant to Oregonians. He increased transparency of Treasury data, pushed for money-saving technology changes, authorized securities fraud lawsuits against firms that misled investors and announced a revamped college savings plan with lower costs and more options for families.

Also as treasurer, he has maintained his commitment to protecting the most vulnerable citizens in Oregon's communities. He convened business leaders and spearheaded a new statewide blueprint dubbed the Oregon Investment Act.

Wheeler was born August 31, 1962, in Portland and graduated from Lincoln High School. He earned a B.A. degree in Economics from Stanford University, an M.B.A. degree from Columbia University and a Masters degree in Public Policy from the John F. Kennedy School of Government at Harvard University. His family has deep Oregon roots. The town of Wheeler, located on Nehalem Bay on the Oregon Coast, is named after his great-grandfather.

Wheeler is a longtime volunteer and has devoted energy to diverse causes including the Oregon Alcohol and Drug Policy Commission, Portland Mountain Rescue and Goose Hollow Family Shelter. He is an Eagle Scout.

As chairman of Multnomah County from 2007 to 2010, Wheeler oversaw a workforce of more than 4,400 and was responsible for reducing and balancing the budget and cutting the county's debt.

When he isn't working, Wheeler enjoys endurance sports. He lives in Southwest Portland with his wife Katrina and their daughter.

State Treasurer Ted Wheeler

159 State Capitol Building, 900 Court St. NE, Salem 97301-4043; 503-378-4329

Ted Wheeler, Portland; Democrat; appointed 2010; elected 2010; reelected 2012; term expires January 2017.

The state treasurer is a constitutional officer and a statewide elected official. The treasurer serves a four-year term and, if reelected, can hold office for two terms.

The treasurer serves as the chief financial officer for the state and is responsible for the prudent financial management of billions of taxpayer dollars. The treasurer also serves as the state's chief investment officer and has the duty of investing the monies of numerous funds such as the Public Employees Retirement Fund, the State Accident Insurance Fund and the Common School Fund.

The treasurer serves on a variety of state financial boards and on the State Land Board, which has a fiduciary duty to manage state trust lands for the benefit of the Common School Fund.

The Office of the State Treasurer is a highly sophisticated organization with a wide range of financial responsibilities, including managing the investment of state funds, issuing state bonds, serving as the central bank for state agencies and administering the Oregon 529 College Savings Network.

The treasurer manages a portfolio of approximately $75 billion with investments diversified across a spectrum of asset classes from stocks to real estate.

For additional information, see page 23.

ELLEN ROSENBLUM *was named Oregon Attorney General on June 29, 2012—the first woman in state history to hold the position. After a 37-year legal career, including more than three decades in public service, Rosenblum won the Democratic primary in May 2012, and was elected to a full four-year term as Attorney General on November 6, 2012.*

Rosenblum arrived in Oregon with her family in 1968 when her father became president of Reed College. Born in Berkeley, California, in 1951 and raised in Evanston, Illinois, she obtained both her undergraduate and Juris Doctor degrees from the University of Oregon. After law school, Rosenblum practiced as an associate and partner in a small Eugene law firm before serving as an assistant U.S. Attorney from 1980 to 1988. She was then appointed to the bench, serving as both a district and circuit court judge for Multnomah County from 1989 to 2005. In 2005, Governor Ted Kulongoski named her to the Oregon Court of Appeals, where she served until 2011.

Rosenblum has received numerous professional honors and has led law-related initiatives in areas of ethics, diversity, access to justice and the rule of law. She was the first sitting judge to serve as an officer of the American Bar Association and she served on the ABA's board of governors for seven years. She currently co-chairs its State Attorney General Committee. She also serves on the board of directors of the American Bar Foundation. She has been active, as well, in the National Association of Women Judges. In 1988, she co-founded Oregon Women Lawyers.

Attorney General Rosenblum lives in Portland with her husband, Richard Meeker. They have two children, Cate Meeker Kent and Will Meeker.

Attorney General Ellen Rosenblum

Justice Building, 1162 Court St. NE, Salem 97301; 503-378-4400

Ellen Rosenblum, Portland; Democrat; appointed June 2012; elected November 2012; term expires January 2017. The attorney general is the chief legal officer of the State of Oregon and heads the Department of Justice and its seven operating divisions.

The attorney general controls and supervises all court actions and legal proceedings in which the state of Oregon is a party or has an interest. The attorney general also has full charge and control of all legal business of all state departments, boards and commissions that require the services of legal counsel. She prepares ballot titles for measures to be voted upon by the people of Oregon and appoints the assistant attorneys general to act as counsel for the various state departments, boards and commissions.

The attorney general gives written opinions upon any question of law in which the state or any public subdivision may have an interest when requested by the governor, by any state agency official or by any member of the Legislature. The attorney general and her assistants are prohibited by law from rendering opinions or giving legal advice to any other persons or agencies.

Services and responsibilities of the attorney general and the Department of Justice are: representation of the state's interests in all civil and criminal cases before the state and federal courts, serving as legal counsel to state agencies and offices, consumer protection and information services, supervision of charitable trusts and solicitations, enforcement of state and federal antitrust laws in Oregon, assistance to the state's district attorneys, administration of the state's crime victims' compensation program, investigations of organized crime and public corruption and the establishment and enforcement of child support obligations for families who receive public assistance.

The term of office for attorney general is four years.

For additional information, see page 25.

BRAD AVAKIAN, Oregon's ninth Commissioner of Labor and Industries, was born February 4, 1961. He attended Beaverton's public schools, received a B.S. degree in Psychology from Oregon State University in 1984 and a J.D. degree from Lewis & Clark Law School in 1990.

Prior to law school, Brad worked as a laborer, counselor and teacher's assistant. After law school, Brad opened a civil rights law practice, serving people statewide who had suffered housing and employment discrimination. Brad was elected to the House of Representatives in 2002, reelected in 2004, and then elected to the Senate in 2006, serving northeast Washington and northwest Multnomah Counties.

During his legislative career, Brad was a strong advocate for public education, Oregon's environment and workers' rights. He served on the Joint Ways and Means, Commerce, Education and Rules Committees and chaired the Senate Environment and Natural Resources Committee. Brad successfully passed the Oregon Renewable Energy Act; the expansion of Oregon's landmark Bottle Bill; the Agriculture and Community Water Act, which will bring desperately needed water to Oregon's farms and rural communities; and expanded the rights of workers to organize and bargain.

In the Legislature, Brad was named "Consensus Builder of the Year" for his ability to bring people together in resolving some of Oregon's most pressing issues. Brad and his wife Debbie and their children, Nathan and Claire, live in northeast Washington County.

Commissioner of Labor and Industries Brad Avakian

State Office Building, 800 NE Oregon St., Suite 1045, Portland 97232; 971-673-0761

Brad Avakian, Beaverton; nonpartisan; appointed April 2008; elected November 2008; reelected 2012; term expires January 2017. The commissioner is chief executive of the Bureau of Labor and Industries. The commissioner also serves as chairperson of the State Apprenticeship and Training Council and executive secretary of the Wage and Hour Commission. The term of the commissioner is four years.

The commissioner enforces state laws prohibiting discrimination in employment, housing, public accommodation and vocational, professional and trade schools and has authority to initiate a "commissioner's complaint" on behalf of victims of discrimination.

Through the Wage and Hour Division, the commissioner administers state laws relating to wages, hours of employment, basic working conditions, child labor and prevailing wage rates; and licenses certain industries to ensure quality professional services. The division administers the Wage Security Fund that covers workers for unpaid wages in certain business closure situations and enforces group-health insurance termination-notification provisions.

The commissioner also oversees the state's registered apprenticeship-training system that gives workers the opportunity to learn a job skill while earning a living. The program benefits employers by providing a pool of skilled workers to meet business and industry demands.

Under the commissioner, agency administrative services include providing public education programs to help employers comply with the law and conducting administrative hearings. A hearings unit convenes administrative law proceedings in contested cases for wage and hour and civil rights determinations. Final orders in contested cases are issued by the commissioner.

For additional information, see page 27.

Office of the Governor

John Kitzhaber, Governor
Address: State Capitol Bldg., 900 Court St. NE, Suite 254, Salem 97301-4047
Phone: 503-378-3111
Fax: 503-378-8970
Web: www.governor.oregon.gov
Statutory Authority: ORS Chapter 176
Duties and Responsibilities: The governor is the chief executive of Oregon. The Oregon Constitution charges the governor with faithfully executing the laws, making recommendations to the Legislature and transacting all necessary business of government. The governor may veto bills of the Legislature and shall fill vacancies by appointment.

Curtis Robinhold is Governor Kitzhaber's Chief of Staff. Policy advisors include: Ben Cannon, Education; Margi Hoffmann, Energy; Kendall Clawson, Executive Appointments; Liani Reeves, General Counsel; Sean Kolmer, Health; Mike Bonetto, Health Care; Scott Nelson, Jobs and Economy; Duke Shepard, Labor and Human Services; Richard Whitman, Natural Resources; Brett Brownscombe, Natural Resources; Gabriela Goldfarb, Natural Resources; Lynn Peterson, Transportation; Cameron Smith, Veterans/Military; Agnes Balassa, Workforce Development; Frank Garcia Jr., Diversity and Inclusion Director; Cheryl Myers, Economic and Business Equity Director; and Dmitri Palmateer, Legislative Director. Tim Raphael is the Communications Director and Jan Murdock is the Executive Assistant.

Arrest and Return (Extradition)

Address: 900 Court St. NE, Salem 97301-4047
Phone: 503-378-3111
Fax: 503-378-3514
Contact: Fran Lushenko, Extradition Officer
Duties and Responsibilities: Arrest and Return provides administrative services for Oregon's extradition program.

Citizens' Representative Office

Address: State Capitol Bldg., 900 Court St. NE, Salem 97301-4047
Phone: 503-378-4582
Fax: 503-378-6827
Contact: Citizens' Representative Office
Duties and Responsibilities: The Citizens' Representative Office provides access and help for citizens who have problems, questions, ideas or suggestions about state government. The citizens' representative reports regularly to the governor, noting issues in state government that need attention. The office aims to treat all inquiries fairly, to examine each situation objectively and to respond in a clear and helpful way.

Diversity and Inclusion Office

Address: 255 Capitol St. NE, Suite 126, Salem 97301
Phone: 503-986-6524
Fax: 503-378-3225
Contact: Frank Garcia Jr., Director
Duties and Responsibilities: The Diversity and Inclusion Office directs and monitors affirmative action programs in all state agencies, a large portion of which is done on the basis of plans developed by state agencies. The director of affirmative action works closely with each state agency to assess its recruitment, placement, promotion and training practices with respect to achieving affirmative action goals. The director recommends and participates in affirmative action and equal opportunity training for state employees at all levels.

Economic and Business Equity

Address: 255 Capitol St. NE, Suite 126, Salem 97301
Phone: 503-986-6522
Fax: 503-378-3225
E-mail: Cheryl.L.Myers@state.or.us
Contact: Cheryl Myers, Director
Duties and Responsibilities: The director is appointed by the governor and serves as a policy advisor on issues related to minority, women and emerging small businesses, and creates access to contracting opportunities for certified firms.

Education

Address: 160 State Capitol Bldg., 900 Court St. NE, Salem 97301
Phone: 503-378-5690
Fax: 503-378-6827
E-mail: Ben.Cannon@state.or.us
Contact: Ben Cannon, Education Policy Advisor
Statutory Authority: Chapter 652, Oregon Laws 1997
Duties and Responsibilities: Oregon is improving its education funding and governance process to deliver better results for students, more resources for teachers and better value for the future of the state. The Education policy advisor is focused on identifying research and policy options to create an efficient and accountable public education system that integrates early childhood development with K–12 and post-secondary education and training. By working closely with the chief education officer and the deputy superintendent of public instruction, the governor's office is pursuing a home-grown system that will help students, teachers and schools set and reach ambitious, but achievable, goals.

Energy

Address: 255 Capitol St. NE, Suite 126, Salem 97301
Phone: 503-986-6545
Fax: 503-378-3225
Contact: Margi Hoffmann, Energy Policy Advisor
Duties and Responsibilities: The energy policy advisor is focused on helping to develop and implement the governor's 10 Year Energy Action Plan. The policy advisor works on strategies for the public and private utility sector, energy transmission, and transportation and infrastructure improvements.

Executive Appointments

Address: 160 State Capitol Bldg., 900 Court St. NE, Salem 97301
Phone: 503-378-3123
Fax: 503-373-0840
E-mail: executive.appointments@das.state.or.us
Contact: Kendall Clawson, Director
Duties and Responsibilities: Governor Kitzhaber makes appointments to nearly 300 boards and commissions representing a broad range of areas and issues for the State of Oregon. Most major state agencies and departments are headed by policy making boards appointed by the governor. These important citizens help the governor in his efforts to highlight advocacy, create innovative community strategies, generate policy and strengthen the responsiveness of governmental agencies.

Health Care

Address: 160 State Capitol Bldg., 900 Court St. NE, Salem 97301
Phone: 503-373-1558
Fax: 503- 378-6827
E-mail: Mike.Bonetto@state.or.us
Contact: Mike Bonetto, Health Care Policy Advisor; Sean Kolmer, Health Policy Advisor
Duties and Responsibilities: Health care is now the single fastest growing cost for state government, both in its capacity as a large employer and also in its responsibility to provide health care for low income and vulnerable citizens through the Oregon Health Plan. The Health Care team is focused on identifying and implementing programs that reduce costs while resulting in better health. Oregon's health care transformation aims to shift the focus from after-the-fact acute care to prevention, wellness and the community-based management of chronic conditions, in turn making health care more affordable for individuals, families and private sector businesses.

Jobs and Economy

Address: 160 State Capitol Bldg., 900 Court St. NE, Salem 97301
Phone: 503-378-5884
Fax: 503-378-6827
E-mail: Scott.Nelson@state.or.us; dan.carol@state.or.us
Contact: Scott Nelson, Jobs and Economy Policy Advisor; Dan Carol, Multi-State Initiatives Director
Duties and Responsibilities: Building Oregon's economy is a top priority for the governor. State government can and must play a key role in creating a favorable environment for the private sector to build a vibrant and innovative economy. The Jobs and Economy advisor is focused on identifying ways to ensure that Oregon companies become more competitive and sustainable and on ensuring that economic recovery touches every part of Oregon, urban and rural. It is also important to maintain connections at the regional, national and international levels. The Multi-State Initiatives director is focused on positioning Oregon at the forefront of the clean economy, on health care transformation and on innovation in building and maintaining public infrastructure.

Labor and Human Services

Address: 160 State Capitol Bldg., 900 Court St. NE, Salem 97301
Phone: 503-373-1558
Fax: 503-378-6827
E-mail: duke.shepard@state.or.us
Contact: Duke Shepard, Labor and Human Services Policy Advisor
Duties and Responsibilities: The Labor and Human Services policy advisor represents the governor on labor and collecting bargaining issues and advises the governor on housing and community services, early learning and early childhood services, and self-sufficiency programs such as SNAP (Supplemental Nutrition Assistance Program) and TANF (Temporary Assistance for Needy Families).

Natural Resources Office

Address: 255 Capitol St. NE, Suite 126, Salem 97301
Phone: 503-986-6549
Fax: 503-378-3225
Web: www.oregon.gov/Gov/GNRO
Contact: Richard Whitman, Brett Brownscombe, Gabriela Goldfarb, Tom Tuchmann, Policy Advisors
Statutory Authority: ORS 173.610
Duties and Responsibilities: The governor's Natural Resources team convenes regular meetings of state natural resources agencies to ensure that state policies are consistently applied across agencies. The office facilitates resolution of policy differences between state agencies, federal agencies, and between agencies and stakeholders and provides direction and coordination for agencies on regulatory, planning and environmental issues that

span multiple agencies. Examples include coordination of species recovery plans, implementation of the Oregon Plan for Salmon and Watersheds, permitting and review of energy facilities, and ocean conservation.

Regional Solutions

Address: 167 State Capitol Bldg., 900 Court St. NE, Salem 97301
Phone: 503-986-6502
Fax: 503-378-6827
E-mail: greg.wolf@state.or.us
Contact: Greg Wolf, Director
Duties and Responsibilities: Regional Solutions is an innovative, collaborative approach to community and economic development in Oregon. The state, in partnership with Oregon colleges and universities, established Regional Solutions Centers throughout Oregon. Each takes a bottom-up approach to development projects, working at the local level to identify priorities, solve problems and seize opportunities to complete projects. These centers integrate state agency work and funding to ensure that projects are completed in the most economical and streamlined process possible.

Transportation and Sustainable Communities

Address: 255 Capitol St. NE, Suite 126, Salem 97301
Phone: 503-986-6545
Fax: 503-378-3225
Contact: Lynn Peterson, Transportation and Sustainable Communities Policy Advisor
Duties and Responsibilities: The Transportation and Sustainable Communities policy advisor is focused on leading the governor's policy efforts to align transportation investments with Oregon's economy, housing needs, health and sustainability.

Veterans/Military and Emergency Management

Address: 255 Capitol St. NE, Suite 126, Salem 97301
Phone: 503-986-6545
Fax: 503-378-3225
Contact: Cameron Smith, Veterans/Military Policy Advisor
Duties and Responsibilities: The Veterans/Military and Emergency Management policy advisor works closely with the leadership of the Oregon National Guard, the Oregon Department of Veteran Affairs and the Office of Emergency Management to achieve the governor's goals on related issues and to link to his other priorities.

Workforce Policy

Address: 255 Capitol St. NE, Suite 126, Salem 97301
Phone: 503-986-6527
Fax: 503-378-3225
Contact: Agnes Balassa, Workforce Policy Coordinator
Duties and Responsibilities: The Workforce Policy coordinator is focused on ensuring Oregon has a skilled workforce ready to meet industry needs and compete in the marketplace with valuable, up-to-date skills. The work emphasizes programs that help people access workforce training and services for career transition and skill development.

Office of the Secretary of State

Kate Brown, Secretary of State
Brian Shipley, Deputy Secretary of State
Address: 136 State Capitol Bldg., Salem 97310-0722
Phone: 503-986-1500
Fax: 503-986-1616
E-mail: oregon.sos@state.or.us
Web: www.sos.state.or.us
Statutory Authority: Oregon Constitution, Article VI, Section 2; ORS Chapters 177, 240
Duties and Responsibilities: The Office of the Secretary of State is one of three constitutional offices established at statehood. The secretary of state is the custodian of the state seal and oversees the functions of seven divisions.

As auditor of public accounts, the secretary of state evaluates and reports on the financial condition and operations of state government and administers the Municipal Audits Law.

The secretary of state is the chief elections officer, responsible for uniformly applying state election laws. She also acts as the filing officer for state offices, initiative and referendum petitions, campaign finance reports and other election documents. In addition, the secretary publishes and distributes the *Voters' Pamphlet* and investigates election law violations.

The secretary of state is the public records administrator for Oregon, a role that includes preserving official acts of the Legislature, state agencies and local governments, as well as supervising the state archivist, publishing administrative rules for state agencies and producing the *Oregon Blue Book*.

The secretary of state registers domestic and foreign corporations' assumed business names, and trade and service marks. The secretary prepares notarial applications and serves as filing officer for Uniform Commercial Code transactions.

The secretary of state serves with the governor and state treasurer on the State Land Board, managing state-owned lands for the benefit of the Common School Fund. The secretary also serves as chair of the Oregon Sustainability Board.

Archives Division

Address: 800 Summer St. NE, Salem 97310
Phone: 503-373-0701
Fax: 503-373-0953
E-mail: archives.info@state.or.us
Web: http://arcweb.sos.state.or.us
Contact: Mary Beth Herkert, State Archivist
Statutory Authority: ORS 192.001, 357.815
Duties and Responsibilities: The Archives Division, established in 1947, houses and provides access to the permanently valuable records of Oregon government. The oldest documents at the archives include records of the provisional and territorial governments and the Oregon Constitution.

The division authorizes disposition of the public records of Oregon government, provides records management advice and assistance to state agencies and political subdivisions, and operates the State Records Center, which provides inexpensive storage for inactive state agency records. The division also files, codifies and publishes state agency administrative rules and publishes the *Oregon Blue Book.*

State Historic Records Advisory Board

Address: 800 Summer St. NE, Salem 97310
Phone: 503-373-0701
Fax: 503-373-0953
Contact: Mary Beth Herkert, State Coordinator

Audits Division

Address: Public Service Bldg., 255 Capitol St. NE, Suite 500, Salem 97310
Phone: 503-986-2255; Hotline: 1-800-336-8218
Fax: 503-378-6767
E-mail: SOS.audits@state.or.us
Web: www.sos.state.or.us/audits/index.html
Contact: Gary Blackmer, Director
Statutory Authority: ORS Chapter 297; 97.810–97.920, 128.400–128.440, 177.170–177.180, 692.285
Duties and Responsibilities: The Audits Division was created in 1929 to carry out the duties of the secretary of state as the constitutional Auditor of Public Accounts. It is the only independent auditing organization in the state with authority to review programs of agencies in all three branches of government: executive, legislative and judicial. The division performs financial, information technology and performance audits of state agencies and state-aided institutions in accordance with professional standards for government audits. The division administers Municipal Audit Law through administrative rules and review of municipal audits and conducts special investigations regarding potential misuse of state resources.

Corporation Division

Address: Public Service Bldg., 255 Capitol St. NE, Suite 151, Salem 97310
Phone: 503-986-2200
Fax: 503-986-6355
Web: http://filinginoregon.com
Contact: Peter Threlkel, Director
Statutory Authority: ORS Chapters 56, 58, 60, 62, 63, 65, 67, 68, 79, 80, 87, 128, 194, 554, 647, 648
Duties and Responsibilities: The Corporation Division assists the public in registering business entities, filing public notices of records of debt, commissions notaries public, investigates notary complaints and provides certifications of records and notarized documents. The division provides the general public and businesses with access to public record information to help them learn more about those with whom they are doing business. The division also publishes the *Oregon Business Guide* and provides information on regulatory requirements and services available to citizens wanting to start a business or hire employees in Oregon.

Elections Division

Address: Public Service Bldg., 255 Capitol St. NE, Suite 501, Salem 97310-0722
Phone: 503-986-1518
Fax: 503-373-7414
E-mail: elections.sos@state.or.us
Web: http://oregonvotes.org
Contact: Stephen N. Trout, Director
Statutory Authority: ORS Chapters 246–260
Duties and Responsibilities: The Elections Division ensures the uniform interpretation and application of Oregon's election laws. The division provides the public, elected officials, candidates, media and interested parties with advice and assistance in all matters related to elections.

The division receives candidate filings for state offices, initiative and referendum petitions, campaign contribution and expenditure reports and other election documents. The division publishes and distributes the state *Voters' Pamphlet* for primary, general and special elections. Complaints of alleged election law violations are investigated by the division.

Internal Support:

Business Services Division

Address: Public Service Bldg., 255 Capitol St. NE, Suite 180, Salem 97310
Phone: 503-986-2204
Fax: 503-378-4991
Contact: Jeff Morgan, Director
Statutory Authority: ORS Chapter 177

Duties and Responsibilities: The Business Services Division provides centralized business and administrative support for the agency including budgeting, payroll, purchasing, safety and risk management and sales of secretary of state publications.

Human Resources Division

Address: Public Service Bldg., 255 Capitol St. NE, Suite 105, Salem 97310
Phone: 503-986-2173
Fax: 503-986-2175
Web: www.sos.state.or.us
Contact: Jackie Steffens, Director
Duties and Responsibilities: The Human Resources Division provides human resource services for the Office of the Secretary of State. This includes staff recruitment and training, policy development, employee relations and compensation.

Information Systems Division

Address: Public Service Bldg., 255 Capitol St. NE, Suite 103, Salem 97310
Phone: 503-986-0521
Fax: 503-986-2249
Contact: Julie Pearson-Ruthven, Director
Statutory Authority: ORS 177.050, 177.120
Duties and Responsibilities: The Information Systems Division provides centralized technology services for the agency which include design, installation, configuration, maintenance and trouble-shooting services for hardware, software and networks. The division also provides security and database administration as well as data back-up and recovery.

Office of the State Treasurer

Ted Wheeler, State Treasurer
Darren Q. Bond, Deputy State Treasurer
Address: 159 State Capitol Bldg., 900 Court St. NE, Salem 97301
Phone: 503-378-4329
Fax: 503-373-7051
E-mail: oregon.treasurer@state.or.us
Web: www.oregon.gov/treasury
Statutory Authority: ORS Chapter 178
Duties and Responsibilities: The state treasurer is a constitutional officer and a statewide elected official. The treasurer serves as the chief financial officer for the state and is responsible for the prudent financial management of billions of tax-payer and trust fund dollars. The Office of the State Treasurer is a sophisticated organization with a range of financial responsibilities, including managing the investment of state funds, issuing all state bonds, serving as the central bank for state agencies, overseeing the protection of public fund deposits in private-sector institutions and administering the Oregon 529 College Savings Network.

Executive Division

Address: 159 State Capitol Bldg., 900 Court St. NE, Salem 97301
Phone: 503-378-4329
Contact: Tom Rinehart, Chief of Staff
Duties and Responsibilities: The Executive Division coordinates policy development, strategic planning, quality initiatives, legislative initiatives, media relations, internal auditing functions, human resource functions and the publication of Treasury financial reports. The state treasurer, by constitutional authority, serves on the State Land Board and, by statute, on a number of public financial boards and councils.

Debt Management Division

Address: 350 Winter St. NE, Suite 100, Salem 97301-3896
Phone: 503-378-4930
Fax: 503-378-2870
Contact: Laura Lockwood-McCall, Director
Duties and Responsibilities: The Debt Management Division provides central coordination and approval for the issuance of all state agency and authority bonds, which totaled $11.9 billion at the end of 2011. This requires monitoring the local and national bond markets and the financing and economic trends that impact bond issuance structures and interest rates. The division staffs the Municipal Debt Advisory Commission, the Private Activity Bond Committee and the State Debt Policy Advisory Commission. The division also provides information to private credit rating agencies.

Facilities Authority, Oregon

Address: 1600 Pioneer Tower, 888 SW 5th Ave., Portland 97204
Phone: 503-802-2102
Contact: Gwendolyn Griffith, Executive Director
Statutory Authority: ORS 289.100
Duties and Responsibilities: The Oregon Facilities Authority (OFA), formerly the Health, Housing, Educational and Cultural Facilities Authority, was created by the Legislature in 1989. OFA assists with the assembling and financing of lands for health, housing, educational and cultural uses and for the construction and financing of facilities for such uses. All bonds issued by the state treasurer upon recommendation of OFA are repaid solely from

revenues generated by the projects or from other sources available to the applying institution.

Interest on the bonds is tax-exempt from federal income taxes and is also exempt from personal income taxes imposed by the state. The state treasurer appoints seven members who serve a term of four years, and an executive director is hired to administer the program.

Municipal Debt Advisory Commission

Address: 350 Winter St. NE, Suite 100, Salem 97301-3896
Phone: 503-378-4930
Fax: 503-378-2870
Contact: Laura Lockwood-McCall, Debt Management Division Director
Statutory Authority: ORS 287.030
Duties and Responsibilities: The commission assists local governments in the issuance of municipal debt and provides information on such debt. The commission promotes methods of reducing the cost of issuing municipal bonds.

Private Activity Bond Committee

Address: 350 Winter St. NE, Suite 100, Salem 97301-3896
Phone: 503-378-4930
Fax: 503-378-2870
Contact: Laura Lockwood-McCall, Debt Management Division Director
Duties and Responsibilities: The 1986 Tax Reform Act limited the number of bonds that each state may issue for "private activity" purposes. The committee has three members including a representative of the Department of Administrative Services, the Office of the State Treasurer and a public member appointed by the governor. The committee allocates a portion of the state private activity bond limit to local governments pursuant to ORS 286.625 and the 1986 Tax Reform Act.

State Debt Policy Advisory Commission

Address: 350 Winter St. NE, Suite 100, Salem 97301-3896
Phone: 503-378-4930
Fax: 503-378-2870
Contact: Laura Lockwood-McCall, Debt Management Division Director
Statutory Authority: ORS 286.550–286.555
Duties and Responsibilities: The commission advises the governor and the Legislature regarding policies and actions that enhance and preserve the state's credit rating. It also maintains the future availability of low-cost capital financing.

Finance Division

Address: 350 Winter St. NE, Suite 100, Salem 97301-3896
Phone: 503-378-4633
Fax: 503-373-1179
Contact: Cora Parker, Director
Duties and Responsibilities: The Finance Division is the central bank for all state agencies. Almost all money that flows to and from Oregon state government passes through this division. Finance responsibilities include the processing of millions of checks and electronic funds transfers annually. The division provides an automated banking system to state agencies to help manage these activities. The division also administers the Local Government Investment Pool, which provides a short-term investment vehicle for local governments' idle cash. The Public Funds Collateralization Program helps to protect deposits of taxpayer funds.

Short Term Fund Board

Address: 350 Winter St. NE, Suite 100, Salem 97301-3896
Phone: 503-378-4633
Fax: 503-373-1179
Contact: Cora Parker, Finance Division Director
Statutory Authority: ORS 294.885
Duties and Responsibilities: In seeking to best serve local governments, the Legislature established the Oregon Short Term Fund Board. The purpose of the board is to advise the state treasurer and the Oregon Investment Council in the management and investments of the Oregon Short Term Fund and the Local Government Investment Pool. The treasurer serves as an ex officio member and appoints three members to the board. The governor appoints the remaining three members.

Investment Division

Address: 350 Winter St. NE, Suite 100, Salem 97301-3896
Phone: 503-378-4000
Contact: John Skjervem, Chief Investment Officer
Duties and Responsibilities: The Investment Division manages the investments of the Oregon Public Employees Retirement Fund, State Accident Insurance Fund, Oregon Short Term Fund, Common School Fund, Oregon Growth Account and numerous smaller funds. The Oregon Public Employees Retirement Fund is the largest fund under the treasurer's management, standing at about $59 billion. The total portfolio managed by the Office of the State Treasurer has a market value of about $75 billion and is diversified across a spectrum of asset classes from stocks to real estate. The Investment Division strives to save taxpayers money by earning the highest risk-

adjusted return on its investments. The division also manages the investment program for the state's deferred compensation plan and staffs the Oregon Investment Council and the Oregon Growth Account Board.

Growth Account Board, Oregon

Address: 6650 SW Redwood Ln., # 190, Tigard 97224
Phone: 971-673-2800
Contact: Michael Mueller, CFA, Deputy Chief Investment Officer
Statutory Authority: ORS 348.702
Duties and Responsibilities: The Oregon Growth Account Board governs the investment of Lottery-generated funds in the Oregon Growth Account, which earns returns for the Education Stability Fund by making investments in, or to provide seed capital for, emerging growth businesses in Oregon. The board selects and oversees management companies to manage the funds. The treasurer or a designee serves as the chair of the board and the governor appoints the remaining six board members.

Investment Council, Oregon

Address: 350 Winter St. NE, Suite 100, Salem 97301-3896
Phone: 503-378-4000
Contact: John Skjervem, Chief Investment Officer
Statutory Authority: ORS 293.706
Duties and Responsibilities: The Oregon Investment Council is responsible for the investment of all state funds. The state treasurer serves as a member of the council. Monies are invested in accordance with the "Prudent Investor Rule" to achieve the investment objectives of the various funds and to make the monies as productive as possible. The governor appoints council members to four-year terms, subject to Senate confirmation.

Other Entities:

Oregon 529 College Savings Network

Address: 900 Court St. NE, Rm. 159, Salem 97301
Phone: 503-373-1903
Web: www.oregon529network.com
Contact: Michael Parker, Executive Director
Duties and Responsibilities: The Oregon 529 College Savings Network was created by the 1999 Legislature to help families save for higher education expenses. The plans are unique investment vehicles that provide significant state and federal tax advantages and more flexibility than many other college savings tools. State law and Section 529 of the Internal Revenue Code govern the plan.

Oregon 529 College Savings Board

Address: 900 Court St. NE, Rm. 159, Salem 97301
Phone: 503-373-1903
Contact: Michael Parker, Executive Director
Statutory Authority: ORS 348.849
Duties and Responsibilities: The Oregon 529 College Savings Board administers plans in the Oregon 529 College Savings Network. The five-member public board includes the state treasurer or a designee, and the staff is located at the Office of the State Treasurer. The board sets investment policies for the plan and oversees the private sector vendors that manage plan assets.

Internal Support:

Information Services Division

Address: 350 Winter St. NE, Suite 100, Salem 97301-3896
Phone: 503-378-3436
Contact: Ron Pope, Chief Information Officer
Duties and Responsibilities: The Information Services Division is the technology management center for the Office of the State Treasurer. The division develops and maintains information technology infrastructures that support business operations of the office. Disaster recovery readiness and management of security controls are key components of the division's efforts to ensure provision of vital services for Oregon citizens.

Oregon Department of Justice

Ellen F. Rosenblum, Attorney General
Address: 1162 Court St. NE, Salem 97301
Phone: 503-378-6002; TTY: 503-378-5938
Fax: 503-378-4017
Web: www.doj.state.or.us
Statutory Authority: ORS Chapter 180
Duties and Responsibilities: The Department of Justice, established by statute in 1891, is Oregon state government's law firm. Administered by the attorney general, it represents and advises all state elected and appointed officials, agencies, boards and commissions. The attorney general has control and supervision of all court actions in which the state is a party or has an interest.

In addition to legal services, the department has various program-service functions, including child-support enforcement, technical and investigative assistance to district attorneys, organized crime investigation, consumer protection and service, charitable trust supervision and crime-victim compensation. In all, the department and attorney general have responsibility and authority under more than 350 state statutes.

Appellate Division

Address: 1162 Court St. NE, Salem 97301
Phone: 503-378-4402
Web: www.doj.state.or.us
Contact: Anna M. Joyce, Solicitor General
Duties and Responsibilities: The Appellate Division generally is responsible for representing the state's interests in all civil, criminal and administrative cases before all state and federal appellate courts. Under supervision of the solicitor general, division attorneys articulate and defend the state's legal policies in written briefs and oral arguments before the Oregon Court of Appeals, the Oregon Supreme Court, the United States Court of Appeals and the Supreme Court of the United States.

Child Support Division

Address: 1215 State St., Salem 97301;
Mail: 1162 Court St. NE, Salem 97301
Phone: 503-947-4388
Web: http://oregonchildsupport.gov
Contact: Kate Cooper Richardson, Administrator
Duties and Responsibilities: The Child Support Division provides child support services to Oregon's citizens, including locating absent parents, establishing paternity, establishing child support orders, modifying and enforcing child support orders and receiving and distributing child support payments. Child support services are provided to all parents regardless of income. The Child Support Division maintains local branches around the state and works in partnership with county district attorneys' offices to deliver Oregon's Child Support Program. The program collects and distributes more than $360 million in child support annually, providing a vital component to the well-being of Oregon families.

Civil Enforcement Division

Address: 1162 Court St. NE, Salem 97301
Phone: 503-934-4400
Web: www.doj.state.or.us
Contact: Frederick M. Boss, Chief Counsel
Duties and Responsibilities: The Civil Enforcement Division is responsible for civil law enforcement. The Charitable Activities Section enforces laws regarding charitable trusts and solicitations and regulates bingo and raffle operations. The Civil Recovery Section is responsible for reducing to judgment and collecting debts owed to state agencies. It also provides legal services to the Child Support Division. The Financial Fraud/Consumer Protection Section protects Oregon consumers from predatory marketplace practices. Its responsibilities include enforcement of laws pertaining to antitrust, securities, civil racketeering, unlawful trade practices and charitable solicitations. The Medicaid Fraud Unit is part of a federally subsidized program for deterring fraud committed by Medicaid health care service providers. It detects and prosecutes cases of criminal abuse or neglect in health care facilities receiving Medicaid funds. The Child Advocacy Section provides legal advice and court representation to the Department of Human Services, Child Welfare Division.

Crime Victims' Services Division

Address: 1162 Court St. NE, Salem 97301
Phone: 503-378-5348; Toll-free 1-800-503-7983
Fax: 503-378-5738
Email: cvsd.email@doj.state.or.us
Web: www.doj.state.or.us/crimev
Contact: Shannon Sivell, Director
Duties and Responsibilities: The mission and goal of the Crime Victims' Services Division is to improve the treatment of all victims of crime. The division strives to reduce the impact of crime on victims' lives by supporting statewide victim services programs, promoting victims' rights, and providing victims access to information and resources in a compassionate, responsive and dedicated manner.

Criminal Justice Division

Address: 1162 Court St. NE, Salem 97301
Phone: 503-378-6347
Fax: 503-373-1936
Web: www.doj.state.or.us
Contact: Darin E. Tweedt, Chief Counsel
Duties and Responsibilities: The Criminal Justice Division is a full-service law enforcement agency that includes prosecuters, special agents and criminal intelligence analysts. It houses the state Criminal Intelligence Unit and maintains the Oregon State Information Network, serves as counsel for the Department of Public Safety Standards and Training, provides assistance to Oregon district attorneys, and investigates and prosecutes organized crime, tobacco smuggling, Internet crimes against children, public corruption and election fraud. The division also conducts the Annual Institute for Prosecutors, the DOJ Law Enforcement and Intelligence Conference and numerous other training programs for law enforcement.

District Attorneys

The Constitution describes the dual functions of the district attorney as the prosecuting attorney and law officer of the state and counties. Elected to four year terms, the district attorney serves as the public prosecutor, represents the state in criminal proceedings and initiates proceedings for punishable offenses. They enforce child support orders, represent the state in juvenile matters and undertake inquests into the cause and manner of certain deaths. Although elected by county voters, the district attorney is a state officer whose salary is paid by the state and, in most cases, who is prohibited from privately practicing law.

District Attorneys by county: Baker – Matthew Shirtcliff; Benton – John Haroldson; Clackamas – John Foote; Clatsop – Joshua Marquis; Columbia – R. Steven Atchison; Coos – R. Paul Frasier; Crook – Daina Vitolins; Curry – Everett Dial; Deschutes – Patrick J. Flaherty; Douglas – Richard Wesenberg; Gilliam – Marion Weatherford; Grant – Ryan Joslin; Harney – Timothy Colahan; Hood River – John T. Sewell; Jackson – Beth Heckert; Jefferson – Steven Lariche; Josephine – Stephen D. Campbell; Klamath – Vacant; Lake – Ulys Stapleton; Lane – Alex Gardner; Lincoln – Robert Bovett; Linn – Doug Marteeny; Malheur – Dan Norris; Marion – Walter Beglau; Morrow – Justin Nelson; Multnomah – Rodney Underhill; Polk – Aaron Felton; Sherman – Wade McLeod; Tillamook – William Porter; Umatilla – Daniel R. Primus; Union – Timothy Thompson; Wallowa – Mona K. Williams; Wasco – Eric J. Nisley; Washington – Robert Hermann; Wheeler – Daniel Ousley; Yamhill – Bradley C. Berry

General Counsel Division

Address: 1162 Court St. NE, Salem 97301
Phone: 503-947-4540
Web: www.doj.state.or.us
Contact: Steven A. Wolf, Chief Counsel
Duties and Responsibilities: The General Counsel Division provides a broad range of legal services to state agencies, boards and commissions, including day-to-day legal advice necessary for the state's operation. The division is composed of the following sections headed by attorneys-in-charge: Business Activities, Business Transactions, Government Services, Human Services, Labor and Employment, Natural Resources, and Tax and Finance.

Trial Division

Address: 158 12th St. NE, Salem 97301;
Mail: 1162 Court St. NE, Salem 97301
Phone: 503-947-4700
Web: www.doj.state.or.us
Contact: Cheryl Pellegrini, Chief Trial Counsel
Duties and Responsibilities: The Trial Division defends the state, its agencies, employees, and elected and appointed officials in civil litigation brought in state and federal courts. The division includes four sections, each with a particular area of focus. The Civil Litigation Section handles a wide variety of cases that may be tried to a jury in state and federal courts. These cases fall into five general categories: torts, employment, commercial disputes, prisoner civil rights lawsuits and real estate condemnation. The Criminal and Collateral Remedies Litigation Section defends convictions secured by county district attorneys against collateral attacks brought by the convicted person. The Defense of Agency Orders Litigation Section defends state agency decisions when they are challenged in circuit court. The Special Litigation Unit defends state statutes and policies against constitutional challenges in state and federal courts and handles complex class-action lawsuits, elections litigation and other high-profile or sensitive matters in which the state or its agencies may be plaintiffs or defendants.

Bureau of Labor and Industries

Brad Avakian, Commissioner of Labor and Industries
Address: 800 NE Oregon St., Suite 1045, Portland 97232
Phone: 971-673-0761; Oregon Relay System TTY: 711
Fax: 971-673-0762
E-mail: BOLI.MAIL@state.or.us
Web: www.oregon.gov/BOLI
Statutory Authority: ORS Chapter 651
Duties and Responsibilities: The Bureau of Labor and Industries (BOLI) was created by the 1903 Legislature, and the first labor commissioner was elected in 1906. The bureau was created to oversee the rapidly developing industrial workplace and to protect workers, especially minors. Its original responsibilities included inspecting mills, factories and schools as well as enforcing pay regulations and helping workers collect wages.

Today, the bureau enforces anti-discrimination laws in workplaces and public accommodations, enforces wage and hour laws and investigates violations, educates employers to avoid unnecessary worker complaints, and partners with labor, business and other organizations to develop a highly-skilled, competitive workforce in Oregon.

BOLI is headquartered in Portland and has regional offices in Bend, Eugene, Medford and Salem.

Commissioner's Office and Program Services Division

Address: 800 NE Oregon St., Suite 1045, Portland 97232
Phone: 971-673-0761; Oregon Relay System TTY: 711
Fax: 971-673-0762
Web: www.oregon.gov/BOLI
Contact: Christine Hammond, Deputy Labor Commissioner
Statutory Authority: ORS Chapter 651

Duties and Responsibilities: The Commissioner's Office and Program Services Division provides policy direction, support and accountability to assist the operating units in encouraging compliance and in enforcing wage and hour and civil rights laws and apprenticeship standards. Administrative services include policy development, strategic planning, intergovernmental relations and public information. Business services include budget management, accounting, data processing and human resources. The Hearings Unit convenes administrative law proceedings in contested case hearings for wage and hour and civil rights determinations. The Technical Assistance for Employers Program provides employers with a telephone information line, pamphlets, handbooks and printed materials, and public or company-based seminars and workshops to keep the business community informed about employment laws.

Apprenticeship and Training Division

Address: Main office: 800 NE Oregon St., Suite 1045, Portland 97232
Phone: 971-673-0761; Oregon Relay System TTY: 711
Fax: 971-673-0768
Web: www.oregon.gov/BOLI
Contact: Stephen Simms
Statutory Authority: ORS Chapter 660; 334.745–334.750
Duties and Responsibilities: The Apprenticeship and Training Division promotes apprenticeship in a variety of occupations and trades and works with business, labor, government and education organizations to increase training and employment opportunities in apprenticeable occupations. Apprenticeship is occupational training that combines on-the-job experience with classroom training. Industry employers design and control the training programs and pay apprentices' wages. The division registers occupational skill standards and agreements between apprentices and employers and works with local apprenticeship committees across the state to ensure that apprenticeship programs provide quality training and equal employment opportunities, particularly for women and minorities in technical and craft occupations.

Regional Offices:

Address: Bend: Worksource Bend, 1645 NE Forbes Rd., Suite 106, Bend 97701-4990
Phone: 541-322-2435
Fax: 541-389-8265

Address: Eugene: 1400 Executive Pkwy., Suite 200, Eugene 97401
Phone: 541-686-7654
Fax: 541-686-7980

Address: Medford: 119 N Oakdale Ave., Medford 97501
Phone: 541-776-6201
Fax: 541-776-6284

Address: Salem: 3865 Woverine St. NE, Bldg. E-1, Salem 97305
Phone: 503-378-2313
Fax: 503-378-7636

State Apprenticeship and Training Council

Address: 800 NE Oregon St., Suite 1045, Portland 97232
Phone: 971-673-0777; Oregon Relay System TTY: 711
Contact: Stephen Simms, Secretary; Brad Avakian, Chair
Statutory Authority: ORS 660.110
Duties and Responsibilities: The Oregon State Apprenticeship and Training Council has eight members appointed by the governor and confirmed by the Senate. The council sets policy for apprenticeship training and registers individual apprenticeship programs.

Two of the council members are from generally apprenticed occupations that have programs registered with the council, four are from the construction occupations and two are from the public. Members are equally divided among employee representatives and management. The council has statutory authority to oversee apprenticeship committees, programs and policies and to approve apprenticeship committee members.

Civil Rights Division

Address: Main office: 800 NE Oregon St., Suite 1045, Portland 97232
Phone: 971-673-0764; Oregon Relay System TTY: 711
Fax: 971-673-0765
Web: www.oregon.gov/BOLI
Contact: Amy Klare
Statutory Authority: ORS 30.670, 30.685, 345.240, 654.062, Chapter 659A
Duties and Responsibilities: The Civil Rights Division enforces laws granting individuals equal access to jobs, career schools, promotions and a work environment free from discrimination and harassment. These laws ensure that workers' jobs are protected when they report worksite safety violations, use family leave or the workers' compensation system. Civil rights laws also provide protection for those seeking housing or using public facilities such as retail establishments or transportation.

Regional Offices:

Address: Eugene: 1400 Executive Pkwy., Suite 200, Eugene 97401

Phone: 541-686-7623
Fax: 541-686-7980

Address: Salem: 3865 Wolverine St. NE, Bldg. E-1, Salem 97305
Phone: 503-378-3292
Fax: 503-373-7636

Wage and Hour Division

Address: Main office: 800 NE Oregon St., Suite 1045, Portland 97232
Phone: 971-673-0761; Oregon Relay System TTY: 711
Fax: 971-673-0769
Web: www.oregon.gov/BOLI
Contact: Gerhard Taeubel, Administrator
Statutory Authority: ORS Chapters 279, 652, 653, 658; ORS 654.251
Duties and Responsibilities: The Wage and Hour Division serves Oregon wage earners by enforcing laws covering state minimum wage and overtime requirements, wage collection, working conditions, child labor, farm and forest labor contracting, and private employment agencies. The division also regulates the employment of workers on public works projects.

Regional Offices:

Address: Eugene: 1400 Executive Pkwy., Suite 200, Eugene 97401
Phone: 541-686-7623
Fax: 541-686-7980

Address: Salem: 3865 Wolverine St. NE, Bldg. E-1, Salem 97305
Phone: 503-378-3292
Fax: 503-373-7636

Prevailing Wage Advisory Committee

Address: 800 NE Oregon St., Suite 1045, Portland 97232
Phone: 971-673-0837
Contact: Gerhard Taeubel, Administrator
Statutory Authority: ORS 279C.820
Duties and Responsibilities: The commissioner of the Bureau of Labor and Industries appoints a committee to assist in the administration of prevailing wage rate laws. This committee includes an equal number of management and labor members who are involved in the building and construction industry and work on public works contracts. The commissioner may also appoint other members from the public.

Wage and Hour Commission

Address: 800 NE Oregon St., Suite 1045, Portland 97232
Phone: 971-673-0837
Contact: Gerhard Taeubel, Administrator
Statutory Authority: ORS 653.505
Duties and Responsibilities: The Wage and Hour Commission sets minimum standards for the working conditions of minors and may grant specific exceptions to child labor laws. The governor appoints the three members of this commission to four-year terms. The commissioner of the Bureau of Labor and Industries acts as executive officer of the commission.

Other State Agencies, Boards and Commissions

Beyond the previous five main executive offices, there are other agencies, boards, commissions and programs that carry out executive branch duties. The following section contains information about these entities. Each description includes basic contact information and when available, a summary of the entity's duties and responsibilities.

In general, the agencies are listed alphabetically by substantive name. For example, the Department of Human Services appears as "Human Services, Department of." Programs under the main agency are listed under that agency's heading. Thus, Self-Sufficiency Programs would appear within the larger entry for Department of Human Services. These subdivisions are also listed alphabetically by substantive name with a few exceptions; such as, when a board or commission is connected directly to the main agency office.

The *Oregon Blue Book* Index is helpful for locating individual agencies, boards, commissions or programs.

Accountancy, Board of

Address: 3218 Pringle Rd. SE, Suite 110, Salem 97302-6307
Phone: 503-378-4181
Fax: 503-378-3575
Web: www.oregon.gov/BOA
Contact: Martin Pittioni, Executive Director; Jessie Bridgham, CPA, Chair
Statutory Authority: ORS Chapter 673
Duties and Responsibilities: The Board of Accountancy assures that approximately 9,500 Certified Public Accountants (CPAs), Public Accountants (PAs), municipal auditors and public accounting firms registered to practice in Oregon demonstrate and maintain knowledge of professional standards and practices to serve the needs of their clients and other users of their services.

The board is authorized to establish and enforce standards and regulations, approve candidates for the Uniform CPA Examination and license qualified applicants in the field of public accounting.

Administrative Services, Department of

Address: 155 Cottage St. NE, U20, Salem 97301-3972
Phone: 503-378-3104; TTY 503-373-3737
Fax: 503-373-7643
E-mail: oregon.info@state.or.us
Web: www.oregon.gov/DAS
Contact: Michael Jordan, Chief Operating Officer and Director
Statutory Authority: ORS 184.305
Duties and Responsibilities: The Department of Administrative Services (DAS) is the central administrative agency of Oregon's state government. DAS works to implement policy and financial decisions made by the governor and the Legislature. DAS sets and monitors standards of accountability, ensuring that tax dollars are used productively. DAS supports state agencies by providing a strong and stable management infrastructure.

Chief Operating Officer, Office of the

Address: 155 Cottage St. NE, U20, Salem 97301-3965
Phone: 503-378-3104
Fax: 503-373-7643
Web: www.oregon.gov/COO
Contact: Michael Jordan, Chief Operating Officer
Duties and Responsibilities: The Office of the Chief Operating Officer (COO) manages statewide initiatives designed to improve state government's efficiency and effectiveness. These initiatives include the 10-Year Plan for Oregon, County Payments, and Regulatory Streamlining. COO staff also provides support to the Enterprise Leadership Team.

Chief Financial Office

Address: 155 Cottage St. NE, U10, Salem 97301-3965
Phone: 503-378-3106
Fax: 503-373-7643
E-mail: CFO.info@das.state.or.us
Web: www.oregon.gov/DAS/CFO
Contact: George Naughton, Administrator
Statutory Authority: ORS 184.335
Duties and Responsibilities: The Chief Financial Office prepares the Governor's Recommended Budget and monitors the development and execution of state agency budgets. The office provides management review services, issues Certificates of Participation to finance capital construction and infrastructure, helps agencies manage about three million acres of public lands and coordinates the state's bonded debt process. The Chief Financial Office also manages the financial system infrastructure for state government, which includes accounting, payroll and financial reporting.

Chief Human Resource Office

Address: 155 Cottage St. NE, U30, Salem 97301-3967
Phone: 503-378-8344
Fax: 503-373-7684
Web: www.oregon.gov/DAS/CHRO
Contact: Clyde Saiki, Interim Administrator
Statutory Authority: ORS 240.055
Duties and Responsibilities: The Chief Human Resource Office is responsible for statewide human resource systems, policies and initiatives; establishes and maintains classification and compensation plans; administers and maintains the central state employee database; and performs PERS reconciliation for all state agencies.

Chief Information Office

Address: 955 Center St. NE, Rm. 470, Salem 97301
Phone: 503-378-3175
Fax: 503-378-3795
Web: www.oregon.gov/DAS/CIO
Contact: Julie Pearson-Ruthven, Interim State Chief Information Officer
Statutory Authority: ORS 182.122, 184.305, 184.475, 184.477, 291.038
Duties and Responsibilities: The Chief Information Office is Oregon's enterprise information technology (IT) strategic planning and policy leader and is responsible for development of enterprise technology architecture and standards. Programs include Oregon E-Government, Enterprise Security, Geospatial Information Systems (GIS) and IT Investment and Planning.

DAS Business Services

Address: 155 Cottage St. NE, U90, Salem 97301-3972
Phone: 503-378-2350, ext. 287
Fax: 503-378-2349
E-mail: donna.haole-valenzuela@state.or.us
Web: www.oregon.gov/DAS/OP
Contact: Donna Haole-Valenzuela, Interim Administrator
Duties and Responsibilities: DAS Business Services provides administrative and operational support to the divisions of the Department of Administrative Services as well as to the Office of the Governor and select commissions and agencies. Functional areas within DAS Business Services are accounting, budgeting, contracts, payroll and employee services, application support and LAN/desktop services.

Enterprise Asset Management

Address: 1225 Ferry St. SE, U100, Salem 97301-4281
Phone: 503-378-2865
Fax: 503-373-7210
E-mail: fac.info@state.or.us
Web: www.oregon.gov/DAS/EAM
Contact: Jeanette Fish, Administrator
Statutory Authority: ORS Chapter 276
Duties and Responsibilities: Enterprise Asset Management acquires and maintains space for state agencies. It provides property management, real property transaction services (buy, sell and lease), project management, space planning, real property sales, building operations and maintenance and landscape maintenance to state agencies. It manages parking and commuter programs for state employees in Salem and Portland.

Enterprise Goods and Services

Address: 1225 Ferry St. SE, Salem 97310
Phone: 503-378-4642
Fax: 503-373-1626
E-mail: ssd.info@state.or.us
Web: www.oregon.gov/DAS/EGS
Contact: Bret West, Administrator
Statutory Authority: ORS 184.305, ORS Chapters 278, 279, 282, 283
Duties and Responsibilities: Enterprise Goods and Services oversees Risk Management, Procurement, Surplus Property, Publishing and Distribution and Statewide Fleet. Risk Management provides risk management advice, coverage, claims management and insurance purchasing for state agencies. Procurement provides statewide buying and procurement services and administers state purchasing and contracting rules. Surplus Property reutilizes and sells surplus government property. Publishing and Distribution provides printing, mail processing and inter-agency delivery services. Statewide Fleet provides statewide fleet management and operates a motor pool in Salem.

Enterprise Human Resource Services

Address: 155 Cottage St. NE, U30, Salem 97301
Phone: 503-378-3622
Web: www.oregon.gov/DAS/EHRS
Contact: Mark Rasmussen, Administrator
Duties and Responsibilities: Enterprise Human Resource Services offers DAS and client agencies a variety of human resource-related services, including human resource consultation, recruitment and position management, and it oversees state government's personnel-related computer systems and databases.

Enterprise Technology Services

Phone: 503-378-2176; Service Desk: 503-373-1000
Fax: 503-378-2736
E-mail: ets.info@state.or.us
Web: www.oregon.gov/DAS/ETS
Contact: Julie Bozzi, Administrator
Statutory Authority: ORS 184.305, ORS Chapters 278, 279
Duties and Responsibilities: Enterprise Technology Services is a 24-hour, seven days a week operation that provides shared information technology infrastructure services to thousands of state and local government programs.

Other Entities:

Economic Analysis, Office of

Address: 155 Cottage St. NE, U20, Salem 97301-3966
Phone: 503-378-3405
Fax: 503-373-7643
E-mail: OEA.info@das.state.or.us
Web: www.oregon.gov/DAS/OEA
Contact: Mark McMullen, State Economist
Duties and Responsibilities: The Office of Economic Analysis prepares state economic and revenue forecasts and the long-term population and employment forecasts. The office assesses long-term economic and demographic trends, evaluates their implications and conducts special economic and demographic studies. The office also prepares state criminal and juvenile population forecasts and manages the Highway Cost Allocation Study.

Governor's Council of Economic Advisors

Address: 155 Cottage St. NE, U20, Salem 97301-3966
Phone: 503-378-3405
Fax: 503-373-7643
Contact: Joseph Cortright, Chair

Public Lands Advisory Committee

Address: 1225 Ferry St. SE, U100, Salem 97301-4281
Phone: 503-373-7063
Fax: 503-373-7210
Web: www.oregon.gov/DAS/CFO/Pages/PLAC.aspx
Contact: Tom Byler, Chair
Statutory Authority: ORS 270.120, 270.100(1)(d)
Duties and Responsibilities: The Public Lands Advisory Committee's primary role is to advise the Department of Administrative Services on all real property acquisitions, exchanges or terminal dispositions valued at $100,000 or more for which the department must give its consent.

Public Officials Compensation Commission

Address: 155 Cottage St. NE, U30, Salem 97301-3967
Phone: 503-378-8344
Fax: 503-373-7684
Statutory Authority: ORS 292.907

Advocacy Commissions Office, Oregon

Address: 1515 SW 5th Ave., Suite 1050-S, Portland 97201; Mail: 1819 SW Fifth Ave., #313, Portland 97201
Phone: 503-302-9725
Fax: 503-473-8519
E-mail: OACO.mail@state.or.us
Web: www.oregon.gov/OAC
Contact: Lucy Baker, Administrator
Statutory Authority: ORS 185.005
Duties and Responsibilities: The Oregon Advocacy Commissions Office (OACO) was created in 2005 to support Oregon's Commission on Asian and Pacific Islander Affairs, Commission on Black Affairs, Commission on Hispanic Affairs and the Commission for Women.

In that role, OACO supports each commission's work advising the governor, Legislature and departmental leadership on policies affecting communities of color and women; growing leadership from their communities within government; and building success for Asian Pacific, Black and Hispanic Oregonians and for women in Oregon.

Asian and Pacific Islander Affairs, Commission on

Address: 1515 SW 5th Ave., Suite 1050-S, Portland 97201; Mail: 1819 SW Fifth Ave., #313, Portland 97201
Phone: 503-302-9725
Fax: 503-473-8519
E-mail: OACO.mail@state.or.us
Web: www.oregon.gov/OCAPIA
Contact: OACO Office
Statutory Authority: ORS 185.610, 185.620
Duties and Responsibilities: The Oregon Commission on Asian and Pacific Islander Affairs (OCAPIA) was established in 1995 and originally had trade and economic development focus. The 1999 Legislature amended the commission's function to place a greater emphasis on advocacy.

The goal of OCAPIA is to facilitate communication and dissemination of information between state government and Asian and Pacific Islander communities. This not only benefits Oregon's Asian and Pacific Islander Americans, but also provides the state with information on how to best provide services to all its citizens. Volunteers who are already leaders in their communities aid the commission with their knowledge and relationships.

The commission is composed of 11 members, nine of whom are appointed by the governor and confirmed by the Senate to serve three-year terms. The president of the Senate and the speaker of the House each appoint a member to serve a two-year term. The commission strives for ethnic as well as geographic diversity in its appointments.

Black Affairs, Commission on

Address: 1515 SW 5th Ave., Suite 1050-S, Portland 97201; Mail: 1819 SW Fifth Ave., #313, Portland 97201
Phone: 503-302-9725
Fax: 503-473-8519
Web: www.oregon.gov/OCBA
E-mail: OACO.mail@state.or.us
Contact: OACO Office
Statutory Authority: ORS 185.410, 185.420
Duties and Responsibilities: The Commission on Black Affairs works for the implementation of economic, social, legal and political equality for Oregon's African American and Black populations.

The commission is authorized by law to monitor existing programs and legislation designed to meet the needs of the African American and Black community, identify and research concerns and issues affecting the community in order to recommend actions and programs to the governor and the Legislature, act as a liaison between the community and Oregon's government, encourage African American and Black representation on state boards and commissions, and establish special committees as needed.

The commission is composed of 11 members, nine of whom are appointed by the governor and confirmed by the Senate to serve three-year terms. The president of the Senate and the speaker of the House each appoint a member to serve a two-year term. The commission strives for ethnic as well as geographic diversity in its appointments.

Hispanic Affairs, Commission on

Address: 1515 SW 5th Ave., Suite 1050-S, Portland 97201; Mail: 1819 SW Fifth Ave., #313, Portland 97201
Phone: 503-302-9725
Fax: 503-473-8519
E-mail: OACO.mail@state.or.us
Web: www.oregon.gov/Hispanic
Contact: Andrea Cano, Chair
Statutory Authority: ORS 185.310, 185.320
Duties and Responsibilities: The Oregon Commission on Hispanic Affairs (OCHA) was created by the 1983 Legislature to work for economic, social, legal and political equality for Hispanics in Oregon. The commission monitors existing pro-

grams and legislation to ensure that the needs of Hispanics are met. The commission researches problems and issues and recommends appropriate action, maintains a liaison between the Hispanic community and government entities and encourages Hispanic representation on state boards and commissions.

In addition, the commission focuses on and responds to the wider statewide context of equity and social well being, identifies and seeks solutions to disparities in services and programs for the ethnically diverse Hispanic/Latino/Indigenous community, and encourages good public policy development. In networking numerous Hispanic community, civic, cultural/ethnic and professional organizations, OCHA also promotes civic engagement, economic development and ongoing mentoring for the next generation of leaders.

The commission is composed of 11 members, nine of whom are appointed by the governor and confirmed by the Senate to serve three-year terms. The president of the Senate and the speaker of the House each appoint a member to serve a two-year term. The commission strives for ethnic as well as geographic diversity in its appointments.

Women, Commission for

Address: 1515 SW 5th Ave., Suite 1050-S, Portland 97201; Mail: 1819 SW Fifth Ave., #313, Portland 97201
Phone: 503-302-9725
Fax: 503-473-8519
E-mail: OACO.mail@state.or.us
Web: www.oregon.gov/Women
Contact: OACO Office
Statutory Authority: ORS 185.510–185.570
Duties and Responsibilities: In 1964, Governor Mark Hatfield established the Governor's Commission on the Status of Women to advise him of the needs and concerns of Oregon women. In 1983, the commission gained independent status as the Commission for Women, with a directive to strive for women's equality through the implementation of beneficial programs and policies. The commission continues this work by advocating for women in the community, providing information on women to the governor and Legislature, serving as a link for women to state agencies and providing services to individual women in Oregon.

The commission is composed of 11 members, nine of whom are appointed by the governor and confirmed by the Senate to serve three-year terms. The president of the Senate and the speaker of the House each appoint a member to serve a two-year term. The commission strives for ethnic as well as geographic diversity in its appointments. It also presents awards annually to honor Oregon's outstanding women.

Agriculture, Department of

Address: 635 Capitol St. NE, Salem 97301-2532
Phone: 503-986-4550
Fax: 503-986-4750
E-mail: info@oda.state.or.us
Web: www.oregon.gov/ODA
Contact: Katy Coba, Director
Statutory Authority: ORS Chapter 576
Duties and Responsibilities: The Oregon Department of Agriculture was created in 1931 to provide leadership, service and regulatory functions for food production and processing. Its mission has been expanded to provide food safety and consumer protection at all levels of production and marketing, to protect the agricultural resource base, and to promote economic development and marketing for agriculture and food products. The governor appoints the department director. A 10-member State Board of Agriculture, also appointed by the governor, advises the director. The department is divided into five major program areas that oversee 36 chapters of Oregon laws.

More information on individual programs and advisory groups can be found at the Web site listed above.

Food and Animal Health Program Area

Contact: Vance Bybee, Director
E-mail: vbybee@oda.state.or.us

Food Safety Program

Phone: 503-986-4720
Duties and Responsibilities: The Food Safety Program's team of field inspectors and staff license and inspect all facets of the food distribution system, except restaurants, to assure consumers that food is safe for consumption.

Animal Health Program (State Veterinarian)

Phone: 503-986-4680
Duties and Responsibilities: The major goal of the Animal Health Program is to enhance economic production of livestock by controlling and eradicating animal diseases, including those transmissible to humans, and to ensure animal feeds meet nutritional and labeling standards.

Livestock Identification Program (Brands)

Phone: 503-986-4681
Duties and Responsibilities: The Livestock Identification Program's goal is to prevent livestock theft by denying a market for stolen animals through recording of brands and inspection of animals.

Executive

Internal Services and Consumer Protection Program Area

Contact: Jason Barber, Director
E-mail: jbarber@ oda.state.or.us

Measurement Standards Program

Phone: 503-986-4670
Duties and Responsibilities: The Measurement Standards Program assures consumers of accurate weight and measure of food and non-food products, services and commodities purchased in Oregon. The program also provides official mass, volume and length standards calibration and ensures motor fuel quality standards.

Laboratory Services

Phone: 503-872-6644
Duties and Responsibilities: The Laboratory Services section, located in the Food Innovation Center in Portland, provides analysis for food and dairy samples, animal feeds, fertilizer and water. The laboratory also certifies food for export.

Natural Resources Program Area

Contact: Ray Jaindl, Director
E-mail: rjaindl@oda.state.or.us

Natural Resources Programs

Phone: 503-986-4700
Duties and Responsibilities: The Natural Resources Programs work to conserve, protect and develop natural resources on public and private lands so agriculture will continue to be productive and economically viable in Oregon. Primary program areas include: water quality, confined animal feeding operations, smoke management, land use, Soil and Water Conservation Districts and plant conservation biology.

Pesticides Program

Phone: 503-986-4635
Duties and Responsibilities: The Pesticides Program seeks to protect people and the environment from adverse effects of pesticide use while maintaining the availability of pesticides for beneficial uses. The division regulates the sale and use of pesticides, provides testing and licensing of all users of restricted-use pesticides, is responsible for fertilizer registration and investigates incidents of pesticide misuse.

Plant Program Area

Contact: Dan Hilburn, Director
E-mail: dhilburn@oda.state.or.us
Phone: 503-986-4636
Duties and Responsibilities: The Plant Programs work to exclude, detect and control or eradicate serious insect pests and plant diseases; to enhance the agricultural value of nursery stock, Christmas trees, seeds and other agricultural products for export through pest and disease inspection and certification; and to oversee statewide noxious weed control efforts.

Market Access and Certification Program Area

Contact: Jim Cramer, Director
E-mail: jcramer@oda.state.or.us

Agricultural Marketing and Development Program

Address: 1207 NW Naito Pkwy., Suite 104, Portland 97209-2832
Phone: 503-872-6600
Duties and Responsibilities: The Agricultural Development and Marketing Program, located in the Food Innovation Center in Portland, works to foster a sustainable, profitable agricultural economy in Oregon through business and market development. The program helps Oregon companies expand markets for value-added food and agricultural products, works to create jobs through expanding value-added agricultural businesses and oversees the state's 23 commodity commissions.

Commodity Inspection Program

Phone: 503-986-4620
Duties and Responsibilities: The Commodity Inspection Program provides services to ensure that Oregon commodities meet or exceed the quality requirements of the marketplace. Quality assurance is provided to Oregon producers, packers and shippers through official sampling, grading, inspection and verification. The program also offers voluntary certification services.

State Board of Agriculture

Address: 635 Capitol St. NE, Salem 97301-2532
Phone: 503-986-4619
Fax: 503-986-4750
Contact: Sherry Kudna, Assistant to the Board
Statutory Authority: ORS Chapter 561
Duties and Responsibilities: The State Board of Agriculture advises the director of the Oregon Department of Agriculture and assists in determining policies. Ten members and two ex officio members are appointed to four-year terms by the governor. Two members must be public members. No more than five members may be from one political party.

Agricultural Commodity Commissions

Most commodity commissions conduct promotional, educational, production and market research projects. The commissions are authorized by ORS chapters 576, 577 and 578. They are funded by assessments on the producers of the commodities. The director of the Oregon Department of Agriculture appoints the members of all 23 commissions.

Albacore Commission

Address: PO Box 983, Lincoln City 97367
Phone/Fax: 541-994-2647
Web: www.oregonalbacore.org
Contact: Nancy Fitzpatrick, Administrator

Alfalfa Seed Commission

Address: PO Box 688, Ontario 97914-0688
Phone: 541-881-1335
E-mail: duanekressly@hotmail.com
Contact: Edith Kressly, Administrator

Beef Council

Address: 1827 NE 44th Ave., Portland 97213
Phone: 503-274-2333
Web: www.orbeef.org
Contact: Will Wise, Administrator

Blueberry Commission

Address: PO Box 3366, Salem 97302-0366
Phone: 503-364-2944
Web: www.oregonblueberry.com
Contact: Bryan Ostlund, Administrator

Clover Commission

Address: PO Box 2042, Salem 97308-2042
Phone: 503-370-7019
Web: www.oregonclover.org
Contact: John McCulley, Administrator

Dairy Products Commission

Address: 10505 SW Barbur Blvd., Portland 97219
Phone: 503-229-5033
Web: www.dairyfarmersor.com
Contact: Pete Kent, Executive Director

Dungeness Crab Commission

Address: PO Box 1160, Coos Bay 97420
Phone: 541-267-5810
Web: www.oregondungeness.org
Contact: Hugh Link, Interim Executive Director

Fine Fescue Commission

Address: PO Box 3366, Salem 97302-0366
Phone: 503-364-2944
Web: www.oregonfinefescue.org
Contact: Bryan Ostlund, Administrator

Hazelnut Commission

Address: 21595-A Dolores Way NE, Aurora 97002-9738
Phone: 503-678-6823
Web: www.oregonhazelnuts.org
Contact: Polly Owen, Administrator

Hop Commission

Address: PO Box 298, Hubbard 97032
Phone: 503-982-7600
Web: www.oregonhops.org
Contact: Nancy Frketich, Administrator

Mint Commission

Address: PO Box 3366, Salem 97302-0366
Phone: 503-364-2944
Fax: 503-581-6819
Contact: Bryan Ostlund, Administrator

Orchardgrass Seed Producers Commission

Address: PO Box 2042, Salem 97308-2042
Phone: 503-370-7019
Web: www.orchardgrass.org
Contact: John McCulley, Administrator

Potato Commission

Address: 9320 SW Barbur Blvd., Suite 130 Portland 97219-5405
Phone: 503-239-4763
Web: www.oregonspuds.com
Contact: Bill Brewer, Administrator

Processed Vegetable Commission

Address: PO Box 2042, Salem 97308-2042
Phone: 503-370-7019
Fax: 503-587-8063
Contact: John McCulley, Administrator

Raspberry and Blackberry Commission

Address: 4845 B SW Dresden Ave., Corvallis 97333-3915
Phone: 541-758-4043
Web: www.oregon-berries.com
Contact: Philip Gütt, Administrator

Ryegrass Growers Seed Commission

Address: PO Box 3366, Salem 97302-0366
Phone: 503-364-2944
Web: www.ryegrass.com
Contact: Bryan Ostlund, Administrator

Salmon Commission

Address: PO Box 983, Lincoln City 97367-0983
Phone/Fax: 541-994-2647
Web: http://oregonsalmon.org
Contact: Nancy Fitzpatrick, Administrator

Sheep Commission

Address: 1270 Chemeketa St. NE, Salem 97301
Phone: 503-364-5462
Fax: 503-585-1921
Contact: Richard Kosesan, Administrator

Strawberry Commission

Address: 4845 B SW Dresden Ave., Corvallis 97333-3915
Phone: 541-758-4043
Web: www.oregon-strawberries.org
Contact: Philip Gütt, Administrator

Sweet Cherry Commission

Address: 2667 Reed Rd., Hood River 97031-9609
Phone: 541-386-5761
Web: www.nwcherries.com
Contact: Dana Branson, Administrator

Tall Fescue Commission

Address: PO Box 3366, Salem 97302-0366
Phone: 503-364-2944
Web: www.oregontallfescue.org
Contact: Bryan Ostlund, Administrator

Trawl Commission

Address: 16289 Hwy. 101 S, Suite C, Brookings 97415
Phone: 541-469-7830
Web: www.ortrawl.org
Contact: Brad Pettinger, Administrator

Wheat Commission

Address: 1200 NW Naito Pkwy., Suite 370, Portland 97209
Phone: 503-467-2161
Web: www.owgl.org
Contact: Blake Rowe, Administrator

Appraiser Certification and Licensure Board

Address: 3000 Market St. NE, Suite 541, Salem 97301
Phone: 503-485-2555
Fax: 503-485-2559
E-mail: bob@oregonaclb.org
Web: http://oregonaclb.org
Contact: Bob Keith, Administrator
Statutory Authority: ORS Chapter 674
Duties and Responsibilities: The Appraiser Certification and Licensure Board (ACLB) is a semi-independent agency that licenses and certifies real estate appraisers in Oregon and develops and establishes appraisal education and experience requirements in accordance with state and federal laws, standards and guidelines. The board also registers and regulates appraisal management companies.

The board was created in 1991. Its regulatory functions are independent of other realty-related regulatory agencies. The ACLB consists of eight members appointed by the governor. Five of these are appraisers, one represents the perspectives of appraisal management companies, one is from the banking industry and one is a member of the public.

Architect Examiners, Board of

Address: 205 Liberty St. NE, Suite A, Salem 97301
Phone: 503-763-0662
Fax: 503-364-0510
E-mail: architectboard@orbae.com
Web: www.orbae.com
Contact: Jim Denno, Administrator
Statutory Authority: ORS 671.010–671.220
Duties and Responsibilities: The Oregon Board of Architect Examiners (OBAE) was established in 1919 and consists of seven members appointed by the governor. Five members are resident architects and two members represent the general public. The main objective of the board is to safeguard the health, safety and welfare of the public through licensing and registration and to ensure Oregon's citizens receive continued competent architectural services. The board ensures that only competent persons and firms are permitted to practice architecture in Oregon and that all practicing architects follow professional standards of conduct set by the board. The board establishes qualifications and examines architects who want to practice in Oregon, registers architectural firms, investigates complaints and alleged violations of the Architectural Practice Act, and is authorized to deny, suspend or revoke registrations and to assess civil penalties.

The OBAE is a semi-independent, self-supporting agency that receives the majority of its revenue from application, registration and renewal fees. The board currently has 2,901 individual architects and 661 architectural firms registered as active in Oregon.

Aviation, Oregon Department of

Address: 3040 25th St. SE, Salem 97302-1125
Phone: 503-378-4880
Fax: 503-373-1688
E-mail: aviation.mail@state.or.us
Web: www.oregon.gov/Aviation
Contact: Mitch Swecker, Director
Statutory Authority: ORS 835.100

Duties and Responsibilities: Established in 1999, the Oregon Department of Aviation works to develop aviation as an integral part of Oregon's transportation network, creating strategies to protect and improve Oregon's aviation system, encouraging aviation related economic development, supporting aviation safety and education and increasing commercial air service and general aviation in Oregon.

The department owns and operates 28 Oregon airports and annually licenses or registers more than 450 public or private airports, heliports and landing areas. It also registers pilots and non-military aircraft based in Oregon, oversees statewide aviation system planning and helps with community airport planning, administers a pavement maintenance program for airports around the state, administers the Statewide Capital Improvements Grant Program in coordination with the Federal Aviation Administration and airport owners/sponsors for 55 federally funded airports, and conducts aviation safety and public education programs.

State Aviation Board

The seven-member State Aviation Board, appointed by the governor, works through the Oregon Department of Aviation to develop airports, state airways, aviation industry and general aviation issues and interests in Oregon. The board provides direction and oversight to the department. Members are appointed with consideration given to geographic divisions within Oregon.

Blind, Commission for the

Address: 535 SE 12th, Portland 97214
Phone: 971-673-1588, Toll-free: 1-888-202-5463; TTY: 971-673-1577
Fax: 503-234-7468
E-mail: ocb.mail@state.or.us
Web: www.oregon.gov/blind
Contact: Linda Mock, Administrator
Statutory Authority: ORS 346.110–346.270
Duties and Responsibilities: Through a state-federal partnership under the Rehabilitation Act, the Commission for the Blind assists blind Oregonians toward full inclusion in society. The commission provides a wide range of individualized services to legally blind Oregonians so that they may prepare for and secure employment. The commission also provides training for blind citizens to maximize their ability to live independently in their homes and communities.

Business Development Department, Oregon

Address: 755 Summer St. NE, Suite 200, Salem 97301-1280
Phone: 503-986-0123; TTY: 1-800-735-2900
Fax: 503-581-5115
Web: www.oregon4biz.com
Contact: Tim McCabe, Director
Statutory Authority: ORS 285A.070
Duties and Responsibilities: The Oregon Business Development Department (Business Oregon) develops and implements Oregon's economic development policy and strategy. The mission of Business Oregon is to create, retain, expand and attract businesses that provide sustainable, family-wage jobs for Oregonians through public-private partnerships, leveraged funding and support of economic opportunities for Oregon companies and entrepreneurs. Business Oregon includes the Infrastructure Finance Authority, where staff and programs assist communities in building infrastructure capacity and community facilities to address public health, safety and compliance issues necessary to improve the quality of life for Oregonians.

The nine-member Oregon Business Development Commission consists of seven members appointed by the governor and confirmed by the Senate plus two members who are non-voting, ex officio members, one appointed by the president of the Senate and one by the speaker of the House. The commission established a framework, intended to work in concert with the Oregon Business Plan, for Business Oregon to further job and wage growth throughout the state. The Infrastructure Finance Authority Board is a nine-member independent board with oversight of the Infrastructure Finance Authority and the state's infrastructure activities. Six board members are appointed by the governor; three are a direct appointment by the treasurer, speaker of the House and president of the Senate.

The department works closely with state and federal agencies, non-profit groups, businesses, industry groups, cities, counties, local economic development districts, ports and others to create opportunities and address challenges pertaining to economic development. Business Oregon also helps communities meet needs and standards for clean water, wastewater disposal and other public facilities; develop telecommunications infrastructure, particularly in rural Oregon; and support community-identified economic development projects. Business Oregon has nine business development officers located throughout the state where they serve as key contacts for accessing department services:

Baker/Grant/Malheur/Morrow/Umatilla/Union/Wallowa: 503-508-3147
Benton/Linn/Lane: 541-346-8620
Clackamas/Washington: 503-229-5117
Clatsop/Columbia/Lincoln/Tillamook: 503-791-2732
Coos/Curry/Douglas: 541-267-4651
Crook/Deschutes/Gilliam/Jefferson/Sherman/Wheeler: 541-322-2036

Executive

Harney/Jackson/Josephine/Klamath/Lake: 541-882-1340

Hood River/Multnomah/Wasco: 503-229-5115

Marion/Polk/Yamhill: 503-837-1808

Business Oregon also provides administrative support to the Oregon Arts Commission and distributes funds to the semi-privatized Film and Video Office.

Arts Commission

Address: 775 Summer St. NE, Suite 200, Salem 97301-1280
Phone: 503-986-0082
Fax: 503-986-0260
E-mail: Oregon.artscomm@state.or.us
Web: www.oregonartscommission.org
Contact: Christine D'Arcy, Executive Director
Statutory Authority: ORS 359.020
Duties and Responsibilities: The Oregon Arts Commission provides leadership, funding and arts programs through grants, special initiatives and services to arts organizations, artists and communities. Commission staff helps build local ability to improve community involvement in the arts and annually undertakes specific projects serving Oregon's cultural community. Nine commissioners, appointed by the governor, determine the needs for the state and establish policies for public support of the arts.

Cultural Trust

Address: 775 Summer St. NE, Suite 200, Salem 97301-1280
Phone: 503-986-0088
Fax: 503-986-0260
E-mail: cultural.trust@state.or.us
Web: www.culturaltrust.org
Contact: Christine D'Arcy, Executive Director
Statutory Authority: ORS 359.020
Duties and Responsibilities: The Cultural Trust is a statewide initiative that raises significant new public and private funds to invest in Oregon's arts, humanities and heritage. In addition to the creation of a long-term, protected endowment, Trust funds are distributed annually through competitive grants to cultural organizations, grants to cultural coalitions in Oregon counties and within federally recognized tribes, and grants to statewide cultural agencies. Oregonians who contribute to the Cultural Trust are eligible for an innovative tax credit.

The Trust works in partnership with the Oregon Arts Commission, Oregon Heritage Commission, Oregon Historical Society, Oregon Humanities and State Historic Preservation Office. The Cultural Trust is governed by a 13-member board, with 11 citizen voting members appointed by the governor and approved by the Senate. There are two non-voting members, one appointed by the speaker of the House and the other by the president of the Senate.

Chiropractic Examiners, Board of

Address: 3218 Pringle Rd. SE, Suite 150, Salem 97302-6311
Phone: 503-378-5816
Fax: 503-362-1260
E-mail: oregon.obce@state.or.us
Web: www.oregon.gov/OBCE
Contact: Dave McTeague, Executive Director
Statutory Authority: ORS Chapter 684
Duties and Responsibilities: The Oregon Board of Chiropractic Examiners (OBCE) was created in 1915 and is responsible for administering the Chiropractic Practice Act and establishing the rules and regulations governing the practice of chiropractic in Oregon. The seven-member board is composed of five chiropractic physicians and two public members who are appointed by the governor to three-year terms.

The OBCE regulates chiropractic practice, promotes quality and ensures competent ethical health care. As of July 2012, the board licenses 1,508 active and 323 inactive chiropractic physicians and 1,391 certified chiropractic assistants. The board's programs include application, examination, continuing education, public information and investigation of complaints. If violations are found, the board issues disciplinary actions and/or rehabilitation plans to meet competency standards.

Columbia River Gorge Commission

Address: PO Box 730, White Salmon, WA 98672
Phone: 509-493-3323
Fax: 509-493-2229
E-mail: info@gorgecommission.org
Web: www.gorgecommission.org
Contact: Nancy Andring, Administrative Assistant
Statutory Authority: ORS 196.150
Duties and Responsibilities: The Columbia River Gorge Commission was established by a bi-state compact between the states of Oregon and Washington in 1987. The commission was created in response to federal legislation that established the 300,000-acre Columbia River Gorge National Scenic Area in 1986. The purposes of the legislation are to protect and provide for the enhancement of the scenic, natural, cultural and recreational resources of the Columbia River Gorge and to protect and support the area's economy by encouraging growth within existing areas and allowing future economic development elsewhere when consistent with the area's important resources.

The commission works in partnership with the U.S. Forest Service, six counties and four tribes to implement a regional management plan.

Community Colleges and Workforce Development, Department of

Address: Public Service Bldg., 255 Capitol St. NE, 3rd Floor, Salem 97310-0001
Phone: 503-378-8648
Fax: 503-378-8434
E-mail: ccwd.info@odccwd.state.or.us
Web: www.oregon.gov/CCWD
Contact: Camille Preus, Commissioner
Statutory Authority: ORS 326.051
Duties and Responsibilities: The Oregon Department of Community Colleges and Workforce Development, with local education and workforce partners, manages state, federal and other funds (including lottery) supporting Oregon's community colleges, workforce development programs, WorkSource Oregon one-stop career centers, Adult Basic Skills Programs, English as a Second Language programs and the Oregon Youth Conservation Corps.

Oregon has 17 independent community colleges and seven Local Workforce Investment Areas. The Workforce Investment Act of 1998 reformed federal job training programs and created a new, comprehensive workforce investment system to help Americans access the tools they need to manage their careers through information and services and to help companies find skilled workers.

Construction Contractors Board

Address: 700 Summer St. NE, Suite 300, PO Box 14140, Salem 97309-5052
Phone: 503-378-4621
Fax: 503-373-2007
E-mail: craig.p.smith@state.or.us
Web: www.oregon.gov/CCB
Contact: Craig P. Smith, Administrator
Statutory Authority: ORS 701.205
Duties and Responsibilities: The Construction Contractors Board (CCB) was created in 1971 and was originally called the Builders Board. The agency licenses and regulates construction contractors, and educates contractors and homeowners on best practices for preventing and resolving construction contracting problems.

The board administers the Oregon Construction Contractors Licensing Act that provides for the licensing of all residential and commercial construction contractors and subcontractors, the investigating and mediating of complaints filed against licensees and the assessing of civil penalties against contractors who are not licensed or who violate laws.

The board tests applicants on the *Oregon Contractors Reference Manual* which includes information on construction laws and business practices. The board also tests and certifies home inspectors and locksmiths. The agency oversees and monitors the continuing education program and develops residential continuing education courses. The board issues licenses for Lead-Based Paint Activities and CCB Certified Lead-Based Paint Renovation contractors and certifies Energy Efficiency and Sustainable Technology contractors.

The board engages in outreach activities aimed at educating homeowners on steps they can take to have a successful construction project and providing information designed to reinforce the agency's key consumer protection messages.

Consumer and Business Services, Department of

Address: 350 Winter St. NE, Salem 97301-3878; PO Box 14480, Salem 97309-0405
Phone: 503-378-4100
Fax: 503-378-6444
E-mail: dcbs.info@state.or.us
Web: www.oregon.gov/DCBS
Contact: Patrick Allen, Director
Statutory Authority: ORS 705.010–705.350
Duties and Responsibilities: The Department of Consumer and Business Services (DCBS) is Oregon's largest business regulatory and consumer protection agency. The department administers state laws and rules in the areas of workers' compensation, occupational safety and health, financial services, insurance, and building codes.

DCBS consists of the Workers' Compensation Division, Oregon Occupational Safety and Health Division, Division of Finance and Corporate Securities, Insurance Division, Building Codes Division and a number of other programs and offices that assist consumers, workers and businesses. These include the Senior Health Insurance Benefits Assistance program, Small Business Ombudsman for Workers' Compensation and Ombudsman for Injured Workers. The department also includes the Workers' Compensation Board. The director of the department is appointed by the governor.

Building Codes Division

Address: 1535 Edgewater St. NW, PO Box 14470, Salem 97309-0404
Phone: 503-378-4133
Fax: 503-378-2322

Executive

Web: www.bcd.oregon.gov
Contact: Mark Long, Administrator
Statutory Authority: ORS Chapters 446, 447, 455, 460, 479, 480, 693
Duties and Responsibilities: The Building Codes Division adopts and enforces a uniform statewide building code relating to construction, reconstruction, alteration and repair of structures, and installation of mechanical, plumbing and electrical devices and equipment. The division certifies inspectors and licenses trade professionals; provides code and rule interpretation and dispute resolution; enforces license, code and permit requirements; and conducts inspections where local entities do not.

The division includes the following seven boards.

Boiler Rules, Board of

Address: PO Box 14470, Salem 97309-0404
Phone: 503-378-4133
Web: www.bcd.oregon.gov/boards.html
Contact: Policy and Technical Services Section Manager
Statutory Authority: ORS 480.535, 705.250
Duties and Responsibilities: The Board of Boiler Rules assists in adopting, amending and enforcing rules, certifications and minimum safety standards for boilers, pressure vessels and pressure piping; approves related division fees and training programs; hears code appeals; approves suspensions or revocations of boiler licenses; and makes scientific and technical findings related to alternate method rulings. The governor appoints the board's 11 members to four-year terms, subject to Senate confirmation.

Building Codes Structures Board

Address: PO Box 14470, Salem 97309-0404
Phone: 503-378-4133
Web: www.bcd.oregon.gov/boards.html
Contact: Policy and Technical Services Section Manager
Statutory Authority: ORS 455.132, 455.144, 705.250
Duties and Responsibilities: The Building Codes Structures Board assists in the administration of commercial structural, prefabricated structure and energy programs, as well as programs which promote accessibility for persons with physical disabilities. The board hears code appeals and makes scientific and technical findings related to alternate method rulings. The governor appoints the board's nine members to four-year terms, subject to Senate confirmation.

Construction Industry Energy Board

Address: PO Box 14470, Salem 97309-0404
Phone: 503-378-4133
Web: www.bcd.oregon.gov/boards.html
Contact: Policy and Technical Services Section Manager
Statutory Authority: ORS 455.492, 705.250
Duties and Responsibilities: The Construction Industry Energy Board may evaluate and recommend or disapprove proposed state building code standards relating to the energy use and energy efficiency aspects of the electrical, structural, prefabricated structure and low-rise residential specialty codes. The proposed standards evaluated by the board may include, but are not limited to, standards regarding energy-conserving technology, construction methods, products and materials. The board forwards any recommended standards to the director of the DCBS for adoption or rejection by the director. The board has seven members.

Electrical and Elevator Board

Address: PO Box 14470, Salem 97309-0404
Phone: 503-378-4133
Web: www.bcd.oregon.gov/boards.html
Contact: Policy and Technical Services Section Manager
Statutory Authority: ORS 455.138, 455.144, 479.680, 705.250
Duties and Responsibilities: The Electrical and Elevator Board assists in administering the state's electrical safety law and advises and approves electrical rules and codes, as well as revocations or suspensions of electrical licenses. The board advises on rules governing elevator safety and hears appeals. The board also approves related division fees and training programs, and makes scientific and technical findings related to alternate method rulings. The governor appoints the board's 15 members, subject to Senate confirmation.

Mechanical Board

Address: PO Box 14470, Salem 97309-0404
Phone: 503-378-4133
Web: www.bcd.oregon.gov/boards.html
Contact: Policy and Technical Services Section Manager
Statutory Authority: ORS 455.140, 705.250
Duties and Responsibilities: The Mechanical Board assists in adopting and administering the state's mechanical code. The board advises on rules governing the mechanical code and approves related division fees and training programs, hears code appeals, and makes scientific and technical findings related to alternate method rulings. The governor appoints the board's nine members, subject to Senate confirmation.

Plumbing Board, State

Address: PO Box 14470, Salem 97309-0404
Phone: 503-378-4133
Web: www.bcd.oregon.gov/boards.html

Contact: Policy and Technical Services Section Manager
Statutory Authority: ORS 693.115, 705.250
Duties and Responsibilities: The State Plumbing Board advises on plumbing products, approves related division fees and training programs, hears code appeals, and makes scientific and technical findings related to alternate method rulings. The board also administers examinations to plumbers and issues licenses and approves revocations or suspensions of plumbing licenses. The governor appoints the board's seven members to four-year terms, subject to Senate confirmation.

Residential and Manufactured Structures Board

Address: PO Box 14470, Salem 97309-0404
Phone: 503-378-4133
Web: www.bcd.oregon.gov/boards.html
Contact: Policy and Technical Services Section Manager
Statutory Authority: ORS 455.135, 705.250
Duties and Responsibilities: The Residential and Manufactured Structures Board assists in adopting and administering the state's residential code. The board advises on rules governing the residential and manufactured structures codes and approves related division fees and training programs, hears code appeals, and makes scientific and technical findings related to alternate method rulings. The governor appoints the board's 11 members, subject to Senate confirmation.

Finance and Corporate Securities, Division of

Address: 350 Winter St. NE, Salem 97301-3881; PO Box 14480, Salem 97309-0405
Phone: 503-378-4140
Fax: 503-947-7862
E-mail: dcbs.dfcsmail@state.or.us
Web: http://dfcs.oregon.gov
Contact: David Tatman, Administrator
Statutory Authority: ORS Chapters 59, 86A, 97, 446, 645, 646, 646A, 650, 697, 705–709, 711, 713–717, 723, 725, 725A, 726
Duties and Responsibilities: The Division of Finance and Corporate Securities regulates Oregon's state-chartered financial institutions, including banks, trust companies, savings and loan associations and credit unions. It also regulates mortgage bankers, brokers and loan originators, and consumer finance companies (including payday and title loan). It regulates and registers public offerings of securities, and licenses securities broker-dealers, investment advisors and salespersons. The division also regulates debt management providers, check-cashing businesses, credit service organizations, money transmitters, pre-need funeral trusts, endowment cemeteries, appraisal management companies and administers the Oregon Identity Theft Protection Act. The division provides information to help consumers make informed decisions about financial transactions and recognize and avoid fraud and inappropriate products and services. The division also investigates consumer complaints relating to areas it regulates.

Insurance Division

Address: 350 Winter St. NE, Salem 97301-3883; PO Box 14480, Salem 97309-0405
Phone: 503-947-7980; Consumer Advocacy Unit: 503-947-7984
Fax: 503-378-4351
E-mail: dcbs.insmail@state.or.us
Web: http://insurance.oregon.gov
Contact: Lou Savage, Commissioner
Statutory Authority: ORS 646.263–646.285, 705.137, 705.139, Chapters 731, 732, 733, 734, 735, 737, 742, 743, 744, 746, 748, 750, 752
Duties and Responsibilities: The Insurance Division works to ensure the financial soundness of insurance companies, the availability and affordability of insurance and the fair treatment of policyholders. The division enforces Oregon's insurance code, licenses insurance companies and producers (agents) doing business in Oregon, examines insurers for solvency and compliance with insurance law and approves insurance products to be offered to the public. The division also reviews rates charged for insurance products, provides information to help consumers make informed decisions about insurance and investigates consumer complaints against insurance companies and producers (agents).

Oregon Occupational Safety and Health Division

Address: 350 Winter St. NE, Rm. 430, Salem 97301-3882; PO Box 14480, Salem 97309-0405
Phone: 503-378-3272 (Voice/TTY); Toll-free in Oregon only: 1-800-922-2689 (Voice/TTY)
Fax: 503-947-7461
E-mail: admin.web@state.or.us
Web: www.orosha.org
Contact: Michael Wood, Administrator
Statutory Authority: ORS 654.001–654.295, 654.750–654.780, 654.991
Duties and Responsibilities: The Oregon Occupational Safety and Health Division (Oregon OSHA) administers the Oregon Safe Employment Act and enforces the state's occupational safety and health rules, which establish minimum safety and health standards for Oregon employers. The division inspects workplaces for occupational safety and health hazards, investigates complaints about safety and health issues on the job and investigates

fatal accidents to determine if the Oregon Safe Employment Act has been violated. The division also provides technical, educational and consultative services to help employers and their employees implement and improve injury and illness prevention plans.

Workers' Compensation Division

Address: 350 Winter St. NE, Salem 97301-3879; PO Box 14480, Salem 97309-0405
Phone: 503-947-7810
Fax: 503-947-7514
E-mail: workcomp.questions@state.or.us
Web: http://wcd.oregon.gov
Contact: John L. Shilts, Administrator
Statutory Authority: ORS Chapter 656
Duties and Responsibilities: The Workers' Compensation Division administers and enforces Oregon's workers' compensation law to ensure that employers provide coverage for their workers, and that workers with occupational injuries or diseases receive timely and accurate benefits and quality medical care. The division facilitates injured workers' early return-to-work through incentive programs funded through the Workers' Benefit Fund; helps resolve medical, vocational, disability and other disputes; and provides consultation services to people and businesses within the system.

Injured Workers, Ombudsman for

Address: 350 Winter St. NE, Salem 97301-3878; PO Box 14480, Salem 97309-0405
Phone: 503-378-3351; Toll-free: 1-800-927-1271
Fax: 503-373-7639
E-mail: oiw.questions@state.or.us
Web: www.oregon.gov/DCBS/OIW
Contact: Jennifer Flood, Ombudsman
Statutory Authority: ORS 656.709
Duties and Responsibilities: The office of the Ombudsman for Injured Workers serves as an advocate for injured workers. The office investigates and attempts to resolve workers' compensation related complaints. In addition, the office provides information to injured workers to enable them to protect their rights and makes recommendations for improving ombudsman services and the workers' compensation system.

Small Business Ombudsman for Workers' Compensation

Address: 350 Winter St. NE, Salem 97301-3878; PO Box 14480, Salem 97309-0405
Phone: 503-378-4209
Fax: 503-373-7639
E-mail: david.waki@state.or.us
Web: www.oregon.gov/DCBS/SBO
Contact: David Waki, Ombudsman
Statutory Authority: ORS 656.709
Duties and Responsibilities: The Small Business Ombudsman for Workers' Compensation serves as a workers' compensation resource center, assisting small businesses in the areas of insurance and claims processing matters. This includes the intervention, investigation and resolution of any workers' compensation related issue. Additionally, the office undertakes an educational role to provide information to employers, trade groups, agents and insurers on relevant workers' compensation issues.

Workers' Compensation Management-Labor Advisory Committee

Address: 350 Winter St. NE, Salem 97301-3878; PO Box 14480, Salem 97309-0405
Phone: 503-947-7867
Fax: 503-378-6444
E-mail: mlac@state.or.us
Web: www.oregon.gov/DCBS/MLAC
Contact: Lou Savage, Administrator
Statutory Authority: ORS 656.790
Duties and Responsibilities: The Workers' Compensation Management-Labor Advisory Committee is charged with reviewing and making recommendations on workers' compensation issues to the director of DCBS and the Legislature. Members of the committee are appointed by the governor and subject to Senate confirmation. The committee consists of five management and five labor representatives and the DCBS director who serves as an ex officio member.

Other Entities:

Senior Health Insurance Benefits Assistance

Address: 350 Winter St. NE, Suite 330, Salem 97301; PO Box 14480, Salem 97309-0405
Phone: 503-947-7979; Toll-free: 1-800-722-4134; TTY: 1-800-735-2900
Fax: 503-947-7092
E-mail: shiba.oregon@state.or.us
Web: www.oregon.gov/DCBS/SHIBA
Contact: Lisa Emerson
Duties and Responsibilities: The Senior Health Insurance Benefits Assistance (SHIBA) program uses trained staff and volunteers to help people with Medicare make health insurance decisions. Volunteers are available in most counties throughout Oregon to assist beneficiaries and their family members understand Medicare benefits, choose a supplemental insurance policy and enroll in a prescription drug benefit. SHIBA counseling services are free of charge.

Workers' Compensation Board

Address: 2601 25th St. SE, Suite 150, Salem 97302-1280
Phone: 503-378-3308
Fax: 503-373-1684
Web: www.wcb.oregon.gov
Contact: Abigail Herman, Chair
Statutory Authority: ORS Chapter 656
Duties and Responsibilities: The Workers' Compensation Board resolves disputes arising under the Workers' Compensation Law and the Oregon Safe Employment Act. The board chair oversees the Hearings Division, whose Administrative Law Judges (ALJs) conduct contested case hearings and provide mediation for workers' compensation matters as well as for Oregon Occupational Safety and Health Division (Oregon OSHA) citations and orders. The board is the appellate body that reviews ALJ workers' compensation orders on appeal, exercises own motion jurisdiction and reviews Claim Disposition Agreements (Compromise and Release of workers' benefits). In addition, the board hears appeals from Oregon Department of Justice decisions regarding applications for compensation under the Crime Victim Assistance Program, and resolves disputes between workers and workers' compensation carriers arising from workers' civil actions against allegedly liable third parties.

The board consists of five full-time members, two of whom are selected from among persons with backgrounds and understanding of the concerns of employers and two of whom are selected from among persons with backgrounds and understanding of the concerns of employees. One member represents the interests of the public and serves as the chair. The members are appointed to four-year terms by the governor and confirmed by the Senate.

Corrections, Department of

Address: 2575 Center St. NE, Salem 97301-4667
Phone: 503-945-0927
Fax: 503-373-1173
E-mail: doc.info@doc.state.or.us
Web: www.oregon.gov/DOC
Contact: Colette S. Peters, Director
Statutory Authority: ORS Chapter 423
Duties and Responsibilities: The Department of Corrections (DOC), created by the Legislature in 1987, has custody of felony offenders sentenced to prison for more than 12 months and operates community corrections in Linn and Douglas Counties. Oregon houses offenders in 14 state prisons statewide. Oregon's recidivism rate is about 30 percent.

The DOC provides administrative oversight and funding for the community corrections activities of the 34 Oregon counties that manage their own offenders who are subject to jail, parole, post-prison supervision and probation. The department provides interstate compact administration and jail inspections, central information and data services regarding felons statewide. It is also responsible for evaluating the performance of community corrections.

Inspector General, Office of the

Address: 2575 Center St. NE, Salem 97301-4667
Phone: 503-945-0945
Fax: 503-373-7092
Web: www.oregon.gov/DOC/INSPEC/pages/index.aspx
Contact: Leonard Williamson, Inspector General
Duties and Responsibilities: The Office of the Inspector General was created in 1990, as recommended by an investigative report to the governor. The inspector general has broad responsibility for oversight of suspected, alleged or actual misconduct within the DOC, reporting to the director and deputy and to other officials as required by law and the DOC Code of Conduct. Specifically, the inspector general investigates suspected wrongdoings by inmates, staff, contractors, volunteers and inmate visitors, and conducts disciplinary hearings in accordance with established rules and relevant case law for inmates accused of rule violations.

Planning and Budget, Office of

Address: 2575 Center St. NE, Salem 97301-4667
Phone: 503-945-9007
Fax: 503-945-7150
Web: www.oregon.gov/DOC/ADMIN/pages/planning.aspx
Contact: Nathan Allen, Administrator
Duties and Responsibilities: The Office of Planning and Budget is responsible for the budget development, budget management and financial analysis activities of the agency, including determining the resources necessary to support existing and growing offender populations. The office develops and executes the department's Long-Range Construction Plan to ensure appropriate institutions are in place to house offenders entering the system.

Population Management, Office of

Address: 2575 Center St. NE, Salem 97301-4667
Phone: 503-378-6174
Fax: 503-378-6191
Web: www.oregon.gov/DOC/ADMIN/pages/population_management.aspx
Contact: Jamie Breyman, Administrator

Duties and Responsibilities: Created in 2006, the Office of Population Management is responsible for developing and implementing agency inmate population management strategies to plan for the forecasted inmate population. The office is responsible for new prison construction, community development, capacity and resource management, inmate classification and the interstate corrections compact.

General Services Division

Address: 2575 Center St. NE, Salem 97301-4667
Phone: 503-945-9017
Fax: 503-373-1173
Web: www.oregon.gov/DOC/GENSVC
Contact: Tami Dohrman, Assistant Director
Duties and Responsibilities: The General Services Division comprises Information Systems, Facilities Services, Central Distribution and Fiscal Services. The Information Systems Unit is responsible for the Department of Corrections' network, desktop technical support, and applications development and maintenance. Other users of the department's automated systems include law enforcement agencies, county corrections agencies, the Board of Parole and Post-Prison Supervision, district attorneys and the courts. The Facilities Services Section oversees new prison construction and maintenance of current institutions. Facilities Services and Central Distribution support the operation of Oregon's prisons and administrative facilities. Fiscal Services manages the accounting, central trust, commissary, purchasing and warehouse operations for the entire department.

Operations Division

Address: 2575 Center St. NE, Salem 97301-0470
Phone: 503-945-0950
Fax: 503-373-1173
Web: www.oregon.gov/DOC/OPS
Contact: Mike Gower, Assistant Director
Duties and Responsibilities: The Operations Division is responsible for the central administration and management of Oregon's prisons, including security, inmate transfers, transportation, security threat group (gang) management, emergency preparedness, most inmate work crew activities and inmate health and mental health treatment.

Emergency Preparedness

Duties and Responsibilities: Emergency preparedness efforts are designed to protect the lives and property of the public, staff and inmates through a well-planned and coordinated system that includes department and community resources. A strong emphasis is placed on prevention of emergencies. The DOC conducts emergency exercises and security audits to sharpen skills and ensure the evolution and effectiveness of the emergency preparedness system.

Health Services

Web: www.oregon.gov/DOC/OPS/HESVC
Duties and Responsibilities: Health Services comprises all medical, dental and mental health services for inmates in the custody of the agency. The state has a moral and legal obligation to provide health care for inmates. The federal courts have mandated that inmates, though incarcerated, remain entitled to community-standard medical care. All DOC health care programs have passed accreditation standards set by the National Commission on Correctional Health Care.

Inmate Work Crews

Web: www.oregon.gov/DOC/OPS/PRISON/pages/inmate_work_activities.aspx
Duties and Responsibilities: The DOC contracts with local, state and federal governmental agencies, and non-profit and private entities for the use of inmate labor and services on work projects. Crews of supervised minimum-custody inmates perform work such as park maintenance, flood control and clean-up, upkeep of parkways, litter control of community roads, groundskeeping, community beautification projects, seasonal gleaning of field crops for use in local food banks, fire fighting, forest lands restoration and hazardous fuels removal.

Government Efficiencies and Communications

Address: 2575 Center St. NE, Salem 97301-4667
Phone: 503-945-9092
Fax: 503-947-1034
Web: www.oregon.gov/DOC/GECO
Contact: Heidi Stewart, Assistant Director
Duties and Responsibilities: Government Efficiencies and Communications is charged with furthering the DOC's mission through close collaboration with internal and external stakeholders. The division is comprised of Project Management, Research, Rules, Central Services and the Office of Public Affairs, which coordinates all media, legislative and legal matters. Key objectives and services include developing and disseminating statistical and narrative information about the DOC's mission, policies, programs and services to a broad array of stakeholders; managing implementation of agency-wide and intra-agency projects requiring the expertise of professional project managers; providing a full range of public affairs and government relations services for the department; providing research and data to support evidence-based programs; and coordinating agency rulemaking.

Offender Management and Rehabilitation Division

Address: 2575 Center St. NE, Salem 97301-4667
Phone: 503-945-9050
Fax: 503-373-7810
Web: www.oregon.gov/DOC/OMR
Contact: Chane Griggs, Assistant Director
Duties and Responsibilities: The Offender Management and Rehabilitation Division develops and delivers effective outcome-based interventions to inmates in Oregon's prisons. Using seven criminogenic risk factors, staff assesses each inmate during the intake process at Coffee Creek Correctional Facility and creates an individualized corrections plan. Correctional programs specified in an inmate's corrections plan may include work skills development, parenting, education, training, thinking changes, health care, mental health care, alcohol and drug treatment, work experience and re-entry services such as job placement and housing to support their transition back into the community. Additionally, all inmates are eligible to participate in religious services. Automated systems track the inmates' progress in pursuing their plans as well as their behavior and conduct.

Community Corrections

Web: www.oregon.gov/DOC/CC
Contact: Jeremiah Stromberg, Assistant Director of Community Corrections
Duties and Responsibilities: Through intergovernmental agreements with 34 of Oregon's counties, the Community Corrections unit oversees, advocates for, and works in partnership with all of the community corrections offices throughout the state. County community corrections agencies provide supervision, services and sanctions to felony offenders in their communities. Parole and probation officers monitor the behavior and compliance of more than 30,000 felony offenders living in Oregon's communities. They enforce conditions of supervision set by the court for those on probation and by the Board of Parole and Post-Prison Supervision for those who have been released from prison. State funding administered through the Community Corrections unit supports both the supervision of felony offenders and the development of community-based sanctions and correctional treatment programs.

Offender Information and Sentence Computation Unit

Duties and Responsibilities: The Offender Information and Sentence Computation Unit (OISC) calculates and updates the length of all prison terms based on information provided by the courts. OISC also is the repository for legal files pertaining to offenders who have been, or currently are, under the custody or supervision of the DOC. The unit is responsible for the maintenance of the department's official offender records.

Religious Services

Web: www.oregon.gov/DOC/OMR/pages/religious_services/rs_home_page.aspx
Duties and Responsibilities: The agency's oldest correctional program, Religious Services provides worship services, study and music programs, serious illness/death notifications, and pastoral counseling to meet mandates of the U.S. Constitution, Oregon Constitution and judicial decisions. Through its chaplains and volunteers, Religious Services provides mandated and innovative services in a cost-effective manner.

State Prisons:

Coffee Creek Correctional Facility

Address: 24499 SW Grahams Ferry Rd., PO Box 9000, Wilsonville 97070-9000
Phone: 503-570-6400
Fax: 503-570-6417
Web: www.oregon.gov/DOC/OPS/PRISON/pages/cccf.aspx
Contact: Kim Brockamp, Superintendent
Duties and Responsibilities: Coffee Creek Correctional Facility is a 1,672-bed dual-mission facility that comprises Oregon Corrections Intake Center for men and women as well as a multi-custody, full-service women's prison. Virtually all inmates entering Oregon's prisons are initially housed at Coffee Creek. During an approximately four-week assessment period, individual corrections plans are designed for each inmate, after which inmates are assigned to a prison.

Columbia River Correctional Institution

Address: 9111 NE Sunderland Ave., Portland 97211-1799
Phone: 503-280-6646
Fax: 503-280-6012
Web: www.oregon.gov/DOC/OPS/PRISON/pages/crci.aspx
Contact: Joe DeCamp, Superintendent
Duties and Responsibilities: Columbia River Correctional Institution is a 540-bed minimum security prison located in northeast Portland. The prison houses 500 male inmates in dormitories. Major program activities for most inmates include community service work projects, institution support and maintenance work, and educational and cognitive skills classes. Inmates may also participate in therapeutic programs designed to address serious addiction and substance abuse problems.

Deer Ridge Correctional Institution

Address: 3920 East Ashwood Rd., Madras 97741
Phone: 541-325-5999
Web: www.oregon.gov/DOC/OPS/PRISON/pages/drci.aspx
Contact: Rick Angelozzi, Superintendent
Duties and Responsibilities: Deer Ridge Correctional Institution, the newest prison in Oregon, is located near Madras in central Oregon. The prison is comprised of a 644-bed minimum security facility and a 1,223-bed medium security facility. The DOC has appointed a Prison Advisory Committee (PAC) consisting of representatives from Jefferson County who provide representation from a cross-section of backgrounds and local interests. The purpose of the PAC is to serve as a citizen advisory group to DOC regarding correctional issues and other DOC activities that may affect communities in Jefferson County.

Eastern Oregon Correctional Institution

Address: 2500 Westgate, Pendleton 97801-9699
Phone: 541-276-0700
Fax: 541-276-1841
Web: www.oregon.gov/DOC/OPS/PRISON/pages/eoci.aspx
Contact: Rick Coursey, Superintendent
Duties and Responsibilities: Eastern Oregon Correctional Institution (EOCI) was authorized in 1983 by the Oregon Legislature as the first medium-security adult male correctional facility outside of Marion County. EOCI facilities were previously a state mental hospital with many of the buildings constructed in 1913. The facility accomodates a maximum of 1,711 inmates and is one of the largest employers in the Pendleton area.

EOCI provides a variety of educational, training and work experiences for inmates as well as programs to prepare indviduals for their return to society. The Prison Blues™ line of denim clothing is manufactured in the garment factory. The institution shops provide work and training for inmates in a number of trades and a commercial laundry meets the needs of the facility as well as a number of local industries and public service agencies. EOCI partners with a local community college to give inmates opportunities to complete the General Education Development (GED) test and participate in other educational programs. A pre-release alcohol and drug treatment program is also available, as well as day treatment and special housing for inmates in need of mental health care.

Mill Creek Correctional Facility

Address: 5465 Turner Rd. SE, Salem 97301-9400
Phone: 503-378-2600, ext. 221
Fax: 503-378-8235
Web: www.oregon.gov/DOC/OPS/PRISON/pages/mccf.aspx
Contact: Jeff Premo, Superintendent
Duties and Responsibilities: Mill Creek Correctional Facility (MCCF) is a minimum-security prison, in operation since 1929, housing 310 inmates. All inmates are within three years of release and most have successfully completed required correctional programs prior to being assigned to MCCF. The facility prepares inmates for transition and release to the community by providing a variety of work programs and training opportunities.

Oregon State Correctional Institution

Address: 3405 Deer Park Dr. SE, Salem 97310-9385
Phone: 503-373-0100
Fax: 503-378-8919
Web: www.oregon.gov/DOC/OPS/PRISON/pages/osci.aspx
Contact: Rob Persson, Superintendent
Duties and Responsibilities: Oregon State Correctional Institution, a men's medium-security transitional release facility located near Salem, was established by the 1955 Legislature and became fully operational in 1959. The 892-bed facility focuses on providing transition programs and work skills to inmates who have less than three years to serve but who are not suitable for housing in a minimum-security environment. Work and skills training opportunities include printing and telecommunication services for state agencies.

Oregon State Penitentiary

Address: 2605 State St., Salem 97310-0505
Phone: 503-378-2445
Fax: 503-378-3897
Web: www.oregon.gov/DOC/OPS/PRISON/pages/osp.aspx
Contact: Jeff Premo, Superintendent
Duties and Responsibilities: Oregon State Penitentiary (OSP), Oregon's first state prison, was originally located in Portland in 1851. In 1866, it was moved to a 26-acre site in Salem. OSP is the state's only maximum-security prison, accommodating up to 2,150 inmates. In addition to general population housing, there is a disciplinary segregation unit, a mental health infirmary and a medical infirmary. The penitentiary's 196-bed, self-contained Intensive Management Unit provides programs, housing and control for maximum-custody male inmates who are disruptive or pose a substantial threat to staff and other inmates, as well as those inmates with a sentence of death. Penitentiary inmates may work in Oregon Corrections Enterprises' shops, including a furniture factory, metal and upholstery shops and a commercial laundry.

Powder River Correctional Facility

Address: 3600 13th St., Baker City 97814-1346
Phone: 541-523-6680
Fax: 541-523-6678
Web: www.oregon.gov/DOC/OPS/PRISON/pages/prcf.aspx
Contact: Brad Cain, Operations Manager
Duties and Responsibilities: Powder River Correctional Facility houses 286 adult male inmates. The facility operates a 178-bed alternative incarceration addictions-treatment program where inmates follow a strict regimen of work, education, treatment, physical exercise and service to the community. Inmates perform institution- or community-based work projects for government, private sector and non-profit organizations in Baker County and surrounding counties. All inmates are expected to participate in and successfully complete transition programming designed to address their individual needs.

Santiam Correctional Institution

Address: 4005 Aumsville Hwy. SE, Salem 97301-9112
Phone: 503-378-5558, ext. 259
Fax: 503-378-8235
Web: www.oregon.gov/DOC/OPS/PRISON/pages/sci.aspx
Contact: Paula Myers, Superintendent
Duties and Responsibilities: Santiam Correctional Institution (SCI) is a minimum-security prison located in southeast Salem that accommodates 400 male inmates in four dormitories. SCI houses inmates who are within six months of release and emphasizes programs that increase the inmates' chances of successful re-entry into their communities. In addition to transitional programs, the prison's work crews provide inmates with work experience at DOC facilities and other government agencies.

Shutter Creek Correctional Institution

Address: 95200 Shutters Landing Ln., North Bend 97459-0303
Phone: 541-756-6666
Fax: 541-756-6888
Web: www.oregon.gov/DOC/OPS/PRISON/pages/scci.aspx
Contact: Tim Causey, Superintendent
Duties and Responsibilities: Shutter Creek Correctional Institution (SCCI) is a 260-bed minimum-security prison located in North Bend. Prior to its conversion to a prison in 1990, the site was an Air National Guard radar station. Staff provides supervision and programming for 100 male general population inmates as well as 150 male inmates in the Oregon SUMMIT Program. SUMMIT is a voluntary alternative incarceration program in which eligible inmates may earn reductions to their prison terms. Those who fail to make adequate progress are removed from the program and returned to general population. Other SCCI programs include work, general education, alcohol and drug education, cognitive restructuring, and anger management.

Snake River Correctional Institution

Address: 777 Stanton Blvd., Ontario 97914-0595
Phone: 541-881-5000
Fax: 541-881-5460
Web: www.oregon.gov/DOC/OPS/PRISON/pages/srci.aspx
Contact: Mark Nooth, Superintendent
Duties and Responsibilities: Snake River Correctional Institution (SRCI) is a multi-security facility that opened in 1991with 648 beds. In 1995, the Legislature approved construction of 1,350 additional beds. SRCI is now Oregon's largest prison with 105 acres inside the perimeter. SRCI has 2,416 medium-security beds, 174 minimum-security beds and 494 special-housing beds. SRCI employs more than 800 corrections professionals. Inmate work programs include a call center, training in building maintenance and a construction technology program in which inmates build modular buildings.

South Fork Forest Camp

Address: 48300 Wilson River Hwy., Tillamook 97141-9799
Phone: 503-842-2811
Fax: 503-842-7943
Web: www.oregon.gov/DOC/OPS/PRISON/pages/sffc.aspx
Contact: Joe DeCamp, Superintendent
Duties and Responsibilities: South Fork Forest Camp (SFFC) was established in 1951, following the catastrophic Tillamook Burn and is operated in partnership with the Department of Forestry. SFFC is located 28 miles east of Tillamook and houses 200 minimum-security inmates. SFFC inmates perform numerous reforestation projects in the Tillamook Burn area and are screened, trained and deployed to fight wildfires throughout the state. SFFC also operates an on-site salmon/steelhead rearing pond in cooperation with the Department of Fish and Wildlife.

Two Rivers Correctional Institution

Address: 82911 Beach Access Rd., Umatilla 97882
Phone: 541-922-2001
Fax: 541-922-2011
Web: www.oregon.gov/DOC/OPS/PRISON/pages/trci.aspx

Contact: Steve Franke, Superintendent

Duties and Responsibilities: Two Rivers Correctional Institution (TRCI) opened in phases between December 1999 and September 2001 and now houses up to 1,802 male inmates. TRCI is designated as an education/work facility for long-term inmates. Its programs focus on Adult Basic Education and the General Educational Development (GED) test. Inside work activities include institution maintenance, commercial laundry and furniture-making. The prison provides minimum-custody inmate work crews for community service and the Oregon Food Bank. It also sends crews for other work projects, primarily under contract with government agencies.

Warner Creek Correctional Facility

Address: 20654 Rabbit Hill Rd., Lakeview 97630
Phone: 541-947-8200
Fax: 541-947-8231
Web: www.oregon.gov/DOC/OPS/PRISON/pages/wccf.aspx
Contact: Steve Brown Superintendent

Duties and Responsibilities: Warner Creek Correctional Facility (WCCF) is a 400-bed dormitory-style minimum security prison for males. All inmates are within four years of release and most have successfully completed required correctional programs prior to being assigned to WCCF. The facility prepares inmates for transition and release to the community by providing a variety of work and training programs. Major activities include community service work projects, institution support and maintenance work, and cognitive skills classes. Activities for skill building include transition preparation classes, parenting education, religious services and general education classes.

Other Entity:

Oregon Corrections Enterprises

Address: 3691 State St., Salem 97301
Phone: 503-428-5500
Fax: 503-363-4170
Web: www.oce.oregon.gov
Contact: Rob Killgore, Administrator

Duties and Responsibilities: Oregon Corrections Enterprises (OCE) was created by the voters in 1999 to streamline the department's efforts to put all inmates to work. OCE is a semi-independent state agency. Its administrator reports to the director of the DOC.

Most DOC inmates are required to participate in work and training assignments 40 hours each week. Inmate work opportunities are divided into three categories: prison industries, private partnerships and inmate work crews. OCE manages the first two. Work is a major component of the Oregon Accountability Model, teaching inmates skills that translate into gainful employment upon release, potentially reducing repeat offenses.

OCE's ventures include commercial laundry operations that serve both public and private institutions and businesses throughout the state; a garment factory that produces the Prison Blues™ line of clothing; a furniture factory producing cabinetry, custom office furniture and other furnishings; a metal shop producing gates, tables, lockers, boat docks and other items; and services to public- and private-sector customers including publishing and printing, telecommunications, mailing and computer-aided design services.

Counselors and Therapists, Oregon Board of Licensed Professional

Address: 3218 Pringle Rd. SE, Suite 250, Salem 97302-6312
Phone: 503-378-5499
E-mail: lpct.board@state.or.us
Web: www.oregon.gov/OBLPCT
Contact: Becky Eklund, Executive Director
Statutory Authority: ORS 675.705–675.835

Duties and Responsibilities: The Oregon Board of Licensed Professional Counselors and Therapists was created in 1989. The primary purpose of the board is consumer protection. The board determines professional standards and issues licenses to counselors and to marriage and family therapists, sets standards for licensees and registered interns working toward licensure, sets and enforces continuing education requirements, publishes an annual directory, and investigates alleged violations and complaints against applicants and licensees.

The board consists of eight members appointed by the governor and confirmed by the Senate, including three licensed professional counselors, two licensed marriage and family therapists, a faculty member and two public representatives. Members serve three year terms.

Criminal Justice Commission, Oregon

Address: 885 Summer St. NE, Salem 97301
Phone: 503-378-4830
Fax: 503-378-4861
E-mail: liz.skinner@state.or.us
Web: www.oregon.gov/CJC
Contact: Craig Prins, Executive Director
Statutory Authority: ORS 137.651–137.673

Duties and Responsibilities: The Criminal Justice Commission's purpose is to improve the efficiency and effectiveness of state and local criminal justice systems by providing a centralized and impartial forum for statewide policy development and planning. The commission administers state and federal grants, conducts research, develops impact estimates of crime-related legislation, acts as a statistical and data clearinghouse, administers Oregon's felony sentencing guidelines and provides staff to the asset forfeiture advisory committee.

Commission members are appointed to four-year terms by the governor and confirmed by the Senate.

Degree Authorization, Office of

Address: 775 Court St. NE, Salem 97301
Phone: 503-373-0072
Fax: 503-378-8395
Web: www.oregonstudentaid.gov/oda
Contact: Jennifer Diallo, Director
Statutory Authority: ORS 348.594–348.615
Duties and Responsibilities: The mission of the Office of Degree Authorization is to assist Oregon students and their families in attaining a post-secondary education and to enhance the value, integrity, and diversity of college programs offered in Oregon.

The office works to ensure the quality of degrees and certificates offered by private degree-granting colleges in Oregon and out-of-state public and private degree-granting colleges; evaluate requests to start new post-secondary degree programs in Oregon or offer academic programs for college credit to Oregon citizens from outside the state; protect existing degree programs offered by private colleges from detrimental duplication by publicly-funded institutions and protect Oregonians from fraudulent use of substandard academic credentials and from "degree mills" offering fraudulent degrees.

Dentistry, Oregon Board of

Address: 1600 SW 4th Ave., Suite 770, Portland 97201-5519
Phone: 971-673-3200
Fax: 971-673-3202
E-mail: information@oregondentistry.org
Web: www.oregon.gov/Dentistry
Contact: Patrick D. Braatz, Executive Director
Statutory Authority: ORS Chapter 679, ORS 680.010–680.205, 680.990
Duties and Responsibilities: The Oregon Board of Dentistry, created in 1887, administers the Dental Practice Act and rules of the board, establishes standards for licensure, and examines and licenses dentists and dental hygienists. The board regulates the use of anesthesia in the dental office and certifies dental assistants in radiologic proficiency and expanded functions. The board investigates alleged violations of the Dental Practice Act and may discipline licensees.

Members of the Board of Dentistry are appointed by the governor, confirmed by the Senate, and serve four-year terms. There are ten board members: six dentists, one of whom must be a specialist, two dental hygienists and two public members.

The board is supported solely by revenues received from licensees, including application, license, permit and certification fees.

Education, Department of

Address: 255 Capitol St. NE, Salem 97310-0203
Phone: 503-947-5600; TDD: 503-378-2892
Fax: 503-378-5156
E-mail: ode.frontdesk@ode.state.or.us
Web: www.ode.state.or.us
Contact: Rob Saxton, Deputy Superintendent of Public Instruction; Dr. Rudy Crew, Chief Education Officer
Statutory Authority: ORS 326.111
Duties and Responsibilities: The Oregon Department of Education (ODE) is directed by the State Board of Education to implement state policies regarding pre-kindergarten through grade 12. ODE serves 197 elementary and secondary school districts and 19 education service districts, and these serve 560,950 Oregon students.

ODE carries out educational policies set by the Legislature and State Board of Education and helps to ensure districts comply with federal and state regulations and laws. ODE is responsible for the development of statewide standards, assessments and school improvement efforts. It reports student performance by school in every district through state report cards. ODE promotes collaboration, professional development and best practices among educators to improve student achievement.

ODE distributes the State School Fund (approximately $5.5 billion in 2011–12) to school districts and education service districts and distributes approximately $1.2 billion (2011–12) to federally-funded programs, which it monitors.

ODE is also responsible for the state School for the Deaf, regional programs for children with disabilities and education programs in Oregon youth correctional facilities.

State Board of Education

Address: 255 Capitol St. NE, Salem 97310-0203
Phone: 503-947-5616
Fax: 503-378-5156
E-mail: jan.mccomb@state.or.us
Web: www.ode.state.or.us/search/results/?id=144
Contact: Jan McComb, Executive Director

Statutory Authority: ORS 326.011–326.075
Duties and Responsibilities: The Oregon Legislature created the State Board of Education in 1951 to oversee the state's schools and community colleges. The board sets educational policies and standards for Oregon's 197 public school districts, 17 community college districts and 19 education service districts. All of these agencies have their own elected governing boards responsible for oversight, budgeting and policy within their jurisdictions.

The board works to ensure that every Oregon public school student has equal access to high quality educational services that promote lifelong learning and prepare students for their next steps following high school graduation, including college, work and citizenship. To this end, the board has raised graduation requirements, including the requirement that students demonstrate proficiency in reading, writing and math through assessments or work samples. It is also focused on easing transitions from pre-kindergarten through high school, college and career.

The board is comprised of seven members appointed by the governor and confirmed by the Senate. Five members represent Oregon's congressional districts, two members represent the state at large, and the secretary of state and state treasurer serve in ex officio capacity. Members serve four-year terms and are limited to two consecutive terms. The board meets about eight times per year and the public is welcome to attend the meetings.

Fair Dismissal Appeals Board

Address: 255 Capitol St. NE, Salem 97310-0203
Phone: 503-947-5651; TDD: 503-378-2892
Fax: 503-378-5156
Web: www.ode.state.or.us/search/page/?id=3676
Contact: Cindy Hunt, Government and Legal Affairs Manager
Statutory Authority: ORS 342.930
Duties and Responsibilities: The Fair Dismissal Appeals Board (FDAB) was created in 1971 to hear appeals of teacher and administrator dismissals and to provide a uniform statewide system of pre- and post-determination due process for these cases. It also provides uniform standards for dismissals.

The 20-member FDAB is appointed by the governor and confirmed by the Senate and is chosen from specific categories: five public school administrators, five contract teachers, five school board members and five who must have no occupational affiliation with a school district. Each category must be further distributed by size of school district. Members serve a term of four years but also serve "at the pleasure" of the governor. A member's term continues to the completion of an appeal, including a motion for reconsideration.

The board meets annually in October. The meeting is subject to the Public Meetings Law and is open to the public.

Quality Education Commission

Address: 255 Capitol St. NE, Salem 97310-0203
Phone: (503) 947-5670; TDD: 503-378-2892
Fax: 503-378-5156
Web: www.ode.state.or.us/search/results/?id=166
Contact: Brian Reeder, Assistant Superintendent
Statutory Authority: ORS 327.497–327.506
Duties and Responsibilities: The 2001 Legislature established the Quality Education Commission to determine the amount of funding needed to meet the state's quality education goals for kindergarten through grade 12 public education. The 11-member board is appointed by the governor and confirmed by the Senate. No more than five members of the commission may be employed by a school district at the time of appointment. Prior to August 1 of each even-numbered year, the commission issues a report to the governor and the Legislative Assembly that identifies current education practices in the state, the costs of continuing those practices and the expected student performance under those practices; and the best practices for meeting the quality goals, the costs of implementing the best practices and the expected student performance under the best practices.

Employment Department

Address: 875 Union St. NE, Salem 97311
Phone: 503-947-1470; Toll-free: 1-800-237-3710
Fax: 503-947-1472
E-mail: info@emp.state.or.us
Web: www.oregon.gov/EMPLOY
Contact: Laurie Warner, Director
Statutory Authority: ORS 657.601
Duties and Responsibilities: The Oregon State Employment Service was created in 1935 as a division of the Unemployment Compensation Commission. In the mid-1950s, the Oregon State Employment Service and the State Unemployment Compensation Commission came together under the Department of Employment. In the late 1960s, the Legislature moved the department to the newly-formed Department of Human Resources, and the agency became the Employment Division. It continued as a division until 1993, when the Legislature made it a separate agency and named it the Employment Department.

Through 38 WorkSource Centers and three Unemployment Centers, the department supports business and promotes employment, helping workers find suitable employment; provides qualified applicants for employers; supplies statewide and local labor market information; provides unemployment insurance benefits to workers temporarily unemployed through no fault of their own; and assures safe and quality child care.

Business and Employment Services

Address: 875 Union St. NE, Salem 97311
Phone: 503-947-1670
Fax: 503-947-1658
Contact: Martin Burrows, Assistant Director
Statutory Authority: ORS 657.601
Duties and Responsibilities: The department serves employers by recruiting workers with skills matching employers' needs and offering an innovative online tool called iMatchSkills® to match qualified candidates to job openings. The department helps job seekers find jobs that match their skills, provides them with information about trends in occupations and skills needed for success in the job market, and works with other agencies to direct job seekers to appropriate training programs.

Veterans' representatives provide the maximum level of employment and training opportunities for veterans of the U.S. Armed Forces, including service-connected disabled veterans, veterans of the Vietnam Era, veterans who are recently separated from military service and other eligible persons.

Child Care Division

Address: 875 Union St. NE, Salem 97311
Phone: 503-947-1400; 1-800-556-6616
Fax: 503-947-1428
E-mail: childcare.emp@state.or.us
Web: www.oregon.gov/EMPLOY/CCD
Contact: Kara Waddell, Administrator
Statutory Authority: ORS 657A.010
Duties and Responsibilities: The Child Care Division is responsible for regulating child care centers and family child care homes. The division also administers the federal Child Care and Development Fund (CCDF) which provides support and assistance to low-income working families, child care resource and referral agencies, community-based child care programs, and training and technical assistance to child care providers. The division also uses CCDF funds to support child care for high risk populations including migrant and seasonal workers, parents in substance abuse treatment, teen and post-secondary student parents, and children with special needs.

Unemployment Insurance Division

Address: 875 Union St. NE, Salem 97311
Phone: 503-947-1330
Fax: 503-947-1668
Web: www.oregon.gov/EMPLOY/UI
Contact: David Gerstenfeld, Assistant Director
Statutory Authority: ORS 657.601
Duties and Responsibilities: Unemployment Insurance benefits replace part of the income lost when workers become unemployed through no fault of their own. This softens the impact job losses have on workers and their communities. The division is responsible for paying benefits to eligible claimants in an accurate and timely manner, deciding eligibility issues, discouraging fraud and collecting taxes to fund the program.

The money used to pay Oregon unemployment insurance benefits comes from Oregon employers' state payroll taxes. The taxes collected are deposited in a trust fund used to pay unemployment insurance benefits to unemployed Oregon workers. Benefit payments totaled over $1.9 billion in 2011.

Workforce and Economic Research Division

Address: 875 Union St. NE, Salem 97311
Phone: 503-947-1229
Fax: 503-947-1210
Web: www.QualityInfo.org
Contact: Graham Slater, Administrator
Statutory Authority: ORS 657.601
Duties and Responsibilities: The division's team of economists, workforce analysts and researchers collect and analyze statewide and regional labor market information and help organizations and businesses apply it. Analysts provide concise, up-to-date information about the local and state economies and their effects on the workforce. Research staff studies labor force and related topics, supplies data and analysis to new and expanding firms, and analyzes occupational supply and demand, which is gathered through surveys sent to employers. Besides offering general information, staff is available to produce special reports upon request. Businesses, in turn, use this labor market information to identify challenges and opportunities. Economic development planners, educators and training providers, job applicants, legislators and the news media also regularly rely on this information to learn about workforce issues that affect Oregonians.

Other Entities:

Administrative Hearings, Office of

Address: 4600 25th Ave. NE, Suite 140, Salem 97301; Mail: PO Box 14020, Salem 97309-4020
Phone: 503-947-1918
Fax: 503-947-1920
E-mail: OAH@emp.state.or.us
Web: www.oregon.gov/OAH

Contact: Karla Forsythe, Chief Administrative Law Judge
Statutory Authority: ORS 183.605
Duties and Responsibilities: The Office of Administrative Hearings was created by the Legislature in 1999 to provide an independent and impartial forum for citizens and businesses to dispute state agency actions against them. Sixty-five professional administrative law judges hold over 30,000 hearings a year for approximately 70 state agencies. By statute, all administrative law judges are required to be "impartial in the performance of [their] duties and shall remain fair in all hearings." Oregon is the 22nd state in the nation with an independent central panel of administrative law judges.

Employment Appeals Board

Address: 875 Union St. NE, Salem 97311
Phone: 503-378-2077
Fax: 503-378-2129
Contact: Sarah Owens, Chair
Statutory Authority: ORS 657.685–657.690
Duties and Responsibilities: The three-member Employment Appeals Board (EAB) is appointed by the governor to review hearing decisions issued in contested unemployment insurance claims cases. The board performs new revisions of 2,500 to 3,000 cases per year, with authority to affirm, modify or reverse the decisions of administrative law judges of the Employment Department or to remand for additional evidence. Final written decisions of the EAB are subject to review by the Oregon Court of Appeals.

Employment Department Advisory Council

Address: 875 Union St. NE, Salem 97311
Phone: 503-947-1732
Fax: 503-947-1878
Contact: Melissa Leoni, Council Staff
Statutory Authority: ORS 657.695
Duties and Responsibilities: The Employment Department Advisory Council includes volunteer representatives of the public, management and labor. Council members are appointed by the governor. The council assists the director of the Employment Department in the effective development of policies and programs with respect to unemployment insurance, employment services, labor market information and child care.

Employer Council, Oregon

Address: 875 Union St. NE, Salem 97311
Phone: 503-947-1305
Fax: 503-947-1309
Contact: Greg Ivers, Coordinator
Duties and Responsibilities: The Oregon Employer Council is a partnership between Oregon employers and the Employment Department. The council brings together volunteer employer representatives who serve as advisors to the department to identify and address employment issues, primarily in the areas of employment services and other business needs. The council also provides educational seminars and job fairs for employers.

Employment Relations Board

Address: 528 Cottage St. NE, Suite 400, Salem 97301-3807
Phone: 503-378-3807
Fax: 503-373-0021
E-mail: Emprel.Board@state.or.us
Web: www.oregon.gov/ERB
Contact: Susan Rossiter, Chair
Statutory Authority: ORS Chapters 240, 663, ORS 243.650–243.795, 662.010–662.455
Duties and Responsibilities: The Employment Relations Board was established in 1977. It consists of three members appointed by the governor for four-year terms. The board administers the Public Employee Collective Bargaining Act, which covers collective bargaining in state and local government; the State Personnel Relations Law, which creates appeal rights for non-union state employees who believe they were treated unfairly in the workplace; and the private sector labor-management relations law, which concerns collective bargaining for private sector employees not covered by federal law.

The Board's Conciliation Service Office provides mediation services for solving collective bargaining disputes in public and private employment and provides lists of arbitrators for the resolution of labor disputes.

Energy, Department of

Address: 625 Marion St. NE, Salem 97301-3737
Phone: 503-378-4040; 1-800-221-8035 (Toll-free in Oregon)
Fax: 503-373-7806
E-mail: energy.in.internet@state.or.us
Web: www.oregon.gov/ENERGY
Contact: Lisa Schwartz, Director
Statutory Authority: ORS Chapters 469, 470
Duties and Responsibilities: The Department of Energy, created in 1975, ensures that Oregon has an adequate supply of reliable and affordable energy, is safe from nuclear contamination, develops clean energy resources, promotes renewable energy and cleans up nuclear waste. To encourage investments in energy efficiency and conservation, the department offers loans, tax credits, information and technical expertise to households, businesses, schools and governments. The department works to ensure

that Oregon's mix of energy resources minimizes harm to the environment and reliably meets the state's needs. To meet this commitment, the department formulates energy policies, advances the development of renewable energy resources, and evaluates whether proposed energy facilities are safe and environmentally acceptable.

The department also oversees the cleanup and safe transport of radioactive waste and develops and implements emergency plans in the event of an accident involving radioactive materials. A major focus is the cleanup of radioactive waste at the Hanford nuclear site on the Columbia River in eastern Washington. The department staffs two energy policy and regulatory boards. The Energy Facility Siting Council is a board of citizens appointed by the governor and confirmed by the Senate. The council determines whether large energy facilities may be built in Oregon. The Hanford Cleanup Board represents Oregon's interests related to the Hanford site.

Energy Facility Siting Council

Address: 625 Marion St. NE, Salem 97301-3737
Phone: 503-378-4040; 1-800-221-8035 (Toll-free in Oregon)
Contact: Bryan Wolfe, Chair

Hanford Cleanup Board

Address: 625 Marion St. NE, Salem 97301-3737
Phone: 503-378-4040; 1-800-221-8035 (Toll-free in Oregon)
Contact: Max Power, Chair

Engineering and Land Surveying, State Board of Examiners for

Address: 670 Hawthorne Ave. SE, Suite 220, Salem 97301
Phone: 503-362-2666
Fax: 503-362-5454
E-mail: osbeels@osbeels.org
Web: www.oregon.gov/OSBEELS
Contact: Mari Lopez, Executive Secretary
Statutory Authority: ORS 672.240
Duties and Responsibilities: The Oregon State Board of Examiners for Engineering and Land Surveying (OSBEELS) regulates the practices of engineering, land surveying and photogrammetry in the state in order to safeguard the life, health and property of the public. OSBEELS accomplishes this by setting standards of qualification for licensure, ensuring only individuals fully qualified by education, experience and examination are granted license to practice engineering, land surveying and photogrammetry in Oregon. The board ensures that licensed practitioners maintain competency, reviews relevant laws and rules and promulgates revisions, enforces regulatory laws and rules by investigating complaints related to violations, and disseminates information about board goals and activities to licensees and the public.

OSBEELS was established in 1919. In 1999, it transitioned to semi-independent status, making the board solely accountable for its performance. There are no tax dollars or general funds used towards the operation of OSBEELS. Activities are supported entirely by fees received from applicants and licensed professionals. OSBEELS currently regulates more than 13,000 licensed professionals in Oregon and is directed by an 11-member board appointed by the governor.

Environmental Quality, Department of

Address: 811 SW 6th Ave., Portland 97204-1390
Phone: 503-229-5696; Toll-free (Oregon only): 1-800-452-4011
Fax: 503-229-6762
Web: www.oregon.gov/DEQ
Contact: Dick Pedersen, Director
Statutory Authority: ORS Chapters 454, 459, 466, 467, 468
Duties and Responsibilities: The Department of Environmental Quality (DEQ) is responsible for protecting and enhancing Oregon's water and air quality, managing the proper disposal of solid and hazardous wastes, providing assistance in cleaning up contaminated properties, and enforcing Oregon's environmental laws. The agency was formed in 1969 to replace the State Sanitary Authority, which had been created in 1938 when citizens overwhelmingly supported an initiative to clean up the Willamette River.

As environmental problems have become more complex, DEQ's roles have expanded. DEQ helps fight climate change with policies to reduce greenhouse gas emissions. It is committed to preventing toxic chemical releases and reducing risks from toxins already in our environment. It is helping Oregonians solve environmental problems by encouraging personal responsibility and providing communities with technical assistance.

DEQ employs a staff of about 700, including scientists, engineers, technicians and environmental specialists. The agency is headquartered in Portland, with regional offices in Bend, Eugene and Portland and field offices in Coos Bay, Medford, Pendleton, Salem and The Dalles. The DEQ director has the authority to issue civil penalties for violations of pollution laws and standards. DEQ relies on several advisory committees of citizens and government officials to help guide its decision-making.

Environmental Quality Commission

Address: 811 SW 6th Ave., Portland 97204
Phone: 503-229-6585
Fax: 503-229-6762
Contact: Joan Stevens-Schwenger
Duties and Responsibilities: The Environmental Quality Commission, DEQ's policy and rulemaking board, adopts administrative rules, issues orders and judges appeals of fines or other department actions, and hires the DEQ director. Commission members are appointed to four-year terms by the governor.

Air Quality Division

Address: 811 SW 6th Ave., Portland 97204-1390
Phone: 503-229-5696
Fax: 503-229-5675
Web: www.oregon.gov/DEQ/AQ
Contact: Andy Ginsburg, Administrator
Duties and Responsibilities: The Air Quality Division's goal is to achieve clean and healthy air for all Oregonians. DEQ works to ensure that federal clean air standards are met, that the public is protected from toxic air pollutants and that our scenic vistas are visible. To meet these goals, DEQ develops and implements strategies to reduce emissions from industry, cars, trucks, burning and other sources of air pollution. Among other strategies, DEQ regulates about 1,200 sources of industrial air pollution through permits, operates a vehicle inspection program in the Portland and Medford areas, and protects the public from asbestos in buildings that are being demolished or remodeled.

Laboratory and Environmental Assessment Division

Address: 3150 NW 229th Ave., Bldg. B, Hillsboro 97124
Phone: (503) 693-5700
Fax: (503) 693-4999
Web: www.oregon.gov/DEQ/LAB
Contact: Greg Pettit, Administrator
Duties and Responsibilities: DEQ opened its Laboratory and Environmental Assessment Division facility in Hillsboro in 2007. DEQ shares the state-of-the-art facility with the Oregon State Public Health Lab. About 70 DEQ employees work at the lab, which was remodeled for energy savings and with the latest lab equipment in mind. The facility allows DEQ to test for toxic compounds at much lower concentrations than previously able, which leads to better environmental protection. The improvements include a special clean room for trace metals analysis at very low concentrations.

Monitoring and assessment programs conducted by the DEQ lab provide the foundation for restoring, maintaining and enhancing Oregon's environmental quality. DEQ scientists maintain monitoring networks for air, water and land and conduct special studies to determine the status, trends and sources of impairment for Oregon's environmental quality.

Land Quality Division

Address: 811 SW 6th Ave., Portland 97204-1390
Phone: 503-229-5696
Fax: 503-229-6977
Web: www.oregon.gov/DEQ/LQ
Contact: Wendy Wiles, Administrator
Duties and Responsibilities: The Land Quality Division oversees agency programs in environmental cleanup and site assessment, hazardous and solid waste, spill response and underground storage tanks.

DEQ inventories and assesses sites contaminated with hazardous waste and supervises development and implementation of cleanup strategies.

The emergency response program provides DEQ's round-the-clock capability to deal with releases of hazardous materials and oil to both land and water and provides on-scene incident commanders for major cleanups.

DEQ oversees Oregon's only hazardous waste landfill, regulates hazardous waste disposal and offers businesses pollution prevention assistance. A separate program regulates underground storage tanks.

Landfills are regulated through DEQ permits that set requirements for design, operation and monitoring. DEQ promotes waste reduction education and waste prevention strategies and implements a state recycling law that requires cities to provide curbside recycling collection and reduce garbage going into landfills. The solid waste program also requires manufacturers selling computers, monitors and televisions in Oregon to provide a system for free, convenient recycling of these products.

The division also operates a program to ensure that ballast water discharges and related maritime activities do not harm the state's water bodies.

Water Quality Division

Address: 811 SW 6th Ave., Portland 97204-1390
Phone: 503-229-5696
Fax: 503-229-5408
Web: www.oregon.gov/DEQ/WQ
Contact: Greg Aldrich, Administrator
Duties and Responsibilities: The Water Quality Division sets and enforces water quality standards and monitors 19 river basins around the state for water quality. The program also monitors and assesses groundwater and implements strategies to protect and enhance Oregon's waters. Oregon law prohibits discharging pollution into state waters without a DEQ-issued permit. DEQ regulates more

than 4,800 waste discharges from city sewage treatment plants, industrial facilities and stormwater-generating activities. DEQ develops strategies to reduce pollution carried by runoff from urban areas, agricultural and forest practices, and construction. The program provides loans to local governments for sewage treatment systems and control of non-regulated pollution sources. DEQ also regulates the installation of septic sewage disposal systems.

Film and Video Office

Address: 1001 SE Water Ave., Suite 430, Portland 97214
Phone: 503-229-5832
Fax: 503-229-6869
E-mail: shoot@oregonfilm.com
Web: www.oregonfilm.org
Contact: Vince Porter, Executive Director
Statutory Authority: ORS 284.305
Duties and Responsibilities: The Oregon Film and Video Office acts as a liaison between production companies and Oregon businesses, citizens and government. The office markets film locations and the film and television workforce within Oregon in addition to promoting Oregon companies and workers in the emerging areas of multimedia. The office also recruits film and video related businesses to relocate to Oregon on a permanent basis and serves as a resource for local communities interested in attracting film production.

Fish and Wildlife, Oregon Department of

Address: 3406 Cherry Ave. NE, Salem 97303-4924
Phone: 503-947-6000; Toll-free: 1-800-720-6339 (ODFW); Licensing: 503-947-6101; Controlled Hunts Hotline (Recorded): 503-947-6102
E-mail: odfw.info@state.or.us
Web: www.dfw.state.or.us

Director's Office

Address: 3406 Cherry Ave. NE, Salem 97303-4924
Phone: 503-947-6044
Fax: 503-947-6042
Contact: Roy Elicker, Director; Curt Melcher, Deputy Director for Fish and Wildlife Programs; Debbie Colbert, Deputy Director for Administration
Statutory Authority: ORS 496.080–496.166
Duties and Responsibilities: The Oregon Department of Fish and Wildlife (ODFW) is responsible for all Oregon fish and wildlife resources and their habitats for use and enjoyment by present and future generations. The agency's responsibilities include managing fish and wildlife populations, conservation policies, operating hatcheries, selling hunting and angling licenses, advising on habitat protection for Oregon's diverse fish and wildlife populations and educating the public on natural resource issues. ODFW works closely with other federal and state agencies, tribes, volunteers, property owners, and hunters and anglers to balance protection of fish and wildlife with the economic, social and recreational needs of Oregonians.

Fish and Wildlife Commission, Oregon

Address: 3406 Cherry Ave. NE, Salem 97303-4924
Phone: 503-947-6044
Web: www.dfw.state.or.us/agency/commission
Contact: Director's Office
Statutory Authority: ORS 496.090
Duties and Responsibilities: The Oregon Fish and Wildlife Commission consists of seven members appointed by the governor for four-year terms, subject to confirmation by the Senate. One commissioner must be from each congressional district, one from east of the Cascades and one from west of the Cascades. All members have a general knowledge of fish and wildlife issues and possess natural resources backgrounds.

Consistent with state law, the commission formulates general state programs and policies concerning management and conservation of fish and wildlife resources, and represents the public interest of the state and makes decisions affecting the wildlife resources of the state for the benefit of those resources. The commission provides for the productive and sustainable utilization of wildlife resources for all groups of users.

Fish Division

Address: 3406 Cherry Ave. NE, Salem 97303-4924
Phone: 503-947-6201
Fax: 503-947-6202
Web: www.dfw.state.or.us/fish
Contact: Edward Bowles, Administrator
Duties and Responsibilities: The Fish Division manages fish populations by setting regulations for gamefish species, monitoring populations and operating 34 fish hatcheries, which produce up to 80 percent of all salmon, trout and steelhead caught in Oregon each year. The division works cooperatively with other state and federal agencies and tribes on habitat and fishery management issues for inland and ocean waters, works with landowners to improve and protect habitat, and coordinates law enforcement needs and activities with the Oregon State Police.

Restoration and Enhancement Board

Address: 3406 Cherry Ave. NE, Salem 97303-4924
Phone: 503-947-6259
Web: www.dfw.state.or.us/fish/RE
Contact: Josie Thompson, Coordinator
Statutory Authority: ORS 496.286–496.291
Duties and Responsibilities: The Oregon Fisheries Restoration and Enhancement Act (R&E) was signed into law in 1989. This act allows the ODFW to undertake a comprehensive program to restore state owned fish hatcheries, enhance natural fish production and provide additional public access to fishing waters. The R&E program increases sport recreational fishing opportunities and supports and improves the commercial salmon fishery. The R&E program also seeks out and funds privately sponsored projects and supports ongoing ODFW programs that are integral to fisheries management. R&E projects create economic stimulus in rural and urban communities throughout Oregon.

Information and Education Division

Address: 3406 Cherry Ave. NE, Salem 97303-4924
Phone: 503-947-6000
Fax: 503-947-6009
Contact: Roger Fuhrman, Administrator
Duties and Responsibilities: The Information and Education Division teaches individuals the skills needed to safely participate in aquatic, angling, hunting and other outdoor activities. The division also informs the public about recreational opportunities throughout the state, fishing and hunting regulations, wildlife viewing opportunities, and other issues related to the state's fish and wildlife resources.

Wildlife Division

Address: 3406 Cherry Ave. NE, Salem 97303-4924
Phone: 503-947-6300
Fax: 503-947-6330
Web: www.dfw.state.or.us/wildlife
Contact: Ron Anglin, Administrator
Duties and Responsibilities: The Wildlife Division manages all game and non-game wildlife species in Oregon. The division manages game species by setting hunting and trapping regulations and relocating wildlife or applying other management techniques. The division manages non-hunted species through the Wildlife Diversity Program, works cooperatively with other state and federal agencies and tribes on habitat and wildlife management issues, works with landowners to improve habitat or manage animal damage complaints, and coordinates law enforcement needs and activities with the Oregon State Police.

Access and Habitat Board

Address: 3406 Cherry Ave. NE, Salem 97303-4924
Phone: 503-947-6087
Web: www.dfw.state.or.us/lands/AH
Contact: Matthew Keenan, Coordinator
Statutory Authority: ORS 496.228
Duties and Responsibilities: The Oregon Department of Fish and Wildlife's Access and Habitat Program was created in 1993 to improve wildlife habitat and public hunting access on private lands throughout the state. The program's motto, "Landowners and Hunters Together for Wildlife," conveys its mission to foster partnership between landowners and hunters for the benefit of the wildlife they all value. To accomplish those objectives, the program provides grants for a variety of cooperative wildlife habitat and hunter access projects.

Internal Support:

Administrative Services Division

Address: 3406 Cherry Ave. NE, Salem 97303-4924
Phone: 503-947-6000
Fax: 503-947-6156
Contact: Shirlene Gonzalez, Administrator
Duties and Responsibilities: The Administrative Services Division oversees the department's fishing and hunting licensing responsibilities, fiscal management, budget and contracts management and economic forecasting for the agency.

Human Resources Division

Address: 3406 Cherry Ave. NE, Salem 97303-4924
Phone: 503-947-6051
Fax: 503-947-6050
Contact: Roxie Burns, Administrator
Duties and Responsibilities: The Human Resources Division serves 1,350 employees statewide, providing programs to recruit, maintain and train a diverse workforce in a safe environment.

Information Systems Division

Address: 3406 Cherry Ave. NE, Salem 97303-4924
Phone: 503-947-6000
Fax: 503-947-6265
Contact: Doug Juergensen, Administrator
Duties and Responsibilities: The Information Systems Division is responsible for developing and supporting information processing systems services and training, and maintaining the Point-of-Sale computer system for license sales.

Forest Resources Institute, Oregon

Address: 317 SW 6th Ave., Suite 400, Portland 97204
Phone: 971-673-2944
Fax: 971-673-2946
Web: http://Oregonforests.org
Contact: Paul F. Barnum, Executive Director
Statutory Authority: ORS 526.600–526.675
Duties and Responsibilities: The Oregon Forest Resources Institute (OFRI) is a non-profit, semi-independent agency dedicated to forestry education and outreach to forest landowners and the general public, including K–12 students. It is governed by a board of directors largely appointed by the state forester and representing small, medium and large forest landowners. Ex officio members of the board include the dean of the Oregon State University College of Forestry and a public representative appointed by the president of the Senate and the speaker of the House. Since its creation by the Legislature in 1991, OFRI has worked to create links among forest landowners, the Oregon State University College of Forestry, Oregon Department of Forestry, federal land managers and non-governmental organizations to promote science-based information about forest management. OFRI is funded by a portion of the harvest tax on forest products.

OFRI's programs include workshops, symposia, conferences, curricula development and scientific research and studies. OFRI develops publications and displays on a wide variety of forestry subjects and its Web site is a source for forestry education materials for the public, forest landowners, and students.

Forestry Department, State

Address: 2600 State St., Salem 97310
Phone: 503-945-7200; TTY: 1-800-437-4490
Fax: 503-945-7212
E-mail: information@odf.state.or.us
Web: www.oregon.gov/ODF
Contact: Doug Decker, State Forester
Statutory Authority: ORS Chapter 526
Duties and Responsibilities: The State Forestry Department was established in 1911. It is under the direction of the state forester who is appointed by the State Board of Forestry. The statutes direct the state forester to act on all matters pertaining to forestry, including collecting and sharing information about the conditions of Oregon's forests, protecting forestlands and conserving forest resources. Specific activities include fire protection for 16 million acres of private, state and federal forests; regulation of forest practices (under the Oregon Forest Practices Act) and promotion of forest stewardship; implementation of the Oregon Plan for Salmon and Watersheds; detection and control of harmful forest insect pests and forest tree diseases on state and private lands; management of 848,000 acres of state-owned forestlands; forestry assistance to Oregon's non-industrial private woodland owners; forest resource planning; and community and urban forestry assistance.

Board of Forestry, State

Contact: John L. Blackwell, Chair
Phone: 503-945-7210
Statutory Authority: ORS Chapter 526
Duties and Responsibilities: The Board of Forestry is a seven-member citizen board appointed by the governor and confirmed by the Senate. The board's duty is to represent the public interest. No more than three members of the board may receive any significant portion of their income from the forest products industry. At least one member must reside in each of the three major forest regions of the state.

The Board of Forestry oversees all matters of forest policy within the state. Additionally, the board appoints the state forester, adopts rules regulating forest practices and other forestry programs, and provides general supervision of the state forester's duties. Thus, the board supervises many actions related to the sustainable management of Oregon's forests. The board does not limit its scope to state or private forestlands. Its policies and leadership are designed to have a positive influence over all of the state's 30.4 million acres of forests.

The board periodically develops a strategic plan called the Forestry Program for Oregon that describes the Board of Forestry's guidance to the state forester, Legislature, governor and the public on matters of forest policy and the use of sound forest management. With nearly half of Oregon's land base covered by forests, the successful implementation of this vision can profoundly affect the lives of all Oregonians.

County Forestland Classification Committees

Address: 2600 State St., Salem 97310
Phone: 503-945-7204
Contact: Nancy Hirsch, Fire Protection Division Chief
Statutory Authority: ORS 526.305–526.350
Duties and Responsibilities: Each county may establish a County Forestland Classification Committee of six persons appointed by the state forester, the director of the Oregon State University Extension Service, the State Fire Marshal and the county governing body. Owners of forestland and grazing land must be represented. These committees are charged with investigating forestlands to

determine how the lands are to be classified. The classifications are used by the Board of Forestry and the state forester in administering Oregon's wildland fire protection laws, promoting the primary use for which that land is classified.

The committee must hold public hearings before final classifications and reclassification. Appeals by landowners may be taken to the circuit court. When no classification of forestland is made by a committee, the state forester may make this determination.

Emergency Fire Cost Committee

Address: 2600 State St., Salem 97310
Phone: 503-945-7449
Contact: Tim Keith, Fund Administrator
Statutory Authority: ORS 477.750–477.775
Duties and Responsibilities: The Emergency Fire Cost Committee supervises and controls the distribution of monies from the Oregon Forest Land Protection Fund which was established for emergency firefighting expenditures in controlling forest fires. Four members are appointed to the committee by the State Board of Forestry to serve four-year terms.

Family Forestlands, Committee for

Address: 2600 State St., Salem 97310
Phone: 503-945-7482
Contact: Peter Daugherty, Private Forests Division Chief
Statutory Authority: ORS 526.016
Duties and Responsibilities: The Committee for Family Forestlands advises the Board of Forestry in matters relating to family forestlands. These include maintaining a viable base of family-owned forestlands; evaluating the effects of forest policy changes on family forestland owners; and maintaining and enhancing the attributes of family forestlands, such as timber availability, watershed health and habitat for fish and wildlife. The Board of Forestry appoints the seven voting members to three-year terms. Six ex officio members represent various organizations, including the Oregon State University College of Forestry and the Oregon Small Woodlands Association.

Forest Resource Trust Advisory Committee

Address: 2600 State St., Salem 97310
Phone: 503-945-7493
Contact: Jim Cathcart
Statutory Authority: ORS 526.700
Duties and Responsibilities: The Forest Resource Trust Advisory Committee was established in 1993. The Forest Resource Trust provides funds for financial, technical and related assistance to private non-industrial forest landowners. This assistance is used for timber stand establishment and improved management of forestlands for timber production as well as for wildlife, water quality and other environmental purposes. The Board of Forestry has responsibility for managing the trust. The committee assists the board in setting policy for the best use and investment of funds available to the trust and otherwise assisting board members in carrying out trustee duties. The state forester is responsible for implementing board policies and trust programs.

Forest Trust Land Advisory Committee

Address: 2600 State St., Salem 97310
Phone: 503-945-7213
Contact: Mike Bordelon, State Forests Division Chief
Statutory Authority: ORS 526.156
Duties and Responsibilities: The 1987 Legislature established the Forest Trust Land Advisory Committee to advise the State Board of Forestry and the state forester on the management of lands subject to the provisions of statutes and on other matters in which the counties may have a responsibility pertaining to forestland. The committee is composed of the Board of Directors of the Council of Forest Trust Land Counties. The council represents the 15 state/county forest trust land counties in policy matters related to the management of the forestlands and distribution of revenues produced from those lands.

Regional Forest Practice Committees

Address: 2600 State St., Salem 97310
Phone: 503-945-7482
Contact: Peter Daugherty, Private Forests Division Chief
Statutory Authority: ORS 527.650
Duties and Responsibilities: The Northwest Oregon, Southwest Oregon and Eastern Oregon Regional Forest Practice Committees make recommendations to the Board of Forestry on forest practice rules appropriate to the forest conditions in their regions. The Board of Forestry appoints nine members to each committee to serve three-year terms.

Geologist Examiners, State Board of

Address: 707 13th St. SE, Suite 114, Salem 97301
Phone: 503-566-2837
Fax: 503-485-2947
E-mail: osbge.info@state.or.us
Web: www.oregon.gov/OSBGE
Contact: Christine Valentine, Administrator
Statutory Authority: ORS 672.615
Duties and Responsibilities: The purpose of the State Board of Geologist Examiners, established in 1977, is to safeguard the health, welfare and property of Oregonians affected by the geologic fields

of ground water, land-use planning, mineral exploration and development, geologic hazards and the further development of the science of geology through the regulation of professional practice.

The board evaluates qualifications, examines and registers geologists, certifies those with engineering geology specialty, and suspends, revokes or refuses to renew registration or certification and assesses civil penalties when warranted. The board practices cooperative registration with other states that register geologists. More than 1,000 geologists are registered in Oregon, with nearly 250 also holding an engineering geology certification.

Geology and Mineral Industries, Oregon Department of

Address: 800 NE Oregon St., Suite 965, Portland 97232
Phone: 971-673-1555
Fax: 971-673-1562
Web: www.oregon.gov/DOGAMI
Contact: Vicki McConnell, State Geologist
Statutory Authority: ORS Chapters 516, 517, 520, 522
Duties and Responsibilities: The Oregon Department of Geology and Mineral Industries was created in 1937 and is Oregon's centralized source of geologic information. The department produces maps and reports that can be used to manage geologic resources, including water, and to reduce the loss of life and property due to geologic hazards. The department helps Oregonians understand and prepare for earthquakes, tsunamis, coastal erosion, landslides, floods and other geologic hazards. It is the lead regulator for geologic resources (oil, gas, geothermal energy, metallic and industrial minerals and sand, gravel and crushed stone), with attention paid to environmental, reclamation, conservation and related economic, engineering and technical issues.

The department provides geologic data to assist in policy development of state, federal and local governmental natural resource agencies as well as with industry and private sector groups. The department's library is a central repository for both published and unpublished state geologic information.

The Mineral Land Regulation and Reclamation Program, located at the Albany field office, is the lead coordinating agency for state mining regulation, operating through an interagency team-permit process. In Oregon, exploration and operating permits and bonds are required to ensure reclamation of land disturbed by mining.

Field Offices:

Albany
Mineral Land Regulation and Reclamation
Address: 229 Broadalbin St. NW, Albany 97321
Phone: 541-967-2039
Fax: 541-967-2075

Baker City
Address: 1995 Third St., Baker City 97814
Phone: 541-523-3133
Fax: 541-523-5992

Newport
Coastal Field Office
Address: 313 SW 2nd St., Suite D, Newport 97365
Phone: 541-574-6658
Fax: 541-265-5241

Geology and Mineral Industries Governing Board

Contact: Larry Givens, Chair
Duties and Responsibilities: The Geology and Mineral Industries Governing Board appoints the state geologist and approves the agency's budget. The governor appoints five members to four-year terms.

The Nature of the Northwest Information Center

Address: 800 NE Oregon St., Suite 965, Portland 97232
Phone: 971-673-2331
Fax: 971-673-1562
E-mail: info@naturenw.org
Web: www.naturenw.org
Contact: Don Haines, Manager
Duties and Responsibilities: The Nature of the Northwest Information Center is operated by the Department of Geology and Mineral Industries. The center provides "one-stop shopping" for natural resource, natural science, and outdoor recreation maps, books and brochures (some for sale, some free), which are primarily produced by state, federal and local government natural resource agencies.

Government Ethics Commission, Oregon

Address: 3218 Pringle Rd. SE, Rm. 220, Salem 97302-1544
Phone: 503-378-5105
Fax: 503-373-1456
E-mail: ogec.mail@state.or.us
Web: www.oregon.gov/OGEC
Contact: Ronald A. Bersin, Executive Director
Statutory Authority: ORS 171.725–171.785, 192.660, 192.685, ORS Chapter 244

Duties and Responsibilities: The Oregon Government Ethics Commission (GEC), established by vote of the people in 1974, is a seven-member citizen commission charged with enforcing government ethics laws. Government ethics laws prohibit public officials from using office for financial gain and require public disclosure of economic conflict of interest. The GEC also enforces state laws which require lobbyists and the entities they represent to register and periodically report their expenditures. The third area of GEC jurisdiction is the executive session provisions of public meetings law. Before 2007, the agency was known as the Oregon Government Standards and Practices Commission.

Health Authority, Oregon

Address: 500 Summer St. NE, E20, Salem 97301-1097
Phone: 503-947-2340; 877-398-9238
Fax: 503-947-2341
E-mail: OHA.DirectorsOffice@state.or.us and OHPB.Info@state.or.us
Web: www.oregon.gov/OHA
Contact: Bruce Goldberg, M.D., Director
Statutory Authority: ORS 413.032
Duties and Responsibilities: The Oregon Health Authority (OHA) was created to transform the state's system to make quality health care accessible and affordable for every Oregonian. OHA works to improve the lifelong health of Oregonians; increase the quality, reliability and availability of care for all Oregonians; and lower or contain the cost of care so it is affordable to everyone. Most health-related programs in the state, including Public Health, Addictions and Mental Health, Oregon State Hospital, Medical Assistance Programs (Oregon Health Plan-Medicaid), the Public Employees' Benefit Board and Oregon Educators Benefit Board, have been joined together under OHA.

Oregon Health Policy Board

Address: 500 Summer St. NE, E20, Salem 97301-1097
Phone: 503-947-2340; 877-398-9238
Fax: 503-947-2341
E-mail: OHPB.Info@state.or.us
Web: www.oregon.gov/OHA/OHPB
Statutory Authority: ORS 413.032
Duties and Responsibilities: The Oregon Health Policy Board serves as the policy-making and oversight body for the Oregon Health Authority. The nine-member, citizen-led board is appointed by the governor and confirmed by the Senate.

Addictions and Mental Health Division

Address: 500 Summer St. NE, E86 Salem 97301-1118
Phone: 503-945-5763; TTY: 1-800-375-2863
Fax: 503-378-8467
Web: www.oregon.gov/OHA/AMH
Contact: Linda Hammond, Interim Director
Duties and Responsibilities: The Addictions and Mental Health Division is responsible for delivering mental health and addiction services to adults and children. These services are delivered locally through community mental health programs and their contracted providers, as well as through state-operated psychiatric hospitals in Salem, Portland and Pendleton. The division is responsible for delivering addiction prevention and treatment services in the areas of alcohol, tobacco, drug addiction and problem gambling.

Addictions and Mental Health Planning and Advisory Council

Address: 500 Summer St. NE, E86, Salem 97301
Phone: 503-945-6196; TTY: 1-800-375-2863
Contact: Marisha L. Johnson, Mental Health Planner
Statutory Authority: 42 USC 300x-3

Alcohol and Drug Policy Commission

Address: 500 Summer St. NE, Salem 97301
Phone: 503-945-9707
Fax: 971-673-3320
Contact: Mary Ellen Glynn, Executive Director
Statutory Authority: ORS 430.240

Blue Mountain Recovery Center

Address: 2600 Westgate, Pendleton 97801
Phone: 503-945-5763; TTY: 800-375-2863
E-mail: Amh.web@state.or.us
Duties and Responsibilities: Blue Mountain Recovery Center (BMRC) is a 60-bed inpatient adult mental health care facility in Pendleton, operated by the Oregon Health Authority's Addictions and Mental Health Division.

Located in the admission and treatment building of the former Eastern Oregon State Hospital, Blue Mountain Recovery Center was built in 1948. BMRC admits clients from all areas of the state and is the primary state hospital resource for Eastern Oregon. BMRC serves civilly committed individuals with severe and persistent mental illness who have been found to be a danger to themselves or others or are unable to care for their basic needs due to a mental illness. In addition, BMRC provides care and treatment for a small number of forensic clients who have close family ties in Eastern Oregon.

Oregon State Hospital

Address: Salem Campus adminstration: 2600 Center St. NE, Salem 97301; Portland Campus: 1121 NE 2nd Ave., Portland 97232
Phone: 503-945-2870, Salem; 503-731-8620, Portland
Duties and Responsibilities: Oregon State Hospital (OSH) operates under the direction of the Oregon Health Authority's Mental Health and Addictions Division.

Adults needing long-term intensive psychiatric treatment for severe and persistent mental illness who are civilly or criminally committed to OSH receive treatment at campuses in Salem and Portland. The mission of OHS is to provide therapeutic, evidence-based, patient-centered treatment focusing on recovery and community reintegration, all in a safe environment.

Medical Assistance Programs

Address: 500 Summer St. NE, E49, Salem 97301
Phone: 503-945-5772; TTY: 711; Toll-free: 1-800-527-5772
Fax: 503-373-7689
Contact: Judy Mohr Peterson, Director
Duties and Responsibilities: Medical Assistance Programs (MAP) oversees the Oregon Health Plan (OHP), Oregon's innovative Medicaid program that has saved $15 billion in state and federal dollars over the past 18 years. MAP is responsible for the budget, policies and systems that support the "triple aim" of better health, better care and lower costs for services to OHP clients. Services are delivered locally through Coordinated Care Organizations, community-based networks of all types of health care providers that coordinate care for each OHP client. MAP also provides daily service to OHP clients, prospective clients, community partners, contracted health plans and providers.

Public Health Division

Address: 800 NE Oregon St., Suite 930, Portland 97232
Phone: 971-673-1222
Fax: 971-673-1299
E-mail: health.webmaster@state.or.us
Web: http://public.health.oregon.gov
Contact: Mel Kohn, M.D., Public Health Director
Duties and Responsibilities: The Public Health Division works to improve lifelong health for all Oregonians by promoting health and preventing the leading causes of death, disease and injury in the state. The division consists of the Office of the State Public Health Director, the Center for Health Protection, the Center for Prevention and Health Promotion and the Center for Public Health Practice. The division oversees health promotion and prevention activities, health care facilities and licensing, environmental health regulation, public health emergency preparedness and epidemiological outbreak investigations. The division oversees the Oregon State Public Health Laboratory, which supports state and local infectious disease control efforts, preventing metabolic disorders detectable at birth and assuring the quality of testing in clinical and environmental laboratories.

Conference of Local Health Officials

Address: 800 NE Oregon St., Suite 930, Portland 97232
Phone: 971-673-1222
Fax: 971-673-1299
Web: http://public.health.oregon.gov/ProviderPartnerResources/LocalHealthDepartmentResources
Contact: Tom Engle
Statutory Authority: ORS 431.330

Healthy Kids, Office of

Address: 500 Summer St. NE, E40, Salem 97301
Phone: 503-945-6809
Fax: 503-945-6871
E-mail: hkp.partners@state.or.us
Web: www.oregonhealthykids.gov
Contact: Cathy Kaufmann, Administrator
Duties and Responsibilities: The Office of Healthy Kids is an expansion of the Oregon Health Plan, providing no-cost, low-cost and full-cost health coverage options for uninsured Oregon children and teens up to 19 years of age. The program office works with community organizations to reach uninsured families across the state.

Public Health Advisory Board

Address: 800 NE Oregon St., Suite 930, Portland 97232
Phone: 971-673-1222; TTY: 971-673-0372
Fax: 971-673-1299
Web: http://public.health.oregon.gov/ProviderPartnerResources/LocalHealthDepartmentResources
Contact: Katy King, Government Relations Manager; Brittany Sande, Staff
Statutory Authority: ORS 431.195
Duties and Responsibilities: Oregon's Public Health Advisory Board (PHAB) serves as an advisory body to the Oregon Health Authority on policy matters related to public health programs, provides a review of statewide public health issues and participates in public health policy development.

Radiation Advisory Committee

Address: 800 NE Oregon St., Suite 640, Portland 97232
Phone: 971-673-0490
Fax: 971-673-0553
Contact: David Howe

Other Entities:

Educators Benefit Board, Oregon

Address: 1225 Ferry St. SE, Suite B, Salem 97301
Phone: 1-888-469-6322
Fax: 503-378-5832
E-mail: oebb.benefits@state.or.us
Web: www.oregon.gov/OHA/OEBB
Contact: Joan M. Kapowich, Administrator
Statutory Authority: ORS 243.864
Duties and Responsibilities: Created in 2007, the Oregon Educators Benefit Board (OEBB) provides health and dental benefits for most of Oregon's school district and education service district (ESD) employees. Community colleges can choose to purchase health care benefit plans through OEBB.

OEBB purchases and pools benefits for school districts, ESDs and community college employees to create administrative savings for educational entities throughout the state. The board consists of 10 members appointed by the governor and confirmed by the Senate.

Public Employees' Benefit Board

Address: 1225 Ferry St. SE, Suite B, Salem 97301
Phone: 503-373-1102
Fax: 503-373-1654
E-mail: inquiries.pebb@state.or.us
Web: www.oregon.gov/DAS/PEBB
Contact: Joan M. Kapowich, Administrator
Statutory Authority: ORS 243.125
Duties and Responsibilities: The Public Employees' Benefit Board (PEBB) is responsible for the design, purchase and administration of benefit plans for approximately 50,000 state employees, 77,000 dependents, 300 COBRA-eligible former state employees and 2,000 pre-Medicare eligible retirees. The benefit plans include contracts for medical, dental, life, accidental death, disability and long-term care insurance and IRS-qualified flexible spending accounts. PEBB is also responsible for providing education, training and ongoing communication to state employees, dependents and agencies regarding benefits, services offered and federal and state health benefit policy.

Health Policy and Research, Office for Oregon

Address: 1225 Ferry St. SE, 1st Floor, Salem 97301
Phone: 503-373-1779
Fax: 503-378-5511
E-mail: Jeanene.Smith@state.or.us
Web: www.oregon.gov/OHA/OHPR
Contact: Jeanene Smith, M.D., MPH, Administrator
Statutory Authority: ORS 442.011
Duties and Responsibilities: The Office for Oregon Health Policy and Research advises the Legislature and governor on health policy issues. The office analyzes and recommends options for Oregon's health care reform efforts and also provides interagency coordination and oversight.

Health Analytics, Office of

Address: 1225 Ferry St. SE, 1st Floor, Salem 97301
Phone: 503-373-1818
Fax: 503-378-5511
E-mail: gretchen.morley@state.or.us
Web: www.oregon.gov/OHA/OHPR
Contact: Gretchen Morley, MPA, Director
Statutory Authority: ORS 442.011, 413.032
Duties and Responsibilities: The Office of Health Analytics conducts research and data analysis critical to improving the health of Oregonians. Health Analytics collects and analyzes data to inform policy development, program implementation and system evaluation. Health Analytics collaborates with professional researchers to develop a body of knowledge that can be used to ensure better health, better health care and lower costs of care.

Major initiatives associated with data collection and dissemination include: Oregon's All-Payer All-Claims database, behavioral health administrative and outcome data, coordinated care organizations and managed care quality metrics, and epidemiological client perception of care and insurance surveys.

Health Evidence Review Commission

Address: 1225 Ferry St. SE, 1st Floor, Salem 97301
Phone: 503-373- 1985
Fax: 503-378-5511
E-mail: Darren.D.Coffman@state.or.us
Web: www.oregon.gov/oha/ohpr/pages/herc/index.aspx
Contact: Darren Coffman, Director
Statutory Authority: ORS 414.688 to 414.704

Medicaid Advisory Committee

Address: 1225 Ferry St. SE, 1st Floor, Salem 97301
Phone: 503-373-2275
Fax: 503-378-5511
E-mail: Oliver.Droppers@state.or.us
Web: www.oregon.gov/oha/OHPR/Pages/mac/MACwelcomepage.aspx

Contact: Oliver Droppers
Statutory Authority: ORS 414.211–414.227

Pain Management Commission

Address: 1225 Ferry St. SE, 1st Floor, Salem 97301
Phone: 503-373-1605
Fax: 503-378-5511
Web: www.oregon.gov/oha/OHPR/Pages/pmc/index.aspx
Contact: Kathy Kirk, Coordinator
Statutory Authority: ORS 413.570–413.599

Prescription Drug Program, Oregon

Address: 500 Summer St. NE, E55, Salem 97301
Phone: 503-945-7834
Fax: 503-378-6842
E-mail: Missy.Dolan@state.or.us
Web: www.oregon.gov/OHA/pharmacy/OPDP
Contact: Missy Dolan, Administrator
Statutory Authority: ORS 414.312–414.318
Duties and Responsibilities: The Oregon Prescription Drug Program (OPDP) was created in 2003 to pool prescription drug purchasing for group purchasers and uninsured or underinsured residents of Oregon. By participating in the OPDP, employer group purchasers and facilities enjoy the leverage offered through a larger negotiating body, as well as transparent contracting with financially guaranteed performance goals. Uninsured or underinsured residents of Oregon may participate in OPDP through a discount program honored at most pharmacies in the state. The discounts they receive are the same provided to group participants, and there is no cost for the individuals enrolled in this discount program. OPDP has joined with Washington's WPDP to form the Northwest Prescription Drug Consortium. Together, they have launched Group Purchasing Organization programs for facilities and eligible employer groups including attractive wholesaler discount programs.

Private Health Partnerships, Office of

Address: 250 Church St. SE, Suite 200, Salem 97301-3921
Phone: 503-373-1692; Toll-free in Oregon: 1-800-542-3104
Fax: 503-378-8365
E-mail: ophp.mail@state.or.us
Web: www.oregon.gov/OHA/OPHP
Contact: Don Myron, Administrator
Statutory Authority: ORS 735.700
Duties and Responsibilities: The Office of Private Health Partnerships (OPHP) was created in 1987 to help Oregonians obtain health benefit coverage. The agency provides information about health insurance to individuals, small employers, civic groups and others. Beginning January 1, 2014, most OPHP programs will no longer be needed due to the full implementation of 2010's federal Affordable Care Act.

Family Health Insurance Assistance Program

Address: PO Box 5880, Salem 97304-0880
Phone: 503-373-7419; Toll-free in Oregon: 1-888-564-9669
Fax: 1-866-843-8936
E-mail: ophp.mail@state.or.us
Web: www.oregon.gov/oha/OPHP/FHIAP
Contact: John McLean, Program Manager
Statutory Authority: ORS 414.841
Duties and Responsibilities: The Family Health Insurance Assistance Program (FHIAP) was created by the 1997 Legislature to help low-income Oregonians afford private health insurance. The program subsidizes or pays up to 95 percent of a member's health insurance premium and 100 percent for children under 19 years old. Due to the implementation of the federal Affordable Care Act, this program will sunset in January 2014.

Healthy KidsConnect and Healthy Kids Employer Sponsored Insurance

Address: 250 Church St. SE, Suite 200, Salem 97301-3921
Phone: 503-378-8631; Toll-free in Oregon: 888-260-4555
Fax: 503-373-7251
E-mail: hkc.info@state.or.us
Web: www.oregon.gov/oha/OPHP/kidsconnect
Contact: Eve Ford, Program Manager
Statutory Authority: ORS 414.231
Duties and Responsibilities: Created by the 2009 Legislature, Healthy KidsConnect and Healthy Kids Employer Sponsored Insurance provide private market coverage for uninsured children through age 18 in families with incomes above the 200 percent federal poverty level (FPL). Families above 200 percent, up to and including 300 percent FPL, receive subsidies based on income. Families above 300 percent FPL also have access to the coverage, but no subsidies are available. As of January 1, 2014, the Healthy KidsConnect Program will continue in as part of the federal Affordable Care Act.

Information, Education and Outreach

Address: 250 Church St. SE, Suite 200, Salem 97301-3921
Phone: 503-373-1692; Toll-free in Oregon: 1-800-542-3104
Fax: 503-378-8365
E-mail: ophp.mail@state.or.us
Web: www.oregon.gov/OHA/OPHP
Contact: Mark I. Jungvirt, Manager

Statutory Authority: ORS 735.700
Duties and Responsibilities: The Information, Education and Outreach (IEO) program supports the Oregon Health Authority's mission by establishing and maintaining relationships with private and public sector partners. IEO trains employers, insurance producers (agents), industry professionals and civic groups and educates consumers and stakeholders on the health care delivery system and state programs.

Medical Insurance Pool, Oregon

Address: C/O Regence BlueCross BlueShield of Oregon, PO Box 1271, Portland 97207-1271
Phone: 503-225-6620; Toll-free: 1-800-848-7280
Fax: 503-225-5474
E-mail: omip.mail@state.or.us
Web: www.oregon.gov/OHA/OPHP/omip
Contact: Don Myron, Administrator
Statutory Authority: ORS 735.600–735.650
Duties and Responsibilities: The Oregon Medical Insurance Pool (OMIP) and the Federal Medical Insurance Pool offer guaranteed-issue health insurance coverage, regardless of income level, for individuals who are unable to obtain medical insurance because of health conditions. OMIP also provides medical insurance for Oregonians who have exhausted their COBRA coverage and do not have any commercial Oregon Portability coverage available through the previous insurance carrier, or for those who qualify to receive a federal subsidy through the Health Coverage Tax Credit program. Due to the implementation of the federal Affordable Care Act, OMIP programs will sunset in January 2014.

Health Licensing Agency, Oregon

Address: 700 Summer St. NE, Suite 320, Salem 97301-1287
Phone: 503-378-8667; TTY: 503-373-2114
Fax: 503-370-9004
E-mail: ohla.info@state.or.us
Web: www.oregon.gov/OHLA
Contact: Holly Mercer, Interim Director
Statutory Authority: ORS 676.600–676.992
Duties and Responsibilities: The Oregon Health Licensing Agency (OHLA) is a state consumer protection agency providing centralized regulatory oversight for multiple volunteer citizen boards of health and related professions. The agency works to promote consumer protection through education, enforcement and partnerships and to promote a positive business environment by reducing barriers to professional practice.

The boards under OHLA's administration set educational and professional scope of practice requirements for their fields of practice. The agency director assumes responsibility for central operations, achieving outcomes, complying with state law and ensuring proper stewardship of agency funds. The director provides overall vision and leadership for the agency budget, legislative agenda and formulation of policy.

The following volunteer citizen boards are under the agency's administrative oversight.

Athletic Trainers, Board of

Web: www.oregon.gov/OHLA/AT
Statutory Authority: ORS 688.701–688.734
Duties and Responsibilities: Oregon law requires athletic trainers to be registered and meet state-established professional standards. This governor-appointed board oversees regulation of athletic training and consists of three practicing athletic trainers, one physician and one public member. Athletic trainers prevent, recognize and evaluate athletic injuries and provide immediate care, rehabilitation and reconditioning services to athletes.

Body Art Practitioners, Board of

Web: www.oregon.gov/OHLA/BAP
Statutory Authority: ORS 690.350–690.992
Duties and Responsibilities: To address public health and safety concerns about emerging body art practices, the 2011 Legislature established the Board of Body Art Practitioners to advise OHLA on the regulation of body piercing, dermal implanting, electrology, scarification and tattooing. Board members are appointed by the governor to four-year terms. There are seven members: two licensed to perform tattooing; two licensed to perform body piercing, dermal implanting or scarification; one licensed to perform electrolysis; one licensed to practice medicine, nursing or naturopathic medicine; and one public member.

Cosmetology, Board of

Web: www.oregon.gov/OHLA/COS
Statutory Authority: ORS 690.005–690.992
Duties and Responsibilities: This governor-appointed board regulates cosmetology practices. The board is made up of six certified practitioners and one public member. Cosmetologists earn certification in one or more of four individual fields of practice: barbering, hair design, esthetics and nail technology.

Denture Technology, Board of

Web: www.oregon.gov/OHLA/DT
Statutory Authority: ORS 680.500–680.990
Duties and Responsibilities: This governor-appointed, Senate-confirmed board oversees the licensing of denturists. The board consists of four denturists, one dentist and two public members. Denturists construct, repair, reline, reproduce,

duplicate, supply, fit or alter removable prosthetic dental appliances, otherwise known as dentures.

Dietitians, Board of Licensed

Web: www.oregon.gov/OHLA/LD
Statutory Authority: ORS 691.405
Duties and Responsibilities: The Board of Licensed Dietitians was created in 1989 and became part of OHLA in 2011. The board oversees the practice of licensed dietitians by determining the qualifications of applicants for licensure and setting standards of practice.

Environmental Health Registration Board

Web: www.oregon.gov/OHLA/EHS
Statutory Authority: ORS 700.005–700.995
Duties and Responsibilities: This governor-appointed board oversees the regulation of environmental health specialists and waste water specialists. The board consists of four registered environmental health specialists, one physician licensed in Oregon to practice medicine or surgery who has an emphasis in public health, one representative of the food or food/alcoholic beverage retail industry and one public member. Environmental health specialists promote the control of infectious disease through environmental hygiene by enforcing health and safety standards relating to food, water and consumer products.

Hearing Aids, Advisory Council on

Web: www.oregon.gov/OHLA/HAS
Statutory Authority: ORS 694.015–694.991
Duties and Responsibilities: This governor-appointed council oversees the licensing of hearing aid specialists. The council consists of four individuals authorized to dispense hearing aids, one licensed physician certified in otolaryngology (ear, nose, throat), one certified audiologist and one public member who is a consumer of hearing aids. With the exception of audiologists and physicians, anyone who sells, leases or rents hearing aids in conjunction with the evaluation or measurement of human hearing must be licensed.

Midwifery, Board of Direct Entry

Web: www.oregon.gov/OHLA/DEM
Statutory Authority: ORS 687.405–687.991
Duties and Responsibilities: This governor-appointed, Senate-confirmed board oversees the regulation of direct entry midwifery. The board consists of four licensed direct entry midwives, two certified nurse midwives, one licensed physician who is involved at the time of appointment in obstetrical care or education, and one public member. Licensure is voluntary, and unlicensed midwives may practice in Oregon. However, state law allows reimbursement under the Oregon Health Plan only if a licensed midwife provides birthing assistance.

Nursing Home Administrators Board

Web: www.oregon.gov/OHLA/NHAB
Statutory Authority: ORS 678.800
Duties and Responsibilities: This governor-appointed, Senate-confirmed board consists of three nursing home administrators, one registered nurse, one physician, one pharmacist and two public members. The board develops and enforces standards for nursing home administrators and formulates appropriate examinations.

Respiratory Therapist and Polysomnographic Technologist Licensing Board

Web: www.oregon.gov/OHLA/RTPT
Statutory Authority: ORS 688.800–688.995
Duties and Responsibilities: This governor-appointed, Senate-confirmed board regulates the licensing of respiratory therapists and polysomnographic technologists. The board consists of three respiratory therapists, two polysomnographic technologists, one qualified medical director for polysomnography or respiratory care, and one public member.

Respiratory therapists, or respiratory care practitioners, provide services to patients with abnormalities associated with the cardiopulmonary system—or breathing disorders—under the direction of a licensed physician. Polysomnographic technologists provide treatment, management, diagnostic testing, education and care of patients with disorders related to sleep.

Sex Offender Treatment Board

Web: www.oregon.gov/OHLA/SOTB
Statutory Authority: ORS 675.360–675.410
Duties and Responsibilities: This governor-appointed board provides certification for clinical sex offender therapists and associate sex offender therapists. The board consists of seven members: two are recommended by the Oregon Association for the Treatment of Sexual Abusers, two are recommended by the Oregon Adolescent Sex Offender Treatment Network, one is recommended by the Oregon Association of Community Corrections Directors, one is recommended by the Oregon Juvenile Department Directors Association and one is recommended by a victims' advocacy organization. Clinical and associate sex offender therapists provide services for the treatment and rehabilitation of sex offenders.

Housing and Community Services Department

Address: 725 Summer St. NE, Suite B, Salem 97301-1266
Phone: 503-986-2000
E-mail: info@hcs.state.or.us
Web: www.oregon.gov/OHCS
Contact: Margaret Van Vliet, Director
Statutory Authority: ORS 456.555
Duties and Responsibilities: Oregon Housing and Community Services Department (OHCS) is the State's affordable housing finance agency and community services program administrator. OHCS provides financial and program support to create and preserve quality, affordable housing for Oregonians of lower and moderate income. The OHCS mission: "Provide leadership that enables Oregonians to gain housing, become self-sufficient, and achieve prosperity."

The department administers 49 unique federal and state programs that support: antipoverty; community services; energy assistance; financing of single-family homes; foreclosure prevention; grants and tax credits to promote affordable housing; homelessness prevention; hunger relief; manufactured housing; new construction, preservation or rehabilitation of multifamily affordable housing developments; volunteerism; and weatherization.

Oregon State Housing Council

Address: 725 Summer St. NE, Suite B, Salem 97301-1266
Phone: 503-986-6703
Fax: 503-986-2020
E-mail: info@hcs.state,or.us
Web: www.oregon.gov/OHCS
Contact: Greg Current, Executive Assistant
Statutory Authority: ORS 456.567

Business Operations Division

Address: 725 Summer St. NE, Suite B, Salem 97301-1266
Phone: 503-986-2000
Fax: 503-986-2020
E-mail: info@hcs.state.or.us
Web: www.oregon.gov/OHCS
Contact: Diana Koppes, Administrator
Statutory Authority: ORS 315.271, 317.097, 446.543, 456.515–456.723, 458.305–458.310, 458.600-458.650, 458.670–458.700
Duties and Responsibilities: The Business Operations Division provides administrative and operational support to the agency. The functional areas within Business Operations include Information Technology, Asset Management, Compliance, Budget, Debt Management, Facilities, and Financial Services such as Accounting, Grants, Payroll, and Procurement and Contracts.

Policy, Strategy and Community Engagement Division

Address: 725 Summer St. NE, Suite B, Salem 97301-1266
Phone: 503-986-2000
Fax: 503-986-2020
E-mail: info@hcs.state.or.us
Web: www.oregon.gov/OHCS
Contact: Karen Tolvstad, Administrator
Statutory Authority: ORS 456.555
Duties and Responsibilities: The Policy, Strategy and Community Engagement Division provides agency support in the areas of strategic planning; legislative, partner and media relations; internal and external communication; and policy development. The division takes the lead in researching, analyzing and recommending policy and strategy for the agency. It serves as the research and development arm of the organization, gathering quantitative and qualitative information; tracking and analyzing data and working closely with internal and external stakeholders.

The division's goal is to address critical housing and anti-poverty issues for the state; direct the development of new programs and policies to create opportunities for quality, affordable housing for low- to moderate-income Oregonians; and promote strategies and programs to assist low-income Oregonians in meeting basic needs for shelter and food and in achieving self-sufficiency.

Program Delivery Division

Address: 725 Summer St. NE, Suite B, Salem 97301-1266
Phone: 503-986-2000
Fax: 503-986-2020
E-mail: info@hcs.state.or.us
Web: www.oregon.gov/OHCS
Contact: Julie Cody, Administrator
Statutory Authority: ORS 90.800–90.840, 317.097, 446.525–446.543, 456.515–456.723, 458.210–458.310, 458.350–458.365, 458.505–458.545,458.600–458.650, 458.670–458.700
Duties and Responsibilities: The Program Delivery Division focuses on effectively and efficiently implementing programs to meet OHSC goals and statutory requirements. The division includes all program areas in the agency: Multi-Family; Single-Family/Weatherization; HUD Contract Administration; Community Services; and Foreclosure Prevention. In all, OHCS administers 49 specific programs which serve, among others, homeless persons, renters, homebuyers, homeowners, and households at-risk of foreclosure

throughout the state. The division also manages a wide variety of other anti-poverty programs which include food assistance, homelessness prevention, energy assistance and weatherization programs. For a full list of programs administered by OHCS, visit the agency's Web site.

Human Services, Department of

Address: 500 Summer St. NE, Salem 97301
Phone: 503-945-5944
Fax: 503-581-6198
E-mail: dhs.info@state.or.us
Web: www.oregon.gov/DHS
Contact: Erinn Kelley-Siel, Director
Statutory Authority: ORS 409.010
Duties and Responsibilities: The Department of Human Services (DHS) is Oregon's principal agency for helping Oregonians achieve well-being and independence through opportunities that protect, empower, respect choice and preserve dignity, especially for those who are least able to help themselves.

The majority of the DHS budget is spent directly in Oregon communities by providing direct services to more than one million Oregonians each year. These services provide a key safety net for those in our society who are most vulnerable or who are at difficult places in their lives.

Services are provided through five program areas: Developmental Disabilities, Aging and People with Disabilities, Child Welfare, Self-Sufficiency and Vocational Rehabilitation.

Director's Office

Address: 500 Summer St. NE, E15, Salem 97301
Phone: 503-945-5600
Fax: 503-581-6198
E-mail: dhs.directorsoffice@state.or.us
Contact: Erinn Kelley-Siel, Director; Jim Scherzinger, Chief Operating Officer
Duties and Responsibilities: The Director's Office provides overall guidance and direction. Key functions include Federal Financial Policy, Governor's Advocacy, Legislative Relations, Media and Communications, Tribal Relations, Community Engagement, Equity and Multi-cultural Services, Finance and Human Resources. The office also includes the chief operating officer responsible for Shared Services, Internal Audits, Business Intelligence, Licensing and Regulatory Oversight, Continuous Improvement, Information Technology Business Supports, Adult Abuse Prevention and Investigations, Performance Excellence and Program Integrity.

Aging and People with Disabilities Program

Address: 500 Summer St. NE, E02, Salem 97301
Phone: 503-945-5811
Fax: 503-373-7823
Contact: Mike McCormick, Director
Duties and Responsibilities: Responsibilities include administering programs that promote independence and protection for aging people and people with disabilities of all ages to achieve well-being through opportunities for community living, employment, family support, and services that promote independence, choice and dignity.

Functions include the Older Americans Act, direct financial support, in-home services, community-based care facilities and nursing facilities. Eligibility determination for federal Social Security disability benefits and help arranging and paying for in-home services are provided through programs such as Oregon Project Independence or support services. Many of the services are provided to clients through local Area Agency on Aging or branch offices throughout the state.

Deaf and Hard of Hearing Services Program

Address: 500 Summer St. NE, E16, Salem 97301
Phone: 503-947-5183; Toll-free: 1-800-521-9615
Fax: 503-947-5184
Contact: Jeff Brownson
Statutory Authority: ORS 185.230
Duties and Responsibilities: Assists state agencies to make sure services and programs are accessible to deaf and hard of hearing people.

Medicaid Long-Term Care Quality and Reimbursement Advisory Council

Address: 500 Summer St. NE, E02, Salem 97301
Phone: 503-945-6465
Fax: 503-373-7823
Contact: Sarah Hansen
Statutory Authority: ORS 410.500

Governor's Commission on Senior Services

Address: 500 Summer St. NE, E02, Salem 97301
Phone: 503-945-6993
Fax: 503-373-7823
Contact: Max Brown
Statutory Authority: ORS 410.320

Child Welfare Program

Address: 500 Summer St. NE, E48, Salem 97301
Phone: 503-945-5600
Fax: 503-581-6198
Web: http://oregon.gov/DHS
Contact: Lois Day, Director
Duties and Responsibilities: Oversees child welfare programs, including child-abuse investigations and intervention, foster care, adoptions and child safety.

Child Welfare Advisory Committee

Address: 500 Summer St. NE, E62, Salem 97301
Phone: 503-945-5650
Fax: 503-581-6198
Contact: Pam Pearson
Statutory Authority: ORS 418.005

Family Services Review Commission

Address: 500 Summer St. NE, E62, Salem 97301
Phone: 503-945-6186
Fax: 503-581-6198
Contact: Mary Anne Camp
Statutory Authority: ORS 411.125

Independent Living Council

Address: 500 Summer St. NE, E87, Salem 97301
Phone: 503-945-6204
Fax: 503-945-8991
Contact: Shelly Emery
Statutory Authority: Exec. Order No. 94-12

Refugee Child Welfare Advisory

Address: 500 Summer St. NE, E48, Salem 97301
Phone: 503-945-6739
Fax: 503-373-7032
Contact: Oscar Herrera
Statutory Authority: ORS 418.941

State of Oregon Rehabilitation Council

Address: 500 Summer St. NE, E87, Salem 97301
Phone: 503-945-6256; Toll-free: 1-877-277-0513
Fax: 503-945-8991
Contact: Rhonda Hunter
Statutory Authority: ORS 344.735

Developmental Disabilities Program

Address: 500 Summer St. NE, E02, Salem 97301
Phone: 503-945-5811; Toll-free:1-800-282-8096
Fax: 503-373-7823
Contact: Trisha Baxter, Chief Operations Officer
Duties and Responsibilities: Provides assistance to people who have a developmental disability that impedes their ability to function independently. Developmental disabilities include mental retardation, cerebral palsy, Down syndrome, autism and other impairments of the brain that occur during childhood. Some people with developmental disabilities also have significant medical or mental health needs. Services are provided through local Community Developmental Disabilities programs.

Oregon Council on Developmental Disabilities

Address: 540 24th St. NE, Salem 97301
Phone: 503-945-9941
Fax: 503-945-9947
Contact: Kathryn Weit, Executive Director
Statutory Authority: 42 USC 15001

Oregon Disabilities Commission

Address: 500 Summer St. NE, Salem 97301
Phone: 503-945-6993 or 503-947-1136
Fax: 503-373-7823
Contact: Becky Murphy or Max Brown, Administrative Support
Statutory Authority: ORS 185.130
Duties and Responsibilities: The commission identifies and publicizes the needs and rights of individuals with disabilities; advises the Legislature, the governor, state agencies and other public and private agencies on disability issues and coordinates inter-agency efforts in the delivery of disability-related services.

Self-Sufficiency Programs

Address: 500 Summer St. NE, E48, Salem 97301
Phone: 503-945-5600
Fax: 503-581-6198
Contact: Jerry Waybrant, Chief Operating Officer
Duties and Responsibilities: Programs in self-sufficiency provide a critical safety net for families and individuals with very low to no income to help them meet their basic needs. Programs include Temporary Assistance for Needy Families, Supplemental Nutrition Assistance Program (food stamps), Employment Related Day Care, Refugee and domestic violence assistance, and some employment and eligibility programs.

Vocational Rehabilitation Programs

Address: 500 Summer St. NE, E87, Salem 97301

Phone: 503-945-5880
Fax: 503-947-5025
Contact: Stephaine Parrish Taylor, Administrator
Statutory Authority: ORS 344.510–344.630
Duties and Responsibilities: Assists youth and adults with disabilities to obtain, maintain or advance in employment and to live as independently as possible. Vocational Rehabilitation Programs assist clients with all disabilities, with the exception of blindness and deaf-blindness. Services are provided through field offices across the state. Programs develop employment opportunities for clients and offer staffing solutions and disability awareness services to employers.

Land Conservation and Development, Department of

Address: 635 Capitol St. NE, Suite 150, Salem 97301-2540
Phone: 503-373-0050
Fax: 503-378-5518
Web: www.oregon.gov/LCD
Contact: Jim Rue, Director
Statutory Authority: ORS Chapters 92, 195, 196, 197, 215, 222, 227, 268, 308
Duties and Responsibilities: The Department of Land Conservation and Development administers Oregon's statewide land use planning program and Oregon's federally approved Coastal Management Program. The department's director is appointed by the Land Conservation and Development Commission, which provides policy direction for the department and has seven members who are appointed by the governor and confirmed by the Senate.

Oregon's statewide planning program was created in 1973 when the Legislature passed the Oregon Land Use Act (Senate Bill 100). Under that program, all cities and counties have adopted comprehensive plans that meet mandatory state standards. The standards are 19 statewide planning goals that deal with issues such as land use, economic development, housing, transportation and conservation of natural resources. Periodic review of comprehensive plans and technical assistance, including grants to local jurisdictions, are key elements of the program.

Citizen Involvement Advisory Committee

Address: 635 Capitol St. NE, Suite 150, Salem 97301-2540
Phone: 503-373-0050
Contact: Bob Rindy
Statutory Authority: ORS 197.160

Local Officials Advisory Committee

Address: 635 Capitol St. NE, Suite 150, Salem 97301-2540
Phone: 503-373-0050
Contact: Leslie Roth
Statutory Authority: ORS 197.165

Community Services Division

Address: 635 Capitol St. NE, Suite 150, Salem 97301-2540 (Regional Offices in Bend, Central Point, La Grande, Newport, Portland and Springfield)
Phone: 503-373-0050
Fax: 503-378-5518
Web: www.oregon.gov/LCD/commserv.shtml
Contact: Rob Hallyburton, Manager
Duties and Responsibilities: The Community Services Division is composed of regional representatives and support staff in eight field and regional solution center offices who provide technical and financial assistance to urban and rural communities. Representatives assist local governments in the implementation of the statewide land use planning program by providing technical assistance to local government planners and officials, the general public and interest groups.

Ocean and Coastal Services Division

Address: 635 Capitol St. NE, Suite 150, Salem 97301-2540 (Field Offices in Portland and Newport)
Phone: 503-373-0050
Fax: 503-378-6033
Web: www.oregon.gov/LCD/OCMP
Contact: Patty Snow, Manager
Duties and Responsibilities: The Ocean and Coastal Services Division works with coastal cities, counties, and state and federal agencies to administer Oregon's federally approved Coastal Management Program, which emphasizes conservation of estuaries, shorelands, beaches, dunes and ocean resources. The division provides financial and planning assistance to local governments, implements a coastal hazards and assessment program, supports the Oregon Ocean Policy Advisory Council, maintains an online Oregon Coastal Atlas, and has authority under federal law to review federal programs and activities for consistency with Oregon's federally approved coastal program standards.

Planning Services Division

Address: 635 Capitol St. NE, Suite 150, Salem 97301-2540
Phone: 503-373-0050
Fax: 503-378-5518
Web: www.oregon.gov/LCD/planserv.shtml

Contact: Matt Crall, Manager

Duties and Responsibilities: The Planning Services Division provides specialized technical assistance and policy consultation to the Department of Land Conservation and Development's regional representatives serving local governments and citizens. The division includes the Transportation and Growth Management Program and specialists dealing with urban development, farm and forest land protection, mineral and aggregate resources, economic development, natural resource management and floodplain management. The division also assists Measure 49 claimants and local jurisdictions in the development of Measure 49 authorizations.

Internal Support:

Administrative Services Division

Address: 635 Capitol St. NE, Suite 150, Salem 97301-2540

Phone: 503-373-0050

Fax: 503-378-6033

Web: www.oregon.gov/LCD/operserv.shtml

Contact: Teddy Leland, Manager

Duties and Responsibilities: The Administrative Services Division provides human resources, labor relations, budget, accounting, purchasing, information systems, landowner notification, agency policy, inventory, property control, and reception.

Land Use Board of Appeals

Address: 550 Capitol St. NE, Suite 235, Salem 97301-2552

Phone: 503-373-1265

Fax: 503-373-1580

Web: www.oregon.gov/LUBA

Contact: Tod A. Bassham, Board Chair; Kelly Burgess, Paralegal

Statutory Authority: ORS 197.810

Duties and Responsibilities: The Land Use Board of Appeals (LUBA) was created by legislation in 1979 and has exclusive jurisdiction to review all governmental land-use decisions, whether legislative or quasi-judicial in nature. LUBA was created to simplify the appeal process, speed resolution of land-use disputes and provide consistent interpretation of state and local land-use laws. The governor appoints the three-member board to serve four-year terms, subject to Senate confirmation. The board members serving on LUBA must be attorneys who are members of the Oregon State Bar.

Landscape Architect Board, State

Address: 707 13th St. SE, Suite 114, Salem 97301

Phone: 503-589-0093

Fax: 503-485-2947

E-mail: oslab.info@state.or.us

Web: www.oregon.gov/LANDARCH

Contact: Christine Valentine, Administrator

Statutory Authority: ORS 671.459

Duties and Responsibilities: Since 1981, the State Landscape Architect Board has registered individuals to practice landscape architecture. Registration as a landscape architect requires a degree, applicable supervised experience and passing national examinations. More than 450 landscape architects and 200 landscape architecture firms are registered in Oregon. The board consists of four registered landscape architects and three public members appointed by the governor to four-year terms. The board oversees the practice and may revoke or suspend a certificate or restrict the scope of practice.

The board safeguards the public health, safety and welfare in the practice of landscape architecture as it relates to engineering, architecture, ground water, land use planning and landscape hazards. Landscape architecture has the dominant purpose of landscape preservation, development and enhancement. This includes reconnaissance, research, planning, landscape and site design, and the preparation of related drawings, construction documents and specifications.

Landscape Contractors Board, State

Address: 2111 Front St. NE, Suite 2-101, Salem 97301

Phone: 503-967-6291

Fax: 503-967-6298

E-mail: lcbinfo@lcb.state.or.us

Web: www.oregon.gov/LCB

Contact: Shelley Sneed, Administrator

Statutory Authority: ORS 671.510–671.760

Duties and Responsibilities: Created in 1972, the State Landscape Contractors Board licenses landscape contracting businesses and individual landscape construction professionals who must demonstrate minimum competency by passing a comprehensive examination. Landscape contracting businesses must post a surety bond, submit evidence of liability insurance and workers' compensation insurance, if applicable. Each landscape contracting business must either be owned by a licensed landscape construction professional or the business must employ a licensed landscape construction professional to supervise the landscape activities of the business and directly supervise all unlicensed employees of the business.

The board receives and investigates consumer complaints which it settles through dispute resolution processes including mediation and arbitration, answers questions from the public and the industry, and enforces compliance to the laws governing the landscape construction industry.

There are approximately 1,100 licensed landscape contracting businesses and approximately 1,300 licensed individual landscape construction professionals in Oregon. The governor appoints the seven-member board to serve three-year terms. Five members are from the landscape construction industry and two are public members.

Library, State

Address: 250 Winter St. NE, Salem 97301-3950
Phone: 503-378-4243
Fax: 503-585-8059
Web: www.oregon.gov/OSL
Contact: MaryKay Dahlgreen, State Librarian
Statutory Authority: ORS Chapter 357
Duties and Responsibilities: The Oregon State Library was established as the Oregon Library Commission in 1905. Since its founding, the library has been governed by an independent board of trustees. The present board consists of seven citizens from throughout the state who are appointed by the governor. The library consists of an administrative team and three programs.

The Government Research Services program provides research and reference assistance to state government and to persons on official state business. Specialized collections include federal and state government publications and a comprehensive collection of materials about Oregon. The library also provides permanent public access to Oregon state government documents. The Genealogical Research Center is a partnership between the library and the Willamette Valley Genealogical Society.

The Library Development Services program includes planning for statewide library development, hosting quality Web sites for public libraries, providing equal access to information resources for K–12 students through the Oregon School Library Information System, collecting and reporting library statistics and administering state and federal library grant programs. Current library development priorities are improving early literacy services to children in public libraries and facilitating access to library services for all Oregonians.

The Talking Book and Braille Services program is the Oregon Regional Library for the Library of Congress' National Library Service for the blind and physically handicapped. Oregonians who are unable to read standard print because of a visual or physical disability are eligible for free library services. Books and magazines are available in audio format and in braille.

Liquor Control Commission, Oregon

Address: 9079 SE McLoughlin Blvd., Portland 97222-7355
Phone: 503-872-5000; Toll-free: 1-800-452-6522
Fax: 503-872-5266
Web: www.oregon.gov/OLCC
Contact: Merle Lindsey, Interim Executive Director
Statutory Authority: ORS Chapters 471, 472, 473
Duties and Responsibilities: Five citizen commissioners set policy for the Oregon Liquor Control Commission (OLCC). Commissioners are appointed by the governor to four-year terms, subject to Senate confirmation. Each represents a state congressional district, with one coming from the food and beverage industry. The OLCC promotes the public interest through the responsible sale and service of alcoholic beverages. It was created in 1933 by a special session of the Legislature after national prohibition ended. Oregon is a "control state" with the exclusive right to sell packaged distilled spirits, dispersed statewide from a 230,000-square-foot distribution center and sold in 248 retail liquor stores operated by contracted agents. The agency is headquartered in Portland with regional offices in Bend, Eugene, Medford and Salem.

The OLCC ensures that only qualified people and businesses are licensed to sell and serve alcoholic beverages. Licenses are issued to private businesses such as grocery stores to sell beer and wine and to restaurants, bars and taverns to sell beer, wine and distilled spirits by the glass.

The OLCC works to control underage drinking and alcohol problems with a balanced blend of liquor law enforcement and outreach education. Much of this is carried out by the agency's Public Safety Services Program. OLCC inspectors work with licensees to help them comply with liquor laws. The agency also administers the Alcohol Education Program, which focuses on responsible alcohol service. All alcohol servers must complete the training course every five years.

In fiscal year 2011–12, the OLCC distributed $194.1 million to Oregon. The state's General Fund received $110.2 million, cities received $34.2 million, $17.1 million went to counties and city revenue sharing received $24 million. Revenue is also distributed to mental health, alcoholism and drug services, as well as to the Oregon Wine Board.

The OLCC also enforces the Bottle Bill under which any malt, carbonated beverage or water container sold in Oregon must have a refund value of at least five cents.

Long-Term Care Ombudsman, Office of the

Address: 3855 Wolverine St. NE, Suite 6, Salem 97305-1251
Phone: 503-378-6533; Toll-free: 1-800-522-2602; TTY: 503-378-5847
Fax: 503-373-0852
E-mail: ltco.contact@ltco.state.or.us
Web: www.oregon.gov/LTCO
Contact: Mary Jaeger, Director/State Long-Term Care Ombudsman
Statutory Authority: ORS 441.100–441.153
Duties and Responsibilities: The Office of the Long-Term Care Ombudsman is charged with enhancing the quality of life and the level of care, protecting the individual rights and promoting the dignity of each Oregon citizen living in a nursing facility, adult foster care home, residential care facility or assisted living facility. The office investigates and resolves complaints made by, or on behalf of, long-term care residents and monitors the long-term care system. The State Ombudsman and Deputy State Ombudsmen work with trained and Certified Ombudsman volunteers who advocate, investigate and educate for over 42,000 residents in long-term care facilities.

The office has oversight from the Long-Term Care Advisory Committee, which is appointed by legislative leadership and the governor. Their role is to advise the governor and Legislature on long-term care issues and the activities of the Ombudsman Office.

In 2011, the agency was selected as the Outstanding Statewide Volunteer Program by the Oregon Governor's Volunteer Awards.

Lottery, Oregon State

Address: PO Box 12649, Salem 97309
Phone: 503-540-1000; TTY: 503-540-1068
Fax: 503-540-1168
E-mail: lottery.webcenter@state.or.us
Web: www.oregonlottery.org
Contact: Larry Niswender, Director
Statutory Authority: ORS Chapter 461
Duties and Responsibilities: The Oregon State Lottery was created through the initiative process in November 1984, when voters amended the Oregon Constitution to establish a state lottery. The lottery is entirely self-financed through its sales and does not receive any General Fund or other tax dollars. It develops, produces and markets its games, pays its winners and operating expenses and turns the remaining net profits over to the state.

The lottery is operated under the direction of a five-member citizen commission. Commissioners are appointed by the governor and confirmed by the Senate. One commissioner must be a certified public accountant and one must have at least five years experience in law enforcement.

Initially, lottery profits were to be used exclusively for economic development and job creation. In May 1995, voters enabled lottery profits to be used to help finance public education and, in November 1998, voters approved another initiative directing 15 percent of lottery net proceeds to go to parks, salmon habitat restoration and watershed enhancement programs. The Legislature is responsible for allocating lottery funds for economic development, public education, parks, and salmon restoration programs. Since 1985, lottery players have won over $23 billion in prizes and over $8 billion in lottery earnings have gone back to public education, economic development, parks, salmon habitat restoration and watershed enhancement programs.

Marine Board, State

Address: PO Box 14145, Salem 97309-5065
Phone: 503-378-8587; TTY: 503-378-8587 (press space bar to begin)
Fax: 503-378-4597
E-mail: marine.board@state.or.us
Web: www.oregon.gov/OSMB
Contact: Scott Brewen, Director
Statutory Authority: ORS 830.105
Duties and Responsibilities: The State Marine Board was established in 1959. It is Oregon's recreational boating agency dedicated to safety, education and access. The board returns user fees (marine fuel tax and title and registration fees) to boaters in the form of boating safety and clean boating educational programs, marine law enforcement and improved boating facilities.

The board titles and registers more than 175,000 recreational vessels, registers outfitters and guides and licenses ocean charterboats. The board establishes statewide boating regulations and contracts with county sheriffs and the State Police to enforce marine laws. The board provides technical training to marine patrol officers and also provides grants and engineering services to local governments (cities, counties, park districts, port districts) to develop and maintain accessible boating facilities and protect water quality.

The board promotes safe and sustainable boating through several programs. The Mandatory Boater Education program requires all powerboat operators to complete a safety course. The Aquatic Invasive Species Prevention program protects Oregon waters from costly, damaging invasive plants and animals. The Clean Marina program is a voluntary incentive-based program encouraging environmental "best practices" at Oregon's marinas.

Massage Therapists, State Board of

Address: 748 Hawthorne Ave. NE, Salem 97301
Phone: 503-365-8657
Fax: 503-385-4465
E-mail: OBMT.info@state.or.us
Web: www.oregon.gov/OBMT
Contact: Kate Coffey, Executive Director
Statutory Authority: ORS 687.011–687.991
Duties and Responsibilities: The Board of Massage Therapists regulates the practice of massage. This is accomplished by licensing, establishing continuing education requirements, promoting education, administering tests to establish minimum competency to practice and enforcing professional behavior and standards. The board consists of seven members appointed by the governor and confirmed by the Senate. Four are licensed massage therapists and three are members of the public, with one public member selected from a health related field.

Medical Board, Oregon

Address: 1500 SW 1st Ave., #620, Portland 97201-5847
Phone: 971-673-2700
Fax: 971-673-2670
E-mail: omb.info@state.or.us
Web: www.oregon.gov/OMB
Contact: Kathleen Haley, Executive Director
Statutory Authority: ORS Chapter 677
Duties and Responsibilities: The Oregon Medical Board, created in 1889, administers the Medical Practice Act and establishes the rules and regulations pertaining to the practice of medicine in Oregon. The board determines requirements for Oregon licensure as a Medical Doctor (MD), Doctor of Osteopathy (DO), Doctor of Podiatric Medicine (DPM), Physician Assistant (PA) and Acupuncturist (LAc); ensures that all applicants granted licensure meet all Oregon requirements; investigates complaints against licensees and takes disciplinary action when a violation of the Medical Practice Act occurs. The board monitors licensees who have come under disciplinary action to ensure compliance with their terms of probation and ensure that it is safe for them to practice medicine, and supports rehabilitation, education and research to further its legislative mandate to protect the citizens of Oregon.

Medical Imaging, Board of

Address: 800 NE Oregon St., Suite 1160A, Portland 97232
Phone: 971-673-0215
Fax: 971-673-0218
E-mail: OBMI.Info@state.or.us
Web: www.oregon.gov/OBMI
Contact: Ed Conlow, Executive Director
Statutory Authority: ORS 688.405–688.605, 688.915
Duties and Responsibilities: The Board of Medical Imaging was established in 1977 as the Board of Radiologic Technology. The board works to ensure the quality of diagnostic radiography, radiation therapy, diagnostic medical sonography, nuclear medicine technology and magnetic resonance imaging (MRI) through ethics and competency standards for licensing radiologic technologists, radiation therapists, sonographers, nuclear medicine technologists and MRI technologists. The board administers limited scope examinations to determine initial competence to practice for limited X-ray machine operators (LXMO) and approves continuing education offerings to technologists, therapists, sonographers and limited X-ray machine operators.

Military Department, Oregon

Address: 1776 Militia Way SE, PO Box 14350, Salem 97309-5047
Phone: 503-584-3980; Toll-Free: 1-800-452-7500
Fax: 503-584-3962
Web: www.oregon.gov/OMD
Contact: Brigadier General Daniel R. Hokanson, The Adjutant General
Statutory Authority: ORS 396.305
Duties and Responsibilities: The Oregon Military Department's purpose is to administer, house, equip and train the Oregon National Guard, a ready force to support the governor during unrest or natural disaster and as a reserve force to the total forces of the United States. The department administers 39 Readiness Centers/Armories, seven Maintenance centers, four training sites, two Army Aviation Support Facilities and two Air Bases. Each community with sufficient population to support guard activities has a National Guard unit assigned to it.

The National Guard is found in both the United States and Oregon Constitutions. Its tradition and history is grounded in its mission statement: "A ready force equipped and trained to respond to any contingency. When we are needed, we are there."

Command Group

Address: AGDD 237, PO Box 14350, Salem 97309-5047
Phone: 503-584-3985
Fax: 503-584-3987
E-mail: agdd@mil.state.or.us
Contact: Brigadier General Daniel R. Hokanson, The Adjutant General

Duties and Responsibilities: The Command Group administers all components of the Oregon National Guard. It consists of The Adjutant General of the Oregon National Guard; the Joint Force Headquarters, including the Assistant Adjutants General for the Air and Army National Guard Components; and the Deputy Director for the State Affairs Component and the Oregon State Defense Force.

The Adjutant General directs the administration, discipline, training and mobilization of the Oregon National Guard, the Oregon State Defense Force and the Joint Force Headquarters. The Adjutant General develops and coordinates policies and programs in cooperation with the governor and the state Legislature.

Financial Administration Division

Address: AGC Rm. 158, PO Box 14350, Salem 97309-5047
Phone: 503-584-3911
E-mail: agc@mil.state.or.us
Contact: Karl Jorgenson, Director
Duties and Responsibilities: The Financial Administration Division is responsible for agency-wide financial accounting and reporting, budget development and execution, purchasing and contracting, risk management and administration of the fiscal and information management system for the Oregon Military Department.

Installations Division

Address: AGI Rm. 155, PO Box 14350, Salem 97309-5047
Phone: 503-584-3914
Fax: 503-584-3584
E-mail: agi-s@mil.state.or.us
Contact: Colonel Christian Rees, Director
Duties and Responsibilities: The Installations Division acquires and maintains the armories, training installations, logistics installations and office space for the Oregon Military Department and the Oregon Army National Guard. The division provides master planning, programming and real estate services on behalf of the agency. The Operations and Maintenance Program provides maintenance and repair of existing facilities as well as energy conservation through centralized energy monitoring and management. The Construction Operations Program provides construction management services for the Army National Guard Construction Program. The Environmental Program provides environmental management services for Army National Guard facilities.

Public Affairs Office

Address: AGPA Rm. 204, PO Box 14350, Salem 97309-5047
Phone: 503-584-3917
Fax: 503-584-3912
E-mail: agpa@mil.state.or.us
Contact: Captain Stephen Bomar, Public Affairs Officer
Duties and Responsibilities: The Public Affairs Office provides information on activities of the Oregon National Guard and responds to requests for information from the public and private sector and from active and retired members of the Oregon National Guard.

Other Entities:

Emergency Management, Office of

Address: 3225 State St., Salem 97301; PO Box 14370, Salem 97309-5062
Phone: 503-378-2911; TTY: 503-373-7857
Fax: 503-373-7833
Web: www.oregon.gov/OMD/OEM
Contact: Martin Plotner, Director
Statutory Authority: ORS Chapter 401
Duties and Responsibilities: The Office of Emergency Management executes the governor's responsibilities to maintain an emergency services system to deal with emergencies or disasters that may present threats to the lives and property of Oregon's citizens. The agency coordinates and facilitates emergency planning, preparedness, response and recovery activities with state and local emergency service agencies and organizations.

State Defense Force, Oregon

Address: Camp Withycombe, 15300 Industrial Way, Clackamas 97015-9372
Phone: 503-683-5458
Fax: 503-683-5255
Web: http://orsdf.org
Contact: Brigadier General J. Michael Caldwell, Commanding General
Statutory Authority: 32 U.S. Code Sec.109, ORS 399.035
Duties and Responsibilities: The Oregon State Defense Force (ORSDF) was established in 1961 to provide Oregon with a trained National Guard Reserve Force. With the governor as Commander-in-Chief, the ORSDF serves within the Military Department. The ORSDF, as an augmentation for the Oregon National Guard, is administered by The Adjutant General and is a force multiplier for the state's emergency operations.

Youth Challenge Program

Address: 23861 Dodds Rd., Bend 97701
Phone: 541-317-9623

Fax: 541-382-6785
Web: www.oycp.com
Contact: Dan Radabaugh, Director
Duties and Responsibilities: The Oregon National Guard Youth Challenge Program is a public alternative high school that operates similar to a military academy. The program is guided by military principles, structure and discipline. It is a residential school where cadets (students) live on site for five and one-half months while attending the school. This period is followed by a mandatory 12-month mentor phase back in the community.

Mortuary and Cemetery Board, State

Address: 800 NE Oregon St., Suite 430, Portland 97232-2195
Phone: 971-673-1500
Fax: 971-673-1501
E-mail: mortuary.board@state.or.us
Web: www.oregon.gov/MortCem
Contact: Michelle Gaines, Executive Director
Statutory Authority: ORS 97.931, 692.300,
Duties and Responsibilities: The Mortuary and Cemetery Board is composed of 11 members appointed by the governor: two funeral service practitioners, one embalmer, three cemetery representatives, one crematory representative and four public members.

The board regulates the practice of individuals and establishments engaged in the sale of funeral, cemetery and crematory goods and services as well as the care, preparation, processing, transportation and final disposition of human remains. The board's licensees include funeral service practitioners, embalmers, apprentices, pre-need sales people, death care consultants, funeral establishments, immediate disposition companies, cemeteries and crematories.

The board's programs include background investigation, apprenticeship, practitioner examination, licensing, facility inspection, complaint investigation and education. The board's financing is derived from licensing, examination and death registration fees.

Naturopathic Medicine, Oregon Board of

Address: 800 NE Oregon St., Suite 407, Portland 97232
Phone: 971-673-0193
Fax: 971-673-0226
E-mail: obnm.info@state.or.us
Web: www.oregon.gov/obnm
Contact: Anne Walsh, Executive Director
Statutory Authority: ORS Chapter 685
Duties and Responsibilities: The Oregon Board of Naturopathic Medicine, consisting of seven members, was established by the 1927 Legislature to protect the public by setting and enforcing standards in the practice of Naturopathic Medicine. It examines, licenses, educates and investigates complaints, taking appropriate action when necessary.

Nursing, Oregon State Board of

Address: 17938 SW Upper Boones Ferry Rd., Portland 97224-7012
Phone: 971-673-0685
Fax: 971-673-0684
E-mail: oregon.bn.info@state.or.us
Web: www.oregon.gov/OSBN
Contact: Holly Mercer, Executive Director
Statutory Authority: ORS 678.010–678.445
Duties and Responsibilities: The Oregon State Board of Nursing was established in 1911 to regulate nursing practice and education to protect the public's health, safety and well-being. The board examines, licenses and renews licenses of qualified Registered Nurses and Licensed Practical Nurses; certifies nursing assistants and establishes standards for their training and certification; licenses nurse practitioners and grants prescriptive and dispensing authority to qualified nurse practitioners and Clinical Nurse Specialists; licenses Certified Registered Nurse Anesthetists and Clinical Nurse Specialists; prescribes essential curricula and standards for nursing education programs; surveys and approves nursing education programs which meet board standards; and investigates complaints about nurses and nursing assistants to determine if there have been violations to laws or standards.

Members are appointed by the governor for three-year terms. License fees finance all board programs.

Occupational Therapy Licensing Board

Address: 800 NE Oregon St., Suite 407, Portland 97232
Phone: 971-673-0198
Fax: 971-673-0226
E-mail: felicia.m.holgate@state.or.us
Web: www.oregon.gov/otlb
Contact: Felicia Holgate, Executive Director
Statutory Authority: ORS 675.210–675.340
Duties and Responsibilities: The Occupational Therapy Licensing Board, created in 1977, regulates occupational therapy practice to ensure that only qualified persons provide occupational therapy services. The board sets the standards of practice and examines applicants for licensure,

issues licenses to qualified applicants, investigates complaints and takes appropriate disciplinary action when violations are found to have occurred.

Optometry, Oregon Board of

Address: 1900 Hines St. SE, Suite 290, Salem 97302
Phone: 503-399-0662
Fax: 503-399-0705
E-mail: board@oregonobo.org
Web: www.oregonobo.org
Contact: Nancy Sellers DeSouza, Executive Director
Statutory Authority: ORS Chapter 683
Duties and Responsibilities: Created in 1905, the Oregon Board of Optometry (OBO) protects the health, safety and welfare of the public by determining the requirements for Oregon licensure, establishing rules and enforcing professional standards for the practice of optometry. The board investigates alleged violations and complaints against licensees and takes disciplinary action for violations of statues and rules, including issuing civil penalties, and has the authority to revoke, suspend or impose probation on a licensee or limit his or her practice. The OBO has authority over only the practice of optometry; opticians are not licensed or regulated by the board.

The OBO is a semi-independent, self-supporting agency that receives the majority of its revenue from application, licensing and renewal fees. The board currently licenses more than 1,200 optometrists. The five members of the Board of Optometry are appointed by the governor and confirmed by the Senate to serve three-year terms and include four optometrists and one public member.

Pacific Northwest Electric Power and Conservation Planning Council

Address: Oregon Office: 851 SW 6th Ave., Suite 1020, Portland 97204-1347
Phone: 503-229-5171
Fax: 503-229-5173
Web: www.nwcouncil.org
Contact: Bill Bradbury, Henry Lorenzen, Oregon Council Members
Statutory Authority: ORS 469.805
Duties and Responsibilities: Through the Northwest Power Act of 1980 (PL 96-502), the U.S. Congress authorized Idaho, Montana, Washington and Oregon to create the Pacific Northwest Electric Power and Conservation Planning Council (commonly known as the Northwest Power and Conservation Council) as a planning and policy-making body. The four state governors each appoint two members to the council. Council members serve three-year terms and can be reappointed.

Congress charged the council with developing a program to protect, mitigate and enhance fish and wildlife affected by the development, operation and management of hydroelectric facilities in the Columbia River Basin while assuring the Pacific Northwest an adequate, efficient, economical and reliable power supply; developing a power plan that included a 20-year demand forecast, an energy conservation program and the fish and wildlife program; and involving the public extensively in the decision-making process.

Pacific States Marine Fisheries Commission

Address: 205 SE Spokane St., Suite 100, Portland 97202
Phone: 503-595-3100
Fax: 503-595-3232
Web: www.psmfc.org
Contact: Randy Fisher, Executive Director
Statutory Authority: Compact entered into by the states with the consent of the United States Congress, July 1947; ORS 507.040
Duties and Responsibilities: The Pacific States Marine Fisheries Commission (PSMFC) is dedicated to resolving fishing issues and represents California, Oregon, Washington, Idaho and Alaska. PSMFC promotes and supports policies and actions directed at the conservation, development and management of fishery resources. PSMFC serves as a primary contractor on state and government funded grants and contracts. In addition, PSMFC collects data and maintains databases on salmon, steelhead and other marine fish for fishery managers and the fishing industry.

Parks and Recreation Department, State

Address: 725 Summer St. NE, Suite C, Salem 97301
Phone: 503-986-0707;
Campground Reservations: 1-800-452-5687;
Parks Information: 1-800-551-6949
Fax: 503-986-0794
E-mail: tim.wood@state.or.us
Web: www.oregon.gov/OPRD
Contact: Tim Wood, Director
Statutory Authority: ORS Chapters 97, 358, 390
Duties and Responsibilities: The State Parks and Recreation Department operates Oregon's state parks, recreation programs, community grants and heritage programs through a headquarters staff in

Salem and three field regions. The department was initially created as a branch of the Highway Department in 1921. The 1989 Legislature created a separate Parks and Recreation Department effective January 1, 1990.

Oregon's state parks are among the most popular in the United States. Their combined day-use and camping attendance of 43.7 million visitors (2010) consistently ranks the system among the ten most visited in the nation. The department also manages the State Historic Preservation Office, Oregon Heritage Commission, Oregon Commission on Historic Cemeteries, Recreation Trails, the Ocean Shores Recreation Area, Scenic Waterways, the Oregon Exposition Center and State Fair and the Willamette River Greenway. Department services are funded primarily by Oregon Lottery dollars, state park user fees and recreation vehicle license fees. Lottery funds were dedicated to parks by Oregon voters in 1998 and reaffirmed in 2010.

Exposition Center and State Fair

Address: 2330 17th St. NE, Salem 97303-3201
Phone: 503-947-3247
Fax: 503-947-3206
Web: www.oregonstateexpo.org; www.oregonstatefair.org
Contact: Toni Payseno, Exposition Center Manager
Statutory Authority: ORS 565.040
Duties and Responsibilities: The Oregon Exposition Center and State Fair operates the business and properties of the center as a year-round exposition center and meeting space. The annual Oregon State Fair event disseminates knowledge about, and encourages the growth and prosperity of, all agricultural, stock raising, horticultural, mining, mechanical, artistic and industrial pursuits in the state.

Heritage Commission

Address: 725 Summer St. NE, Suite C, Salem 97301
Phone: 503-986-0673
Fax: 503-986-0793
E-mail: kyle.jansson@state.or.us
Web: www.oregon.gov/OPRD/HCD/OHC
Contact: Kyle Jansson, Coordinator
Statutory Authority: ORS 358.570
Duties and Responsibilities: The mission of the Oregon Heritage Commission is to secure, sustain and enhance Oregon's heritage by coordinating heritage initiatives by public and private organizations, advocating for all levels of support for heritage, educating the public about its extent and value and promoting and celebrating its diversity. It carries out its mission with Heritage and Museum grants, technical assistance to heritage organizations, declarations of statewide heritage celebrations, a statewide conference and an inventory of state-owned historic artifacts.

Established by the Oregon Legislature in 1995, the Heritage Commission is comprised of nine gubernatorial appointments, who represent the geographic and cultural diversity of the state, and nine ex officio members. The ex officio commissioners represent the Oregon Historical Society, State Library, State Archives, State Historic Preservation Office, State Historical Records Advisory Board, Department of Education, Oregon University System, Land Conservation and Development Department and Oregon Business Development Department.

The commission is housed within the Oregon Parks and Recreation Department and is a statewide partner of the Oregon Cultural Trust.

Historic Cemeteries, Commission on

Address: 725 Summer St. NE, Suite C, Salem 97301
Phone: 503-986-0685
Fax: 503-986-0793
E-mail: kuri.gill@state.or.us
Web: www.oregon.gov/OPRD/HCD/OCHC
Contact: Kuri Gill, Coordinator
Duties and Responsibilities: The Oregon Commission on Historic Cemeteries (OCHC) consists of seven citizens with broad knowledge of the issues relating to preservation, restoration, upkeep and advocacy for historic burial sites and the importance of historic burial grounds in Oregon history. The OCHC coordinates the restoration, renovation and maintenance of historic cemeteries statewide.

Historic Preservation, State Advisory Committee on

Address: 725 Summer St. NE, Suite C, Salem 97301
Phone: 503-986-0677
Fax: 503-986-0793
E-mail: roger.roper@state.or.us
Web: www.oregon.gov/OPRD/HCD/NATREG/pages/nrhp_sachphome.aspx
Contact: Roger Roper, Deputy State Historic Preservation Officer
Statutory Authority: ORS 358.622
Duties and Responsibilities: The State Advisory Committee on Historic Preservation is a nine-member committee appointed by the governor that reviews nominations to the National Register of Historic Places in Oregon and votes on their eligibility. When the committee determines that a nomination is eligible, it recommends that the state historic preservation officer sign the nomination and forward it to the National Register office in Washington, D.C., for review and listing. The committee meets three times a year to review

nominations brought forward by the State Historic Preservation Office's (SHPO) National Register coordinator. The committee also advises SHPO on matters of program policy and budget.

Historic Preservation Office, State

Address: 725 Summer St. NE, Suite C, Salem 97301
Phone: 503-986-0677
Fax: 503-986-0793
E-mail: roger.roper@state.or.us
Web: www.oregon.gov/OPRD/HCD/SHPO
Contact: Roger Roper, Deputy State Historic Preservation Officer
Duties and Responsibilities: The State Historic Preservation Office (SHPO) was established in 1967 under the terms of the National Historic Preservation Act of 1966. Under a mandate from the federal government as well as state administrative rules and laws, the office manages programs that allow Oregonians as individuals, organizations and local governments to become directly involved in the protection of significant historic and cultural resources. State and federal grants are available for the rehabilitation of historic properties as well as for other preservation related activities.

Programs of the SHPO include: National Register of Historic Places, Certified Local Governments, Historic/Prehistoric Survey and Inventory, Archaeological Permit Process, Historic Preservation Special Assessment for Historic Properties, Federal Historic Rehabilitation Tax Credit, Historic Preservation Comprehensive Planning, Section 106 Review and Compliance.

Historic Trails Advisory Council

Address: 725 Summer St. NE, Suite C, Salem 97301
Phone: 503-986-0579
Fax: 503-986-0793
E-mail: tracy.zeller@state.or.us
Web: www.oregon.gov/OPRD/HCD/ohtac.shtml
Contact: Tracy Zeller, Administrative Specialist
Statutory Authority: Executive Order 98-16
Duties and Responsibilities: The Oregon Historic Trails Advisory Council is composed of nine volunteer citizens appointed by the governor to oversee and provide advice on Oregon's 16 historic trails, including locating, preserving and encouraging the use of these historic trails, evaluating and recording trail conditions and discussing opportunities for the marking and interpretation of the trails. Goals include collecting and sharing information on locating and marking trails; encouraging local communities and agencies to develop directional and interpretive signs, brochures and maps; and helping them find the resources to protect and share these corridors of history.

Recreation Trails Advisory Council

Address: 725 Summer St. NE, Suite C, Salem 97301
Phone: 503-986-0750
Fax: 503-986-0792
E-mail: rocky.houston@state.or.us
Web: www.oregon.gov/OPRD/PLANS/ORTAC.shtml
Contact: Rocky Houston, State Trails Coordinator
Statutory Authority: ORS 390.950–390.989
Duties and Responsibilities: The 1971 Legislature created the Oregon Recreation Trails Program and the Oregon Recreation Trails Advisory Council. This seven-member council, appointed by the State Parks and Recreation Commission, meets four times a year and advises the State Parks and Recreation Department and the commission on statewide trail matters. The council also makes recommendations to other trail managing agencies and non-governmental groups. The council focuses on trails for hiking, equestrian use, bicycling, cross-country skiing and non-motorized boating.

Parole and Post-Prison Supervision, State Board of

Address: 2575 Center St. NE, Suite 100, Salem 97301-4621
Phone: 503-945-9009
Fax: 503-373-7558
Web: www.oregon.gov/BOPPPS
Contact: Jay Scroggin, Executive Director; Kristin Winges-Yanez, Board Chair
Statutory Authority: ORS Chapter 144
Duties and Responsibilities: The Board of Parole and Post-Prison Supervision works in partnership with the Department of Corrections and local supervisory authorities to protect the public and reduce the risk of repeat criminal behavior. The board imposes prison terms and makes release decisions on offenders whose criminal conduct occurred prior to November 1, 1989. The board sets conditions of supervision for all offenders being released from prison, imposes sanctions for violations of supervision and determines whether discharge from parole supervision is compatible with public safety. Discharge from supervision for offenders sentenced under sentencing guidelines occurs automatically upon expiration of the statutory period of post-prison supervision. The board's decisions are based on applicable laws, victims' interests, public safety and the recognized principles of offender behavioral change.

The governor appoints the members for four-year terms and also determines the chair and vice-chair. The full-time board was authorized in 1969.

In 1975, the board was enlarged to five members, with the stipulation that at least one member must be a woman. The membership was reduced to three in 1992.

Patient Safety Commission, Oregon

Address: PO Box 285, Portland 97207-0285
Phone: 971-266-8079
Fax: 503-224-9150
E-mail: info@oregonpatientsafety.org
Web: http://oregonpatientsafety.org
Contact: Bethany Higgins, Executive Director
Statutory Authority: ORS 442.820–442.835, Chapter 686
Duties and Responsibilities: The Oregon Patient Safety Commission is a semi-independent state agency charged by the Oregon Legislature with reducing the risk of serious adverse events occurring in Oregon's health care system and encouraging a culture of patient safety. To accomplish this mission, the commission has established a confidential, voluntary reporting program for Oregon ambulatory surgery centers, hospitals, nursing homes and pharmacies and supports evidence-based prevention practices and quality improvement efforts in Oregon's health care organizations.

Pharmacy, State Board of

Address: 800 NE Oregon St., Suite 150, Portland 97232-2162
Phone: 971-673-0001
Fax: 971-673-0002
E-mail: pharmacy.board@state.or.us
Web: www.oregon.gov/Pharmacy
Contact: Gary Schnabel, Executive Director
Statutory Authority: ORS Chapters 475, 689
Duties and Responsibilities: The Board of Pharmacy was created in 1891, and regulates pharmacy practice to ensure that only qualified individuals practice pharmacy in Oregon. The board licenses pharmacists by examination or through reciprocity with other states, and it registers and inspects hospital and retail pharmacies, drug wholesalers and manufacturers and over-the-counter drug outlets. It investigates drug diversion and violations of its rules and regulates the quality and distribution of controlled substances, prescription and over-the-counter drugs within the state. The board enforces compliance by administrative procedures and by court action. Board activities are financed by license fees.

Physical Therapist Licensing Board

Address: 800 NE Oregon St., Suite 407, Portland 97232-2187
Phone: 971-673-0200
Fax: 971-673-0226
Web: www.oregon.gov/PTBrd
Contact: James Heider, Executive Director
Statutory Authority: ORS 688.160
Duties and Responsibilities: The Physical Therapist Licensing Board was created in 1971 to regulate the practice of physical therapy in Oregon. The board's purpose is public protection and to establish professional standards of practice which assure that physical therapists and physical therapist assistants are properly educated, hold valid, current licenses, practice within their scope of practice and continue to receive ongoing training throughout their careers. Physical therapy practice is governed by state statutes and rules, which define the scope of practice.

The board validates credentials, issues licenses, promulgates rules, monitors continuing education, investigates complaints, issues civil penalties for violations and may revoke, suspend or impose probation on a licensee or limit his or her practice. The board is composed of eight volunteer members: five physical therapists, one physical therapist assistant and two public members. Each member is appointed by the governor and may serve a four-year term, with a maximum of two terms. The board is self-supporting and activities are financed solely from licensure and related fees.

Police, Department of State

Address: 255 Capitol St. NE, 4th Floor, Salem 97310
Phone: 503-378-3720
Fax: 503-378-8282
E-mail: ask.osp@state.or.us
Web: www.oregon.gov/OSP
Contact: Richard Evans, Jr., Superintendent
Statutory Authority: ORS 181.020
Duties and Responsibilities: The Department of State Police was created in 1931 to serve as a rural patrol and to assist local city police and sheriffs' departments.

The department is organized into two bureaus, Police Services Bureau and Public Safety Services Bureau, and has two professional divisions. Some of the agency's specialized programs and services include: transportation safety, major crime investigations, forensic services, automated fingerprint identification and computerized criminal history files, drug investigation, fish and wildlife enforcement, gaming enforcement and regulation, state emergency response coordination, state Fire Marshal services, statewide Criminal Justice Information services, Medical Examiner services and Special Weapons and Tactics (SWAT).

Criminal Investigation Division

Address: 255 Capitol St. NE, 4th Floor, Salem 97310
Phone: 503-378-3720
Fax: 503-378-8282
E-mail: ask.osp@state.or.us
Web: www.oregon.gov/OSP/CID
Contact: Captain Calvin Curths
Statutory Authority: ORS 181.030
Duties and Responsibilities: The Criminal Investigation Division provides specialized investigative services in support of criminal justice agencies statewide through innovative programs and highly trained, dedicated personnel.

The division is composed of several sections: Major Crimes, Drug Enforcement, Arson/Explosives and Investigative Reports. Service delivery is done through participation in interagency task forces, such as the child sex abuse multi-disciplinary teams, major crime teams, drug enforcement task forces and interagency fire investigation teams. As a statewide law enforcement agency, the division has the ability to mobilize resources for major criminal investigations. This may be a police officer-involved shooting, a major criminal investigation involving a large public government agency or entity, or other major crime incident requiring extensive investigative resources in a short time period.

Law Enforcement Data Systems

Address: 3225 State St., Salem 97301; PO Box 14360, Salem 97309-5074
Phone: 503-378-3055
Fax: 503-364-2661
E-mail: terry.oconnell@state.or.us
Web: www.oregon.gov/OSP/CJIS
Contact: Terry O'Connell, Director
Statutory Authority: ORS 181.730
Duties and Responsibilities: Law Enforcement Data Systems (LEDS) plans, develops, manages and operates statewide information systems to enhance police officer safety and to assist law enforcement and criminal justice agencies in the investigation of crimes; the location, apprehension, adjudication and supervision of criminal offenders; location of missing persons; identification of stolen property; and the measurement of the type, extent and effect of crime in the state.

Fish and Wildlife Division

Address: 255 Capitol St. NE, 4th Floor, Salem 97310
Phone: 503-378-3720
Fax: 503-378-8282
E-mail: osp.fwd@state.or.us
Web: www.oregon.gov/OSP/FW
Contact: Captain Jeff Samuels
Statutory Authority: ORS 181.020
Duties and Responsibilities: The Fish and Wildlife Division ensures compliance with the laws and regulations that protect and enhance the long-term health and equitable utilization of Oregon's fish and wildlife resources and the habitats upon which they depend. The division provides public safety and enforcement of boating, criminal and traffic laws and the protection of the state's natural resources.

Forensic Services Division

Address: 255 Capitol St. NE, 4th Floor, Salem 97310
Phone: 503-378-3720
Fax: 503-363-5475
E-mail: osp.forensics@state.or.us
Web: www.oregon.gov/OSP/FORENSICS
Contact: Captain Mike Dingeman
Statutory Authority: ORS 181.066–181.080
Duties and Responsibilities: The Forensic Services Division is a nationally accredited forensic laboratory system serving all state and local law enforcement agencies, medical examiners and prosecuting attorneys in Oregon. The division also performs forensic analysis on criminal cases for a defendant upon a court order.

The division operates Oregon's only full service forensic laboratory system. Analysts provide technical assistance and training, evaluate and analyze evidence, interpret results, and provide expert testimony related to the full spectrum of physical evidence recovered from crime scenes.

This forensic analysis utilizes six regional laboratories designed to provide optimum crime scene response and interaction with local law enforcement. The labs are in Bend, Central Point, Pendleton, Portland and Springfield.

Gaming Enforcement Division

Address: 3400 State St., G-750, Salem 97301
Phone: 503-378-6999
Fax: 503-378-6878
E-mail: ask.osp@state.or.us
Web: www.oregon.gov/OSP/GAMING
Contact: Major Joel Lujan
Statutory Authority: ORS 181.050, Chapter 463
Duties and Responsibilities: The Gaming Enforcement Division was created to ensure the fairness, honesty, integrity and security of gaming operations in Oregon. The division oversees the

Oregon State Athletic Commission, the Lottery Gaming Section and the Tribal Gaming Section.

The Oregon State Athletic Commission regulates boxing, entertainment wrestling and mixed martial arts events. The Lottery Gaming Section ensures that lottery gaming activities are conducted in a fair, honest and secure manner with the highest level of integrity. The Tribal Gaming Section ensures that tribal gaming activities are conducted in a fair, honest and secure manner in accordance with Tribal/State compact agreements.

Medical Examiner Division

Address: 13309 SE 84th Ave., Suite 100, Clackamas 97015
Phone: 971-673-8200
E-mail: eugene.gray@state.or.us
Web: www.oregon.gov/OSP/SME
Contact: Dr. Karen Gunson, Medical Examiner
Statutory Authority: ORS Chapter 146
Duties and Responsibilities: The Medical Examiner Division provides direction and support to the state death investigation program. The medical examiner manages all aspects of the state medical examiner program and has responsibility for technical supervision of county offices in each of the 36 counties of Oregon. The division is staffed by five full-time forensic pathologists, supported by five staff personnel located in the Portland Metropolitan area. Further administrative support and oversight are provided by the Department of State Police. The division certifies the cause and manner of a death requiring investigation within the authority of ORS Chapter 146. This includes post mortem examination and alcohol and drug analyses. The division also maintains appropriate records and provides lectures and training on legal medicine and death investigation to medical school physicians and students, attorneys, law students, police officers, emergency medical technicians and other persons associated with the death investigation system.

Patrol Services Division

Address: 255 Capitol St. NE, 4th Floor, Salem 97310
Phone: 503-378-3720
Fax: 503-378-8282
E-mail: osp.psd@state.or.us
Web: www.oregon.gov/OSP/PATROL
Contact: Captain Craig Durbin
Statutory Authority: ORS Chapter 181
Duties and Responsibilities: The Patrol Services Division provides a uniform police presence and law enforcement services throughout the state, with a primary responsibility for traffic safety and response to emergency calls-for-service on Oregon's 7,000 miles of state and federal highways. Some of the services provided include augmenting and supporting local enforcement and meeting the needs of the public for criminal investigation and transportation safety.

Other Entity:

State Fire Marshal, Office of

Address: 4760 Portland Rd. NE, Salem 97305-1760
Phone: 503-378-3473
Fax: 503-373-1825
E-mail: oregon.sfm@state.or.us
Web: www.oregon.gov/OSP/SFM
Contact: Mark Wallace, State Fire Marshal
Statutory Authority: ORS 476.020
Duties and Responsibilities: The Office of State Fire Marshal was created in 1917 and was consolidated in 1993 into the Department of State Police. The office is charged with reducing the loss of life and property from fire, explosion and hazardous materials and minimizing the fire and life-safety hazards of structures, equipment and materials exposed to fire risks. Program areas cover fire prevention and investigation; uniform fire and life safety code development, adoption and interpretation; Community Right to Know; public education and firesetter intervention; industry licensing and permits relating to liquefied petroleum gas, fireworks and explosives; licensing and surveying non-retail gasoline dispensing; Regional Hazardous Materials Response Team system; and the All Incident Reporting system.

Psychiatric Security Review Board

Address: 610 SW Alder St., Suite 420, Portland 97204
Phone: 503-229-5596
Fax: 503-229-5085
E-mail: psrb@psrb.org
Contact: Mary Claire Buckley, J.D., Executive Director
Statutory Authority: ORS 161.327, ORS Chapter 419C
Duties and Responsibilities: The Psychiatric Security Review Board (PSRB) was created in 1978 to assume jurisdiction over persons in Oregon found to be "guilty except for insanity" of a crime. The board's jurisdiction is equal to the maximum sentence provided by statute for such a crime. In 2005, the Legislature created a juvenile panel of the PSRB to assume jurisdiction over youths who are found "responsible except for insanity" of a crime. Both panels monitor the progress of those placed under its jurisdiction and determine their appropriate placement.

Ten board members, appointed by the governor and confirmed by the Senate to four-year terms, have authority to commit a person to a state hospital designated by the Department of Human Services or, in the case of a youth, to a secure adolescent inpatient rehabilitation program; conditionally release a person from a state hospital or secure facility to a community-based program with close supervision; discharge a person from its jurisdiction; and, when appropriate, revoke the conditional release of a person under its jurisdiction and order the person's return to a state hospital or secure adolescent inpatient rehabilitation program.

Since 2009, in order to keep the national database updated for those prohibited from possessing a firearm, the PSRB has provided information to the Oregon State Police regarding persons who are, or have been, under PSRB's jurisdiction.

Psychologist Examiners, State Board of

Address: 3218 Pringle Rd. SE, Suite 130, Salem 97302-6309
Phone: 503-378-4154
Fax: 503-378-4404
Web: www.oregon.gov/OBPE
Contact: Debra Orman McHugh, Executive Director
Statutory Authority: ORS 675.010–675.150
Duties and Responsibilities: The State Board of Psychologist Examiners was created in 1973 to determine qualifications, examine and license individuals to practice psychology in Oregon. The board may deny, suspend, revoke or restore licenses. It investigates alleged violations of the statutes and imposes appropriate sanctions, adopts a code of ethics and enforces continuing education requirements.

Public Employees Retirement System

Address: 11410 SW 68th Pkwy., Tigard 97223; PO Box 23700, Tigard 97281-3700
Phone: 503-598-7377; Toll-free: 1-888-320-7377; TTY: 503-603-7766
Fax: 503-598-1218
Web: www.oregon.gov/PERS
Contact: Paul R. Cleary, Executive Director
Statutory Authority: ORS 237.350–237.980, 238.005–238.750, 238A.005–238A.475, 243.401–243.507
Duties and Responsibilities: The Public Employees Retirement System (PERS) was established in 1946 to provide retirement, disability and death benefits to Oregon public employees. Membership includes state, school district and local government employees. On December 31, 2010, there were approximately 233,000 PERS members and 113,000 retired members or beneficiaries. PERS is administered by a five-member Board of Trustees, appointed by the governor and confirmed by the Senate for three-year terms. Three are from the private sector and two are from the public sector representing public employees and employers. The PERS Board also administers the retiree Health Insurance Program and the Oregon Savings Growth Plan, a deferred compensation program available to Oregon public employees. Investment of the PERS fund is managed by the Oregon State Treasury with oversight by the Oregon Investment Council.

Public Employees Retirement Board

Address: PO Box 23700, Tigard 97281-3700
Phone: 503-598-7377
Contact: James Dalton, Chair
Statutory Authority: ORS 238.630

Oregon Savings Growth Plan Advisory Committee

Address: 800 Summer St. NE, Suite 200, Salem 97301
Phone: 503-378-3730
Web: www.oregon.gov/PERS/OSGP
Contact: Gay Lynn Bath

Public Safety Standards and Training, Department of

Address: 4190 Aumsville Hwy. SE, Salem 97317
Phone: 503-378-2100
Fax: 503-378-3306
Web: www.oregon.gov/DPSST
Contact: Eriks Gabliks, Director
Statutory Authority: ORS 181.610–181.991, 206.010–206.015, 243.950–243.974, 703.010–703.325
Duties and Responsibilities: The Department of Public Safety Standards and Training (DPSST) implements minimum standards established by the Board on Public Safety Standards and Training for recruitment and training of city, county and state police, corrections officers, parole and probation officers, fire service personnel, emergency telecommunicators and private security providers. DPSST conducts public safety training throughout Oregon and at the central academy in Salem, certifies qualified officers at levels from basic through executive, certifies qualified instructors and inspects and accredits training programs throughout the state based on standards established by the board.

Public Safety Standards and Training, Board on

Address: 4190 Aumsville Hwy. SE, Salem 97317
Phone: 503-378-2100

Web: www.oregon.gov/DPSST/BD
Contact: Kent Barker, Chair; Scott Stanton, Vice Chair
Duties and Responsibilities: The 24-member Board on Public Safety Standards and Training includes members representing city, county and state administrators; professionals representing each of the public safety disciplines; and a private citizen appointed by the governor. The board establishes minimum standards for recruitment and training of city, county and state police; corrections officers; parole and probation officers; fire service personnel; emergency telecommunicators; and private security providers. The board operates in partnership with the DPSST which implements the standards set by the board. The board is supported by six advisory and policy committees representing the public safety disciplines.

Public Utility Commission

Address: 550 Capitol St. NE, Suite 215, Salem 97301-2551; Mail: PO Box 2148, Salem 97308-2148
Phone: 503-378-6611
Fax: 503-378-6163
E-mail: puc.commission@state.or.us
Web: www.puc.state.or.us
Contact: Michael Dougherty, Interim Executive Director; Susan Ackerman, Chair
Statutory Authority: ORS Chapters 756, 757, 758, 759, 772
Duties and Responsibilities: Since 1911, the Public Utility Commission of Oregon (PUC) has regulated customer rates and services of the state's investor-owned electric, natural gas and telephone utilities and certain water companies. The PUC does not regulate people's utility districts, cooperatives or municipally-owned utilities except in matters of safety. The PUC conducts its business at public hearings and in public meetings scheduled every two weeks at its headquarters in Salem. The PUC encourages public involvement in its decisions. The PUC's regulatory responsibilities are carried out by a staff of about 129 employees. Each year, the PUC issues a variety of reports about utility companies.

Maritime Pilots, Board of

Address: 800 NE Oregon St., #15, Portland 97232
Phone: 971-673-1530
Fax: 971-673-1531
Web: www.oregon.gov/PUC/BMP
Contact: Susan Johnson, Administrator
Duties and Responsibilities: The Board of Maritime Pilots is an independent occupational licensing and regulatory agency for state maritime pilots who navigate ships on certain territorial waters of the state. Established in 1846, the board exists today as Oregon's oldest state agency. A maritime pilot is a local navigational and ship-handling expert, engaging in a professional occupation that requires education, experience and licensure.

Racing Commission, Oregon

Address: 800 NE Oregon St., Suite 310, Portland 97232
Phone: 971-673-0207
Fax: 971-673-0213
E-mail: randy.evers@state.or.us
Web: www.oregon.gov/RACING
Contact: Randy Evers, Executive Director
Statutory Authority: ORS 462.210
Duties and Responsibilities: The mission of the Oregon Racing Commission is to regulate and facilitate all aspects of the pari-mutuel industry in Oregon for the benefit of the citizenry, the licensees, the participants and the economy of Oregon. The commission was established in 1933 as part of the Pari-Mutuel Wagering Act. The commission currently regulates all horse racing where pari-mutuel wagering is conducted. Regulation occurs both on track and at off-track wagering facilities and covers all aspects of the operation.

In addition, the commission regulates the multi-jurisdictional hubs licensed in the state. Under current statute, one-third of the funds that come to the commission from pari-mutuel wagering of the multi-jurisdictional hubs are allocated to the state General Fund. The remaining two-thirds of the proceeds are distributed to the racing industry participants to support the commercial race meet in Portland and the local community summer fair race meets throughout the state.

The commission's five-member governing board is appointed by the governor and confirmed by the Senate.

Real Estate Agency

Address: 1177 Center St. NE, Salem 97301-2505
Phone: 503-378-4170
Fax: 503-378-2491
E-mail: orea.info@state.or.us
Web: www.rea.state.or.us
Contact: Gene Bentley, Commissioner
Statutory Authority: ORS 696.375
Duties and Responsibilities: The Real Estate Agency, established in 1919, is administered by the real estate commissioner who is appointed by the governor. The agency is responsible for the licensing, education and enforcement of Oregon's real estate laws applicable to brokers, property

managers, real estate marketing organizations; licensing and regulation of escrow agents (ORS chapter 696); and subdivision (ORS chapter 92), condominium (ORS chapter 100), timeshare and campground (ORS chapter 94) registration/public report issuance.

Each year, the agency processes and tests more than 2,500 license applicants and monitors regulated activities in over 4,400 escrow and real estate offices. Land developers with offerings to Oregon citizens have thousands of disclosure filings with the agency.

The agency provides educational material and seminars for real estate professionals, and conducts investigations and hearings when complaints are filed against licensees, registrants and real property developers.

Real Estate Board

Address: 1177 Center St. NE, Salem 97301-2505
Phone: 503-378-4407
Contact: Dean Owens
Statutory Authority: ORS 696.405
Duties and Responsibilities: The Oregon Real Estate Board consists of seven industry members and two public members, and meets six times a year. Board members are appointed by the governor for four-year terms, which may be extended.

Board duties include providing advice to the real estate commissioner and the governor's office regarding real estate industry matters, reviewing proposed rulemaking, approving experience waiver requests of real estate licensing applicants and overseeing the license examination process.

Revenue, Department of

Address: 955 Center St. NE, Salem 97301-2555
Phone: 503-378-4988; Toll-free 800-356-4222; TTY: 800-886-7204
Fax: 503-945-8738
E-mail: questions.dor@state.or.us
Web: www.oregon.gov/DOR
Contact: Jim Bucholz, Director
Statutory Authority: ORS 305.025
Duties and Responsibilities: The Department of Revenue administers personal income tax and more than 30 Oregon tax programs. These programs include corporation income and excise taxes, inheritance tax and tobacco tax. The department also collects revenues for some local governments, including Tri-County Metropolitan Transportation District (TriMet) and Lane Transit District. In the fiscal year ending in June 2012, $6.3 billion was raised through personal and corporation income taxes.

The department processes five million documents each year. More than 1.8 million of those are personal income tax returns. The department collects delinquent and liquidated accounts for nearly 300 public agencies, commissions and boards. A few of these include the Oregon Judicial Department, Oregon University System, community colleges, corrections departments and the Department of Human Services. In fiscal year 2012, collections totaled more than $52.5 million. This revenue helps fund the services these agencies, commissions and boards provide.

Although the department doesn't collect property taxes, it ensures that property tax laws are applied fairly in all of Oregon's 36 counties. It also provides training and assistance for county assessors, tax collectors, treasurers and local government budget officials. The department appraises utility property, timberland and most large industrial property, providing valuations for county tax rolls. It collects timber privilege taxes for distribution to local districts.

Social Workers, State Board of Licensed

Address: 3218 Pringle Rd. SE, Suite 240, Salem 97302-6130
Phone: 503-378-5735
Fax: 503-373-1427
E-mail: martin.pittioni@state.or.us
Web: www.oregon.gov/BLSW
Contact: Martin Pittioni, Executive Director
Statutory Authority: ORS 675.510–675.600
Duties and Responsibilities: The State Board of Licensed Social Workers, created in 1979, is composed of four licensed clinical social workers and three public members. The board regulates licensed social workers and issues four license and certification types: Registered Bachelor of Social Work (RBSW), Licensed Master of Social Work (LMSW), Clinical Social Work Associate (CSWA) and Licensed Clinical Social Worker (LCSW). The board sets policy, writes and adopts rules, renews licenses and audits continuing education requirements. The board investigates allegations of misconduct by licensed social workers, unauthorized use of protected titles and the unlicensed practice of clinical social work. The board has the authority to discipline licensees; to deny, revoke, suspend or refuse to renew a certificate or license; and to impose civil penalties. Board meetings are held in Salem and are open to the public.

Speech-Language Pathology and Audiology, State Board of Examiners for

Address: 800 NE Oregon St., Suite 407, Portland 97232-2162
Phone: 971-673-0220; TDD: 503-731-4031

Fax: 971-673-0226
E-mail: speechaud.board@state.or.us
Web: www.oregon.gov/BSPA
Contact: Sandy Leybold, Executive Director
Statutory Authority: ORS 681.205–681.991
Duties and Responsibilities: The Board of Examiners for Speech-Language Pathology and Audiology was established in 1973 to license and regulate the performance of speech-language pathologists and audiologists for consumer protection.

State Lands, Department of

Address: 775 Summer St. NE, Suite 100, Salem 97301-1279
Phone: 503-986-5200
Fax: 503-378-4844
E-mail: dsl@dsl.state.or.us
Web: www.oregon.gov/DSL
Contact: Mary M. Abrams, Director
Statutory Authority: ORS Chapter 273
Duties and Responsibilities: The Department of State Lands, established in 1878, is one of Oregon's oldest agencies, managing more than 630,000 acres of grazing and agricultural land; 120,000 acres of forest land; 7,000 acres of industrial, commercial and residential land; and 1.26 million acres of off-shore land, estuarine tidelands, and submerged and submersible lands of the state's extensive navigable waterway system. The agency also manages two million acres of mineral rights owned by other state agencies and 774,000 acres of mineral and energy resources under land owned by other parties. Proceeds from management of lands and waterways and other activities become part of the Common School Fund principal. The fund's market value was $1.1 billion as of June 2012. Earnings from fund investments are distributed semi-annually to school districts through the Department of Education.

The Department of State Lands also administers the state's removal-fill law, which protects Oregon's waterways and wetlands from uncontrolled alteration. Under the Unclaimed Property Act, the department director serves as trust agent for "abandoned funds" such as bank accounts and uncashed checks. Oregon's probate law designates the director as representative for the estate of a deceased person with no will nor known heirs.

Other department responsibilities include leasing state-owned mineral rights for exploration and production of oil, gas, hard minerals and geothermal energy; providing opportunities to lease or buy state land; maintenance of historical records related to early land transactions; management oversight for the South Slough National Estuarine Research Reserve; oversight for protection and maintenance of Oregon's wetlands; and management of coastal resources seaward of the mean high tide line.

State Land Board

Statutory Authority: ORS 273.031
Duties and Responsibilities: The State Land Board is composed of the secretary of state and the state treasurer and is chaired by the governor. Under constitutional and statutory guidelines, the board is responsible for managing the assets of the Common School Fund (land and money) and has additional duties assigned by the Legislature.

The Common School Fund was established as a constitutional trust when Oregon was admitted to The Union on February 14, 1859. At that time, the federal government granted to the state the 16th and 36th sections of every township, or other lands "in lieu" of these sections, to support Oregon's public schools.

South Slough National Estuarine Research Reserve

Address: PO Box 5417, Charleston 97420
Phone: 541-888-5558
Fax: 541-888-5559
Web: www.oregon.gov/DSL/SSNERR
Contact: Mike Graybill, Manager
Statutory Authority: ORS 273.554
Duties and Responsibilities: Established in 1974, the South Slough National Estuarine Research Reserve was the first created under the 1972 federal Coastal Zone Management Act. The reserve is a 5,000 acre natural area located in the Coos estuary on Oregon's south coast. Under policy guidance from the Department of State Lands, the reserve is managed through a cooperative agreement between the state and federal governments, with the goal of improving understanding and stewardship of Pacific Northwest estuaries and coastal watersheds through programs focused on scientific research, education and interpretive facilities. A nine-member South Slough National Estuarine Research Reserve Management Commission, appointed by the governor, provides management oversight. The director of the Department of State Lands chairs the commission.

Student Access Commission, Oregon

Address: 1500 Valley River Dr., Suite 100, Eugene 97401
Phone: 541-687-7400; Toll-free: 1-800-452-8807
Fax: 541-687-7414
E-mail: public_information@osac.state.or.us
Web: www.OregonStudentAid.gov
Contact: Bob Brew, Interim Executive Director

Statutory Authority: ORS Chapter 348

Duties and Responsibilities: The Oregon Student Access Commission (OSAC), created by the 1959 Legislature, administers a variety of state, federal and privately funded student financial aid programs for the benefit of Oregonians attending institutions of postsecondary education. The agency works to create a college-going culture for all Oregonians by providing access through information, mentoring and financial support.

ASPIRE and Outreach Programs

Address: 1500 Valley River Dr., Suite 100, Eugene 97401
Phone: 541-687-7400
Fax: 541-687-7414
Web: www.OregonStudentAid.gov
Contact: Lorianne Ellis, Administrator
Duties and Responsibilities: ASPIRE (Access to Student assistance Programs In Reach of Everyone) is the state's official mentoring program to help students access education and training beyond high school. Trained volunteers mentor middle school and high school students on options for post-secondary education and training beyond high school. Outreach activities include financial aid trainings and workshops throughout the state to financial aid professionals, school counselors and the public.

Oregon Opportunity Grant and Public Programs

Address: 1500 Valley River Dr., Suite 100, Eugene 97401
Phone: 541-687-7400
Fax: 541-687-7414
E-mail: susan.r.degen@state.or.us
Web: www.OregonStudentAid.gov
Contact: Susan Degen, Administrator
Duties and Responsibilities: The Oregon Opportunity Grant is Oregon's largest state-funded, need-based program for students planning to go to college. The program was established by the Legislature in 1971 to assist financially needy students in attaining a postsecondary education at an Oregon community college, public university or four-year private nonprofit institution. Funding sources include the state General Fund and interest earnings from the Lottery-supported Education Stability Fund. Students apply for the grant by completing the Free Application for Federal Student Aid, which is also the gateway for all federal student financial aid. This unit also oversees a number of publicly funded programs to assist former foster youth, students with childcare expenses, and children of deceased and disabled public safety officers.

Scholarship Program

Address: 1500 Valley River Dr., Suite 100, Eugene 97401
Phone: 541-687-7400
Fax: 541-687-7414
E-mail: holly.j.willeford@state.or.us
Web: www.OregonStudentAid.gov
Contact: Holly Willeford, Administrator
Duties and Responsibilities: OSAC works in partnership with the state's largest foundations, private individuals, financial institutions, employers, membership organizations and private individuals to administer scholarships for the benefit of Oregon students. Through the OSAC common application, students can apply for scholarships by selecting from more than 450 scholarship funds administered by OSAC.

Tax Practitioners, State Board of

Address: 3218 Pringle Rd. SE, Suite 120, Salem 97302-6308
Phone: 503-378-4034
Fax: 503-585-5797
E-mail: tax.bd@state.or.us
Web: www.oregon.gov/OBTP
Contact: Ron Wagner, Executive Director; Janis Salisbury, Chair
Statutory Authority: ORS 673.605–673.740
Duties and Responsibilities: The Board of Tax Practitioners issues license credentials, conducts a program of examination and continuing education, and conducts compliance enforcement activities. All persons who prepare, advise or assist in the preparation of personal income tax returns for a fee must be licensed. Licensed Tax Consultants must prove their competency through experience and examination. Licensed Tax Preparers are apprentice-level practitioners who must work under the supervision of Licensed Tax Consultants.

Teacher Standards and Practices Commission

Address: 250 Division St. NE, Salem 97301
Phone: 503-378-3586
Fax: 503-378-3758
E-mail: contact.tspc@state.or.us
Web: www.oregon.gov/tspc
Contact: Victoria Chamberlain, Executive Director
Statutory Authority: ORS 342.350
Duties and Responsibilities: The Teacher Standards and Practices Commission was established in 1965 and made an independent agency in 1973. It is one of 11 independent educator licensure boards in the nation. The commission accredits all educator licensure preparation programs in colleges

and universities who wish to do business in Oregon; licenses teachers, administrators, school counselors and school psychologists in Oregon public and charter schools; certifies school nurses; and takes disciplinary actions against licensees, applicants and student teachers when found to have been convicted of crimes or engaged in misconduct by violating ethical standards of professional practices.

Tourism Commission, Oregon

Address: 250 Church St. SE, Suite 100, Salem 97301
Phone: 503-967-1560
Fax: 503-967-1579
E-mail: info@traveloregon.com
Web: www.TravelOregon.com
Contact: Todd Davidson, CEO
Statutory Authority: ORS 285A.261
Duties and Responsibilities: The Oregon Tourism Commission (dba Travel Oregon), created in 1995 and made semi-independent by the 2003 Legislature, encourages economic growth by strengthening tourism throughout the state. The nine-member commission, appointed by the governor, provides leadership for Oregon's tourism industry and works to market the state with advertising, publications, public relations, research, tourism development and the state's Welcome Centers.

Travel Oregon works to enhance visitors' experiences by providing information and trip planning tools that inspire travel and convey the uniqueness of Oregon. The commission works to strengthen economic benefits of the state's $7.7 billion tourism industry.

Transportation, Department of

Address: 355 Capitol St. NE, Salem 97301-3871
Phone: 503-986-3200; 1-888-ASK-ODOT (275-6368) for questions and concerns
Fax: 503-986-3432
Web: www.oregon.gov/ODOT
Contact: Matthew L. Garrett, Director
Statutory Authority: ORS 184.615
Duties and Responsibilities: The mission of the Oregon Department of Transportation (ODOT) is to provide Oregonians with a safe, efficient transportation system that supports economic opportunity and livable communities. ODOT develops Oregon's system of highways and bridges; supports public transit services, passenger rail, statewide freight systems, bicycle/pedestrian and other multimodal programs; and manages driver licensing and vehicle registration programs, motor carrier operations and transportation safety programs.

Office of the Director

Address: MS 11, 355 Capitol St. NE, Salem 97301-3871
Phone: 503-986-4214
Fax: 503-986-3432
Contact: Dale Hormann, Chief of Staff
Duties and Responsibilities: The Office of the Director oversees the agency's biennial budget and manages Oregon's statewide transportation policy and development of surface transportation, driver and vehicle safety and licensing, and motor carrier programs. The chief of staff directs the activities of the ODOT executive team in setting overall policy and strategic direction. The Government Relations Section analyzes local, state and federal laws and rules that affect transportation. The Office of Employee Safety develops employee safety and risk management programs. The Office of Civil Rights manages ODOT's federal and state regulatory civil rights programs. The Office of Innovative Partnerships and Alternative Funding creates opportunities for innovation and creativity and provides the option to use flexible financing for speedy delivery of transportation projects through partnerships with private business and other units of government.

Transportation Commission, Oregon

Address: MS 11, 355 Capitol St. NE, Salem 97301-3871
Phone: 503-986-3450
Fax: 503-986-3432
Contact: Jacque Carlisle, Commission Assistant
Statutory Authority: ORS 184.615–184.620
Duties and Responsibilities: The Oregon Transportation Commission is a five-member, volunteer citizens' board, appointed by the governor and approved by the Senate. Members serve a four-year term and may be re-appointed. When making appointments, the governor considers the geographic regions of the state and ensures that at least one member is a resident east of the Cascade Mountains. In addition, not more than three members may belong to any one political party.

Central Services Division

Address: MS 11, 355 Capitol St. NE, Salem 97301-3871
Phone: 503-986-4399
Fax: 503-986-3432
Contact: Clyde Saiki, Deputy Director
Statutory Authority: ORS 184.615
Duties and Responsibilities: Eight branches provide core services to support ODOT operations: Financial Services ensures that resources are directed to the priority needs of ODOT; Human

Resources provides staffing and development support; Information Systems is responsible for technology solutions; Business Services provides records, information and forms management, and photo, video and design services; Facilities provides security, access, maintenance and construction management for ODOT facilities; Audit Services performs internal and external audits to ensure appropriate functioning; Budget Office coordinates ODOT's legislative budget development process; and Procurement Office provides procurement, risk management and training services.

Communications Division

Address: MS 11, 355 Capitol St. NE, Salem 97301-3871
Phone: 503-986-3455
Fax: 503-986-3432
Web: www.oregon.gov/ODOT/COMM
Contact: Patrick Cooney, Administrator
Duties and Responsibilities: The Communications Division helps citizens understand transportation programs and issues through ODOT's outreach and information efforts, which include community relations, public information, employee and emergency communications, and media relations. The division also provides support for the Office of the Director, the Oregon Transportation Commission and numerous citizen advisory committees.

Driver and Motor Vehicle Division

Address: 1905 Lana Ave. NE, Salem 97314-0100
Phone: 503-945-5000;
Toll-free (Portland): 503-299-9999
Fax: 503-945-0893
Web: www.oregon.gov/ODOT/DMV
Contact: Tom McClellan, Administrator
Statutory Authority: ORS 184.615(3)
Duties and Responsibilities: The Driver and Motor Vehicle Division (DMV) contributes to public safety by licensing only qualified persons and vehicles to drive on Oregon roads. DMV issues titles to protect the financial and ownership interests in vehicles. There are currently more than 3.5 million licensed drivers and over 4.2 million registered vehicles in Oregon. The fees collected for licensing and registration are dedicated to the Oregon Highway Fund. Law enforcement uses DMV computer records thousands of times throughout the year. DMV also licenses commercial driving schools and instructors, snowmobile dealers and instructors, and vehicle dealers and wreckers. Each day, DMV serves about 12,000 customers statewide, and each year, 1.8 million customers served by telephone. Many transactions can be performed online at the DMV Web site.

Motor Carrier Transportation Division

Address: 550 Capitol St. NE, Salem 97301-2530
Phone: 503-378-5849
Fax: 503-373-1940
Web: www.oregontruckingonline.com
Contact: Gregg Dal Ponte, Administrator
Statutory Authority: ORS Chapters 803, 810, 818, 823, 825, 826
Duties and Responsibilities: The Motor Carrier Transportation Division is responsible for issuing operating authority to motor carriers; collecting highway use taxes; conducting motor carrier tax, International Fuel Tax Agreements and International Registration Plan audits; registering heavy vehicles; enforcing motor carrier safety regulations; and enforcing truck size and weight laws, all aimed at protecting motorists and Oregon's highways, roads and bridges.

Highway Division

Address: 4040 Fairview Industrial Dr. SE, Salem 97302-1142
Phone: 503-986-3819
Fax: 503-986-3150
Web: www.oregon.gov/ODOT/HWY
Contact: Paul Mather, Administrator
Statutory Authority: ORS 184.615(3)
Duties and Responsibilities: The Highway Division is responsible for design, construction, maintenance and operation of more than 8,000 miles of state highways. The division's activities include identifying highway needs; maintaining state highway routes; acquiring rights of way; designing highways, bridges and related structures; awarding highway construction contracts; supervising contractors; obtaining federal highway funds; testing materials; evaluating environmental impacts of proposed projects; and conducting traffic studies and other research.

ODOT has five regional offices which are responsible for a wide variety of transportation operations in those geographic areas. In addition, each region has several district offices that maintain transportation systems in those areas. These regions are transitioning from highway-centric to multimodal as the industry moves to offer more options for transportation.

Region 1 (Portland metro area)
Address: 123 NW Flanders, Portland 97209-4012
Phone: 503-731-8200
Fax: 503-731-8259

Region 2 (Willamette Valley, North and Central Coast, Western Cascades)
Address: 455 Airport Rd. SE, Salem 97301-5395

Phone: 503-986-2600
Fax: 503-986-2630

Region 3 (Southwest Oregon)
Address: 3500 NW Stewart Pkwy., Roseburg 97470-1687
Phone: 541-957-3500
Fax: 541-957-3547

Region 4 (Central Oregon)
Address: 63055 N Hwy. 97, Bend 97701-5765
Phone: 541-388-6180
Fax: 541-388-6231

Region 5 (Eastern Oregon)
Address: 3012 Island Ave., La Grande 97850-9497
Phone: 541-963-3177
Fax: 541-963-9079

Bicycle and Pedestrian Advisory Committee

Address: 555 13th ST NE, Suite 2, Salem 97301-4178
Phone: 503-986-3555
Web: http://www.oregon.gov/ODOT/HWY/BIKEPED
Contact: Sheila Lyons, Program Manager
Statutory Authority: ORS 366.112

Historic Columbia River Highway Advisory Committee

Address: 123 NW Flanders, Portland 97209-4037
Phone: 503-731-4957
Contact: Kristen Stallman, Scenic Area Coordinator

Public Transit Division

Address: 555 13th St. NE, Suite 3, Salem 97301-4179
Phone: 503-986-4077
Fax: 503-986-3183
Web: www.oregon.gov/ODOT/PT
Contact: Hal Gard, Administrator
Statutory Authority: ORS 184.615(3)
Duties and Responsibilities: The Public Transit Division develops and supports the use of public transportation, ridesharing, telecommuting and other alternatives to driving alone. The division provides financial and technical help to urban, small-city and rural transit service providers; to providers of transportation for elderly people and people with disabilities; and to rural inter-city passenger service providers. Planning staff supports statewide and metropolitan transit planning.

Rail Division

Address: 555 13th St. NE, Suite 3, Salem 97301-4179
Phone: 503-986-4077
Fax: 503-986-3183
Web: www.oregon.gov/ODOT/Rail
Contact: Hal Gard, Administrator
Statutory Authority: ORS 184.615(3)
Duties and Responsibilities: The Rail Division represents and advocates for customers of railroads, both passenger and freight, to ensure a safe, efficient and reliable rail transportation system. It regulates the industry for safety and service and has jurisdiction over all public highway-rail grade crossings. The division also manages Oregon's inter-city passenger rail service and supports investment in railroad improvement projects.

Transportation Development Division

Address: 555 13th St. NE, Suite 2, Salem 97301-4178
Phone: 503-986-3421
Fax: 503-986-4173
Web: www.oregon.gov/ODOT/TD
Contact: Jerri Bohard, Administrator
Statutory Authority: ORS 184.615
Duties and Responsibilities: The Transportation Development Division is responsible for research, data collection and analysis, planning and related activities that inform current and future transportation systems. Staff provides technical and planning assistance to local governments and organizations; employs Geographic Information Systems technology in project planning and implementation; compiles crash data, roadway and traffic information; supports multimodal project planning and implementation; facilitates freight planning, and coordinates multiple funding and grant programs.

Transportation Safety Division

Address: MS 3, 4040 Fairview Industrial Dr. SE, Salem 97302-1142
Phone: 503-986-4190
Fax: 503-986-3143
Web: www.oregon.gov/ODOT/TS
Contact: Troy E. Costales, Administrator
Statutory Authority: ORS 184.615(3), 802.300
Duties and Responsibilities: The Transportation Safety Division organizes, plans and conducts a statewide transportation safety program that focuses on occupant protection, driving under the influence of intoxicants, speeding, youthful drivers, pedestrians, bicyclists, motorcyclists and driver education. The division operates these programs by

annually awarding more than 500 grants and contracts to service providers.

Oregon Transportation Safety Committee

Address: MS 3, 4040 Fairview Industrial Dr. SE, Salem 97302-1142
Phone: 503-986-4188
Contact: Mike Laverty, Chair

Governor's Advisory Committee on DUII

Address: MS 3, 4040 Fairview Industrial Dr. SE, Salem 97302-1142
Phone: 503-986-4188
Contact: Chuck Hayes, Chair

Governor's Advisory Committee on Motorcycle Safety

Address: MS 3, 4040 Fairview Industrial Dr. SE, Salem 97302-1142
Phone: 503-986-4188
Contact: David Peterson, Chair

Travel Information Council

Address: 1500 Liberty St. SE, Salem 97302
Phone: 503-378-4508; Toll-free: 1-800-574-9397
Fax: 503-378-6282
Web: http://ortravelexperience.com
Contact: Kyle K. Walker, Chief Executive Officer
Statutory Authority: ORS 377.835
Duties and Responsibilities: The Travel Information Council, doing business as Oregon Travel Experience (OTE), administers the State Highway Logo program, the Tourist Oriented Directional Sign program, and museum signs. OTE also offers signs for the Interstate Oasis program for facilities that provide increased opportunities for stopping to rest, using restroom facilities and obtaining basic services. OTE manages 13 Travel Information kiosks in rest areas, the Travel Plaza program, and administers the Historical Marker and Heritage Tree programs for Oregon. OTE manages five interstate rest areas throughout the state.

University System, Oregon

Address: PO Box 3175, Eugene 97403
Phone: 541-346-5794
Fax: 541-346-5764
Web: www.ous.edu
Contact: George P. Pernsteiner, Chancellor
Statutory Authority: ORS 352.002
Duties and Responsibilities: The Oregon University System is headed by the chancellor and consists of staff who provide services to the seven campuses of the Oregon University System. Staff also link the system to the other agencies of Oregon state government and discharge those duties that the State Board of Higher Education has not explicitly delegated to the campuses.

Oregon has seven public universities: the University of Oregon, Eugene; Oregon State University, Corvallis; Portland State University, Portland; Eastern Oregon University, La Grande; Southern Oregon University, Ashland; Western Oregon University, Monmouth; and Oregon Institute of Technology, Klamath Falls.

Higher Education, State Board of

Address: PO Box 3175, Eugene 97403-0175
Phone: 541-346-5749
Fax: 541-346-5790
E-mail: marcia_stuart@ous.edu
Web: www.ous.edu/state_board
Contact: Marcia Stuart, Associate Board Secretary
Statutory Authority: ORS 351.010
Duties and Responsibilities: The Oregon State Board of Higher Education is the statutory governing board of the Oregon University System. It has 12 members appointed by the governor and confirmed by the Senate. Eight lay members are appointed for four-year terms, two faculty members are appointed for two-year terms and two students are appointed for two-year terms.

Veterans' Affairs, Department of

Address: 700 Summer St. NE, Salem 97301-1285
Phone: 503-373-2000; Toll-free: 1-800-828-8801; TTY: 503-373-2217
Fax: 503-373-2362
Web: www.oregon.gov/ODVA
Contact: Edward Van Dyke, Deputy Director
Statutory Authority: ORS 406.020
Duties and Responsibilities: The Department of Veterans' Affairs has been serving Oregon's military veterans since 1945. The Legislature created the department in answer to the citizens' mandate to provide veterans' benefits and services for Oregon soldiers, sailors, airmen and marines returning from duty in World War II. Since then, benefits managed by the department have been extended to include veterans of later eras.

In addition to providing veterans' benefits counseling, claims preparation and conservatorship services to veterans, their dependents and survivors, the department administers the Veterans' Home Loan and Oregon Educational and Emergency Aid programs. The loan program provides equity for returning war veterans. As stated by the Oregon Senate Concurrent Resolution #2, 1943: "Let it be in the declared policy of the State of Oregon to place our returning military and naval forces as nearly as possible on the same economic equality as those who remained at home."

That policy, resulting in the program to provide below-market home loans to qualified veterans, has not changed, although the program itself has been revised and expanded.

Advisory Committee to the Director of Veterans' Affairs

Address: 700 Summer St. NE, Salem 97301-1285
Phone: 503-373-2383
Contact: Gerard Lorang, Chair
Statutory Authority: ORS 406.210

Veterans' Services Division

Address: 700 Summer St. NE, Salem 97301-1285
Phone: 503-373-2249
Contact: Tom Mann, Administrator
Duties and Responsibilities: The Veterans' Services Division provides a variety of services to Oregon's veterans, their dependents and survivors through its Veterans' Benefits Counseling and Claims, Veterans' Home Loans, Conservatorship and Oregon Educational Aid programs. Through the Counseling and Claims program, veterans' service officers (VSO) provide assistance to veterans, their dependents and survivors with obtaining federal, state and local veterans benefits. VSOs are located in Salem and Portland and offer outreach to nursing homes, correctional facilities, other state institutions and private residences. The Veterans' Loan program provides home acquisition and home improvement loans to veterans at favorable interest rates. Through the Conservatorship Program, the director provides conservatorship service, including total estate management to certain veterans and their survivors who are legally determined to be "protected persons" by various Oregon probate courts. The Oregon Educational Aid Program provides a financial benefit to help offset the educational expenses of honorably discharged Oregon veterans.

Salem Claims and Counseling

Address: 700 Summer St. NE, Salem 97301-1285
Phone: 503-373-2085; Toll-free: 1-800-692-9666
Fax: 503-373-2392
Contact: Mitch Sparks

Portland Claims and Counseling

Address: 1220 SW 3rd Ave., Suite 1610, Portland 97204
Phone: 503-412-4777
Fax: 503-412-4785
Contact: Edward Van Dyke

Conservatorship Program

Address: 700 Summer St. NE, Salem 97301-1289
Phone: 503-373-2085; Toll-free: 1-800-692-9666
Fax: 503-373-2391
Contact: Kelly Breshears

Loan Program

Address: 700 Summer St. NE, Salem 97301-1285
Phone: 503-373-2051; Toll-free: 1-800-828-8801, 1-888-673-8387 (within Oregon)
Fax: 503-373-2393
Contact: Steve Schlag

Other Entity:

Oregon Veterans' Home

Address: 700 Veterans Dr., The Dalles 97058
Phone: 541-296-7190; Toll-free: 1-800-846-8460
Web: www.oregon.gov/ODVA/VETSHOME
Contact: Dallas Swafford, Admissions and Liaison Officer
Statutory Authority: ORS 408.360
Duties and Responsibilities: Opening its doors in 1997, the Oregon Veterans' Home is a state-of-the-art, 151-bed long-term health care facility that provides professional Alzheimer and other dementia care, nursing, rehabilitative, recreational, social and other support services for Oregon veterans, for veterans' spouses, widows and widowers, and for parents whose children have died while serving in the Armed Forces of the United States. The home is the first and only state-mandated nursing home to provide comprehensive nursing care specifically for Oregon's veterans. The Oregon Veterans' Home is a tax-exempt organization and accepts donations to help meet operating expenses.

VETERINARY MEDICAL EXAMINING BOARD

Address: 800 NE Oregon St., Suite 407, Portland 97232
Phone: 971-673-0224
Fax: 971-673-0226
E-mail: ovmeb.info@state.or.us
Web: www.oregon.gov/OVMEB
Contact: Lori Makinen, Executive Director

Statutory Authority: ORS 686.210
Duties and Responsibilities: The Veterinary Medical Examining Board regulates veterinary professionals through enforcement of the Veterinary Practice Act. The board establishes licensing requirements and monitors the professional conduct of veterinarians, veterinary technicians, euthanasia shelters and euthanasia technicians. The board investigates consumer complaints and takes appropriate remedial or disciplinary action. The board monitors consumer issues and identifies and establishes minimum practice standards to ensure that quality veterinary care is provided to the public.

Water Resources Department

Address: 725 Summer St. NE, Suite A, Salem 97301
Phone: 503-986-0900
Fax: 503-986-0904
Web: www.oregon.gov/OWRD
Contact: Phillip C. Ward, Director
Statutory Authority: ORS 536.039
Duties and Responsibilities: The Water Resources Department (WRD) was established in 1909 and is authorized by the Water Rights Act. By law, all surface and ground water in Oregon belongs to the public. WRD protects existing water rights, facilitates voluntary streamflow restoration, increases understanding of the demands on the state's water resources, provides accurate and accessible water resource data and facilitates water supply solutions.

As administrative chief of WRD, the director carries out water management policies set by the Water Resources Commission and oversees the enforcement of Oregon's water laws. The director is appointed by the governor to a four-year term, subject to confirmation by the Senate.

WRD employs a wide variety of experts, including hydrologists, engineers, geologists, technicians and administrative specialists. Agency staff monitors streamflows at hundreds of gaging stations, maps and studies ground water aquifers and helps develop Oregon's Integrated Water Resources Strategy. Staff supplies local governments and citizen groups with information and technical assistance to carry out their own water programs.

WRD is represented throughout the state by a network of five regional and 15 field offices. Among other duties, regional managers meet with user groups to explain current water laws and how they affect local practices. Watermasters, under the direction of regional managers, enforce water laws and measure the waters of the state.

Water Resources Commission

Address: 725 Summer St. NE, Suite A, Salem 97301
Phone: 503-986-0900
Contact: Cindy Smith, Commission Assistant
Statutory Authority: ORS 536.022
Duties and Responsibilities: This seven-member citizen board oversees the activities of WRD. Consistent with state law, the commission sets water policy.

Through WRD, the commission authorizes diversions and appropriations of surface and ground water; issues and records permits, licenses and certificates allowing use of water; establishes instream water rights; and determines critical ground water areas.

Commission members are appointed by the governor for four-year terms, subject to confirmation by the Senate.

Ground Water Advisory Committee

Address: 725 Summer St. NE, Suite A, Salem 97301
Phone: 503-986-0900
Contact: Ivan Gall, Department Liaison; Rob Turkisher, Chair
Statutory Authority: ORS 536.090

Klamath River Basin Compact

Address: 6600 Washburn Way, Klamath Falls 97603
Phone: 541-880-2576
Contact: Debra Crisp, Chair, Klamath Falls, federal government representative; Phillip C. Ward, Oregon representative; Curtis Anderson, California representative
Statutory Authority: 542.610
Duties and Responsibilities: Members facilitate and promote intergovernmental cooperation to assist in the development and proper use of the water resources of the Klamath River Basin.

Western States Water Council

Address: 5296 S. Commerce Dr., Suite 202, Murray, UT 84107
Phone: 801-685-2555
Web: www.westgov.org/wswc
Contact: Tony Willardson, Executive Director
Duties and Responsibilities: The Western States Water Council was established by the Western Governors' Conference to foster cooperation among western states in the management of their water resources. Member states are Alaska, Arizona, California, Colorado, Idaho, Kansas, Montana, Nebraska, Nevada, New Mexico, North Dakota, Oklahoma, Oregon, South Dakota, Texas, Utah, Washington and Wyoming. Delegates to the council are appointed by, and serve at the discretion of, the governors. Oregon's delegate is Phillip C. Ward, who also serves as chair of the council.

Watershed Enhancement Board, Oregon

Address: 775 Summer St. NE, Suite 360, Salem 97301-1290
Phone: 503-986-0178
Fax: 503-986-0199
E-mail: bonnie.ashford@state.or.us
Web: www.oregon.gov/OWEB
Contact: Tom Byler, Executive Director
Statutory Authority: ORS Chapter 541
Duties and Responsibilities: Since 1999, the Oregon Constitution has dedicated 7.5% of Lottery proceeds to restore and protect native fish and wildlife, watersheds and water quality in Oregon. The majority of these funds are allocated to a grant program which supports these objectives. The Oregon Watershed Enhancement Board (OWEB) has been the state agency directed to administer these grant funds.

OWEB's grants help Oregonians take care of local streams, rivers, wetlands and natural areas. Community members and landowners use scientific criteria to decide jointly what needs to be done to conserve and improve local rivers and natural habitat. OWEB maintains a Watershed Restoration Inventory of funded projects, tracking local restoration efforts and investment results, and monitors watershed conditions and provides leadership for natural resource data management. Progress of the Oregon Plan for Salmon and Watersheds is reported to the governor and Legislature biennially.

The agency is led by a 17-member citizen board made up of 11 voting members and six advisory members. Five voting members represent five state natural resource agency boards and commissions: Board of Forestry, Board of Agriculture, Water Resources Commission, Environmental Quality Commission and Fish and Wildlife Commission. Six public voting members represent all regions of the state. Nonvoting, advisory members represent federal natural resource agencies and other concerns: U.S. Forest Service, Bureau of Land Management, Environmental Protection Agency, Natural Resources Conservation Service, National Marine Fisheries Service, the Tribes and the Oregon State University Extension Service. The board allocates funds for watershed restoration activities and is responsible for establishing Oregon's long-term strategy for sustainable watershed health.

OWEB is administered by an executive director and staff in Salem with six regional field offices.

Wine Board, Oregon

Address: 1200 NW Naito Pkwy., Suite 400, Portland 97209
Phone: 503-228-8336
Fax: 503-228-8337
E-mail: info@oregonwine.org
Web: www.oregonwine.org
Contact: Tom Danowski, Executive Director
Statutory Authority: ORS 576.753
Duties and Responsibilities: The Oregon Wine Board, established as a semi-independent agency in 2003, supports enological, viticultural and economic research and promotes grape growing and winemaking in Oregon. Funding comes from a mandatory tax of $25 per ton on grapes used to make wine and 2¢ per gallon on certain wines sold in Oregon.

The board is appointed by the governor and is composed of nine industry leaders, owners or officers of a winery or vineyard organized or registered to do business in Oregon.

Youth Authority, Oregon

Address: 530 Center St. NE, Suite 200, Salem 97301-3765
Phone: 503-373-7205
Fax: 503-373-7622
E-mail: oya.info@oya.state.or.us
Web: www.oregon.gov/OYA
Contact: Fariborz Pakseresht, Director
Statutory Authority: ORS Chapters 419A, 419C, 420, 420A
Duties and Responsibilities: The Oregon Youth Authority (OYA) holds youth offenders accountable and provides opportunities for reformation. OYA exercises legal and physical custody of offenders committed to OYA by juvenile courts, and physical custody of young offenders committed to the Oregon Department of Corrections by adult courts. The agency serves the state's most delinquent youth ages 12 through 24 who commit crimes before their 18th birthday.

OYA manages the supervision and administration of youth correctional facilities, state youth probation and parole services, and community out-of-home placements for youth. OYA also provides funding for community-delivered delinquency prevention and intervention initiatives.

Through evidence-based treatment and rehabilitation programs, classroom education, vocational training, and assistance with daily living skills, OYA helps youths successfully transition back into their communities.

OYA operates close custody or secure transition facilities in Albany, Burns, Florence, Grants Pass, La Grande, Salem, Tillamook, Warrenton and Woodburn and provides probation and parole services in all of Oregon's 36 counties. During 2012, approximately 750 youths were in OYA's close custody or secure transition programs and 1,050 were under OYA's supervision on probation or parole. An additional 20,000 youth offenders were served by Oregon's counties.

Judicial

A boy plays on the beach at Seal Rock State Park—Oregon State Archives Scenic Photograph lincDA0055b

Oregon's judicial branch of government helps individuals, businesses and government groups resolve disputes, protect their rights and enforce their legal duties. Oregon judges review cases for compliance with federal, state and local laws. This section describes the judicial system and introduces Oregon's judges.

Oregon Supreme Court

Address: Supreme Court Bldg., 1163 State St., Salem 97301-2563
Records and Case Information: 503-986-5555; Oregon Relay 711
Fax: 503-986-5560

The Supreme Court of Oregon has seven justices, elected by nonpartisan, statewide ballot, to serve six-year terms. Justices elected to the Supreme Court must be United States citizens, members of the Oregon State Bar and residents of Oregon for at least three years. The court has its offices and courtroom in the Supreme Court Building one block east of the State Capitol in Salem. The members of the court elect one of their number to serve as chief justice for a six-year term.

Powers and Authority

The Supreme Court was created, and its role largely defined, by Article VII of the Oregon Constitution, as amended. It is primarily a court of review in that it reviews the decisions of the Court of Appeals in selected cases. The Supreme Court usually selects cases with significant legal issues calling for interpretation of laws or legal principles affecting many citizens and institutions of society. When the Supreme Court decides not to review a Court of Appeals case, the Court of Appeals' decision becomes final. In addition to its discretionary review function, the Supreme Court hears direct appeals in death penalty, lawyer and judicial discipline, and Oregon Tax Court cases. It may accept original jurisdiction in mandamus, quo warranto and habeas corpus proceedings. It also reviews ballot measure titles, prison siting disputes, reapportionment of legislative districts, and legal questions on Oregon law referred by federal courts.

Administrative Authority

The chief justice is the administrative head of the Judicial Department and, as such, exercises administrative authority over and supervises the appellate, circuit and tax courts. The chief justice makes rules and issues orders to carry out necessary duties and requires appropriate reports from judges and other officers and employees of the courts. As head of the Judicial Department, the chief justice appoints the chief judge of the Court of Appeals and the presiding judges of all state trial courts from the judges elected to those courts. The chief justice adopts certain rules and regulations respecting procedures for state courts. The chief justice also supervises a statewide plan for budgeting, accounting and fiscal management of the judicial department.

The chief justice and the Supreme Court have the authority to appoint lawyers, elected judges and retired judges to serve in temporary judicial assignments.

Admission and Discipline of Lawyers and Judges

The Supreme Court has responsibility for admitting lawyers to practice law in Oregon and the power to reprimand, suspend or disbar lawyers whose actions have been investigated and prosecuted by the Oregon State Bar. In admitting lawyers, the Supreme Court acts on the recommendation of the Board of Bar Examiners, which conducts examinations for lawyer applicants each February and July and which screens applicants for character and fitness to practice law. The Supreme Court appoints at least 14 members to the Board of Bar Examiners. The board includes two "public" members who are not lawyers. The Supreme Court also has the power to censure, suspend or remove judges after investigation and recommendation by the Commission on Judicial Fitness and Disability.

Oregon Court of Appeals

Address: Supreme Court Bldg., 1163 State St., Salem 97301-2563
Records and Case Information: 503-986-5555; Oregon Relay 771
Fax: 503-986-5865

Created in 1969 as a five-judge court, the Court of Appeals was expanded to six judges in 1973 and to ten in 1977. The 2012 House Bill 4026B amended ORS 2.540 to increase the number of Court of Appeals judges from 10 to 13. The bill provides that the new positions become operative on October 1, 2013, and that they should be filled by gubernatorial appointment. The judges, otherwise elected on a statewide, nonpartisan basis for six-year terms, must be United States citizens, members of the Oregon State Bar and qualified electors of their county of residence. The chief justice of the Supreme Court appoints a chief judge from among the judges of the Court of Appeals.

Court of Appeals judges have their offices in the Justice Building in Salem and usually hear cases in the courtroom of the Supreme Court Building. The court ordinarily sits in panels of three judges. The Supreme Court has authority to appoint a Supreme Court justice, a circuit court judge or an Oregon Tax Court judge to serve as a judge pro tempore of the Court of Appeals. The 1997 Legislature created an appellate mediation program called the Appellate Settlement Conference Program; see ORS 2.560(3).

Jurisdiction

The Court of Appeals has jurisdiction to review appeals of most civil and criminal cases and most state administrative agency actions. The exceptions are appeals in death penalty, lawyer and judicial

continued on page 98

Supreme Court

Balmer, Thomas A.
Chief Justice
Position 1
Served since 2001
Term expires 1/2015

Baldwin, Richard
Associate Justice
Position 3
Served since 2013
Term expires 1/2019

Brewer, David
Associate Justice
Position 2
Served since 2013
Term expires 1/2019

Kistler, Rives
Associate Justice
Position 4
Served since 2003
Term expires 1/2017

Landau, Jack L.
Associate Justice
Position 5
Served since 2011
Term expires 1/2017

Linder, Virginia L.
Associate Justice
Position 6
Served since 2007
Term expires 1/2019

Walters, Martha Lee
Associate Justice
Position 7
Served since 2006
Term expires 1/2015

continued from page 96

disciplinary, and Oregon Tax Court cases, which go directly to the Oregon Supreme Court.

Reviews and Decisions

A party aggrieved by a decision of the Court of Appeals may petition the Supreme Court for review within 35 days after the Court of Appeals issues its decision. The Supreme Court determines whether to review the case. The Supreme Court allows a petition for review whenever at least one fewer than a majority of the Supreme Court judges participating vote to allow it.

Oregon Tax Court

Address: Robertson Bldg., 1241 State St., 4th Floor, Salem 97301-2563
Phone: 503-986-5645; TTY: 503-986-5651
Fax: 503-986-5507

The Oregon Tax Court has exclusive, statewide jurisdiction in all questions of law or fact arising under state tax laws, including income taxes, corporate excise taxes, property taxes, timber taxes, cigarette taxes, local budget law and property tax limitations.

Magistrate Division

Address: Robertson Bldg., 1241 State St., 3rd Floor, Salem 97301-2563
Phone: 503-986-5650

The Oregon Tax Court consists of two divisions: the Magistrate Division and the Regular Division. The judge of the Oregon Tax Court appoints a presiding magistrate and one or more other magistrates to serve in the Magistrate Division.

Trials in the Magistrate Division are informal proceedings. Statutory rules of evidence do not apply, and the trials are not reported. The proceedings may be conducted by telephone or in person. A taxpayer may be represented by a lawyer, public accountant, real estate broker or appraiser.

The filing fee is $240. All decisions of the magistrates may be appealed to the Regular Division of the Oregon Tax Court.

Regular Division

Appeals from the Magistrate Division are made directly to the Regular Division of the Oregon Tax Court. The judge of the Oregon Tax Court presides over trials in the Regular Division. The Regular Division is comparable to a circuit court and exercises equivalent powers. All trials are before the judge only (no jury) and are reported. The parties may either represent themselves or be represented by an attorney. Appeals from the judge's decision are made directly to the Oregon Supreme Court. The filing fee is $240.

The judge serves a six-year term and is elected on the statewide, nonpartisan judicial ballot.

Circuit Courts

The circuit courts are the state trial courts of general jurisdiction. The circuit courts have juvenile jurisdiction in all counties except Gilliam, Morrow, Sherman and Wheeler, where the county court exercises juvenile jurisdiction except for termination of parental rights proceedings, over which the circuit courts have exclusive jurisdiction. The circuit courts also exercise jurisdiction in probate, adoptions, guardianship and conservatorship cases in all counties except Gilliam, Grant, Harney, Malheur, Sherman and Wheeler.

Circuit court judges are elected on a nonpartisan ballot for a term of six years. They must be citizens

continued on page 100

Court of Appeals

Haselton, Rick T.
Chief Judge
Position 5
Served since 1994
Term expires 1/2019

Armstrong, Rex
Associate Judge
Position 10
Served since 1995
Term expires 1/2019

Duncan, Rebecca
Associate Judge
Position 2
Served since 2010
Term expires 1/2015

Egan, James
Associate Judge
Position 6
Served since 2013
Term expires 1/2019

Hadlock, Erika L.
Associate Judge
Position 9
Served since 2011
Term expires 1/2019

Nakamoto, Lynn
Associate Judge
Position 8
Served since 2011
Term expires 1/2019

Ortega, Darleen
Associate Judge
Position 3
Served since 2003
Term expires 1/2017

Schuman, David
Associate Judge
Position 1
Served since 2001
Term expires 1/2015

Sercombe, Timothy
Associate Judge
Position 4
Served since 2007
Term expires 1/2015

Wollheim, Robert D.
Associate Judge
Position 7
Served since 1998
Term expires 1/2017

Oregon Tax Court

Breithaupt, Henry C.
Tax Judge
Served since 2001
Term expires 1/2015

Cases Filed in Oregon Courts 2006–2011

	2006	2007	2008	2009	2010	2011
Oregon Supreme Court	1,347	1,274	1,321	1,368	1,271	1,191
Oregon Court of Appeals	3,517	3,317	3,224	3,419	3,093	2,943
Oregon Tax Court, Regular	27	26	73	50	53	71
Oregon Tax Court, Magistrate	827	915	1,237	1,641	1,374	1,310
Circuit Courts	602,896	605,753	610,334	599,605	565,397	552,601

continued from page 98

of the United States, members of the Oregon State Bar, residents of Oregon for at least three years and residents of their judicial district for at least one year (except Multnomah County judges, who may reside within ten miles of the county). Since January 1, 2007, there are 173 circuit judges serving the 36 Oregon counties. The circuit judges are grouped in 27 geographical areas called judicial districts. Multnomah County district has 38 circuit judges; Lane, 15; Marion, 14; Washington, 14; Clackamas, 11; Jackson, 9; Deschutes, 7; Coos-Curry, 6; four districts have five judges, three districts have four judges, six districts have three judges, three districts have two judges and three districts have one judge.

To expedite judicial business, the chief justice of the Supreme Court may assign any circuit judge to sit in any judicial district in the state.

Senior Judges

Under Oregon law, a judge who retires from the circuit court, Oregon Tax Court, Court of Appeals or Supreme Court, except a judge retired under the provisions of ORS 1.310, may be designated a senior judge of the state by the Supreme Court, and is eligible for temporary assignment by the Supreme Court to any state court at or below the level in which he or she last served as a full-time judge. The current roster of senior judges follows:

From the Supreme Court: Wallace P. Carson Jr., Paul J. De Muniz, Robert D. Durham, W. Michael Gillette, Ralph M. Holman, Susan M. Leeson, Hans Linde, Edwin Peterson, R. William Riggs, Richard L. Unis, George Van Hoomissen

From the Court of Appeals or Oregon Tax Court: Carl N. Byers, Mary J. Deits, Walter Edmonds, William L. Richardson, John Warden, Edward H. Warren

From the circuit courts: Pamela L. Abernethy, Philip T. Abraham, Ted Abram, T Marshall L. Amiton, Fred Avera, Raymond Bagley, Glen D. Baisinger, Richard D. Barber, Frank L. Bearden, Mary Ann Bearden, John C. Beatty, William Beckett, Douglas G. Beckman, Linda Bergman, Jack A. Billings, Alan C. Bonebrake, Sid Brockley, Nancy W. Campbell, H. Ted Carp, Joseph F. Ceniceros, Ronald E. Cinniger, Allan H. Coon, Ross Davis, Don A. Dickey, Henry R. Dickinson Jr., Jim Donnell, Hugh C. Downer Jr., James R. Ellis, Greg Foote, Kimberly C. Frankel, Karl W. Freerksen Jr., Jackson L. Frost, Stephen A. Gallagher, Mark Gardner, Robert S. Gardner, David Gernant, James C. Goode, Joe Guimond, David Hantke, James Hargreaves, Wayne R. Harris, Bryan T. Hodges, Janet S. Holcomb, William Horner, Robert J. Huckleberry, Don Hull, Dale Jacobs, Nely L. Johnson, Donald Kalberer, Mitchell A. Karaman, John V. Kelly, Karla J. Knieps, Frank D. Knight, Dale R. Koch, Thomas Kolberg, Kristena La Mar, Darryl Larson, William Lasswell, Terry A. Leggert, Kip Leonard, John B. Lewis, William O. Lewis, Paul J. Lipscomb, Charles P. Littlehales, John Lowe, Jon B. Lund, Charles E. Luukinen, William S. Mackay, Steven Maurer, Robert B. McConville, John A. McCormick, Rick J. McCormick, Michael J. McElligott, Keith E. Meisenheimer, L. A. Merryman, Richard Mickelson, Rodney W. Miller, Robert Millikan, Douglas Mitchell, Robert J. Morgan, Thomas M. Mosgrove, Thomas Moultrie, Rudy M. Murgo, George W. Neilson, Gerald C. Neufeld, Joseph V. Ochoa, Loyd O'Neal, Clifford Olsen, Jack F. Olsen, Rebecca Orf, Edward L. Perkins, Hollie M. Pihl, Milo Pope, J. Burdette Pratt, Steven Price, William G. Purdy, Richard Rambo, Robert Redding, Garry L. Reynolds, Rick W. Roll, Don H. Sanders, Mark S. Schiveley, Joan G. Seitz, Robert Selander, Lane W. Simpson, Berkeley Smith, Bernard L. Smith, William C. Snouffer, Douglas R. Spencer, Michael C. Sullivan, Ronald D. Thom, Stephen Tiktin, Wendell H. Tompkins, Gary S. Thompson, Eric Valentine, Pierre Van Rysselberghe, Lyle Velure, Robert Walberg, Jeff M. Wallace, Elizabeth Welch, C. Gregory West, Raymond B. White, Darrell J. Williams, Janice R. Wilson, John Wilson, George Woodrich, Jan Wyers, Frank J. Yraguen

From the district courts:* H. Aaron Brown Jr., Anthony L. Casciato, Richard J. Courson, Robert L. Gilliland, Robert E. Jones, Winfrid K. Liepe, Charles H. Reeves, Joseph J. Thalhofer

continued on page 124

Circuit Court

(P) = Presiding Judge

Abar, Donald D.
Marion
District 3, Position 11

Adkisson, Marci W.
Klamath
District 13, Position 3

Adler, A. Michael
Deschutes
District 11, Position 4

Ahern, Daniel J.
Crook, Jefferson (P)
District 22, Position 2

Albrecht, Cheryl
Multnomah
District 4, Position 31

Ambrosini, George
Douglas
District 16, Position 5

Arnold, G. Philip
Jackson
District 1, Position 3

Ashby, Wells B.
Deschutes
District 11, Position 6

Avera, Sally
Polk
District 12, Position 1

Bachart, Sheryl
Lincoln
District 17, Position 1

Bagley, Beth
Deschutes
District 11, Position 2

Bailey, Charlie
Washington
District 20, Position 6

Baker, Lindi L.
Josephine (P)
District 14, Position 4

Barnack, Tim
Jackson
District 1, Position 6

Barron, Richard L.
Coos, Curry (P)
District 15, Position 2

Baxter, Greg
Baker (P)
District 8, Position 1

Beaman, Cynthia
Coos, Curry
District 15, Position 6

Bechtold, Paula M.
Coos, Curry
District 15, Position 5

Bergstrom, Eric
Multnomah
District 4, Position 8

Bispham, Carol R.
Linn
District 23, Position 1

Bloch, Eric J.
Multnomah
District 4, Position 20

Bloom, Benjamin M.
Jackson
District 1, Position 7

Brady, Alta J.
Deschutes (P)
District 11, Position 1

Branford, Thomas O.
Lincoln (P)
District 17, Position 3

Brauer, Christopher R.
Morrow, Umatilla
District 6, Position 5

Brownhill, Paula J.
Clatsop
District 18, Position 1

Bunch, Dan
Klamath
District 13, Position 5

Burge, Frances
Douglas
District 16, Position 4

Burton, Claudia M.
Marion
District 3, Position 4

Bushong, Stephen
Multnomah
District 4, Position 21

Butterfield, Eric
Washington
District 20, Position 4

Campbell, Monte S.
Polk (P)
District 12, Position 2

Carlson, Charles D.
Lane
District 2, Position 2

Carlson, Cynthia D.
Lane
District 2, Position 13

Chanti, Suzanne
Lane
District 2, Position 9

Cobb, Rita B.
Washington
District 20, Position 12

Collins, John L.
Yamhill (P)
District 25, Position 1

Connell, David B.
Benton
District 21, Position 3

Conover, R. Curtis
Lane
District 2, Position 12

Crain, Patricia
Jackson
District 1, Position 4

Cramer, William D., Jr.
Grant, Harney (P)
District 24, Position 1

Crowley, Paul G.
Gilliam, Hood River,
Sherman, Wasco,
Wheeler (P)
District 7, Position 3

Dailey, Kathleen M.
Multnomah
District 4, Position 25

Darling, Deanne L.
Clackamas
District 5, Position 9

Day, Vance D.
Marion
District 3, Position 5

DeHoog, Roger J.
Deschutes
District 11, Position 3

Dretke, Brian C.
Union, Wallowa
District 10, Position 1

Easterday, Cynthia
Yamhill
District 25, Position 3

Erwin, Andrew R.
Washington
District 20, Position 7

Forte, Stephen P.
Deschutes
District 11, Position 7

Frantz, Julie
Multnomah
District 4, Position 10

Fuchs, Alicia A.
Multnomah
District 4, Position 15

Fun, James Lee, Jr.
Washington
District 20, Position 13

Garcia, Oscar
Washington
District 20, Position 9

Garrison, Randolph Lee
Douglas (P)
District 16, Position 3

Gerking, Timothy
Jackson
District 1, Position 5

Geyer, Courtland
Marion
District 3, Position 12

Gillespie, Michael J.
Coos, Curry
District 15, Position 4

Grant, Jenefer
Columbia (P)
District 19, Position 3

Graves, Dennis J.
Marion
District 3, Position 7

Greif, Lisa
Jackson
District 1, Position 8

Grensky, Ron
Jackson
District 1, Position 9

Photo Not Submitted

Grove, Ted
Columbia
District 19, Position 2

Hampton, Lynn W.
Morrow, Umatilla
District 6, Position 1

Harris, Daniel L.
Jackson
District 1, Position 2

Hart, Thomas M.
Marion
District 3, Position 13

Haslinger, Barbara A.
Deschutes
District 11, Position 5

Henry, Eveleen
Lane
District 2, Position 15

Herndon, Robert D.
Clackamas (P)
District 5, Position 7

Hill, Daniel J.
Morrow, Umatilla
District 6, Position 3

Hill, Jonathan R.
Tillamook
District 27, Position 1

Hill, Norman R.
Polk
District 12, Position 3

Hillman, Annette
Crook, Jefferson
District 22, Position 1

Hodson, Jerry
Multnomah
District 4, Position 3

Holland, Lauren S.
Lane
District 2, Position 11

Hull, Thomas M.
Josephine
District 14, Position 1

Hung, Lung S.
Malheur
District 9, Position 2

Immergut, Karin
Multnomah
District 4, Position 26

Isaacson, Rodger J.
Klamath
District 13, Position 1

James, Mary
Marion
District 3, Position 6

Jones, Edward J.
Multnomah
District 4, Position 23

Jones, Jeffrey S.
Clackamas
District 5, Position 1

Kantor, Henry
Multnomah
District 4, Position 30

Kasubhai, Mustafa
Lane
District 2, Position 3

Knapp, Rick
Washington
District 20, Position 14

Kohl, Thomas W.
Washington
District 20, Position 1

Kurshner, Paula J.
Multnomah
District 4, Position 35

LaBarre, Jerome
Multnomah
District 4, Position 7

Leith, David E.
Marion
District 3, Position 8

Letourneau, Donald R.
Washington
District 20, Position 3

Litzenberger, Marilyn
Multnomah
District 4, Position 38

Lopez, Angel
Multnomah
District 4, Position 22

Photo
Not
Submitted

Love, Valeri L.
Lane
District 2, Position 8

Loy, Michael S.
Multnomah
District 4, Position 33

Margolis, Jesse
Coos, Curry
District 15, Position 3

Marshall, Christopher J.
Multnomah
District 4, Position 5

Marshall, William A.
Douglas
District 16, Position 2

Matarazzo, Judith H.
Multnomah
District 4, Position 28

Matyas, Cindee S.
Clatsop
District 18, Position 3

Maurer, Jean Kerr
Multnomah
District 4, Position 24

McAlpin, Jay A.
Lane
District 2, Position 7

McHill, Thomas
Linn
District 23, Position 5

McKnight, Maureen H.
Multnomah
District 4, Position 13

McShane, Michael J.
Multnomah
District 4, Position 19

Mejia, Lorenzo A.
Jackson (P)
District 1, Position 1

Merten, Maurice K.
Lane
District 2, Position 6

Miller, Eve L.
Clackamas
District 5, Position 2

Mooney, Josephine H.
Lane
District 2, Position 10

Murphy, Daniel R.
Linn (P)
District 23, Position 3

Nachtigal, Gayle A.
Washington
District 20, Position 8

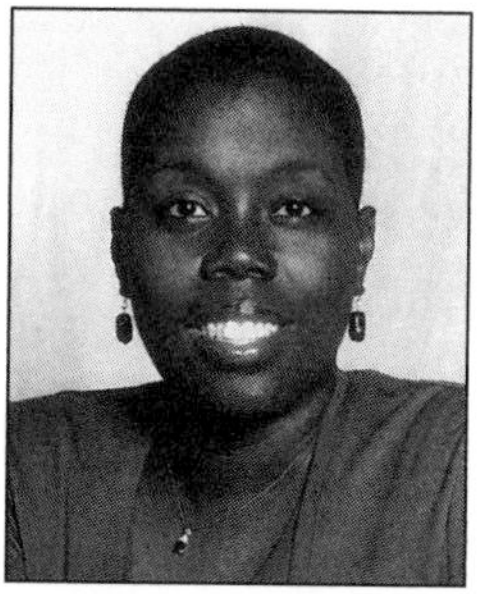

Nelson, Adrienne C.
Multnomah
District 4, Position 4

Nelson, Philip L.
Clatsop (P)
District 18, Position 2

Newman, Michael
Josephine
District 14, Position 3

Norblad, Albin W.
Marion
District 3, Position 3

Norby, Susie
Clackamas
District 5, Position 11

Novotny, DeAnn L.
Linn
District 23, Position 4

Olson, John A.
Gilliam, Hood River,
Sherman, Wasco, Wheeler
District 7, Position 1

Osborne, Roxanne B.
Klamath
District 13, Position 2

Pahl, Ronald J.
Morrow, Umatilla (P)
District 6, Position 2

Partridge, Lindsay R.
Marion
District 3, Position 10

Penn, Dale
Marion
District 3, Position 9

Photo
Not
Submitted

Poole, Ronald
Douglas
District 16, Position 1

Prall, Tracy A.
Marion
District 3, Position 2

Raines, Keith R.
Washington
District 20, Position 5

Rasmussen, Karsten H.
Lane (P)
District 2, Position 1

Rastetter, Thomas
Clackamas
District 5, Position 10

Reed, Steven B.
Columbia
District 19, Position 1

Rees, David
Multnomah
District 4, Position 9

Rhoades, Jamese L.
Marion (P)
District 3, Position 1

Roberts, Leslie
Multnomah
District 4, Position 37

Rooke-Ley, Ilisa
Lane
District 2, Position 5

Ryan, Thomas
Multnomah
District 4, Position 18

Sanders, Paulette
Lincoln
District 17, Position 2

Skye, Kelly
Multnomah
District 4, Position 17

Stauffer, Janet L.
Gilliam, Hood River,
Sherman, Wasco, Wheeler
District 7, Position 2

Steele, Kathie F.
Clackamas
District 5, Position 6

Stone, Martin E.
Coos, Curry
District 15, Position 1

Stone, Ronald W.
Yamhill
District 25, Position 2

Stuart, Diane
Multnomah
District 4, Position 27

Sullivan, Patricia
Malheur (P)
District 9, Position 1

Svetkey, Susan M.
Multnomah
District 4, Position 16

Temple, Eva J.
Morrow, Umatilla
District 6, Position 4

Tennyson, Katherine
Multnomah
District 4, Position 1

Thompson, Kirsten E.
Washington (P)
District 20, Position 2

Tichenor, Carroll J.
Yamhill
District 25, Position 4

Trevino, Mari
Tillamook (P)
District 27, Position 2

Tripp, Susan
Marion
District 3, Position 14

Upton, Suzanne
Washington
District 20, Position 10

Van Dyk, Douglas V.
Clackamas
District 5, Position 4

Villa-Smith, Kathryn L.
Multnomah
District 4, Position 29

Vogt, Debra
Lane
District 2, Position 14

Walker, Kenneth
Multnomah
District 4, Position 11

Waller, Nan G.
Multnomah (P)
District 4, Position 2

Weber, Katherine
Clackamas
District 5, Position 5

West, Russell B.
Union, Wallowa (P)
District 10, Position 2

Wetzel, Michael
Clackamas
District 5, Position 3

Williams, Gary
Crook, Jefferson
District 22, Position 3

Williams, Locke A.
Benton (P)
District 21, Position 1

Wipper, Janelle F.
Washington
District 20, Position 11

Wittmayer, John
Multnomah
District 4, Position 36

Wogan, Cameron F.
Klamath (P)
District 13, Position 4

Wolf, John A.
Gilliam, Hood River,
Sherman, Wasco, Wheeler
District 7, Position 4

Wolke, Pat
Josephine
District 14, Position 2

Wyatt, Merri Souther
Multnomah
District 4, Position 32

You, Youlee Yim
Multnomah
District 4, Position 6

Zennaché, Charles
Lane
District 2, Position 4

Circuit Court Judges

newly appointed at press time:

Allen, Beth
Multnomah
District 4, Position 34

Holmes Hehn, Amy
Multnomah
District 4, Position 14

Circuit Court Judges by District

District 1—Jackson

Jackson County Justice Bldg., Medford 97501

Arnold, G. Philip
Pos. 3, Exp. 1-4-17, 541-776-7171 x173

Barnack, Tim
Pos. 6, Exp. 1-5-15, 541-776-7171 x168

Bloom, Benjamin M.
Pos. 7, Exp. 1-7-19, 541-776-7171 x230

Crain, Patricia
Pos. 4, Exp. 1-4-17, 541-776-7171 x112

Gerking, Timothy
Pos. 5, Exp. 1-7-19, 541-776-7171 x163

Greif, Lisa
Pos. 8, Exp. 1-5-15, 541-776-7171 x108

Grensky, Ron
Pos. 9, Exp. 1-7-19, 541-776-7171 x169

Harris, Daniel L.
Pos. 2, Exp. 1-4-17, 541-776-7171 x172

Mejia, Lorenzo A. (presiding judge)
Pos. 1, Exp. 1-5-15, 541-776-7171 x164

District 2—Lane

Lane County Courthouse, Eugene 97401

Carlson, Charles D.
Pos. 2, Exp. 1-5-15, 541-682-4257

Carlson, Cynthia D.
Pos. 13, Exp. 1-7-19, 541-682-4218

Chanti, Suzanne
Pos. 9, Exp. 1-4-17, 541-682-4254

Conover, R. Curtis
Pos. 12, Exp. 1-7-19, 541-682-4497

Henry, Eveleen
Pos. 15, Exp. 1-5-15, 541-682-4753

Holland, Lauren S.
Pos. 11, Exp. 1-4-17, 541-682-4415

Kasubhai, Mustafa
Pos. 3, Exp. 1-5-15, 541-682-4256

Love, Valeri L.
Pos. 8, Exp. 1-7-19, 541-682-4250

McAlpin, Jay A.
Pos. 7, Exp. 1-4-17, 541-682-4240

Merten, Maurice K.
Pos. 6, Exp. 1-4-17, 541-682-4258

Mooney, Josephine H.
Pos. 10, Exp. 1-7-19, 541-682-3601

Rasmussen, Karsten H. (presiding judge)
Pos. 1, Exp. 1-7-19, 541-682-4253

Rooke-Ley, Ilisa
Pos. 5, Exp. 1-5-15, 541-682-4300

Vogt, Debra
Pos. 14, Exp. 1-7-19, 541-682-4027

Zennaché, Charles
Pos. 4, Exp. 1-5-15, 541-682-4259

District 3—Marion

Marion County Courthouse, Salem 97309-0869

Abar, Donald D.
Pos. 11, Exp. 1-7-19, 503-373-4467

Burton, Claudia M.
Pos. 4, Exp. 1-4-17, 503-584-7713

Day, Vance D.
Pos. 5, Exp. 1-7-19, 503-588-5026

Geyer, Courtland
Pos. 12, Exp. 1-7-19, 503-373-4445

Graves, Dennis J.
Pos. 7, Exp. 1-7-19, 503-585-4939

Hart, Thomas M.
Pos. 13, Exp. 1-4-17, 503-584-7749

James, Mary
Pos. 6, Exp. 1-4-17, 503-373-4303

Leith, David E.
Pos. 8, Exp. 1-7-19, 503-588-5160

Norblad, Albin W.
Pos. 3, Exp. 1-7-19, 503-588-5028

Partridge, Lindsay R.
Pos. 10, Exp. 1-7-19, 503-588-5030

Penn, Dale
Pos. 9, Exp. 1-4-17, 503-588-5492

Prall, Tracy A.
Pos. 2, Exp. 1-5-15, 503-588-5020

Rhoades, Jamese L. (presiding judge)
Pos. 1, Exp. 1-7-19, 503-588-7950

Tripp, Susan
Pos. 14, Exp. 1-5-15, 503-373-4361

District 4—Multnomah

Multnomah County Courthouse, Portland 97204

Albrecht, Cheryl
Pos. 31, Exp. 1-7-19, 503-988-3835

Allen, Beth
Pos. 34, Exp. 1-5-15, 503-988-3250

Bergstrom, Eric
Pos. 8, Exp. 1-7-19, 503-988-5029

Bloch, Eric J.
Pos. 20, Exp. 1-4-17, 503-988-3954

Bushong, Stephen
Pos. 21, Exp. 1-5-15, 503-988-3546

Dailey, Kathleen M.
Pos. 25, Exp. 1-4-17, 503-988-3062

Frantz, Julie
Pos. 10, Exp. 1-5-15, 503-988-3045

Fuchs, Alicia A.
Pos. 15, Exp. 1-4-17, 503-988-5544

Holmes Hehn, Amy
Pos. 14, Exp. 1-5-15, 503-988-3052

Hodson, Jerry
Pos. 3, Exp. 1-7-19, 503-988-5101

Immergut, Karin
Pos. 26, Exp. 1-4-17, 503-988-5008

Jones, Edward J.
Pos. 23, Exp. 1-7-19, 503-988-3540

Kantor, Henry
Pos. 30, Exp. 1-5-15, 503-988-3972

Kurshner, Paula J.
Pos. 35, Exp. 1-7-19, 503-988-5010

LaBarre, Jerome
Pos. 7, Exp. 1-7-19, 503-988-3348

Litzenberger, Marilyn
Pos. 38, Exp. 1-5-15, 503-988-3365

Lopez, Angel
Pos. 22, Exp. 1-4-17, 503-988-3068

Loy, Michael S.
Pos. 33, Exp. 1-5-15, 503-988-3813

Marshall, Christopher J.
Pos. 5, Exp. 1-5-15, 503-988-3274

Matarazzo, Judith Hudson
Pos. 28, Exp. 1-7-19, 503-988-3227

Maurer, Jean Kerr
Pos. 24, Exp. 1-5-15, 503-988-3668

McKnight, Maureen H.
Pos. 13, Exp. 1-5-15 503-988-3986

McShane, Michael J.
Pos. 19, Exp. 1-5-15 503-988-3214

Nelson, Adrienne C.
Pos. 4, Exp. 1-7-19, 503-988-5047

Rees, David
Pos. 9, Exp. 1-4-17, 503-988-3803

Roberts, Leslie
Pos. 37, Exp. 1-7-19, 503-988-6760

Ryan, Thomas
Pos. 18, Exp. 1-5-15, 503-988-3008

Skye, Kelly
Pos. 17, Exp. 1-5-15, 503-988-3204

Stuart, Diane
Pos. 27, Exp. 1-5-15, 503-988-3201

Svetkey, Susan M.
Pos. 16, Exp. 1-7-19, 503-988-3060

Tennyson, Katherine
Pos. 1, Exp. 1-5-15, 503-988-3078

Villa-Smith, Kathryn L.
Pos. 29, Exp. 1-7-19, 503-988-3985

Walker, Kenneth
Pos. 11, Exp. 1-5-15, 503-988-3041

Waller, Nan G. (presiding judge)
Pos. 2, Exp. 1-3-15, 503-988-3846

Wittmayer, John
Pos. 36, Exp. 1-5-15, 503-988-3165

Wyatt, Merri Souther
Pos. 32, Exp. 1-7-19, 503-988-3029

You, Youlee Yim
Pos. 6, Exp. 1-5-15, 503-988-3404

Vacant
Pos. 12, Exp. 1-7-19, 503-988-3069

District 5—Clackamas

Clackamas County Courthouse, Oregon City 97045

Darling, Deanne L.
Pos. 9, Exp. 1-5-15, 503-557-2841

Herndon, Robert D. (presiding judge)
Pos. 7, Exp. 1-4-17, 503-655-8644

Jones, Jeffrey S.
Pos. 1, Exp. 1-7-19, 503-655-8687

Miller, Eve L.
Pos. 2, Exp. 1-4-17, 503-655-8686

Norby, Susie
Pos. 11, Exp. 1-7-19, 503-650-8902

Rastetter, Thomas
Pos. 10, Exp. 1-4-17, 503-655-8432

Steele, Kathie F.
Pos. 6, Exp. 1-5-15, 503-655-8678

Van Dyk, Douglas V.
Pos. 4, Exp. 1-4-17, 503-655-8688

Weber, Katherine
Pos. 5, Exp. 1-4-17, 503-655-8233

Wetzel, Michael
Pos. 3, Exp. 1-7-19, 503-655-8685

Vacant
Pos. 8, Exp. 1-7-19, 503-655-8643

District 6—Morrow, Umatilla

Umatilla County Courthouse, Pendleton 97801

Brauer, Christopher R.
Pos. 5, Exp. 1-7-19, 541-278-0341 x222

Hampton, Lynn W.
Pos. 1, Exp. 1-5-15, 541-278-0341 x232

Pahl, Ronald J. (presiding judge)
Pos. 2, Exp. 1-4-17, 541-278-0341 x225

Stafford Hansell Gov't Center, Hermiston 97838

Hill, Daniel J.
Pos. 3, Exp. 1-4-17, 541-667-3034

Temple, Eva J.
Pos. 4, Exp. 1-4-17, 541-667-3031

District 7—Gilliam, Hood River, Sherman, Wasco, Wheeler

Hood River Co. Courthouse, Hood River 97031

Crowley, Paul G. (presiding judge)
Pos. 3, Exp. 1-4-17, 541-386-1862

Olson, John A.
Pos. 1, Exp. 1-7-19, 541-386-2676

Wasco County Courthouse, The Dalles 97058

Stauffer, Janet L.
Pos. 2, Exp. 1-4-17, 541-506-2710

Wolf, John A.
Pos. 4, Exp. 1-4-17, 541-506-2717

District 8—Baker

Baker County Courthouse, Baker City 97814

Baxter, Greg (presiding judge)
Pos. 1, Exp. 1-7-19, 541-523-6303

District 9—Malheur

Malheur County Courthouse, Vale 97918

Hung, Lung S.
Pos. 2, Exp. 1-5-15, 541-473-5568

Sullivan, Patricia (presiding judge)
Pos. 1, Exp. 1-7-19, 541-473-5178

District 10—Union, Wallowa

Union County Courthouse, La Grande 97850
Wallowa County Courthouse, Enterprise 97828

Dretke, Brian C.
Pos. 1, Exp. 1-7-19, 541-962-9500 x2231; 541-426-4991

West, Russell B. (presiding judge)
Pos. 2, Exp. 1-5-15, 541-962-9500 x2225; 541-426-4991

District 11—Deschutes

Deschutes County Courthouse, Bend 97701

Adler, A. Michael
Pos. 4, Exp. 1-4-17, 541-388-5300 x2490

Ashby, Wells B.
Pos. 6, Exp. 1-4-17, 541-388-5300 x2520

Bagley, Beth
Pos. 2, Exp. 1-7-19, 541-388-5300 x2410

Brady, Alta J. (presiding judge)
Pos. 1, Exp. 1-7-19, 541-388-5300 x2450

DeHoog, Roger J.
Pos. 3, Exp. 1-7-19, 541-388-5300 x2370

Forte, Stephen P.
Pos. 7, Exp. 1-5-15, 541-388-5300 x2580

Haslinger, Barbara A.
Pos. 5, Exp. 1-5-15, 541-388-5300 x2550

District 12—Polk

Polk County Courthouse, Dallas 97338

Avera, Sally
Pos. 1, Exp. 1-7-19, 503-831-1776

Campbell, Monte S. (presiding judge)
Pos. 2, Exp. 1-4-17, 503-623-9245

Hill, Norman R.
Pos. 3, Exp. 1-4-19, 503-623-5235

District 13—Klamath

Klamath Co. Courthouse, Klamath Falls 97601

Adkisson, Marci Warner
Pos. 3, Exp. 1-4-17, 541-883-5503 x251

Bunch, Dan
Pos. 5, Exp. 1-4-17, 541-883-5503 x255

Isaacson, Rodger J.
Pos. 1, Exp. 1-5-15, 541-883-5503 x247

Osborne, Roxanne Burgett
Pos. 2, Exp. 1-4-17, 541-883-5503 x257

Wogan, Cameron F. (presiding judge)
Pos. 4, Exp. 1-4-17, 541-883-5503 x244

District 14—Josephine

Josephine County Courthouse, Grants Pass 97526

Baker, Lindi L. (presiding judge)
Pos. 4, Exp. 1-4-17, 541-476-2309 x243

Hull, Thomas M.
Pos. 1, Exp. 1-7-19, 541-476-2309 x232

Newman, Michael
Pos. 3, Exp. 1-4-17, 541-476-2309 x250 & 314

Wolke, Pat
Pos. 2, Exp. 1-7-19, 541-476-2309 x218

District 15—Coos, Curry

Coos County Courthouse, Coquille 97423

Barron, Richard L. (presiding judge)
Pos. 2, Exp. 1-4-17, 541-396-4095

Beaman, Cynthia
Pos. 6, Exp. 1-5-15, 541-247-2742
Curry County Courthouse, PO Box H, Gold Beach 97444

Bechtold, Paula M.
Pos. 5, Exp. 1-7-19, PO Box 324, North Bend Courthouse Annex, 97459, 541-396-2337

Gillespie, Michael J.
Pos. 4, Exp. 1-4-17, 541-396-4115

Margolis, Jesse
Pos. 3, Exp. 1-7-19, 541-247-2742
Curry County Courthouse, PO Box H, Gold Beach 97444

Stone, Martin E.
Pos. 1, Exp. 1-4-17, 541-396-4117

District 16—Douglas

Douglas County Justice Bldg., Roseburg 97470

Ambrosini, George
Pos. 5, Exp. 1-7-19, 541-957-2422

Burge, Frances
Pos. 4, Exp. 1-4-17, 541-957-2420

Garrison, Randolph Lee (presiding judge)
Pos. 3, Exp. 1-4-17, 541-957-2433

Marshall, William A.
Pos. 2, Exp. 1-4-17, 541-957-2436

Poole, Ronald
Pos. 1, Exp. 1-5-15, 541-957-2430

District 17—Lincoln

Lincoln County Courthouse, Newport 97365

Bachart, Sheryl
Pos. 1, Exp. 1-5-15, 541-265-4236 x252

Branford, Thomas O. (presiding judge)
Pos. 3, Exp. 1-7-19, 541-265-4236 x223

Sanders, Paulette
Pos. 2, Exp. 1-7-19, 541-265-4236 x224

District 18—Clatsop

Clatsop County Courthouse, Astoria 97103

Brownhill, Paula J.
Pos. 1, Exp. 1-5-15, 503-325-8555 x304

Matyas, Cindee S.
Pos. 3, Exp. 1-7-19, 503-325-8555 x339

Nelson, Philip L. (presiding judge)
Pos. 2, Exp. 1-4-17, 503-325-8555 x318

District 19—Columbia

Columbia County Courthouse, St. Helens 97051

Grant, Jenefer (presiding judge)
Pos. 3, Exp. 1-5-15, 503-397-2327 x317

Grove, Ted
Pos. 2, Exp. 1-5-15, 503-397-2327 x314

Reed, Steven B.
Pos. 1, Exp. 1-5-15; 503-397-2327 x313

District 20—Washington

Washington County Courthouse, Hillsboro 97124

Bailey, Charlie
Pos. 6, Exp. 1-7-19, 503-846-4403

Butterfield, Eric
Pos. 4, Exp. 1-4-17, 503-846-6204

Cobb, Rita B.
Pos. 12, Exp. 1-7-19, 503-846-3443

Erwin, Andrew R.
Pos. 7, Exp. 1-5-15, 503-846-8009

Fun, James Lee, Jr.
Pos. 13, Exp. 1-7-19, 503-846-3615

Garcia, Oscar
Pos. 9, Exp. 1-7-19, 503-846-4840

Knapp, Rick
Pos. 14, Exp. 1-5-15, 503-846-8832

Kohl, Thomas W.
Pos. 1, Exp. 1-4-17, 503-846-3589

Letourneau, Donald R.
Pos. 3, Exp. 1-7-19, 503-846-3418

Nachtigal, Gayle A.
Pos. 8, Exp. 1-4-17, 503-846-4562

Raines, Keith R.
Pos. 5, Exp. 1-5-15, 503-846-3457

Thompson, Kirsten E. (presiding judge)
Pos. 2, Exp. 1-5-15, 503-846-8872

Upton, Suzanne
Pos. 10, Exp. 1-4-17, 503-846-3590

Wipper, Janelle F.
Pos. 11, Exp. 1-7-19, 503-846-3852

District 21—Benton

Benton County Courthouse, Corvallis 97330

Connell, David B.
Pos. 3, Exp. 1-4-17, 541-766-6830

Williams, Locke A. (presiding judge)
Pos. 1, Exp. 1-5-15, 541-766-6827

Vacant
Pos. 2, Exp. 1-4-17, 541-766-6843

District 22—Crook, Jefferson

Jefferson Co. Courthouse, Madras 97741-1794
Crook County Courthouse, Prineville 97754

Ahern, Daniel J. (presiding judge)
Pos. 2, Exp. 1-5-15, 541-475-3317; 541-447-6541

Hillman, Annette
Pos. 1, Exp. 1-7-19, 541-475-3317; 541-447-6541

Williams, Gary
Pos. 3, Exp. 1-5-15, 541-475-3317; 541-447-6541

District 23—Linn

Linn County Courthouse, Albany 97321

Bispham, Carol R.
Pos. 1, Exp. 1-4-17, 541-812-8767

McHill, Thomas
Pos. 5, Exp. 1-7-19, 541-812-8765

Murphy, Daniel R. (presiding judge)
Pos. 3, Exp. 1-7-19, 541-812-8769

Novotny, DeAnn L.
Pos. 4, Exp. 1-7-19, 541-812-8768

Vacant
Pos. 2, Exp. 1-4-17, 541-812-8766

District 24—Grant, Harney

Grant County Courthouse, Canyon City 97820
Harney County Courthouse, Burns 97720

Cramer, William D., Jr. (presiding judge)
Pos. 1, Exp. 1-5-15, 541-573-5207; 541-575-1438

District 25—Yamhill

Yamhill County Courthouse, McMinnville 97128

Collins, John L. (presiding judge)
Pos. 1, Exp. 1-4-17, 503-434-7497

Easterday, Cynthia
Pos. 3, Exp. 1-4-17, 503-434-7486

Stone, Ronald W.
Pos. 2, Exp. 1-7-19, 503-434-7485

Tichenor, Carroll J.
Pos. 4, Exp. 1-5-15, 503-434-3054

District 26—Lake

Lake County Courthouse, Lakeview 97630

Vacant (presiding judge)
Pos. 1, Exp. 1-5-15, 541-947-6051

District 27—Tillamook

Tillamook County Courthouse, Tillamook 97141

Hill, Jonathan R.
Pos. 1, Exp. 1-4-17, 503-842-2598 x112

Trevino, Mari (presiding judge)
Pos. 2, Exp. 1-5-15, 503-842-2598 x114

Circuit Judges Association:

President—Hon. Daniel R. Murphy
Vice President—Hon. Paula J. Brownhill
Secretary—Hon. Christopher J. Marshall
Treasurer—Hon. Josephine H. Mooney
Immediate Past Pres.— Hon. A. Michael Adler

---

continued from page 100

*Effective January 15, 1998, all district courts were abolished and the powers, functions and judges of the district courts were transferred to the circuit courts.

Judicial Conference

The Oregon Judicial Conference, created under ORS 1.810, is composed of all judges of the Supreme Court, Court of Appeals, Tax Court, circuit courts and all senior judges certified under ORS 1.300. The chief justice of the Supreme Court is chair of the conference, and the state court administrator acts as executive secretary. Under ORS 1.820, the conference may make a continuous survey and study of the organization, jurisdiction, procedure, practice and methods of administration and operation of the various courts within the state.

The Judicial Conference meets annually to conduct their business meeting, attend educational seminars, issue committee reports and adopt resolutions, if any.

State Court Administrator, Office of the

Source: Kingsley W. Click, Administrator
Address: 510 Justice Bldg. (mail: Supreme Court Bldg., 1163 State St., Salem 97301-2563)
Phone: 503-986-5500; Oregon Relay 711
Fax: 503-986-5503
Web: http://courts.oregon.gov/OJD/OSCA

The state court administrator position was statutorily created in 1971 to assist the chief justice in exercising administrative authority and supervision over the state courts. In 1983, with unification and state funding of the trial and appellate courts, the duties of the position expanded to include supervision of the personnel plan for nonjudge staff and human resources; supervision of the accounting system for the state courts; preparation and management of the consolidated budget, revenue, and collections system; management of the legislative program requirements; inventory of state court property and procurement; internal audit; provision of legal contracts and services; collection and compilation of state court statistics; maintenance of a statewide automated information system; continuing education programs for judges and nonjudge staff; development of statewide administrative, personnel, fiscal and records policies and procedures concerning the courts, public information, and long-range planning for the future needs of the courts. (See ORS 8.110 and 8.125 primarily.)

In addition, the state court administrator oversees staff responsible for managing records of all cases filed with the Court of Appeals, Supreme Court and Oregon Tax Court. The administrator publishes the opinions of the Supreme Court, Court of Appeals and Oregon Tax Court and oversees the State Law Library. The administrator also has responsibility for administrative management of the Office of the

State Court Administrator, including the State Court Security program, State Court Interpreter program, Certified Shorthand Reporters program and the State Citizen Review Board program. Under ORS 30.273, the state court administrator also calculates and posts the annual adjustment to the liability limitations under the Oregon Tort Claims Act.

State of Oregon Law Library

Source: Cathryn Bowie, State Law Librarian
Address: 1163 State St., Supreme Court Bldg., Salem 97301-2563
Phone: 503-986-5640; TTY: 503-986-5561
Fax: 503-986-5623
Web: www.oregon.gov/SOLL

The State of Oregon Law Library traces its origins to the organization of the territorial government of Oregon. The Territorial Act of 1848 provided for the establishment of a library "to be kept at the seat of government." An 1851 act provided for the appointment of a librarian and defined the librarian's duties. The library served a broad constituency from its beginnings: "Members of the legislature, and its clerks and officers; Judges of the Supreme and District Courts, and their clerks; Attorney-general and marshall of the Territory; attorneys-at-law, secretary of the Territory; and all other persons, shall have access to the library, and the privileges allowed by law." This inclusive policy was continued with statehood in 1859 and after charge and control of the library was transferred to the Supreme Court in 1905.

Today, the mission of the library is to provide the comprehensive legal resources that the executive, legislative and judicial branches of state government require to serve the public effectively and to afford all Oregonians access to legal information.

The library provides access to the largest collection of legal information resources in state government, including the primary law of all U.S. jurisdictions, historical and current, secondary material in virtually all areas of law, and many legal periodicals.

The library operates under the administrative authority of the State Court Administrator.

Related Organizations

Board of Bar Examiners

Source: Charles Schulz, Interim Executive Director
Address: 16037 SW Upper Boones Ferry Rd., PO Box 231935, Tigard 97281-1935
Phone: 503-620-0222
Web: www.osbar.org/admissions

Hon. Mustafa Kasubhai, Chair, Eugene, 2013; Renee Starr, Vice-Chair, Portland, 2013; Jennifer Lloyd, Salem, 2013; David White, Portland, 2013; Dr. Shane Hayden, Ph.D., public member, Salem, 2013; Randall Green, Ph.D., public member, Salem, 2013; John Schroedel, Portland, 2014; David Reese, Portland, 2014; Caroline Wong, Portland, 2014; Tanya O'Neil, Portland, 2014; Jeffrey Howes, Portland, 2015; Hon. Jill Tanner, Salem, 2015; Stephanie Tuttle, Portland, 2015; Nicole Robbins, Portland, 2015

The Board of Bar Examiners, established in 1913, acts for the Supreme Court in evaluating an applicant's qualifications to practice law in Oregon. Board activities in determining an applicant's qualifications for admission to the Bar include preparation, grading and evaluation of a bar examination; and investigation and evaluation of the character and fitness of each applicant.

Oregon State Bar

Source: Sylvia Stevens, Executive Director
Address: 16037 SW Upper Boones Ferry Rd., PO Box 231935, Tigard 97281-1935
Phone: 503-620-0222; Toll-free: 1-800-452-8260
Fax: 503-684-1366
Web: www.osbar.org

Board of Governors: Michael E. Haglund, President, Portland, 2013; Tom Kranovich, President-Elect, Lake Oswego, 2014; Jenifer S. Billman, Public Member, Salem, 2014; Patrick Joseph Ehlers, Jr., Portland, 2014; Hunter B. Emerick, Salem, 2014; R. Ray Heysell, Medford, 2016; Matthew H. Kehoe, Hillsboro, 2014; Ethan D. Knight, Portland, 2013; Theresa M. Kohlhoff, Portland, 2015; Audrey T. Matsumonji, Public Member, Gresham, 2015; Caitlin J. Mitchel-Markley, McMinnville, 2016; Maureen Claire O'Connor, Public Member, Portland, 2013; Travis S. Prestwich, Salem, 2015; Joshua L. Ross, Portland, 2016; Richard G. Spier, Portland, 2015; and David Wade, Eugene, 2013; Charles A. Wilhoite, Public Member, Portland, 2016; Timothy L. Williams, Bend, 2016.

Established in 1935 to license and discipline lawyers, the Oregon State Bar is a large public corporation with diverse programs benefitting the public, lawyers, government and the courts. The state bar oversees the admission and discipline of Oregon's lawyers. It also operates a lawyer referral service and Tel-Law program, conducts continuing legal education programs, publishes legal and public service material, sponsors a legislative program to improve the laws and judicial system of Oregon, provides malpractice coverage for lawyers in private practice, and funds and supports law-related and public service programs through the Oregon Law Foundation.

The Oregon State Bar is a full-service professional organization having regulatory, public service and law improvement responsibilities.

Council on Court Procedures

Source: Mark A. Peterson, Executive Director
Address: 1018 Board of Trade Bldg., 310 SW 4th Ave., Portland 97204
Phone: 503-768-6500
Fax: 503-768-6540
E-mail: ccp@lclark.edu

Established in 1977 by ORS 1.725 to 1.750, the council promulgates rules governing pleading, practice and procedure in all civil proceedings in the circuit courts of the state. Promulgated amendments to the rules are submitted to the Legislature in January of odd-numbered years and go into effect on January 1 of the following even-numbered year unless amended, repealed or supplemented by the Legislature. The following is a list of members, term-expiration dates and the statutory appointing authority:

Judicial member appointed by the Oregon Supreme Court: Justice Rives Kistler, Salem, 2013

Judicial member appointed by the Oregon Court of Appeals: Rex Armstrong, Salem, 2013

Circuit judge members appointed by the Executive Committee of the Circuit Court Judges Association: Hon. Timothy Gerking, Medford, 2015; Hon. Robert D. Herndon, Oregon City, 2013; Hon. Jerry B. Hodson, Portland, 2015; Hon. Lauren S. Holland, Eugene, 2013; Hon. Eve L. Miller, Oregon City, 2015; Hon. David F. Rees, Portland, 2013; Hon. Locke A. Williams, Corvallis, 2013; Hon. Charles Zennaché, Eugene, 2013

Practitioners appointed by the Board of Governors of the Oregon State Bar: Brooks F. Cooper, Chair, Portland, 2013; Kristen S. David, Vice-Chair, Oregon City, 2015; John Bachofner, Vancouver, WA, 2013; Jay Beattie, Portland, 2015; Michael Brian, Medford, 2013; Eugene H. Buckle, Portland, 2013; Brian Campf, Portland, 2015; Jennifer Gates, Portland, 2013; Robert Keating, Portland, 2015; Maureen Leonard, Portland, 2013; Leslie W. O'Leary, Portland, 2013; Mark R. Weaver, Medford, 2015

Public member appointed by the Oregon Supreme Court: Arwen Bird, Portland, 2013

Commission on Judicial Fitness and Disability

Source: Susan D. Isaacs, Executive Director
Address: PO Box 1130, Beaverton 97075-1130
Phone: 503-626-6776
Fax: 503-626-6787
Web: http://courts.oregon.gov/CJFD/

2013 Chair Eugene Hallman 2016; J. Patricia Sullivan 2013, J. Steven Maurer 2013; J. Robert Wollheim 2014; Patricia Smith 2014; Annabelle Jaramillo 2015; Judy Snyder 2015; Robert Thuemmel 2015; and Linda M. Collins 2016.

Commission members, serving four-year terms, include three judges appointed by the Supreme Court, three lawyers appointed by the Oregon State Bar and three citizens appointed by the governor subject to Senate confirmation.

Pursuant to ORS 1.410 to 1.480, the Oregon Constitution and the Rules of Judicial Conduct, the commission investigates complaints regarding Oregon judges. If the commission believes there is substantial evidence of misconduct, a public hearing is held. The commission makes recommendations regarding disciplinary actions to the Supreme Court. A judge may be censured, suspended or removed from office by the Supreme Court. The commission cannot change the decision of a judge and does not have jurisdiction over arbitrators, mediators or municipal court judges.

County Courts

At one time, county courts existed in all 36 Oregon counties. The title "county judge" is retained in some counties as the title of the chair of the board of county commissioners. There is no requirement that county judges be members of the bar.

Where a county judge's judicial function still exists, it is limited to juvenile and probate matters and occupies only a portion of the judge's time, which is primarily devoted to nonjudicial administrative responsibilities as a member of the county board.

Only seven counties, all east of the Cascades, now have county judges who retain any judicial authority: Gilliam, Sherman and Wheeler (both juvenile and probate jurisdiction); Grant, Harney, and Malheur (probate only); and Morrow (juvenile only).

Municipal Court

Oregon Municipal Judge's Association

Source: Karen Brisbane, President
Address: 16217 SE McLoughlin Blvd., Bldg. B, Oak Grove 97267
Phone: 503-794-3802
E-mail: karenbrisbin@comcast.net
Web: www.omjaonline.com

The Oregon Municipal Judges Association participates in arranging continuing educational training sessions for Municipal Judges. It maintains a listserv for judges to gain access to other

Municipal Court Judges and Justices of the Peace. The two associations trade off on annual conferences in Oregon. And, it coordinates with the Oregon Department of Transportation which has its own annual conference for judges.

Many incorporated cities in Oregon have a municipal court, as authorized by charter and state law. Municipal courts have concurrent jurisdiction with circuit and justice courts over all violations and misdemeanors committed or triable in the city in which the court is located. They do not have jurisdiction over felonies. Municipal courts primarily hear traffic violations and crimes; violations of municipal codes and ordinances, including animal, high grass and trash nuisances; vehicle impoundments and forfeitures; and parking and pedestrian violations. They also hear certain minor tobacco, liquor and drug violations. Municipal courts may be a court of record, although most are not, due to the additional cost of a court reporter or audio equipment. Municipal court procedures are controlled to a large extent by state law.

A municipal judge need not be an attorney, although most are. Municipal judges are usually appointed by, and serve at the pleasure of, the city council. Several Oregon cities have elected judges. Qualifications for office are determined by the city council or charter. A municipal judge may perform weddings anywhere within the state of Oregon.

Justice Courts

Source: Joe Charter, President
Address: 505 Oak St., Central Point 97502
Phone: 541-774-1286
Web: www.ojpa.org

Justice court is held by a justice of the peace within the district for which he or she is elected. The county commissioners have power to establish justice court district boundaries. The justice of the peace is a remnant of territorial days when each precinct of the state was entitled to a justice court. Thirty-two justice courts currently administer justice in 21 counties.

Justice courts have jurisdiction within their county concurrent with the circuit court in all criminal prosecutions, except felony trials. Actions at law in justice courts are conducted using the mode of proceeding and rules of evidence similar to those used in the circuit courts, except where otherwise specifically provided.

Justice courts have jurisdiction over traffic, boating, wildlife and other violations occurring in their county. Justices of the peace also perform weddings at no charge if performed at their offices during regular business hours.

The justice court has small claims/civil jurisdiction where the money or damages claimed does not exceed $7,500, except in actions involving title to real property, false imprisonment, libel, slander or malicious prosecution.

A justice of the peace must be a citizen of the United States, a resident of Oregon for three years, and a resident of the justice court district for one year prior to becoming a nonpartisan candidate for election to that office. They are elected to 6-year terms. The names of the Oregon justices of the peace can be found in the Local Government chapter in the section titled "County Government."

Office of Public Defense Services

Source: Nancy Cozine, Executive Director
Address: 1175 Court St. NE, Salem 97301-4030
Phone: 503-378-3349
Fax: 503-378-2163
Web: www.oregon.gov/OPDS

The Public Defense Services Commission (PDSC) is an independent body that governs the Office of Public Defense Services (OPDS). The chief justice of the Oregon Supreme Court appoints the seven commission members to four year terms. The commission's primary charge is to establish "a public defense system that ensures the provision of public defense services in the most cost efficient manner consistent with the Oregon Constitution, the United States Constitution and Oregon and national standards of justice[.]" The current chair is Barnes Ellis, Portland.

The PDSC appoints the executive director for OPDS. The Office of Public Defense Services has two divisions: Contract and Business Services (CBS) and the Appellate Division (AD), formerly known as the State Public Defender.

CBS is responsible for administering the public defense contracts that provide legal representation for financially eligible persons in criminal, civil commitment and juvenile proceedings, and for processing requests and payments for non-contract fees and expenses. Contracts provide trial-level representation and appellate representation on cases not handled by AD.

AD is the appellate arm of OPDS. The division provides constitutionally mandated representation in the appellate courts to financially eligible persons in criminal cases (misdemeanor and felony criminal offenses, including capital offenses), parents in juvenile dependency cases, and inmates appealing administrative decisions from the Board of Parole and Post-Prison Supervision.

Legislative

An antique car on display on the Capitol Mall in Salem—Oregon State Archives Scenic Photograph marDB0029a

Oregon's Provisional Legislature first met formally in 1845 in Oregon City. They were a unicameral body that operated on an uncertain schedule. The present bicameral system — two houses with senators and representatives — was adopted in 1859 upon statehood. Today's legislators meet annually in Salem and deal with complex matters and busy schedules. This section introduces the members of the Legislature and describes how the Legislature is organized.

Oregon's Legislative Assembly

Source: Legislative Administration
Address: 900 Court St. NE, Rm. 140-A, Salem 97301
Phone: 503-986-1848
Web: www.leg.state.or.us

Senate President

Peter Courtney, Senate President
Address: 900 Court St. NE, Rm. S-201, Salem 97301
Phone: 503-986-1600

The Senate president is elected by members of the Senate to select committee chairs and membership, preside over its daily sessions and coordinate its administrative operations. Subject to the rules of the Senate, the president refers measures to committees, directs Senate personnel and mediates questions on internal operations.

The Senate president's staff assists in carrying out official duties, helps coordinate Senate operations and provides a variety of public information services. In cooperation with the speaker of the House, the president coordinates and supervises the work product of the legislative branch of Oregon state government and represents that branch in contacts with the executive and judicial branches. The president's office works closely with all political parties to ensure that session goals are met.

Secretary of the Senate

Robert Taylor, Secretary of the Senate
Address: 900 Court St. NE, Rm. 233, Salem 97301
Phone: 503-986-1851

The secretary of the Senate is an elected officer of the state Senate. The secretary is responsible for and supervises Senate employees engaged in keeping measures, papers and records of proceedings and actions of the Senate. The secretary supervises preparation of the daily agenda, all measures, histories, journals and related publications and is in charge of publication of documents related to the Senate. In addition, the secretary has custody of all measures, official papers and records of the Senate, except when released to authorized persons by signed receipt. The secretary also serves as parliamentary consultant to the Senate, advises officers of the Senate on parliamentary procedure and manages the Honorary Page program.

During the interim, the secretary receives messages from the governor announcing executive appointments requiring Senate confirmation, prepares the agenda for the convening of the Senate and supervises publication of the official record of proceedings.

Speaker of the House of Representatives

Tina Kotek, Speaker of the House
Address: 900 Court St. NE, Rm. 269, Salem 97301
Phone: 503-986-1200

The speaker of the House is elected by House members to preside over the deliberations of the House, preserve order and decorum and decide questions of order. The speaker appoints chairs and members to each committee and refers measures to appropriate committees in accordance with provisions of the rules of the House.

The House speaker's staff coordinates operations of the speaker's office, assists the presiding officer in performing official duties, provides research and policy support in issue areas, provides information to the news media and assists legislators in solving constituent problems. In conjunction with the Senate president's office, the speaker's office coordinates and supervises operations of the legislative branch of government, joint statutory committees and joint interim committees and task forces.

Chief Clerk of the House of Representatives

Ramona Line, Chief Clerk
Address: 900 Court St. NE, Rm. H-271, Salem 97301
Phone: 503-986-1870

The chief clerk, elected by members of the House of Representatives, supervises and keeps a correct journal and is the official custodian of all other records of House proceedings. The chief clerk notifies the Senate of all acts of the House, certifies and transmits all bills, resolutions and papers requiring Senate concurrence immediately upon their passage or adoption, and secures proper authentication of bills that have passed both houses and transmits them to the governor.

The chief clerk prepares the agenda, coordinates details for the opening organization of the House and acts as parliamentarian as directed by House rules. In addition, the chief clerk supervises and authenticates the revision and printing of the *Senate and House Journal* at the end of the legislative session, and prepares all legislative records that are to be permanently filed with the state archivist.

Caucus Offices

Diane Rosenbaum, Senate Majority Leader
Address: 900 Court St. NE, Rm. S-223, Salem 97301
Phone: 503-986-1700

Ted Ferrioli, Senate Minority Leader
Address: 900 Court St. NE, Rm. S-323, Salem 97301
Phone: 503-986-1950

Val Hoyle, House Majority Leader
Address: 900 Court St. NE, Rm. H-395, Salem 97301
Phone: 503-986-1900

Mike McLane, House Minority Leader
Address: 900 Court St. NE, Rm. H-354, Salem 97301
Phone: 503-986-1400

Caucus offices provide many services to their members during session and interim periods. Each office is directed by a leader chosen by the respective political party. The operations of the four offices are not identical, but typical services include conducting research, writing speeches and press releases, providing public information services, serving as liaison to state and federal agencies to help solve constituent problems, organizing caucus activities and circulating information about legislative business among caucus members during both session and interim periods.

Organization

Oregon's Legislative Assembly is composed of two chambers, the Senate and House of Representatives. The Senate consists of 30 members elected to four-year terms. Half of the Senate seats are up for election every two years. The House consists of 60 representatives elected to two-year terms. Except in cases of persons selected to fill vacancies, legislators are elected in even-numbered years from single-member districts. Election by single-member district means that each Oregonian is represented by one senator and one representative. To qualify for a seat in the Legislature, one must be at least 21 years of age, a U.S. citizen and reside in the legislative district for at least one year prior to election. Each chamber elects presiding officers to oversee daily sessions and operations and perform other duties set by rule, custom and law. These officers are known as the president of the Senate and speaker of the House.

Functions

The primary functions of the Legislature are to enact new laws and revise existing ones, make decisions that keep the state in good economic and environmental condition and provide a forum for discussion of public issues.

The Legislature reviews and revises the governor's proposed budget and passes tax laws to provide needed revenue. The Oregon Constitution requires that the state must not spend money in excess of revenue.

The Legislature also influences executive and judicial branch decisions. Laws enacted by the Legislature, along with adoption of the budget, establish state policy that directs all state agency activity and impacts the courts. The Senate confirms gubernatorial appointments to certain offices. To ensure that legislative intent is followed, the Legislative Counsel Committee reviews administrative rules of state agencies.

Legislative Process

During the 2011 regular session, 732 of 2,805 introduced bills became law. During the 2012 regular session, 112 of 275 introduced bills became law. Most of the discussion and revisions of bills and other measures are done in committees. The process begins when a measure is introduced and referred to a committee. The committee may hear testimony on the measure, frequently from members of the public, and may amend the measure and send it to the floor of its respective chamber for debate. The committee can also table the measure and end its consideration. Unlike many state legislatures, Oregon does not amend measures during floor debate.

After a measure has been considered by a committee and passed by the chamber in which it was introduced, it is sent to the other chamber where a similar procedure is followed.

If both chambers pass a bill in identical form, including any amendments approved by the other chamber, it is enrolled (printed in final form) for the signatures of the presiding officers and governor. The governor may sign the bill, veto it or let it become law without signature. The governor may also veto line items of appropriation bills, but may not veto an act referred for a vote of the people or an act initiated by the people.

The Oregon Constitution and state law require that deliberations of the Legislative Assembly and its committees be open to the public. The law also requires public notice of meetings and maintenance of public meeting records. These practices ensure that the legislative process is open to public scrutiny.

Effective Date of Laws

The regular effective date of a measure is January 1, of the year following passage of the measure. Some measures may contain a provision, such as an emergency clause, that specifies an earlier effective date.

The Oregon Constitution prohibits tax measures from having an emergency clause. This ensures that the people have the right to refer a tax measure for a vote by petition before it goes into effect.

Session Schedule

In 2010, voters approved a ballot measure referred by the Legislature requiring the Legislature to meet annually. Beginning in 2011, the Legislature convenes in February at the State Capitol in Salem, but sessions may not exceed 160 days in odd-numbered years and 35 days in even-numbered years. Five-day extensions are allowed by a two-thirds vote in both houses. In addition, the Legislature may hold an organizational session to swear in newly elected officials, elect legislative leaders, adopt rules, organize and appoint committees and begin introducing bills.

Special sessions to deal with emergencies may be called by the governor or by a majority of each chamber. For example, the Legislative Assembly called itself into a special session in 2002, 2006, 2008 and 2010, Governor Ted Kulongoski called for a special session in 2006, and Governor John Kitzhaber called for a special session in 2012.

Contacting a Legislator and Obtaining Legislative Information

During session, the following numbers are available to reach your legislator or for legislative information:

- Outside Salem: 1-800-332-2313
- Within Salem: 503-986-1187

During the interim, individual legislators may be reached by calling the telephone numbers listed on pages 141–143 and 149–153. Legislative information may be obtained by calling the legislative liaison at 503-986-1000.

Chronology of Regular Legislative Sessions in Oregon

Leg. Assembly	Year	Dates	Length in Days	Leg. Assembly	Year	Dates	Length in Days
1	1860	Sept. 10–Oct. 19	40	42	1943	Jan. 11–March 10	59
2	1862	Sept. 8–Oct. 17	40	43	1945	Jan. 8–March 17	69
3	1864	Sept. 12–Oct. 22	41	44	1947	Jan. 13–April 5	83
4	1866	Sept. 10–Oct. 20	41	45	1949	Jan. 10–April 16	100
5	1868	Sept. 14–Oct. 28	44	46	1951	Jan. 8–May 3	116
6	1870	Sept. 12–Oct. 20	39	47	1953	Jan. 12–April 21	100
7	1872	Sept. 9–Oct. 23	45	48	1955	Jan. 10–May 4	115
8	1874	Sept. 14–Oct. 21	38	49	1957	Jan. 14–May 21	128
9	1876	Sept. 11–Oct. 20	40	50	1959	Jan. 12–May 6	115
10	1878	Sept. 9–Oct. 18	40	51	1961	Jan. 9–May 10	124
11	1880	Sept. 13–Oct. 23	41	52	1963	Jan. 14–June 3	143
12	1882	Sept. 11–Oct. 19	39	53	1965	Jan. 11–May 14	127
13	1885	Jan. 12–Feb. 21	40	54	1967	Jan. 11–June 14	157
14	1887	Jan. 10–Feb. 18	39	55	1969	Jan. 13–May 23	131
15	1889	Jan. 14–Feb. 22	39	56	1971	Jan. 11–June 10	151
16	1891	Jan. 12–Feb. 20	39	57	1973	Jan. 8–July 6	180
17	1893	Jan. 9–Feb. 17	39	58	1975	Jan. 13–June 14	153
18	1895	Jan. 14–Feb. 23	40	59	1977	Jan. 10–July 5	177
19	1897	Jan. 11–March 2	*	60	1979	Jan. 8–July 4	178
20	1899	Jan. 9–Feb. 18	40	61	1981	Jan. 13–August 1	202
21	1901	Jan. 14–March 4	50	62	1983	Jan. 10–July 15	187
22	1903	Jan. 12–Feb. 20	39	63	1985	Jan. 14–June 21	159
23	1905	Jan. 9–Feb. 17	40	64	1987	Jan. 12–June 28	168
24	1907	Jan. 14–Feb. 23	41	65	1989	Jan. 9–July 4	177
25	1909	Jan. 11–Feb. 20	41	66	1991	Jan. 14–June 30	168
26	1911	Jan. 9–Feb. 18	41	67	1993	Jan. 11–August 5	207
27	1913	Jan. 13–March 5	51	68	1995	Jan. 9–June 10	153
28	1915	Jan. 11–Feb. 20	41	69	1997	Jan. 13–July 5	174
29	1917	Jan. 8–Feb. 19	43	70	1999	Jan. 11–July 24	195
30	1919	Jan. 13–Feb. 27	46	71	2001	Jan. 8–July 7	181
31	1921	Jan. 10–Feb. 23	45	72	2003	Jan. 13–August 27	227
32	1923	Jan. 8–Feb. 22	46	73	2005	Jan. 10–August 5	208
33	1925	Jan. 12–Feb. 26	46	74	2007	Jan. 8–June 28	172
34	1927	Jan. 10–Feb. 25	47	75	2009	Jan. 12–June 29	169
35	1929	Jan. 14–March 5	50	76	2011	Feb. 1–June 30	150
36	1931	Jan. 12–March 6	54	77	2012	Feb. 1–March 5	34
37	1933	Jan. 9–March 9	60	78	2013	Feb. 14–	
38	1935	Jan. 14–March 13	59				
39	1937	Jan. 11–March 8	57				
40	1939	Jan. 9–March 15	66				
41	1941	Jan. 13–March 15	62				

**The House of Representatives never formally convened because its members failed to reach agreement on organization.*

Session Interim

After adjournment of regular or special sessions, the work of the Legislature continues. Legislators study issues likely to be important during future sessions, become acquainted with new issues, prepare drafts of legislation and exercise legislative oversight.

Convening of the Senate to Act on Executive Appointments

The Legislative Assembly may require that appointments to state public office made by the governor be subject to Senate confirmation.

During the legislative session, the Senate president refers executive appointments to a standing or special committee to review the background and qualifications of appointees, ensuring that statutory requirements are met. Appointees may be asked to come before the committee for personal interviews. The committee submits its recommendations to the full Senate for confirmation votes.

During the interim, the secretary of the senate receives the governor's announcements of executive appointments requiring Senate confirmation. Generally, gubernatorial appointments made during a regular or special session of the Legislature are acted upon by the Senate prior to adjourning sine die (final adjournment).

History

Oregon's Provisional Legislature met formally for the first time in Oregon City, December 2–19, 1845. An earlier pre-provisional committee met in August of the same year after the formal ratification of Oregon's Organic Articles and Laws of 1843 and the inauguration of George Abernethy as governor. The first Provisional Legislature, a unicameral body with autonomous powers, conducted its sessions in a rather casual manner and frequently suspended its rules to take care of unexpected situations. It met annually or more frequently until February 1849, five months before the first Territorial Legislature met during July 16–24, 1849, also in Oregon City.

The Territorial Legislature was bicameral. It had an upper council of nine members and a lower house of 18 members elected from the eight existing counties that had regular annual meetings. Unlike the Provisional Legislature, its actions were subject to review in Washington, D.C. At the time of statehood and adoption of the constitution in 1859, the present bicameral system was adopted. The Legislature then met in the fall of even-numbered years until 1885 when the sessions were moved to the early winter months of odd-numbered years to accommodate members who farmed.

Statistical Summary of the Seventy-sixth Legislative Assembly

Source: Legislative Counsel

2011 Regular Session

Session Length	150 Calendar Days
Convened	February 1, 2011
Adjourned	June 30, 2011
Bills Introduced	2,805
Other Measures	216
Total	3,021
Senate Total Membership	30
Democrats	16
Republicans	14
President: Peter Courtney (D), Salem	
House Total Membership	60
Democrats	30
Republicans	30
Co-Speakers: Bruce Hanna (R), Roseburg, and Arnie Roblan (D), Coos Bay	

Bills	**House**	**Senate**	**Total**
Introduced	1,752	1,053	2,805
Passed Both Houses	427	306	733
Vetoed	1*	0	1*
Became Law	426+	306#	732+#
Unsigned by Governor	0	0	0
Resolutions and Memorials			
Introduced	132	84	216
Adopted	50	24	74

* HB 2212

+ Totals include HB 2649 and HB 3405 (which voters approved as Ballot Measures 66 and 67 on 1/26/10 after successful referendum petitions).

Totals include SB 545 and SB 897 (which were vetoed in 2009 and overridden at the 2010 special session on 2/23/10 and 2/8/10, respectively).

Senate and Representative District Numbers

Senate	House Dist.	Senate	House Dist.	Senate	House Dist.	Senate	House Dist.
1	1 and 2	9	17 and 18	17	33 and 34	25	49 and 50
2	3 and 4	10	19 and 20	18	35 and 36	26	51 and 52
3	5 and 6	11	21 and 22	19	37 and 38	27	53 and 54
4	7 and 8	12	23 and 24	20	39 and 40	28	55 and 56
5	9 and 10	13	25 and 26	21	41 and 42	29	57 and 58
6	11 and 12	14	27 and 28	22	43 and 44	30	59 and 60
7	13 and 14	15	29 and 30	23	45 and 46		
8	15 and 16	16	31 and 32	24	47 and 48		

2012 Regular Session

Session Length	34 Calendar Days
Convened	February 1, 2012
Adjourned	March 5, 2012
Bills Introduced	275
Other Measures	27
Total	302
Senate Total Membership	30
Democrats	16
Republicans	14
President: Peter Courtney (D), Salem	
House Total Membership	60
Democrats	30
Republicans	30
Co-Speakers: Bruce Hanna (R), Roseburg, and Arnie Roblan (D), Coos Bay	

Bills	**House**	**Senate**	**Total**
Introduced	179	96	275
Passed Both Houses	68	44	112
Vetoed	0	0	0
Became Law	68	44	112
Unsigned by Governor	0	0	0
Resolutions and Memorials			
Introduced	9	18	27
Adopted	7	14	21

Statutory Committees and Interim Offices

Source: Legislative Administration
Address: 900 Court St. NE, Rm. 140-A, Salem 97301
Phone: 503-986-1848
Web: www.leg.state.or.us/comm/legadmin/

Legislative Administration Committee

Kevin Hayden, Legislative Administrator

The Legislative Administration Committee (LAC) provides services to the Legislative Assembly, its support staff and the public. The committee, authorized by ORS 173.710, includes the president of the Senate, the speaker of the House, members of the Senate appointed by the president and members of the House appointed by the speaker. The committee appoints an administrator to serve as its executive officer. The administrator's office coordinates and oversees the operation of the following administrative units:

Committee Services

Address: Room 453
Phone: 503-986-1813

Committee Services provides professional services to legislative committees, legislators, legislative offices and staff, government agencies and the public. Services include organizing and administering committee meetings, researching current issues and requested topics and reviewing implementation of legislation. Committee Services includes Committee Records and the Legislative Library and Public Access Room.

Special Legislative Sessions in Oregon[1]

Year	Date	Length in Days
1860	Oct. 1–Oct. 2	2
1865	Dec. 5–Dec. 18	14
1885	Nov. 11–Nov. 24	14
1898	Sept. 26–Oct. 15	20
1903	Dec. 21–Dec. 23	3
1909	Mar. 15–Mar. 16	2
1920	Jan. 12–Jan. 17	6
1921	Dec. 19–Dec. 24	6
1933	Jan. 3–Jan. 7	5
1933	Nov. 20–Dec. 9	20
1935	Oct. 21–Nov. 9	20
1957	Oct. 28–Nov. 15	19
1963	Nov. 11–Dec. 2	13[2]
1965	May 21–May 25	5
1967	Oct. 30–Nov. 21	23
1971	Nov. 16–Nov. 22	7
1974	Jan. 24–Feb. 24	14
1975	Sept. 16–Sept. 16	1
1978	Sept. 5–Sept. 9	5[3]
1980	Aug. 4–Aug. 8	5
1981	Oct. 24–Oct. 24	1
1982	Jan. 18–Mar. 1	37
1982	June 14–June 14	1
1982	Sept. 3–Sept. 3	1
1983	Sept. 14–Oct. 4	21
1984	July 30–July 30	1
1990	May 7–May 7	1
1992	July 1–July 3	3
1995	July 28–Aug. 4	8
1996	Feb. 1–Feb. 1	1
2002	Feb. 8–Feb. 11	4
2002	Feb. 25–Mar. 2	6
2002	June 12–June 30	19
2002	Aug. 16–Aug. 20	5
2002	Sept. 1–Sept. 18	18
2006	April 20–April 20	1
2008	Feb. 4–Feb. 22	19
2010	Feb. 1–Feb. 25	25
2012	Dec. 14–Dec. 14	1

[1]Historical records are not consistent on actual dates.
[2]Nine-day recess, Nov. 22 to Dec. 2, due to death of President Kennedy.
[3]Does not include recess from Jan. 24 to Feb. 11.

Employee Services

Address: Room 140-B
Phone: 503-986-1373

Employee Services provides human resource administration to all legislative employees and legislative job seekers.

Facility Services

Address: Room 49
Phone: 503-986-1360

Facility Services manages the infrastructure of the Capitol including maintenance, capital improvement projects and space planning. The staff also provides centralized purchasing, mail handling and distribution of legislative publications.

Financial Services

Address: Room 140-C
Phone: 503-986-1695

Financial Services provides budgeting, accounting and financial reporting services to the Legislature.

Information Services

Address: Room 141
Phone: 503-986-1914

Information Services supports the Legislature by providing computer and mainframe programs and services, legislative publications, electronic access to legislative information and maintenance of computer equipment.

Legislative Media

Address: Room 35
Phone: 503-986-1195

Legislative Media, a division of Information Services, provides audio and video coverage of legislative events, production videos, and maintains audio and video equipment in the Capitol.

Visitor Services

Address: Capitol Rotunda Area
Phone: 503-986-1388
Web: www.leg.state.or.us/capinfo

Visitor Services provides guided tours and information on the legislative process and Capitol history. It also operates the Capitol Gift Shop.

Legislative Counsel Committee

Dexter Johnson, Legislative Counsel
Address: 900 Court St. NE, Rm. S-101, Salem 97301
Phone: 503-986-1243

The Legislative Counsel Committee is a joint legislative committee established under ORS 173.111, consisting of the president of the Senate and senators appointed by the president, the speaker of the House of Representatives and representatives appointed by the speaker. The legislative counsel, who is selected by the committee, serves as executive officer to the committee. The legislative counsel manages the Office of the Legislative Counsel and employs a legal and professional staff.

The Office of the Legislative Counsel is responsible for drafting legislative measures for legislators, legislative committees and state agencies. The office also provides legal opinions and other legal services to legislators, legislative committees and legislative staff. During legislative sessions, the office prepares amendments to measures that are considered by the Legislative Assembly.

The Office of the Legislative Counsel prepares indexes and tables for all measures introduced during a legislative session and those introduced by iniative petition of the citizens of Oregon. At the end of each session, the office publishes the official compilation of that session's laws, *Oregon Laws*. The office also prepares and publishes every two years, the official codification of Oregon's statute laws, *Oregon Revised Statutes* (ORS). Each edition of ORS incorporates the new statutory provisions and amendments to statutory provisions passed by the Legislative Assembly in the preceding two years. As part of the ORS set, subscribers receive a supplement of laws enacted during the short, even-year regular legislative session. The office also incorporates any new sections or amendments into the Constitution of Oregon.

Pursuant to ORS 183.710 to 183.725, the Office of Legislative Counsel conducts a review of all new administrative rules adopted by state agencies. This review allows the Legislative Assembly to monitor whether an agency's rules are consistent with the agency's constitutional and statutory authority.

Oregon Law Commission

Lane P. Shetterly, Chair
Jeffrey Dobbins, Executive Director
Address: Willamette University College of Law, 245 Winter St. SE, Salem 97301
Phone: 503-370-6973
Web: www.willamette.edu/wucl/centers/ok/

The Oregon Law Commission, established in 1997, studies Oregon law and makes suggestions for reforming, correcting or revising the law.

The Oregon Law Commission consists of 15 commissioners: two persons appointed by the president of the Senate (one of whom must be a senator), two persons appointed by the speaker of the House of Representatives (one of whom must be a representative), the deans or an appointee from each of Oregon's three law schools, three persons appointed by the Oregon State Bar, the attorney general, the chief justice of the Supreme Court, the chief judge of the Court of Appeals, a circuit court judge and one person appointed by the governor.

The commission submits a biennial report to the Legislative Assembly. Pursuant to ORS 173.335, the Office of the Legislative Counsel assists the commission in carrying out its duties.

Legislative Fiscal Office

Ken Rocco, Legislative Fiscal Officer

Address: 900 Court St. NE, Rm. H-178, Salem 97301

Phone: 503-986-1828

The Legislative Fiscal Office is a permanent, nonpartisan legislative agency created in 1959, pursuant to ORS 173.410 to 173.450, to serve legislators and committees on matters related to the state's fiscal affairs. The office provides research, analysis, evaluation and recommendations concerning state expenditures, budget issues, agency organization and program administration. It also provides fiscal impact assessment of proposed legislation and provides staff assistance to the Joint Legislative Committee on Information Management and Technology and the Joint Legislative Audit Committee. The office staffs the Joint Committee on Ways and Means during the session and the Emergency Board during the interim.

Emergency Board

Ken Rocco, Legislative Fiscal Officer

Address: 900 Court St. NE, Rm. H-178, Salem 97301

Phone: 503-986-1828

The Emergency Board, authorized by section 3, Article III of the Oregon Constitution and established by ORS 291.324, consists of the president of the Senate, the speaker of the House of Representatives, the co-chairs of the Joint Committee on Ways and Means, and eight Senate and eight House members, totaling 20 members. Between sessions, the Emergency Board may allocate to state agencies, out of emergency funds appropriated to the board, additional monies to carry on activities required by law for which appropriations were not made. The board may authorize an agency to expend from funds dedicated or continuously appropriated for the purpose of the agency sums in excess of the amount budgeted for the agency, may approve a budget for a new activity coming into existence, and may revise budgets of state agencies to the extent of authorizing transfers between expenditure classifications within an agency.

Joint Committee on Ways and Means

Ken Rocco, Legislative Fiscal Officer

Address: 900 Court St. NE, Rm. H-178, Salem 97301

Phone: 503-986-1828

The Joint Committee on Ways and Means, created under ORS 171.555, is the legislative appropriations committee that determines state budget policy. Staffed by the Legislative Fiscal Office and made up of both Senate and House members appointed by the president of the Senate and the speaker of the House, the committee works to resolve budgetary differences. This appropriation process structure, employed in Oregon and several other states, is especially effective in resolving budgetary differences.

Legislative Revenue Office

Paul Warner, Legislative Revenue Officer

Address: 900 Court St. NE, Rm. 143, Salem 97301

Phone: 503-986-1266

Pursuant to ORS 173.810 to 173.850, the Legislative Revenue Office, established by the 1975 Oregon Legislature, provides nonpartisan analysis of tax and school finance issues.

The legislative revenue officer is appointed by, and responsible to, the House and Senate committees that deal with revenue and school finance.

The office staffs the House and Senate Revenue Committees, writes revenue impact statements for proposed legislation and researches tax and other revenue related issues.

Legislative Commission on Indian Services

Karen Quigley, Executive Officer

Address: 900 Court St. NE, Rm. 167, Salem 97301

Phone: 503-986-1067

E-mail: karen.m.quigley@state.or.us

Web: www.leg.state.or.us/cis

The Commission on Indian Services, an advisory body created in 1975 by ORS 172.100 to 172.140, operates as a small agency within the legislative branch. It consists of 13 members appointed by legislative leadership to two-year terms: one member from each of Oregon's nine federally-recognized tribal governments, one each from the Portland area and Willamette Valley tribal communities, one state senator and one state representative.

Commission responsibilities include compiling information about services for tribal peoples; developing and sponsoring programs that inform tribal people of available services and that make the needs and concerns of tribal people known to the public and private agencies whose activities affect the tribes and their members; and encouraging and supporting agencies to expand and improve services. The commission reports biennially to the governor and the Legislature on matters concerning Oregon's tribes, and is the primary point of contact for the state of Oregon for questions about Oregon's tribal people and their issues.

Senate Districts

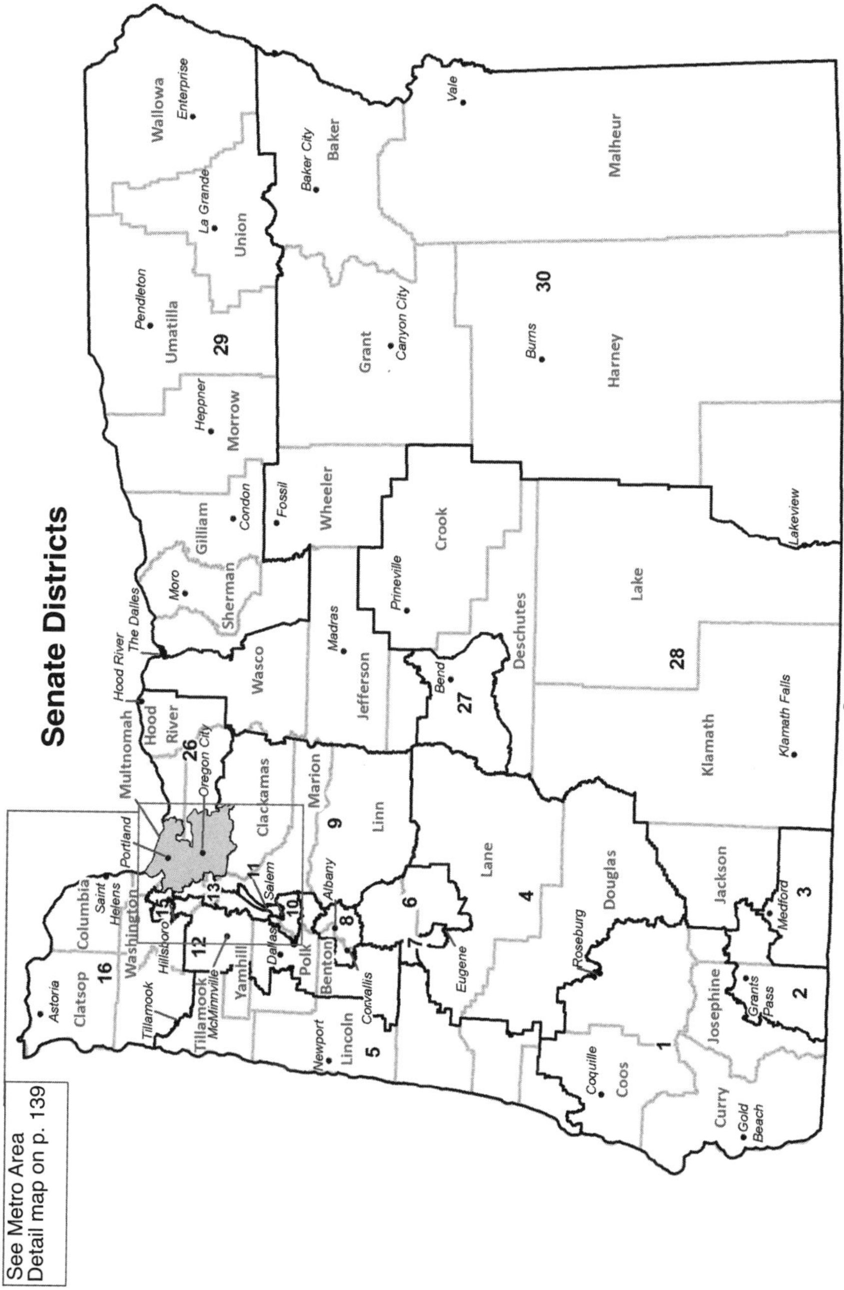

Source: Oregon Department of Administrative Services, Geospatial Enterprise Office

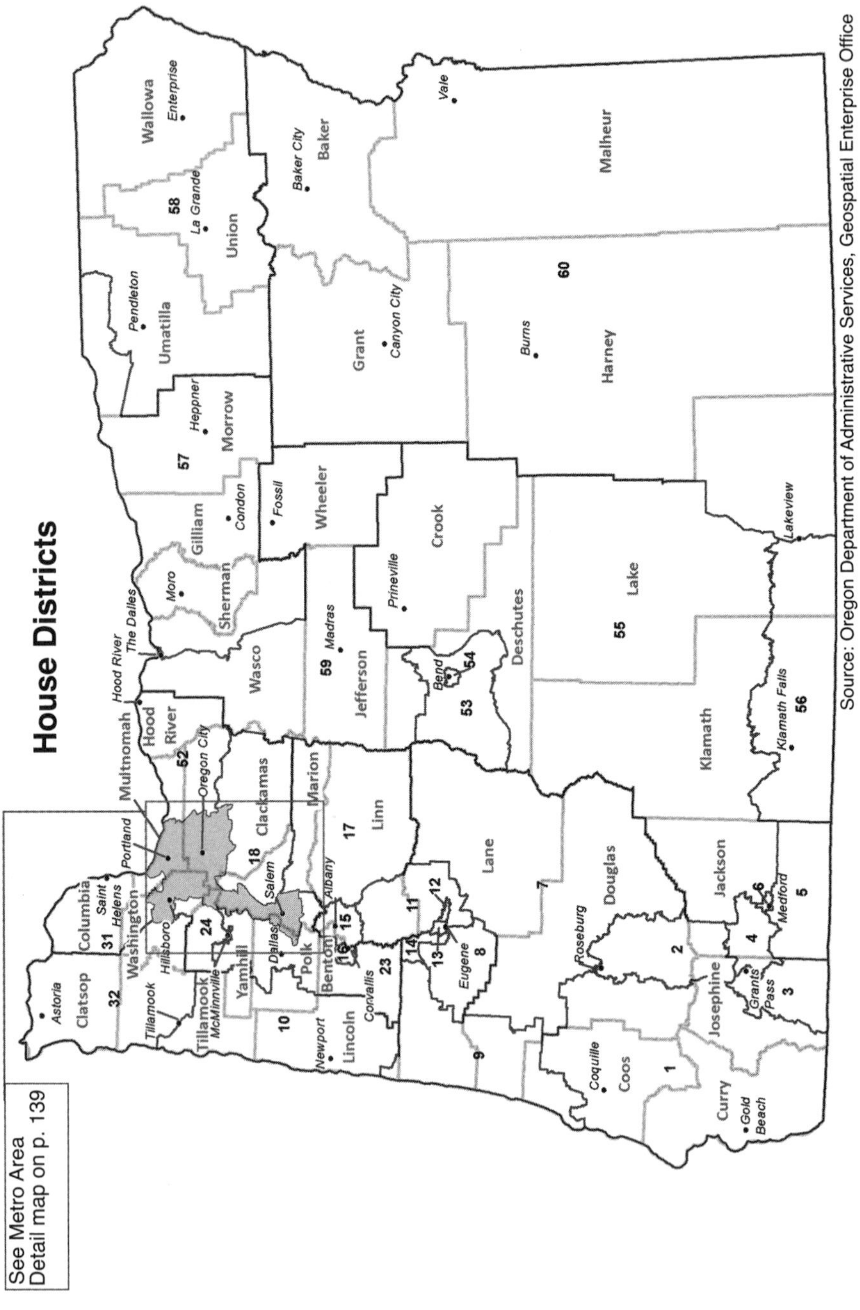
House Districts
See Metro Area
Detail map on p. 139
Wallowa
Enterprise
58
La Grande
Union
Baker City
Baker
Vale
Malheur
Pendleton
Umatilla
Grant
Canyon City
60
Burns
Harney
Heppner
Morrow
57
Condon
Gilliam
Fossil
Wheeler
Crook
Prineville
Moro
Sherman
The Dalles
Hood River
Wasco
Madras
59
Jefferson
Deschutes
Bend
54
53
Lake
55
Lakeview
Klamath Falls
56
Klamath
Multnomah
Hood River
52
Oregon City
Clackamas
Marion
Portland
Saint Helens
Columbia
31
Washington
Hillsboro
24
Yamhill
McMinnville
Tillamook
Astoria
Clatsop
32
18
Salem
Dallas
Polk
Albany
17
Linn
15
16
Benton
Corvallis
23
Lincoln
Newport
10
9
14
13
11
12
Eugene
8
Lane
7
Douglas
Roseburg
2
Jackson
6
Medford
5
4
Josephine
Grants Pass
3
Coos
Coquille
1
Curry
Gold Beach
Source: Oregon Department of Administrative Services, Geospatial Enterprise Office

Metro Area Detail Maps

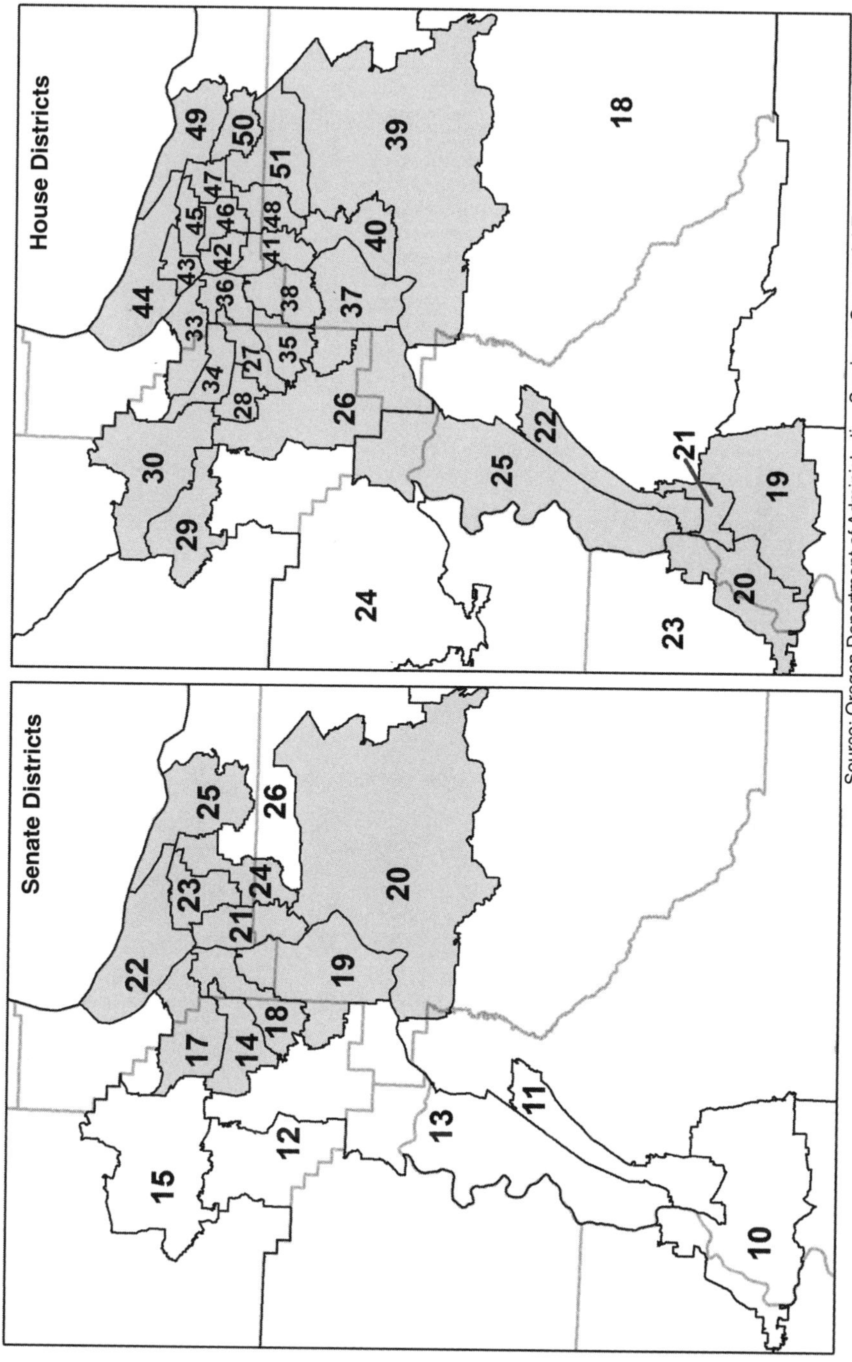

Source: Oregon Department of Administrative Services, Geospatial Enterprise Office

Legislative

President of the Senate

Peter Courtney (Democrat, District 11) was born in Philadelphia, Pennsylvania on June 18, 1943. He graduated with Bachelor and Master degrees from the University of Rhode Island and received a law degree from Boston University. Courtney was first elected to the Salem City Council in 1974 where he served until 1981. He began serving in the House of Representatives in 1981 and was first elected to the Senate in 1998. He has now served a record five terms as President of the Oregon Senate.

Courtney has worked at Western Oregon University since 1985, where he is an adjunct professor and serves as assistant to University President Mark D. Wiess. He has served on the Salem Mass Transit Board, the United Way Board, and the Board of Directors for the YMCA, and he has coached for the Boys and Girls Club.

Courtney has worked as a political commentator for *The 10 O'Clock News* at KPTV, Channel 12, Portland, and at KSLM Radio, Salem. He married his wife Margie in 1976. They have three sons, Peter, Sean and Adam.

Peter Courtney

Baertschiger, Herman
R—District 2

Bates, Alan
D—District 3

Beyer, Lee
D—District 6

Boquist, Brian
R—District 12

Burdick, Ginny
D—District 18

Close, Betsy
R—District 8

Courtney, Peter
D—District 11

Devlin, Richard
D—District 19

Dingfelder, Jackie
D—District 23

Edwards, Chris
D—District 7

Ferrioli, Ted
R—District 30

George, Larry
R—District 13

Girod, Fred
R—District 9

Hansell, Bill
R—District 29

Hass, Mark
D—District 14

Johnson, Betsy
D—District 16

Knopp, Tim
R—District 27

Kruse, Jeff
R—District 1

Monnes Anderson, Laurie
D—District 25

Monroe, Rod
D—District 24

Olsen, Alan R.
R—District 20

Prozanski, Floyd
D—District 4

Roblan, Arnie
D—District 5

Rosenbaum, Diane
D—District 21

Shields, Chip
D—District 22

Starr, Bruce
R—District 15

Steiner Hayward, Elizabeth
D—District 17

Thomsen, Chuck
R—District 26

Whitsett, Doug
R—District 28

Winters, Jackie
R—District 10

State Senators by District

District/Counties	Name/Address/Phone	Occupation/Yr. Elected*	Birthplace/Year
1. Curry and portions of Coos, Douglas, Jackson and Josephine	Jeff Kruse (R) 636 Wild Iris Lane Roseburg 97470 541-673-7201	Co-owner Kruse Farms 2005/2009/2013 (1997–2003)	Oregon 1951
2. Portions of Jackson and Josephine	Herman Baertschiger, Jr. (R) 900 Court St. NE, S-403 Salem, 97301 503-986-1702	Forester/Rancher 2013	California 1959
3. Portion of Jackson	Alan Bates (D) 2859 State St., Ste. 101 Medford 97504 541-282-6502	Family Physician 2005/2011 (2001/2003)	Washington 1945
4. Portions of Douglas and Lane	Floyd Prozanski (D) PO Box 11511 Eugene 97440 541-342-2447	Attorney 2005/2009 (1995–2003)	Texas 1954
5. Lincoln and portions of Coos, Douglas, Lane, Polk, Tillamook and Yamhill	Arnie Roblan (D) PO Box 1410 Coos Bay 97420 503-986-1705	Retired School Principal 2013 (2005/2007/2009/2011)	Washington 1948
6. Portions of Lane and Linn	Lee Beyer (D) PO Box 131 Springfield 97477 541-726-2533	Retired Business Advisor 1999/2011 (1991–1997)	Nebraska 1948
7. Portion of Lane	Chris Edwards (D) PO Box 42082 Eugene 97404 503-986-1707	Owner, Export Trade Company 2009/2011 (2007/2009)	Oregon 1973
8. Portions of Benton and Linn	Betsy Close (R) 900 Court St. NE, S-303 Salem, 97301 503-986-1708	Teacher 2013 (1999–2003)	Washington 1950
9. Portions of Clackamas, Linn and Marion	Fred Girod (R) 101 Fern Ridge Rd. SE Stayton 97383 503-769-4321	Dentist 2008/2009/2013 (1993–2007)	Oregon 1951
10. Portions of Marion and Polk	Jackie Winters (R) 900 Court St. NE, S-301 Salem 97301 503-986-1710	Retired Business Owner and Agency Administrator 2003/2007/2011 (1999/2001)	Kansas 1937
11. Portion of Marion	Peter Courtney (D) 900 Court St. NE, S-201 Salem 97301 503-986-1600	Asst. to Western Oregon University President 1999/2003/2007/2011 (1981–1997)	Pennsylvania 1943
12. Portions of Benton, Marion, Polk, Washington and Yamhill	Brian Boquist (R) 900 Court St. NE, S-305 Salem 97301 503-986-1712	Businessman/Rancher 2009/2013 (2005/2007)	Oregon 1958

**Senate terms are four years, and House terms (in parentheses) are two years, unless appointed mid-term.*

District/Counties	Name/Address/Phone	Occupation/Yr. Elected*	Birthplace/Year
13. Portions of Clackamas, Marion, Washington and Yamhill	Larry George (R) 900 Court St. NE, S-307 Salem, 97301 503-986-1713	Business Owner 2007/2011	California 1968
14. Portion of Washington	Mark Hass (D) 900 Court St. NE, S-207 Salem 97301 503-986-1714	Brand Manager 2008/2009/2013 (2001–2005)	Rhode Island 1956
15. Portion of Washington	Bruce Starr (R) 900 Court St. NE, S-411 Salem 97301 503-986-1715	Small Business Owner 2003/2007/2011 (1999/2001)	Oregon 1969
16. Clatsop, Columbia and portions of Multnomah, Tillamook and Washington	Betsy Johnson (D) PO Box R Scappoose 97056 503-543-4046	Former Business Owner 2007/2011 (2001/2003)	Oregon 1951
17. Portions of Multnomah and Washington	Steiner Hayward, Elizabeth (D) PO Box 990 Beaverton 97075 503-627-0246	OHSU Associate Professor of Family Medicine 2011/2013	New York 1963
18. Portions of Multnomah and Washington	Ginny Burdick (D) 6227 SW 18th Dr. Portland 97239 503-986-1718	Communications Consultant/Legislator 1997/2001/2005/2009/2013	Oregon 1947
19. Portions of Clackamas and Multnomah	Richard Devlin (D) 10290 SW Anderson Ct. Tualatin 97062 503-691-2026	Civil/Criminal Investigations, Legislator 2003/2007/2011 (1997– 2001)	Oregon 1952
20. Portions of Clackamas and Marion	Alan R. Olsen (R) PO Box 820 Canby 97013 503-936-8605	General Contractor 2011	Illinois 1948
21. Portions of Clackamas and Multnomah	Diane Rosenbaum (D) 1125 SE Madison St. #100B Portland 97214 503-231-9970	Legislator 2009/2013 (1999–2007)	California 1949
22. Portion of Multnomah	Chip Shields (D) 5313 N Vancouver Ave. Portland 97217 503-231-2564	Consultant 2009/2013 (2005–2009)	Missouri 1967
23. Portion of Multnomah	Jackie Dingfelder (D) PO Box 13432 Portland 97213 503-493-2804	Environmental Consultant/Legislator 2009/2013 (2001–2007)	New York 1960
24. Portions of Clackamas and Multnomah	Rod Monroe (D) 7802 SE 111th Ave. Portland 97266 503-760-4310	Small Business Owner/ Legislator 1981/1985/2007/2011 (1977–1981)	British Columbia, Canada 1942
25. Portion of Multnomah	Laurie Monnes Anderson (D) PO Box 1531 Gresham 97030 503-618-3071	Retired Nurse 2005/2009/2013 (2001/2003)	California 1945

District/Counties	Name/Address/Phone	Occupation/Yr. Elected*	Birthplace/Year
26. Hood River and portions of Clackamas and Multnomah	Chuck Thomsen (R) 900 Court St NE, S-316 Salem 97301 503-986-1726	Orchardist 2011	Oregon 1957
27. Portion of Deschutes	Tim Knopp (R) 900 Court St NE, S-309 Salem 97301 503-986-1727	Exec. Vice President Non-Profit Trade Assoc. 2013	Oregon 1965
28. Crook, Klamath and portions of Deschutes, Jackson and Lake	Doug Whitsett (R) 23131 North Poe Valley Rd. Klamath Falls 97603 541-882-1315	Retired Veterinarian 2005/2009/2013	California 1943
29. Gilliam, Morrow, Sherman, Umatilla, Union and Wallowa and portion of Wasco	Bill Hansell (R) 900 Court St NE, S-423 Salem 97301 503-986-1729	Former County Commissioner 2013	Washington 1945
30. Baker, Grant, Harney, Jefferson, Malheur, Wheeler and portions of Deschutes, Lake and Wasco	Ted Ferrioli (R) 900 Court St NE, S-323 Salem 97301 503-986-1730	Retired Association Director and Rancher 1997/2001/2005/2009/2013	Washington 1951

Members of the Oregon House of Representatives

Tina Kotek

Speaker of the House

Tina Kotek (Democrat, District 44) holds a B.S. in religious studies from the University of Oregon and an M.A. in international studies from the University of Washington.

Before her election to the Oregon House of Representatives in 2006, Representative Kotek worked as the policy director for the non-profit advocacy organization Children First for Oregon. Prior to joining Children First, she was a public policy advocate for the Oregon Food Bank.

Some of Representative Kotek's legislative accomplishments include: helping to pass landmark legislation that ended discrimination based on sexual orientation and created domestic partnerships for same-sex couples; championing the redesign of the state's welfare program maintaining funding for the Temporary Assistance for Needy Families Program (TANF); leading the fight to establish statewide nutrition standards for food sold in schools; passing a statewide menu labeling bill to provide consumers with calorie information in fast food restaurants; restricting the use of a job applicant's credit history when making hiring decisions through the passage of the Job Applicant Fairness Act; and implementing a vision screening demonstration project to explore the best ways to ensure every child receives routine vision screening.

She lives in North Portland with her partner Aimee Wilson and their dogs Wickett and Rudy.

Bailey, Jules
D—District 42

Barker, Jeff
D—District 28

Barnhart, Phil
D—District 11

Barton, Brent
D—District 40

Bentz, Cliff
R—District 60

Berger, Vicki
R—District 20

Boone, Deborah
D—District 32

Buckley, Peter
D—District 5

Cameron, Kevin
R—District 19

Clem, Brian L.
D—District 21

Conger, Jason
R—District 54

Davis, John
R—District 26

Dembrow, Michael E.
D—District 45

Doherty, Margaret
D—District 35

Esquivel, Sal
R—District 6

Fagan, Shemia
D—District 51

Frederick, Lew
D—District 43

Freeman, Tim
R—District 2

Gallegos, Joseph
D—District 30

Garrett, Chris
D—District 38

Gelser, Sara
D—District 16

Gilliam, Vic
R—District 18

Gomberg, David
D—District 10

Gorsek, Chris
D—District 49

Greenlick, Mitch
D—District 33

Hanna, Bruce
R—District 7

Harker, Chris
D—District 34

Hicks, Wally
R—District 3

Holvey, Paul
D—District 8

Hoyle, Val
D—District 14

Huffman, John E.
R—District 59

Jenson, Bob
R—District 58

Johnson, Mark
R—District 52

Kennemer, Bill
R—District 39

Keny-Guyer, Alissa
D—District 46

Komp, Betty
D—District 22

Kotek, Tina
D—District 44

Krieger, Wayne
R—District 1

Lively, John
D—District 12

Matthews, Greg
D—District 50

McKeown, Caddy
D—District 9

McLane, Mike
R—District 55

Nathanson, Nancy
D—District 13

Olson, Andy
R—District 15

Parrish, Julie
R—District 37

Read, Tobias
D—District 27

Reardon, Jeff
D—District 48

Richardson, Dennis
R—District 4

Smith, Greg
R—District 57

Sprenger, Sherrie
R—District 17

Thatcher, Kim
R—District 25

Thompson, Jim
R—District 23

Tomei, Carolyn
D—District 41

Unger, Ben
D—District 29

Vega Pederson, Jessica
D—District 47

Weidner, Jim
R—District 24

Whisnant, Gene
R—District 53

Whitsett, Gail
R—District 56

Williamson, Jennifer
D—District 36

Witt, Bradley
D—District 31

State Representatives by District

District/Counties	Name/Address/Phone	Occupation/Yr. Elected*	Birthplace/Year
1. Curry and portions of Coos, Douglas and Josephine	Wayne Krieger (R) 95702 Skyview Ranch Rd. Gold Beach 97444 541-247-7990	Legislator 2001/2003/2005/2007/ 2009/2011/2013	Oregon 1940
2. Portions of Douglas, Jackson and Josephine	Tim Freeman (R) 792 NW Garden Vly. Blvd. Roseburg 97471 503-986-1402	Small Business Owner 2009/2011/2013	California 1965
3. Portion of Josephine	Wally Hicks (R) 900 Court St. NE, H-378 Salem 97301 503-986-1403	Deputy District Attorney 2011/2013	Eugene 1976
4. Portions of Jackson and Josephine	Dennis Richardson (R) 55 S 5th St. Central Point 97502 541-601-0083	Businessman/Attorney 2003/2005/2007/2009/ 2011/2013	California 1949
5. Portion of Jackson	Peter Buckley (D) 71 Dewey St. Ashland 97520 503-986-1405	Writer 2005/2007/2009/2011/ 2013	California 1957
6. Portion of Jackson	Sal Esquivel (R) 711 Medford Center #178 Medford 97504 541-734-4369	Real Estate Broker 2005/2007/2009/2011/ 2013	California 1948
7. Portions of Douglas and Lane	Bruce Hanna (R) 900 Court St. NE, H-382 Salem 97301 503-986-1407	Business Owner 2005/2007/2009/2011/ 2013	Oregon 1960
8. Portion of Lane	Paul Holvey (D) PO Box 51048 Eugene 97405 541-344-5636	Carpenters' Union Representative 2005/2007/2009/2011/ 2013	Oregon 1954
9. Portions of Coos, Douglas, Lane and Lincoln	Caddy McKeown (D) 900 Court St. NE, H-376 Salem 97301 503-986-1409	Port Commissioner/ Retired Agency Supervisor 2013	Oregon 1951
10. Portions of Lincoln, Polk, Tillamook and Yamhill	David Gomberg (D) 900 Court St. NE, H-371 Salem 97301 503-986-1410	Small Business Owner 2013	Oregon 1953
11. Portions of Lane and Linn	Phil Barnhart (D) PO Box 71188 Eugene 97401 503-986-1411	State Representative 2001/2003/2005/2007/ 2009/2011/2013	New York 1946
12. Portion of Lane	John Lively (D) 900 Court St. NE, H-488 Salem 97301 503-986-1412	Account Manager 2013	Oregon 1946

**House terms are two years, and Senate terms (in parentheses) are four years, unless appointed mid-term.*

District/Counties	Name/Address/Phone	Occupation/Yr. Elected*	Birthplace/Year
13. Portion of Lane	Nancy Nathanson (D) PO Box 41895 Eugene 97404 541-343-2206	Library Program Staff 2007/2009/2011/2013	Texas 1951
14. Portion of Lane	Val Hoyle (D) PO Box 70795 Eugene 97401 541-747-8436	United Way of Lane Co. Director of Health Access Initiative 2009/2011/2013	California 1964
15. Portions of Benton and Linn	Andy Olson (R) PO Box 891 Albany 97321 541-967-6576	Retired Law Enforcement 2005/2007/2009/2011/2013	Nebraska 1952
16. Portion of Benton	Sara Gelser (D) 4030 Glen Eden Dr. Corvallis 97330 503-986-1416	Educator/Civil Servant 2007/2009/2011/2013	Nevada 1973
17. Portions of Linn and Marion	Sherrie Sprenger (R) 900 Court St. NE, H-473 Salem 97301 503-986-1417	Small Business Owner 2008/2009/2011/2013	Oregon 1965
18. Portions of Clackamas and Marion	Vic Gilliam (R) PO Box 158 Silverton 97381 503-986-1418	Self-Employed; Real Estate and Media 2007/2009/2011/2013	Ohio 1953
19. Portion of Marion	Kevin Cameron (R) 900 Court St. NE, H-384 Salem 97301 503-986-1419	Small Business Owner 2005/2007/2009/2011/2013	California 1956
20. Portions of Marion and Polk	Vicki Berger (R) 805 Kingwood Dr. NW Salem 97304 503-581-9969	Retired Business Owner 2003/2005/2007/2009/2011/2013	Oregon 1949
21. Portion of Marion	Brian L. Clem (D) 396 Hoyt St. SE Salem 97302 503-391-9770	Small Business Owner 2007/2009/2011/2013	Oregon 1972
22. Portion of Marion	Betty Komp (D) 885 Garfield St. Woodburn 97071 503-986-1422	Retired School Administrator 2005/2007/2009/2011/2013	Oregon 1949
23. Portions of Benton, Marion, Polk and Yamhill	Jim Thompson (R) 3380 Mistletoe Rd. Dallas 97338 503-986-1423	Allergy Consultant 2009/2011/2013	Washington 1947
24. Portions of Washington and Yamhill	Jim Weidner (R) 900 Court St. NE, H-387 Salem 97301 503-986-1424	Small Business Owner 2009/2011/2013	Oregon 1968
25. Portion of Marion	Kim Thatcher (R) PO Box 9111 Salem 97305 503-932-6382	Small Business Owner 2005/2007/2009/2011/2013	Idaho 1964

District/Counties	Name/Address/Phone	Occupation/Yr. Elected*	Birthplace/Year
26. Portions of Clackamas, Washington and Yamhill	John Davis (R) 900 Court St. NE, H-372 Salem 97301 503-986-1426	Attorney 2013	Oregon 1982
27. Portion of Washington	Tobias Read (D) PO Box 2101 Beaverton 97075 503-641-6800	Footwear Developer, Nike Inc. 2007/2009/2011/2013	Montana 1975
28. Portion of Washington	Jeff Barker (D) PO Box 6751 Aloha 97007 503-986-1428	Retired Police Lieutenant 2003/2005/2007/2009/2011/2013	Oregon 1943
29. Portion of Washington	Ben Unger (D) 900 Court St. NE, H-377 Salem 97301 503-986-1429	Small Business Owner 2013	Oregon 1976
30. Portion of Washington	Joseph Gallegos (D) 900 Court St. NE, H-484 Salem 97301 503-986-1430	Small Business Owner 2013	Texas 1941
31. Columbia and portions of Multnomah and Washington	Bradley Witt (D) 900 Court St. NE, H-374 Salem 97301 503-986-1431	Labor Official 2005/2007/2009/2011/2013	Massachusetts 1952
32. Clatsop and portions of Tillamook and Washington	Deborah Boone (D) PO Box 928 Cannon Beach 97110 503-986-1432	Business Owner 2005/2007/2009/2011/2013	Oregon 1951
33. Portions of Multnomah and Washington	Mitch Greenlick (D) 712 NW Spring Ave. Portland 97229 503-297-2416	Professor Emeritus, OHSU 2003/2005/2007/2009/2011/2013	Michigan 1935
34. Portion of Washington	Chris Harker (D) 900 Court St. NE, H-485 Salem 97301 503-986-1434	High Technology Entrepreneur 2008/2009/2011/2013	New Jersey 1954
35. Portions of Multnomah and Washington	Margaret Doherty (D) 16200 SW Pacific Hwy. H-273 Tigard 97224 503-986-1435	Teacher/Small Business Owner 2009/2011/2013	California 1950
36. Portion of Multnomah	Jennifer Williamson (D) 900 Court St. NE, H-389 Salem 97301 503-986-1436	Attorney 2013	Oregon 1973
37. Portions of Clackamas and Washington	Julie Parrish (R) 1980 Willamette Falls Dr., #120 West Linn 97068 971-227-6541	CEO and Business Owner 2011/2013	Oregon 1974
38. Portions of Clackamas and Multnomah	Chris Garrett (D) PO Box 132 Lake Oswego 97034 503-210-2474	Attorney 2009/2011/2013	Oregon 1973

District/Counties	Name/Address/Phone	Occupation/Yr. Elected*	Birthplace/Year
39. Portion of Clackamas	Bill Kennemer (R) 900 Court St. NE, H-380 Salem 97301 503-986-1439	Psychologist/County Commissioner 2009/2011/2013	California 1946
40. Portion of Clackamas	Brent Barton (D) 900 Court St. NE, H-275 Salem 97301 503-986-1440	Attorney 2013	Oregon 1980
41. Portions of Clackamas and Multnomah	Carolyn Tomei (D) PO Box 22147 Milwaukie 97269 503-653-5180	Legislator/Psychiatric Social Worker 2001/2003/2005/2007/2009/2011/2013	West Virginia 1936
42. Portion of Multnomah	Jules Bailey (D) PO Box 42429 Portland 97242 503-986-1442	Economic Consultant 2009/2011/2013	Oregon 1979
43. Portion of Multnomah	Lew Frederick (D) 900 Court St. NE, H-276 Salem 97301 503-986-1443	Strategic Communications Consultant 2009/2011/2013	Washington 1951
44. Portion of Multnomah	Tina Kotek (D) 7930 N Wabash Ave. Portland 97217 503-986-1444	Legislator/Consultant 2007/2009/2011/2013	Pennsylvania 1966
45. Portion of Multnomah	Michael E. Dembrow (D) 900 Court St. NE, H-487 Salem 97301 503-986-1445	College Teacher 2009/2011/2013	Connecticut 1951
46. Portion of Multnomah	Alissa Keny-Guyer (D) 900 Court St. NE, H-281 Salem 97301 503-986-1446	Nonprofit Management 2011/2013	New York 1959
47. Portion of Multnomah	Jessica Vega Pederson (D) 900 Court St. NE, H-490 Salem 97301 503-986-1447	Technical Project Mgr. 2013	Indiana 1973
48. Portions of Clackamas and Multnomah	Jeff Reardon (D) 900 Court St. NE, H-491 Salem 97301 503-986-1448	Teacher 2013	Washington 1947
49. Portion of Multnomah	Chris Gorsek (D) 900 Court St. NE, H-486 Salem 97301 503-378-1449	Teacher 2013	Oregon 1958
50. Portion of Multnomah	Greg Matthews (D) 900 Court St. NE, H-379 Salem 97301 503-986-1450	Fire Fighter 2009/2011/2013	Oregon 1964
51. Portions of Clackamas and Multnomah	Shemia Fagan (D) 900 Court St. NE, H-492 Salem 97301 503-986-1451	Attorney 2013	Oregon 1981

District/Counties	Name/Address/Phone	Occupation/Yr. Elected*	Birthplace/Year
52. Hood River and portions of Clackamas and Multnomah	Mark Johnson (R) PO Box 1047 Hood River 97031 503-986-1452	Builder 2011/2013	California 1957
53. Portion of Deschutes	Gene Whisnant (R) PO Box 3565 Sunriver 97707 541-598-7560	USAF Colonel, Retired 2003/2005/2007/2009/ 2011/2013	North Carolina 1943
54. Portion of Deschutes	Jason Conger (R) PO Box 2058 Bend 97709 541-317-5076	Attorney 2011/2013	California 1968
55. Crook and portions of Deschutes, Jackson, Klamath and Lake	Mike McLane (R) 900 Court St. NE, H-395 Salem 97301 541-233-4411	Attorney 2011/2013	Alaska 1965
56. Portions of Klamath and Lake	Gail Whitsett (R) 900 Court St. NE, H-474 Salem 97301 503-986-1456	Geologist/Legislator 2013	Territory of Hawaii 1956
57. Gilliam, Morrow, Sherman and portions of Umatilla and Wasco	Greg Smith (R) PO Box 219 Heppner 97836 541-676-8719	Small Business Owner/Legislator 2001/2003/2005/2007/ 2009/2011/2013	Oregon 1968
58. Union, Wallowa and portion of Umatilla	Bob Jenson (R) 2126 NW Despain Ave. Pendleton 97801 541-276-5821	Educator/Legislator 1997/1999/2001/2003/ 2005/2007/2009/2011/ 2013	Nebraska 1931
59. Jefferson, Wheeler and portions of Deschutes and Wasco	John E. Huffman (R) PO Box 104 The Dalles 97058 541-298-5959	Commercial Property Owner/Manager 2007/2009/2011/2013	Missouri 1957
60. Baker, Grant, Harney, Malheur and portion of Lake	Cliff Bentz (R) 900 Court St. NE, H-475 Salem 97301 503-986-1460	Attorney 2008/2009/2011/2013	Oregon 1952

Government Finance

"The Volunteer" statue by Gareth Curtiss in Salem's Veterans' Heritage Park represents the volunteer spirit of the Oregon National Guard—Oregon State Archives Scenic Photograph marDA0039

Government finance—where government gets its money and how it spends it—affects all Oregonians. The connections between state and local government revenues and state and local government services are important. This section describes revenue sources and distribution.

State and Local Government Finance

State Government

Oregon has a biennial budget. Budgets begin July 1 of odd-numbered years and continue for two years. Oregon law requires all state and local governments to balance their budgets. How does the state government's budget work? The state receives money from a variety of sources which are grouped into funds. These funds are known as the General Fund, the Lottery Fund, Other Funds and Federal Funds.

The total "Legislatively Approved Budget" for the 2011–13 biennium was $58.8 billion. This is 2.4 percent more than the 2009–11 total actual expenditures of $57.5 billion. The General and Lottery Funds portions of the 2011–13 budget amounted to $14.8 billion, which is $1.3 billion more than actual expenditures in 2009–11.

General Fund

The 2011–13 Legislatively Approved Budget included approximately $13.7 billion in the General Fund for a 23.3 percent share of the total budget. The General Fund is largely made up of personal and corporate income taxes collected by the Oregon Department of Revenue. The personal income tax makes up the largest share of General Fund revenue. It accounts for about 87 percent of projected revenue for 2011–13 as of the June 2012 quarterly revenue forecast. Corporate income taxes are about 6 percent of the total revenue amount. Other sources make up the remainder. The largest of these are the cigarette tax, estate tax and the liquor apportionment transfer.

General Fund appropriations provide funding to agencies that do not generate revenues, receive federal funds or generate sufficient other funds to support their approved programs. Agencies do not actually receive money from the General Fund. Instead, they expend against an appropriation from the General Fund that is established for general government purposes up to the amount approved in their budget bill. Because General Fund monies can be used for any public purpose and the amount of the General Fund is limited, competition for these monies is keen.

In 1990, voters approved Ballot Measure 5. This reduced local property tax rates, which reduced local revenue and, in turn, shifted much of the responsibility for funding public schools to the state's General Fund. The 2011–13 Legislatively Approved Budget had $7.4 billion, or 50 percent, of the General and Lottery Funds being spent on education.

General Fund revenues for the 2011–13 biennium are expected to total $14 billion. There was no balance carried over from the prior biennium. As of June 2012, the revenue forecast was $200 million below the "Close of Session" forecast, bringing total resources to $13.8 billion. The updated projected ending balance for 2011–13 is $95 million.

Lottery Fund

The Lottery Fund derives from the sale of lottery game tickets and from Video Lottery. After prizes and lottery expenses are paid, revenue flows to the Economic Development Fund. A portion of the Lottery Fund is constitutionally dedicated to be spent in specific ways. The remainder is distributed at the discretion of the Legislature for economic development.

The 2011–13 Legislatively Approved Budget included $1.1 billion of expenditures from the Lottery Fund, which is about 1.8 percent of the total budget. Dedicated spending accounted for about 38 percent of that amount, and debt service accounted for another 24 percent. The remainder was distributed to the State School Fund and a variety of other projects. Overall, about 60 percent of the Lottery Fund is dedicated to education.

2011-13 Legislatively Approved Budget Expenditures

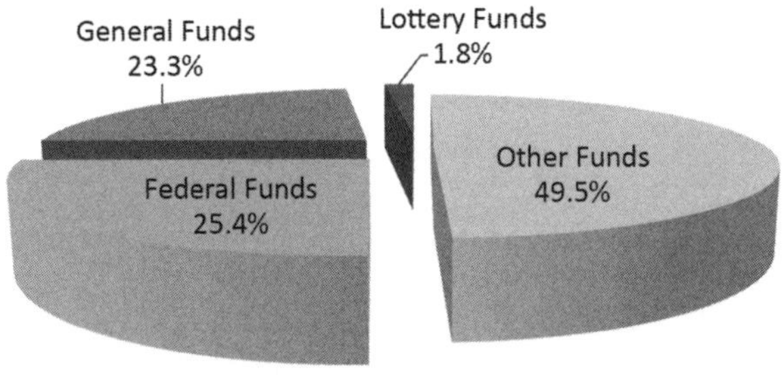

Source: Department of Administrative Services, Budget and Management Division

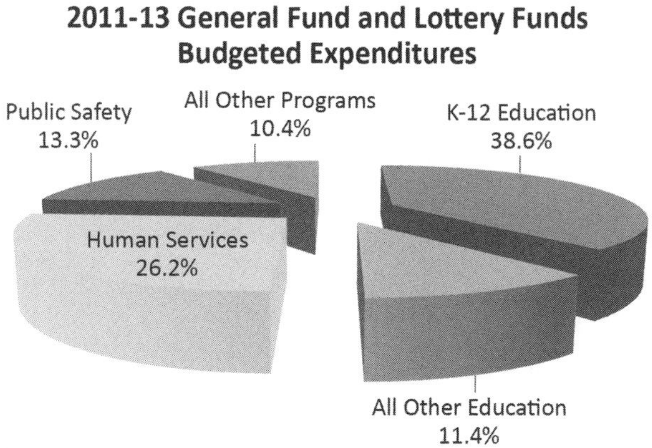

Source: Department of Administrative Services, Budget and Management Division

Other Funds

The 2011–13 Legislatively Approved Budget included $29.1 billion in Other Funds for a 49.5 percent share of the total budget. Other Funds revenue generally refers to money collected by agencies in return for services. Legislative actions may allow an agency to levy taxes, provide services for a fee, license individuals or otherwise earn revenues to pay for programs. These Other Funds are often separate and distinct from monies collected for general government purposes (General Fund), and they may be based on statutory language, federal mandate and legal requirements or for specific business reasons. Some funds are "dedicated" in that the income and disbursements are limited by the state's constitution or by another law (for example, the Highway Fund). Other Funds may not be moved from one major program to another. Consequently, competition for these monies is limited.

Federal Funds

The 2011–13 Legislatively Approved Budget included $14.9 billion in Federal Funds for a 25.4 percent share of the total budget. Federal Funds are monies received from the federal government. Federal Funds increased substantially in 2009–11 due to infusions of American Recovery and Reinvestment Act stimulus funds. As expected, these one-time funds decreased by $1.1 billion in the 2011–13 biennium. The Legislative Assembly may authorize receipt of Federal Funds for specific purposes. Federal Funds may be used to match General

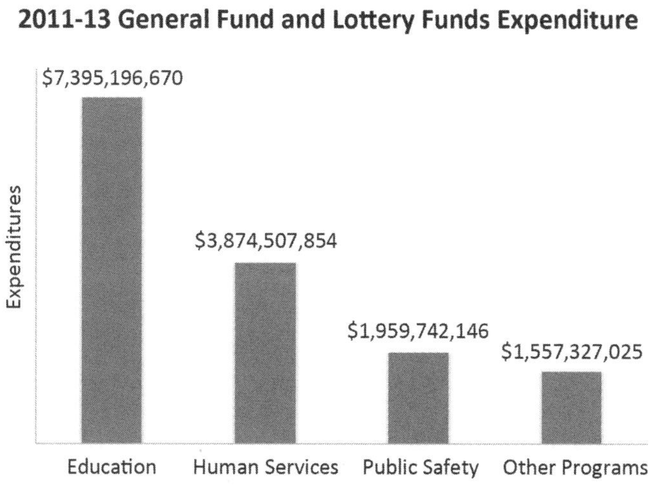

Source: Department of Administrative Services, Budget and Management Division

Government Finance

Fund dollars, used for specific programs, or passed through to local governments.

State Budget Process

Oregon state agencies develop biennial budgets according to instructions provided by the Department of Administrative Services, Budget and Management Division. This budget development process begins in even-numbered years, well before the Legislative Assembly convenes in January of the odd-numbered years. Agencies are required to prepare and submit their budget requests for review by the Budget and Management Division by September 1. These budget requests consist of narrative descriptions of agency programs, completed forms, and reports from the Oregon Budget Information and Tracking System (ORBITS).

Agencies begin by building a current program budget, which is the amount of money needed in the new biennium to continue all existing programs. An agency may request changes to this budget through policy packages, which describe the purpose and the amount needed. Agencies also must identify program reductions and performance targets. For their 2011–13 budget requests, agencies began in March 2010 and submitted their completed requests by September 2010. An agency's budget provides an outline of what an agency does, what it costs, and how many people are involved.

After they pass a review by the Governor's Office and the Budget and Management Division, the budget requests become part of the Governor's Recommended Budget. Because the governor has a legal obligation to submit a balanced budget for all of state government, the Governor's Recommended Budget includes the proposed budgets for the Legislative Assembly and the Judicial Department. However, because of separation of power principles, the governor's budget recommendations are advisory only for the other two branches. The governor presents the Recommended Budget to the Legislative Assembly when it convenes in January of odd-numbered years.

When the Legislative Assembly is in session, a subcommittee of the Joint Ways and Means Committee hears each agency's budget. At the budget hearings, an agency presents its budget request and answers questions asked by members of the committee. Staff members from the Legislative Fiscal Office and the Budget and Management Division are also present at the budget hearings. Members of the public may attend the hearings and request an opportunity to testify. At the end of an agency's budget hearings, the agency's budget goes to the full Ways and Means Committee for a vote and then on to the full House and Senate for a vote. The agency's budget may be amended at any point in this process, although changes typically occur during the subcommittee hearings. After passage by both houses, an agency's budget becomes its Legislatively Adopted Budget for the biennium, and it goes into effect July 1 of odd-numbered years. If the Legislature makes changes to the adopted budget in special sessions or through the Emergency Board, it becomes known as the "Legislatively Approved Budget."

Kicker Provision

The Oregon Constitution requires the governor to provide an estimate of biennial General Fund revenues.

In 1979, the Legislature placed a condition on those revenue estimates that required excess funds to be "kicked back" to taxpayers if actual revenues exceeded estimated revenues by 2 percent or more.

For revenues from corporate income and excise taxes, the provision had required that the excess be returned to taxpayers who paid corporate income and excise taxes. However, this provision was amended in November 2012 by the citizen initiative process. Ballot Measure 85 requires that this excess be retained in the General Fund to provide additional funding for public education, kindergarten through twelfth grade. This measure is applicable to biennial estimates on or after July 1, 2013.

For General Fund revenues from all other sources where the actual revenues exceed the estimated revenues by 2 percent or more, the excess is "kicked back" to taxpayers who paid personal income tax. Ballot Measure 85 did not affect this provision. These taxpayers receive the refund by December 1 of the year the biennium ends, which is an odd-numbered year. The refund is an identical proportion of each taxpayer's personal income tax liability for the prior year.

During 2007–09, $1.1 billion was refunded to personal income tax payers; however, the Legislature required that $319.3 million be placed in the Oregon Rainy Day Fund rather than refunding that excess to corporate income and excise tax payers.

Rainy Day Fund and Education Stability Fund

Established in 2007, the Oregon Rainy Day Fund is essentially a savings account for state government. Withdrawals can be made only if at least one of three requirements is met: a decline in statewide employment, a projected budgetary shortfall, or declaration of a state of emergency plus a three-fifths vote of the members of both houses. Given the economic conditions in 2009 and 2010, the fund needed to be used. The fund balance is expected to be $61.7 million at the end of the current biennium.

The Education Stability Fund (ESF) was created through a constitutional amendment approved

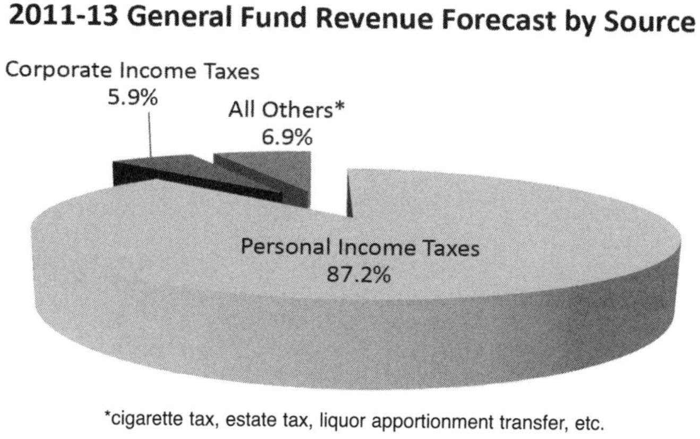

Source: Department of Administrative Services, Budget and Management Division

by voters in 2002. The ESF receives 18 percent of lottery earnings deposited on a quarterly basis. The ESF has similar triggers as the Rainy Day Fund. Just as the Rainy Day Fund had been drawn down during the last economic downturn, the ESF was used to balance budgets in the 2009–11 and 2011–13 biennia. Based on the June 2012 revenue forecast, the fund is projected to have a balance of $10.5 million at the end of the 2011–13 biennium.

State Spending Limit

The state spending limit was first enacted by the 1979 Legislative Assembly. It limited the growth of General Fund appropriations to the growth of personal income in Oregon. The 2001 Legislative Assembly replaced this spending limit with one tying appropriations for a biennium to personal income for that biennium. The appropriations subject to this limit may not exceed 8 percent of projected personal income for the same biennium. The 2003–05 Legislatively Adopted Budget authorized an expenditure limit of 7.6 percent of projected personal income for the biennium based on the May 2003 revenue forecast. The limit may be exceeded if the governor declares an emergency and three-fifths of the members of both houses vote to exceed it.

Local Government

Local government in Oregon is predominantly financed by the property tax, although there are other local taxes, such as hotel-motel taxes, transit taxes and, in Multnomah County, a business income tax.

Most local governments must prepare and adopt an annual budget. This includes schools, counties, cities, ports, rural fire protection districts, water districts, urban renewal agencies and special districts. Oregon's Local Budget Law establishes standard budget procedures and requires citizen participation in budget preparation and public disclosure of the budget before it is formally adopted. A budget officer must be appointed and a budget committee formed. The budget officer prepares a draft budget and the budget committee reviews and revises it before it is approved. Notices are then published, copies of the budget are made available for public review and at least two opportunities for public comment are provided.

Local government budgets are usually for a fiscal year beginning July 1 and ending June 30. However, local governments have the option of creating a two-year biennial budget like the state. The governing body must enact a resolution or an ordinance to formally adopt the budget, make appropriations, and levy and categorize any tax. This must be done no later than June 30. Budget revenues are divided into ensuing year property tax and non-property tax revenues.

The Oregon Constitution allows a local government to levy annually the amount that would be raised by its permanent rate limit without further authorization from the voters. When a local government has to increase the permanent rate limit or when the rate limit does not provide enough revenue to meet estimated expenditures, the government may request a local option levy from the voters. Approval requires a "double majority." This means that at least 50 percent of the registered voters must vote, and a majority of those who vote must approve the levy. Since 1991, the constitution has limited the maximum amount of taxes to support the public schools to $5 per $1,000 of real market value. The maximum amount to support other government operations is $10 per $1,000 of real market value.

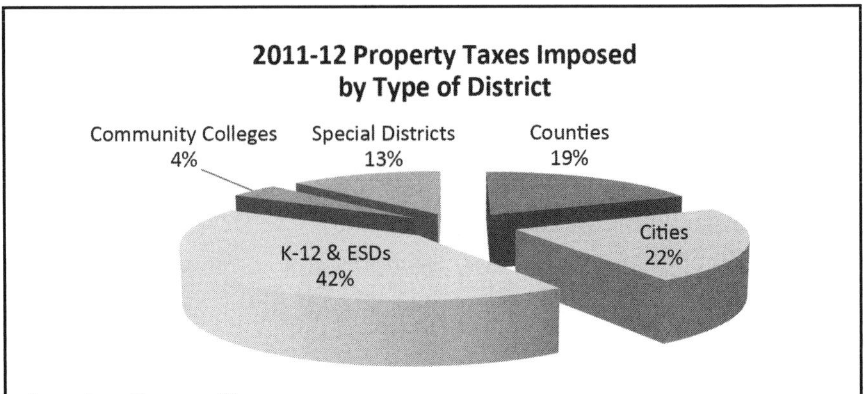

Source: Oregon Department of Revenue

Taxes

Personal Income Tax

Oregon residents and nonresidents who earn income in Oregon pay personal income tax. Oregon's taxable income is the same as federal taxable income with some adjustments. Tax rates range from 5 percent to 11 percent of taxable income. After deductions and credits, the average effective tax rate is about 5.7 percent of adjusted gross income. Since 1993, the income tax brackets have been indexed to changes in the *Consumer Price Index*. The current standard deduction is $3,895 on a joint return, $1,945 on single and married filing separate returns, and $3,135 for a head of household return.

The personal income tax is the largest source of state tax revenue. In January 2010, Oregon voters approved Ballot Measure 66, which made two changes to personal income tax calculations. First, it established new tax brackets for adjusted gross incomes above $125,000 (single filers) and $250,000 (joint filers) and phased out the federal tax subtraction for these same filers. Second, it allowed a one-year tax exclusion of the first $2,400 of unemployment benefits, as does federal tax law.

Business Taxes

Corporations that do, or are authorized to do, business in Oregon pay an excise tax. Corporations not doing, or that are not authorized to do, business in Oregon, but that have income from an Oregon source, pay income tax. The tax rate is 6.6 percent of Oregon net income. There is a minimum excise tax of $150.

The corporate excise and income tax is the second largest source of state tax revenue. Oregon voters approved Ballot Measure 67 in January 2010. The measure made three changes to Oregon corporate taxation. First, it increased the minimum corporate tax from $10 to $150. Second, it instituted a new corporate income tax rate structure that applies a marginal rate of 7.9 percent to corporate net income above $250,000 in tax years 2009 and 2010. For 2011 and 2012, the rate drops to 7.6 percent. In 2013, the marginal rate is 7.6 percent for net income above $10 million and 6.6 percent for net income below $10 million. Third, it established higher rates for corporate filing fees with the secretary of state.

Property Tax

Property tax rates differ across Oregon. The rate depends on the tax rate approved by local voters and the limits established by the Oregon Constitution. Most properties are taxed by a number of districts, such as a city, county, school district, community college, fire district or port. The total tax rate on any particular property is calculated by adding all the local taxing district rates in the area. The total tax rate is then multiplied by the assessed value of the property. The county assessor verifies the tax rates and levies submitted by each local taxing district on an annual basis. The county tax collector collects the taxes and distributes the funds to the local districts.

Taxable property includes real property, mobile homes and some tangible personal property used by business. The state and each county assessor determine the value of property in each county. Measure 5, which was passed by the voters in November 1990, restricted non-school taxes on any property to $10 per $1,000 of real market value. It restricted school taxes on any property to $5 per $1,000 of real market value.

Measure 50 was passed by the voters in May 1997. Measure 50 added another limit to the Measure 5 limits. Now, each property has a real market value and an assessed value. Each taxing district has a fixed, permanent tax rate for operations. Districts may not increase this rate. Voters can approve local option levies for up to five years for operations and up to 10 years or the useful life of capital projects, whichever is less. Local option levies require a "double majority" for approval. Measure 50 established the 1997–98 maximum assessed value as 90 percent of a property's 1995–96 real market value. In subsequent tax years, the assessed value is limited to 3 percent annual growth until it reaches real market value. The assessed value can never exceed real market value. New property is assessed at the average county ratio of assessed to real market value of existing property of the same class. For 2008–09, for all classes of property statewide, total assessed value was about 56 percent of real market value.

Resources

Legislative Fiscal Office

www.leg.state.or.us/comm/lfo
The Legislative Fiscal Office publishes detailed analyses of the *Legislatively Adopted Budget* and the *Governor's Recommended Budget*.

Legislative Revenue Office

www.leg.state.or.us/comm/lro
The Legislative Revenue Office publishes reports on revenue-related issues including *Oregon Public Finance: Basic Facts,* which serves as an introduction to how Oregon government is financed.

Department of Administrative Services, Chief Financial Office

www.oregon.gov/DAS/CFO/Pages/index.aspx
The Chief Financial Office publishes *The Budget Process Overview* and *Governor's Recommended Budget.*

Department of Administrative Services, Office of Economic Analysis

www.oregon.gov/DAS/OEA/Pages/index.aspx
The Office of Economic Analysis publishes periodic *Economic and Revenue Forecasts,* as well as related demographic data.

Department of Revenue

www.oregon.gov/DOR/index.shtml
The Department of Revenue publishes information about taxes in Oregon.

Education

hitectural detail above the entrance to Inlow Hall on the Eastern Oregon University campus in La Grande—Oregon State Archives Scenic Photograph uniDB0440

As Oregon's population grows and our economy evolves, the strength of our educational institutions is an important public policy issue. This section describes public education in Oregon and also lists independent colleges and universities.

Public Education in Oregon

In the 2010–11 school year, Oregon had 197 public school districts, which administered a total of 1,296 public schools. These schools enrolled a total of 561,328 K–12 students. 28,109 (full time equivalent) teachers worked in Oregon's public schools for a student to teacher ratio of 20.3 to 1 (2010 national average: 16 to 1). Student demographics show a minority enrollment of 33.7 percent (2010 national average: 47.6 percent).

Students who qualified for free and reduced-price lunch made up 50.7 percent of all students in 2010–2011 (2010–11 national average: 48 percent). Special education students made up 14.2 percent of the total in 2010–2011 (2010–11 national average: 13 percent). In 2009–10, there were 61,625 students in English language learning programs. This number is 11 percent of the total student population (2009–10 national average: 9.7 percent).

The state's budget for K–12 education in fiscal year 2009 was $6.1 billion, of which the federal government provided $671 million (revenues).

Source: National figures are from the U.S. Department of Education, National Center for Education Statistics.

Education in Oregon

Never has education been more important to the lives and fortunes of Oregonians and our communities. Yet, Oregon is falling behind. In most other states – and countries – the younger generation of adults is more educated than their elders. In Oregon, adults aged 25–34 are less educated than their parents' generation, with fewer earning certificates or degrees beyond high school. Almost a third of Oregon students are failing to graduate with a regular diploma after four or even five years in high school.

The state — through legislation passed in 2011 and 2012 — has embarked on the most significant education reform in 20 years, reshaping governance, priorities and budgeting all with a strong focus on investing in better educational outcomes for Oregon's students.

Ambitious Goals

The 2011 Oregon Legislature passed Senate Bill 253, which established the most aggressive high school and college completion goals of any state in the country: By 2025, we must ensure that 40 percent of adult Oregonians have earned a bachelor's degree or higher, that 40 percent have earned an associate's degree or post-secondary credential, and that the remaining 20 percent or less have earned a high school diploma or its equivalent. Those targets form Oregon's "40/40/20" goal.

Key Strategies

Oregon's education reform plan is founded on three key strategies:

1. Creating a coordinated public education system, from preschool through college and career readiness, to enable all Oregon students to learn at their best pace and achieve their full potential. At the state level, this will require better integration of education agencies' capacities and smarter use of resources to encourage and support successful teaching and learning across the education continuum.

2. Focusing state investment on achieving student outcomes. The Oregon Education Investment Board has defined core educational outcomes that matter for students, their families, and the state at key stages in a student's learning. For example: Are entering kindergarten students ready for school? Are they reading at grade level by third grade? How many students graduate from high school, and how many earn college credits before graduation? Do they go on to college and further training? How many earn their college degrees?

Under 2012's Senate Bill 1581, the Oregon Education Investment Board is entering into achievement compacts with every K–12 school

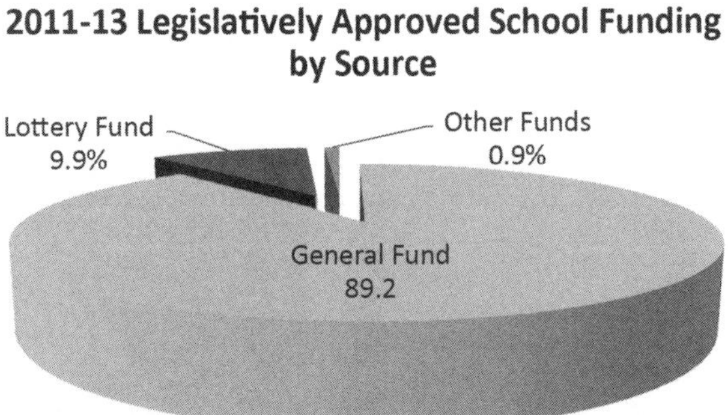

Source: Legislative Fiscal Office

district, education service district, community college, the university system and public universities, and Oregon Health Sciences University. These two-way partnership agreements challenge educators across Oregon to set targets on key student outcomes and encourage broad collaboration to adopt transformational practices, policies and budgets (at the state and local level) to help Oregon students achieve the educational outcomes.

3. Build statewide support systems. The state will continue to set standards, provide guidance, and conduct assessments, coordinated along the education pathway. To enhance these efforts, 2011's Senate Bill 909 commits the state to build a longitudinal data system—tracking important data on student progress and returns on statewide investments from preschool through college and into careers. These data will help guide investment decisions and spotlight programs that are working or failing. Beyond data systems, the state will expand on the successful local model of professional learning communities to increase support for collaboration among schools and teachers.

Education Funding

Oregon has struggled with funding public education since Measure 5 passed in 1990. The property tax limitations enacted under Measure 5 and the later Measures 47 and 50 shifted the primary burden of paying for K–12 education from local property tax payers to the state General Fund. That shift led the Legislature in 1991 to establish a school funding equalization formula. That funding formula, largely based on student enrollment numbers and student demographics, determines how much money each school district will get from the State School Fund to fill the gap between the district's local revenue and its equalization target under the formula.

In the 1990s, as Measure 5 phased in, more of the state General Fund went to pay for education. However, in recent years, funding for education – K–12 and post-secondary – has been squeezed, both as the result of general budget cuts during the recession and also as the costs of corrections and social services grow.

In 1999, legislation passed allowing local school districts' voters to approve additional "local option" property tax levies for up to five years of operational funding to supplement the State School Fund appropriation. Starting in 2000, voters have passed these temporary school funding levies in 26 different school districts – ranging in size from tiny Camas Valley, with 124 students, to Portland Public Schools, the state's largest at 47,000 students. This has helped those districts maintain their programs, but also has limited the ability of the state to equalize funding among districts.

Overall, under the state's current revenue system and the economic recession, education at all levels is widely recognized to be underfunded:

• Early learning: The state has expanded the Oregon pre-kindergarten program to serve thousands more children, complementing the federal Head Start program. Even so, those programs reach only a small share of the young children who need support to be ready for kindergarten.

• K–12 schools: State support for K–12 schools has fluctuated over the years, but in general has not kept pace with inflation. As school districts face increased costs – particularly for their employees' health care and retirement – and real reductions in actual dollars available, most Oregon districts have resorted to cost-cutting measures. Those have included strategies such as increasing class sizes, cutting administrative and teaching staff, pay freezes, consolidating small schools and cutting days from the school calendar.

• Post-secondary: Oregon's community colleges and public universities have faced dwindling state funding. While they have cut costs, limited employee compensation, and served record numbers of students in recent years, students have taken on more and more of the share of college costs through increased tuition as a result of the state's funding challenges. For example, in 1989–90,

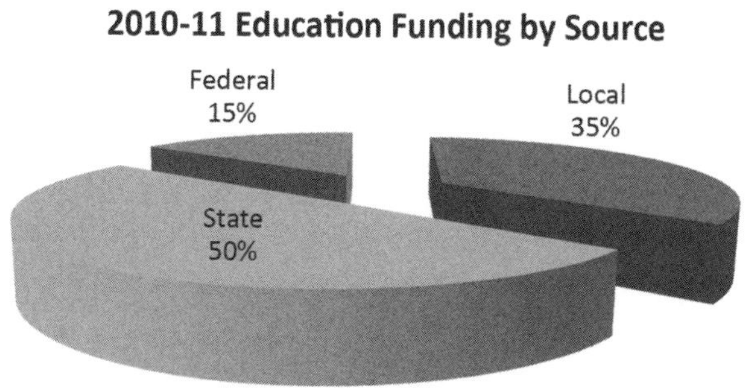

Source: Oregon Department of Education

student tuition and fees covered 29 percent of the costs of instruction in Oregon's public universities, and the state paid 62 percent of the costs, with the remaining from other funds. Twenty years later, in 2009–10, those numbers had essentially reversed, with tuition and fees paying close to 63 percent of the costs and state support covering less than a third (29 percent).

Early Childhood Education

2011 Senate Bill 909 created the Early Learning Council, appointed by the Governor, to coordinate, streamline and improve early childhood services. It replaces more than two dozen programs in six different state agencies providing early childhood services.

In 2012, the Legislature passed House Bill 4165, to:

• Streamline administration, policy, and planning of the state's early childhood services;

• Promote collaboration, competition, and local creativity based on meaningful outcomes for children;

• Preserve Head Start as well as early intervention/early childhood education for special needs students;

• Improve screening and assessment so that children receive support in order to thrive in kindergarten; and

• Provide incentives for child care quality and a rating system to give parents useful information when choosing care.

A new statewide kindergarten readiness assessment will help answer critical questions: When Oregon children enter kindergarten, are they ready to learn? How can the state direct its investment in early childhood services – whether prekindergarten, health care, child care or early intervention – to help more at-risk children start school with the skills and support they need to succeed? The Oregon Early Learning Council will select one assessment to test in up to 15 pilot schools across Oregon in the fall of 2012. In 2013, every kindergarten classroom will use the assessment.

The federal government has recognized Oregon's work in early learning, inviting Oregon to join four other states in applying for a second round of its Race to the Top Early Learning Challenge Grant, to be awarded in the fall of 2012.

K–12 Schools

At the state level, the State Board of Education sets policy for K–12 schools. The Department of Education implements educational policies and helps districts comply with the appropriate state and federal regulations.

Significant reforms underway include:

Rigorous state standards. The State Board of Education in 2010 adopted the Common Core State Standards — rigorous, national learning expectations aligned with international standards. These common standards will prepare Oregon students to compete, not just here, but nationally and internationally as well. Oregon is one of more than 45 states to adopt these standards and will phase them into classroom instruction over several years. Oregon is in the forefront in the development of national assessments designed to test students on these new standards.

Higher expectations for achievement. The State Board of Education has adopted more

Average Oregon SAT Results Compared Nationally

Critical Reading	Oregon	National
2011	520	497
2010	523	501
2009	523	501
2008	523	502
2007	522	502
2006	523	503
2005	526	508
2004	527	508
2003	526	507
2002	524	504
2000	527	505
1998	528	505
1996	523	505

Writing	Oregon	National
2011	499	489
2010	499	492
2009	499	493
2008	502	494
2007	502	494
2006	503	497

Mathematics	Oregon	National
2011	521	514
2010	524	516
2009	525	515
2008	527	515
2007	529	515
2006	529	518
2005	528	520
2004	528	518
2003	527	519
2002	528	516
2000	527	514
1998	528	512
1996	521	508

18,461 graduating seniors (53%) took the Scholastic Achievement Test (SAT) in Oregon in 2011.

Source: Oregon Department of Education

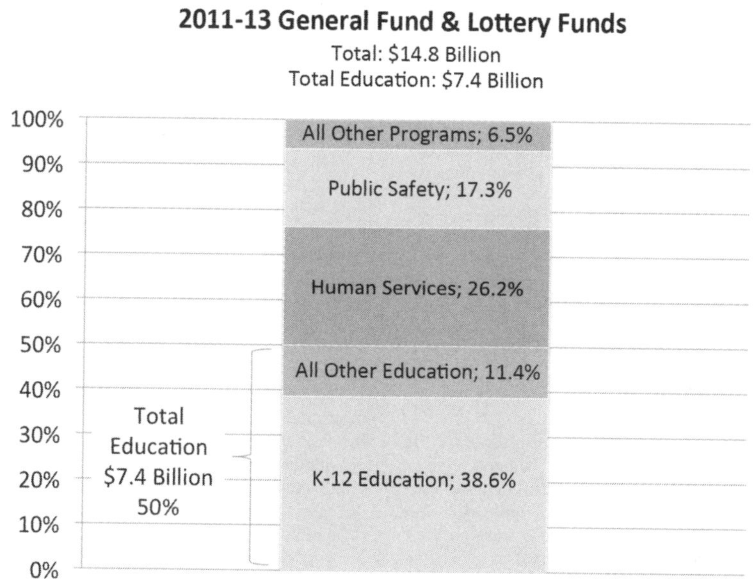

Source: Legislative Fiscal Office

rigorous math achievement standards (in effect in 2010–11), and reading and science achievement standards (in effect 2011–12). These higher state achievement standards will better prepare students to meet Oregon's graduation requirements and will help pave the way for the higher expectations of the Common Core.

New diploma requirements. Oregon schools continue to work toward full implementation of the Oregon Diploma and the Essential Skills requirements that will ensure all graduates leave high school college- and work-ready. The graduates of 2012 were the first required to demonstrate proficiency in reading. The Oregon Department of Education helps students and schools prepare, by providing tools including the Oregon K–12 Literacy Framework and the Assessment of Essential Skills Tool Kit. Graduates in future years will be asked to demonstrate additional skills: writing in 2013 and math in 2014.

Full-day kindergarten. Oregon's state funding formula only pays for a half-day of kindergarten for students. But many districts have decided to offer full-day kindergarten, particularly for disadvantaged students. They generally pay for these programs by shifting funding from other grades, using federal Title I anti-poverty dollars, or by charging parents a fee to cover half the day. 2011 Senate Bill 248 determined that the state should cover the costs of full-day kindergarten starting in 2015. That will bring greater opportunity for Oregon's youngest students and put an end to the inequity the patchwork of funding solutions has brought.

Federal flexibility in accountability system. Oregon plans to apply for a waiver from certain provisions of the Elementary and Secondary Education (ESEA)/No Child Left Behind (NCLB) Act. The ESEA Flexibility Waiver offers an opportunity to obtain relief from the rigid Adequate Yearly Progress targets and one-size-fits-all sanctions that NCLB mandated. Oregon's waiver proposal includes measures that are consistent with (though more detailed than) the K–12 achievement compacts, and a state system of support and interventions aimed at improving student achievement.

The waiver also provides an opportunity to align the state's system of accountability. The 2011 Legislature appointed a Joint Task Force on Accountable Schools (House Bill 2289) to examine Oregon's school and district report cards, the state's primary tool to communicate student achievement and other information to students, families, and the broader school community. The task force and governor's office are coordinating efforts to ensure that the achievement compacts, accountability system, and state report cards are consistent, aligned, and mutually reinforcing.

The ODE Web site is www.ode.state.or.us. Much information about public education in Oregon may be found there.

The National Center for Educational Statistics (NCES), www.nces.ed.gov, a program of the U.S. Department of

Education, collects data from states and provides analytical tools for users. NCES allows users to view data in graphic representation as well and provides the means to assess how well other states are doing in the same areas.

SchoolMatters, www.schoolmatters.com, a service of Standard and Poor's, relies on much the same data collected by NCES and again provides the ability to compare districts within a state or different states. Both sites should be used with caution, since data is notoriously difficult to compare accurately. However, they do provide the means to get a sense of how Oregon school children and Oregon school districts are performing and how Oregon compares with other states.

Oregon School for the Deaf

Patti Togioka, Director
Address: 999 Locust St. NE, Salem 97301-5254
Phone: 503-378-3825 (Voice/TDD)
Fax: 503-373-7879
Web: http://www.osd.oregonk-12.net/

Established in 1870, the Oregon School for the Deaf (OSD) enrolls students who, because of hearing impairment, need a more comprehensive level of service and/or a more communication-rich environment than can be provided through their regular public school. OSD is funded by legislative appropriation and is operated by the Oregon Department of Education. In 2012–13, 109 students were enrolled at the school at no cost to their families.

Teachers certified to teach the deaf use American Sign Language (ASL) or Total Communication in all instructional settings which uses a variety of modes depending on individual student needs. Modes may include: American Sign Language, English-like signing, spoken English or print. The academic curriculum includes regular state of Oregon diploma credits as well as specialized classes for those students who may benefit from them. It is enhanced by courses in computer-aided design, robotics, culinary arts, graphic arts, deaf culture and ASL, speech, art, and drama. OSD's high school is Oregon's only residential, comprehensive, secondary program designed exclusively for deaf students. OSD is fully accredited by the Northwest Association of Accredited Schools and Programs and the Conference of Educational Administrators of Schools and Programs for the Deaf.

State Board of Education

The State Board of Education, with seven members appointed to four-year terms by the governor, is charged with establishing policy for the administration and operation of the public elementary and secondary schools and the public community colleges in Oregon.

Board members are Artemio Paz, Jr., Chair (term ends 2013); Samuel Henry, Vice Chair (2016); Angela Bowen (2016); Gerald Hamilton (2016); Serilda Summers-McGee (2015) and Duncan Wyse (2012). One position is vacant.

The State Board of Education adopted new graduation requirements that will require students to take more rigorous levels of mathematics and science. Additionally, all students must demonstrate proficiency in the Essential Skills beginning with reading in 2012, writing in 2013 and math in 2014. Students are given multiple opportunities and assessment options to demonstrate Essential Skills proficiency. Assessment options include:

1) achieving a passing score on the Oregon Assessment of Knowledge and Skills (OAKS) state tests, or

2) passing a local assessments such as work samples, using state approved scoring guides, or

3) achieving a passing score on approved national assessments, such as ACT, SAT, PSAT or WorkKeys.

The state will monitor the numbers of students meeting the Essential Skills requirements through local assessments. Accommodations will be provided to students with disabilities.

Students may also earn credit toward graduation on the basis of demonstrated proficiency rather than on attendance only. Proficiency-based credit must be aligned to rigorous standards for student achievement.

Community Colleges

Source: Camille Preus, Commissioner
Address: Department of Community Colleges and Workforce Development, 255 Capitol St. NE, Salem 97310-0001
Phone: 503-378-8648
Fax: 503-378-3365
E-mail: ccwd.info@odccwd.state.or.us
Web: www.oregon.gov/ccwd/Pages/index.aspx

Oregon has 17 community colleges. Although community colleges receive state money, each college is governed by a local board. In 2011, full-time equivalent (FTE) community college enrollment was 124,888. Approximately 35.8% percent of 2010 Oregon high school graduates attended an Oregon community college the year following graduation. However, in the 2010–11 academic year, 61 percent of community college students are older than 24. This reflects the fact that many students are either seeking retraining for different jobs or delaying enrollment in postsecondary education. Average tuition and fees for 2010–11 was $3,720.

Oregon community colleges currently (2011–12) have the third highest tuition in the 15 Western states. Tuition and fees for 2012–13 at Oregon community colleges rose to $4,369 statewide, an increase of nearly 30 percent in five years. According to the National Center for Public Policy and Higher Education (June 2011), 68 percent of community college students report that they chose their college because of cost.

Another important factor impacting student enrollment and retention is financial aid. In

2011–12, there were 112,701 community college students eligible for the Oregon Opportunity Grant. However, only 13.4 percent actually received those grant funds.

Department of Community Colleges and Workforce Development

The Department of Community Colleges and Workforce Development (CCWD) coordinates Oregon's 17 community colleges. It has responsibility for monitoring the programs, services, and effectiveness of local community colleges and for reporting to the Legislative Assembly. The commissioner is appointed by the State Board of Education.

Direct state support to community colleges is funded in the CCWD budget, primarily through the Community College Support Fund (CCSF). The agency also coordinates and provides statewide administration of the federally funded Workforce Investment Act (WIA), Title IB Adult, Youth, Dislocated Worker programs, WIA Title II Adult Education and Family Literacy programs, Carl Perkins Career and Technical Education Programs, the Oregon Youth Conservation Corps (OYCC) and the General Education Development (GED) program. During the 2009–11 biennium, WIA served over 340,626 adult Oregonians.

The 2011–13 legislatively-adopted budget for CCWD was $568 million. The state provided $418 million from the General Fund and $14 million in other funds. Federal funds amounted to $136 million. In general, state money is distributed to community colleges on the basis of enrollment. The General Fund supports 31 percent of the college costs. The General Fund support is distributed to community colleges through a formula adopted by the State Board of Education. Another 24 percent of college operating revenue is provided through property tax collections. Tuition and fees, which are not included in the state agency budget, are projected to provide the remaining 45 percent of college operating revenues.

Blue Mountain Community College

Address: 2411 NW Carden Ave., PO Box 100, Pendleton 97801-1000
Phone: 541-276-1260
Web: www.bluecc.edu
2010–11 FTE enrollment: 2,987

Central Oregon Community College

Address: 2600 NW College Way, Bend 97701-5998
Phone: 541-383-7700
Web: www.cocc.edu
2010–11 FTE enrollment: 6,987

Chemeketa Community College

Address: 4000 Lancaster Dr. NE, PO Box 14007, Salem 97309-7070
Phone: 503-399-5000
Web: www.chemeketa.edu
2010–11 FTE enrollment: 14,311

Clackamas Community College

Address: 19600 S Molalla Ave., Oregon City 97045-7998
Phone: 503-657-6958
Web: www.clackamas.edu
2010–11 FTE enrollment: 8,942

Clatsop Community College

Address: 1653 Jerome Ave., Astoria 97103-3698
Phone: 503-325-0910
Web: www.clatsopcc.edu
2010–11 FTE enrollment: 1,550

Columbia Gorge Community College

Address: 400 E Scenic Dr., The Dalles 97058-3434
Phone: 541-506-6000
Web: www.cgcc.cc.or.us
2010–11 FTE enrollment: 1,262

Klamath Community College

Address: 7390 S Sixth St., Klamath Falls 97603-7121
Phone: 541-882-3521
Web: https://www.klamathcc.edu
2010–11 FTE enrollment: 2,005

Lane Community College

Address: 4000 E 30th Ave., Eugene 97405-0640
Phone: 541-463-3000
Web: www.lanecc.edu
2010–11 FTE enrollment: 15,822

Linn-Benton Community College

Address: 6500 Pacific Blvd. SW, Albany 97321-3779
Phone: 541-917-4999
Web: www.linnbenton.edu
2010–11 FTE enrollment: 8,303

Mt. Hood Community College

Address: 26000 SE Stark St., Gresham 97030-3300
Phone: 503-491-6422
Web: www.mhcc.edu
2010–11 FTE enrollment: 10,716

Oregon Coast Community College

Address: 400 SE College Way, Newport 97366
Phone: 541-265-2283
Web: http://www.oregoncoastcc.org/
2010–11 FTE enrollment: 519

Portland Community College

Address: 12000 SW 49th Ave., PO Box 19000, Portland 97280-0990
Phone: 503-244-6111
Web: www.pcc.edu
2010–11 FTE enrollment: 32,768

Rogue Community College

Address: 3345 Redwood Hwy., Grants Pass 97527-9298
Phone: 541-956-7500
Web: www.roguecc.edu
2010–11 FTE enrollment 6,358

Southwestern Oregon Community College

Address: 1988 Newmark Ave., Coos Bay 97420-2971
Phone: 541-888-2525
Web: www.socc.edu
2010–11 FTE enrollment: 3,390

Tillamook Bay Community College

Address: 2510 First St., Tillamook 97141-2599
Phone: 503-842-8222
Web: www.tbcc.cc.or.us
2010–11 FTE enrollment: 519

Treasure Valley Community College

Address: 650 College Blvd., Ontario 97914-3498
Phone: 541-881-8822
Web: www.tvcc.cc.or.us
2010–11 FTE enrollment: 3,627

Umpqua Community College

Address: 1140 Umpqua College Rd., PO Box 967, Roseburg 97470
Phone: 541-440-4600
Web: www.umpqua.edu
2010–11 FTE enrollment: 4,925

Higher Education in Oregon

State Board of Higher Education

Address: PO Box 751, Portland 97207
Phone: 503-725-5717
Fax: 503-725-5709
E-mail: charles_triplett@ous.edu
Web: www.ous.edu/state_board

The Oregon State Board of Higher Education is the statutory governing board of the Oregon University System (OUS). It has 15 members appointed by the governor and confirmed by the Senate. Eleven lay members are appointed for four-year terms; two faculty members are appointed for two-year terms; and two students are appointed for two-year terms. The board has three standing committees: Finance and Administration; Academic Strategies; and Governance and Policy.

Members: Matthew W. Donegan, President, Portland, 2013 (term expires); Jill W. Eiland, Vice President, Portland, 2013; Dr. Lynda M. Ciuffetti, Corvallis, 2014; Brianna R. Coulombe, La Grande, 2013; Dr. Orcilia Z. Forbes, Portland, 2014; Allyn C. Ford, Roseburg, 2013; James L. Francesconi, Portland, 2016; Farbodd A. Ganjifard, Corvallis, 2013; Paul J. Kelly, Jr., Portland, 2015; Dr. James Middleton, Bend, 2016; Dr. Emily J. Plec, Monmouth, 2013; Kirk E. Schueler, Bend, 2013; David V. Yaden, Portland, 2016.

Oregon University System

George P. Pernsteiner, Chancellor
Address: PO Box 751, Portland 97207-0751
Phone: 503-725-5700
Fax: 503-725-5709
Web: www.ous.edu

The Oregon University System (OUS) is headed by the chancellor and consists of staff who provide services to Oregon's public universities. The State Board of Higher Education entrusts the Chancellor's Office to carry out all legislatively identified and required duties and Board policies, and to ensure effective oversight of OUS institutions on behalf of the state and the public. The system office ensures that the higher education needs of the entire state are being met; the programs and services are developed and implemented efficiently; and optimal collaboration occurs among universities, education entities, and other public and private organizations for the benefit of Oregon and its citizens.

The Board sets undergraduate admission requirements for OUS institutions, which include high school graduation; some specific subject requirements — three to four years of math, English, science and social studies, plus two years of the same foreign language — minimum high school GPA; and SAT or ACT test results. For more specific information see the OUS website: http://ous.edu/stucoun/prospstu/fadmissions.

Oregon has seven public universities, including one branch campus: University of Oregon, Eugene; Oregon State University, Corvallis and Bend; Portland State University, Portland; Eastern Oregon University, La Grande; Southern Oregon University, Ashland; Western Oregon University, Monmouth; and Oregon Institute of Technology, Klamath Falls.

Oregon faces formidable challenges in the coming decades: the globalization of the knowledge economy, the need for a bachelor's degree to compete for family wage jobs, and a dramatically changing demographic landscape, which combine

Enrollment at Oregon University System Institutions

Fall 2011 Student Enrollment

Eastern Oregon University	4,298
Oregon Institute of Technology	3,911
Oregon State University (includes Cascades Campus)	25,741
Portland State University	28,958
Southern Oregon University	6,744
University of Oregon	24,447
Western Oregon University	6,217
Total Oregon University System enrollment, Fall 2011	**100,316**

to create a set of new and compelling demands. The OUS's long-range plan is framed around four broad goals:

1. Create in Oregon an educated citizenry to support responsible roles in a democratic society and provide a globally competitive workforce to drive the state's economy, while ensuring access for all qualified Oregonians to a quality postsecondary education;
2. Ensure high-quality student learning leading to subsequent student success;
3. Create original knowledge and advance innovation; and
4. Contribute positively to the economic, civic, and cultural life of communities in all regions of Oregon.

State support for higher education was reduced greatly after the passage of Measure 5 in 1990. Oregon met the requirements to support K–12 education by limiting funding for many programs, but OUS was particularly affected. State support for the Education and General Services program not only failed to grow enough to cover inflation, but it actually declined in nominal dollars. General Fund support of Education and General Services for the 2011–13 biennium was less than it was a decade ago in 2001–03, while enrollment grew by over 25,000 students during this period. As state support for higher education has declined, more of college costs have shifted from the state to students and their families in the form of tuition increases. The Board of Higher Education works with its education and state partners to reinvest in Oregon's university system to keep tuition increases as low as possible, provide student support services, retain quality faculty and invest in research that positively affects Oregon's economy.

2012–13 Annual Tuition and Fee Rates
Resident Undergraduate — 15 Credit Hours

University:	EOU	OIT	OSU	PSU	SOU	UO	WOU
Total Tuition and Fees[1]:	$7,238	$8,308	$8,139	$7,653	$7,521	$9,310	$7,989[2]
Full-time Instructional Faculty:	113	134	833	711	209	856	204
All Faculty[3]:	134	157	2,181	1,750	353	1,855	471
Student to Full-time Faculty Ratio[4]:	26.3:1	20.3:1	26.2:1	29.6:1	23.8:1	26.6:1	26.2:1

[1]Excludes programmatic resource fees

[2]WOU's Tuition Promise rate is $8,529. This program guarantees the tuition rate will not increase for four years.

[3]All faculty, both full- and part-time, including instructional, research, and public service categories

[4]Student:Faculty ratio is the ratio of fall FTE (calculated as full-time plus one-third part-time students) to full-time instructional faculty.

Source: Oregon University System

Eastern Oregon University

Dr. Robert Davies, President
Address: One University Blvd., La Grande 97850-2899
Phone: 541-962-3512; Toll-free: 1-800-452-8639
Fax: 541-962-3113
Web: www.eou.edu

Oregon Institute of Technology

Dr. Christopher Maples, President
Address: 3201 Campus Dr., Klamath Falls 97601-8801
Phone: 541-885-1000
Fax: 541-885-1101
Web: www.oit.edu

Oregon State University

Dr. Edward J. Ray, President
Address: 634 Kerr Administration Building, Corvallis 97331-2128
Phone: 541-737-4133
Fax: 541-737-3033
Web: http://oregonstate.edu

Portland State University

Dr. Wim Wiewel, President
Address: PO Box 751, Portland 97207-0751
Phone: 503-725-4419; Toll-free: 1-800-547-8887
Fax: 503-725-4499
Web: www.pdx.edu

Southern Oregon University

Dr. Mary Cullinan, President
Address: 1250 Siskiyou Blvd., Ashland 97520
Phone: 541-552-7672
Fax: 541-552-6337
Web: www.sou.edu

University of Oregon

Dr. Michael R. Gottfredson, President
Address: 110 Johnson Hall, Eugene 97403
Phone: 541-346-3036
Fax: 541-346-3017
Web: www.uoregon.edu

Western Oregon University

Mark D. Weiss, President
Address: 345 N Monmouth Ave., Monmouth 97361
Phone: 503-838-8888
Fax: 503-838-8474
Web: www.wou.edu

Oregon Health and Science University

Joseph E. Robertson, MD, MBA, President
Address: 3181 SW Sam Jackson Park Rd., Portland 97239-3098
Phone: 503-494-8311
Fax: 503-494-8935
Web: www.ohsu.edu/xd/

The Oregon Health and Science University (OHSU) occupies a unique status in Oregon higher education. OHSU has been organized as a public corporation since 1995. It is not a part of OUS. OHSU is governed by a Board of Directors that is appointed by the governor and confirmed by the Senate. The public policy of the university is delineated in statute. OHSU includes Oregon's only academic health center and has schools of medicine, dentistry, nursing, and science and engineering. The state continues to support OHSU through grants, primarily for its educational activities. These grants totaled $65,534,636 in the 2011–13 biennium.

Western Interstate Commission for Higher Education

Address: PO Box 3175, Eugene 97403
Phone: 541-346-5729
Web: www.wiche.edu

The Western Interstate Commission for Higher Education (WICHE) is a regional organization created by the Western Regional Education Compact, adopted in the 1950s by 15 western states. WICHE was created to facilitate resource sharing among the higher education systems of the West. It has implemented a number of regional activities to accomplish its objectives. Fifteen states are members of WICHE, which is governed by three gubernatorially-appointed commissioners from each state. Under terms of the Compact, each state commits to support WICHE's basic operations through annual dues established by the full commission. Oregon's three commissioners are Ryan Deckart, Portland; Cam Preus, Salem; and Tim Nesbitt, Portland.

Independent Colleges and Universities

Oregon Alliance of Independent Colleges and Universities

Source: Larry D. Large, President
Address: 16101 SW 72nd Ave., Suite 10, Portland 97224
Phone: 503-639-4541
Fax: 503-639-4851
Web: www.oaicu.org

The mission of the Oregon Alliance of Independent College and Universities is to represent and serve its member institutions, all of which are regionally accredited, not-for-profit, independent colleges and universities in Oregon. This is accomplished through public advocacy, institutional cooperation, and strategic collaboration with the public sector, including business, philanthropy, and government. The organization seeks to strengthen Oregon's intellectual, creative, and economic resources.

As representatives of the independent, not-for-profit higher education sector, the Alliance invests in diverse students, committed educators, and relevant learning by partnering with leaders from business and industry, philanthropy, and public sector agencies and institutions, getting an excellent return on Oregon's behalf—a highly educated workforce, a significant contribution to Oregon's economy, and Oregon's next generation of active leaders and contributing citizens.

Following is a list of Oregon's 20 independent, nonprofit higher education institutions accredited by Northwest Commission on Colleges and Universities.

Concordia University

Dr. Charles Schlimpert, President
Address: 2811 NE Holman St., Portland 97211-6099
Phone: 503-288-9371
Web: www.cu-portland.edu
Fall 2011 enrollment: 2,509

Corban University

Reno Hoff, President
Address: 5000 Deer Park Dr. SE, Salem 97317-9392
Phone: 503-581-8600
Web: www.corban.edu
Fall 2011 enrollment: 1,251

George Fox University

Robin Baker, President
Address: 414 N Meridian St., Newberg 97132
Phone: 503-538-8383
Web: www.georgefox.edu
Fall 2011 enrollment: 3,502

Lewis & Clark College

Barry Glassner, President
Address: 0615 SW Palatine Hill Rd., Portland 97219-7899
Phone: 503-768-7000
Web: www.lclark.edu/
Fall 2011 enrollment: 3,713

Linfield College

Thomas L. Hellie, President
Address: 900 SE Baker St., McMinnville 97128-6894
Phone: 503-883-2200
Web: www.linfield.edu
Fall 2011 enrollment: 2,664

Marylhurst University

Judith A. Johansen, President
Address: 17600 Pacific Hwy., Hwy. 43, Marylhurst 97036-0261
Phone: 503-636-8141
Web: www.marylhurst.edu
Fall 2011 enrollment: 1,796

Mount Angel Seminary

Rev. Joseph Betschart, President
Address: 1 Abbey Dr., Saint Benedict 97373-0505
Phone: 503-845-3951
Web: www.mountangelabbey.org
Fall 2011 enrollment: 183

Multnomah University

Daniel R. Lockwood, President
Address: 8435 NE Glisan St., Portland 97220
Phone: 503-255-0332
Web: www.multnomah.edu
Fall 2011 enrollment: 932

National College of Natural Medicine

David J. Schleich, PhD, President
Address: 049 SW Porter St., Portland 97201-4848
Phone: 503-552-1555
Web: www.ncnm.edu
Fall 2011 enrollment: 551

Northwest Christian University

Joseph Womack, President
Address: 828 E 11th Ave., Eugene 97401-3745
Phone: 541-343-1641
Web: www.nwcu.edu/
Fall 2011 enrollment: 610

Oregon College of Art and Craft

Denise Mullen, President
Address: 8245 SW Barnes Rd., Portland 97225
Phone: 503-297-5544
Web: www.ocac.edu
Fall 2011 enrollment: 151

Oregon College of Oriental Medicine

Michael Gaeta, President
Address: 75 NW Couch St., Portland 97209
Phone: 503-253-3443
Web: http://ocom.edu
Fall 2011 enrollment: 315

Pacific Northwest College of Art

Thomas Manley, President
Address: 1241 NW Johnson St., Portland 97209-3023
Phone: 503-226-4391
Web: www.pnca.edu
Fall 2011 enrollment: 596

Pacific University

Dr. Lesley Hallick, President
Address: 2043 College Way, Forest Grove 97116
Phone: 877-722-8648
Web: www.pacificu.edu
Fall 2011 enrollment: 3,293

Reed College

John Kroger, President
Address: 3203 SE Woodstock Blvd., Portland 97202-8199
Phone: 503-771-1112
Web: www.reed.edu
Fall 2011 enrollment: 1,474

University of Portland

Rev. E. William Beauchamp, President
Address: 5000 N Willamette Blvd., Portland 97203-5798
Phone: 503-943-7911
Web: www.up.edu
Fall 2011 enrollment: 3,973

University of Western States

Joseph Brimhall, D.C., President
Address: 2900 NE 132nd Ave., Portland 97230-3099
Phone: 503-256-3180
Web: www.uws.edu
Fall 2011 enrollment: 531

Warner Pacific College

Andrea Cook, PhD., President
Address: 2219 SE 68th Ave., Portland 97215-4026
Phone: 503-517-1000
Web: www.warnerpacific.edu
Fall 2011 enrollment: 1,679

Western Seminary

Randal Roberts, President
Address: 5511 SE Hawthorne Blvd., Portland 97215-3367
Phone: 503-517-1800
Web: www.westernseminary.edu
Fall 2011 enrollment: 684

Willamette University

Stephen Thorsett, President
Address: 900 State St., Salem 97301
Phone: 503-370-6300
Web: www.willamette.edu
Fall 2011 enrollment: 2,968

Arts, History and Sciences

Weddle Covered Bridge in Sweet Home—Oregon State Archives Scenic Photograph linnDA0010a

Through the organizations described in this section, we are fortunate to have many opportunities to gain greater understanding and appreciation for the arts and culture, history and heritage, earth sciences and technology of Oregon.

Arts and Culture in Oregon

Source: Oregon Arts Commission
Address: 775 Summer St. NE, Suite 200, Salem 97301-1280
Phone: 503-986-0082; TDD: 503-986-0123
Fax: 503-986-0260
Web: www.oregonartscommission.org
Contact: Christine D'Arcy, Executive Director

Oregon citizens greatly value culture, education and the arts. Throughout the state, individuals, organizations and local communities collaborate to promote artistic and cultural activities and venues for residents and visitors.

The Oregon Arts Commission works to promote the arts by providing grant support, technical assistance and cultural planning. The commission works to see that access to the arts exists all around the state.

Oregon Cultural Trust

Address: 775 Summer St. NE, Suite 200, Salem 97301-1280
Phone: 503-986-0088; TDD: 503-986-0123
Fax: 503-986-0260
Web: www.culturaltrust.org
Contact: Christine D'Arcy, Executive Director

The Oregon Cultural Trust is a statewide cultural plan to raise significant new funds to invest in Oregon's arts, humanities and heritage.

The Trust works in partnership with the Oregon Arts Commission, the Oregon Heritage Commission, the Oregon Historical Society, Oregon Humanities, and the State Historic Preservation Office. It is governed by a 13-member board of directors appointed by the governor, the president of the Senate and the speaker of the House of Representatives.

Oregon Humanities

Cara Ungar, Executive Director
Address: 813 SW Alder, Suite 702, Portland 97205
Phone: 503-241-0543; Toll-free: 1-800-735-0543
Fax: 503-241-0024
Web: http://oregonhumanities.org

Oregon Humanities is an independent, nonprofit affiliate of the National Endowment for the Humanities. Oregon Humanities, formerly the Oregon Council for the Humanities, was established in 1971 and is one of five statewide partners of the Oregon Cultural Trust. Programs include the *Oregon Humanities* magazine, Conversation Project, Humanity in Perspective, Idea Lab, Think & Drink and grants programs.

Oregon Humanities connects Oregonians to ideas that change lives and transform communities. Oregon Humanities' programs and publications provide a forum for individuals and communities to raise questions, challenge assumptions, listen to others, and think critically about the issues that directly affect their lives and those of the people around them.

The impact of this work is profound — participants listen, question, rethink and consider more deeply and, as a result, act from a place of knowledge, compassion, connectedness and personal responsibility.

Oregon's Major Arts Organizations

Oregon Shakespeare Festival

Bill Rauch, Artistic Director; Paul Nicholson, Executive Director
Address: 15 S Pioneer St., PO Box 158, Ashland 97520
Phone: 1-800-219-8161
Fax: 541-482-0446
Web: www.osfashland.org

The Oregon Shakespeare Festival is one of the largest non-profit theaters in the country. Established in 1935, it has an annual attendance of almost 400,000. It annually presents more than 760 performances of eleven plays in repertory from mid-February through October on its three stages. The festival also offers backstage tours, classes, lectures, concerts and play readings.

Oregon Symphony Association

Mary Christ and Janet Plummer, Interim Co-Presidents
Address: 923 SW Washington St., Portland 97205
Phone: 503-228-1353
Fax: 503-416-6302
Web: www.orsymphony.org

Led by Music Director Carlos Kalmar, the Oregon Symphony is one of the largest performing arts organizations in the Pacific Northwest. Its many performances each year include the classical concert series, pops concerts, youth and educational concerts, family concerts and special performances at its home in Portland, as well as in Salem and elsewhere in Oregon.

Portland Art Museum

Brian Ferriso, Executive Director
Address: 1219 SW Park Ave., Portland 97205
Phone: 503-226-2811
Fax: 503-226-4842
Web: www.portlandartmuseum.org

The Portland Art Museum, founded in 1892, is the region's oldest and largest visual and media arts center and one of the state's greatest cultural assets. The museum is a premier venue for education in the visual arts and for the collection and preservation of art for the enrichment of present and future generations.

The internationally renowned museum presents special exhibitions drawn from the world's finest collections. The permanent collection showcases unique American tribal objects, and Japanese, Chinese, and Korean objects up to 3000 years old. European, modern and contemporary art, Northwest art, photography and graphic arts round out the collection. Located in downtown Portland's cultural district, the Museum offers lectures, tours and family activities. Admission is free to children ages 17 and under.

Portland Opera

Christopher Mattaliano, General Director
Address: 211 SE Caruthers St., Portland 97214
Phone: 503-241-1407 ext. 4
Fax: 503-241-4212
Web: www.portlandopera.org

Internationally renowned singers perform with the Portland Opera Orchestra and Chorus in a four-production season of exciting opera at the Keller Auditorium in Portland. Although sung in their original languages, the operas are easily understood by an avid and growing audience, thanks to the opera's projected English translations. The opera's efforts are not limited to the Keller Auditorium stage. The Portland Opera Studio Artist program, a training ground for up and coming young singers from around the nation, is featured in its own opera production in the Newmark Theater. In addition, the opera's Education and Outreach programs continue year-round, including fully staged traveling opera productions that tour the state, in-school programs, student dress rehearsals, pre- and post-performance lectures, public presentations, radio shows, as well as costume shop and backstage tours.

In addition to its opera productions, the company also presents the Broadway Across America Portland series which delights regional audiences with nationally touring Broadway productions.

Regional Arts Councils

The Arts Center

David Huff, Executive Director
Address: 700 SW Madison Ave., Corvallis 97333
Phone: 541-754-1551
Fax: 541-754-1552
Web: http://theartscenter.net
Serving Benton and Linn Counties

Arts Central

Cate O'Hagan, Executive Director
Address: 15 SW Colorado Ave., Bldg. II, Ste. 100, Bend 97702
Phone: 541-749-2291
Web: www.artscentraloregon.org
Serving Crook, Deschutes and Jefferson Counties

Arts Council of Southern Oregon

Arlis Dincan, Board President
Address: 206 N 5th St., Jacksonville 97530
Phone: 541-779-2820
E-mail: office@artscouncilso.org
Web: www.artscouncilso.org
Serving Jackson and Josephine Counties

ArtsEast

Deena Heath, Executive Director
Address: PO Box 541, La Grande 97850
Phone: 541-962-3624
Web: http://artseast.org
Serving Baker, Gilliam, Grant, Harney, Malheur, Morrow, Umatilla, Union, Wallowa and Wheeler Counties

Columbia Center for the Arts

Kyle DeVaul, Executive Director
Address: 215 Cascade Ave., PO Box 1543, Hood River 97031
Phone/Fax: 541-387-8877
Web: www.columbiaarts.org
Serving Hood River, Sherman and Wasco Counties

Lane Arts Council

Liora Sponko, Executive Director
Address: 1590 Willamette St., Suite 200, Eugene 97401
Phone: 541-485-2278
Web: www.lanearts.org
Serving Lane County

Oregon Coast Council for the Arts

Catherine Rickbone, Executive Director
Address: PO Box 1315, Newport 97365-0101
Phone: 541-265-2787; Toll-free: 1-888-701-7123
Fax: 541-265-9464
Web: www.coastarts.org
Serving Clatsop, Coos, Curry, Lincoln and Tillamook Counties

Regional Arts and Culture Council

Eloise Damrosch, Executive Director
Address: 411 NW Park Ave., Suite 101, Portland 97209-3318
Phone: 503-823-5111; TDD: 503-823-6868
Fax: 503-823-5432
Web: www.racc.org
Serving Clackamas, Multnomah and Washington Counties

Umpqua Valley Arts Association

Kathy Henderson, Executive Director
Address: 1624 W Harvard Ave., Roseburg 97470
Phone: 541-672-2532
Fax: 541-672-7696
Web: http://uvarts.com
Serving Douglas County

Local and Regional Arts Agencies in Oregon

Astoria

Astor Street Opry Company
Address: 129 W Bond St., PO Box 743, Astoria 97103
Phone: 503-325-6104
Web: www.shanghaiedinastoria.com

Baker City

Crossroads Carnegie Art Center
Address: 2020 Auburn Ave., Baker City 97814
Phone/Fax: 541-523-5369
Web: www.crossroads-arts.org

Beaverton

Beaverton Arts Commission
Address: 4755 SW Griffith Dr., PO Box 4755, Beaverton 97076
Phone: 503-526-2288
Fax: 503-526-2479
Web: www.beavertonarts.org

Brookings

Manley Art Center
Address: 433 Oak St., Brookings 97415
Phone: 541-469-1807

Pelican Bay Arts Association
Address: 433 Oak St., PO Box 2568, Brookings 97415
Phone/Fax: 541-469-1807
E-mail: manlyart@charter.net

Cannon Beach

Cannon Beach Arts Association
Address: 1064 S Hemlock St., PO Box 684, Cannon Beach 97110
Phone: 503-436-0744
Web: www.cannonbeacharts.org

Condon

Greater Condon Arts Association
Address: 403 W Walnut St., PO Box 165, Condon 97823
Phone/Fax: 541-384-5114

Coos Bay

Coos Art Museum
Address: 235 Anderson Ave., Coos Bay 97420
Phone: 541-267-3901
Fax: 541-267-4877
Web: www.coosart.org

Coquille

Coquille Valley Art Association
Address: 10144 Hwy. 42, Coquille 97423
Phone: 541-396-3294

Coquille Performing Arts Council
Address: PO Box 53, Coquille 97423

Elgin

Elgin Opera House Theatre
Address: 104 N 8th St., Elgin 97827
Phone: 541-663-6324
Web: www.elginoperahouse.com

Florence

Florence Artists
Phone: 541-902-1489
Web: http://florenceartists.com

Forest Grove

Valley Art Association
Address: 2022 Main St., PO Box 333, Forest Grove 97116
Phone: 503-357-3703
Web: www.valleyart.org

Grants Pass

Grants Pass Museum of Art
Address: PO Box 966, Grants Pass 97528
Phone: 541-479-3290
Web: www.gpmuseum.com

Halfway

Cornucopia Arts Council
Address: PO Box 353, Halfway 97834
Phone: 541-742-7280

Hillsboro

Hillsboro Arts & Culture Council
Address: 527 E Main St., Hillsboro 97123
Phone: 503-615-3497
Web: www.ci.hillsboro.or.us/Arts/HACC/index.aspx

Hillsboro Community Arts
Address: PO Box 3303, Hillsboro 97123
Phone: 503-577-5459
Web: www.showtimeatshute.com

Hood River

Columbia Gorge Arts in Education
Address: 1009 Eugene St., Hood River 97031
Phone: 541-387-5031
Fax: 541-386-7198
Web: http://cgaie.org

Joseph

Wallowa Valley Arts Council
Address: PO Box 526, Joseph 97846

Keizer

Keizer Art Association
Address: 980 Chemawa Rd. NE, Keizer 97303
Phone: 503-390-3010
Web: www.keizerarts.com

Klamath Falls

Klamath Art Association
Address: 120 Riverside Dr., Klamath Falls 97601
Phone: 541-883-1833
Web: http://klamathartgallery.blogspot.com

Klamath Arts Council
Address: PO Box 1706, Klamath Falls 97601
Phone: 541-883-2009

Ross Ragland Theater
Address: 218 N 7th St., Klamath Falls 97601
Phone: 541-884-0651
Fax: 541-884-8574
Web: http://rrtheater.org

Lake Oswego

Arts Council of Lake Oswego
Address: 520 First St., Lake Oswego 97034
Phone: 503-675-3738
Fax: 503-534-5247
Web: www.artscouncillo.org

Lakewood Center for the Arts
Address: 368 S State St., Lake Oswego 97034
Phone: 503-635-3901
Fax: 503-635-2002
Web: www.lakewood-center.org

Lincoln City

Lincoln City Cultural Center
Address: PO Box 752, Lincoln City 97367
Gallery: 540 NE Hwy. 101
Phone: 541-994-9994
Web: www.lincolncity-culturalcenter.org

Madras

Jefferson County Arts Association
Address: PO Box 376, Madras 97741
Phone: 541-475-7701
E-mail: coraleepoppy@yahoo.com

McMinnville

Arts Alliance of Yamhill County
Address: PO Box 898, McMinnville 97128
Phone: 503-472-3784
Web: www.artsallianceyamhillco.org

Medford

Arts Council of Southern Oregon
Address: 33 N Central Ave., Suite 421, Medford 97501
Phone: 541-779-2820
Web: www.artscouncilso.org

Medford Parks and Recreation Department
Address: 701 N Columbus Ave., Medford 97501
Phone: 541-774-2400
Fax: 541-774-2560
Web: www.ci.medford.or.us/SectionIndex.asp

Rogue Gallery & Arts Center
Address: 40 S Bartlett St., Medford 97501
Phone: 541-772-8118
Fax: 541-772-0294
Web: www.roguegallery.org

Milwaukie

North Clackamas Art Guild
Address: PO Box 220004, Milwaukie 97269
Phone: 503-653-2142

Monmouth

Monmouth/Independence Community Arts Association
Address: PO Box 114, Monmouth 97361
Phone: 503-838-2779

Nehalem

The Art Ranch
Address: 39450 Northfork Rd., Nehalem 97131
Phone: 503-368-7160
Fax: 503-368-7656
E-mail: lortiz@nehalemtel.net

Newport

Yaquina Art Association and Gallery
Address: 789 NW Beach Dr., Newport 97365
Phone: 541-265-5133
Web: www.yaquinaart.org

Ontario

Four Rivers Cultural Center
Address: 676 SW 5th Ave., Ontario 97914
Phone: 541-889-8191
Fax: 541-889-7628
Web: www.4rcc.com/index.php/en/

Oregon City

Arts Action Alliance of Clackamas County
Address: PO Box 2181, Oregon City 97045
Phone: 503-655-0525
Web: www.clackamasartsalliance.org

Pendleton

Pendleton Center for the Arts
Address: 214 N Main St., Pendleton 97801
Phone: 541-278-9201
Web: www.pendletonarts.org

Salem

Salem Art Association
Address: 600 Mission St. SE, Salem 97302
Phone: 503-581-2228
Fax: 503-371-3342
Web: http://salemart.org

Silverton

Silverton Arts Association
Address: 303 Coolidge St., Silverton 97381
Phone/Fax: 503-873-2480
Web: www.silvertonarts.org

Springfield

Emerald Empire Art Association
Address: 500 Main St., Springfield 97477
Phone: 541-726-8595

Fax: 541-726-2954
Web: www.emeraldartcenter.org

Springfield Arts Commission
Address: 225 Fifth St., Springfield 97477
Phone: 541-726-2237
Fax: 541-726-3747
Web: www.springfieldartscommission.org

Tillamook

Tillamook County Art Association
Address: 1000 Main Ave. N, Suite 7, Tillamook 97141
Phone: 503-842-1244

Tualatin

Tualatin Arts Advisory Committee
Address: 18880 SW Martinazzi Ave., Tualatin 97062
Phone: 503-691-3060
Fax: 503-691-9786
Web: www.tualatinoregon.gov/

Welches

Wy'East Artisans Guild
Address: PO Box 682, Sandy 97055
E-mail: wyeast@gmx.com
Web: http://wyeastartisansguild.com

Wilsonville

Wilsonville Arts and Culture Council
Address: PO Box 861, Wilsonville 97070
Phone: 503-638-6933
Web: www.wilsonvillearts.org

Woodburn

Woodburn Art Center
Address: 2551 N Boones Ferry Rd., Woodburn 97071
Phone: 503-982-6450
Web: www.woodburnartcenter.com

Oregon History Organizations

Oregon's Major History and Heritage Organizations

Oregon State Archives

Mary Beth Herkert, State Archivist
Address: 800 Summer St. NE, Salem 97310
Phone: 503-373-0701
Fax: 503-378-4118
E-mail: archives.info@state.or.us
Web: http://arcweb.sos.state.or.us

The Archives Division, established in 1947, houses and provides public access to the permanently valuable records of Oregon government. Oldest documents at the archives include records of the provisional and territorial governments and the Oregon Constitution.

The division authorizes disposition of the public records of Oregon government, provides records management advice and assistance to state agencies and local governments, and operates the State Records Center which provides inexpensive storage for inactive state agency records. The division also files, codifies and publishes state agency administrative rules and publishes the *Oregon Blue Book*.

National Historic Oregon Trail Interpretive Center

Sarah LeCompte, Center Director
Address: 22267 Hwy 86, PO Box 987, Baker City 97814
Phone: 541-523-1843
Fax: 541-523-1834
Web: www.blm.gov/or/oregontrail

Operated by the U.S. Department of Interior's Bureau of Land Management (BLM), the National Historic Oregon Trail Interpretive Center is located at Flagstaff Hill on Highway 86, five miles east of Baker City. The 509-acre site features a 23,000 square-foot facility with permanent exhibits offering audio, video, dioramas and artifacts to recreate the experiences of Oregon Trail emigrants. The Interpretive Center also includes exhibits on American tribal culture, mining and history of the BLM. A 150-seat theater hosts an active schedule of lectures and performances.

From atop Flagstaff Hill, visitors see more than 13 miles of the Oregon Trail route. Visitors may also view close-up trail ruts at the base of Flagstaff Hill. During the summer, living history characters interpret pioneer life at a wagon encampment.

Please check the web site or call for admission prices and hours of operation.

Oregon Commission on Historic Cemeteries

Kuri Gill, Coordinator
Address: 725 Summer St. NE, Suite C, Salem 97301
Phone: 503-986-0685
Fax: 503-986-0793
E-mail: kuri.gill@state.or.us
Web: www.oregon.gov/OPRD/HCD/OCHC/

Established in 1999, the Oregon Commission on Historic Cemeteries (OCHC) consists of seven citizens with broad knowledge of the issues relating to preservation, restoration, upkeep and advocacy for historic burial sites and their importance in Oregon history. An historic cemetery in Oregon is one in which a burial occurred before February 14, 1909, or in which someone who died before that date is buried.

The OCHC coordinates the restoration, renovation and maintenance of historic cemeteries statewide.

The OCHC develops and maintains a listing of historic cemeteries and gravesites in Oregon; awards grants to protect and develop historic cemeteries; provides technical assistance on the care of grave markers, structures, railings and curbs, ironwork, fencing and plantings; and develops legislation that would benefit historic cemeteries.

Oregon Geographic Names Board

Sharon Nesbit, President
Address: 1200 SW Park Ave., Portland 97205
Phone: 503-306-5203
Fax: 503-221-2035
Web: www.ohs.org/research/oregon-geographic-names-board/

Founded in 1908, the board is an advisor to the United States Board on Geographic Names and is associated with the Oregon Historical Society which maintains the board's correspondence and records. It is composed of 25 appointed board members representing all geographic areas of the state and is served by advisors from government agencies and the private sector.

The board supervises the naming of all geographic features within the state to standardize geographic nomenclature, prevent confusion and duplication in naming geographic features, and correct previous naming errors. The board's recommendations are submitted to the U.S. board in Washington, D.C., for final action.

Oregon Heritage Commission

Kyle Jansson, Coordinator
Address: 725 Summer St. NE, Suite C, Salem 97301
Phone: 503-986-0673
Fax: 503-986-0794
Web: www.oregonheritage.org

Oregon's heritage is more than history, and it is more than historic artifacts or documents in a museum. It is brick on an historic downtown building, hand-hewn beams in a homestead barn, smoke rising from a powwow campfire and sounds from a community celebration. Heritage is stories about people and places and traditions handed down by elders.

The mission of the Oregon Heritage Commission is to secure, sustain and enhance Oregon's heritage by coordinating heritage initiatives by public and private organizations; advocating for all levels of support for heritage; educating the public about its extent and value and promoting and celebrating its diversity.

Established by the 1995 Legislature, the commission is composed of nine gubernatorial appointments, who represent the geographic and cultural diversity of the state, and nine ex officio members. The ex officio commissioners represent the Oregon Historical Society, the State Library, the State Archives, the State Historic Preservation Office, the State Historical Records Advisory Board, the Department of Education, the Oregon University System, the Land Conservation and Development Department, and the Business Development Department.

The commission is housed within the Oregon Parks and Recreation Department and is a statewide partner of the Oregon Cultural Trust.

Oregon Historical Society

Kerry Tymchuk, Executive Director
Address: 1200 SW Park Ave., Portland 97205
Phone: 503-222-1741; TDD: 503-306-5194
Fax: 503-221-2035
Web: www.ohs.org

For more than 100 years, the Oregon Historical Society (OHS) has provided a place for history—a home for Oregon heritage, culture, beginnings, and future. The society has expanded far beyond its original mission of collecting, preserving, publishing, and sharing Oregon's rich history. Attractions include exhibits covering a wide range of historical topics, lectures and special events, a museum store, its peer-reviewed journal the *Oregon Historical Quarterly*, and research library with a wealth of books, maps, documents, oral histories, photographs and film footage. OHS also operates educational programs for children and adults, and provides smaller exhibits that travel around the state. Web site content is also available across the state through the OHS historical time-line entitled TIMEWEB. The museum is open Monday through Saturday, 10 a.m. to 5 p.m., and Sunday, 12 p.m. to 5 p.m. The admission fee covers entrance to both the museum and library (OHS members are free). Multnomah County residents are also admitted free due to the passing of a modest levy in November 2010.

Oregon Historic Trails Advisory Council

Roger Roper, Deputy State Historic Preservation Officer
Address: 725 Summer St. NE, Suite C, Salem 97301
Phone: 503-986-0677
Fax: 503-986-0794
Web: www.oregonheritage.org

The Oregon Historic Trails Advisory Council (OHTAC) was established by Executive Order 98-16 to recognize all Oregon historic trails as outlined in ORS 358.057. The council is a nine-member committee appointed by the governor and formed to promote public awareness of the significance of Oregon's historic trails as well as to advise a variety of public and private agencies and organizations on policy matters. The council is Oregon's official liaison to other states, associations and federal agencies in acquiring national as well as state recognition of Oregon's historic trails.

The OHTAC represents three National Historic Trails in Oregon—the Lewis and Clark Trail, the

Applegate Trail and the Nez Perce Trail—as well as five alternative routes to the Oregon Trail, and seven other major Oregon historic trails.

State Historic Preservation Office

Roger Roper, Deputy State Historic Preservation Officer
Address: 725 Summer St. NE, Suite C, Salem 97301
Phone: 503-986-0677
Fax: 503-986-0794
Web: www.oregonheritage.org

The State Historic Preservation Office (SHPO) works in partnership with individuals, organizations and government entities to help identify various ways to preserve and use historic sites and places.

The SHPO was established in 1967 to manage and administer programs for the protection of the state's historic and cultural resources. When these resources disappear, Oregonians not only lose the tangible and educational value they contribute to our heritage, we can also lose a real monetary value to our economy and intangible, yet quite meaningful, aspects of Oregon's culture.

SHPO's program coordinators and representatives assist city planners and other officials, property owners and preservation groups in finding forward-thinking solutions to better protect and preserve our past.

By wisely planning for growth and change while respecting and ultimately protecting historic buildings and other important sites, state agencies, local governments and community organizations can play key leadership roles in safeguarding Oregon's cultural heritage resources. By becoming involved in historic preservation efforts at the local level, Oregonians can gain a greater understanding and appreciation of our shared heritage in all its variations.

Tamástslikt Cultural Institute

Roberta Conner, Director
Address: 47106 Wildhorse Blvd., Pendleton 97801
Phone: 541-429-7700
Fax: 541-429-7705
Web: www.tamastslikt.org

Tamástslikt Cultural Institute is dedicated to the accurate depiction and perpetuation of the culture and history of the Cayuse, Umatilla and Walla Walla Tribes. Located on the Umatilla Indian Reservation, Tamástslikt is the only tribally owned and operated interpretive center along the National Historic Oregon Trail, and Tamástslikt is a National Park Service certified interpretive site for both the Lewis and Clark and Oregon National Historic Trails. The institute is open daily April through September; and from Monday through Saturday October through March.

Visitors to Tamástslikt hear horses rumbling across a grassy plateau, Coyote saving the plants and animals from an ancient monster, generations-old songs in the winter lodge, the bell and translated hymns in the church. They see the brilliant color of dances at a competition powwow, poignant interviews with Tribal warriors and stories from families who have long participated in the Pendleton Round-Up. Ancient tools and art forms, ambient sounds and voices, along with historical photographs and contemporary video footage, combine to create an intriguing experience. One visit yields a new understanding of these peoples and their Eastern Oregon and Southeastern Washington homeland. The Outdoor Living Culture Village is open from Memorial Day through Labor Day.

Local native arts and crafts are available in the spacious museum store. The Kinship Café offers lunch and spectacular views.

Willamette Heritage Center at the Mill

John R. Hawkins, Interim Executive Director
Address: 1313 Mill St. SE, Salem 97301
Phone: 503-585-7012
Fax: 503-588-9902
Web: www.willametteheritage.org

The Willamette Heritage Center (WHC) brings together Mission Mill Museum, established in 1964, and Marion County Historical Society, established in 1950. Both organizations were leaders in the preservation and interpretation of mid-Willamette Valley history. The WHC continues on that tradition as it interprets the lives of the people who lived and worked in the Willamette Valley.

The five-acre campus is home to 14 historic structures that present the saga and richness of Oregon's past. Buildings include the 1841 Jason Lee house, arguably the oldest standing wooden framed house in Oregon, and the 1896 Thomas Kay Woolen Mill, one of the best-preserved Victorian-age factories in the West and designated an American Treasure by the National Park Service.

Permanent exhibits at WHC explore pre-Oregon Trail pioneer life in the Willamette Valley, reflect on life in the industrializing Northwest, present the story of the Kalapuya and discuss the import of agriculture in the Willamette Valley. Changing exhibits will tell the many different histories found throughout the region. The Research Library at WHC holds valuable photographs, records and documents that are centered on Marion County. The center offers beginning and advanced classes in various fiber arts through its Textile Learning Center. WHC hosts educational programs and events year-round. These include Sheep to Shawl, held the third Saturday in May, honoring the agricultural heritage of the Valley, and Magic at the Mill, held December 19th to 23rd, which celebrates the holidays with lights, music and activities. Other events include Family Fun Saturdays, summer outdoor concerts on the lawn, Quilt Show and Handweavers Sale, historical lectures and Spooky Mill tours.

WHC is open Monday through Saturday, 10 a.m. to 5 p.m. and most holidays except Thanksgiving, Christmas and New Year's Day. The Research Library is open Tuesday through Friday, 12 p.m. to 4 p.m. and on Saturday by appointment.

Regional Historical Societies and Heritage Organizations

Baker Heritage Museum

Address: 2480 Grove St., Baker City 97814-2719
Phone: 541-523-9308
Web: www.bakerheritagemuseum.com

Benton County Historical Society

Address: 1101 Main St., PO Box 35, Philomath 97370
Phone: 541-929-6230
Fax: 541-929-6261
Web: www.bentoncountymuseum.org

Clackamas County Historical Society and Museum of the Oregon Territory

Address: 211 Tumwater Dr., Oregon City 97045
Phone: 503-655-5574
Fax: 503-655-0035
Web: www.ClackamasHistory.org

Clatsop County Historical Society

Address: 714 Exchange St., PO Box 88, Astoria 97103
Phone: 503-325-2203
Fax: 503-325-7727
Web: www.cumtux.org

Columbia Gorge Discovery Center and Wasco County Historical Museum

Address: 5000 Discovery Dr., The Dalles 97058
Phone: 541-296-8600
Fax: 541-298-8660
Web: www.gorgediscovery.org

Columbia River Maritime Museum

Address: 1792 Marine Dr., Astoria 97103
Phone: 503-325-2323
Fax: 503-325-2331
Web: www.crmm.org

Coos Historical and Maritime Museum

Address: 1220 Sherman Ave., North Bend 97459
Phone: 541-756-6320
Web: www.cooshistory.org

Crook County Historical Society and Bowman Museum

Address: 246 N Main St., Prineville 97754
Phone: 541-447-3715
Fax: 541-447-3715
Web: www.bowmanmuseum.org

Curry Historical Society

Address: 29419 S Ellensberg Ave., PO Box 1598, Gold Beach 97444
Phone: 541-247-9396
Web: www.curryhistory.com

Deschutes County Historical Society

Address: 129 NW Idaho Ave., Bend 97701
Phone: 541-389-1813
Fax: 541-317-9345
Web: www.deschuteshistory.org

Douglas County Natural and Cultural Museum

Address: 123 Museum Dr., Roseburg 97471
Phone: 541-957-7007
Fax: 541-957-7017
Web: www.douglasmuseum.com

Four Rivers Cultural Center and Museum

Address: 676 SW Fifth Ave., Ontario 97914
Phone: 541-889-8191
Fax: 541-889-7628
Web: http://4rcc.com/index.php/en/

Genealogical Forum of Oregon

Address: 2505 SE 11th Ave., Suite B18, Portland 97242
Phone: 503-963-1932
Web: www.gfo.org

Gilliam County Historical Society

Address: Hwy. 19 at Burns Park, PO Box 377, Condon 97823
Phone: 541-384-4233

Grant County Historical Society

Address: 101 S Canyon City Blvd., Canyon City 97820
Phone: 541-575-0362
Web: www.gchistoricalmuseum.com

Harney County Historical Society

Address: 18 W D St., PO Box 388, Burns 97720
Phone: 541-573-5618
Web: http://ww2.burnsmuseum.com

Hood River County Historical Society

Address: 300 E Port Marina Way, Hood River 97031
Phone/Fax: 541-386-6772

Josephine County Historical Society
Address: 512 SW Fifth St., Grants Pass 97526
Phone: 541-479-7827
Fax: 888-488-5410
Web: www.jocohistorical.org

Lake County Museum
Address: 118 S E St., Lakeview 97630
Phone: 541-947-2220

Lane County Historical Society and Museum
Address: 740 W 13th Ave., Eugene 97402
Phone: 541-682-4242
Fax: 541-682-7361
Web: www.lanecountyhistoricalsociety.org

Lincoln County Historical Society and Oregon Coast History Center
Address: 545 SW 9th St., Newport 97365
Phone: 541-265-7509
Fax: 541-265-3992
Web: www.oregoncoasthistory.org

Linn County Historical Museum
Address: 101 Park Ave., Brownsville 97327
Phone: 541-466-3390
Web: www.linnparks.com

Malheur County Historical Society
Address: PO Box 691, Ontario 97914
E-mail: malheurcountyhist@gmail.com
Web: https://sites.google.com/site/malheurcountryhistorical/

Museum at Warm Springs
Address: 2189 Hwy. 26, Warm Springs 97761
Phone: 541-553-3331
Fax: 541-553-3338
Web: www.museumatwarmsprings.org

North Lincoln County Historical Museum
Address: 4907 SW Hwy. 101, Lincoln City 97367
Phone: 541-996-6614
Fax: 541-996-1244
Web: www.northlincolncountyhistoricalmuseum.org

Oregon Jewish Museum
Address: 1953 NW Kearney St., Portland 97209
Phone: 503-226-3600
Fax: 503-226-1800
Web: www.ojm.org

Oregon Nikkei Legacy Center
Address: 121 NW Second Ave., Portland 97209
Phone: 503-224-1458
Fax: 503-224-1459
Web: www.oregonnikkei.org

Polk County Historical Society
Address: 650 S Pacific Hwy., PO Box 67, Rickreall 97361
Phone: 503-623-6251
Web: www.polkcountyhistoricalsociety.com

Sherman County Historical Society and Museum
Address: 200 Dewey St., Moro 97039
Phone: 541-565-3232
Web: www.shermanmuseum.org

Southern Oregon Historical Society
Address: 106 N Central Ave., Medford 97501
Phone: 541-773-6536
Web: www.sohs.org

Tillamook County Pioneer Museum
Address: 2106 Second St., Tillamook 97141
Phone: 503-842-4553
Fax: 503-842-4553
Web: www.tcpm.org/

Troutdale Historical Society
Address: 473 E Historic Columbia River Hwy., Troutdale 97060
Phone: 503-661-2164
Fax: 503-674-2995
Web: http://troutdalehistory.org

Umatilla County Historical Society
Address: 108 SW Frazer Ave., Pendleton 97801
Phone: 541-276-0012
Fax: 541-276-7989
Web: www.heritagestationmuseum.org

Washington County Museum
Address: 17677 NW Springville Rd., Portland 97229
Phone: 503-645-5353
Fax: 503-645-5650
Web: www.washingtoncountymuseum.org

Yamhill County Historical Society and Museum
Address: 605 Market St., Lafayette 97127
Phone: 503-864-2308
Web: http://yamhillcountyhistory.org/

Earth Sciences and Technology

Along with the many state and national parks and forest centers, other organizations have facilities that teach visitors about our natural world and encourage us to explore further.

Oregon's Major Industry, Science and Technology Organizations

Columbia Gorge Discovery Center

Carolyn Purcell, Executive Director
Address: 5000 Discovery Dr., The Dalles 97058
Phone: 541-296-8600
Fax: 541-298-8660
Web: www.gorgediscovery.org

The Columbia Gorge Discovery Center is the official interpretive center for the Columbia River Gorge National Scenic Area. The 26,100 square-foot exhibit wing holds interactive displays which bring to life the tremendous volcanic upheavals and raging floods that created the Gorge, the theories of why ice ages occur, the mighty river which sculpted patterns for a unique and spectacular diversity of vegetation, wildlife and ancient life ways, and the currents that shape our futures in the Gorge.

Live raptor programs daily. Open seven days a week, 9 a.m. to 5 p.m.

Evergreen Aviation & Space Museum

Delford M. Smith, Chairman
Address: 500 NE Captain Michael King Smith Wy., McMinnville 97128
Phone: 503-434-4180
Web: www.evergreenmuseum.org

The Evergreen Aviation & Space Museum is best known as the home of the world's largest wooden flying boat, the "Spruce Goose," the SR-71 "Blackbird," the Titan II SLV Missile and Oregon's largest IMAX 3D theater. In addition, there are more than 200 historic aircraft, spacecraft and exhibits on display, along with artwork and traveling exhibits.

In June 2011, the museum opened the 70,000 square-foot Wings & Waves Waterpark, an educational waterpark that includes 10 waterslides, a wave pool and a children's museum dedicated to teaching students about the power of water.

The museum is open 9 a.m. to 5 p.m. daily, except when it is closed for Thanksgiving, Christmas Day and Easter. The museum is located about three miles southeast of McMinnville on Highway 18, across from the McMinnville Airport. Check the web site for admission prices and waterpark hours.

The High Desert Museum

Janeanne A. Upp, President
Address: 59800 S Hwy. 97, Bend 97702-7963
Phone: 541-382-4754
Fax: 541-382-5256
Web: www.highdesertmuseum.org

The High Desert Museum is nationally acclaimed for its close-up wildlife encounters, living history performances, Tribal and Western art, and cultural exhibits and special programs for all ages. The museum and its nature trails on 135 forested acres feature indoor and outdoor exhibits and natural animal habitats. It is renowned for inspiring stewardship of High Desert cultural and natural resources.

Major permanent exhibits include the Earle A. Chiles Center on the Spirit of the West, the Henry J. Casey Hall of Plateau Indians, and the Donald M. Kerr Birds of Prey Center, which is the home of many raptors, including North America's only pair of northern spotted owls to have bred in captivity.

Outdoor wildlife viewing areas include the "Wind, Earth, and Fire" interpretive fire trail. A North American river otter can be found frolicking in the pond at the naturalistic Autzen Otter Exhibit, and a family of porcupines, badgers, a bobcat, lynx, fox and reptiles are among the museum's wildlife collection of more than 100 animals.

The museum's 1910 working sawmill and 1880 High Desert Homestead Ranch offer authentic settings for its living history performers.

The High Desert Museum is just five minutes south of Bend and is open every day except Thanksgiving, Christmas and New Year's Day. The museum is funded by visitors, members, donors and grants.

Malheur Field Station

Duncan Evered and Lyla Messick, Directors
Address: 34848 Sodhouse Ln., Princeton 97721
Phone: 541-493-2629
E-mail: mfs@highdesertair.com
Web: www.malheurfieldstation.org

Malheur Field Station is an environmental education and research center located in the northern Great Basin region in southeastern Oregon. It is operated by the Great Basin Society, a non-profit organization founded in 1985. Its mission is dedicated to the concept that learning is a lifelong process. This philosophy is achieved by providing public lectures, accredited and non-accredited courses, professional development workshops, Elderhostel programs, in-service teacher education and scout projects. It also serves as host to individuals, families, birding groups, K–12 school groups, and other organizations and agencies. A member-based consortium of 19 northwest universities, colleges, and education organizations guides the academic programs. Individual and Family Membership (Friends of Malheur) benefits include newsletters, bookstore and lodging discounts.

Located on Malheur National Wildlife Refuge, 32 miles south of Burns, the field station is a unique and diverse setting of extensive marshland, desert basins, alkali playas, upland desert scrub steppe, volcanic and glacial landforms, and fault block mountains. As such, the Malheur Field Station provides a rich outdoor classroom for the biologist, geologist, archaeologist, artist, astronomer, environmental science student or visitor interested in the cultural or natural history of the region.

Lodging and food services can be arranged. Basic accommodations range from dormitories and kitchenettes to trailers and RV hook-ups. The dining hall serves cafeteria-style breakfasts and dinners and offers sack lunches for field trips.

The field station's Natural History Museum exhibits and bookstore are open to the public.

Oregon Coast Aquarium

Carrie E. Lewis, President and CEO; W. Brent Denham, Board Chair

Address: 2820 SE Ferry Slip Rd., Newport 97365
Phone: 541-867-3474
Fax: 541-867-6846
Web: http://aquarium.org

The Oregon Coast Aquarium, located in Newport, is a non-profit institution occupying a 32-acre site on Yaquina Bay, adjacent to the Oregon State University Mark O. Hatfield Marine Science Center. Aquarium exhibits are housed in an 80,000 square-foot building and on six acres of elaborately rocked pools, caves, cliffs and bluffs.

Indoor exhibits include four galleries replicating habitats found in coastal wetlands, sandy and rocky shores, and off Oregon's coast in deeper waters. Also indoors are a demonstration lab, Whale Theater, changing exhibit area, full-service cafe and gift shop. Outdoor exhibits include sea otters, harbor seals and sea lions, wave-pummeled tide pools, a coastal cave featuring a giant Pacific octopus, the largest walk-through seabird aviary in North America, a nature trail and a children's play area. The aquarium is open every day except Christmas and is handicap accessible.

Oregon Museum of Science and Industry (OMSI)

Nancy Stueber, President; Don Vollum, Board Chair

Address: 1945 SE Water Ave., Portland 97214-3354
Phone: 503-797-4000
Fax: 503-797-4566
Web: www.omsi.edu

Established in 1944, the Oregon Museum of Science and Industry is an independent, non-tax-based educational and cultural resource center with an international reputation for excellence in science exhibitry and informal science education. OMSI is dedicated to improving the public's understanding of science and technology through a wide variety of innovative and interactive science programming. More than one million people visit the museum and participate in OMSI's programs every year.

Since 1992, OMSI has occupied a 18.5-acre riverside campus on the east bank of the Willamette River in downtown Portland. The complex includes five exhibit halls; eight inter¬active science labs; a planetarium; a 300-seat, five-story, domed OMNIMAX Theater; and the 219-foot U.S.S. *Blueback* submarine moored just outside the building in the river. The museum has river view dining, a science store stocked with hundreds of educational fun toys and an extensive bookstore.

In addition to the exhibits on permanent display, OMSI researches, designs and builds science exhibits for travel to other science centers around the globe. Boasting the largest museum-based, traveling science exhibits program in North America, OMSI has an international reputation for producing popular exhibits.

OMSI also has the largest science outreach education programs in the United States, reaching more than 220,000 students across seven western states. OMSI provides eucation programs to more than 1,900 each year, and OMSI camps serve more than 10,000 children and provide approximately 328,000 hours of science instruction annually. OMSI's education programs include science classes and camp-ins.

OMSI is open Tuesday through Sunday from 9:30 a.m. to 5:30 p.m. from Labor Day through mid-June and is open daily from 9:30 a.m. to 7:00 p.m. from mid-June through Labor Day. Open all holidays except Thanksgiving and Christmas.

Oregon State University Hatfield Marine Science Center

Dr. George W. Boehlert, Director

Address: 2030 SE Marine Science Dr., Newport 97365
Phone: 541-867-0212
Fax: 541-867-0138
Web: http://hmsc.oregonstate.edu

The Hatfield Marine Science Center (HMSC) is the hub of Oregon State University's coastal research, teaching and marine extension activities. The center was built on the shores of Yaquina Bay in 1965 with the help of the Port of Newport and the federal government, which granted the initial construction funds. Since that time, HMSC facilities have expanded to accommodate over 300 researchers and students from many departments at OSU and from six state and federal agencies. Facilities include a Visitor Center, research and teaching laboratories including seawater wet lab facilities, and on-site housing for undergraduate and graduate students in residence and visiting scientists. HMSC also serves as a base for oceanographic research vessels and is adjacent to the site of the National Oceanic and Atmospheric Administration (NOAA) Marine Operations Center – Pacific.

Agencies located at the HMSC include the Oregon Department of Fish and Wildlife (Marine Resources Program), U.S. Environmental Protection Agency (Pacific Coastal Ecology Branch), U.S. Fish and Wildlife Service (Oregon Coast National Wildlife Refuge Complex), the U.S. Geological Survey, the USDA's Agricultural Research Service, and NOAA, which includes elements of the Alaska Fisheries Science Center, Northwest Fisheries Science Center and the Pacific Marine Environmental Laboratory. Collaboration between university and agency scientists and community partners is a hallmark of research and education activities at HMSC which aim to increase understanding of coastal and ocean ecosystems and foster sustainable management of marine resources.

The HMSC Visitor Center, managed by Oregon Sea Grant, offers the opportunity to explore over 15,000 square feet of exhibit space featuring interactive hands-on exhibits and aquaria. The public wing with its beloved touch pool and octopus tank features frequently changing exhibits, including a wave tank exhibit installed in 2012. Computer simulations enable visitors to play the role of scientific explorers while learning about some of the current research underway at the center, and a new webcam features the giant Pacific octopus: http://hmsc.oregonstate.edu/visitor/octocam. The Visitor Center doubles as a living laboratory for OSU's Free-Choice Learning Lab, which researches self-paced, leisure-time lifelong learning to understand what informal science education venues can do to enhance visitors' learning experience. Informal education programs are offered in the auditorium, along the Yaquina Bay estuary nature trail, beside the docks and in occasional workshops. Hands-on laboratories are available for school and organized groups with prior reservations, and a dedicated corps of trained volunteers assists visitors with their individual explorations.

Admission to the Visitor Center is by donation. Summer hours are 10 a.m. to 5 p.m. daily, Memorial Day through Labor Day. Winter hours are 10 a.m. to 4 p.m., Thursday through Monday (closed Tuesday and Wednesday). For more information, see web site.

The HMSC was named in 1983 in honor of Mark O. Hatfield, who served Oregon as a state legislator and two-term governor before joining the U.S. Senate in 1966, where he served more than 30 years.

Oregon Zoo

Jani Iverson, Director
Address: 4001 SW Canyon Rd., Portland 97221
Phone: 503-226-1561
Fax: 503-226-6836
Web: www.oregonzoo.org

Nestled on 64 acres in the forested hills of Washington Park, the Oregon Zoo is just five minutes from downtown Portland, easily accessible by MAX light rail, TriMet bus #63 or by auto on Highway 26 West, the Sunset Highway. Parking charges apply.

The Oregon Zoo is home to more than 2,000 animals from around the world. The Great Northwest exhibit welcomes visitors to the zoo. The mountain village atmosphere of the entry plaza is complete with visitor amenities including the Cascade Grill and the Cascade Outfitters Gift Shop. The Cascade Crest exhibit is home to shaggy mountain goats living among a jumble of boulders, green grass and a crystal clear pond.

Steller Cove is home to sea lions and sea otters. Visitors can get an underwater view of these graceful animals and explore the diversity of a kelp forest and tide pool.

The Eagle Canyon exhibit surrounds visitors with the splendors of a natural watershed. Visitors have a fish-eye view of salmon, sturgeon and other native fish. Farther up the trail, magnificent bald eagles appear. Visitors discover the importance of rivers and streams and the interconnectedness of animals and the ecosystem.

Trillium Creek Family Farm, a re-creation of an Oregon Century Farm complete with farmhouse and barn, allows visitors of all ages a chance to interact with sheep, goats, chickens and other farm animals.

The zoo is a perfect place to explore more exotic habitats. Red Ape Reserve showcases orangutans and white-cheeked gibbons. Predators of the Serengeti houses lions, cheetah and African wild dogs, while the Africa Savanna is home to rhinos, hippos, zebras, giraffes and more. The Africa Rainforest features fruit bats, monkeys, crocodiles, and many bright and colorful birds. The Amazon Flooded Forest gives visitors a peek at some of the many animals living in the most diverse ecosystem in the world. Other zoo residents include black bears, cougars, polar bears, penguins, lorikeets, Amur tigers and leopards all living in lush exhibits recreating their natural habitats.

Visitors can hop aboard the Washington Park and Zoo Railway for a ride through the forested hillsides surrounding the zoo. During the summer, visitors may enjoy the four-mile loop or get off at the Rose Garden and take a stroll, enjoying a view of the city, and catch a later train back to the zoo. The zoo is Oregon's most popular paid attraction.

The Oregon Zoo is committed to conservation, research and education and is home to more than 20 endangered and 50 threatened species. The zoo participates in more than 40 conservation breeding programs sponsored by the Association of Zoos and Aquariums. The zoo is a leader in animal environmental enrichment and is internationally recognized for its successful Asian elephant breeding program with 28 elephant births to date. The most recent is a baby girl elephant named Lily. She was born on November 30, 2012, and is the second offspring of 18-year-old Rose-Tu.

In recent years, the zoo has partnered with other conservation organizations to help with the preservation of Pacific Northwest species. The zoo is taking an active role in rearing Oregon silverspot and Taylor's checkerspot butterflies, Columbia Basin pygmy rabbits, western pond turtles and Oregon spotted frogs. In 2001, the Oregon Zoo joined the California condor recovery program. In 2004, the first two condor eggs were laid in Oregon in more than 100 years!

Education programs involve participants from three years old to senior citizens. A–Z Preschool classes, Zoomobile outreach, Wildlife Live! shows, Conservation Lecture Series, Zoo Animal Presenters, Urban Nature Overnights, ZooCamp and many others reach over 150,000 people each year.

University of Oregon Museum of Natural and Cultural History

Jon Erlandson, Director
Address: 1680 E 15th Ave., Eugene 97403-1224
Phone: 541-346-3024
Fax: 541-346-5334
Web: http://natural-history.uoregon.edu

Founded in 1935-36 by the state Legislature, the Museum of Natural and Cultural History at the University of Oregon has a remarkable collection of archaeological, anthropological, historical, paleontological and other natural history from Oregon, the broader Pacific Northwest, and around the world. Museum research staff and associates are actively engaged in cutting-edge archaeological and paleontological research which is interpreted for audiences through interactive exhibits and educational programs.

The museum's main exhibit hall, "Oregon—Where Past is Present," highlights millions of years of geological history and 15,000 years of the human record in Oregon's diverse and dynamic landscapes. This cultural history is told through a combination of archaeological specimens, including the 10,000 year old sagebrush sandals from Fort Rock Cave, "America's oldest shoes," numerous historical tribal baskets, as well as scientific discoveries. Traditional replicas of a longhouse, wikiup, and fishing net, all made by Oregon tribal members, and seasonal round murals can be viewed in each of the geographical regions.

Changing exhibits showcase the museums' extensive collections of fossils and traditional artifacts from around the globe.

Currently, the museum is undergoing a Landmark Expansion with a new collections center and public galleria already completed and a new exhibit hall on the natural history of Oregon and a research wing in progress.

Located adjacent to historic Hayward Field, the museum is open Wednesday (Free Day) through Sunday, 11:00 a.m. to 5:00 p.m. Don't forget to visit the museum store—Past & Presents.

World Forestry Center

Gary Hartshorn, Ph.D., President and CEO
Address: 4033 SW Canyon Rd., Portland 97221
Phone: 503-228-1367
Fax: 503-228-4608
Web: www.worldforestry.org

The World Forestry Center, located in Portland's Washington Park, is a private, non-profit forestry education organization. Through classes, tours, museum exhibits and demonstrations, it illustrates and interprets benefits of the forest environment and promotes appreciation and understanding of forests and forest resources worldwide. The center's Discovery Museum re-opened in 2005 with over 100 new exhibits. The museum won the 2006 POVA (Portland Oregon Visitors Association) president's award for valued contributions to the visitor industry.

Merlo Hall, added to the center's campus in 1989, houses the World Forest Institute. This facility was designed as an international forest information clearinghouse, as well as hosting an international fellowship program.

The center also operates the Magness Tree Farm, an 80-acre demonstration forest near Wilsonville, with a visitors' center and log bunkhouses used for summer camps. The area is also a wildlife sanctuary. Individuals and groups of all ages are welcome to visit and take advantage of the farm's varied educational activities, many of which are free of charge.

Economy

sign for the Liberty Theater in Astoria—Oregon State Archives Scenic Photograph clatDA0090a

Historically, Oregon's economy was based on natural resources: timber, fishing and agriculture. Today, the economy is in transition to add manufacturing and service industries, with an emphasis on technology. This section describes Oregon's economy.

Oregon's Economy

Source: Employment Department, Workforce & Economic Research Division

Oregon's economy shadowed the national "Great Recession" that took hold in 2008. The seasonally adjusted unemployment rate for Oregon bottomed out at 5 percent in the spring of 2007 and climbed during the next two years to a near-record high of 11.6 percent. The national unemployment rate fluctuated around 4.5 percent in the first half of 2007 and then climbed to 10 percent near the end of 2009, the highest level seen in decades. Both the Oregon and national unemployment rates fell from their peaks but stayed persistently high. Oregon's unemployment rate averaged 9.5 percent in 2011, slightly higher than the U.S. unemployment rate of 8.9 percent.

During the past two decades, Oregon made the transition from a resource based economy to a more mixed manufacturing and marketing economy, with an emphasis on high technology. Oregon's hard times of the early 1980s signaled basic changes had occurred in traditional resource sectors — timber, fishing and agriculture — and the state worked to develop new economic sectors to replace older ones. Most important, perhaps, was the state's growing high-tech sector, centered in the three counties around Portland. However, rural Oregon counties were generally left out of any shift to a new economy.

As with the nation, Oregon's expansion from 2004 through 2007 was fueled by growth in construction and services. The recession erased construction's job gains and devastated the economy to the extent that employment in 2010 was at roughly the same level as in 2000. Job growth since the end of the recession has been slow. The private sector has carried the recovery so far, including growth in private educational and health services, professional and business services, and retail trade. Government job cuts and the lack of recovery in construction and financial activities are contributing to the state's slow job growth.

Oregon is one of the most trade dependent states in the nation and, to some extent, economic activity in other countries helps drive the state's economy. The value of exports from Oregon to foreign countries was $18.3 billion in 2011. The state's largest trading partners are China, Canada, Malaysia, Japan, and South Korea. Of course, Oregon's trade with other U.S. states far exceeds its trade with foreign nations.

The aging population will factor into the future of Oregon's economy. The eldest members of the Baby Boom generation are becoming eligible for Social Security benefits, and many are considering retirement. More than one out of five workers in Oregon is already 55 years or older. As the generation ages, employers will need to find new workers with the skills to replace their retiring workforce. At the same time, the growing number of retirees will demand more leisure and health care services.

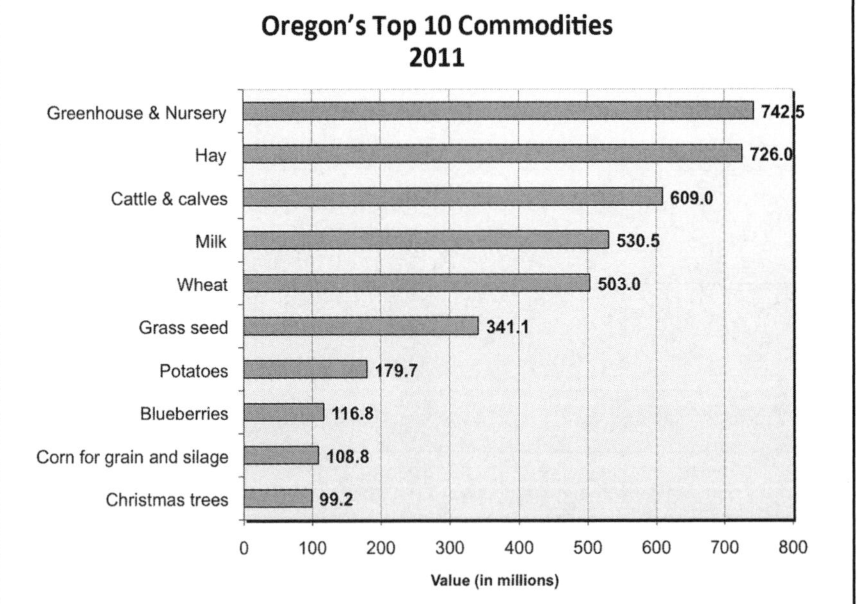

Source: Oregon Department of Agriculture

Employment

Oregon's labor force is nearly two million strong. Four out of five of the state's working age population is involved in the labor force. Some are currently looking for a job, many are working for themselves, and more than 1.6 million are employees working at the nearly 130,000 business establishments and government entities across the state. Employment in trade, transportation and utilities accounts for nearly one out of five Oregon jobs, making them the state's largest industries. Federal, state and local government jobs are the next largest group, followed by private education and health services, and professional and business services.

Nearly every industry in Oregon was hit hard by the Great Recession, but a few were able to grow despite the turbulent economy. Private education, driven by the growing population, and health services, driven by an aging population, added a combined 51,000 jobs during the decade, growing at an average annual rate of 3 percent. Leisure and hospitality, which includes restaurants, hotels and recreational activities, added 15,000 jobs and grew at an average annual rate of 1 percent. Other services, which include businesses such as repair and maintenance shops, personal and laundry services, and religious and membership organizations, was the only other industry to add jobs. Government added 21,000 jobs during the decade, the bulk of which were local education, state education or tribal jobs.

Mining and logging, an industry with employment in steady yet slow decline for decades, lost 30 percent of its jobs. The manufacturing industry shed one-quarter of its jobs during the decade. Wood products workers lost the most jobs, followed by computer and electronic workers and then transportation equipment workers. Food manufacturing was the only manufacturing sector that was able to add jobs in the midst of the recession. The information industry was hit hard by both recessions of the decade and lost 17 percent of its workers since 2000.

The construction industry rode a wave of housing demand starting in 2004 that led to growth beyond its historical share of total employment. The growth peaked in 2007 and then crashed with the bursting of the "housing bubble." This brought construction employment back down to near its traditional share of employment, but still nearly 10,000 fewer jobs than at the start of the decade. The financial activities industry, which is closely tied to the real estate market, experienced a boom and bust in employment similar to the construction industry, and employment levels in 2010 were about equal to where they were at the beginning of the decade.

By the end of 2011, Oregon had added back about one-fourth of the jobs lost in the recession. That means an additional 110,000 are needed before the state reaches the peak level of employment seen prior to the recession. Forecasts suggest that Oregon will return to pre-recession employment levels at the end of 2014.

Oregon's top 10 industries by employment in 2011:

1. Food services and drinking places (122,000)
2. Administrative and support services (77,900)
3. Ambulatory health care services (71,500)
4. Hospitals (53,700)
5. Nursing and residential care facilities (43,900)
6. Specialty trade contractors (42,200)
7. Food and beverage stores (38,300)
8. General merchandise stores (38,300)
9. Computer and electronic product manufacturing (36,300)
10. Social assistance (30,700)

Wages

Oregon has the second highest minimum wage rate in the nation. In 2013, the minimum wage was $8.95 per hour. Ballot Measure 25, enacted by Oregon voters in 2002, requires a minimum wage adjustment annually based on changes in inflation as measured by the U.S. City Average Consumer Price Index for All Urban Consumers for All Items (CPI-U). Oregon was one of 10 states that adjusts minimum wage based on inflation. Washington has the highest minimum wage rate of any state at $9.19 per hour. Nevada's minimum wage is $8.25 per hour and California's minimum wage is $8.00 per hour. Idaho's minimum wage is $7.25 per hour, which is equal to the federal minimum wage rate.

Although Oregon has a high minimum wage, average wage earnings are below the national level. Workers at Oregon businesses earned an average of $735 in weekly wages in 2011, which is below the national average earnings of $802 per week.

Oregon workers earned an annual average of $43,091 in 2011, but the wages workers earn vary widely by industry. The average annual earnings in the information industry were $66,163, the most of any broad sector, followed by manufacturing ($60,265) and financial activities ($53,329). On the low earnings end were jobs in leisure and hospitality, where workers averaged $17,236 per year.

Of course, the average wage for an industry does not reveal how many low- or high-wage jobs are in an industry. Roughly 20 percent of Oregon jobs have an average wage of less than $10 per hour. Another 25 percent are between $10 and $15 per hour. This suggests that more than half of all jobs pay at least $15 per hour.

Income

Per capita personal income, a broader measure of the income all Oregonians receive from all sources, was $37,909 per person in 2011, which is $1,527 more per person than in 2001 after adjusting for inflation. In addition to wages, personal income includes proprietors' income, income from dividends, interest, and rent, and transfer receipts.

The national per capita personal income outperformed Oregon over the decade, increasing by $2,909 over the same period and reaching $41,663 in 2011. Oregon's per capita personal income is just 91 percent of the nation's and ranks 33rd among the states and Washington, D.C.

Despite lower average incomes than the nation as a whole, Oregon's poverty rate is better than average. According to the U.S. Census Bureau, 12.7 percent of Oregon residents lived in families with incomes below the poverty threshold during 2008–2010. The U.S. poverty rate was higher at 14.2 percent. Oregon ranked roughly 30th among the states with the lowest percentage of people living in poverty.

Revenue and Taxes

Oregon collects personal income taxes, corporate income taxes, property taxes and gasoline taxes. It does not have a state sales tax. The personal income tax rate ranges from 5 percent to 9.9 percent of taxable income. The corporate income tax rate is 6.6 percent or 7.6 percent of taxable business income. The minimum corporate tax ranges from $150 to $100,000. In 2009, voters increased the minimum tax from a flat $10. In tax year 2009, almost 78 percent of all C corporation Oregon taxpayers paid the minimum tax.

Property tax rates vary from community to community. Voters passed tax initiatives limiting the growth of property tax values to 3 percent a year. In addition, voters shifted much of the responsibility for funding public schools from property taxes to the state's general fund. This has depleted resources for other programs that are also dependent on the general fund. When the 2001 recession struck, public education and human services were hit particularly hard. A significant part of the reason for the intensity of the downturn, at least as experienced by those who lost employment, was the restructuring of Oregon's tax system in the early 1990s. The demands on the state's general fund, when faced with a decline in revenues, meant pervasive truncation of government services. Perhaps the most conspicuous victim was public education. School districts throughout Oregon were faced with shorter school years, larger class sizes and elimination of programs.

Landowners who harvest timber from lands in Oregon pay a tax on the timber harvested. The tax rate for 2012 and 2013 is $3.6841 per thousand board feet of timber harvested. This rate is set biennially by the Legislature based on the budgetary needs of the recipients. The recipients are the Oregon Department of Forestry for fire protection and monitoring forest practices, Oregon State University for forestry research and Oregon Forest Resources Institute for forestry education.

Measure 37 was approved by voters in November 2004. The law allowed owners of private real property to file claims against the state and local governments that enacted or enforced land use regulations that restricted the use and reduced the fair market value of their property. After establishing that a claim was valid, the government entity could pay compensation or waive the restrictive regulations so that the property owner could apply for a use that was allowed when the property was acquired. Approximately 7,000 Measure 37 claims were filed with the state, and, in all cases, the state waived land use regulations back to the date of acquisition. These claims included uses ranging from farm partitions and non-farm dwellings to 100-lot subdivisions, strip malls and gravel mining operations.

Measure 49 — which amended the scope of Measure 37 and clarified many of its terms — was drafted by the 2007 Legislature. Measure 49 was referred to the voters and passed. The compensation for claims that were filed under Measure 37, whether or not a waiver had been issued, was amended to limited residential development. Under Measure 49, claimants could elect for supplemental review of their claim by the Department of Land Conservation and Development (DLCD) if they had not already "vested" the use authorized in a Measure 37 waiver. Review under Section 6 of Measure 49 provided maximum relief of a total of three home sites. Section 7 allowed for up to 10 home sites, but required the claimant to submit an extensive appraisal demonstrating the loss of value due to the restrictive land use regulations.

Under Measure 49, DLCD has reviewed 4,660 claims involving 239,099 acres of rural land. Approximately 80 percent of those claims have been approved and home site authorizations are transferrable to new owners.

Going forward, Measure 49 also provides for claims based on new land use regulations restricting residential use, or farm or forest practices that reduce the fair market value of private real property.

Additional Information

Department of Agriculture
www.oregon.gov/ODA/Pages/index.aspx

Department of Consumer and Business Services
www.oregon.gov/DCBS/Pages/index.aspx

Department of Education
www.ode.state.or.us/

Department of Environmental Quality
www.oregon.gov/DEQ/Pages/index.aspx

Department of Human Services
www.oregon.gov/DHS/Pages/index.aspx

Forestry Department
www.oregon.gov/ODF/Pages/index.aspx

Housing and Community Services Department
www.oregon.gov/OHCS/Pages/index.aspx

Land Conservation and Development Department
www.oregon.gov/LCD/Pages/index.aspx

Department of Revenue
http://www.oregon.gov/DOR/Pages/index.aspx

U.S. Department of Labor
www.dol.gov/esa/minwage/america.htm

Media Directories

Tommy Tucker Veterans Memorial Statue by Rip Caswell at Friendship Park in Madras—Oregon State Archives Scenic Photograph jefDB1549

Oregon's long tradition of open government and citizen involvement depends in part on its citizens receiving accurate and timely information. The media play an important role in providing this information to Oregonians. This section lists Oregon's media resources.

Newspapers Published in Oregon

The following newspapers are published at least once a week. See "Selected Periodicals" following this section for other magazines and journals.

Source: Oregon Newspaper Publishers Association (ONPA)*

Executive Director: Laurie Hieb

Address: 7150 SW Hampton St., Suite 111, Portland 97223

Phone: 503-624-6397

Fax: 503-624-9811

E-mail: onpa@orenews.com

*For newspapers that are not ONPA members, information was provided independently.

Key: (P) = Publisher, (E) = Editor

Albany

Albany Democrat-Herald

Mon–Fri p.m., Sat–Sun a.m.; Rick Parrish (P); Mike McInally (E); Circ. 14,092 (Mon–Sat), 14,779 (Sun); Estab. 1865

PO Box 130, Albany 97321; 541-926-2211; Fax: 541-926-7209

Web: www.democratherald.com

Ashland

Ashland Daily Tidings

Mon–Sat p.m.; J. Grady Singletary (P); Robert L. Hunter (E); Circ. 1,916; Estab. 1876

PO Box 1108, Medford 97501; 541-776-4411; Fax: 541-776-4376

Web: www.dailytidings.com

Astoria

The Daily Astorian

Mon–Fri p.m.; Steve Forrester (P/E); Circ. 7,001; Estab. 1873

PO Box 210, Astoria 97103; 503-325-3211; Fax: 503-325-6573

Web: www.dailyastorian.com

Baker City

Baker City Herald

Mon, Wed, Fri p.m.; Kari Borgen (P); Jayson Jacoby (E); Circ. 2,615; Estab. 1870

PO Box 807, Baker City 97814; 541-523-3673; Fax: 541-523-6426

Web: www.bakercityherald.com

The Record-Courier

Thur; Greg Brinton (P); Debby Schoeningh (E); Circ. 2,301; Estab. 1901

PO Box 70, Baker City 97814; Phone/Fax: 541-523-5353

Web: www.therconline.com

Bandon

Bandon Western World

Wed; Clark Walworth (P/E); Circ. 1,537; Estab. 1912

PO Box 248, Bandon 97411-0248; 541-347-2423; Fax: 541-347-2424

Web: http://theworldlink.com/bandon

Beaverton

Beaverton Valley Times

Thur; Mark Garber (P); Christina Lent (E); Circ. 3,857; Estab. 1921

PO Box 22109, Portland 97269; 503-684-0360; Fax: 503-620-3433

Web: http://portlandtribune.com/beaverton-valley-times-news

Bend

The Bulletin

Mon–Sun a.m.; Gordon Black (P); John Costa (E); Circ. 27,547 (Mon–Fri), 28,924 (Sat), 29,997 (Sun); Estab. 1903

PO Box 6020, Bend 97708-6020; 541-382-1811; Fax: 541-385-5802

Web: www.bendbulletin.com

Brookings

Curry Coastal Pilot

Wed, Sat; Charles R. Kocher (P); Scott Graves (E); Circ. 6,168; Estab. 1946

PO Box 700, Brookings 97415; 541-469-3123; Fax: 541-469-4679

Web: www.currypilot.com

Brownsville

The Times

Wed; Don and Wannell Ware (P); Don Ware (E); Circ. 783; Estab. 1888

PO Box 278, Brownsville 97327; 541-466-5311; Fax: 541-466-5312

Burns

Burns Times-Herald

Wed; Sue Pedersen (P); Debbie Raney (E); Circ. 3,445; Estab. 1887

355 N Broadway, Burns 97720; 541-573-2022; Fax: 541-573-3915

Web: www.burnstimesherald.info

Canby

Canby Herald

Wed, Sat; William D. Cassel (P); John Baker (E); Circ. 5,388; Estab. 1906

PO Box 1108, Canby 97013; 503-266-6831; Fax: 503-266-6836

Web: www.canbyherald.com

Cave Junction

Illinois Valley News

Wed; Dan Mancuso (P); Kevan Moore (E); Circ. 2,459; Estab. 1937

PO Box 1370, Cave Junction 97523; 541-592-2541; Fax: 541-592-4330
Web: www.illinois-valley-news.com

Clatskanie

The Clatskanie Chief

Thur; Deborah Steele Hazen (P/E); Circ. 2,407; Estab. 1891
PO Box 8, Clatskanie 97016; Phone/Fax: 503-728-3350
Web: www.clatskaniechiefnews.com

Condon

The Times-Journal

Thur; McLaren and Janet Stinchfield (P); McLaren Stinchfield (E); Circ. 1,467; Estab. 1886
PO Box 746, Condon 97823; 541-384-2421; Fax: 541-384-2411

Coos Bay

The World

Mon–Thur, Sat; Clark Walworth (P/E); Circ. 9,272 (Mon–Thur) 10,393 (Sat); Estab. 1878
PO Box 1840, Coos Bay 97420; 541-269-1222; Fax: 541-267-0294
Web: www.theworldlink.com

Coquille

The Sentinel

Wed; Jean Ivey (P/E); Circ. 3,010; Estab. 1882
61 E First, Coquille 97423; 541-396-3191; Fax: 541-396-3624

Corvallis

Corvallis Gazette-Times

Mon–Sun a.m.; Rick Parrish (P); Mike McInally (E); Circ. 9,802 (Mon–Sat), 10,158 (Sun); Estab. 1862
PO Box 368, Corvallis 97339; 541-753-2641; Fax: 541-758-9505
Web: www.gazettetimes.com

Cottage Grove

Cottage Grove Sentinel

Wed; Jessica Baker (P); Jon Stinnett (E); Circ. 3,210; Estab. 1889
PO Box 35, Cottage Grove 97424; 541-942-3325; Fax: 541-942-3328
Web: www.cgsentinel.com

Creswell

The Creswell Chronicle

Thur; Scott Olson (P/E); Circ. 754; Estab. 1965
PO Box 428, Creswell 97426; 541-895-2197; Fax: 541-895-2361
Web: www.thecreswellchronicle.com

Dallas

Polk County Itemizer-Observer

Wed; Nancy J. Adams (P); Kurt Holland (E); Circ. 4,751; Estab. 1875
PO Box 108, Dallas 97338; 503-623-2373; Fax: 503-623-2395
Web: www.polkio.com

Drain

The Drain Enterprise

Thur; Sue Anderson (P/E); Circ. 764; Estab. 1950
PO Box 26, Drain 97435; 541-836-2241; Fax: 541-836-2243

Enterprise

Wallowa County Chieftain

Wed; Marissa Williams (P); Robert Ruth (E); Circ. 2,962; Estab. 1884
PO Box 338, Enterprise 97828; 541-426-4567; Fax: 541-426-3921
Web: www.wallowa.com

Estacada

Estacada News

Thur; Mark Garber (P); Steve Brown (E); Circ. 1,520; Estab. 1904
PO Box 549, Estacada 97023; 503-630-3241; Fax: 503-630-5840
Web: http://portlandtribune.com/estacada-news-news

Eugene

Eugene Weekly

Thur; Ted Taylor (P/E); Circ. 39,000; Estab. 1982
1251 Lincoln St., Eugene 97401; 541-484-0519; Fax: 541-484-4044
Web: www.eugeneweekly.com

The Register-Guard

Mon–Sun a.m.; Alton F. Baker III (P/E); Circ. 51,889 (Mon–Fri), 59,057 (Sat), 59,672 (Sun); Estab. 1862
3500 Chad Dr., Eugene 97408; 541-485-1234; Fax: 541-984-4699
Web: www.registerguard.com

Florence

Siuslaw News

Wed, Sat; John Bartlett (P); Theresa Baer (E); Circ. 4,903; Estab. 1890
PO Box 10, Florence 97439; 541-997-3441; Fax: 541-997-7979
Web: www.thesiuslawnews.com

Forest Grove

News-Times

Wed; John Schrag (P/E); Circ. 3,096; Estab. 1886
2038 Pacific Ave., Forest Grove 97116; 503-357-3181; Fax: 503-359-8456
Web: http://portlandtribune.com/forest-grove-news-times-news

Gold Beach

Curry County Reporter

Wed; Matt Hall (P/E); Circ. 2,351; Estab. 1914

PO Box 766, Gold Beach 97444; 541-247-6643; Fax: 541-247-6644

Web: www.currycountyreporter.com

Grants Pass

Grants Pass Daily Courier

Mon–Sat p.m.; Dennis Mack (P); Dennis Roler (E); Circ. 14,073; Estab. 1885

PO Box 1468, Grants Pass 97528-0330; 541-474-3700; Fax: 541-474-3814

Web: www.thedailycourier.com

Gresham

The Outlook

Tue, Fri; Mark Garber (P); Tiffaney O'Dell (E); Circ. 7,434; Estab. 1911

PO Box 747, Gresham 97030; 503-665-2181; Fax: 503-665-2187

Web: http://portlandtribune.com/gresham-outlook-news

Halfway

Hells Canyon Journal

Wed; Steve Backstrom (P/E); Circ. 1,099; Estab. 1984

PO Box 646, Halfway 97834; 541-742-7900; Fax: 541-742-7933

Heppner

Heppner Gazette-Times

Wed; David Sykes (P); Andrea Di Salvo (E); Circ. 1,421; Estab. 1883

PO Box 337, Heppner 97836; 541-676-9228; Fax: 541-676-9211

Hermiston

The Hermiston Herald

Wed, Fri; Randy Thompson (E); Circ. 1,301; Estab. 1906

333 E Main St., Hermiston 97838; 541-567-6457; Fax: 541-567-1764

Web: www.hermistonherald.com

Hillsboro

Hillsboro Argus

Tue, Fri; Chris Anderson (P); Tom Maurer (E); Circ. 6,539; Estab. 1873

PO Box 588, Hillsboro 97123; 503-648-1131; Fax: 503-648-9191

Web: www.oregonlive.com/argus

Hood River

Hood River News

Wed, Sat; Joe Petshow (P); Kirby Neumann-Rea (E); Circ. 4,678; Estab. 1905

PO Box 390, Hood River 97031; 541-386-1234; Fax: 541-386-6796

Web: www.hoodrivernews.com

John Day

Blue Mountain Eagle

Wed; Marissa Williams (P); Scotta Callister (E); Circ. 2,572; Estab. 1898

195 N Canyon Blvd., John Day 97845; 541-575-0710; Fax: 541-575-1244

Web: www.bluemountaineagle.com

Keizer

Keizertimes

Fri; Lyndon Zaitz (P); Jason Cox (E); Circ. 2,320; Estab. 1979

142 Chemawa Road N, Keizer 97303; 503-390-1051; Fax: 503-390-8023

Web: www.keizertimes.com

Klamath Falls

Herald and News

Tue–Sun a.m.; Heidi Wright (P); Steve Miller (E); Circ. 13,119; Estab. 1906

PO Box 788, Klamath Falls 97601; 541-885-4410; Fax: 541-885-4456

Web: www.heraldandnews.com

La Grande

The Observer

Mon, Wed, Fri; Kari Borgen (P); Glenn Rabinowitz (E); Circ. 5,259; Estab. 1896

1406 Fifth St., La Grande 97850; 541-963-3161; Fax: 541-963-7804

Web: www.lagrandeobserver.com

Lake Oswego

Lake Oswego Review

Thur; J. Brian Monihan (P); Martin Forbes (E); Circ. 5,831; Estab. 1920

PO Box 548, Lake Oswego OR 97034; 503-635-8811; Fax: 503-635-8817

Web: http://portlandtribune.com/lake-oswego-review-news

Lakeview

Lake County Examiner

Wed; Tillie Flynn (P/E); Circ. 2,409; Estab. 1880

739 N 2nd St., Lakeview 97630; 541-947-3378; Fax: 541-947-4359

Web: www.lakecountyexam.com

Lebanon

Lebanon Express

Wed; Mike McInally (P/E); Circ. 1,913; Estab. 1887

90 E Grant, Lebanon 97355; 541-258-3151; Fax: 541-259-3569

Web: www.lebanon-express.com

Lincoln City

The News Guard

Wed; Samantha Swindler (P/E); Circ. 3,236; Estab. 1927

PO Box 848, Lincoln City 97367; 541-994-2178; Fax: 541-994-7613

Web: www.thenewsguard.com

Madras

The Madras Pioneer

Wed; Tony Ahern (P); Susan Matheny (E); Circ. 3,773; Estab. 1904

345 SE Fifth St., Madras 97741; 541-475-2275; Fax: 541-475-3710

Web: www.madraspioneer.com

McKenzie Bridge

McKenzie River Reflections

Thur; Ken Engelman (P); Louise Engelman (E); Circ. 713; Estab. 1978

59059 Old McKenzie Hwy., McKenzie Bridge 97413; Phone: 541-822-3358; Fax: 541-663-4558

Web: http://mckenzieriverreflectionsnewspaper.com

McMinnville

News-Register

Wed, Sat; Jeb Bladine (P); Steve Bagwell (E); Circ. 8,808; Estab. 1866

PO Box 727, McMinnville 97128; 503-472-5114; Fax: 503-472-9151

Web: www.newsregister.com

Medford

Mail Tribune

Mon–Sun a.m.; J. Grady Singletary (P); Robert L. Hunter (E); Circ. 22,731 (Mon–Fri), 23,089 (Sat), 24,864 (Sun); Estab. 1906

PO Box 1108, Medford 97501; 541-776-4411; Fax: 541-776-4376

Web: www.mailtribune.com

Mill City

Independent Press

Wed; William Downer (P); Circ. 1,000; Estab. 1998

PO Box 108, Mill City 97360; 503-897-4216

E-mail: indypress@frontier.com

Milton-Freewater

Valley Herald

Fri; Melanie Hall (P/E); Circ. 751; Estab. 2001

PO Box 664, Milton-Freewater 97862; 541-938-6688; Fax: 541-938-6689

Web: www.mfvalleyherald.com

Molalla

Molalla Pioneer

Wed; Joe Wilson (P); Bethany Monroe (E); Circ. 3,495; Estab. 1913

PO Box 168, Molalla 97038; 503-829-2301; Fax: 503-829-2317

Web: www.molallapioneer.com

Myrtle Creek

The Douglas County Mail

Thur; Robert L. Chaney, Sr. (P/E); Circ. 1,038; Estab. 1902

PO Box 729, Myrtle Creek 97457; 541-863-5233; Fax: 541-863-5234

Myrtle Point

Myrtle Point Herald

Thur; Sherry Anderson (P); Mary Schamehorn (E); Circ. 1,700; Estab. 1889

PO Box 606, Myrtle Point 97458; 541-572-2717; Fax: 541-572-2828

Newberg

The Newberg Graphic

Wed, Sat; Al Herriges (P); Gary Allen (E); Circ. 4,960; Estab. 1888

PO Box 700, Newberg 97132; 503-538-2181; Fax: 503-538-1632

Web: www.newberggraphic.com

Newport

News-Times

Wed, Fri; Jeremy Burke (P); Steve Card (E); Circ. 7,011; Estab. 1882

PO Box 965, Newport 97365; 541-265-8571; Fax: 541-265-3103

Web: www.newportnewstimes.com

Oakridge

Dead Mountain Echo

Thur; Larry Roberts (P/E); Circ. 456; Estab. 1973

PO Box 900, Oakridge 97463; 541-782-4241; Fax: 541-782-3323

Ontario

Argus Observer

Tue–Fri p.m., Sun a.m.; John Dillon (P); Scott McIntosh (E); Circ. 6,837; Estab. 1896

1160 SW Fourth St., Ontario 97914; 541-889-5387; Fax: 541-889-3347

Web: www.argusobserver.com

Pendleton

East Oregonian

Tue–Sun; Tom Brown (P&E); Circ. 7,343; Estab. 1875

211 SE Byers Ave., Pendleton 97801; 541-276-2211; Fax: 541-276-8314

Web: www.eastoregonian.com

Pendleton Record

Thur; Marguerite Maznaritz (P); Sam Westover (E); Circ. 876; Estab. 1911

PO Box 69, Pendleton 97801; 541-276-2853; Fax: 541-278-2916

Port Orford

Port Orford News

Wed; Matt Hall (P/E); Circ. 982; Estab. 1958
PO Box 5, Port Orford 97465; 541-260-3638
Web: www.portorfordnews.net

Portland

Daily Journal of Commerce

Mon–Fri a.m.; Stephanie Basalyga (E); Circ. 2,278; Estab. 1872
921 SW Washington St., Suite 210, Portland 97205; 503-226-1311; Fax: 503-226-1315
Web: www.djcoregon.com

Portland Tribune

Thur; Mark Garber (P/E); Circ. 102,500; Estab. 2001
6605 SE Lake Rd., Portland 97222; 503-226-6397; Fax: 503-226-7042
Web: www.portlandtribune.com

The Asian Reporter

Bi-monthly (1st and 3rd Mon); Jaime Lim (P/E); Circ. 26,000; Estab. 1990
922 N. Killingsworth St., Portland 97217; 503-283-4440; Fax: 503-283-4445
Web: www.asianreporter.com

The Oregonian

Mon–Sun a.m.; Chris Anderson (P); Peter Bhatia (E); Circ. 247,833 (Mon–Fri), 238,883 (Sat), 306,712 (Sun); Estab. 1850
1320 SW Broadway, Portland 97201; 503-221-8327; Fax: 503-227-5306
Web: www.oregonlive.com/oregonian

The Skanner

Wed; Bernie Foster (P); Circ. 75,000; Estab. 1975
PO Box 5455, Portland 97228; 503-285-5555; Fax: 503-285-2900
Web: www.theskanner.com

Willamette Week

Wed; Richard Meeker (P) Mark Zusman (E); Circ. 85,000; Estab. 1974
2220 NW Quimby St., Portland 97210; 503-243-2122; Fax: 503-243-1115
Web: www.wweek.com

Prineville

Central Oregonian

Tue, Fri; Vance W. Tong (P/E); Circ. 2,829; Estab. 1881
558 N Main St., Prineville 97754; 541-447-6205; Fax: 541-447-1754
Web: www.centraloregonian.com

Redmond

The Redmond Spokesman

Wed; Steve Hawes (P); Leslie Pugmire Hole (E); Circ. 2,385; Estab. 1910
PO Box 788, Redmond 97756; 541-548-2184; Fax: 541-548-3203
Web: http://redmondspokesman.blogspot.com

Reedsport

The Umpqua Post

Wed; Clark Walworth (P); Sarah Haase (E); Circ. 1,101; Estab. 1996
PO Box 145, Reedsport 97467; 541-271-7474; Fax: 541-271-2821
Web: www.theumpquapost.com

Rogue River

Rogue River Press

Wed; Teresa Pearson (P); Tammy Asnicar (E); Circ. 1,582; Estab. 1962
PO Box 1485, Rogue River 97537; 541-582-1707; Fax: 541-582-0201
Web: www.rogueriverpress.com

Roseburg

The News-Review

Mon–Fri p.m., Sun a.m.; Jeff Ackerman (P); Vicki Menard (E); Circ. 16,549; Estab. 1867
PO Box 1248, Roseburg 97470; 541-672-3321; Fax: 541-957-4265
Web: www.nrtoday.com

Salem

Capital Press

Fri; Mike O'Brien (P); Joe Beach (E); Circ. 38,765; Estab. 1928
PO Box 2048, Salem 97308-2048; 503-364-4431; Fax: 503-370-4383
Web: www.capitalpress.com

Statesman Journal

Mon–Sun a.m.; Steve Silberman (P); Michelle Maxwell (Interim Editor); Circ. 36,629 (Mon–Fri); 38,168 (Sat); 46,059 (Sun); Estab. 1851
PO Box 13009, Salem 97309; 503-399-6611; Fax: 503-399-6706
Web: www.statesmanjournal.com

Sandy

The Sandy Post

Wed; Mark Garber (P); Steve Brown (E); Circ. 2,722; Estab. 1937
PO Box 68, Sandy 97055; 503-668-5548; Fax: 503-668-0748
Web: http://portlandtribune.com/sandy-post-news

Scappoose

The South County Spotlight

Wed; Darryl Swan (P); Stover E. Harger III (E); Circ. 3,410; Estab. 1961
PO Box C, Scappoose 97056; 503-543-6387; Fax: 503-543-6380
Web: http://portlandtribune.com/south-county-spotlight-news

Seaside

Seaside Signal

Thur; Jeremy C. Ruark (P/E); Circ. 1,032; Estab. 1905

PO Box 848, Seaside 97138; 503-738-5561; Fax: 503-738-9285

Web: www.seasidesignal.com

Sheridan

The Sun

Wed; Clinton Vining (P/E); Circ. 1,070; Estab. 1890

PO Box 68, Sheridan 97378; 503-843-2312; Fax: 503-843-3830

Web: www.sheridansun.com

Silverton

Appeal Tribune

Wed; Steve Silberman (P/E); Circ. 1,067; Estab. 1880

PO Box 35, Silverton 97381; 503-873-8385; Fax: 503-873-8064

Web: www.statesmanjournal.com/section/silverton

Springfield

Springfield Times

Fri; Scott J. Olson (P); Craig Murphy (E); Circ. 1,443; Estab. 2008

PO Box 1859, Springfield 97477, 541-741-7368; Fax: 541-741-7380

Web: www.springfieldtimes.net

St. Helens

The Chronicle

Wed; Don Patterson (P); Shari Phiel (E); Circ. 4,092; Estab. 1881

PO Box 1153, St. Helens 97051; 503-397-0116; Fax: 503-397-4093

Web: www.thechronicleonline.com

Stayton

The Stayton Mail

Wed; Steve Silberman (P/E); Circ. 790; Estab. 1894

PO Box 400, Stayton 97383; 503-769-6338; Fax: 503-769-6207

Web: www.statesmanjournal.com/section/stayton

Sutherlin

Douglas County News

Wed; Becky Holm (P/E); Circ. 2,124; Estab. 2002

352 S Calapooia, Suite A, Sutherlin 97479; 541-459-0716; Fax: 541-459-0283

Web: www.douglascountynews.info

Sweet Home

The New Era

Wed; Scott Swanson (P/E); Circ. 1,851; Estab. 1929

PO Box 39, Sweet Home 97386; 541-367-2135; Fax: 541-367-2137

Web: http://sweethomenews.com

The Dalles

The Dalles Chronicle

Tue–Fri p.m., Sun a.m., Marilyn Roth (P); Kathy Ursprung (E); Circ. 3,530; Estab. 1890

PO Box 1910, The Dalles 97058; 541-296-2141; Fax: 541-298-1365

Web: www.gorgenews.com

Tigard/Tualatin/Sherwood

The Times

Thur; Christine Moore (P); Christina Lent (E); Circ. 2,976; Estab. 1956

PO Box 22109, Portland 97269; 503-684-0360; Fax: 503-620-3433

Web: http://portlandtribune.com/the-times-news

Tillamook

Headlight-Herald

Wed; Samantha Swindler (P/E); Circ. 6,176; Estab. 1888

PO Box 444, Tillamook 97141; 503-842-7535; Fax: 503-842-8842

Web: www.tillamookheadlightherald.com

Vale

Malheur Enterprise

Wed; Rick Nelson (P/E); Circ. 1,253; Estab. 1909

PO Box 310, Vale 97918; 541-473-3377; Fax: 541-473-3268

Warrenton

The Columbia Press

Fri; Gary Nevan (P/E); Circ. 862; Estab. 1922

PO Box 130, Warrenton 97146; 503-861-3331; Fax: 503-325-1477

Web: www.thecolumbiapress.com

West Linn

West Linn Tidings

Thur; Mark Garber (P); Lori Hall (E); Circ. 2,731; Estab. 1981

PO Box 548, Lake Oswego 97034; 503-635-8811; Fax: 503-635-8817

Web: http://portlandtribune.com/west-linn-tidings-news

Wilsonville

Wilsonville Spokesman

Wed; William D. Cassel (P); Michelle Te (E); Circ. 3,338; Estab. 1985

PO Box 1108, Canby 97013; 503-682-3935; Fax: 503-266-6836

Web: www.wilsonvillespokesman.com

Woodburn

Woodburn Independent

Wed, Sat; Nikki DeBuse (P); Jason Horton (E); Circ. 3,490; Estab. 1888

PO Box 96, Woodburn 97071; 503-981-3441; Fax: 503-981-1253

Web: www.woodburnindependent.com

Selected Periodicals Published in Oregon

The State Library has compiled a representative sample of the many periodicals published in Oregon. The first year of each periodical's publication follows its title and publication schedule.

Key: A = Annual; BM = Bi-monthly; BW = Bi-weekly; M = Monthly; Q = Quarterly; SA = Semi-annual; SM = Semi-monthly; W = Weekly

Agri-Times Northwest (SM) 1984: Sterling Ag, LLC, PO Box 1626, Pendleton 97801-0189; 541-276-6202; Web: www.agritimesnw.com

Animal Law Review (SA) 1995: Lewis & Clark Law School, 10015 SW Terwilliger Blvd., Portland 97219; 503-768-6798; Fax: 503-768-6671;
Web: http://law.lclark.edu/law_reviews/animal_law_review

Backwoods Home Magazine (BM) 1989: PO Box 712, Gold Beach 97444; 541-247-8900; Fax: 541-247-8600; Web: www.backwoodshome.com

Book Dealers World (Q) 1980: North American Exchange, PO Box 606, Cottage Grove 97424; Phone/Fax: 541-942-7455;
Web: www.bookmarketingprofits.com

Calyx (SA) 1976: PO Box B, Corvallis 97339; 541-753-9384/1-888-336-2665; Fax: 541-753-0515; Web: www.calyxpress.org

Central Oregon Magazine (Q) 2010: 63088 NE 18th St., Suite 200 Bend 97701; 541-385-3560; Fax: 541-388-0456;
Web: www.centraloregonmagazine.com

Dialogue (BM) 1961: Blindskills, Inc., PO Box 5181, Salem 97304-0181; 503-581-4224/1-800-860-4224; Fax: 503-581-0178;
Web: www.blindskills.com

Digger (M) 1988: Oregon Association of Nurseries, 29751 SW Town Center Loop W, Wilsonville 97070; 503-682-5089/1-800-342-6401; Fax: 503-682-5099; Web: www.oan.org

El Hispanic News (W) 1981: PO Box 306, Portland 97207-0306; 503-228-3139; Fax: 503-228-3384; Web: www.elhispanicnews.com

El Latino de Hoy: Semanario Latinoamericano de Oregon (W) 1991: 7112 NE Sandy Blvd., Portland 97213; 503-493-1106; 503-493-1126; Fax: 503-493-1107; Web: www.ellatinodehoy.com

Environmental Law (Q) 1970: Lewis & Clark Law School, 10015 SW Terwilliger Blvd., Portland 97219; 503-768-6700; Fax: 503-768-6671;
Web: http://law.lclark.edu/law_reviews/environmental_law

Eugene Magazine (Q) 2006: Olive Tree, LLC., 1400 High St, Suite C-3, Eugene 97401; 541-686-6608; Fax 541-686-8008;
Web: www.eugenemagazine.com

Flyfishing and Tying Journal (Q) 1978: Frank Amato Publications, PO Box 82112, Portland 97282; 503-653-8108/1-800-541-9498; Fax: 503-653-2766; Web: www.amatobooks.com

Glimmer Train (Q) 1992: Glimmer Train Press, Inc., PO Box 80430, Portland 97280-1430; 503-221-0836; Fax: 503-221-0837;
Web: www.glimmertrain.com/index.html

Heritage Newsletter (M) 1987: Linn County Genealogical Society, PO Box 1222, Albany 97321-0537; 541-791-1618;
Web: www.lgsoregon.org

High Desert Journal (SA) 2005: PO Box 7647, Bend 97708; 541-419-9836;
Web: http://highdesertjournal.com

Home Power (BM) 1987: Home Power, PO Box 520, Ashland 97520-0520; 541-512-0201/1-800-707-6585; Fax: 541-512-0343;
Web: https://homepower.com/home

Journal of Environmental Law and Litigation (SA) 1985: University of Oregon, 138 Knight Law Center, 1515 Agate St., Eugene 97403; 541-346-3844; Web: http://law.uoregon.edu/org/jell

Learning and Leading with Technology (8x yr) 1995: International Society for Technology in Education, 180 West 8th Ave. Suite 300, Eugene 97401-2916; 1-800-336-5191; Fax: 541-302-3778;
Web: www.iste.org/learn/publications/learning-leading

Metroscape (SA) 1995: Institute of Portland Metropolitan Studies, Portland State University, PO Box 751, Portland 97207-0751; 503-725-5170; Fax: 503-725-5199;
Web: www.pdx.edu/ims/metroscape

Midwifery Today (Q) 1987: PO Box 2672, Eugene 97402; 541-344-7438/1-800-743-0974; Fax: 541-344-1422;
Web: www.midwiferytoday.com

Northwest Labor Press (SM) 1987: PO Box 13150, Portland 97213; 503-288-3311;
Web: http://nwlaborpress.org

Northwest Palate (BM) 1987: PO Box 10860, Portland 97296; 503-224-6039/1-800-398-7842; Fax: 503-222-5312;
Web: http://northwestpalate.com

Noticias Latinas! Latin News! (Q) 1995: 524 SE 14th Ave., Portland 97214; 503-227-7780; Fax: 503-227-7790;
Web: www.latinmedianw.com

OLA Quarterly (Q) 1995: Oregon Library Association, PO Box 3067, La Grande, OR 97850; 541-962-5824; Web: www.olaweb.org

Open Spaces: Views From the Northwest (Q) 1998: Open Spaces Publishing, 6327-C SW Capitol Hwy., PMB 134, Portland 97239-1937; 503-227-5764; Fax: 503-227-3401;
Web: www.open-spaces.com

Oregon Business Magazine (M) 1981: MIF Publications, Inc., 715 SW Morrison St., Suite 800, Portland 97205; 888-881-5861, 503-223-0304; Fax: 503-221-6544;
Web: www.oregonbusiness.com

Oregon Coast (BM) 1982: Northwest Regional Magazines, 4969 Hwy. 101, #2, Florence 97439; 541-997-8401/1-800-348-8401; Fax: 541-997-1124;
Web: www.northwestmagazines.com

Oregon Grange Bulletin (M) 1990: Oregon State Grange, 643 Union St. NE, Salem 97301; 503-316-0106; Fax: 503-316-0109;
Web: www.orgrange.org/bulletin.htm

Oregon Historical Quarterly (Q) 1900: Oregon Historical Society, 1200 SW Park Ave., Portland 97205; 503-306-5198; Fax: 503-221-2035;
Web: www.ohs.org/research/quarterly/index.cfm

Oregon Home (BM) 1997: MediAmerica, 610 SW Broadway, Suite 200, Portland 97205; 503-223-0304; Fax: 503-221-6544;
Web: www.oregonhomemagazine.com

Oregon Hunter (BM) 1983: Oregon Hunters Association, PO Box 1706, Medford 97501; 541-772-7313;
Web: www.oregonhunters.org/magazine.htm

Oregon Law Review (Q) 1921: University of Oregon, 139A Knight Law Center, 1515 Agate St., Eugene 97403; 541-346-3844;
Web: http://law.uoregon.edu/org/olr

Oregon Review of International Law (A) 1999: University of Oregon, 137A Knight Law Center, 1515 Agate St., Eugene 97403; 541-346-3849; Fax: 541-346-1596;
Web: http://law.uoregon.edu/org/oril

Oregon Wheat (7x yr) 1962: Oregon Wheat Growers League, 115 SE 8th St., Pendleton 97801-2319; 541-276-7330; Fax: 541-276-1723;
Web: www.owgl.org

Oregon's Agricultural Progress (Q) 1953: Oregon State University, Agricultural Experiment Station, 422 Kerr Admin. Bldg., Corvallis 97331-2119; 541-737-3311; Fax: 541-737-0817;
Web: http://oregonprogress.oregonstate.edu

Parenting Now! (Q) 1978: 86 Centennial Loop, Eugene 97401; 541-484-5316; Fax: 541-484-1449;
Web: http://info.parentingnow.org

Peaceworker (M) 2003: 104 Commercial St. NE Salem 97301; 503-585-2767; Fax: 503-588-0088;
Web: http://peaceworker.org

Portland Monthly (M) 2003: Portland Monthly Magazine, 921 SW Washington St., Suite 750, Portland 97205; 503-222-5144; Fax: 503-227-8777;
Web: www.portlandmonthlymag.com

Random Lengths (W) 1944: PO Box 867, Eugene 97440-0867; 541-686-9925; Fax: 1-800-874-7979; Web: www.randomlengths.com

Resource Recycling (M) 1982: Resource Recycling, PO Box 42270, Portland 97242-0270; 503-233-1305; Fax: 503-233-1356;
Web: www.resource-recycling.com

Rubberstampmadness (BM) 1980: RSM Enterprises, Inc., PO Box 610, Corvallis 97339-0610; 541-752-0075/1-877-782-6762;
Web: www.rsmadness.com

Ruralite (M) 1953: Ruralite Services, Inc., PO Box 558, Forest Grove 97116-2333; 503-357-2105; Fax: 503-357-8615; Web: www.ruralite.org

Skipping Stones (BM) 1988: PO Box 3939, Eugene 97403-0939; 541-342-4956;
Web: www.skippingstones.org

Small Farmers Journal (Q) 1976: PO Box 1627, Sisters 97759-1627; 541-549-2064/1-800-876-2893; Fax: 541-549-4403;
Web: http://smallfarmersjournal.com

Tinnitus Today (Q) 1975: American Tinnitus Association, PO Box 5, Portland 97207-0005; 503-248-9985/1-800-634-8978; Fax: 503-248-0024;
Web: www.ata.org/home

Travel Oregon (Q) 2002: Oregon Tourism Commission, PO Box 14070, Portland 97293-0070; 1-800-547-7842; Web: http://traveloregon.com

Western Places (SA) 1992: PO Box 2093, Lake Grove 97035; 503-635-1379
Web: www.westernplaces.net

Willamette Journal of International Law and Dispute Resolution (A) 1997: Willamette University College of Law, 245 Winter St. SE, Rm. 226, Salem 97301; 503-370-6632; Fax: 503-370-6579;
Web: http://willamette.edu/wucl/wjildr

Willamette Law Review (Q) 1978: Willamette University College of Law, 245 Winter St. SE, Salem 97301; 503-370-6186; Fax: 503-375-5463;
Web: www.willamette.edu/wucl/resources/journals/wjildr

Oregon Radio Stations

Source: Oregon Association of Broadcasters
Contact: Bill Johnstone, President/CEO
Address: 9020 SW Washington Square Rd., Suite 140, Portland 97223-4433
Phone: 503-443-2299; 800-843-6221
Fax: 503-443-2488
Web: www.theoab.org

Albany

KHPE-FM (107.9) Contemporary Christian Music;
KWIL-AM (790) Christian Bible Teaching
PO Box 278, Albany 97321; 541-926-2233; Fax: 541-926-3925; Randy Davison

KRKT-FM (99.9) Country;
KTHH-AM (990) Comedy
2840 Marion St. SE, Albany 97321; 541-926-8628; Fax: 541-928-1261; Larry Rogers

Astoria

KAST-AM (1370) News/Talk;
KCRX-FM (102.3) Classic Rock;
KLMY-FM (99.7) Hot Adult Contemporary;
KVAS-AM (1230) Classic Country;
KVAS-FM (103.9) Country
285 SW Main Ct., Suite 200, Warrenton 97146; 503-861-6620; Fax: 503-861-6630; Trila Bumstead

KCYS-FM (98.1) Hot Country
PO Box 1258, Astoria 97103; 503-717-9643; Fax: 503-717-9578; Dave Heick

Baker City

KBKR-AM (1490) Talk;
KKBC-FM (95.3) Classic Hits
2510 E Cove Ave., La Grande 97850; 541-963-4121; Fax: 541-963-3117; Becky Hunter

KCMB-FM (104.7) Country
1009-C Adams Ave., La Grande 97850; 541-963-3405; Fax: 541-963-5090; Randy McKone

Bandon

KBDN-FM (96.5) Classic Country
PO Box 180, Coos Bay 97420; 541-267-2121; Fax: 541-267-5229; George Feola

Bend/Redmond

KBND-AM (1110) News/Talk;
KLRR-FM (101.7) Adult Contemporary/Adult Album Alternative;
KMTK-FM (99.7) Country;
KTWS-FM (98.3) Classic Rock;
KWXS-FM (107.7) Contemporary Hit Radio
PO Box 5037, Bend 97708; 541-382-5263; Fax: 541-388-0456; Chuck Chackel

KBNW-AM (1340/104.5 translator in Bend) News/Talk/Information;
KLTW-FM (95.7) Adult Contemporary;
KQAK-FM (105.7) Classic Hits;
KWLZ-FM (96.5) News/Talk/Information;
KWPK-FM (104.1) Hot Adult Contemporary
854 NE 4th St., Bend 97701; 541-383-3825; Fax: 541-383-3403; Keith Shipman

KICE-AM (940) Sports/Talk;
KMGX-FM (100.7) Adult Contemporary;
KRXF-FM (92.7) Modern Rock;
KSJJ-FM (102.9) Country;
KXIX-FM (94.1) Contemporary Hit Radio
345 SW Cyber Dr., Suites 101–103, Bend 97702; 541-388-3300; Fax: 541-388-3303; Jim Gross

KNLR-FM (97.5) Contemporary Christian;
KNLX-FM (104.9) Contemporary Christian/Spanish Christian
PO Box 7408, Bend 97708; 541-389-8873; Fax: 541-389-5291; Terry Cowan

KRCO-AM (690/96.9 translator in Prineville) Classic Country
PO Box 690, Prineville 97754; 541-447-6770; Fax: 541-383-3403; Keith Shipman

Brookings

KURY-AM (910) Adult Standards;
KURY-FM (95.3) Classic Hits
PO Box 1029, Brookings 97415; 541-469-2111; Fax: 541-469-6397; Brian Papstein

Burns

KBNH-AM (1230) True Country
PO Box 877, Burns 97720; 541-573-2055; Fax: 541-573-5223; Leighton (Linc) Reed-Nickerson

KORC-FM (92.7) Classic Hits
PO Box 877, Burns 97720; 541-573-2055; Fax: 866-541-5390; Leighton (Linc) Reed-Nickerson

Cave Junction

KCNA-FM (102.7)

Coos Bay/North Bend

KBBR-AM (1340) Progressive News/Talk;
KOOS-FM (107.3/107.7) Hot Adult Contemporary;
KTEE-FM (94.9/95.7) Adult Album Alternative
PO Box 180, Coos Bay 97420; 541-267-2121; Fax: 541-267-5229; George Feola

KDCQ-FM (92.9) Classic Hits/Oldies
PO Box 478, Coos Bay 97420; 541-269-0929; Fax: 541-269-9376; Stephanie Kilmer

KHSN-AM (1230)

KYSJ-FM (105.9) Smooth Jazz
580 Kingwood Ave., Coos Bay 97420; 541-266-8531; Fax: 541-267-0114; Rick Stevens

KYTT-FM (98.7) Contemporary Christian
580 Kingwood Ave., Coos Bay 97420; 541-269-2022; Fax: 541-267-0114; Rick Stevens

Coquille

KSHR-FM (97.3) Hot Country;
KWRO-AM (630) Conservative News/Talk
PO Box 180, Coos Bay 97420; 541-267-2121; Fax: 541-267-5229; George Feola

Corvallis

KEJO-AM (1240) Sports Talk;
KLOO-AM (1340) News/Talk;
KLOO-FM (106.3) Classic Rock
2840 Marion St. SE, Albany 97322; 541-926-8628; Fax: 541-928-1261; Larry Rogers

Cottage Grove

KNND-AM (1400)

Dallas

KWIP-AM (880) Regional Mexican
PO Box 469, Dallas 97338; 503-623-0245; Fax: 503-623-6733; Ayesh Shannah

Elgin

KRJT-FM (105.9) Classic Hits
2510 E Cove Ave., La Grande 97850; 541-963-4121; Fax: 541-963-3117; Becky Hunter

Enterprise

KWVR-AM (1340) Talk/Sports/News;
KWVR-FM (92.1) Country
220 W Main St., Enterprise 97828; 541-426-4577; Fax: 541-426-4578; David Frasch

Eugene/Springfield

KDUK-FM (104.7) Top 40 Hits;
KFLY-FM (101.5) Mainstream Rock;
KOOL-FM (99.1) Classic Hits;
KPNW-AM (1120) News/Talk/Sports
1500 Valley River Dr., Suite 350, Eugene 97401; 541-284-3600; Fax: 541-484-5769; Larry Rogers

KEHK-FM (102.3) Bright Adult Contemporary;
KNRQ-FM (97.9) Alternative Rock/Active Rock;
KSCR-AM (1320) Talk Network;
KUGN-AM (590) News/Talk;
KUJZ-FM (95.3) Sports/Talk;
KZEL-FM (96.1) Quality/Classic Rock
1200 Executive Pkwy., Suite 440, Eugene 97401; 541-284-8500; Fax: 541-485-0969; B. J. O'Brien

KEUG-FM (105.5) Adult Hits
KKNU-FM (93.3) New Country;
KMGE-FM (94.5) Adult Contemporary
925 Country Club Rd., Suite 200, Eugene 97401; 541-484-9400; Fax: 541-344-9424; John Tilson

KKNX-AM (840) Hits of the '60s through '80s, CBS News, OSU Sports
1142 Willagillespie Rd. #28, Eugene 97401; 541-342-1012; Fax: 541-342-6201; John S. Mielke

KLZS-AM (1450)

KORE-AM (1050) Christian Programs/Talk
2080 Laura St., Springfield 97477-2197; 541-747-5673; Larry Knight

KQFE-FM (88.9)

Florence

KCFM-AM (1250) Adult Standards/Music of Your Life;
KCFM-FM (104.1/103.1 in Mapleton) Adult Standards;
KCST-FM (106.9) Adult Contemporary Gold
PO Box 20000, Florence 97439; 541-997-9136; Fax: 541-997-9165; Jon Thompson

Gold Beach

KGBR-FM (92.7) Hot Adult Contemporary
PO Box 787, Gold Beach 97444-0787; 541-247-7211; Fax: 541-247-4155; Dale St. Marie

Grants Pass

KAJO-AM (1270) Full Service/Talk/Music
888 Rogue River Hwy., Grants Pass 97527; 541-476-6608; Fax: 541-476-4018; Carl Wilson

KCMD-FM (99.3) Classical Hits
820 NE 7th St., Suite 1, Grants Pass 97526 503-476-2137; Don Monette

KLDR-FM (98.3) Hot Modern Adult Contemporary
888 Rogue River Hwy., Grants Pass 97527; 541-474-7292; Fax: 541-474-7300; Carl Wilson

KROG-FM (97.1)

KRRM-FM (94.7) Classic Country/Bluegrass/ Cowboy Music and Poetry
225 Rogue River Hwy., Grants Pass 97527; 541-479-6497; Fax: 541-479-5726; Herb Bell

Hermiston

KLKY-FM (96.1)

KOHU-AM (1360) Country;
KQFM-FM (100.1) Adult Contemporary
PO Box 145, Hermiston 97838-0145; 541-567-6500; Fax: 541-567-6068; Angela Pursel

Hood River

KCGB-FM (105.5/96.9) Adult Contemporary;
KIHR-AM (1340/98.3) Country/Information
PO Box 360, Hood River 97031; 541-386-1511; Fax: 541-386-7155; Gary Grossman

Jacksonville

KAPL-AM (1300)

John Day

KJDY-AM (1400) Country;
KJDY-FM (94.5) Country
PO Box 399, John Day 97845; 541-575-1400; Fax: 541-575-2313; Phil Gray

Junction City

KXOR-AM (660)

Klamath Falls

KAGO-AM (1150) News/Talk;
KAGO-FM (99.5) Rock;
KLAD-AM (960) Country Legends;
KLAD-FM (92.5) Country Legends
404 Main St., Suite 4, Klamath Falls 97601; 541-882-8833; Fax: 541-882-8836; Rob Siems

KFEG-FM (104.7) Classic Rock;
KFLS-AM (1450) News/Talk/Sports;
KFLS-FM (96.5) Country;
KKRB-FM (106.9) Adult Contemporary
1338 Oregon Ave., Klamath Falls 97601; 541-882-4656; Fax: 541-884-2845; Robert Wynne

KKKJ-FM (105.5) Rythmic Contemporary Hit Radio
1338 Oregon Ave., Klamath Falls 97601; 541-850-5242; Fax: 541-884-2845; Robert Wynne

KRAM-AM (1070)

La Grande

KLMB-AM (1450) News/Talk;
KUBQ-FM (98.7) Classic Rock
2510 E Cove Ave., La Grande 97850; 541-963-4121; 541-963-3117; Becky Hunter

KWRL-FM (99.9) Adult Contemporary
1009-C Adams Ave., La Grande 97850; 541-963-3405; Fax: 541-963-5090; Randy McKone

Lakeview

KORV-FM (93.5) Real Country
PO Box 877, Burns 97720; 541-573-2055; Fax: 541-573-5223; Marcie Wade

KQIK-AM (1230)

Lebanon

KGAL-AM (1580) News/Talk/Sports;
KSHO-AM (920) Adult Standards
PO Box 749, Albany 97321; 541-451-5425; Fax: 541-451-5429; Charlie Eads

Lincoln City

KBCH-AM (1400) Adult Standards/Talk/Sports;
KCRF-FM (96.7) Classic Rock
PO Box 1430, Newport 97365; 541-265-2266; Fax: 541-265-6397; Dave Miller

McMinnville

KLYC-AM (1260) Classic Hits
PO Box 1099, McMinnville 97128; 503-472-1260; Fax: 503-472-3243; Dick Mason

Medford/Ashland/Phoenix

KAKT-FM (105.1) Country;
KBOY-FM (95.7) Classic Rock;
KCMX-AM (880) News/Talk;
KCMX-FM (101.9) Adult Contemporary;
KTMT-AM (580) ESPN Sports;
KTMT-FM (93.7) Hit Adult Contemporary
1438 Rossanley Dr., Medford 97501; 541-779-1550; Fax: 541-776-2360; Joe Mussio

KDOV-FM (91.7) News/Talk/Christian
1236 Disk Dr., Suite E, Medford 97501; 541-776-5368; Fax: 541-842-4334; Perry Atkinson

KIFS-FM (107.5) Contemporary Hits Radio;
KLDZ-FM (103.5) Classic Hits;
KRWQ-FM (100.3) Country
3624 Avion Dr., Medford 97504; 541-772-4170; Fax: 541-857-0326; Susu Mahood

KLVB-AM (730)

KMED-AM (1440) News/Talk
3624 Avion Dr., Medford 97504; 541-773-1440; Fax: 541-857-0326; Susu Mahood

KRTA-AM (610)

KZZE-FM (106.3) Rock
3624 Avion Dr., Medford 97504; 541-857-0340; Fax: 541-857-0326; Susu Mahood

Milton-Freewater

KTHK-FM (97.9)

Newport

KCUP-AM (1230) News/Talk;
KPPT-FM (100.7) Hits of '60s, '70s and Beyond
PO Box 456, Newport 97365; 541-265-5000 Fax: 541-265-9576; Cheryl Harle

KNCU-FM (92.7) Country;
KNPT-AM (1310/98.3 translator) News/Talk/Sports;
KYTE-FM (102.7) Adult Contemporary
PO Box 1430, Newport 97365; 541-265-2266; Fax: 541-265-6397; Dave Miller

KSHL-FM (97.5)

Ontario

KSRV-AM (1380) Country/Agricultural News
PO Box 129, Ontario 97914; 541-889-8651; Fax: 541-889-8733; Darrell Calton

KSRV-FM (96.1) Adult Hits
5660 Franklin Rd., Suite 200, Nampa, ID 83687 208-465-9966; Fax: 208-465-2922; Darrell Calton

Pendleton

KTIX-AM (1240) Sports;
KUMA-AM (1290) News/Talk;
KUMA-FM (92.1) Adult Contemporary
2003 NW 56th Dr., Pendleton 97801;
541-276-1511; Fax: 541-276-1480;
Julie Thompson

KWHT-FM (103.5) Country;
KWVN-FM (107.7) Variety
13 1/2 E Main St., Suite 202, Walla Walla, WA 99362; 509-522-1383; Fax: 509-522-0211;
Colleen Brady

Portland

KBFF-FM (95.5) Adult Contemporary;
KUFO-AM (970) Talk;
KUPL-FM (98.7) Country;
KXL-FM (101.1) News/Talk/Sports;
KXTG-AM (750) Sports
1211 SW Fifth Ave., 6th Floor, Portland 97204;
503-517-6000; Fax: 503-517-6401; Bob Proffitt

KBMS-AM (1480)

KBNP-AM (1410)

KDZR-AM (1640) Family Hits
3030 SW Moody St., Suite 210, Portland 97201; 503-228-4322; Fax: 503-228-4325;
Stacey Bailey

KEX-AM (1190) News/Talk;
KEX-FM (102.3) News/Talk;
KFWB-FM (105.9) Classic Rock;
KLTH-FM (106.7) Classic Rock;
KPOJ-AM (620) Fox Sports;
KXJM-FM (107.5) Contemporary Hits
13333 SW 68th Pkwy., Suite 310, Tigard 97223;
503-323-6400; Fax: 503-323-6660;
Robert Dove

KFXX-AM (1080) Sports Talk;
KGON-FM (92.3) Classic Rock;
KNRK-FM (94.7) Alternative Rock;
KRSK-FM (105.1) Hot Adult Contemporary;
KWJJ-FM (99.5) Country;
KWOD-AM (1390) ESPN (simulcast);
KYCH-FM (97.1) Variety Hits
0700 SW Bancroft St., Portland 97239;
503-223-1441; Fax: 503-223-6909;
Tim McNamara

KGDD-AM (1520) "La GranD" Spanish Regional Variety;
KOOR-AM (1010) Russian Radio 7;
KQRR-AM (1130) Russian Religious;
KXET-FM (93.5) Mexican Regional;
KZZR-FM (94.3) Mexican Regional
5110 SE Stark, Portland 97215; 503-234-5550;
Fax: 503-234-5583; Amador Bustos

KINK-FM (101.9) Adult Album Alternative
1211 SW Fifth Ave., 6th Floor, Portland 97204; 503-517-6000; Fax: 503-517-6130;
Bob Proffitt

KKCW-FM (103.3) Adult Contemporary;
KKRZ-FM (100.3) Hot Adult Contemporary
13333 SW 68th Pkwy., Suite 310, Tigard 97223;
503-323-6400; Fax: 503-241-1033;
Robert Dove

KKOV-AM (1550) Talk;
KPAM-AM (860) News/Talk
6605 SE Lake Rd., Portland 97222-2161;
503-223-4321; Fax: 503-294-0074;
Jeanne Winter

KKPZ-AM (1330)

KKSL-AM (1290)

KLVP-AM (1040)

KLVP-FM (88.7)

KPDQ-AM (800)

KPDQ-FM (93.7)

KRYN-AM (1230) Christian Music
9834 17th St. NW, Seattle, WA 98106;
206-439-1188; Fax: 206-658-3135;
Amador Bustos

KUIK-AM (1360) News/Talk/Sports
PO Box 566, Hillsboro 97123; 503-640-1360;
Fax: 503-640-6108; Don McCoun

Redmond

KRDM-AM (1240)

Reedsport

KDUN-AM (1030) Oldies
136 N 7th St., Reedsport 97467; 541-271-5386;
Fax: 541-271-5140; Kent Abendroth

KJMX-FM (99.5/100.3) Classic Rock
PO Box 180, Coos Bay 97420; 541-267-2121;
Fax: 541-267-5229; George Feola

Roseburg

KKMX-FM (104.3) Adult Contemporary;
KQEN-AM (1240) News/Talk;
KRSB-FM (103.1) Contemporary Country;
KSKR-AM (1490) Sports;
KSKR-FM (101.1) Top 40
1445 W Harvard Blvd., Roseburg 97471;
541-672-6641; Fax: 541-673-7598;
Pat Markham

St. Helens

KOHI-AM (1600) News/Talk/Sports
36200 Pittsburg Rd., Suite C, St. Helens 97051;
503-397-1600; Fax: 503-397-1601; Marty Rowe

Salem

KBZY-AM (1490)

KPJC-AM (1220)

KYKN-AM (1430) News/Talk
PO Box 1430, Salem 97303; 503-390-3014;
Fax: 503-390-3728; Mike Frith

Scappoose

KFIS-FM (104.1)

Seaside

KCBZ-FM (96.5) Hot Adult Contemporary
PO Box 354, Seaside 97138; 503-738-8668; Fax: 503-738-8778; Cal Brady

KCYS-FM (98.1) Hot Country
PO Box 1258, Astoria 97103; 503-717-9643; Fax: 503-717-9578; Dave Heick

KSWB-AM (840) Classic Rock Oldies
PO Box 682, Seaside 97138; 503-717-5533; Fax: 503-717-5500; John Chapman

Stayton

KCKX-AM (1460) Traditional Country Music
PO Box 158, Woodburn 97071; 503-769-1460; Fax: 503-981-3561; Donald Coss

Sweet Home

KFIR-AM (720) News/Talk
PO Box 720, Sweet Home 97386; 541-367-5115; Fax: 541-367-5233; Michael Astalis

The Dalles

KACI-AM (1300/103.9 FM) News/Talk;
KACI-FM (93.5) Classic Hits;
KMSW-FM (92.7) Rock Classics
PO Box 1517, The Dalles 97058; 541-296-2211; Fax: 541-296-2213; Gary Grossman

KLCK-AM (1400) Talk;
KYYT-FM (102.3) Contemporary Country
PO Box 1023, The Dalles 97058; 541-296-9102; Fax: 541-298-7775; Shannon Milburn

KODL-AM (1440) Adult Standards
PO Box 1488, The Dalles 97058; 541-296-2101; Fax: 541-296-3766; Al Wynn

KWCQ-FM (106.1)

Tillamook

KDEP-FM (105.5) Oldies;
KRKZ-FM (94.3) Rock;
KTIL-AM (1590) News/Talk;
KTIL-FM (95.9) Mainstream Country
170 Third St. W, Tillamook 97141; 503-842-4422; Fax: 503-842-2755; Shaena Peterson

Umatilla

KLWJ-AM (1090)

Waldport

KWDP-AM (820) Adult Standards/Sports
PO Box 1430, Newport 97365; 541-265-2266; Fax: 541-265-6397; Dave Miller

Walla Walla, WA

KTEL-AM (1490) News/Talk
13-1/2 E Main St., Suite 202, Walla Walla, WA 99362; 509-522-1383; 509-522-0211; Colleen Brady

Winston

KGRV-AM (700)

Woodburn

KSND-FM (95.1) Spanish Language International Romantica/Oldies;
KWBY-AM (940) Spanish Language Music Regional Mexican/News/Sports
PO Box 158, Woodburn 97071; 503-981-9400; Fax: 503-981-3561; Donald Coss

Oregon Commercial Television Stations

Source: Oregon Association of Broadcasters
Contact: Bill Johnstone, President/CEO
Address: 9020 SW Washington Square Rd., Suite 140, Portland 97223-4433
Phone: 503-443-2299; 800-843-6221
Fax: 503-443-2488
Web: www.theoab.org

Bend

KBNZ-LD (7) CBS
63090 Sherman Rd., Bend 97701; 541-312-6567; Fax: 541-312-3926; Tim Olson; Web: www.kbnztv.com

KFXO-LP (39) Fox
PO Box 6038, Bend 97701; 541-382-2121; Fax: 541-382-1616; Bob Singer; Web: www.ktvz.com/kfxo

KOHD-TV (51) ABC
63049 Lower Meadow Dr., Bend 97702; 541-749-5151; Fax: 541-749-4633; Mike Boring; Web: www.kohd.com

KTVZ-TV (21) NBC
62990 O. B. Riley Rd., Bend 97701; 541-383-2121; Fax: 541-382-1616; Bob Singer; Web: www.ktvz.com

Brookings

KBSC-TV (49)

Coos Bay

KCBY-TV (11) CBS
PO Box 1156, Coos Bay 97420; 541-269-1111; Fax: 541-269-7464; Greg Raschio; Web: www.kcby.com

KMCB-TV (23) NBC (See KMTR-TV, Eugene)
Sub-channel: NMCB (23.2) CW

Eugene

KEVU-TV (23) My Network TV
2940 Chad Dr., Eugene 97408; 541-683-2525;
Fax: 541-683-8016; Mark Metzger;
Web: www.kevutv.com

KEZI-TV (9) ABC
PO Box 7009, Eugene 97401; 541-485-5611;
Fax: 541-342-1568; Michael Boring;
Web: www.kezi.com
Sub-channel: KEZI 9+ (9.2) Non-Stop News

KLSR-TV (34) Fox
2940 Chad Dr., Eugene 97408; 541-683-3434;
Fax: 541-683-8016; Mark Metzger;
Web: www.OregonsFOX.com

KMTR-TV (16) NBC
3825 International Ct., Springfield 97477;
541-746-1600; Fax: 541-747-0866;
Cambra Ward; Web: www.kmtr.com
Sub-channel: NMTR (16.2) CW Network

KVAL-TV (13) CBS
PO Box 1313, Eugene 97440; 541-342-4961;
Fax: 541-342-2635; Greg Raschio;
Web: www.kval.com
Sub-channel: KVAL2 (13.2) This TV

Klamath Falls

KDKF-TV (31) ABC
231 E Main St., Klamath Falls 97601;
541-883-3131; Fax: 541-883-8931;
Mark J. Hatfield; Web: www.kdkf.com

KOTI-TV (2) NBC
PO Box 2K, Klamath Falls 97601;
541-882-2222; Fax: 541-883-7664; Bob Wise;
Web: www.koti2.com

Medford

KDOV-LP (44) Faith and Family
1236 Disk Dr., Suite E, Medford 97501;
541-776-5368; Fax: 541-842-4334;
Perry Atkinson; Web: www.TheDove.us

KDRV-TV (12) ABC
PO Box 4220, Medford 97501; 541-773-1212;
Fax: 541-779-9261; Mark J. Hatfield;
Web: www.kdrv.com

KFBI-TV (48) My Network TV
300 Main St., Chico, CA 95928;
530-893-1234, ext. 204; Fax: 530-899-5475;
Rob Castro

KMCW-TV (14) Telemundo
1236 N Riverside Ave., Medford 97501;
541-245-5244; Fax: 541-245-5274; Rob Castro

KMVU-TV (26) Fox
820 Crater Lake Ave., #105, Medford 97504;
541-772-2600; Fax: 541-772-7364;
Dave Olmsted
Sub-channel: KMVU D2 (26.2) MeTV

KOBI-TV (5) NBC
PO Box 1489, Medford 97501; 541-779-5555;
Fax: 541-779-8888; Bob Wise;
Web: www.kobi5.com

KTVL-TV (10) CBS
1440 Rossanley Dr., Medford 97501;
541-773-7373; Fax: 541-779-0451;
Kingsley Kelley; Web: www.ktvl.com
Sub-channel: KTVL.D2 (10.2) CW

Pendleton

KFFX-TV (11)

Portland

KATU-TV (2) ABC
2153 NE Sandy Blvd., Portland 97232;
503-231-4222; Fax: 503-231-4233;
John Tamerlano; Web: www.katu.com

KGW-TV (8) NBC
1501 SW Jefferson St., Portland 97201;
503-226-5000; Fax: 503-226-5059; DJ Wilson;
Web: www.kgw.com

KOIN-TV (6) CBS
222 SW Columbia St., Suite 102, Portland
97201-6601; 503-464-0600; Fax: 503-464-0717;
Tim Perry; Web: www.koin.com

KPDX-TV (49) My Network TV
14975 NW Greenbrier Pkwy., Beaverton 97006;
503-906-1249; Fax: 503-548-6915;
Patrick McCreery; Web: www.kpdx.com

KPTV-TV (12) Fox
14975 NW Greenbrier Pkwy., Beaverton 97006;
503-906-1249; Fax: 503-548-6915;
Patrick McCreery; Web: www.kptv.com

KRCW-TV (32) CW
10255 SW Arctic Dr., Beaverton 97005;
503-644-3232; Fax: 503-626-3576;
Pam Pearson; Web: www.portlandscw32.com
Sub-channel: KRCW (32.2) Antenna TV
Sub-channel: KRCW (32.3) This TV

Roseburg

KPIC-TV (4) CBS
PO Box 1345, Roseburg 97470; 541-672-4481;
Fax: 541-672-4482; Connie Williamson;
Web: www.kpic.com

KTCW-TV (22) NBC (See KMTR-TV, Eugene)
Sub-channel: NTCW (46.2) CW

Salem

KPWC-TV (37.1 Eugene to Wilsonville/
37.2 Wilsonville to Longview, WA)
Azteca Oregon (Azteca America)
17980 Brown Rd., Dallas 97338;
503-930-7228; Ken Lewetag

KPXG-TV (27) ION Media Networks
811 SW Naito Pkwy., Suite 100, Portland
97204; 503-222-2221; Aisha Figilis

KSLM-TV (27.1 Eugene to Wilsonville/ 27.2 Wilsonville to Longview, WA) Retro TV Oregon (Independent);

KWVT-TV (17.1 Eugene to Wilsonville/17.2 Wilsonville to Longview, WA) Independent 17980 Brown Rd., Dallas 97338; 503-930-7228; Ken Lewetag

The Dalles

KRHP-LD (14) Christian and Family
3350 Columbia View Dr., The Dalles 97058; 541-296-2711; Fax: 541-296-6158; Bob Pettitt
Sub-channels:
KRHP-LD (14.2) National Association of Religious Broadcasters TV
KRHP-LD (14.3) E/I Children's TV
KRHP-LD (14.4) JCTV (ages 13–35)

Oregon Public/ Educational Radio and Television Stations

Source: Oregon Association of Broadcasters
Contact: Bill Johnstone, President/CEO
Address: 9020 SW Washington Square Rd., Suite 140, Portland 97223-4433
Phone: 503-443-2299; 800-843-6221
Fax: 503-443-2488
Web: www.theoab.org

Ashland

KSMF-FM (89.1);
KSOR-FM (90.1);
KSRG-FM (88.3)
Southern Oregon University, 1250 Siskiyou Blvd., Ashland 97520; 541-552-6301; Fax: 541-552-8565; Paul Westhelle; Web: www.ijpr.org

Astoria

KMUN-FM (91.9);
KTCB-FM (89.5 - Tillamook)
PO Box 269, Astoria 97103; 503-325-0010; Fax: 503-325-3956; David Hammock; Web: www.kmun.org

Bend

KLBR-FM (88.1)
Lane Community College, 136 W 8th Ave., Eugene 97401; 541-463-6000; Fax: 541-463-6046; Steve Barton; Web: www.klcc.org

KOAB-FM (91.3);
KOAB-TV (3)
PO Box 509, Bend 97709; 541-382-1571; Steven M. Bass, OPB President; sbass@obp.org

Burney/Redding, CA

KNCA-FM (89.7)
Southern Oregon University, 1250 Siskiyou Blvd., Ashland 97520; 541-552-6301; Paul Westhelle; Web: www.ijpr.org

Coos Bay

KSBA-FM (88.5)
Southern Oregon University, 1250 Siskiyou Blvd., Ashland 97520; 541-552-6301; Paul Westhelle; Web: www.ijpr.org

Corvallis

KBVR-FM (88.7);
KBVR-TV (26 - cable)
Oregon State University, Memorial Union East, Rm. 210, Corvallis 97331; 541-737-6323; Fax: 541-737-4545; Jeremy Tricola/Carl Leniger

KOAC-AM (550);
KOAC-TV (7)
Oregon State University, 239 Covell Hall, Corvallis 97331; 541-737-4311; Fax: 541-737-4314; Lynne Clendenin; Web: www.opb.org

Eugene

KLCC-FM (89.7)
Lane Community College, 136 W 8th Ave., Eugene 97401; 541-463-6000; Fax: 541-463-6046; Steve Barton; Web: www.klcc.org

KRVM-AM (1280)
Southern Oregon University, 1250 Siskiyou Blvd., Ashland 97520; 541-552-6301; Fax: 541-552-8565; Randy Larson; Web: www.ijpr.org

KRVM-FM (91.9)
Eugene Public School District 4J, 1574 Coburg Rd.; PMB 237, Eugene 97401; 541-687-3370; Fax: 541-687-3573; Randy Larson; Web: www.krvm.org

KWAX-FM (91.1)
University of Oregon, 75 Centennial Loop, Eugene 97401; 541-345-0800/1-800-422-4301; Paul Bjornstad; Web: www.kwax.com

Florence

K211BP (90.1)
Eugene School District 4J, 1574 Coburg Rd., PMB 237, Eugene 97401; 541-687-3370; Fax: 541-687-3573; Randy Larson

KLFO-FM (88.1)
Lane Community College, 4000 E 30th Ave., Eugene 97405; 541-463-6000; Fax: 541-463-6046; Steve Barton; Web: www.klcc.org

Forest Grove

KPUR-FM (94.5)
Pacific University, 2043 College Way, Forest Grove 97116; 503-352-2822; Mike Geraci

Grants Pass

KAGI-AM (930)
Southern Oregon University, 1250 Siskiyou Blvd., Ashland 97520; 541-552-6301; Paul Westhelle; Web: www.ijpr.org

Gresham

KMHD-FM (89.1)
7140 SW Macadam Ave., Portland 97219; 800-241-8123; Web: www.kmhd.org

Klamath Falls

KFTS-TV (22)
34 S Fir St., Medford 97501; 541-779-0808; Fax: 541-779-2178; Mark Stanislawski

KLMF-FM (88.5);
KSKF-FM (90.9)
Southern Oregon University, 1250 Siskiyou Blvd., Ashland 97520; 541-552-6301; Paul Westhelle; Web: www.ijpr.org

KTEC-FM (89.5)
Oregon Institute of Technology, PO Box 2009, Klamath Falls 97601; 541-885-1840; Fax: 541-885-1857; Christie Wuerst; Web: www.oit.edu/ktec

La Grande

KEOL-FM (91.7)
Eastern Oregon University, One University Blvd., La Grande 97850; 541-962-3698; Charlie Johnson; Web: www.eou.edu/keol

KTVR-TV (13)
PO Box R, La Grande 97850; 541-963-3900; Fax: 541-963-7742; Steven M. Bass, OPB President; sbass@obp.org

McMinnville

KSLC-FM (90.3)
Linfield College, #A587, 900 SE Baker St., McMinnville 97128; 503-883-2271; Fax: 503-883-2360; Nancy Cornwell

Medford

KSYS-TV (8)
34 S Fir St., Medford 97501; 541-779-0808; Fax: 541-779-2178; Mark Stanislawski

Mendocino, CA

KPMO-AM (1300)
Southern Oregon University, 1250 Siskiyou Blvd., Ashland 97520; 541-552-6301; Paul Westhelle; Web: www.ijpr.org

Mt. Shasta, CA

KMJC-AM (620);
KNSQ-FM (88.1)
Southern Oregon University, 1250 Siskiyou Blvd., Ashland 97520; 541-552-6301; Paul Westhelle; Web: www.ijpr.org

Myrtle Point

KOOZ-FM (94.1)
Southern Oregon University, 1250 Siskiyou Blvd., Ashland 97520; 541-552-6301; Paul Westhelle; Web: www.ijpr.org

Newberg

KFOX-AM (1650)
George Fox University, Sub Box F, Newberg 97132; 503-554-3012; James Wolfer

Newport

KLCO-FM (90.5)
Lane Community College, 4000 E 30th Ave., Eugene 97405; 541-463-6000; Fax: 541-463-6046; Steve Barton; Web: www.klcc.org

Oakridge

KAVE-FM (88.5);
KMKR-FM (92.1)
Eugene School District 4J, 1574 Coburg Rd., PMB 237, Eugene 97401; 541-687-3370; Fax: 541-687-3573; Randy Larson

Ontario

KMBA-TV (19)
Treasure Valley Community College, Weese Bldg., 650 College Blvd., Ontario 97914; 541-889-6493, ext. 343; Fax: 541-881-2717; Russell Strawn

Pendleton

KRBM-FM (90.9)
Blue Mountain Community College, PO Box 100, Pendleton, OR 97801; 541-276-1260; Fax: 541-276-6119; Steven M. Bass, OPB President; sbass@obp.org

Portland

KBOO-FM (90.7)
20 SE 8th Ave., Portland 97214; 503-231-8032; Fax: 503-231-7145; Erin Yanke; Web: www.kboo.fm

KBPS-AM (1450)
515 NE 15th Ave., Portland 97232-2897; 503-916-5828; Fax: 503-916-2690; Kevin Flink

KBVM-FM (88.3)
PO Box 5888, Portland 97228; 503-285-5200; Fax: 503-285-3322; Tony Galati

KDUP-AM (1580)
University of Portland Communications Dept., 5000 N Willamette Blvd., Portland 97203; 503-943-7284; Jeremy Kossler

KOPB-FM (91.5);
KOPB-TV (10)
Oregon Public Broadcasting, 7140 SW Macadam Ave., Portland 97219; 503-244-9900; Fax: 503-293-4165; Steven M. Bass, OPB President; Web: www.opb.org

KQAC-FM (89.9)
515 NE 15th Ave., Portland 97232-2897; 503-943-5828; Fax: 503-802-9456; Jack Allen; Web: www.allclassical.org

Reedsport

KLFR-FM (89.1)
Lane Community College, 4000 E 30th Ave., Eugene 97405; 541-463-6000; Fax: 541-463-6046; Steve Barton; Web: www.klcc.org

KSYD-FM (92.1)
Eugene School District 4J, 1574 Coburg Rd., PMB 237, Eugene 97401; 541-687-3370; Fax: 541-687-3573; Randy Larson

Rio Dell/Eureka, CA

KNHM-FM (91.5)
Southern Oregon University, 1250 Siskiyou Blvd., Ashland 97520; 541-552-6301; Fax: 541-552-8565; Paul Westhelle; Web: www.ijpr.org

KNHT-FM (107.3)
Southern Oregon University, 1250 Siskiyou Blvd., Ashland 97520; 541-552-6301; Paul Westhelle; Web: www.ijpr.org

Roseburg

KMPQ-FM (88.1)
Lane Community College, 4000 E 30th Ave., Eugene 97405; 541-463-6000; Fax: 541-463-6046; Steve Barton; Web: www.klcc.org

KSRS-FM (91.5);
KTBR-AM (950)
Southern Oregon University, 1250 Siskiyou Blvd., Ashland 97520; 541-552-6301; Paul Westhelle; Web: www.ijpr.org

Talent

KSJK-AM (1230)
Southern Oregon University, 1250 Siskiyou Blvd., Ashland 97520; 541-552-6301; Paul Westhelle; Web: www.ijpr.org

Warm Springs

KWSO-FM (91.9)
PO Box 489, Warm Springs 97761; 541-553-1968; Fax: 541-553-3348; Sue Matters

Yreka, CA

KNYR-FM (91.3);
KSYC-AM (1490)
Southern Oregon University, 1250 Siskiyou Blvd., Ashland 97520; 541-552-6301; Paul Westhelle; Web: www.ijpr.org

National, International and Tribal Governments

Fly fishing on the Deschutes River—Oregon State Archives Scenic Photograph jefDB1496

The citizens of the United States, through our federal government, own more than half the land in Oregon. Oregon's position on the Pacific Rim has resulted in strong ties between Oregon and other nations. Oregon has nine federally recognized tribes, who have distinct relationships with state government. This section contains information about the federal government, representatives of other nations, and tribes in Oregon.

Jeff Merkley

Democrat. Born in Myrtle Creek, October 24, 1956. Stanford University, B.A., 1979; master's degree in Public Policy from Woodrow Wilson School at Princeton University, 1982. He was Executive Director of Portland Habitat for Humanity before serving as President of the World Affairs Council of Oregon for seven years, where he continues to serve on the Board of Trustees. He and his wife Mary have two children.

Elected to the Oregon House of Representatives, 1999; became speaker of the House in 2007. Elected to the U.S. Senate, 2008. Committee member: Appropriations; Banking, Housing and Urban Development; Budget; and Environment and Public Works. Term expires 2015.

Washington, D.C., Office: 313 Hart Senate Office Bldg., Washington, D.C. 20510; 202-224-3753; Fax: 202-228-3997; Web and e-mail: www.merkley.senate.gov

District Offices: Bend: 131 NW Hawthorne Ave., Suite 208, Bend 97701; 541-318-1298

Eugene: 405 East 8th Ave., Suite 2010, Eugene 97401; 541-465-6750

Medford: 10 South Bartlett St., Suite 201, Medford 97501; 541-608-9102

Pendleton: 310 SE Second St., Suite 105, Pendleton 97801; 541-278-1129

Portland: One World Trade Center, 121 SW Salmon St., Suite 1400, Portland 97204; 503-326-3386; Fax: 503-326-2900

Salem: 495 State St., Suite 330, Salem 97301; 503-362-8102

Ron Wyden

Democrat. Born in Wichita, Kansas, May 3, 1949. Stanford University, A.B. in Political Science, 1971; University of Oregon School of Law, J.D., 1974. Co-director, Oregon Gray Panthers, 1974–80; director, Oregon Legal Services for the Elderly, 1977–79; public member, Oregon Board of Examiners of Nursing Home Administrators, 1978–79.

Elected to Congress, 1980; reelected 1982, 1984, 1986, 1988, 1990, 1992 and 1994. Elected to the U.S. Senate, 1996; reelected 1998, 2004 and 2010. Committee member: Budget; Finance, Chairs its Subcommittee on International Trade, Customs and Global Competitiveness; Committee Chair: Energy and Natural Resources; Select Committee on Aging; Select Committee on Intelligence. Term expires 2017.

Washington, D.C., Office: 221 Dirksen Senate Office Bldg., Washington, D.C. 20510-3703; 202-224-5244; Fax: 202-228-2717; Web and e-mail: http://wyden.senate.gov

District Offices: Bend: Jamison Bldg., 131 NW Hawthorne Ave., Suite 107, Bend 97701; 541-330-9142; Fax: 541-330-6266

Eugene: The Center Court Bldg., 151 W 7th Ave., Suite 435, Eugene 97401; 541-431-0229; Fax: 541-431-0610

La Grande: Sac Annex Bldg., 105 Fir St., Suite 201, La Grande 97850; 541-962-7691; Fax: 541-963-0885

Medford: The Federal Courthouse, 310 W 6th St., Rm. 118, Medford 97501; 541-858-5122; Fax: 541-858-5126

Portland: 911 NE 11th Ave., Suite 630, Portland 97204; 503-326-7525; Fax: 503-326-7528

Salem: 707 13th St. SE, Suite 285, Salem 97301; 503-589-4555; Fax: 503-589-4749

Suzanne Bonamici—First District

Counties: Clatsop, Columbia, Washington, Yamhill and part of Multnomah

Democrat. Born in Detroit, Michigan, October 14, 1954. University of Oregon, B.A., 1980; University of Oregon School of Law, J.D., 1983. Before going into private practice in Portland, she was a consumer protection attorney for the Federal Trade Commission in Washington, D.C. She and her husband Michael Simon have two children.

Elected to the Oregon House of Representatives, 2006. Appointed to the Oregon State Senate, 2008; elected 2008; reelected 2010. Elected to the U.S. House of Representatives, 2012. Committee member: Education and the Workforce; and Science, Space and Technology. Term expires 2015.

Washington, D.C., Office: 439 Cannon House Office Bldg., Washington, D.C. 20515; 202-225-0855; Fax: 202-225-9497; Web and E-mail: www.house.gov/bonamici/

District Office: 12725 SW Millikan Way, Suite 220, Beaverton 97005; 503-469-6010; Toll-free: 800-422-4003; Fax: 503-326-5066

Greg Walden—Second District

Counties: Baker, Crook, Deschutes, Gilliam, Grant, Harney, Hood River, Jackson, Jefferson, Grants Pass area of Josephine, Klamath, Lake, Malheur, Morrow, Sherman, Umatilla, Union, Wallowa, Wasco and Wheeler

Republican. Born January 10, 1957 in The Dalles, Oregon. University of Oregon, B.S. Small-business owner, Columbia Gorge Broadcasters. Press Secretary and Chief of Staff, Congressman Denny Smith, 1981–1987. He and his wife Mylene have one child.

Elected to Oregon House of Representatives, 1988; served as House Majority Leader, 1991–93; appointed to Oregon Senate, 1995; served as Assistant Majority Leader.

Elected to the U.S. House of Representatives, 1998; reelected 2000, 2002, 2004, 2006, 2008, 2010 and 2012. Chair: Subcommittee on Communications and Technology; Committee member: Energy and Commerce; Chair: National Republican Congressional Committee. Term expires 2015.

Washington, D.C., Office: 2182 Rayburn House Office Bldg., Washington, D.C. 20515; 202-225-6730; Fax: 202-225-5774; Web and e-mail: www.walden.house.gov/

District Offices: Bend: Jamison Bldg., 1051 NW Bond St., Suite 400, Bend 97701; 541-389-4408; Fax: 541-389-4452

La Grande: 1211 Washington Ave., La Grande 97850; 541-624-2400; Fax: 541-624-2402

Medford: 843 E Main St., Suite 400, Medford 97504; 541-776-4646; Fax: 541-779-0204

Earl Blumenauer—Third District

Counties: Most of Multnomah and the northern part of Clackamas

Democrat. Born in Portland, August 16, 1948. Attended Lewis & Clark College and Kennedy School of Government at Harvard. Received B.A. degree, political science, 1970; law degree, 1976.

Elected to Oregon House of Representatives, 1972; reelected 1974 and 1976. Elected to Multnomah County Board of Commissioners, 1978; reelected 1982. Elected to Portland City Council, 1986; reelected 1990 and 1994.

Elected to Congress, 1996; reelected 1998, 2000, 2002, 2004, 2006, 2008, 2010 and 2012. Committee member: Ways and Means, and its Subcommittees on Health and Trade. Term expires 2015.

Washington, D.C., Office: 1111 Longworth House Office Bldg., Washington, D.C. 20515; 202-225-4811; Fax: 202-225-8941; Web and e-mail: http://blumenauer.house.gov

District Office: 729 NE Oregon, Suite 115, Portland 97232; 503-231-2300; Fax: 503-230-5413

Peter DeFazio—Fourth District

Counties: Coos, Curry, Douglas, Lane, Linn, and most of Benton and Josephine

Democrat. Born in Needham, Massachusetts, May 27, 1947. Tufts University, B.A., 1969; University of Oregon, M.A., 1977. Honorable discharge, U.S. Air Force Reserve, 1971. Aide to Congressman Jim Weaver, 1977–82; elected to Lane County Board of Commissioners, 1982. He and his wife Myrnie L. Daut own a home and live in Springfield.

Elected to the U.S. House of Representatives, 1986; reelected 1988, 1990, 1992, 1994, 1996, 1998, 2000, 2002, 2004, 2006, 2008, 2010 and 2012. Committee member: Natural Resources; and Transportation and Infrastructure; and serves as ranking member on its Highway and Transit Subcommittee. Term expires 2015.

Washington, D.C., Office: 2134 Rayburn House Office Bldg., Washington, D.C. 20515; 202-225-6416; Fax: 202-225-0032; Web and e-mail: http://www.defazio.house.gov

District Offices: Coos Bay: 125 Central Ave., Rm. 350, Coos Bay 97420; 541-269-2609; Fax: 541-269-5760

Eugene: 405 E 8th Ave., Suite 2030, Eugene 97401; 541-465-6732; Toll-free: 800-944-9603; Fax: 541-465-6458

Roseburg: 612 SE Jackson, Rm. 9, Roseburg 97470; 541-440-3523; Fax: 541-440-3525

Kurt Schrader—Fifth District

Counties: All of Lincoln, Marion, Polk and Tillamook, parts of northern Benton, most of Clackamas and parts of southwestern Multnomah

Democrat. Born in Bridgeport, Connecticut, October 19, 1951. Cornell University, NY, B.A., 1973; University of Illinois, D.V.M., 1977. Owner, Clackamas County Veterinary Clinics. He and his wife Martha raised five children.

Elected to Oregon House of Representatives, 1996; served through 2002; elected to Oregon Senate, 2002; served through 2008.

Elected to the U.S. House of Representatives, 2008; reelected 2010 and 2012. Committee member: Agriculture; and Small Business. Term expires 2015.

Washington, D.C., Office: 108 Cannon House Office Bldg., Washington, D.C. 20515; 202-225-5711; Fax: 202-225-5699; Web and e-mail: http://schrader.house.gov

District Offices: Oregon City: 621 High St., Oregon City 97045; 503-557-1324; Fax: 503-557-1981

Salem: 494 State St., Suite 210, Salem 97301; 503-588-9100; Toll Free: 877-301-KURT (5878); Fax: 503-588-5517

Congressional Districts

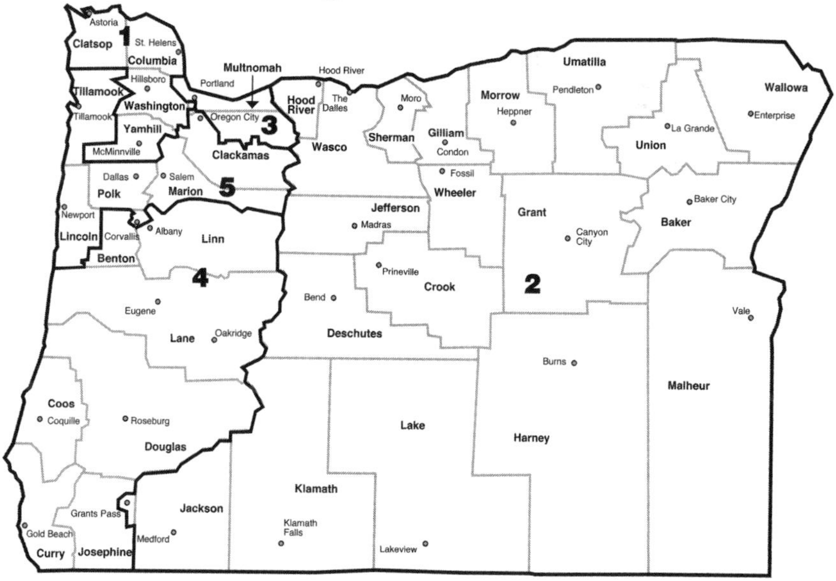

U.S. Government Officials

President of the United States
Barack Obama

Address: The White House, 1600 Pennsylvania Ave., Washington, D.C. 20500
Phone: 202-456-1414
Fax: 202-456-2461
Web: www.whitehouse.gov

Occupational Background: Attorney; author; professor of constitutional law; U.S. Senator. **Educational Background:** Columbia University, bachelor's degree, 1983; Harvard Law School, law degree, 1991. **Governmental Experience:** Illinois State Senate, 1996–2004; U.S. Senate, 2005–2008; U.S. Senate Committee member: Environment and Public Works; Foreign Relations; European Affairs Subcommittee, Chair, 2007; Veterans' Affairs

Vice President of the United States
Joseph R. Biden

Occupational Background: Attorney; U.S. Senator. **Educational Background:** University of Delaware, bachelor's degree, 1965; Syracuse University, law degree, 1968. **Governmental Experience:** U.S. Senate 1972–2008; U.S. Senate Committee member: Foreign Relations 1975–2008, Chair, 2001–2003 and 2007–2008; Judiciary, Chair, 1987–1995

The Cabinet:

Chief of Staff
Denis McDonough
Address: The White House, 1600 Pennsylvania Ave., Washington, D.C. 20500
Phone: 202-456-1414
Web: www.whitehouse.gov

Department of Agriculture
Thomas J. Vilsack, Secretary
Address: 1400 Independence Ave. SW, Washington, D.C. 20250
Phone: 202-720-2791
Web: www.usda.gov

Department of Commerce
Rebecca Blank, Acting Secretary
Address: 1401 Constitution Ave. NW, Washington, D.C. 20230
Phone: 202-482-2000
Web: www.commerce.gov

Department of Defense
Chuck Hagel, Secretary Designate*
Address: 1000 Defense Pentagon, Washington, D.C. 20301-1000
Phone: 703-428-0711
Web: www.defenselink.mil

Department of Education
Arne Duncan, Secretary
Address: 400 Maryland Ave. SW, Washington, D.C. 20202
Phone: 202-401-3000
Web: www.ed.gov

Department of Energy
Steven Chu, Secretary
Address: 1000 Independence Ave. SW, Washington, D.C. 20585
Phone: 800-DIAL-DOE
Web: www.energy.gov

Department of Health and Human Services
Kathleen Sebelius, Secretary
Address: 200 Independence Ave. SW, Washington, D.C. 20201
Phone: 877-696-6775
Web: www.hhs.gov

Department of Homeland Security
Janet A. Napolitano, Secretary
Address: Washington, D.C. 20528
Phone: 202-282-8000
Web: www.dhs.gov

Department of Housing and Urban Development
Shaun L.S. Donovan, Secretary
Address: 451 7th St. SW, Washington, D.C. 20410
Phone: 202-708-1112
Web: www.hud.gov

Department of Interior
Secretary: awaiting presidential appointment at press time
Address: 1849 C St. NW, Washington, D.C. 20240
Phone: 202-208-3100
Web: www.doi.gov/index.cfm

Department of Justice
Eric H. Holder, Jr. Attorney General
Address: 950 Pennsylvania Ave. NW, Washington, D.C. 20530
Phone: 202-514-2000
Web: www.usdoj.gov

Department of Labor
Hilda L. Solis, Secretary
Address: Frances Perkins Bldg., 200 Constitution Ave. NW, Washington, D.C. 20210
Phone: 1-866-4-USA-DOL
Web: www.dol.gov

Department of State
John Kerry, Secretary of State
Address: 2201 C St. NW, Washington, D.C. 20520
Phone: 202-647-4000
Web: www.state.gov

Department of Transportation
Secretary: awaiting presidential appointment at press time
Address: 400 7th St. SW, Washington, D.C. 20590
Phone: 202-366-4000
Web: www.dot.gov

Department of the Treasury
Jack Lew, Secretary Designate*
Address: 1500 Pennsylvania Ave. NW, Washington, D.C. 20220
Phone: 202-622-2000
Web: www.treasury.gov

Department of Veterans Affairs
General Eric K. Shinseki, Secretary
Address: 810 Vermont Ave. NW, Washington, D.C. 20420
Phone: 1-800-827-1000
Web: www.va.gov

Environmental Protection Agency
Administrator: awaiting presidential appointment at press time
Address: 1200 Pennsylvania Ave. NW, Washington, D.C. 20460
Phone: 202-564-4700
Web: www.epa.gov

Office of Management and Budget
Jeffrey Zients, Acting Director
Address: 725 17th St. NW, Washington, D.C. 20503
Phone: 202-395-7254
Web: www.whitehouse.gov/omb

United Nations Ambassador
Susan Rice, Ambassador
Address: 140 E 45th St., New York, NY 10017
Phone: 212-415-4000
Web: www.usunnewyork.usmission.gov

United States Trade Representative
Ronald Kirk, Ambassador
Address: 600 17th St. NW, Washington, D.C. 20508
Phone: 202-395-7360
Web: www.ustr.gov

*Presidential appointee, not yet confirmed by the Senate at press time

U.S. Government in Oregon

For information about U.S. Government in Oregon, contact the Federal Citizen Information Center at 1-800-FED-INFO (1-800-333-4636) or go to: www.loc.gov/rr/news/fedgov.html.

U.S. District Courts in Oregon

Main Office:
U.S. Courthouse
Address: 1000 SW Third Ave., Portland 97204

Eugene Divisional Office:
Wayne L. Morse U.S. Courthouse
Address: 405 E 8th Ave., Suite 2100, Eugene 97401

Medford Divisional Office:
James A. Redden U.S. Courthouse
Address: 310 W 6th, Room 201, Medford 97501

Pendleton Divisional Office:
John F. Kilkenny U.S. Courthouse
Address: 104 SW Dorian, Pendleton 97801

Major Political Parties in Oregon

Democratic National Committee
Address: 430 S Capitol St. SE, Washington, D.C. 20003
Phone: 202-863-8000
Web: www.democrats.org

Democratic State Central Committee of Oregon
Address: 232 NE 9th Ave., Portland 97232-2915
Phone: 503-224-8200
Web: www.dpo.org

Republican National Committee
Address: 310 1st St. SE, Washington, D.C. 20003
Phone: 202-863-8500
Web: www.gop.com

Republican State Central Committee of Oregon
Address: PO Box 25406, Portland 97298-0406
Phone: 503-595-8881
Web: www.oregonrepublicanparty.org

Tribal Peoples of Oregon

Source: Legislative Commission on Indian Services
Address: 900 Court St. NE, Rm. 167, Salem 97301
Phone: 503-986-1067
Fax: 503-986-1071
Web: www.leg.state.or.us/cis
Statutory Authority: ORS 182.162–182.168

Oregon's tribal members speak of being in this area "from time immemorial." Villages and traditional lifeways are known to date back many thousands of years.

Tribal governments are separate sovereign nations with powers to protect the health, safety and welfare of their members and to govern their lands. This tribal sovereignty predates the existence of the U.S. government and the state of Oregon. The members residing in Oregon are citizens of their tribes, of Oregon and, since 1924, of the United States of America.

Oregon's tribal population, according to the 2010 U.S. Census, included 109,223 people who identified themselves as being "American Indian or Alaskan Native" alone or in combination with one or more other races. Oregon's tribal peoples live in all 36 counties, and make up about 2.8 percent of the total Oregon population.

The U.S. Department of the Interior, Bureau of Indian Affairs, oversees tribal interests and administers the federal government's trust obligations. At times, the federal government has been supportive of tribal self-determination and, in other periods, has adopted policies and passed legislation having a negative impact on the ability of tribes to govern as viable sovereigns. "Termination," one such policy in the 1950s, was an attempt to sever federal trusteeship and support for tribal sovereignty. Of the 109 tribes and bands terminated nationwide, 62 were located in Oregon. In 1975, the federal government recognized the failure of its termination policy and passed the Indian Self Determination and Education Assistance Act. Several tribes began the process to restore their sovereign nations. In 1977, the Confederated Tribes of Siletz was the second tribe in the nation to achieve restoration. Following them were the Cow Creek Band of Umpqua Tribe of Indians in 1982, the Confederated Tribes of Grand Ronde in 1983, the Confederated Tribes of Coos, Lower Umpqua and Siuslaw in 1984, the Klamath Tribes in 1986 and the Coquille Tribe in 1989.

Three additional federally recognized tribal governments exist in Oregon: the Confederated Tribes of Warm Springs (Treaty of 1855), the Confederated Tribes of Umatilla (Treaty of 1855) and the Burns Paiute Tribe (established by Executive Order in 1972). Also, Ft. McDermitt Paiute Shoshone Tribe is a federally-recognized tribal government in Nevada with reservation lands in Oregon, and Celilo Village is a federally-recognized tribal government near The Dalles, jointly administered by the Confederated Tribes of Warm Springs, the Confederated Tribes of Umatilla and the Yakama Indian Nation (Washington).

All Oregon tribal governments have reservation or trust lands created by treaties or federal acts. These are lands over which tribal governments have regulatory authority unless that authority has been removed by Congress. Over 875,000 acres, or at least 1.4 percent of land within Oregon's boundaries, are held in trust by the federal government or are designated reservation lands. Like other sovereigns, tribal governments have the authority to decide their own membership or citizenship qualifications and have a right to exclude individuals from their reservations. Just as the state does not collect tax on federal lands nor tax federal or local governments or non-profit corporations, Oregon does not tax tribal governments. However, all tribal members as individual citizens pay federal taxes and most pay state taxes, with the exception of those who live and work on a reservation or earn money on reservation/trust lands or from trust resources.

Public Law 280 gave the state certain civil and criminal jurisdiction over tribes, with the exception of the Confederated Tribes of Warm Springs and the Confederated Tribes of Umatilla which are "non Public Law 280" tribes. Notwithstanding Public Law 280, all Oregon tribes have the authority to elect their own governments and adopt laws and ordinances. Oregon tribal governments have their own departments dealing with governmental services and programs in the areas of natural resources, cultural resources, education, health and human services, public safety, housing, economic development, administration and other areas. Oregon maintains a government-to-government relationship with the tribal governments as directed in ORS 182.162 to 182.168.

Passage of the National Indian Gaming Regulatory Act (NIGRA) in 1988 created the opportunity to build gaming centers on reservation or trust lands. Besides providing employment opportunities for tribal members and citizens of surrounding communities, revenues from these tribal enterprises fund health clinics, education, scholarships, housing and other services. All Oregon tribal governments are striving to diversify their revenue streams and are actively pursuing other avenues for generating revenue. These gaming and other enterprises have made these tribal governments some of the largest employers in their respective counties—generating employment for tax-paying employees. This benefits local communities and the entire state.

Most Oregon tribes are "confederations" of three or more tribes and bands. Each tribe's area of interest may extend far beyond its tribal governmental center or reservation location. The federal government acknowledges that many tribal members do not live on tribal lands and, therefore, allows for tribes to provide certain governmental programs in specified service areas. For example, the Confederated Tribes of Siletz service area includes 11 Oregon counties: Benton, Clackamas, Lane, Lincoln, Linn, Marion, Multnomah, Polk, Tillamook, Washington and Yamhill.

Burns Paiute Tribe

Address: HC-71 100 Pasigo St., Burns 97720
Phone: 541-573-2088
E-mail: dlteeman.burnspaiute@gmail.com
Web: www.burnspaiute-nsn.gov
Restoration: by Executive Order October 13, 1972
Number of Members: 349
Land Base Acreage: 13,736 acres
Number of people employed by the Tribe: 54

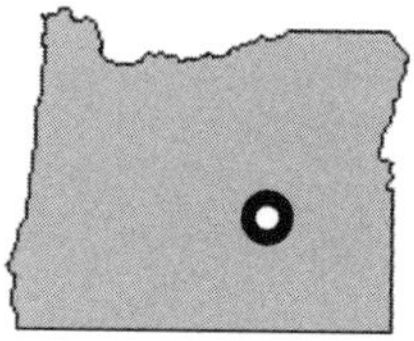

Economy: The Old Camp Casino and RV Park

Points of Interest: Steens Mountain recreational area, Malheur National Wildlife Refuge, Reservation Day Pow Wow occurs two days each fall on or around October 13; annual Mothers' Day Pow Wow.

History and Culture: The Burns Paiute Reservation is located north of Burns in Harney County. Today's tribal members are primarily the descendants of the "Wadatika" band of Paiutes who roamed central and eastern Oregon. The Wadatika, named for the wada seeds collected near Malheur Lake shores, lived on seeds, berries, roots and vegetation they gathered and wild animals they hunted. Their original territory included the area from the Cascade Mountains to Boise, Idaho, and the Blue Mountains to the Steens Mountains. Paiute legends say that the Paiutes have lived in this area since before the Cascade Mountains were formed, coming from the south as part of a migration throughout the Great Basin. People of the Burns Paiute Tribe were basket makers who used fibers of willow, sagebrush, tule plant and Indian hemp to weave baskets, sandals, fishing nets and traps. Archeologists have found clothing made from deer, animal and bird hides, and sandals made from sagebrush fibers believed to be close to 10,000 years old. The tribe continues to hunt and gather traditional foods and berries, and do beadwork and drum-making in traditional ways.

Tribal Court: Tribal Judge Christie Timko; Associate Judge Patricia Davis, 100 Pasigo St., Burns 97720; 541-573-2793

Tribal Council: Chairperson Charisse Soucie (2014); Vice-Chair Charlotte Roderique (2014); Secretary-Treasurer Vacant; Sergeant at Arms DeWayne Hoodie (2016); Members at Large Cecil Dick (2016), Eric Hawley (2015), Garrett Sam (2016), Lanada Teton (2015)

Confederated Tribes of Coos, Lower Umpqua and Siuslaw

Address: 1245 Fulton Ave., Coos Bay 97420
Phone: 541-888-9577
E-mail: Bgarcia@ctclusi.org
Web: http://ctclusi.org
Restoration Date: October 17, 1984
Number of Members: 953
Land Base Acreage: about 415 acres
Number of people employed by the Tribes: 542

Economy: Three Rivers Casino & Hotel; Restoration Forest Plan

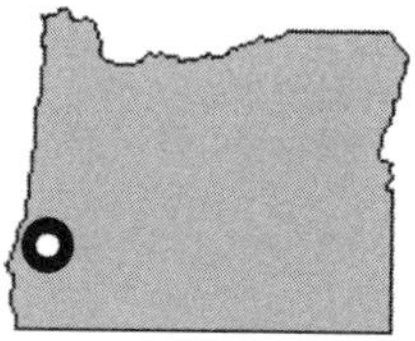

Points of Interest: Three Rivers Casino & Hotel; Salmon Ceremony, held on the first Sunday in August at the Tribal Hall in Coos Bay; Annual Restoration Day celebrated on or about October 17 each year. The Confederated Tribes of Coos, Lower Umpqua and Siuslaw observe summer and winter solstices and sponsor seasonal events for hunting and gathering.

History and Culture: Indians of western Oregon understood the land to be the Spirit expressing itself in the natural world. The people were connected to the land with certainty and gratitude. It sustained and nurtured and made life possible while supporting all the spirits which share this world. The tribal economy reflected the relationship of the Creator to the People. Acquiring objects of both aesthetic and utilitarian value was a measure of an individual's wealth and status, yet acquisition was not an end in itself. The annual Potlatch became the setting for individuals to give their possessions to others, further mirroring the Creator's relationship to the People. The spiritual act of gifting your earthly possessions to others remains a powerful personal experience and a statement of faith and trust.

The tribes administered laws with transparency and a focus on the collective rights of the people. Individualism at the expense of community was not tolerated. Victims of an offense participated in the forming of appropriate punishments in a public arena where justice and fairness were, like other decision making processes, a group affair.

By 1854, white settlers began taking Donation Land Claims around Coos Bay. In 1856, the U.S. Army forcibly removed the tribal people to the new 18,000 acre Great Coast Reservation established on a windswept spit on the north side of the mouth of the Umpqua River.

Tribal Court: Tribal Judge J. D. Williams, 1245 Fulton Ave., Coos Bay 97420; 541-888-9577

Tribal Council: Chief Warren A. Brainard (2020); Council: Bob Garcia (2015), Beverly Bowen (2014), Mark Ingersoll (2015), Ron Brainard (2014), Arron McNutt (2014)

Coquille Indian Tribe

Address: 3050 Tremont St., North Bend 97459
Phone: 541-756-0904
E-mail: cit@coquilletribe.org
Web: www.coquilletribe.org
Restoration Date: June 28, 1989
Number of Members: 963
Land Base Acreage: 6,468 (Trust Land)
Number of people employed by the Tribe: 705

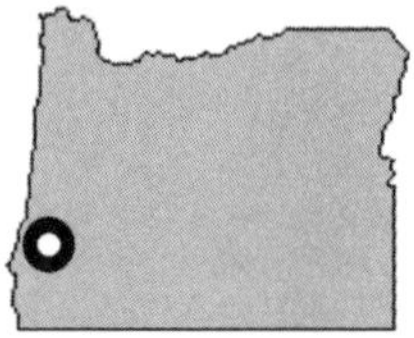

Economy: The Tribe contributes to the economy of Coos County and its other service area counties, Curry, Douglas, Jackson and Lane, through business ventures including, timber operations, the Mill Casino, Hotel and RV Park, Heritage Place Assisted Living, ORCA Communications, and Coquille Cranberries, making it the second largest employer in Coos County.

Points of Interest: Dune rides and shipwrecks at Oregon Dunes National Recreation Area; Charleston Harbor; charter fishing for tuna and salmon; crabbing; storm watching; beachcombing; tide pooling; canoeing; and the holiday lights showcase at Shore Acres State Park.

History and Culture: The Coquilles' ancestral homelands, more than one million acres of lower Coos Bay and the Coquille River watershed, were ceded by treaties to the U.S. government in 1851 and 1855 in exchange for reservation land that never materialized because the treaties were never ratified by the U.S. Senate. No permanent tribal land existed until 1989 when Congress passed Public Law 101-42 re-establishing the Coquilles as a federally recognized Indian Tribe.

After regaining federal recognition, the Coquille tribal government created programs to provide housing, health care, education, elder care, law enforcement and judicial services to its members. Cultural preservation efforts include learning and teaching oral histories and traditions to members of the tribe.

A congressional act in 1996 restored 5,410 acres of forest land to the Tribe. The Tribe operates a multi-discipline natural resources progam to manage its forest lands under certification standards of the Forest Stewardship Council.

Tribal Court: Chief Judge Don Owen Costello, 3050 Tremont Street, North Bend 97459; 541-756-0904

Tribal Council: Chief Ken Tanner (2014); Chairperson Brenda Meade (2015); Vice-Chairperson Toni Ann Brend (2014) Secretary/Treasurer Joan Metcalf (2015); Tribal Representatives: Kippy Robbins (2015) and Sharon Parrish (2014)

Cow Creek Band of Umpqua Tribe of Indians

Address: 2371 NE Stephens St., Suite 100, Roseburg 97470
Phone: 541-672-9405
Web: www.cowcreek.com
Treaty Date: September 19, 1853
Restoration Date: December 29, 1982
Number of Members: 1,536
Land Base Acreage: 1,840 acres (in trust)
Number of people employed by the Tribe: 1,100

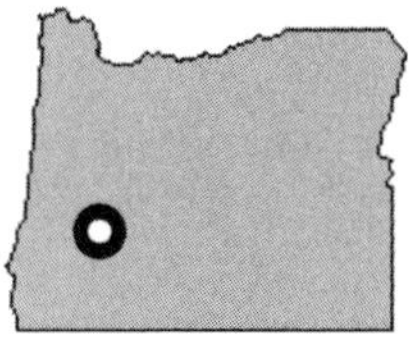

Economy: The Cow Creeks were restored without reservation land in 1982. All land held by the tribe has been by purchase. The tribe's main economy is dependent upon revenues generated from its Seven Feathers Casino Resort in Canyonville. The Resort features a casino, hotels, restaurants and entertainment venues. Several other businesses have been acquired in their economic diversification program. Since Recognition, the tribe has developed housing, education and social services programs, business corporations, a utility cooperative, a charitable foundation, a tribal court system, and is one of the largest employers in Douglas County.

Points of Interest: Oregon's Interstate-5 passes through Canyonville and the heart of Cow Creek's homeland and the Seven Feathers Resort. The area is one of natural beauty and includes the Umpqua Rivers, the Cascade Mountains, the Pacific Ocean and dunes and a growing wine industry.

History and Culture: The Cow Creeks lived between the Cascade and Coast Ranges in southwestern Oregon, along the South Umpqua River. They hunted deer and elk and fished silver salmon and steelhead as far north as the Columbia River, east to Crater Lake, and south to the Klamath Marsh.

Except for the purpose of the Termination Act in 1954, which called for the immediate termination of federal relations with more than 60 tribes in western Oregon, the Cow Creek's Treaty of 1853 was ignored by the U.S. government for over 128 years until Federal Recognition in 1982.

Tribal Court: Tribal Judge Ronald Yockim, 2371 NE Stephens St., Suite 100, Roseburg 97470; 541-672-9405

Tribal Council 2012-2015: Chairman Dan Courtney; Vice Chairman Gary Jackson; Secretary Yvonne McCafferty; Treasurer Robert Van Norman; Council: Jessica Bochart, Tom Cox, Robert Estabrook, Steve Jackson, Shirley Roane, George T. Rondeau, and Tom Rondeau, Sr.

Confederated Tribes of The Grand Ronde Community

Address: 9615 Grand Ronde Rd., Grand Ronde 97347
Phone: 503-879-5211 or 1-800-422-0232
E-mail: publicaffairs@grandronde.org
Web: www.grandronde.org
Restoration Date: November 22, 1983
Number of Members: 5,200
Land Base Acreage: approx. 11,288 acres
Number of people employed by the Tribes: 1,600

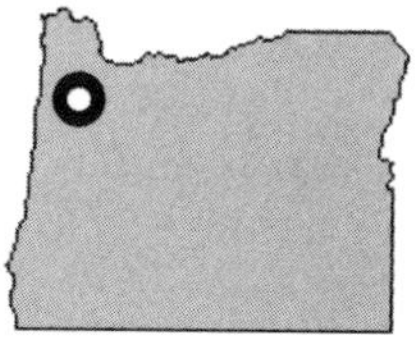

Economy: Spirit Mountain Casino; over 10,000 acres of forest lands; and wildfire fighting crew.

Points of Interest: Spirit Mountain Casino is Oregon's most successful casino and the tribe dedicates 6 percent of the profits to its Spirit Mountain Community Fund, which supports charitable organizations in an 11-county area of western Oregon. The fund has given more than $55 million to area charities since 1997. The West Valley Veterans Memorial, four granite pillars representing the four branches of the armed services, holds the names of tribal members and area veterans who fought and served their country.

The tribe hosts a Veterans' Powwow each July and a Competition Powwow on the third weekend each August. Fort Yamhill Heritage Area nearby tells the story of the relocation, transition and sadness for Grand Ronde's people when they were forced from their ancestral homelands, which extended from the banks of the Columbia River to the Oregon–California border, on to the Grand Ronde Reservation under military guard.

History and Culture: The tribes include Athabaskan speaking Chasta, Rogue River and Upper Umpqua from southern Oregon. Molalla tribes are from the western Cascade mountains, Kalapuya Tribes are from the Willamette Valley and Chinookan speaking Tumwater, Clackamas, Watlala and Multnomah are from the lower Willamette and Columbia Rivers. Chinuk Wawa became the Tribes' common language. Traditional basket making and weaving, skills still practiced today, were important tribal utility and cultural skills.

Tribal Court: Tribal Judge Suzanne Ojibway-Townsend, 9615 Grand Ronde Rd., Grand Ronde 97347; 503-879-2303

Tribal Council: Chairman Reyn Leno (2014); Vice Chair Jack Giffen Jr. (2013); Secretary Toby McClary (2015); Council: Steven L. Bobb, Sr. (2013), Cheryle A. Kennedy (2015), Chris Mercier (2013), June Sherer (2014), Jon A. George (2015) and Kathleen Tom (2014)

Klamath Tribes

Address: PO Box 436, 501 Chiloquin Blvd., Chiloquin 97624
Phone: 541-783-2219 or 800-524-9787
E-mail: taylor.david@klamathtribes.com
Web: www.klamathtribes.org
Restoration Date: August 27, 1986
Number of Members: 3,700
Land Base Acreage: no reservation land
Number of people employed by the Tribes: Over 300

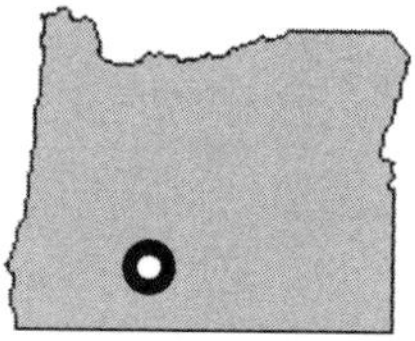

Economy: Kla-Mo-Ya Casino, a full service travel center and wellness center

Points of Interest: Kla-Mo-Ya Casino, Crater Lake National Park, Lava Beds National Monument, and Tulelake History Museum. Named by *Sunset Magazine* as one of the nation's five best birding hotspots, the Klamath Basin, in the Pacific Flyway, is a migratory flyway for more than 350 species of birds, including Bald Eagles, Clarke's Grebes and Black Terns.

History and Culture: Traditionally, every March, the c'waam (Lost River Suckerfish) swims up the Sprague River to spawn. A certain snowfall at this time of year heralds the c'waam's return, and the evening sky reveals the fish constellation (three stars in line making "Orion's Belt") on the southwestern horizon. Klamath traditions state that watchmen, or swaso.llalalYampgis, monitored the riverbanks to see exactly when the fish would return. The head "shaman" would then give thanks for their return. Tribal elders continue this ceremony to ensure the survival of a species, tribal traditions, and mankind. The celebration includes traditional dancing, drumming, feasting and releasing of a pair of c'waam into the river. Other annual events include the Restoration Celebration held the fourth weekend in August and the New Year's Eve Sobriety Pow Wow.

The Klamath Tribes, the Klamath, Modoc and Yahooskin Paiute people, have lived in the Klamath Basin from time beyond memory. Legends and oral history tell about when the world and the animals were created, when the animals and gmok'am'c, the Creator, sat together and discussed the creation of man. According to tribal sayings, if stability defines success, their presence here has been, and always will be, essential to the economic well-being of their homeland.

Tribal Court: Tribal Judge James D. Hill, 116 E. Chocktoot St., PO Box 1260, Chiloquin 97624; 541-783-3020

Tribal Council 2011-2013: Chairman Gary D. Frost; Vice-Chairman Don Gentry; Secretary Torina Case; Treasurer Brandi Decker; Council: Anna Bennett, Shawn Jackson, Georgene Wright-Nelson, Jeff C. Mitchell, Charles E Kimbol, Sr. and Frank Summers

Confederated Tribes of Siletz Indians

Address: 201 Swan Ave SE, PO Box 549, Siletz 97380
Phone: 541-444-2532
Web: www.ctsi.nsn.us
Restoration Date: November 18, 1977
Number of Members: 4,677
Land Base Acreage: 15,204 acres
Number of people employed by the Tribes: 1,069

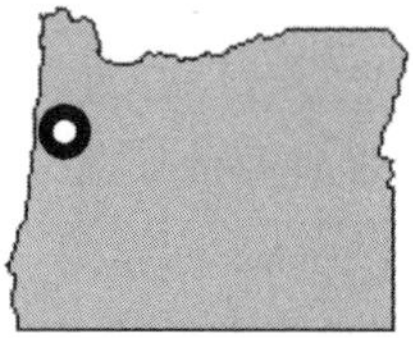

Economy: The Confederated Tribes of Siletz Indians owns and operates the Chinook Winds Casino Resort in Lincoln City. The Siletz Tribal Business Corporation manages several tribal businesses, including Hee Hee Illahee RV Resort; Logan Road RV Park; Imprints Print Shop; The tribe also owns and leases office space in Eugene, Salem and Portland.

Points of Interest: Chinook Winds Casino and Resort including an ocean-front hotel, restaurants, childcare and arcade, and 18-hole golf course in Lincoln City; Nesika Illahee Pow Wow each August; and the Tribes' Restoration Pow Wow each November.

History and Culture: The Confederated Tribes of Siletz Indians is a diverse confederation of 27 Western Oregon, Northern California and Southern Washington bands. A 1.1 million acre reservation was established by President Franklin Pierce on November 9, 1855, fulfilling the stipulations of eight treaties. Over time, reservation lands were drastically reduced and the CTSI were terminated as a tribe in 1954. In 1977, the CTSI was the second tribe in the nation to achieve restoration. In 1980, some reservation lands were reestablished. In spite of mistreatment and displacement, the CTSI continues work to recover as much as possible of what was lost.

Since 1980, the Tribe has increased its land base to 15, 204 acres of timberland and land for cultural preservation, housing, operations, economic purposes, wildlife habitat enhancement and 3666 acres of reservation land in Lincoln County. The tribe provides homes for nearly 150 members and their families, and over 1,000 jobs.

Tribal Court: Tribal Chief Judge Calvin E. Gantenbein, PO Box 549, Siletz 97380, 541-444-8228

Tribal Council: Delores Pigsley, Chairman (2013); Alfred 'Bud' Lane III, Vice-Chairman (2013); Jessie Davis, Treasurer (2015); Tina Retasket, Secretary (2014); Members Lillie Butler (2013), Loraine Butler (2014), Reggie Butler Sr. (2015), Robert Kentta (2014) and Sharon Edenfield (2015)

Confederated Tribes of the Umatilla Indian Reservation

Address: 46411 Ti'mine Way, Pendleton 97801
Phone: 541-276-3165
E-mail: info@ctuir.org
Web: www.ctuir.org
Treaty Date: June 9, 1855; 12 Stat. 945
Number of Members: 2,893
Land Base Acreage: 172,000 acres
Number of people employed by the Tribes: 1,734

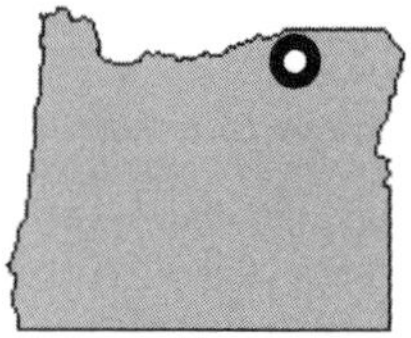

Economy: Prior to the 1855 Treaty, the Tribes' economy consisted primarily of intertribal trade, livestock, trade with fur companies, hunting, fishing and gathering. Today, the economy includes agriculture, livestock, tourism, a travel plaza, grain elevator, the Wildhorse Resort (casino, hotel, RV Park, golf course), Tamástslikt Cultural Institute, Cayuse Technologies, and Coyote Business Park, a 520 acre commercial and light industrial business development on Interstate 84. The reservation is also home to the Umatilla National Forest Supervisor's Office.

Points of Interest: Tamástslikt Cultural Institute, Wildhorse Resort & Casino, Wildhorse Golf Course, Nix-yá-wii Warriors Memorial, Crow's Shadow Institute of the Arts, Indian Lake Recreation Area, seasonal upland gamebird and turkey hunting.

History and Culture: Three tribes make up the CTUIR: Cayuse, Umatilla, and Walla Walla. They have lived on the Columbia River Plateau for over 10,000 years, an area of about 6.4 million acres in what is now northeastern Oregon and southeastern Washington. In 1855, the tribes and the United States Government negotiated a treaty in which the tribes ceded 6.4 million acres of land in exchange for reservation land. The CTUIR reserved rights in the treaty, including fishing and hunting rights and the right to gather traditional foods and medicines on public lands within the ceded areas.

The traditional religion of the tribes is called "Washat" or "Seven Drums." Native languages are still spoken by some and a language preservation program is helping to re-establish the languages.

Tribal Court: Tribal Judge William Johnson, 46411 Ti'mine Way, Pendleton 97801, 541-276-2046

Tribal Council 2011-2013: Les Minthorn, Chairman; Aaron Hines, General Council Chairman; Leo Stewart, Vice-Chairman; Rosenda Shippentower, Treasurer; N. Kathryn Brigham, Secretary; Members: Fred Hill Sr., Armand Minthorn, Bob Shippentower and Woodrow Star

Confederated Tribes of Warm Springs Reservation

Address: PO Box 1299, Warm Springs 97761
Phone: 541-553-3257
E-mail: rsuppah@wstribes.org
Web: www.warmsprings.com
Treaty Date: June 25, 1855
Number of Members: 4,306
Land Base Acreage: 644,000 acres
Number of people employed by the Tribes: 525

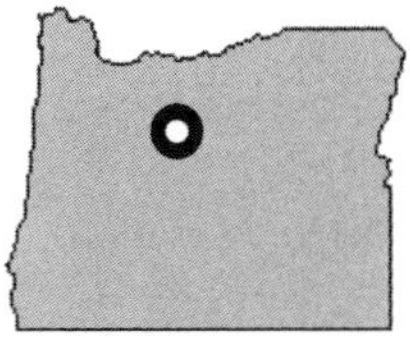

Economy: Under the Corporate Charter, the tribes have established a number of enterprises owned by the tribes, but operated independently of tribal government, that contribute to the economy of the reservation. These include Warm Springs Power & Water, Warm Springs Forest Products and Kah-Nee-Ta Resort and Casino.

Points of Interest: Kah-Nee-Ta Resort Lodge and Casino, Kah-Nee-Ta Village, RV Park and golf course, Indian Head Casino and the Museum at Warm Springs

History and Culture: Long before Europeans set foot on the North American continent, the three tribes of the Warm Springs Reservation – the Wasco, the Walla Walla (later called the Warm Springs), and the Paiute – had developed societies beside the Columbia River, the Cascade Mountains, and other parts of Oregon. Prior to settling on the reservation, natural food resources were so plentiful that agriculture was unnecessary for the three tribes of the Warm Springs Reservation. Salmon from the nearby Columbia was a staple for the Wasco and Warm Springs bands. The high-plains Paiutes depended more on deer and other large game. All three tribes took advantage of assorted roots, fruits and other plant-life. Salmon were hauled out of the Columbia with long-handled dip nets. Roots were pulled from the ground with specialized digging sticks called kapns. Berries were gathered in ornately-woven baskets. Centuries of practice perfected these methods.

Tribal Court: Chief Tribal Judge Anita Jackson, PO Box 850, Warm Springs 97761, 541-553-3454

Tribal Council 2011-2013: Chairman Stanley 'Buck' Smith; Vice Chair Ron Suppah; Representatives Austin Greene Jr. and Lola Sohappy; Paiute Chief Joseph Moses; Seekseequa Reps Reuben Henry and Scott Moses; Warm Springs Chief Delvis Heath; Simnasho Reps Olney JP Patt and Raymond Tsumpti; Wasco Chief - vacant

Oregon Consular Corps

A number of foreign nations maintain consulates in Oregon. A consul is an official appointed by a government to live in a foreign city to look after the business and other interests of the home country and to assist and protect its nationals within the consular territory.

A consular representative promotes a country's trade within the assigned area; assists and protects shipping interests, legalizes ships' papers, assists native seamen in distress and adjudicates on some shipping matters; administers oaths, legalizes foreign documents as required by a country's laws, issues passports and visas and explains a country's policies, cultural achievements and its attractions for tourism.

For assistance from a Consul General or an Honorary Consul, please consult the listing of countries below for a representative of the country in which you have an interest.

Austria
Christopher R. Hermann, Honorary Consul
Address: 900 SW 5th Ave., Ste. 2600, Portland 97204
Phone: 503-552-9733
E-mail: crhermann@stoel.com

Barbados
H. Desmond Johnson, M.D., Honorary Consul
Address: 4750 SW Trail Rd., Tualatin 97062
Phone: 503-638-4707
E-mail: bajandoc@hotmail.com

Belgium
John H. Herman, Honorary Consul
Address: 1024 SW Myrtle Dr., Portland 97201
Phone: 503-228-0465
E-mail: jacherman@aol.com

Canada
Jim Baumgartner, Honorary Consul
Address: 805 SW Broadway, Ste. 1900, Portland 97205
Phone: 503-417-2166
E-mail: honconcanada@bhlaw.com

Cyprus
Alexander Christy, Honorary Consul
Address: 1130 SW Morrison St., Ste. 510, Portland 97205
Phone: 503-248-0500
E-mail: alex@alexchristy.com

Czech Republic
Marie R. Amicci, Honorary Consul
Address: 320 A Ave., Ste. 5, Lake Oswego 97034
Phone: 503-293-9545
E-mail: fcz_consul_pdx@msn.com

Denmark
Ingolf Noto, Honorary Consul
Address: 1600 Pioneer Tower, 888 SW 5th Ave., Portland 97204

Phone: 503-802-2131
E-mail: ingolf.noto@tonkon.com

France
Francoise Aylmer, Honorary Consul
Address: 1600 SW 4th Ave., Portland 97201
Phone: 503-725-5037
E-mail: francoise@pdx.edu

Germany
Robert T. Manicke, Honorary Consul
Address: 200 SW Market St., Ste. 1775, Portland 97201
Phone: 503-222-0490
E-mail: portland-OR@hk-diplo.de

Guatemala
Marta Isabel Guembes Herrera, Consul a.h.
Address: 7304 N Campbell Ave., Portand 97217
Phone: 503-530-0046
E-mail: guembes@yahoo.com

Iceland
Les Swanson, Honorary Consul
Address: 900 SW 83rd Ave., Portland 97225
Phone: 503-228-1838
E-mail: lesswanson@comcast.net

Italy
Andrea Bartoloni, Honorary Consul
Address: 1331 NW Lovejoy St., Ste. 900, Portland 97209
Phone: 503-226-8622
E-mail: ab@aterwynne.com

Japan
Hirofumi Murabayashi, Consul General
Address: 1300 SW 5th Ave., Ste. 2700, Portland 97201
Phone: 503-221-1811
E-mail: hirofumi.murabayashi@mofa.go.jp

Korea, Republic of
John E. Bates, Honorary Consul General
Address: 11626 SW Military Ln., Portland 97219
Phone: 503-636-0039
E-mail: koreanconsulate.pdx@gmail.com

Latvia, Republic of
Uldis J. Berzins, M.D., Honorary Consul
Address: 655 Medical Center Dr. NE, Salem 97301
Phone: 503-581-5287
E-mail: ujberzins@aol.com

Liechtenstein, The Principality of
Mary Jean Thompson, Honorary Consul
Address: 2846 NW Fairfax TER, Portland 97210
Phone: 503-221-3000
E-mail: mjthompson@tdaportland.com

Lithuania
Randolph L. Miller, Honorary Consul
Address: 333 SE 2nd Ave., Portland 97214
Phone: 503-234-5000
E-mail: randy@mooreco.com

Luxembourg
Bill Failing, Honorary Consul
Address: 2649 SW Georgian Pl., Portland 97201
Phone: 503-224-5268
E-mail: bfailing@europa.com

Malaysia
John L. Blackwell, Honorary Consul General
Address: 4708 SW Fairview Blvd., Portland 97221
Phone: 503-243-4472
E-mail: JohnLBlackwell1@gmail.com

Mexico
Enrique A. Romero Cuevas, Consul General
Address: 1305 SW 12th Ave., Portland 97201
Phone: 503-274-1442
E-mail: eromeroc@sre.gob.mx

The Netherlands
Hans van Alebeek, Honorary Consul
Address: 1 Bowerman Dr., Beaverton 97005
Phone: 503-716-1500
E-mail: portland@ncla.org

New Zealand
Charles Swindells, Honorary Consul
Address: 500 NW Hilltop Rd., Portland 97210
Phone: 503-803-7129
E-mail: cjs@theswindells.org

Norway
Larry K. Bruun, Honorary Consul
Address: 4380 SW Macadam, Ste. 120, Portland 97239
Phone: 503-221-0870
E-mail: lbruun@wbgatty.com

Philippines, Republic of the
Richard K. Woodling, Consul General, a.h.
Address: 2662 SW Georgian Pl., Portland 97201
Phone: 971-679-6682
E-mail: Richard.Woodling@comcast.net

Romania
James H. Rudd, Honorary Consul
Address: 888 SW Fifth Ave., Ste. 1200, Portland 97204
Phone: 503-382-5165
E-mail: rudd@fergwell.com

Thailand
Nicholas J. Stanley, Honorary Consul General
Address: 1136 NW Hoyt St., Ste. 210, Portland 97209
Phone: 503-221-0440
E-mail: thai@siaminc.com

United Kingdom
Andrew MacRitchie, Honorary Consul
Address: 1 Sansome St., Ste. 850, San Francisco, CA 94104
Phone: 503-227-5669
E-mail: UKHonConsul@aol.com

Source: Michou Jardini, Oregon Consular Corps, 503-808-0974; www.oregoncc.us

Oregon State Symbols

State Flag: The front of the Oregon ceremonial flag. Navy blue and gold are the state colors.
(Oregon State Archives)

State Flag: The reverse of the ceremonial flag. Oregon is the only United States state to have different designs on the two sides of the flag.
(Oregon State Archives)

State Seal: The seal of the State of Oregon.
(Oregon State Archives)

State Animal: American Beaver *(Castor canadensis)*
(Oregon Department of Fish and Wildlife)

State Gemstone: Oregon Sunstone
(Oregon Department of Geology and Mineral Industries)

State Insect: Oregon Swallowtail *(Papilio oregonius)*
(Oregon State Capitol)

State Mushroom: Pacific Golden Chanterelle *(Cantharellus formosus)*
(Richard F. Bishop)

State Nut: Hazelnut *(Corylus avellana)*
(Oregon State Archives)

State Shell: Hairy Triton *(Fusitriton oregonesis)*
(Bill Hanshumaker, Hatfield Marine Science Center)

State Crustacean: Dungeness Crab
(Metacarcinus magister)
(Dungeness Crab Commission)

State Bird: Western Meadowlark *(Sturnella neglecta)*
(Noah Strycker)

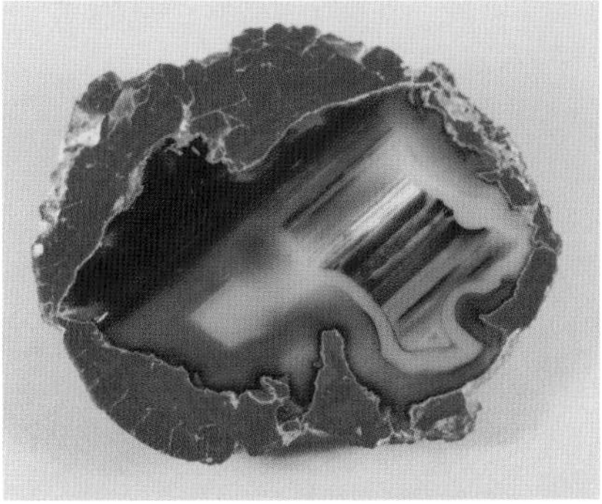

State Rock: Thunderegg (geode)
(Oregon Department of Geology and Mineral Industries)

State Fruit: Pear *(Pyrus communis)*
(Pear Bureau Northwest)

State Flower: Oregon Grape
(Mahonia Aquifolium)
(Oregon State Archives)

State Fossil: Dawn redwood
(Metasequoia glyptostroboides)
(National Park Service, John Day Fossil Beds National Monument)

State Fish: Chinook Salmon *(Oncorhynchus tshawytscha)*
(Oregon Department of Fish and Wildlife)

State Tree: Douglas-fir *(Pseudotsuga menziesii)*
(Oregon State Archives)

Dr. John McLoughlin,
Father of Oregon

Tabitha Moffatt Brown,
Mother of Oregon

Paulann Petersen,
Poet Laureate
(Sabina Samiee)

Oregon's Capitol

Oregon's present Capitol has its origins in two fires. On December 30, 1855, fire swept through a newly occupied Statehouse, completely destroying the structure. The Holman Building, in the business section of Salem, served as a temporary Capitol from 1859 until another one was completed in 1876 (right). On April 25, 1935, fire again destroyed the elegant Statehouse patterned after the U.S. Capitol.

Francis Keally, with the New York firm of Trowbridge & Livingston, designed the current building, which was dedicated on October 1, 1938. A four-story structure of modern Greek architecture, it was completed at a cost of $2.5 million and is the fourth newest Capitol in the United States. The exterior is faced with white Danby Vermont marble. The rotunda, halls and all of the lobby areas are lined with a warm, delicately polished, rose travertine from Montana. The floor and staircases of the rotunda utilize large squares of Phoenix Napoleon grey marble from Missouri, with borders of Radio Black marble from Vermont.

Capitol Entrances

A Capitol "Wings" project, completed in 1977 at a cost of $12.5 million, added further space for legislative offices, hearing rooms, support services, a first floor galleria and underground parking.

The beauty of the entire Capitol plan is enhanced by its utility. The building houses several elected state officials—the governor, secretary of state and state treasurer—in addition to the entire legislative branch of state government. Spacious hearing rooms provide Oregonians an opportunity to participate in legislative decision making and to view state government at work.

The massive Vermont marble sculptures flanking the main entrance, by Leo Friedlander, depict The Covered Wagon (west) and Lewis and Clark led by Sacajawea (east). Intaglio maps outlining the Old Oregon Trail and the routes of Lewis and Clark appear on the backsides of these sculptures. Ulric Ellerhusen sculpted five relief marble works for the exterior of the building. Above the south entrance is a work by Oregon sculptor Tom Morandi. A wheelchair ramp is outside the east entrance. A Liberty Bell replica distinguishes the west entrance.

Capitol Rotunda

In the center of the rotunda, embedded in the floor, is a large bronze replica of the Oregon State Seal sculpted by Ulric Ellerhusen, who also created the six cast bronze sculptures over the main entrance doors—three outside and three inside. Eight medallions painted near the top of the walls of the rotunda represent the eight objects in the state seal.

The Capitol dome rises 106 feet above the state seal in the floor of the spacious rotunda. The ceiling, painted by Frank H. Schwarz, features a design of 33 stars symbolizing Oregon as the 33rd state in The Union.

Capitol Murals and Art

The rotunda and both the House and Senate chambers feature large, colorful Depression-Era murals illustrating events in Oregon history painted by Barry Faulkner and Frank H. Schwarz.

The first wagon train migration in 1843 (rotunda mural detail).

People in Salem celebrate news of statehood in 1859 (Senate chamber mural).

The historic 1843 Champoeg meeting where trappers and settlers voted to form a provisional government for the Oregon Country (House chamber mural).

Dr. John McLoughlin welcomes the first women to cross the continent by covered wagon in 1836 (rotunda mural detail).

Four smaller murals alongside the stairways, including this one representing dairying and ranching, are symbolic of Oregon industries. The seal of the provisional government (1843–1848) is above the grand staircase leading to the Senate Chamber. The territorial seal (1848–1859) is above the opposite staircase leading to the House of Representatives.

Display cases containing exhibits relating to Oregon history, hearing rooms, traveling art exhibits and the visitors' information center highlight the galleria. The visitors' information center provides information to the public about the Capitol, the Legislative Assembly and Oregon. Historical building tours and videos are available. The Tower is open for tours seasonally.

These cast bronze sculptures by Ulric Ellerhusen greet visitors at the outside of the north entry.

These reliefs by Ulric Ellerhusen, representing historical land transportation modes, grace the inside of the north entry.

Portraits of former Oregon governors, such as this one of Governor Vic Atiyeh, hang in the Capitol.

Capitol Rotunda Engraving

"In the souls of its citizens will be found the likeness of the state which if they be unjust and tyrannical then will it reflect their vices but if they be lovers of righteousness confident in their liberties so will it be clean in justice bold in freedom."

House and Senate Chambers

The paneling and furniture in Oregon's 60-member House of Representatives is fashioned entirely of golden oak. Symbolic of Oregon's important wood products industry is the specially designed carpet featuring the Douglas-fir, Oregon's state tree.

Oregon's 30 state senators meet in the Senate Chamber. The room features paneling and furniture of matched black walnut. Alternating designs of wheat and salmon, symbolizing Oregon's agricultural and fishing industries, are woven into the carpeting.

Above the galleries in both the House and Senate Chambers are friezes inscribed with the names of 158 people prominent in the history and development of Oregon.

Governor's Suite

Between the two legislative chambers on the second floor is the Governor's Suite with a reception room, a public ceremonial office and private staff offices. The paneling is matched black walnut. The map of Oregon's geography above the fireplace in the ceremonial office is a work of Barry Faulkner. The ornate table in the reception area is made of 40 different types of wood and depicts the previous Capitol. It was created and given to the citizens of Oregon by the architectural firm employing Francis Keally. The reception area and ceremonial office are used frequently for art exhibits. The ceremonial office was extensively damaged by a fire in 2008 but has been completely renovated.

Tower and Oregon Pioneer

The Oregon Pioneer statue that tops the building is another work by Ulric Ellerhusen. This heroic figure represents the spirit of Oregon's early white settlers. Cast in bronze and finished in gold leaf, it weighs 8.5 tons and is hollow inside. The base of the 23-foot high statue is 140 feet above the ground.

The statue is reached by 121 steps spiraling up into the tower from the fourth floor of the building out onto a deck providing a spectacular view of Salem.

Capitol Grounds

Ornamental and native trees and shrubs are featured in the landscaped areas surrounding the Capitol. To the east, Capitol Park is also the setting of three statues representing major forces in Oregon history: The Circuit Rider (above, right) by A. Phimister Proctor is symbolic of the many missionaries who came to Oregon; Gifford Proctor sculpted both Reverend Jason Lee (above, left) and Dr. John McLoughlin (not shown). Lee, a minister, played a major role in the American colonization of Oregon. He was also the founder of Oregon's oldest university, Willamette University, located south of the Capitol. McLoughlin was the chief factor of the Hudson's Bay Company and was the first man to govern the Oregon territory, although he held no official title. Recent additions to the Capitol Park are fragments of Corinthian columns salvaged from the Capitol destroyed by fire in 1935.

Willson Park, to the west, was a city park from 1853 until 1965 when it officially became part of the Capitol grounds. The park is named after William H. Willson, preacher, physician and founder of Salem who donated the land for the Capitol and the surrounding land.

It is the setting for the Waite Fountain, Parade of Animals sculpture, a Liberty Bell replica and a gazebo constructed in 1982.

Capitol tour credits:
Photographs: Oregon State Archives
Text: Legislative Administration; Additional text: Oregon State Archives

Protecting Oregon Beaches

Explore some of the many public uses of the state's beaches over the decades and efforts to protect them from privatization

Governor Tom McCall looks at Cannon Beach's Surfsand Motel in 1967. The owner wanted this beach area for the use of motel guests only, sparking a legislative conflict about public access. *(Oregon Historical Society)*

Oregon Beaches: Public Uses and Public Access

Oregon has a long history of public beaches. But that history has seen challenges that threatened to privatize and fence off the beaches in ways all too familiar to Californians. For centuries Native Americans regularly used the beaches for transportation, food gathering and other communal activities before the arrival of white settlers in the 1800s. The new inhabitants found that headlands and other geographic obstacles made roadbuilding difficult. This naturally attracted wagon traffic to the wide, flat beaches for much of the north-south transportation. The Oregon Legislature recognized this practice in 1899 when it mandated that the shore between low and high tides in Clatsop County would forever be a public highway.

Meanwhile, the State Land Board was selling tidelands to private upland owners—totaling about 23 miles by 1901. Seeing the threat to public use if this trend toward private ownership continued, Governor Oswald West successfully urged passage of a 1913 bill that declared the entire Oregon shore from low to high tides to be a public highway. This creative solution worked for over 50 years, even as the legislature changed the designation from "highway" to "recreation area" in 1947.

A new threat came in 1966 when the owner of the Surfsand Motel in Cannon Beach instructed his employees to tell non-guest beachgoers to leave a stretch of the dry sand beach in front of the motel (above). This move exposed a flaw in the 1913 bill, which technically protected only the wet sands. The Oregon Highway Department aimed to fix the loophole with a bill in the 1967 legislature. Soon dubbed the "Beach Bill," it triggered a political drama replete with grassroots citizen action, backroom power plays and public posturing that climaxed with Governor Tom McCall's dramatic helicopter ride between two beaches. McCall had surveyors pound stakes in the sand to show Oregonians the stark boundary line choices in competing proposals. The media gleefully covered the event, the public loudly supported McCall's position and the bill passed easily.

Still, that bill relied on zoning laws to protect the beaches and many, including State Treasurer Bob Straub, wanted more solid protections. He and a citizens' group, Beaches Forever, pushed initiative Measure 6 in 1968 proposing a temporary one-cent-a-gallon gas tax for the state to purchase outright the dry sand beaches. After leading in the polls, the measure lost. However, over the next few years, all legal challenges to the Beach Bill also lost, leaving a legacy of public access to some of the most beautiful beaches in the world.

Titled "Rock Oyster Queen," this photograph shows a Native American woman, Annie Ditallo, gathering oysters at Newport in the late-18th or early-19th century. The sledgehammer and prybar were used to extract the oysters, which were then carried in the traditional basket on her back. *(Lincoln County Historical Society, LCHS #1195)*

Siletz Indians pose on Nye Beach. The ocean, tidelands and forests sustained rich tribal cultures all along the Oregon Coast before white settlement. *(Lincoln County Historical Society, LCHS #1867)*

A wagon climbs the road at Hug Point circa 1915. The roadbed was cut in the rock so that wagons could avoid the beach surf at the edge of Hug Point. *(OSU Libraries, Special Collections & Archives)*

Stagecoaches and a wagon on the beach circa 1910. The Beach Stage Line ran from Marshfield, now Coos Bay, inland to Drain. *(Coos Historical & Maritime Museum, CHMM 992-8-0017)* Right: Governor Oswald West's 1913 bill defined the entire Oregon shore as a public highway. *(Oregon State Archives)*

Model T Fords sit on the beach in Coos County circa 1915. The ubiquitous Model Ts led the transition from horse-drawn traffic to automobiles. *(Coos Historical & Maritime Museum, CHMM 992-8-0025)*

The Bayocean Natatorium was built on the edge of the sand in 1914. It was part of a larger resort community that the town founder hoped would become the "Atlantic City of the West." *(PDXHistory.com)*

An early advertisement for Gearhart. The Hotel Gearhart, built in 1890, was a popular retreat for wealthy Portlanders who, by 1898, could travel completely by train from home to resort. *(PDXHistory.com)*

Top: A car bearing military officers drives down the Gearhart beach during a review of troops circa 1914. *(Library of Congress)* Middle: The Seaside Turnaround at the edge of the beach, shown here in a vintage postcard, has long been a popular place to mingle. *(PDXHistory.com)* Bottom: A composite photograph appears to show a man and a woman flying over Newport's Nye Beach in 1911. *(PDXHistory.com)*

Top: A vintage image boasts that the "steam heated" Hotel Gearhart features "surf bathing" on the beach. *(PDXHistory.com)* Middle: A circa late-1920s truck carries a giant old-growth log near a Coos County beach. *(Coos Historical & Maritime Museum, CHMM 978-1.8)* Bottom: A late-1920s postcard shows the Seaside Promenade on the edge of the beach near Trail's End. *(PDXHistory.com)*

A young woman on a bicycle talks with two young women riding horses on the beach at Cannon Beach in 1939. By then, the entire Oregon Coast Highway (U.S. Highway 101) had been completed and the transportation rationale for public beaches had dwindled. Eight years later, the legislature recognized this evolution by changing the designation from "highway" to "recreation area." *(Oregon State Archives)*

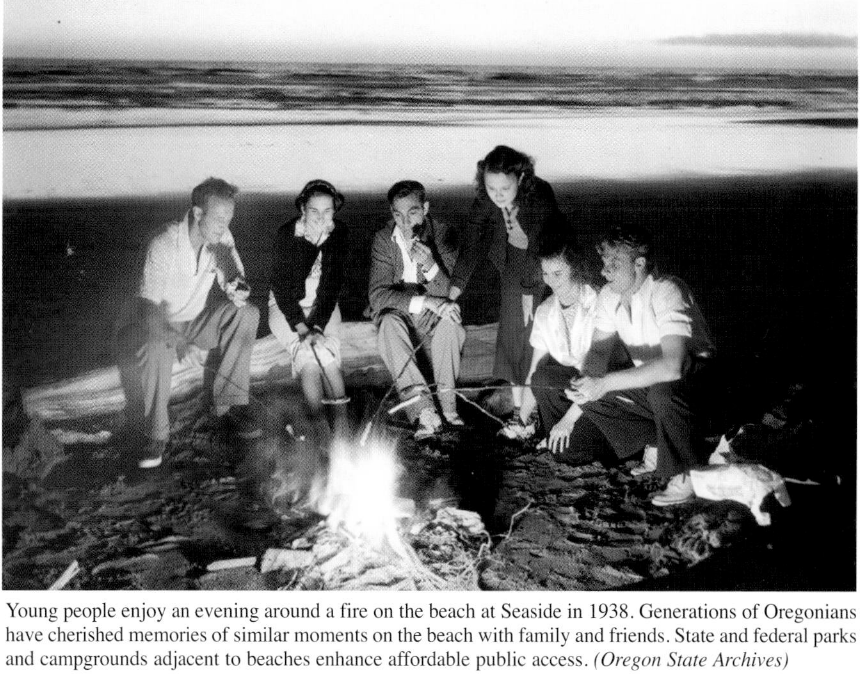

Young people enjoy an evening around a fire on the beach at Seaside in 1938. Generations of Oregonians have cherished memories of similar moments on the beach with family and friends. State and federal parks and campgrounds adjacent to beaches enhance affordable public access. *(Oregon State Archives)*

Boys perch atop an old car badly stuck in the surf at Nye Beach. Getting trapped in the sand by the tide has been a common peril of beach travel. *(Lincoln County Historical Society, LCHS #32)*

Young people drive down the beach in a Chevrolet at Haystack Rock in 1940. *(Oregon State Archives)*

Top: A vintage postcard shows a car rounding the bend at Hug Point with Haystack Rock in the inset. *(PDXHistory.com)* Middle: Young people with a British MG sports car and scooters on the beach at Cannon Beach in 1958. *(Oregon State Archives)* Bottom: Fisherman use a Willys Jeep to pull a boat onto the beach at Cape Kiwanda in 1958. The man to the right is holding two salmon. *(Oregon State Archives)*

Republican Governor Tom McCall (left) and Democratic State Treasurer Bob Straub were often political rivals but agreed on the need to protect public access to Oregon beaches. Both were prime figures in the effort. *(Oregon Historical Society)*

Governor Tom McCall (center) stands next to a survey stake on the beach at Rockaway during a 1967 trip to tout his method of determining the legal boundary between public and private ownership. *(Oregon Historical Society)*

Governor Tom McCall peers through survey equipment on the beach at Rockaway in 1967 as part of his effort to highlight the public access risks if the version of the Beach Bill he favored did not pass. State Representative Sidney Bazett (left) was a key ally in passing the bill. Oregon State University engineer, Robert Schultz (center) helped with the formula to determine the public right of way. The media extensively covered the event and the resulting public response helped pass the Beach Bill. *(Oregon Historical Society)*

After the passage of the Beach Bill, doubts lingered about whether it would withstand legal challenges related to property rights and other issues. Looking for more solid protections, the Beaches Forever citizens' group teamed with Bob Straub to back Measure 6 in 1968. The measure authorized a temporary gas tax to buy privately-owned beach land. Advocates mounted a strong grassroots campaign.

Clara Barefoot-Sehorn, a grade school teacher in the Portland area, supported the effort and mobilized her students to share their feelings about the beach through their drawings. She then presented the Beach Book shown here to Bob Straub.

Measure 6 was defeated by a well-funded and clever anti-gas tax campaign with the slogan "Beware of Tricks in No. 6."

Students Cinda (top) and Louis, both six years old, contributed two of many colorful drawings for the Beach Book. Learn more: Robert W. Straub Oregon Beaches Digital Collection at http://digitalcommons.wou.edu/straub/ *(All images: Western Oregon University Archives, Robert W. Straub Collection)*

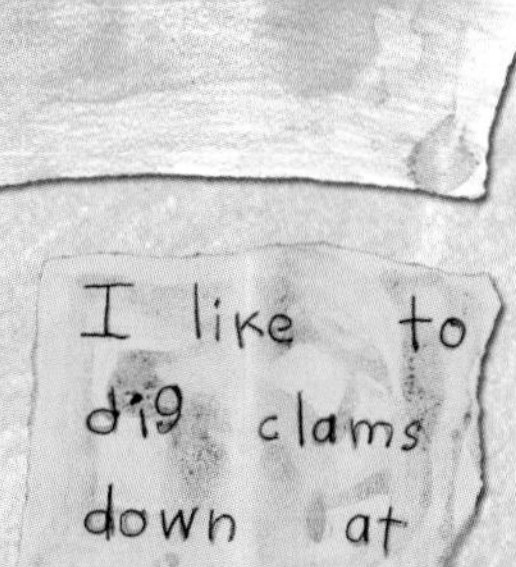

Top: "Mini-Marchers" on the beach to show support for Measure 6 in 1968. *(Oregon Historical Society)*
Middle: Children were a key part of the campaign by supporters of Measure 6 in 1968. *(The Oregonian)*
Bottom: Bob Straub stands on a van to speak to a Yes on Measure 6 rally on the beach. *(The Oregonian)*

The legacy of public access to Oregon beaches... Top: Bob Straub and his wife, Pat, at the state park in Pacific City named in his honor. *(Western Oregon University Archives, Robert W. Straub Collection)* Left: The Tom McCall portrait in the Oregon State Capitol includes Beach Bill symbols. This image: An Oceanside sunset. Below: The beach at Ecola State Park. *(Three images Oregon State Archives)*

Following pages: Nehalem Bay State Park. *(Oregon State Archives)* ▸

Physical Features Map

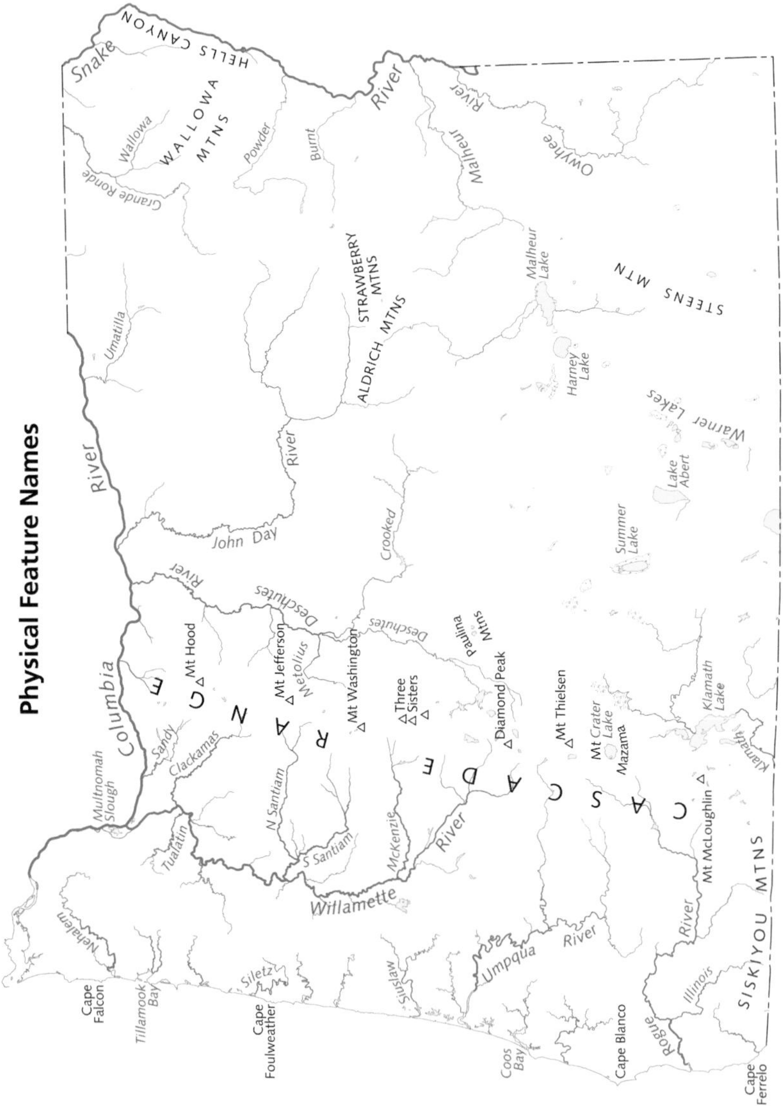

Image reproduced from the *Atlas of Oregon, Second Edition* courtesy of the University of Oregon Press.

Local Governments

The Oregon City Municipal Elevator, built in 1954, is the only "vertical street" in North America—Oregon State Archives Scenic Photograph clacDA0106

Oregon offers us a place of rich geographic diversity to establish our communities — from the Pacific Ocean beaches and Coast Range eastward to the Willamette Valley, Klamath Mountains and southwest valleys; on to the Cascade Range; then further east to the Columbia River Plateau, Blue Mountains, the southeast Basin and ranges; and on to the Snake River at our eastern border. This section identifies incorporated cities and towns, counties, regional governments and special districts.

Salem—Oregon's Capital

Salem, with a population of 155,710, is Oregon's state capital and the third largest city. Salem is also the county seat of Marion County, but a small portion contained within its corporate limits of 44 square miles lies across the Willamette River in Polk County. Salem is situated on the 45th geographic parallel in the center of the Willamette Valley—one of the most fertile and agriculturally productive regions in the world—47 miles south of Portland and 64 miles north of Eugene.

Salem serves as the hub of both state government and the surrounding farming communities. State government is the largest employer, with approximately 17,222 state employees and offices for 74 state agencies located in Salem. Salem is also one of the largest food-processing centers in the United States.

In addition, Salem is one of Oregon's oldest cities. The tribal name for the locality was Chemeketa, said to mean "meeting or resting place." It may also have been the name of one of the bands of the Kalapuya Tribe. In 1840–41, the Jason Lee Mission was moved from the banks of the Willamette River upstream to a site on Mill Creek. In 1842, the missionaries established the Oregon Institute. When the mission was dissolved in 1844, it was decided to lay out a townsite on the Oregon Institute lands. Either David Leslie, one of the trustees who came to Oregon from Salem, Massachusetts, or W. H. Willson, who filed plats in 1850–51 for what is now the main part of the city, selected the name "Salem." Salem is the Anglicized form of the Hebrew word shalom, meaning peace.*

The location of the Oregon capital caused a spirited contest that lasted nearly 15 years. By a legislative act in 1851, the territorial government moved the capital to Salem from Oregon City. In 1855, it was moved to Corvallis, only to move back to Salem the same year. Destruction of the Capitol Building at Salem on December 31, 1855, was considered an incendiary part of this controversy.

The close proximity of government provides Salem citizens with a distinct opportunity to be involved in the decision-making processes of the state. The citizens of Salem also have a long history of commitment to community improvement, a committment recognized nationally through the presentation of two All-America City Awards in 1960–61 and 1982–83.

*Early Salem history from *Oregon Geographic Names* by Lewis A. McArthur.

State Buildings

Agriculture Building (1966)*
635 Capitol St. NE, Salem 97301

Barbara Roberts Human Services Bldg. (1992)
550 Summer St. NE, Salem 97301

Capitol Mall Parking Structure (1991)
900 Chemeketa St. NE, Salem 97301

Cecil Edwards Archives Building (1991)
800 Summer St. NE, Salem 97310

Commerce Building (1931)
158 12th St. NE, Salem 97301

Commission for the Blind (1977)
535 SE 12th Ave., Portland 97204

Employment Building (1974)
875 Union St. NE, Salem 97311

Executive Building (1979)
155 Cottage St. NE, Salem 97301

Fish and Wildlife Building (2003)
3406 Cherry Ave. NE, Salem 97303

Forestry Buildings (1938)
2600 State St., Salem 97310

General Services Building (1954)
1225 Ferry St. SE, Salem 97301

General Services Building Annex (1967)
1257 Ferry St. SE, Salem 97301

Justice Building (1930)
1162 Court St. NE, Salem 97301

Labor and Industries Building (1961)
350 Winter St. NE, Salem 97301

Liquor Control Commission Building (1955)
9201 SE McLoughlin Blvd., Milwaukie 97222

North Capitol Mall Office Building (2003)
725 Summer St. NE, Salem 97301

Public Employees' Retirement System Building (1998)
11410 SW 68th Pkwy., Tigard 97281

Public Service Building (1949)
255 Capitol St. NE, Salem 97310

Public Utility Commission Building (1992)
550 Capitol St. NE, Salem 97301

Real Estate Building (1990)
1177 Center St. NE, Salem 97301

Revenue Building (1981)
955 Center St. NE, Salem 97301

State Capitol Building (1938)
900 Court St. NE, Salem 97301

State Fair Buildings, State Fairgrounds
2330 17th St. NE, Salem 97303

State Hospital Building (1883)
2600 Center St. NE, Salem 97301

State Lands Building (1990)
775 Summer St. NE, Salem 97301

State Library (1939)
250 Winter St. NE, Salem 97301

State Lottery Building (1996)
500 Airport Rd. SE, Salem 97301

State Office Building, Eugene (1961)
165 7th St. E, Eugene 97401

State Office Building, Pendleton (1963)
700 SE Emigrant St., Pendleton 97801

State Office Building, Portland (1992)
800 NE Oregon St., Portland 97232

State Printing Plant (1980)
550 Airport Rd. SE, Salem 97301

Supreme Court Building (1914)
1163 State St., Salem 97301

Transportation Building (1951)
355 Capitol St. NE, Salem 97301

Veterans' Building (1984)
700 Summer St. NE, Salem 97301

*Year is the date the building was constructed, purchased or occupied by the state.

Incorporated Cities and Towns

Source: Michael McCauley, Executive Director, League of Oregon Cities
Address: 1201 Court St. NE, Suite 200, Salem 97301, PO Box 928, Salem 97308
Phone: 503-588-6550
Fax: 503-399-4863
E-mail: loc@orcities.org
Web: www.orcities.org

There are 242 incorporated cities in Oregon. Cities provide a variety of services to residents and serve as centers of population, commerce, education and services. Seventy percent of Oregonians live in cities. Just under 70 percent of Oregon's property value is in cities. Economic activity within cities generates 83 percent of the state's income tax receipts as more than 82 percent of jobs are located in cities. There are almost 11,000 miles of city roads. Cities employ more than 3,600 police officers, comprising 60 percent of all law enforcement officers in Oregon. All of the public institutions of higher education are located in cities, as well as all but two private colleges. All but one of Oregon's 60 hospitals is located within a city. Cities form the heart of Oregon's cultural, educational, service and economic activity.

Among the services city governments typically provide are fire and police protection, streets and street maintenance, sewer and water treatment and collection systems, building permit activities, libraries, parks and recreation activities, and other numerous social services determined locally. Cities also have considerable responsibilities for land use planning within their city limits and urban growth boundaries.

City councils serve as the highest authority within city governments in deciding issues of public policy. In open public forums, city councils pass laws (ordinances), adopt resolutions and generally conduct discussions involving the governance of their communities and the welfare of their citizens.

Four forms of city government determine the administrative role of any city council. Most Oregon cities with populations over 2,500 have the council/manager or council/administrator form, in which the council hires a chief executive officer to be responsible for the daily supervision of city affairs. Portland has a commission form of government, where the elected commissioners function collectively as the city council and serve as administrators of city departments. Smaller Oregon cities typically have the mayor/council form, in which the legislative and policy-making body is a popularly elected council.

City administrators and other city employees often participate in the policy development process but are primarily responsible for effective delivery of municipal services and programs. Under home rule, cities have latitude in managing their affairs, except where the subject matter has been preempted by state government.

Regardless of the form of government, cities find their strength in a cooperative relationship between the citizens, city officials, the private sector and other government entities. Cities recognize the positive impact of working together, both regionally and on a statewide basis, to enhance community livability.

City name origins are available from *Oregon Geographic Names* by Lewis A. McArthur.

Incorporation dates listed are based on information available.

***County seat**

Adair Village
County: Benton
Address: 6030 NE Wm. R. Carr Ave., 97330
Phone: 541-745-5507
Fax: 541-230-5219
Web: www.adairvillage.org
Elevation: 328'
Incorporated: 5/25/1976
Mayor: Nicole Real

Adams
County: Umatilla
Address: PO Box 20, 97810
Phone: 541-566-9380
Fax: 541-566-2077
E-mail: cityofadams@uci.net
Elevation: 1,526'
Incorporated: 2/10/1893
Mayor: Patrick Bryson

Adrian
County: Malheur
Address: PO Box 226, 97901
Phone: 541-372-2179
Fax: 541-372-2179
Elevation: 2,225'
Incorporated: 7/10/1972
Mayor: Clay Webb

*Albany
County: Benton/Linn
Address: PO Box 490, 97321
Phone: 541-917-7500
Fax: 541-917-7511
Web: www.cityofalbany.net
Elevation: 210'
Incorporated: 10/10/1864
Mayor: Sharon Konopa

Amity
County: Yamhill
Address: PO Box 159, 109 Maddox Ave., 97101
Phone: 503-835-3711
Fax: 503-835-3780
Web: www.ci.amity.or.us
Elevation: 162'
Incorporated: 10/19/1880
Mayor: Michael Cape

Antelope
County: Wasco
Address: PO Box 105, 97001
Phone: 541-489-3201
E-mail: cityofantelope@live.com
Elevation: 2,685'
Incorporated: 11/12/1896
Mayor: Chandler Cruise

Arlington
County: Gilliam
Address: PO Box 68, 97812
Phone: 541-454-2743
Fax: 541-454-2753
E-mail: cityofa@gorge.net
Elevation: 285'
Incorporated: 11/20/1885
Mayor: Jeff Bufton

Ashland
County: Jackson
Address: 20 E Main St., 97520
Phone: 541-488-6002
Fax: 541-488-5311
Web: www.ashland.or.us
Elevation: 1,895'
Incorporated: 10/13/1874
Mayor: John Stromberg

*Astoria
County: Clatsop
Address: 1095 Duane St., 97103
Phone: 503-325-5821
Fax: 503-325-2997
Web: www.astoria.or.us
Elevation: 23'
Incorporated: 10/20/1876
Mayor: Willis L. Van Dusen

Athena
County: Umatilla
Address: PO Box 686, 302 E Currant St., 97813
Phone: 541-566-3862
Fax: 541-566-2781
E-mail: cityhall@cityofathena.com
Elevation: 1725'
Incorporated: 2/20/1889
Mayor: John Shafer

Aumsville
County: Marion
Address: 595 Main St., 97325
Phone: 503-749-2030
Fax: 503-749-1852
Web: www.aumsville.us
Elevation: 366'
Incorporated: 8/3/1911
Mayor: Harold L. White

Aurora
County: Marion
Address: 21420 Main St. NE, 97002
Phone: 503-678-1283, ext. 2
Fax: 503-678-2758
Web: www.ci.aurora.or.us
Elevation: 136'
Incorporated: 2/20/1893
Mayor: Greg Taylor

*Baker City
County: Baker
Address: PO Box 650, 97814
Phone: 541-523-6541
Fax: 541-524-2024
Web: www.bakercity.com
Elevation: 3,451'
Incorporated: 10/13/1874
Mayor: Richard Langrell

Bandon
County: Coos
Address: PO Box 67, 97411
Phone: 541-347-2437
Fax: 541-347-1415
Web: www.ci.bandon.or.us
Elevation: 20'
Incorporated: 2/18/1891
Mayor: Mary Schamehorn

Banks
County: Washington
Address: 13680 NW Main St., 97106
Phone: 503-324-5112
Fax: 503-324-6674
Web: www.cityofbanks.org
Elevation: 250'
Incorporated: 1/16/1920
Mayor: John Kinsky

Barlow
County: Clackamas
Address: 106 N Main St., 97013-9191
Phone: 503-266-1330
Fax: 503-266-1330
Elevation: 101'
Incorporated: 2/13/1903
Mayor: Mike Lundsten

Bay City
County: Tillamook
Address: PO Box 3309, 97107
Phone: 503-377-2288
Fax: 503-377-4044
Web: www.ci.bay-city.or.us
Elevation: 17'
Incorporated: 9/13/1910
Mayor: Shaena Peterson

Beaverton
County: Washington
Address: PO Box 4755, 97076-4755
Phone: 503-526-2222
Fax: 503-526-2479
Web: www.beavertonoregon.gov
Elevation: 189'
Incorporated: 2/10/1893
Mayor: Denny Doyle

*Bend
County: Deschutes
Address: PO Box 431, 97709
Phone: 541-388-5505
Fax: 541-385-6676
Web: www.ci.bend.or.us
Elevation: 3,628'
Incorporated: 1/19/1905
Mayor: Jim Clinton

Boardman
County: Morrow
Address: PO Box 229, 97818
Phone: 541-481-9252
Fax: 541-481-3244
Web: www.cityofboardman.com
Elevation: 298'
Incorporated: 5/20/1921
Mayor: Sandy Toms

Bonanza
County: Klamath
Address: PO Box 297, 97623
Phone: 541-545-6566
Fax: 541-545-1027
E-mail: bonanza@fireserve.net
Elevation: 4,120'
Incorporated: 2/20/1901
Mayor: Betty Tyree

Brookings
County: Curry
Address: 898 Elk Dr., 97414
Phone: 541-469-2163
Fax: 541-469-3650
Web: www.brookings.or.us
Elevation: 129'
Incorporated: 10/15/1951
Mayor: Ron Hedenskog

Brownsville
County: Linn
Address: PO Box 188, 97327
Phone: 541-466-5666
Fax: 541-466-5118
Web: www.ci.brownsville.or.us
Elevation: 265'
Incorporated: 10/19/1876
Mayor: Don Ware

*Burns
County: Harney
Address: 242 S Broadway Ave., 97720
Phone: 541-573-5255
Fax: 541-573-5622
Web: www.ci.burns.or.us
Elevation: 4,148'
Incorporated: 2/18/1891
Mayor: Craig LaFollette

Butte Falls
County: Jackson
Address: PO Box 268, 97522
Phone: 541-865-3262
Fax: 541-865-3777
E-mail: bfcityhall@gmail.com
Elevation: 2,536'
Incorporated: 8/21/1911
Mayor: Frederick Phillips

Canby
County: Clackamas
Address: PO Box 930, 97013
Phone: 503-266-4021
Fax: 503-266-7961
Web: www.ci.canby.or.us
Elevation: 153'
Incorporated: 2/15/1893
Mayor: Brian Hodson

Cannon Beach
County: Clatsop
Address: PO Box 368, 97110
Phone: 503-436-1581
Fax: 503-436-2050
Web: www.ci.cannon-beach.or.us
Elevation: 30'
Incorporated: 3/5/1957
Mayor: Mike Morgan

*Canyon City
County: Grant
Address: PO Box 276, 97820
Phone: 541-575-0509
Fax: 541-575-0515
E-mail: bremnert@grantcounty-or.gov
Elevation: 3,194'
Incorporated: 10/19/1864
Mayor: Steve Fischer

Canyonville
County: Douglas
Address: PO Box 765, 97417
Phone: 541-839-4258
Fax: 541-839-4680
Web: www.cityofcanyonville.com
Elevation: 750'
Incorporated: 1/29/1901
Mayor: Bob Deaton

Carlton
County: Yamhill
Address: 191 E Main St., 97111
Phone: 503-852-7575
Fax: 503-852-7761
Web: www.ci.carlton.or.us
Elevation: 198'
Incorporated: 2/17/1899
Mayor: Kathie Oriet

Cascade Locks
County: Hood River
Address: PO Box 308, 97014
Phone: 541-374-8484
Fax: 541-374-8752
Web: www.cascade-locks.or.us
Elevation: 170'
Incorporated: 6/19/1935
Mayor: Tom Cramblett

Cave Junction
County: Josephine
Address: PO Box 1396, 222 W Lister St.,97523
Phone: 541-592-2156
Fax: 541-592-6694
Web: www.cavejunctionoregon.us
Elevation: 1,350'
Incorporated: 9/23/1946
Mayor: Carl Jacobson, Jr.

Central Point
County: Jackson
Address: 140 S 3rd St., 97502
Phone: 541-664-3321
Fax: 541-664-6384
Web: www.centralpointoregon.gov
Elevation: 1,272'
Incorporated: 2/25/1889
Mayor: Hank Williams

Chiloquin
County: Klamath
Address: PO Box 196, 97624
Phone: 541-783-2717
Fax: 541-783-2035
E-mail: chiloquin@centurylink.net
Elevation: 4,200'
Incorporated: 3/3/1926
Mayor: Patricia Ann Twamley

Clatskanie
County: Columbia
Address: PO Box 9, 95 S Nehalem St., 97016
Phone: 503-728-2622
Fax: 503-728-3297
Web: www.cityofclatskanie.com
Elevation: 59'
Incorporated: 2/18/1891
Mayor: Diane Pohl

Coburg
County: Lane
Address: PO Box 8316, 97408
Phone: 541-682-7850
Fax: 541-485-0655
Web: www.coburgoregon.org
Elevation: 398'
Incorporated: 2/10/1893
Mayor: Jae Pudewell

Columbia City
County: Columbia
Address: PO Box 189, 97018
Phone: 503-397-4010
Fax: 503-366-2870
Web: www.columbia-city.org
Elevation: 71'
Incorporated: 6/7/1926
Mayor: Cheryl Young

*Condon
County: Gilliam
Address: PO Box 445, 97823
Phone: 541-384-2711
Fax: 541-384-2700
Web: www.cityofcondon.com
Elevation: 2,900'
Incorporated: 2/10/1893
Mayor: N. Dale Thompson

Coos Bay
County: Coos
Address: 500 Central Ave., 97420
Phone: 541-269-1181
Fax: 541-267-5912
Web: www.coosbay.org
Elevation: 10'
Incorporated: 10/24/1874
Mayor: Crystal Shoji

*Coquille
County: Coos
Address: 851 N Central Blvd., 97423
Phone: 541-396-2115
Fax: 541-396-5125
Web: www.cityofcoquille.org
Elevation: 40'
Incorporated: 2/25/1885
Mayor: Matt Rowe

Cornelius
County: Washington
Address: 1355 N Barlow St., 97113
Phone: 503-357-9112
Fax: 503-357-7775
Web: www.ci.cornelius.or.us
Elevation: 175'
Incorporated: 2/10/1893
Mayor: Jeffrey C. Dalin

*Corvallis
County: Benton
Address: PO Box 1083, 97339
Phone: 541-766-6900
Fax: 541-766-6780
Web: www.ci.corvallis.or.us
Elevation: 224'
Incorporated: 1/28/1857
Mayor: Julie Manning

Cottage Grove
County: Lane
Address: 400 E Main St., 97424
Phone: 541-942-5501
Fax: 541-942-1267
Web: www.cottagegrove.org
Elevation: 640'
Incorporated: 2/11/1887
Mayor: Thomas C. Munroe

Cove
County: Union
Address: PO Box 8, 97824
Phone: 541-568-4566
Fax: 541-568-7747
E-mail: citycove@uci.net
Elevation: 2,870'
Incorporated: 3/10/1904
City Council President: Lyndon Rose

Creswell
County: Lane
Address: PO Box 276, 97426
Phone: 541-895-2531
Fax: 541-895-3647
Web: www.ci.creswell.or.us
Elevation: 542'
Incorporated: 7/16/1909
Mayor: David Strom

Culver
County: Jefferson
Address: 200 First Ave., 97734
Phone: 541-546-6494
Fax: 541-546-3624
Web: http://cocls.a-difference.com
Elevation: 2,640'
Incorporated: 6/27/1946
Mayor: Shawna Clanton

*Dallas
County: Polk
Address: 187 SE Court St., 97338
Phone: 503-623-2338
Fax: 503-623-2339
Web: www.ci.dallas.or.us
Elevation: 312'
Incorporated: 2/20/1874
Mayor: Brian Dalton

Damascus
County: Clackamas
Address: 19920 SE Hwy. 212, 97089
Phone: 503-658-8545
Fax: 503-658-5786
Web: www.ci.damascus.or.us
Elevation: 530'
Incorporated: 2/28/2005
Mayor: Steve Spinnett

Dayton
County: Yamhill
Address: PO Box 339, 97114-0339
Phone: 503-864-2221
Fax: 503-864-2956
Web: www.ci.dayton.or.us
Elevation: 280'
Incorporated: 10/15/1880
Mayor: Jolie White

Dayville
County: Grant
Address: PO Box 321, 97825
Phone: 541-987-2188
Fax: 541-987-2187
E-mail: dville@ortelco.net
Elevation: 2,348'
Incorporated: 10/25/1913
Mayor: Jody Winkelman

Depoe Bay
County: Lincoln
Address: PO Box 8, 97341
Phone: 541-765-2361
Fax: 541-765-2129
Web: www.cityofdepoebay.org
Elevation: 56’
Incorporated: 12/14/1973
Mayor: A. J. (Jim) Mattila

Detroit
County: Marion
Address: PO Box 589, 97342
Phone: 503-854-3496
Fax: 503-854-3232
E-mail: detroit@wbi.com
Elevation: 1,595'
Incorporated: 9/29/1952
Mayor: Sharyl Flanders

Donald
County: Marion
Address: PO Box 388, 97020
Phone: 503-678-5543
Fax: 503-678-2750
E-mail: donaldcity@centurylink.net
Elevation: 198'
Incorporated: 12/6/1912
Mayor: Daroll Nicholson

Drain
County: Douglas
Address: PO Box 158, 97435
Phone: 541-836-2417
Fax: 541-836-7330
Web: www.cityofdrain.org
Elevation: 290'
Incorporated: 2/9/1887
Mayor: Suzanne Anderson

Dufur
County: Wasco
Address: PO Box 145, 97021
Phone: 541-467-2349
Fax: 541-467-2353
Web: www.cityofdufur.org
Elevation: 1,345'
Incorporated: 2/10/1893
Mayor: Arthur Smith

Dundee
County: Yamhill
Address: PO Box 220, 97115-0220
Phone: 503-538-3922
Fax: 503-538-1958
Web: www.dundeecity.org
Elevation: 189'
Incorporated: 2/21/1895
Mayor: Ted Crawford

Dunes City
County: Lane
Address: PO Box 97, Westlake 97493, 82877 Spruce St., Dunes City 94739
Phone: 541-997-3338
Fax: 541-997-5751
Web: www.dunescity.com
Elevation: 39'
Incorporated: 6/13/1963
Mayor: Rebecca Rueda

Durham
County: Washington
Address: 17160 SW Upper Boones Ferry Rd., 97224
Phone: 503-639-6851
Fax: 503-598-8595
Web: www.durham-oregon.us
Elevation: 197'
Incorporated: 7/20/1966
Mayor: Gery Schirado

Eagle Point
County: Jackson
Address: PO Box 779, 97826
Phone: 541-826-4212
Fax: 541-826-6155
Web: www.cityofeaglepoint.org
Elevation: 1,310'
Incorporated: 2/16/1911
Mayor: Bob Russell

Echo
County: Umatilla
Address: PO Box 9, 97826
Phone: 541-376-8411
Fax: 541-376-8218
Web: www.echo-oregon.com
Elevation: 635'
Incorporated: 3/9/1904
Mayor: Richard Winter

Elgin
County: Union
Address: PO Box 128, 97827
Phone: 541-437-2253
Fax: 541-437-0131
Web: www.cityofelginor.org
Elevation: 2,670'
Incorporated: 2/18/1891
Mayor: Brent Linville

Elkton
County: Douglas
Address: PO Box 508, 97436
Phone: 541-584-2547
Fax: 541-584-2547
Web: www.elkton-oregon.com
Elevation: 130'
Incorporated: 11/4/1948
Mayor: Rebecca Swearingen

*Enterprise
County: Wallowa
Address: 108 NE 1st St., 97828
Phone: 541-426-4196
Fax: 541-426-3395
Web: www.enterpriseoregon.org
Elevation: 3,757'
Incorporated: 2/21/1889
Mayor: Margie Shaw

Estacada
County: Clackamas
Address: PO Box 958, 97023-0958
Phone: 503-630-8270
Fax: 503-630-8280
Web: www.cityofestacada.org
Elevation: 426'
Incorporated: 1/31/1905
Mayor: Brent Dodrill

*Eugene
County: Lane
Address: 125 E 8th Ave., 2nd Floor, 97401
Phone: 541-682-5010
Fax: 541-682-5414
Web: www.eugene-or.gov
Elevation: 426'
Incorporated: 10/17/1862 or 10/22/1864
Mayor: Kitty Piercy

Fairview
County: Multnomah
Address: PO Box 337, 97024
Phone: 503-665-7929
Fax: 503-666-0888
Web: www.fairvieworegon.gov
Elevation: 114'
Incorporated: 5/11/1908
Mayor: Mike Weatherby

Falls City
County: Polk
Address: 299 Mill St., 97344
Phone: 503-787-3631
Fax: 503-787-3023
Web: www.fallscityoregon.gov
Elevation: 370'
Incorporated: 2/13/1893
Mayor: Amy Houghtaling

Florence
County: Lane
Address: 250 Hwy. 101, 97439
Phone: 541-997-3436
Fax: 541-997-6814
Web: www.ci.florence.or.us
Elevation: 14'
Incorporated: 2/10/1893
Mayor: Nola Xavier

Forest Grove
County: Washington
Address: PO Box 326, 97116
Phone: 503-992-3200
Fax: 503-992-3207
Web: www.forestgrove-or.gov
Elevation: 210'
Incorporated: 10/5/1872
Mayor: Pete Truax

*Fossil
County: Wheeler
Address: PO Box 467, 97830
Phone: 541-763-2698
Fax: 541-763-2124
Web: www.cityoffossil.org
Elevation: 2,654'
Incorporated: 2/18/1891
Mayor: Jack Lorts

Garibaldi
County: Tillamook
Address: PO Box 708, 97118
Phone: 503-322-3327
Fax: 503-322-3737
Web: www.ci.garibaldi.or.us
Elevation: 22'
Incorporated: 4/8/1946
Mayor: Suzanne McCarthy

Gaston
County: Washington
Address: PO Box 129, 97119
Phone: 503-985-3340
Fax: 503-985-1014
E-mail: gaston.city@comcast.net
Elevation: 300'
Incorporated: 12/7/1911
Mayor: Rick Lorenz

Gates
County: Marion
Address: 101 Sorbin St., 97346
Phone: 503-897-2669
Fax: 503-897-5046
E-mail: ctygtes@wbcable.net
Elevation: 945'
Incorporated: 7/7/1955
Mayor: Mike Higgs

Gearhart
County: Clatsop
Address: PO Box 2510, 97138
Phone: 503-738-5501
Fax: 503-738-9385
Web: www.ci.gearhart.or.us
Elevation: 16'
Incorporated: 1/28/1918
Mayor: Dianne Widdop

Gervais
County: Marion
Address: 592 4th St., 97026
Phone: 503-792-4900
Fax: 503-792-3791
Web: www.gervaisoregon.org
Elevation: 184'
Incorporated: 10/29/1874
Mayor: Shanti M. Platt

Gladstone
County: Clackamas
Address: 525 Portland Ave., 97027
Phone: 503-656-5225
Fax: 503-650-8938
Web: www.ci.gladstone.or.us
Elevation: 57'
Incorporated: 1/5/1911
Mayor: Wade Byers

Glendale
County: Douglas
Address: PO Box 361, 97442
Phone: 541-832-2106
Fax: 541-832-3221
Web: www.cityofglendaleor.com
Elevation: 1,410'
Incorporated: 2/23/1901
Mayor: Fred Jensen

*Gold Beach
County: Curry
Address: 29592 Ellensburg Ave., 97444
Phone: 541-247-7029
Fax: 541-247-2212
Web: www.goldbeachoregon.gov
Elevation: 50'
Incorporated: 9/24/1945
Mayor: Ken Popoff

Gold Hill
County: Jackson
Address: PO Box 308, 97525
Phone: 541-855-1525
Fax: 541-855-4501
Web: www.ci.goldhill.or.us
Elevation: 1,085'
Incorporated: 2/12/1895
Mayor: Jan Fish

Granite
County: Grant
Address: 1378 Main St., 97877
Phone: 541-755-5100
Fax: 541-755-5100
E-mail: granitecity@pinetel.com
Elevation: 4,660'
Incorporated: 5/17/1900
Mayor: Delores Schnitzer

*Grants Pass

County: Josephine
Address: 101 NW A St., 97526
Phone: 541-450-6000
Fax: 541-479-0812
Web: www.grantspassoregon.gov
Elevation: 960'
Incorporated: 2/18/1891
Mayor: Darin Fowler

Grass Valley

County: Sherman
Address: PO Box 191, 97029
Phone: 541-333-2434
Fax: 541-333-2276
E-mail: cityofgv@embarqmail.com
Elevation: 2,257'
Incorporated: 10/8/1900
Mayor: Neil Pattee

Greenhorn

County: Baker
Address: PO Box 1142, Mill City 97360
Phone: 503-523-8200
Fax: 541-523-8201
Web: www.bakercounty.org
Elevation: 6,300'
Incorporated: 2/20/1903
Mayor: Baker County Board of Commissioners

Gresham

County: Multnomah
Address: 1333 NW Eastman Pkwy., 97030
Phone: 503-661-3000
Fax: 503-665-7692
Web: www.greshamoregon.gov
Elevation: 301'
Incorporated: 6/3/1904
Mayor: Shane Bemis

Haines

County: Baker
Address: PO Box 208, 97833
Phone: 541-856-3366
Fax: 541-856-3812
Web: www.cityofhainesor.org
Elevation: 3,341'
Incorporated: 3/11/1902
Mayor: Dennis Anthony

Halfway

County: Baker
Address: PO Box 738, 97834-0738
Phone: 541-742-4741
Fax: 541-742-4742
E-mail: halfwaycity@gmail.com
Elevation: 2,651'
Incorporated: 5/27/1909
Mayor: Sheila Farwell

Halsey

County: Linn
Address: PO Box 10, 97348
Phone: 541-369-2522
Fax: 541-369-2521
Web: www.cityofhalsey.com
Elevation: 280'
Incorporated: 10/20/1876
Mayor: Cynthia Choat

Happy Valley

County: Clackamas
Address: 16000 SE Misty Dr., 97086-6299
Phone: 503-783-3800
Fax: 503-658-5174
Web: www.ci.happy-valley.or.us
Elevation: 497'
Incorporated: 12/4/1965
Mayor: Lori DeRemer

Harrisburg

County: Linn
Address: 120 Smith St., 97446
Phone: 541-995-6655
Fax: 541-995-9244
Web: www.ci.harrisburg.or.us
Elevation: 309'
Incorporated: 10/24/1866
Mayor: Robert Duncan

Helix

County: Umatilla
Address: PO Box 323, 97835
Phone: 541-457-2521
E-mail: cityofhelix@helixtel.com
Elevation: 1,754'
Incorporated: 1/9/1903
Mayor: Jack Bascomb

*Heppner

County: Morrow
Address: PO Box 756, 97836
Phone: 541-676-9618
Fax: 541-676-9650
Web: www.cityofheppner.com
Elevation: 1,955'
Incorporated: 2/9/1887
Mayor: Joe Perry

Hermiston

County: Umatilla
Address: 180 NE 2nd St., 97838
Phone: 541-567-5521
Fax: 541-567-5530
Web: www.hermiston.or.us
Elevation: 450'
Incorporated: 7/23/1907
Mayor: David Drotzemann

*Hillsboro

County: Washington
Address: 150 E Main St., 97123
Phone: 503-681-6100
Fax: 503-681-6213
Web: www.ci.hillsboro.or.us
Elevation: 196'
Incorporated: 10/19/1876
Mayor: Jerry Willey

Hines
County: Harney
Address: PO Box 336, 97738
Phone: 541-573-2251
Fax: 541-573-5827
Web: www.hinesoregon.com
Elevation: 4,155'
Incorporated: 12/13/1930
Mayor: Nikki Morgan

*Hood River
County: Hood River
Address: PO Box 27, 211 2nd St., 97031
Phone: 541-386-1488
Fax: 541-387-5289
Web: www.ci.hood-river.or.us
Elevation: 160'
Incorporated: 2/15/1895
Mayor: Arthur Babitz

Hubbard
County: Marion
Address: PO Box 380, 97032
Phone: 503-981-9633
Fax: 503-981-8743
Web: www.cityofhubbard.org
Elevation: 181'
Incorporated: 2/18/1891
Mayor: Jim Yonally

Huntington
County: Baker
Address: PO Box 369, 97907
Phone: 541-869-2202
Fax: 541-869-2550
E-mail: hun1891@netscape.net
Elevation: 2,110'
Incorporated: 2/18/1891
Mayor: Travis Young

Idanha
County: Linn/Marion
Address: PO Box 430, 97350
Phone: 503-854-3313
Fax: 503-854-3114
E-mail: cityofid@bni.net
Elevation: 1,718'
Incorporated: 3/15/1950
Mayor: Karen Clark

Imbler
County: Union
Address: PO Box 40, 97841-0040
Phone: 541-534-6095
Fax: 541-534-2343
Web: www.imbleroregon.com
Elevation: 2,725'
Incorporated: 3/20/1922
Mayor: Mike McLean

Independence
County: Polk
Address: PO Box 7, 97351
Phone: 503-838-1212
Fax: 503-606-3282
Web: www.ci.independence.or.us
Elevation: 168'
Incorporated: 10/20/1874
Mayor: John McArdle

Ione
County: Morrow
Address: PO Box 361, 97843
Phone: 541-422-7414
Fax: 541-422-7179
E-mail: cityofione@centurytel.net
Elevation: 1,080'
Incorporated: 7/14/1899
Mayor: Linda LaRue

Irrigon
County: Morrow
Address: PO Box 428, 97844
Phone: 541-922-3047
Fax: 541-922-9322
Web: http://cityofirrigon.org
Elevation: 297'
Incorporated: 2/28/1957
Mayor: David Burns

Island City
County: Union
Address: 10605 Island Ave., 97850
Phone: 541-963-5017
Fax: 541-963-3482
E-mail: judy@islandcityhall.com
Elevation: 2,743'
Incorporated: 2/12/1904
Mayor: Dale De Long

Jacksonville
County: Jackson
Address: PO Box 7, 97530
Phone: 541-899-1231
Fax: 541-899-7882
Web: www.jacksonvilleor.us
Elevation: 1,569'
Incorporated: 10/19/1860
Mayor: Paul Becker

Jefferson
County: Marion
Address: PO Box 83, 97352-0083
Phone: 541-327-2768
Fax: 541-327-3120
E-mail: jeffersonrecorder@peak.org
Elevation: 240'
Incorporated: 10/29/1870
Mayor: Ben Pickett

John Day
County: Grant
Address: 450 E Main St., 97845
Phone: 541-575-0028
Fax: 541-575-3668
Web: www.cityofjohnday.com
Elevation: 3,120'
Incorporated: 5/9/1900
Mayor: Ron Lundbom

Johnson City
County: Clackamas
Address: 16121 SE 81st Ave., 97267
Phone: 503-655-9710
Fax: 503-723-0317
E-mail: johnson.city@hotmail.com
Elevation: 60'
Incorporated: 6/23/1970
Mayor: Kay Mordock

Jordan Valley
County: Malheur
Address: PO Box 187, 97910
Phone: 541-586-2460
Fax: 541-586-2460
Web: www.cityofjordanvalley.com
Elevation: 4,385'
Incorporated: 3/21/1911
Mayor: Jake Roe

Joseph
County: Wallowa
Address: PO Box 15, 97846
Phone: 541-432-3832
Fax: 541-432-3832
Web: www.josephoregon.org
Elevation: 4,200'
Incorporated: 2/9/1887
Mayor: Dennis Sands

Junction City
County: Lane
Address: PO Box 250, 97448-0250
Phone: 541-998-2153
Fax: 541-998-3140
Web: www.junctioncityoregon.gov
Elevation: 325'
Incorporated: 10/29/1872
Mayor: David Brunscheon

Keizer
County: Marion
Address: PO Box 21000, 97307-1000
Phone: 503-390-3700
Fax: 503-393-9437
Web: www.keizer.org
Elevation: 132'
Incorporated: 11/16/1982
Mayor: Lore Christopher

King City
County: Washington
Address: 15300 SW 116th Ave., 97224
Phone: 503-639-4082
Fax: 503-639-3771
Web: www.ci.king-city.or.us
Elevation: 213'
Incorporated: 7/14/1966
Mayor: Ron Shay

*Klamath Falls
County: Klamath
Address: PO Box 237, 97601
Phone: 541-883-5316
Fax: 541-883-5399
Web: www.ci.klamath-falls.or.us
Elevation: 4,099'
Incorporated: 2/6/1893
Mayor: Todd Kellstrom

*La Grande
County: Union
Address: PO Box 670, 97850
Phone: 541-962-1309
Fax: 541-963-3333
Web: www.cityoflagrande.org
Elevation: 2,785'
Incorporated: 12/18/1865
Mayor: Daniel Pokorney

La Pine
County: Deschutes
Address: PO Box 3055, 97739
Phone: 541-536-1432
Fax: 541-536-1462
Web: www.ci.la-pine.or.us/
Elevation: 4232'
Incorporated: 12/11/2006
Mayor: Ken Mulenex

Lafayette
County: Yamhill
Address: PO Box 55, 97127
Phone: 503-864-2451
Fax: 503-864-4501
Web: www.ci.lafayette.or.us
Elevation: 160'
Incorporated: 10/17/1878
Mayor: Chris Heisler

Lake Oswego
County: Clackamas
Address: PO Box 369, 97034
Phone: 503-635-0215
Fax: 503-697-6594
Web: www.ci.oswego.or.us
Elevation: 100'
Incorporated: 1/15/1910
Mayor: Kent Studebaker

Lakeside
County: Coos
Address: PO Box L, 97449
Phone: 541-759-3011
Fax: 541-759-3711
E-mail: citymail@cityoflakeside.org
Elevation: 28'
Incorporated: 6/26/1974
Mayor: Ed Gowan

*Lakeview
County: Lake
Address: 525 N 1st St., 97630
Phone: 541-947-2029
Fax: 541-947-2952
Web: www.lakevieworegon.org
Elevation: 4,802'
Incorporated: 2/10/1893
Mayor: Mike Patrick

Lebanon
County: Linn
Address: 925 Main St., 97355
Phone: 541-258-4900
Fax: 541-258-4950
Web: www.ci.lebanon.or.us
Elevation: 347'
Incorporated: 10/17/1878
Mayor: Paul Aziz

Lexington
County: Morrow
Address: PO Box 416, 97839
Phone: 541-989-8515
Fax: 541-989-8515
Web: www.lexingtonoregon.com
Elevation: 1,454'
Incorporated: 2/3/1903
Mayor: Jean Brazell

Lincoln City
County: Lincoln
Address: PO Box 50, 97367
Phone: 541-996-2152
Fax: 541-994-7232
Web: www.lincolncity.org
Elevation: 11'
Incorporated: 2/24/1965
Mayor: Dick Anderson

Lonerock
County: Gilliam
Address: Lonerock Rte., 104 SE Main St., Condon 97823
Phone: 541-384-3196
Elevation: 2,800'
Incorporated: 2/20/1901
Mayor: Paul O'Dell

Long Creek
County: Grant
Address: PO Box 489, 97856
Phone: 541-421-3601
Fax: 541-421-3075
Web: www.cityoflongcreek.com
Elevation: 3,754'
Incorporated: 2/18/1891
Mayor: Don Porter

Lostine
County: Wallowa
Address: PO Box 181, 97857
Phone: 541-569-2415
Fax: 541-569-5116
Elevation: 3,200'
Incorporated: 12/28/1903
Mayor: Krag Norton

Lowell
County: Lane
Address: PO Box 490, 97452
Phone: 541-937-2157
Fax: 541-937-2936
Web: www.ci.lowell.or.us
Elevation: 742'
Incorporated: 11/24/1954
Mayor: Stephen Paulson

Lyons
County: Linn
Address: 449 Fifth St., 97358
Phone: 503-859-2167
Fax: 503-859-5167
Web: www.cityoflyons.org
Elevation: 660'
Incorporated: 12/17/1958
Mayor: Danny Ray Burroughs

*Madras
County: Jefferson
Address: 71 SE D St., 97741-1605
Phone: 541-475-2344
Fax: 541-475-7061
Web: www.ci.madras.or.us
Elevation: 2,242'
Incorporated: 3/29/1910
Mayor: Melanie Widmer

Malin
County: Klamath
Address: PO Box 61, 97632
Phone: 541-723-2021
Fax: 541-723-2011
Web: www.cityofmalin.org
Elevation: 4,058'
Incorporated: 2/22/1922
Mayor: Gary Zieg

Manzanita
County: Tillamook
Address: PO Box 129, 97130-0129
Phone: 503-368-5343
Fax: 503-368-4145
Web: www.ci.manzanita.or.us
Elevation: 78'
Incorporated: 4/15/1946
Mayor: Garry Bullard

Maupin
County: Wasco
Address: PO Box 308, 97037
Phone: 541-395-2698
Fax: 541-395-2499
Web: www.cityofmaupin.com
Elevation: 1,047'
Incorporated: 4/17/1922
Mayor: Karen Dupuis

Maywood Park
County: Multnomah
Address: 10100 NE Prescott St., Suite 147, Portland 97220
Phone: 503-255-9805
Fax: 503-251-0366
Web: www.cityofmaywoodpark.com
Elevation: 77'
Incorporated: 10/25/1967
Mayor: Mark Hardie

*McMinnville

County: Yamhill
Address: 230 NE 2nd St., 97128
Phone: 503-434-7301
Fax: 503-472-7405
Web: www.ci.mcminnville.or.us
Elevation: 157'
Incorporated: 10/20/1876
Mayor: Richard Olson

*Medford

County: Jackson
Address: 411 W 8th St., 97501
Phone: 541-774-2000
Fax: 541-618-1700
Web: www.ci.medford.or.us
Elevation: 1,382'
Incorporated: 2/24/1885
Mayor: Gary Wheeler

Merrill

County: Klamath
Address: PO Box 487, 97633
Phone: 541-798-5808
Fax: 541-798-0145
E-mail: cityofmerrill@centurytel.net
Elevation: 4,067'
Incorporated: 7/16/1908
Mayor: Tim Saunders

Metolius

County: Jefferson
Address: 636 Jefferson Ave., 97741
Phone: 541-546-5533
Fax: 541-546-8809
E-mail: comet@crestviewcable.com
Elevation: 2,530'
Incorporated: 12/16/1912
Mayor: William A. Reynolds, Jr.

Mill City

County: Linn/Marion
Address: PO Box 256, 97360
Phone: 503-897-2302
Fax: 503-897-3499
Web: www.ci.mill-city.or.us
Elevation: 832'
Incorporated: 10/15/1947
Mayor: Tim Kirsch

Millersburg

County: Linn
Address: 4222 NE Old Salem Rd., Albany 97321
Phone: 541-928-4523
Fax: 541-928-8945
Web: www.albany-millersburg.com/millersburg.htm
Elevation: 235'
Incorporated: 11/4/1974
Mayor: Clayton Wood

Milton-Freewater

County: Umatilla
Address: PO Box 6, 97862
Phone: 541-938-5531
Fax: 541-938-8224
Web: www.mfcity.com
Elevation: 1,071'
Incorporated: 12/4/1950
Mayor: Lewis Key

Milwaukie

County: Clackamas
Address: 10722 SE Main St., 97222
Phone: 503-786-7555
Fax: 503-786-7565
Web: www.ci.milwaukie.or.us/
Elevation: 39'
Incorporated: 2/4/1903
Mayor: Jeremy Ferguson

Mitchell

County: Wheeler
Address: PO Box 97, 97750
Phone: 541-462-3121
Fax: 541-462-3121
E-mail: cityofmitchell@gmail.com
Elevation: 2,777'
Incorporated: 2/18/1891
Mayor: Carol Sweet

Molalla

County: Clackamas
Address: PO Box 248, 97038
Phone: 503-829-6855
Fax: 503-829-3676
E-mail: city@molalla.com
Elevation: 371'
Incorporated: 8/23/1913
Mayor: Debbie Rogge

Monmouth

County: Polk
Address: 151 W Main St., 97361
Phone: 503-838-0722
Fax: 503-838-0725
Web: www.ci.monmouth.or.us
Elevation: 214'
Incorporated: 10/19/1880
Mayor: John Oberst

Monroe

County: Benton
Address: PO Box 486, 97456
Phone: 541-847-5175
Fax: 541-847-5177
E-mail: cmonroe.verna@99w.us
Elevation: 288'
Incorporated: 5/16/1913
Mayor: Clifford "Frank" Thayer

Monument

County: Grant
Address: PO Box 426, 97864
Phone: 541-934-2025
Fax: 541-934-2025
E-mail: cityofmonument@centurytel.net
Elevation: 2,000'
Incorporated: 3/6/1905
Mayor: Mike Osborne

*Moro
County: Sherman
Address: PO Box 231, 97039
Phone: 541-565-3535
Fax: 541-565-3535
E-mail: moro@embarqmail.com
Elevation: 1,799'
Incorporated: 2/17/1899
Mayor: Andy Anderson

Mosier
County: Wasco
Address: PO Box 456, 97040
Phone: 541-478-3505
Fax: 541-478-3810
Web: www.cityofmosier.com
Elevation: 164'
Incorporated: 10/14/1914
Mayor: Andrea Rogers

Mt. Angel
County: Marion
Address: PO Box 960, 97362
Phone: 503-845-9291
Fax: 503-845-6261
Web: www.ci.mt-angel.or.us
Elevation: 168'
Incorporated: 2/10/1893
Mayor: Andrew (Andy) Otte

Mt. Vernon
County: Grant
Address: PO Box 647, 97865
Phone: 541-932-4688
Fax: 541-932-4222
Elevation: 2,865'
Incorporated: 5/13/1949
Mayor: Susan Horn

Myrtle Creek
County: Douglas
Address: PO Box 940, 97457
Phone: 541-863-3171
Fax: 541-863-6851
Web: www.cityofmyrtlecreek.com
Elevation: 660'
Incorporated: 2/13/1893
Mayor: Daniel E. Jocoy

Myrtle Point
County: Coos
Address: 424 5th St., 97458
Phone: 541-572-2626
Fax: 541-572-3838
E-mail: cityofmyrtlepoint@yahoo.com
Elevation: 90'
Incorporated: 2/4/1887
Mayor: Michael P. Johnson

Nehalem
County: Tillamook
Address: PO Box 143, 97131
Phone: 503-368-5627
Fax: 503-368-4175
Web: www.ci.nehalem.or.us
Elevation: 11'
Incorporated: 2/2/1899
Mayor: Shirley Kalkhoven

Newberg
County: Yamhill
Address: PO Box 970, 97132
Phone: 503-538-9421
Fax: 503-538-5393
Web: www.newbergoregon.gov
Elevation: 175'
Incorporated: 2/21/1889
Mayor: Bob Andrews

*Newport
County: Lincoln
Address: 169 SW Coast Hwy., 97365
Phone: 541-574-0603
Fax: 541-574-0609
Web: www.thecityofnewport.net
Elevation: 134'
Incorporated: 10/23/1882
Mayor: Sandra Roumazoux

North Bend
County: Coos
Address: PO Box B, 97459
Phone: 541-756-8500
Fax: 541-756-8527
Web: www.northbendcity.org
Elevation: 41'
Incorporated: 7/6/1903
Mayor: Rick Wetherell

North Plains
County: Washington
Address: 31360 NW Commercial St., 97133
Phone: 503-647-5555
Fax: 503-647-2031
Web: www.northplains.org
Elevation: 176'
Incorporated: 10/1/1963
Mayor: David Hatcher

North Powder
County: Union
Address: PO Box 309, 97867
Phone: 541-898-2185
Fax: 541-898-2647
E-mail: cityofnp@eoni.com
Elevation: 3,256'
Incorporated: 7/28/1902
Mayor: Bonita Hebert

Nyssa
County: Malheur
Address: 301 Main St., 97913
Phone: 541-372-2264
Fax: 541-372-3737
Web: www.nyssacity.org
Elevation: 2,175'
Incorporated: 2/24/1903
Mayor: Mark Stringer

Oakland
County: Douglas
Address: 637 NE Locust St., 97462
Phone: 541-459-4531
Fax: 541-459-4472
E-mail: oaklandcityclerk@qwestoffice.net
Elevation: 430'
Incorporated: 10/17/1878
Mayor: Bette Keehley

Oakridge
County: Lane
Address: PO Box 1410, 97463
Phone: 541-782-2258
Fax: 541-782-1081
Web: www.ci.oakridge.or.us
Elevation: 1,240'
Incorporated: 1/22/1934
Mayor: Gerald Glenn Shorey

Ontario
County: Malheur
Address: 444 SW 4th St., 97914
Phone: 541-889-7684
Fax: 541-889-7121
Web: www.ontariooregon.org
Elevation: 2,150'
Incorporated: 9/9/1896
Mayor: Joe Dominick

*Oregon City
County: Clackamas
Address: 625 Center St., 97045
Phone: 503-657-0891
Fax: 503-657-7026
Web: www.orcity.org
Elevation: 55'
Incorporated: 12/24/1844
Mayor: Doug Neeley

Paisley
County: Lake
Address: PO Box 100, 97636
Phone: 541-943-3173
Fax: 541-943-3982
E-mail: cityof_paisley@yahoo.com
Elevation: 4,369'
Incorporated: 11/18/1911
Mayor: Mark Douglas

*Pendleton
County: Umatilla
Address: 500 SW Dorion Ave., 97801
Phone: 541-966-0200
Fax: 541-966-0231
Web: www.pendleton.or.us
Elevation: 1,200'
Incorporated: 10/25/1880
Mayor: Phillip Houk

Philomath
County: Benton
Address: PO Box 400, 97370
Phone: 541-929-6148
Fax: 541-929-3044
Web: www.ci.philomath.or.us
Elevation: 279'
Incorporated: 10/20/1882
Mayor: Rocky Sloan

Phoenix
County: Jackson
Address: PO Box 330, 112 W 2nd St., 97535
Phone: 541-535-1955
Fax: 541-535-5769
Web: www.phoenixoregon.net
Elevation: 1,543'
Incorporated: 10/13/1910
Mayor: Jeff Bellah

Pilot Rock
County: Umatilla
Address: PO Box 130, 97868
Phone: 541-443-2811
Fax: 541-443-2253
Web: www.cityofpilotrock.org
Elevation: 1,637'
Incorporated: 1/10/1902
Mayor: Virginia Carnes

Port Orford
County: Curry
Address: PO Box 310, 97465
Phone: 541-332-3681
Fax: 877-281-5307
Web: www.portorford.org
Elevation: 59'
Incorporated: 12/21/1911
Mayor: James Auborn

*Portland
County: Clackamas/Multnomah/Washington
Address: 1221 SW 4th Ave., Rm. 110, 97204
Phone: 503-823-4000
Fax: 503-823-3050
Web: www.portlandonline.com
Elevation: 77'
Incorporated: 1/23/1851
Mayor: Charlie Hales

Powers
County: Coos
Address: PO Box 250, 97466
Phone: 541-439-3331
Fax: 541-439-5555
E-mail: cityofpowers@msn.com
Elevation: 286'
Incorporated: 12/26/1945
Mayor: Edward Hamlett

Prairie City
County: Grant
Address: PO Box 370, 97869
Phone: 541-820-3605
Fax: 541-820-3566
Web: www.prairiecityoregon.com
Elevation: 3,535'
Incorporated: 2/19/1891
Mayor: Tim Cooley

Prescott
County: Columbia
Address: 72742 Blakely St., Rainier 97048
Phone: 503-556-4116
E-mail: jl.oswald@hotmail.com
Elevation: 17'
Incorporated: 5/9/1949
Mayor: Lynette Oswald

*Prineville
County: Crook
Address: 387 NE 3rd St., 97754
Phone: 541-447-5627
Fax: 541-447-5628
Web: www.cityofprineville.com
Elevation: 2,868'
Incorporated: 10/23/1880
Mayor: Betty Jean Roppe

Rainier
County: Columbia
Address: PO Box 100, 97048-0100
Phone: 503-556-7301
Fax: 503-556-3200
Web: www.cityofrainier.com
Elevation: 51'
Incorporated: 11/25/1885
Mayor: Jerry Cole

Redmond
County: Deschutes
Address: 716 SW Evergreen Ave., 97756
Phone: 541-923-7710
Fax: 541-548-0706
Web: www.ci.redmond.or.us
Elevation: 3,077'
Incorporated: 7/16/1910
Mayor: George Endicott

Reedsport
County: Douglas
Address: 451 Winchester Ave., 97467
Phone: 541-271-3603
Fax: 541-271-2809
Web: www.cityofreedsport.org
Elevation: 10'
Incorporated: 8/6/1919
Mayor: Keith Tymchuk

Richland
County: Baker
Address: PO Box 266, 97870
Phone: 541-893-6141
Fax: 541-893-6267
E-mail: richcity@eagletelephone.com
Elevation: 2,231'
Incorporated: 8/8/1902
Mayor: Gloria Wilson

Riddle
County: Douglas
Address: PO Box 143, 97469
Phone: 541-874-2571
Fax: 541-874-2625
Web: www.RiddleOregon.com
Elevation: 700'
Incorporated: 1/30/1893
Mayor: William G. Duckett

Rivergrove
County: Clackamas/Washington
Address: PO Box 1104, Lake Oswego 97035
Phone: 503-639-6919; 503-807-5560
Fax: 503-624-8498
Web: rivergrove.home.comcast.net
Elevation: 132'
Incorporated: 3/11/1971
Mayor: Heather Kibbey

Rockaway Beach
County: Tillamook
Address: PO Box 5, 97136
Phone: 503-355-2291
Fax: 503-355-8221
Web: www.rockawaybeachor.us
Elevation: 17'
Incorporated: 7/14/1943
Mayor: Danell Marit Boggs

Rogue River
County: Jackson
Address: PO Box 1137, 97537
Phone: 541-582-4401
Fax: 541-582-0937
Web: www.cityofrogueriver.org
Elevation: 1,000'
Incorporated: 10/8/1910
Mayor: Fred English

*Roseburg
County: Douglas
Address: 900 SE Douglas Ave., 97470-3397
Phone: 541-492-6700
Fax: 541-673-2856
Web: www.cityofroseburg.org
Elevation: 480'
Incorporated: 10/26/1868
Mayor: Larry Rich

Rufus
County: Sherman
Address: PO Box 27, 97050
Phone: 541-739-2321
Fax: 541-739-2460
Web: www.cityofrufus.net
Elevation: 235'
Incorporated: 11/3/1964
Mayor: Clifford Jett

*Salem
County: Marion/Polk
Address: 555 Liberty St. SE, 97301
Phone: 503-588-6255
Fax: 503-588-6354
Web: www.cityofsalem.net
Elevation: 154'
Incorporated: 1/13/1857
Mayor: Anna M. Peterson

Sandy
County: Clackamas
Address: 39250 Pioneer Blvd., 97055
Phone: 503-668-5533
Fax: 503-668-8714
Web: www.ci.sandy.or.us
Elevation: 1,000'
Incorporated: 9/11/1911
Mayor: Bill King

Scappoose
County: Columbia
Address: 33568 E Columbia Ave., 97056
Phone: 503-543-7146
Fax: 503-543-7182
Web: www.ci.scappoose.or.us
Elevation: 62'
Incorporated: 8/13/1921
Mayor: Scott Burge

Scio
County: Linn
Address: PO Box 37, 97374-0037
Phone: 503-394-3342
Fax: 503-394-2340
E-mail: scio@smt-net.com
Elevation: 317'
Incorporated: 10/24/1866
Mayor: Earl D. Wilson

Scotts Mills
County: Marion
Address: 265 4th St., PO Box 220, 97375
Phone: 503-873-5435
Fax: 503-873-3931
Web: www.scottsmills.org
Elevation: 426'
Incorporated: 8/2/1916
Mayor: Ronald Bielenberg

Seaside
County: Clatsop
Address: 989 Broadway, 97138
Phone: 503-738-5511
Fax: 503-738-5514
Web: www.cityofseaside.us
Elevation: 17'
Incorporated: 2/17/1899
Mayor: Don Larson

Seneca
County: Grant
Address: PO Box 208, 97873
Phone: 541-542-2161
Fax: 541-542-2161
E-mail: cityseneca@centurytel.net
Elevation: 4,690'
Incorporated: 8/6/1970
Mayor: Warren Wilson

Shady Cove
County: Jackson
Address: PO Box 1210, 97539
Phone: 541-878-2225
Fax: 541-878-2226
Web: www.shadycove.net
Elevation: 1,406'
Incorporated: 11/8/1972
Mayor: Ronald Holthusen

Shaniko
County: Wasco
Address: PO Box 17, 97057
Phone: 541-489-3226
Fax: 541-489-3226
Web: www.shanikooregon.com
Elevation: 3,344'
Incorporated: 3/13/1901
Mayor: Goldie Roberts

Sheridan
County: Yamhill
Address: 120 SW Mill St., 97378
Phone: 503-843-2347
Fax: 503-843-3661
E-mail: fsheridan@wbcable.net
Elevation: 189'
Incorporated: 10/25/1880
Mayor: Val Adamson

Sherwood
County: Washington
Address: 22560 SW Pine St., 97140
Phone: 503-625-5522
Fax: 503-625-5524
Web: www.sherwoodoregon.gov
Elevation: 193'
Incorporated: 2/10/1893
Mayor: Bill Middleton

Siletz
County: Lincoln
Address: PO Box 318, 97380
Phone: 541-444-2521
Fax: 541-444-7371
Web: www.cityofsiletz.org
Elevation: 130'
Incorporated: 3/31/1947
Mayor: John Robinson

Silverton
County: Marion
Address: 306 S Water St., 97381
Phone: 503-873-5321
Fax: 503-874-2260
Web: www.silverton.or.us
Elevation: 252'
Incorporated: 2/16/1885
Mayor: Stu Rasmussen

Sisters
County: Deschutes
Address: PO Box 39, 97759
Phone: 541-549-6022
Fax: 541-549-0561
Web: www.ci.sisters.or.us
Elevation: 3,182'
Incorporated: 4/9/1946
Mayor: Brad Boyd

Sodaville
County: Linn
Address: 30723 Sodaville Rd., 97355
Phone: 541-258-8882
Fax: 541-258-8882
E-mail: sodaville@centurytel.net
Elevation: 492'
Incorporated: 10/25/1880
Mayor: James L. Wilson

Spray
County: Wheeler
Address: PO Box 83, 97874
Phone: 541-468-2069
Fax: 541-468-2044
Web: www.sprayoregon.us
Elevation: 1,795'
Incorporated: 9/18/1958
Mayor: Valerie Howell

Springfield
County: Lane
Address: 225 5th St., 97477
Phone: 541-726-3700
Fax: 541-726-2363
Web: www.springfield-or.gov
Elevation: 454'
Incorporated: 2/25/1885
Mayor: Christine Lundberg

*St. Helens
County: Columbia
Address: PO Box 278, 275 Strand St., 97051
Phone: 503-397-6272
Fax: 503-397-4016
Web: www.ci.st-helens.or.us
Elevation: 39'
Incorporated: 2/25/1889
Mayor: Randy Peterson

St. Paul
County: Marion
Address: PO Box 7, 97137
Phone: 503-633-4971
Fax: 503-633-4972
E-mail: stpaulcity@stpaultel.com
Elevation: 169'
Incorporated: 2/16/1901
Mayor: Steve Manners

Stanfield
County: Umatilla
Address: PO Box 369, 97875
Phone: 541-449-3831
Fax: 541-449-1828
Web: www.cityofstanfield.com
Elevation: 592'
Incorporated: 5/13/1910
Mayor: Thomas J. McCann

Stayton
County: Marion
Address: 362 N 3rd Ave., 97383
Phone: 503-769-3425
Fax: 503-769-1456
Web: www.staytonoregon.gov
Elevation: 452'
Incorporated: 2/13/1901
Mayor: Scott Vigil

Sublimity
County: Marion
Address: PO Box 146, 97385
Phone: 503-769-5475
Fax: 503-769-2206
Web: www.cityofsublimity.org
Elevation: 551'
Incorporated: 2/3/1903
Mayor: Eugene C. Ditter

Summerville
County: Union
Address: PO Box 92, 97876
Phone: 541-534-6701
E-mail: summerville@eoni.com
Elevation: 2,705'
Incorporated: 11/24/1885
Mayor: Sheri Rogers

Sumpter
County: Baker
Address: PO Box 68, 97877
Phone: 541-894-2314
Fax: 541-894-2314
Web: www.sumpter.org
Elevation: 4,437'
Incorporated: 5/5/1898
Mayor: John Young

Sutherlin
County: Douglas
Address: 126 E Central Ave., 97479
Phone: 541-459-2856
Fax: 541-459-9363
Web: www.ci.sutherlin.or.us
Elevation: 520'
Incorporated: 5/4/1911
Mayor: Denny Cameron

Sweet Home
County: Linn
Address: 1140 12th Ave., 97386
Phone: 541-367-5128
Fax: 541-367-5113
Web: www.ci.sweet-home.or.us
Elevation: 537'
Incorporated: 2/10/1893
Mayor: James Gourley

Talent

County: Jackson
Address: PO Box 445, 97540-0445
Phone: 541-535-1566
Fax: 541-535-7423
Web: www.cityoftalent.org
Elevation: 1,635'
Incorporated: 11/25/1910
Mayor: Bill Cecil

Tangent

County: Linn
Address: PO Box 251, 97389
Phone: 541-928-1020
Fax: 541-928-4920
Web: www.cityoftangent.org
Elevation: 245'
Incorporated: 2/10/1893
Mayor: Seaton McLennan

*The Dalles

County: Wasco
Address: 313 Court St., 97058
Phone: 541-296-5481
Fax: 541-296-6906
Web: www.ci.the-dalles.or.us
Elevation: 109'
Incorporated: 1/26/1857
Mayor: Steve Lawrence

Tigard

County: Washington
Address: 13125 SW Hall Blvd., 97223
Phone: 503-639-4171
Fax: 503-684-7297
Web: www.tigard-or.gov
Elevation: 169'
Incorporated: 10/3/1961
Mayor: John Cook

*Tillamook

County: Tillamook
Address: 210 Laurel Ave., 97141
Phone: 503-842-2472
Fax: 503-842-3445
Web: www.tillamookor.gov
Elevation: 24'
Incorporated: 2/18/1891
Mayor: Suzanne Weber

Toledo

County: Lincoln
Address: PO Box 220, 97391
Phone: 541-336-2247
Fax: 541-336-3512
Web: www.cityoftoledo.org
Elevation: 59'
Incorporated: 10/11/1893
Mayor: Ralph Grutzmacher

Troutdale

County: Multnomah
Address: 104 SE Kibling Ave., 97060
Phone: 503-665-5175
Fax: 503-667-6403
Web: www.troutdale.info
Elevation: 30'–200'
Incorporated: 10/3/1907
Mayor: Doug Daoust

Tualatin

County: Clackamas/Washington
Address: 18880 SW Martinazzi Ave., 97062
Phone: 503-692-2000
Fax: 503-692-5421
Web: www.tualatinoregon.gov
Elevation: 123'
Incorporated: 5/8/1913
Mayor: Lou Ogden

Turner

County: Marion
Address: PO Box 456, 97392
Phone: 503-743-2155
Fax: 503-743-4010
Web: www.cityofturner.org
Elevation: 287'
Incorporated: 2/10/1905
Mayor: Paul Thomas

Ukiah

County: Umatilla
Address: PO Box 265, 97880
Phone: 541-427-3900
Fax: 541-427-3902
Web: www.cityofukiahoregon.com
Elevation: 3,400'
Incorporated: 5/23/1972
Mayor: Clint Barber

Umatilla

County: Umatilla
Address: PO Box 130, 97882
Phone: 541-922-3226
Fax: 541-922-5758
Web: www.umatilla-city.org
Elevation: 296'
Incorporated: 10/24/1864
Mayor: Pat Lafferty

Union

County: Union
Address: PO Box 529, 97883
Phone: 541-562-5197
Fax: 541-562-5196
Web: www.cityofunion.com
Elevation: 2,791'
Incorporated: 10/19/1878
Mayor: Bill Lindsley

Unity

County: Baker
Address: PO Box 7, 97884
Phone: 541-446-3544
Fax: 541-446-3544
Web: bakercounty.org
Elevation: 4,040'
Incorporated: 7/31/1972
Mayor: Baker County Board of Commissioners

*Vale
County: Malheur
Address: 252 B St. W, 97918
Phone: 541-473-3133
Fax: 541-473-3895
Web: www.vale.or.us
Elevation: 2,243'
Incorporated: 2/21/1889
Mayor: Mike McLaughlin

Veneta
County: Lane
Address: PO Box 458, 97487
Phone: 541-935-2191
Fax: 541-935-1838
Web: www.ci.veneta.or.us
Elevation: 418'
Incorporated: 5/4/1962
Mayor: Sandra H. Larson

Vernonia
County: Columbia
Address: 1001 Bridge St., 97064
Phone: 503-429-5291
Fax: 503-429-4232
Web: www.vernonia-or.gov
Elevation: 630'
Incorporated: 2/18/1891
Mayor: Josette Mitchell

Waldport
County: Lincoln
Address: PO Box 1120, 97394
Phone: 541-264-7417
Fax: 541-563-5810
Web: www.waldport.org
Elevation: 12'
Incorporated: 3/11/1911
Mayor: Susan Woodruff

Wallowa
County: Wallowa
Address: PO Box 487, 97885
Phone: 541-886-2422
Fax: 541-886-4215
Web: www.wallowaoregon.com
Elevation: 2,950'
Incorporated: 1/18/1909
Mayor: Vikki Knifong

Warrenton
County: Clatsop
Address: PO Box 250, 97146
Phone: 503-861-2233
Fax: 503-861-2351
Web: www.ci.warrenton.or.us
Elevation: 8'
Incorporated: 2/11/1899
Mayor: Mark Kujala

Wasco
County: Sherman
Address: PO Box 26, 97065
Phone: 541-442-5515
Fax: 541-442-5001
E-mail: wascocity@embarqmail.com
Elevation: 1,281'
Incorporated: 4/14/1898
Mayor: Scott Miller

Waterloo
County: Linn
Address: PO Box 1066, Lebanon 97355
Phone: 541-451-2245
Fax: 541-451-3133
E-mail: cityofwaterloo@centurytel.net
Elevation: 402'
Incorporated: 2/15/1893
Mayor: James Cripe

West Linn
County: Clackamas
Address: 22500 Salamo Rd., #100, 97068
Phone: 503-657-0331
Fax: 503-650-9041
Web: www.westlinnoregon.gov
Elevation: 105'
Incorporated: 8/15/1913
Mayor: John Kovash

Westfir
County: Lane
Address: PO Box 296, 97492
Phone: 541-782-3733
Fax: 541-782-3983
E-mail: westfircity@qwestoffice.net
Elevation: 1,075'
Incorporated: 2/6/1979
Mayor: Robert DeHarpport

Weston
County: Umatilla
Address: PO Box 579, 97886
Phone: 541-566-3313
Fax: 541-566-2792
E-mail: westsamp@qwestoffice.net
Elevation: 1,796'
Incorporated: 10/19/1878
Mayor: Duane Thul

Wheeler
County: Tillamook
Address: PO Box 177, 97147
Phone: 503-368-5767
Fax: 503-368-4273
E-mail: cityofwheeler@nehalemtel.net
Elevation: 37'
Incorporated: 6/11/1913
Mayor: Stevie Stephens Burden

Willamina

County: Polk/Yamhill
Address: PO Box 629, 97396
Phone: 503-876-2242
Fax: 503-876-1121
Web: www.ci.willamina.or.us
Elevation: 225'
Incorporated: 2/13/1903
Mayor: Corey Adams

Wilsonville

County: Clackamas
Address: 29799 SW Town Center Lp. E, 97070
Phone: 503-682-1011
Fax: 503-682-1015
Web: www.ci.wilsonville.or.us
Elevation: 175'
Incorporated: 2/4/1969
Mayor: Tim Knapp

Winston

County: Douglas
Address: 201 NW Douglas Blvd., 97496
Phone: 541-679-6739
Fax: 541-679-0794
Web: www.winstoncity.org
Elevation: 545'
Incorporated: 6/29/1953
Mayor: Sharon Harrison

Wood Village

County: Multnomah
Address: 2055 NE 238th Dr., 97060
Phone: 503-667-6211
Fax: 503-669-8723
Web: www.ci.wood-village.or.us
Elevation: 90'–330'
Incorporated: 2/9/1951
Mayor: Patricia Smith

Woodburn

County: Marion
Address: 270 Montgomery St., 97071
Phone: 503-982-5222
Fax: 503-980-2482
Web: www.woodburn-or.gov
Elevation: 186'
Incorporated: 2/20/1889
Mayor: Kathryn Figley

Yachats

County: Lincoln
Address: PO Box 345, 97498
Phone: 541-547-3565
Fax: 541-547-3063
Web: www.ci.yachats.or.us
Elevation: 45'
Incorporated: 7/18/1966
Mayor: Ronald Brean

Yamhill

County: Yamhill
Address: PO Box 9, 97148
Phone: 503-662-3511
Fax: 503-662-4589
Web: www.cityofyamhill.com
Elevation: 182'
Incorporated: 2/20/1891
Mayor: Paula Terp

Yoncalla

County: Douglas
Address: PO Box 508, 97499
Phone: 541-849-2152
Fax: 541-849-2552
Web: www.cityofyoncalla.com
Elevation: 360'
Incorporated: 2/27/1901
Mayor: Gerald Cross

City Populations: 1980–2011

Source: Population Research Center, Portland State University
Phone: 503-725-3922

*Change in population between 2010 and 2011

"t" means there is a tie with another city in the most recent population numbers.

Rank	City	% Change*	2011	2010	2000	1990	1980
169 t	Adair Village	0.0	840	840	536	554	589
204	Adams	4.3	365	350	297	223	240
225 t	Adrian	1.7	180	177	147	131	162
11	Albany	0.7	50,520	50,158	40,852	29,540	26,511
134	Amity	0.1	1,615	1,614	1,478	1,175	1,092
238	Antelope	-2.2	45	46	59	34	39
187	Arlington	-.02	585	586	524	425	521
27	Ashland	0.9	20,255	20,078	19,522	16,252	14,943
52	Astoria	0.2	9,495	9,477	9,813	10,069	9,996
154	Athena	-0.1	1,125	1,126	1,221	997	965
85	Aumsville	2.7	3,680	3,584	3,003	1,650	1,432
164	Aurora	0.2	920	918	655	523	306
47	Baker City	0.6	9,890	9,828	9,860	9,140	9,471
97	Bandon	0.6	3,085	3,066	2,833	2,215	2,311
126	Banks	-0.1	1,775	1,777	1,286	563	489
231 t	Barlow	0.0	135	135	140	118	105
144	Bay City	0.7	1,295	1,286	1,149	1,027	986
6	Beaverton	1.1	90,835	89,803	76,129	53,307	31,962
7	Bend	0.4	76,925	76,639	52,029	20,447	17,260
91	Boardman	0.5	3,235	3,220	2,855	1,387	1,261
193	Bonanza	12.0	465	415	415	323	270
69	Brookings	0.4	6,360	6,336	5,447	4,400	3,384
132 t	Brownsville	0.1	1,670	1,668	1,449	1,281	1,261
100	Burns	0.0	2,805	2,806	3,064	2,913	3,579
197	Butte Falls	1.4	425	423	439	252	428
35	Canby	0.0	15,830	15,829	12,790	8,990	7,659
130	Cannon Beach	0.6	1,700	1,690	1,588	1,221	1,187
176 t	Canyon City	1.0	710	703	669	648	639
120 t	Canyonville	0.1	1,885	1,884	1,293	1,219	1,288
114	Carlton	1.4	2,035	2,007	1,514	1,289	1,302
150	Cascade Locks	1.8	1,165	1,144	1,115	930	838
120 t	Cave Junction	0.1	1,885	1,883	1,363	1,126	1,023
30	Central Point	0.4	17,235	17,169	12,493	7,512	6,357
175	Chiloquin	0.1	735	734	716	673	778
128	Clatskanie	0.2	1,740	1,737	1,528	1,629	1,648
157 t	Coburg	1.0	1,045	1,035	969	763	699
117	Columbia City	0.2	1,950	1,946	1,571	1,003	678
180 t	Condon	1.2	690	682	759	635	783
33	Coos Bay	0.3	16,010	15,967	15,374	15,076	14,424
83	Coquille	0.0	3,865	3,866	4,184	4,121	4,481
42	Cornelius	0.4	11,915	11,869	9,652	6,148	4,402
10	Corvallis	0.1	54,520	54,462	49,322	44,757	40,960

Rank	City	% Change*	2011	2010	2000	1990	1980
49	Cottage Grove	0.6	9,745	9,686	8,445	7,403	7,148
189	Cove	-0.4	550	552	594	507	451
76	Creswell	-0.3	5,015	5,031	3,579	2,431	1,770
140	Culver	1.0	1,370	1,357	802	570	514
37	Dallas	0.3	14,620	14,583	12,459	9,422	8,530
45	Damascus	0.3	10,575	10,539	--	--	--
103	Dayton	-0.2	2,530	2,534	2,119	1,526	1,409
230	Dayville	0.7	150	149	138	144	199
138	Depoe Bay	0.1	1,400	1,398	1,174	870	723
219 t	Detroit	1.5	205	202	262	331	367
161	Donald	0.1	980	979	625	316	267
152	Drain	0.3	1,155	1,151	1,021	1,086	1,148
185 t	Dufur	0.2	605	604	588	527	560
94	Dundee	0.4	3,175	3,162	2,598	1,663	1,223
143	Dunes City	0.2	1,305	1,303	1,241	1,081	1,124
141	Durham	0.7	1,360	1,351	1,382	748	707
58	Eagle Point	0.6	8,520	8,469	4,797	3,008	2,764
179	Echo	0.1	700	699	650	500	624
129	Elgin	0.8	1,725	1,711	1,654	1,586	1,701
222 t	Elkton	0.0	195	195	147	172	155
118	Enterprise	0.0	1,940	1,940	1,895	1,905	2,003
99	Estacada	5.8	2,850	2,695	2,371	2,016	1,419
2	Eugene	0.5	157,010	156,185	137,893	112,733	105,664
56	Fairview	0.0	8,920	8,920	7,561	2,391	1,749
162	Falls City	-0.2	945	947	966	818	804
59	Florence	0.0	8,470	8,466	7,263	5,171	4,411
24	Forest Grove	0.9	21,275	21,083	17,708	13,559	11,499
191 t	Fossil	0.4	475	473	469	399	535
173	Garibaldi	0.8	785	779	899	886	999
183	Gaston	0.5	640	637	600	563	471
191 t	Gates	0.8	475	471	471	499	455
137	Gearhart	0.2	1,465	1,462	995	1,027	967
104	Gervais	2.3	2,520	2,464	2,009	992	799
43	Gladstone	0.0	11,495	11,497	11,438	10,152	9,500
167	Glendale	0.1	875	874	855	707	712
107	Gold Beach	0.1	2,255	2,253	1,897	1,546	1,515
146	Gold Hill	0.0	1,220	1,220	1,073	964	904
239	Granite	5.3	40	38	24	8	17
15	Grants Pass	0.4	34,660	34,533	23,003	17,503	15,032
227	Grass Valley	0.6	165	164	171	160	164
242	Greenhorn	200.0	2	0	0	0	0
4	Gresham	0.2	105,795	105,594	90,205	68,249	33,005
200 t	Haines	-0.2	415	416	426	405	341
210	Halfway	0.7	290	288	337	311	380
165	Halsey	1.2	915	904	724	667	693
39	Happy Valley	3.1	14,330	13,903	4,519	1,519	1,499
86	Harrisburg	0.5	3,585	3,567	2,795	1,939	1,881
224	Helix	0.5	185	184	183	150	155

Rank	City	% Change*	2011	2010	2000	1990	1980
145	Heppner	-0.1	1,290	1,291	1,395	1,412	1,498
31	Hermiston	0.7	16,865	16,745	13,154	10,047	8,408
5	Hillsboro	0.8	92,350	91,611	70,186	37,598	27,664
135	Hines	0.1	1,565	1,563	1,623	1,452	1,632
64	Hood River	2.1	7,320	7,167	5,831	4,632	4,329
93	Hubbard	0.2	3,180	3,173	2,483	1,881	1,640
195	Huntington	0.0	440	440	515	522	539
231 t	Idanha	0.7	135	134	232	289	319
209	Imbler	-0.3	305	306	284	299	292
57	Independence	0.1	8,600	8,590	6,035	4,425	4,024
206	Ione	0.3	330	329	321	255	345
125	Irrigon	0.2	1,830	1,826	1,702	737	700
160	Island City	2.1	1,010	989	916	696	477
101	Jacksonville	0.5	2,800	2,785	2,235	1,896	2,030
95 t	Jefferson	1.2	3,135	3,098	2,487	1,805	1,702
127	John Day	0.6	1,755	1,744	1,821	1,836	2,012
188	Johnson City	-0.2	565	566	634	586	378
225 t	Jordan Valley	-0.6	180	181	239	364	473
155	Joseph	0.8	1,090	1,081	1,054	1,073	999
73	Junction City	1.0	5,445	5,392	4,721	3,670	3,320
14	Keizer	0.6	36,715	36,478	32,203	21,884	--
95 t	King City	0.8	3,135	3,111	1,949	2,060	1,853
25	Klamath Falls	1.3	21,120	20,840	19,460	17,737	16,661
40	La Grande	0.1	13,095	13,082	12,327	11,766	11,354
132 t	La Pine	1.0	1,670	1,653	--	--	--
84	Lafayette	-0.1	3,740	3,742	2,586	1,292	1,215
13	Lake Oswego	0.3	36,725	36,619	35,278	30,576	22,527
131	Lakeside	-0.2	1,695	1,699	1,421	1,437	1,453
106	Lakeview	0.3	2,300	2,294	2,474	2,526	2,770
36	Lebanon	0.3	15,565	15,518	12,950	10,950	10,413
215	Lexington	0.8	240	238	263	286	307
61	Lincoln City	0.4	7,960	7,930	7,437	5,908	5,469
241	Lonerock	-4.8	20	21	24	11	26
222 t	Long Creek	-1.0	195	197	228	249	252
218	Lostine	0.9	215	213	263	231	250
157 t	Lowell	0.0	1,045	1,045	880	785	661
151	Lyons	-0.1	1,160	1,161	1,008	938	877
70	Madras	3.0	6,225	6,046	5,078	3,443	2,235
171 t	Malin	0.0	805	805	640	725	539
185 t	Manzanita	1.2	605	598	564	513	443
198 t	Maupin	0.5	420	418	411	456	495
174	Maywood Park	-0.3	750	752	777	781	845
16	McMinnville	0.3	32,270	32,187	26,499	17,894	14,080
8	Medford	0.4	75,180	74,907	63,687	47,021	39,746
168	Merrill	0.1	845	844	897	837	822
176 t	Metolius	0.0	710	710	729	450	451
123	Mill City	0.5	1,865	1,855	1,537	1,555	1,565
139	Millersburg	3.5	1,375	1,329	651	715	562

Rank	City	% Change*	2011	2010	2000	1990	1980
65	Milton-Freewater	0.1	7,055	7,050	6,470	5,533	5,086
26	Milwaukie	0.5	20,400	20,291	20,490	18,670	17,931
234 t	Mitchell	0.0	130	130	170	163	183
60	Molalla	0.0	8,110	8,108	5,647	3,651	2,992
50	Monmouth	2.0	9,720	9,534	7,741	6,288	5,594
184	Monroe	-0.3	615	617	607	448	412
234 t	Monument	1.6	130	128	151	162	192
207	Moro	0.3	325	324	337	292	336
196	Mosier	0.5	435	433	410	244	340
89	Mt. Angel	0.0	3,285	3,286	3,121	2,778	2,876
190	Mt. Vernon	-0.4	525	527	595	549	569
88	Myrtle Creek	0.0	3,440	3,439	3,419	3,063	3,365
105	Myrtle Point	0.0	2,515	2,514	2,451	2,712	2,859
211	Nehalem	-0.4	270	271	203	232	258
22	Newberg	0.7	22,230	22,068	18,064	13,086	10,394
46	Newport	0.8	10,065	9,989	9,532	8,437	7,519
51	North Bend	0.2	9,710	9,695	9,544	9,614	9,779
116	North Plains	2.2	1,990	1,947	1,605	997	715
194	North Powder	1.4	445	439	489	448	430
90	Nyssa	0.1	3,270	3,267	3,163	2,629	2,862
163	Oakland	-0.2	925	927	954	844	886
92	Oakridge	0.0	3,205	3,205	3,172	3,063	3,680
44	Ontario	0.1	11,375	11,366	10,985	9,394	8,814
17	Oregon City	1.1	32,220	31,859	25,754	14,698	14,673
214	Paisley	0.8	245	243	247	350	343
32	Pendleton	0.1	16,625	16,612	16,354	15,142	14,521
78 t	Philomath	0.6	4,610	4,584	3,838	2,983	2,673
80	Phoenix	0.3	4,550	4,538	4,060	3,239	2,309
136	Pilot Rock	0.2	1,505	1,502	1,532	1,478	1,630
153	Port Orford	0.2	1,135	1,133	1,153	1,025	1,061
1	Portland	0.4	585,845	583,776	529,121	438,802	366,383
180 t	Powers	0.1	690	689	734	682	819
166	Prairie City	0.1	910	909	1,080	1,117	1,106
237	Prescott	0.0	55	55	72	63	73
54	Prineville	0.1	9,260	9,253	7,358	5,355	5,276
119	Rainier	0.0	1,895	1,895	1,687	1,674	1,655
18	Redmond	0.3	26,305	26,215	13,481	7,165	6,452
81	Reedsport	-0.2	4,145	4,154	4,378	4,796	4,984
228 t	Richland	2.6	160	156	147	161	181
148	Riddle	0.0	1,185	1,185	1,014	1,143	1,265
203	Rivergrove	29.8	375	289	324	294	314
142	Rockaway Beach	0.6	1,320	1,312	1,267	970	906
108	Rogue River	0.4	2,140	2,131	1,851	1,759	1,308
23	Roseburg	2.4	21,690	21,181	20,017	17,069	16,644
213	Rufus	0.4	250	249	268	295	352
41	St. Helens	0.1	12,890	12,883	10,019	7,535	7,064
198 t	St. Paul	-0.2	420	421	354	322	312
3	Salem	0.7	155,710	154,637	136,924	107,793	89,091

Rank	City	% Change*	2011	2010	2000	1990	1980
48	Sandy	2.2	9,780	9,570	5,385	4,152	2,905
67	Scappoose	1.1	6,665	6,592	4,976	3,529	3,213
169 t	Scio	0.2	840	838	695	623	579
205	Scotts Mills	0.8	360	357	312	283	249
68	Seaside	0.5	6,490	6,457	5,900	5,359	5,193
221	Seneca	0.5	200	199	223	191	285
98	Shady Cove	0.2	2,910	2,904	2,307	1,351	1,097
240	Shaniko	-2.8	35	36	26	26	30
71	Sheridan	0.0	6,125	6,127	5,561	3,979	2,249
29	Sherwood	0.3	18,255	18,194	11,791	3,093	2,386
147	Siletz	-0.2	1,210	1,212	1,133	992	1,001
53	Silverton	0.5	9,265	9,222	7,414	5,635	5,168
111 t	Sisters	0.8	2,055	2,038	959	708	696
208	Sodaville	0.6	310	308	290	192	171
228 t	Spray	0.0	160	160	140	149	155
9	Springfield	0.5	59,695	59,403	52,864	44,664	41,621
111 t	Stanfield	0.6	2,055	2,043	1,979	1,568	1,568
63	Stayton	0.2	7,660	7,644	6,816	5,011	4,396
102	Sublimity	0.0	2,680	2,681	2,148	1,491	1,077
231 t	Summerville	0.0	135	135	117	142	143
219 t	Sumpter	0.5	205	204	171	119	133
62	Sutherlin	0.9	7,880	7,810	6,669	5,020	4,560
55	Sweet Home	0.9	9,005	8,925	8,016	6,850	6,921
72	Talent	0.5	6,095	6,066	5,589	3,274	2,577
149	Tangent	1.4	1,180	1,164	933	556	478
38	The Dalles	6.0	14,440	13,620	12,156	11,021	10,820
12	Tigard	0.8	48,415	48,035	41,223	29,435	14,799
77	Tillamook	-0.6	4,905	4,935	4,352	4,001	3,991
87	Toledo	0.6	3,485	3,465	3,472	3,174	3,151
34	Troutdale	0.2	16,000	15,962	13,777	7,852	5,908
19	Tualatin	0.3	26,120	26,054	22,791	14,664	7,483
124	Turner	0.3	1,860	1,854	1,199	1,281	1,116
216 t	Ukiah	23.7	230	186	255	250	249
66	Umatilla	1.1	6,980	6,906	4,978	3,046	3,199
108 t	Union	0.9	2,140	2,121	1,926	1,847	2,062
236	Unity	-1.4	70	71	131	87	115
122	Vale	0.1	1,875	1,874	1,976	1,491	1,558
78 t	Veneta	1.1	4,610	4,561	2,762	2,519	2,449
110	Vernonia	-1.9	2,110	2,151	2,228	1,808	1,785
113	Waldport	0.3	2,040	2,033	2,050	1,595	1,274
171 t	Wallowa	-0.4	805	808	869	748	847
75	Warrenton	1.2	5,050	4,989	4,096	2,681	2,493
202	Wasco	0.0	410	410	381	374	415
216 t	Waterloo	0.4	230	229	239	191	211
20	West Linn	0.6	25,250	25,109	22,261	16,389	11,358
212	Westfir	0.8	255	253	280	278	312
182	Weston	1.2	675	667	717	606	719
200 t	Wheeler	0.2	415	414	391	335	319
115	Willamina	0.0	2,025	2,025	1,844	1,748	1,749

Rank	City	% Change*	2011	2010	2000	1990	1980
28	Wilsonville	0.3	19,565	19,509	13,991	7,106	2,920
74	Winston	0.1	5,385	5,379	4,613	3,773	3,359
82	Wood Village	0.2	3,885	3,878	2,860	2,814	2,253
21	Woodburn	0.0	24,090	24,080	20,100	13,404	11,196
176 t	Yachats	2.9	710	690	617	533	482
159	Yamhill	-0.4	1,020	1,024	794	867	690
156	Yoncalla	0.8	1,055	1,047	1,052	919	805

County Populations: 1980–2011

Rank	County	% Change*	2011	2010	2000	1990	1980
28	Baker	0.5	16,215	16,134	16,741	15,317	16,134
11	Benton	0.5	85,995	85,579	78,153	70,811	68,211
3	Clackamas	0.7	378,480	375,992	338,391	278,850	241,911
19	Clatsop	0.3	37,145	37,039	35,630	33,301	32,489
17	Columbia	0.6	49,625	49,351	43,560	37,557	35,646
16	Coos	-0.1	62,960	63,043	62,779	60,273	64,047
27	Crook	-0.6	20,855	20,978	19,182	14,111	13,091
25	Curry	-0.1	22,335	22,364	21,137	19,327	16,992
7	Deschutes	0.7	158,875	157,733	115,367	74,958	62,142
9	Douglas	0.1	107,795	107,667	100,399	94,649	93,748
34	Gilliam	0.5	1,880	1,871	1,915	1,717	2,057
31	Grant	0.1	7,450	7,445	7,935	7,853	8,210
32	Harney	-0.6	7,375	7,422	7,609	7,060	8,314
24	Hood River	1.2	22,625	22,346	20,411	16,903	15,835
6	Jackson	0.4	203,950	203,206	181,269	146,389	132,456
26	Jefferson	0.6	21,845	21,720	19,009	13,676	11,599
12	Josephine	0.1	82,820	82,713	75,726	62,649	58,855
15	Klamath	0.3	66,580	66,380	63,775	57,702	59,117
30	Lake	-0.1	7,885	7,895	7,422	7,186	7,532
4	Lane	0.4	353,155	351,715	322,959	282,912	275,226
18	Lincoln	0.3	46,155	46,034	44,479	38,889	35,264
8	Linn	0.6	117,340	116,672	103,069	91,227	89,495
20	Malheur	0.4	31,445	31,313	31,615	26,038	26,896
5	Marion	0.9	318,150	315,335	284,834	228,483	204,692
29	Morrow	0.9	11,270	11,173	10,995	7,625	7,519
1	Multnomah	0.9	741,925	735,334	660,486	583,887	562,647
14	Polk	0.7	75,965	75,403	62,380	49,541	45,203
35	Sherman	0.0	1,765	1,765	1,934	1,918	2,172
23	Tillamook	0.0	25,255	25,250	24,262	21,570	21,164
13	Umatilla	0.9	76,580	75,889	70,548	59,249	58,861
21	Union	0.9	25,980	25,748	24,530	23,598	23,921
33	Wallowa	-0.2	6,995	7,008	7,226	6,911	7,273
22	Wasco	0.3	25,300	25,213	23,791	21,683	21,732
2	Washington	1.3	536,370	529,710	445,342	311,554	245,860
36	Wheeler	-0.4	1,435	1,441	1,547	1,396	1,513
10	Yamhill	0.7	99,850	99,193	84,992	65,551	55,332
	Oregon	**0.7**	**3,857,625**	**3,831,074**	**3,421,399**	**2,842,321**	**2,633,156**

*Change in population between 2010 and 2011

County Government

The word "county" is from the Middle English word *conte*, meaning the office of a count. However, a county within the United States, defined by Merriam-Webster's dictionary as "the largest territorial division for local government within a state," is based on the Anglo-Saxon shire, which corresponds to the modern county. Counties were brought to the United States by the English colonists and were established in the central and western parts of the United States by the pioneers as they moved westward.

Early county governments in Oregon were very limited in the services they provided. Their primary responsibilities were forest and farm-to-market roads, law enforcement, courts, care for the needy and tax collections. In response to demands of a growing population and a more complex society, today's counties provide a wide range of important public services including: public health, mental health, community corrections, juvenile services, criminal prosecution, hospitals, nursing homes, airports, parks, libraries, land-use planning, building regulations, refuse disposal, elections, air-pollution control, veterans services, economic development, urban renewal, public housing, vector control, county fairs, museums, dog control, civil defense and senior services.

Originally, counties functioned almost exclusively as agents of the state government. Their every activity had to be either authorized or mandated by state law. However, in 1958, an amendment to the Oregon Constitution authorized counties to adopt "home rule" charters, and a 1973 state law granted all counties power to exercise broad "home rule" authority. As a result, the national Advisory Commission on Intergovernmental Relations has identified county government in Oregon as having the highest degree of local discretionary authority of any state in the nation.

Nine counties have adopted "home rule" charters, wherein voters have the power to adopt and amend their own county government organization. Lane and Washington were the first to adopt "home rule" in 1962, followed by Hood River (1964), Multnomah (1967), Benton (1972), Jackson (1978), Josephine (1980), Clatsop (1988) and Umatilla (1993).

Twenty-four of Oregon's 36 counties, including the nine with charters, are governed by a board of commissioners comprised of three to five elected members. The remaining 12 less populated counties are governed by a "county court" consisting of a county judge and two commissioners.

Baker County

County Seat: 1995 3rd St., Baker City 97814
Phone: 541-523-8203 (General); 541-523-8207 (County Clerk)
Fax: 541-523-8240
E-mail: tgreen@bakercounty.org
Web: www.bakercounty.org
Established: Sept. 22, 1862
Elev. at Baker City: 3,471'
Area: 3,089 sq. mi.
Average Temp.: January 25.2° July 66.6°
Assessed Value: $1,245,463,000

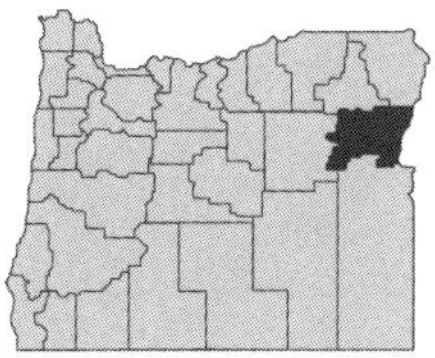

Real Market Value: $1,536,244,322
Annual Precipitation: 10.63"
Economy: Agriculture, forest products, manufacturing and recreation
Points of Interest: The Oregon Trail Interpretive Center and Old Oregon Trail, Sumpter Gold Dredge Park and ghost towns, Sumpter Valley Railroad, Baker City Restored Historic District (including Geiser Grand Hotel), Anthony Lakes Ski Resort and summer picnic areas, camping and hiking trails, Eagle Cap Wilderness area, Brownlee, Oxbow and Hells Canyon Reservoirs and Hells Canyon

Baker County was established from part of Wasco County and named after Colonel Edward D. Baker, a U.S. Senator from Oregon. A Union officer and close friend of President Lincoln, Colonel Baker was the only member of Congress to die in the Civil War. He was killed at Ball's Bluff, Virginia. Auburn, which no longer exists, was the first county seat. Baker City became the county seat in 1868. It was incorporated in1874, and it is the 17th oldest city in Oregon.

Before 1861, the majority of immigrants only paused in Baker County on their way west, unaware of its vast agricultural and mineral resources. Then the great gold rush began, and Baker County became one of the Northwest's largest gold producers. Farming, ranching, logging and recreation have become the chief economic bases for an area that displays spectacular scenery, including the world's deepest gorge, Hells Canyon; an outstanding museum with the famous Cavin-Walfel rock collection; and numerous historic buildings with interesting architectural features.

County Officials: Commissioners—Tim L. Kerns (R) 2017, Carl E. Stiff (R) 2015, Fred Warner Jr. (D) 2015; Dist. Atty. Matthew Shirtcliff 2017; Assess. Kerry Savage 2017; Clerk Tami Green 2015; Justice of the Peace Don Williams 2019; Sheriff Mitch Southwick 2017; Surv. Tom Hanley 2017; Treas. Alice Durflinger 2015; Co. Admin. Christena Cook; CIO Bill Lee

Benton County

County Seat: 408 SW Monroe Ave., Corvallis 97333, 205 NW 5th St., Corvallis 97330
Phone: 541-766-6800 (General); 541-766-6859 (Court Administrator)
Fax: 541-766-6675
E-mail: webmaster@co.benton.or.us
Web: www.co.benton.or.us
Established: Dec. 23, 1847
Elev. at Corvallis: 224'
Area: 679 sq. mi.
Average Temp.: January 39.3° July 65.6°

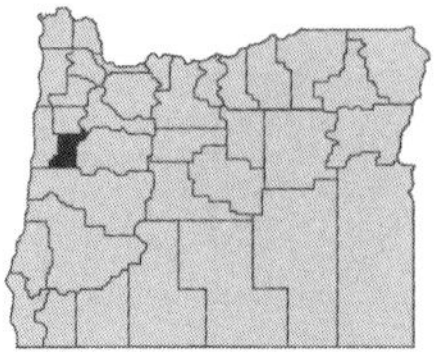

Assessed Value: $6,940,432,924
Real Market Value: $9,082,988,302
Annual Precipitation: 42.71"
Economy: Agriculture, forest products, research and development, electronics and wineries
Points of Interest: Benton County Courthouse, Oregon State University Campus, Benton County Museum (Philomath), Alsea Falls, Mary's Peak, William L. Finley National Wildlife Refuge, Peavy Arboretum, McDonald Forest, Jackson Frazier Wetland

Benton County was created from Polk County by an act of the Provisional Government of Oregon in 1847. It is one of seven counties in the United States to be named after Senator Thomas Hart Benton of Missouri, a longtime advocate of the development of the Oregon Territory. The county was created out of an area originally inhabited by the Klickitat Tribe, who rented it from the Kalapuya Indians for use as hunting grounds. At that time, the boundaries began at the intersection of Polk County and the Willamette River, ran as far south as the California border and as far west as the Pacific Ocean. Later, portions of Benton County were taken to form Coos, Curry, Douglas, Jackson, Josephine, Lane and Lincoln Counties, leaving it in its present form with 679 square miles of land area.

Oregon State University, agriculture, and lumber and wood products manufacturing form the basis of Benton County's economy. A substantial portion of the nation's research in forestry, agriculture, engineering, education and the sciences takes place at OSU.

County Officials: Commissioners—Jay Dixon (D) 2017, Annabelle Jaramillo (D) 2017, Linda Modrell (D) 2015; Dist. Atty. John Haroldson 2017; Assess. Tami Woodward; Clerk James Morales; Sheriff Diana Simpson 2015; Surv. Joe Mardis; Finance Manager Mary Otley; Public Information Officer Rick Osborn

Clackamas County

County Seat: County Courthouse, 2051 Kaen Rd., Oregon City 97045
Phone: 503-650-5686 (General); 503-655-8670 (Court Administrator)
Fax: 503-650-5687 (Records)
E-mail: sherryhal@co.clackamas.or.us
Web: www.clackamas.us
Established: July 5, 1843
Elev. at Oregon City: 55'
Area: 1,879 sq. mi.
Average Temp.: January 40.2° July 68.4°

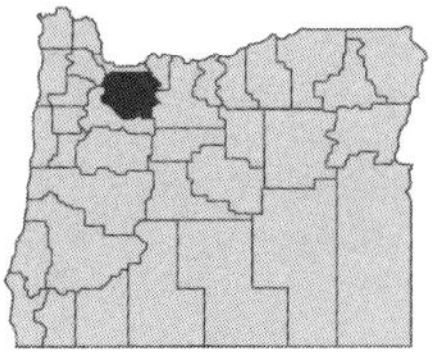

Assessed Value: $38,868,044,294
Real Market Value: $44,029,803,115
Annual Precipitation: 48.40"
Economy: Agriculture, metals manufacturing, trucking and warehousing, nursery stock, retail services, wholesale trade and construction
Points of Interest: Mt. Hood and Timberline Lodge, Willamette Falls and navigation locks, McLoughlin House, Canby Ferry, Molalla Buckaroo, driving tour of Old Barlow Road, Clackamas Town Center, Museum of the Oregon Territory, North Clackamas Aquatic Park

Clackamas County was named for the resident Clackamas Tribe and was one of the four original Oregon counties created in 1843. Oregon City, the county seat, was the first incorporated city west of the Rocky Mountains, the first capital of the Oregon Territory, and the site of the first legislative session.

In 1849, when the city of San Francisco was platted, Oregon City was the site of the only federal court west of the Rockies. The plat was filed in 1850 in the first plat book of the first office of records on the West Coast and is still in Oregon City. The area's early history is featured at the Clackamas County Historical Society and Museum of the Oregon Territory.

From its 55-foot elevation at Oregon City, the county rises to 11,235 feet at the peak of Mt. Hood, the only year-round ski resort in the United States, and the site of Timberline Lodge National Historical Landmark. The mountains, rivers and forests offer excellent outdoor recreation activities, from skiing and rafting to fishing and camping.

County Officials: Commissioners—Jim Bernard 2015, John Ludlow, chair 2017, Paul Savas 2015, Martha Schrader 2017, Tootie Smith 2017; Dist. Atty. John Foote 2017; Assess. Bob Vorman 2017; Clerk Sherry Hall 2015; Justice of the Peace Karen Brisbin 2017; Sheriff Craig Roberts 2017; Surv. R. Charles Pearson; Treas. Shari Anderson 2015; Co. Admin. Steve Wheeler

Clatsop County

County Seat: 820 Exchange St., Suite 410, Astoria 97103
Phone: 503-325-1000 (General); 503-325-8555 (Court Administrator)
Fax: 503-325-8325
E-mail: clerk@co.clatsop.or.us
Web: www.co.clatsop.or.us
Established: June 22, 1844
Elev. at Astoria: 19'
Area: 843 sq. mi.
Average Temp.: January 41.9° July 60.1°
Assessed Value: $5,248,683,735

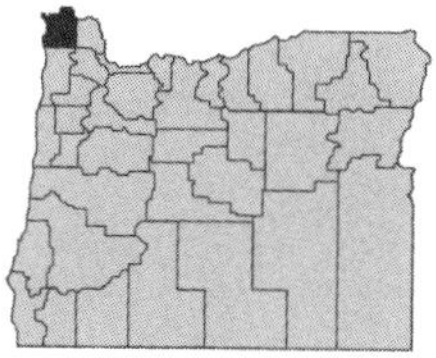

Real Market Value: $7,254,191,848
Annual Precipitation: 66.40"
Economy: Fishing, tourism and forest products
Points of Interest: Astoria Column, Port of Astoria, Flavel Mansion Museum, Lewis and Clark Expedition Salt Cairn, Fort Clatsop, Fort Stevens, Columbia River Maritime Museum

Clatsop County was created from the original Tuality District in 1844 and named for the Clatsop Tribe, one of the many Chinook tribes living in Oregon. *The Journals of Lewis and Clark* mention the tribe. Fort Clatsop, Lewis and Clark's winter headquarters in 1805 and now a national memorial near the mouth of the Columbia River, also took the tribe's name.

Astoria, Oregon's oldest city, was established as a fur trading post in 1811 and named after John Jacob Astor. The first U.S. Post Office west of the Rocky Mountains was also established in Astoria in 1847. The first county courthouse was completed in 1855. The present courthouse was erected in 1904. Records show that the summer resort of Seaside was founded by Ben Holladay, pioneer Oregon railroad builder, in the early 1870s when he constructed the Seaside House, a famous luxury hotel for which the city was finally named. The Lewis and Clark Expedition reached the Pacific Ocean at this spot.

County Officials: Commissioners—Debra Birkby 2015, Peter Huhtala 2015, Scott Lee 2015, Sarah Nebeker 2017, Dirk Rohne 2017; Dist. Atty. Joshua Marquis 2015; Assess. Mike Robison; Clerk Maeve Grimes; Sheriff Thomas J. Bergin 2017; Surv. Steven Thornton; Treas. Mike Robison; County Manager Scott Somers

Columbia County

County Seat: Courthouse, 230 Strand St., St. Helens 97051
Phone: 503-397-3796 (General); 503-397-2327 (Court Administrator)
Fax: 503-397-7266
E-mail: Betty.Huser@co.columbia.or.us
Web: www.co.columbia.or.us
Established: Jan. 16, 1854
Elev. at St. Helens: 42'
Area: 687 sq. mi.
Average Temp.: January 39.0° July 68.4°
Assessed Value: $4,113,111,742

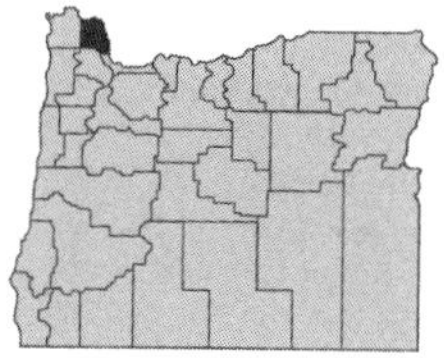

Real Market Value: $5,492,574,239
Annual Precipitation: 44.60"
Economy: Agriculture, forest products, manufacturing, surface mining and tourism
Points of Interest: Lewis and Clark Heritage Canoe Trail, Vernonia/Banks Linear State Park, Jewell Elk Refuge, Sauvie Island Wildlife Area, Sand Island Park, Jones Beach near Clatskanie, Prescott Beach Park, St. Helens Golf Course, Vernonia Golf Course, Lewis and Clark Bridge at Rainier, Columbia County Fairgrounds

Chinook and Clatskanie Tribes inhabited this bountiful region centuries before Captain Robert Gray, commanding the *Columbia Rediviva,* landed on Columbia County's timbered shoreline in 1792. The Corps of Discovery expedition, led by Lewis and Clark, traveled and camped along the Columbia River shore in the area later known as Columbia County in late 1805 and early 1806.

The county has 62 miles of Columbia riverfront and contains deep water ports and some of the finest industrial property in the Pacific Northwest. The Columbia River is a major route for ocean-going vessels and is a popular playground for fishing, boating, camping and windsurfing. The county has two marine parks, Sand Island and J. J. Collins Memorial Marine Park. Columbia County has a strong economic and cultural heritage centered around industries such as forest products, shipbuilding, mining and agriculture. The rural lifestyle and scenic beauty of Columbia County, coupled with its proximity to Portland, have drawn many new residents to the area.

County Officials: Commissioners— Earl Fisher (D) 2017, Henry Heimuller (D) 2015, Anthony (Tony) Hyde (R) 2017; Dist. Atty. R. Steven Atchison 2015; Assess. Sue Martin 2015; Clerk Betty Huser 2015; Justice of the Peace Wally Thompson 2015; Sheriff Jeff Dickerson 2017; Surv. Nathan Woodward; Treas. Jennifer Cuellar-Smith 2017

Coos County

County Seat: Courthouse, 250 N Baxter, Coquille 97423
Phone: 541-396-3121 (General); 541-396-3121, ext. 344 (Court Administrator)
Fax: 541-396-4861
E-mail: coosclerk@co.coos.or.us
Web: www.co.coos.or.us
Established: Dec. 22, 1853
Elev. at Coquille: 40'
Area: 1,629 sq. mi.
Average Temp.: January 44.2° July 60.9°

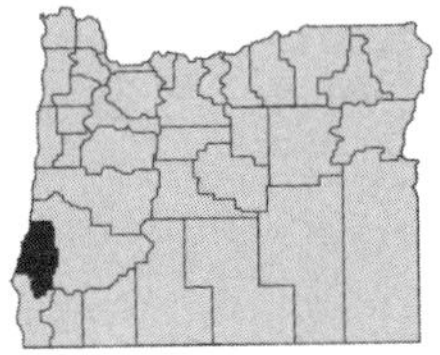

Assessed Value: $4,719,920,398
Real Market Value: $5,999,172,278
Annual Precipitation: 56.8"
Economy: Forest products, fishing, agriculture, shipping, recreation and tourism
Points of Interest: Lumber port, myrtlewood groves, Shore Acres State Park and Botanical Gardens, beaches, Oregon Dunes National Recreation Area, museums, fishing fleets, boat basins, scenic golf courses

Coos County was created by the Territorial Legislature from parts of Umpqua and Jackson Counties in 1853, and included Curry County until 1855. The county seat was Empire City until 1896 when it was moved to Coquille. Although trappers had been in the area a quarter-century earlier, the first permanent settlement in present Coos County was at Empire City, now part of Coos Bay, by members of the Coos Bay Company in 1853. The name "Coos" derives from the Coos tribe and translates to "lake" or "place of pines."

Forest products, tourism, fishing and agriculture dominate the Coos County economy. Boating, dairy farming, myrtlewood manufacturing, shipbuilding and repair, and agriculture specialty products, including cranberries, also play an important role. The International Port of Coos Bay, considered the best natural harbor between Puget Sound and San Francisco, is the world's largest forest products shipping port.

County Officials: Commissioners—Melissa Cribbins 2015, Robert (Bob) Main 2013, John Sweet 2015; Dist. Atty. R. Paul Frasier 2017; Assess. Steve Jansen 2017; Clerk Terri Turi 2015; Sheriff Craig Zanni 2015; Surv. Michael Dado 2017; Treas. Mary Barton 2017

Crook County

County Seat: Courthouse, 300 NE 3rd St., Room 23, Prineville 97754
Phone: 541-447-6553 (General); 541-447-6555 (Court Administrator)
Fax: 541-416-2145
E-mail: dee.berman@co.crook.or.us
Web: www.co.crook.or.us
Established: Oct. 24, 1882
Elev. at Prineville: 2,868'
Area: 2,991 sq. mi.
Average Temp.: January 31.8° July 64.5°

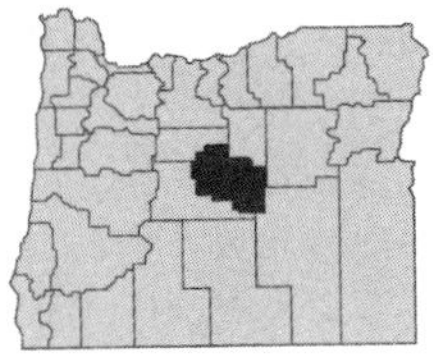

Assessed Value: $1,526,999,365
Real Market Value: $1,701,510,450
Annual Precipitation: 10.50"
Economy: Livestock, forest products, recreation, agriculture, manufacturing and wholesale trade
Points of Interest: Pine Mills, Crooked River Canyon, Ochoco Mountains, Prineville and Ochoco Reservoirs, rockhound areas, county courthouse, Steins Pillar, Wildland Firefighter's Monument, and geological formations

Crook County was formed from Wasco County in 1882, and named for Major General George Crook, U.S. Army. Geographically, the county is in the center of Oregon. It is unique in that it has only one incorporated population center, the city of Prineville, founded in 1868. Prineville's colorful past was the scene of tribal raids, range wars between sheep and cattle ranchers and vigilante justice. Other communities in this sparsely settled region are Powell Butte, Post and Paulina.

Forest products, agriculture, livestock raising and recreation/tourism services constitute most of Crook County's economy. Thousands of hunters, fishers, boaters, sightseers and rockhounds are annual visitors to its streams, reservoirs and the Ochoco Mountains. Rockhounds can dig for agates, limb casts, jasper and thundereggs on more than 1,000 acres of mining claims provided by the Prineville Chamber of Commerce. Major annual events include the Prineville Rockhound Powwow, Crooked River Roundup, Crook County Fair, Old Fashioned Fourth of July Celebration, High Desert Celtic Festival and the Lord's Acre Sale.

County Officials: Commissioners—Seth Crawford (R) 2015, Ken Fahlgren (D) 2017, Judge Mike McCabe, chair (R) 2017; Dist. Atty. Daina Vitolins 2017; Assess. Tom Green 2015; Clerk Deanna (Dee) Berman (R) 2015; Sheriff Jim Hensley 2015; Surv. David Armstrong 2017; Treas. Kathy Gray 2017; CIO Judge Scott Cooper

Curry County

County Seat: PO Box 746, Gold Beach 97444
Phone: 541-247-3295 (General); 541-247-4511 (Court Administrator)
Fax: 541-247-6440 (Elections Division)
E-mail: kolenr@co.curry.or.us
Web: www.co.curry.or.us
Established: Dec. 18, 1855
Elev. at Gold Beach: 60'
Area: 1,648 sq. mi.
Average Temp.: January 45.0° July 65.0°
Assessed Value: $2,533,799,094

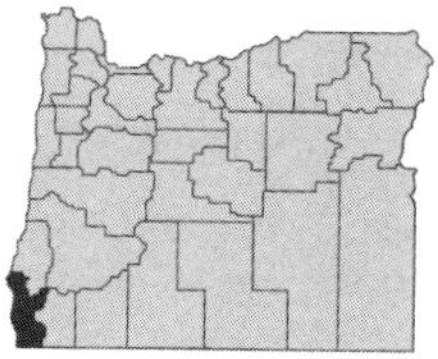

Real Market Value: $3,024,475,157
Annual Precipitation: 82.67"
Economy: Forest products, agriculture, commercial and sport fishing, recreation and tourism
Points of Interest: Cape Blanco Lighthouse, Cape Sebastian and Samuel H. Boardman State Parks, Rogue River Japanese Bomb Site and coastal ports

Named after Territorial Governor George L. Curry, the county was a part of "Coose" [sic] County until it was created in 1855. Port Orford was the county seat until 1859 when it was replaced by Ellensburg (later renamed Gold Beach).

Curry County contains valuable standing timber and also offers spectacular coastal scenery, clamming and crabbing, excellent fishing (freshwater and saltwater), upriver scenic boat trips, hiking trails, and gold for the fun of panning. The Port of Brookings is considered one of the safest harbors on the coast.

Agricultural products include sheep and cattle, cranberries, blueberries, Easter lilies and horticultural nursery stock. Curry County is also a prolific producer of myrtlewood.

County Officials: Commissioners—Susan Brown 2017, David G. Itzen 2015, David Brock Smith 2017; Dist. Atty. Everett Dial 2017; Assess. James V. Kolen 2017; Clerk Renee Kolen 2017; Sheriff John Bishop 2017; Surv. Bryan M. Flavin 2017; Treas. Debra Crumley 2017

Deschutes County

County Seat: 1300 NW Wall St., Suite 202, Bend 97701-1947
Phone: 541-388-6549 (General); 541-388-5300 (Court Administrator)
Fax: 541-389-6830
Web: www.deschutes.org
Established: Dec. 13, 1916
Elev. at Bend: 3,628'
Area: 3,055 sq. mi.
Average Temp.: January 30.5° July 65.5°
Assessed Value: $16,973,332,673

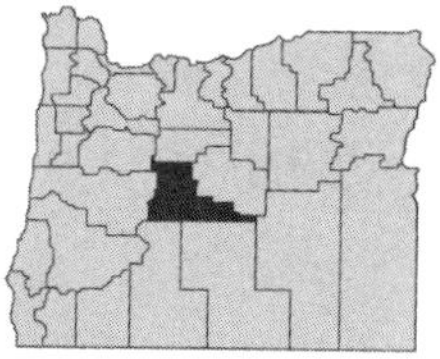

Real Market Value: $20,102,207,973
Annual Precipitation: 12"
Economy: Tourism, retail trade, forest products, recreational equipment, aviation, software and high technology
Points of Interest: Smith Rock State Park, Mt. Bachelor ski area, High Desert Museum, Lava Lands, Cascade Lakes Highway, Lava River Caves State Park, Lava Cast Forests, Newberry Crater, Pilot Butte, Three Sisters Wilderness, Central Oregon Community College, Deschutes County Fairgrounds, Redmond Airport, Pine Mountain Observatory

French-Canadian fur trappers of the Hudson's Bay Company gave the name Riviere des Chutes (River of the Falls) to the Deschutes River, from which Deschutes County took its name. In 1916, Deschutes County was created from a part of Crook County.

Deschutes County, outdoor recreation capital of Oregon, with noble, snow-capped peaks dominating the skyline to the west and the wide-open high desert extending to the east, captures the awe of locals and visitors alike. Deschutes County has grown into a bustling, exciting place where progress and growth are hallmarks.

Deschutes County has experienced rapid growth largely due to its climate and year-round recreation activities. Central Oregon offers downhill and cross-country skiing, snowboarding, fishing, hunting, hiking, rockclimbing, whitewater rafting and golfing. Deschutes County is the host of diverse annual events including the Cascade Festival of Music, the Art Hop, Cascade Children's Festival, Pole Pedal Paddle, Sisters Rodeo, Sunriver Sunfest and the Cascade Cycling Classic.

County Officials: Commissioners—Tammy Baney (R) 2015, Anthony (Tony) De Bone (R) 2015, Alan Unger (D) 2017; Dist. Atty. Patrick J. Flaherty 2015; Assess. Scot Langton 2015; Clerk Nancy Blankenship (D) 2015; Sheriff Larry Blanton 2017; Surv. Mike Berry; Treas. Marty Wynne 2015; Justice of the Peace Charles Fadeley 2017; Co. Admin. Dave Kanner

Douglas County

County Seat: Courthouse, 1036 SE Douglas Ave., Roseburg 97470
Phone: 541-440-4323 (General); 541-957-2409 (Court Administrator)
Fax: 541-440-6292
E-mail: HR@co.douglas.or.us
Web: www.co.douglas.or.us
Established: Jan. 7, 1852
Elev. at Roseburg: 479'
Area: 5,071 sq. mi.
Average Temp.: January 41.2° July 68.4°

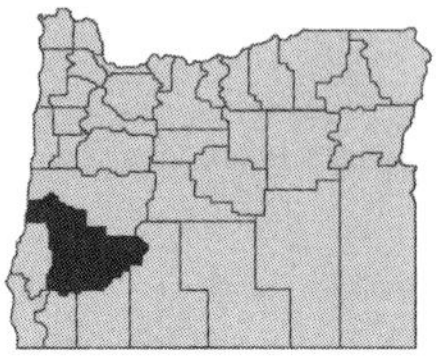

Assessed Value: $7,944,030,545
Real Market Value: $13,567,485,267
Annual Precipitation: 33.35"
Economy: Forest products, mining, agriculture, fishing and recreation
Points of Interest: Winchester Bay, Salmon Harbor, Oregon Dunes National Recreation Area, North Umpqua River, Diamond Lake, historic Oakland, Wildlife Safari, Douglas County Museum, wineries

Douglas County was named for U.S. Senator Stephen A. Douglas, Abraham Lincoln's opponent in the presidential election of 1860, and an ardent congressional advocate for Oregon. Douglas County was created in 1852 from the portion of Umpqua County which lay east of the Coast Range summit. In 1862, Douglas County absorbed what remained of Umpqua County.

Douglas County extends from sea level at the Pacific Ocean to 9,182-foot Mt. Thielsen in the Cascade Range. The Umpqua River marks the dividing line between northern and southern Oregon, and its entire watershed lies within the county's boundaries. The county contains nearly 2.8 million acres of commercial forest lands and the largest stand of old growth timber in the world, which still provides the region's main livelihood. Approximately 25 percent of the labor force is employed in the forest products industry. Agriculture includes field crops, orchards and livestock. Over 50 percent of the land area of the county is federal public land.

County Officials: Commissioners—Joe Laurance 2015, Susan Morgan 2017, Doug Robertson 2017; Dist. Atty. Richard Wesenberg 2017; Assess. Susan Acree 2015; Clerk Patricia Hitt 2017; Justices of the Peace Candace Hissong 2019, Stephen H. Miller 2019, Carol Roberts 2019, Russell Trump 2015; Sheriff John Hanlin 2017; Surv. Randy Smith 2015; Treas. James Rudolph 2017

Gilliam County

County Seat: Courthouse, 221 S Oregon St., Condon 97823-0427
Phone: 541-384-2311 (General); 541-384-3303 (Court Administrator)
Fax: 541-384-2166
E-mail: leanne.durfey@co.gilliam.or.us
Web: www.co.gilliam.or.us
Established: Feb. 25, 1885
Elev. at Condon: 2,844'
Area: 1,223 sq. mi.
Average Temp.: January 31.9° July 71.3°

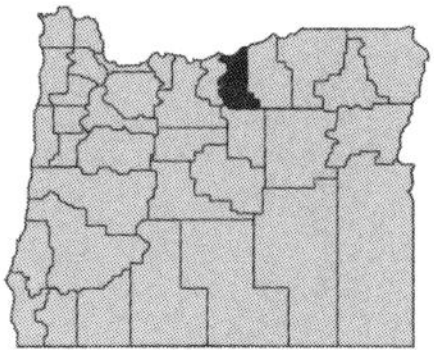

Assessed Value: $783,497,172
Real Market Value: $2,132,111,579
Annual Precipitation: 11.39"
Economy: Agriculture, recreation, environmental services and wind power generation
Points of Interest: Old Oregon Trail, Arlington Bay and Marina, Lonerock area, Condon historic district, tribal pictographs

Gilliam County was established in 1885 from a portion of Wasco County and was named after Colonel Cornelius Gilliam, a veteran of the Cayuse Indian War. The first county seat was at Alkali, now Arlington. In 1890, voters chose to move the county seat to Condon, known then as "Summit Springs." A brick courthouse was built in Condon in 1903 which was destroyed by fire in 1954. The present courthouse was built on the same site in 1955.

Gilliam County is in the heart of the Columbia Plateau wheat area. The economy is based mainly on agriculture, with an average farm size of about 4,200 acres. Wheat, barley and beef cattle are the principal crops. The largest individual employers in the county, Chemical Waste Management of the Northwest and Oregon Waste Systems, subsidiaries of Waste Management Inc., are regional waste disposal landfills.

With elevations of over 3,000 feet near Condon, in the south of the county, and 285 feet at Arlington, 38 miles north, the county offers a variety of climates. Hunting, fishing and tourism are secondary industries. Two major rivers, the John Day and Columbia, and Interstate 84 traverse the area east to west. Highway 19 connects the county's major cities north to south and serves as the gateway to the John Day Valley.

County Officials: Commissioners—Dennis Gronquist (D) 2017, Judge Steve Shaffer 2019, Mike Weimar (R) 2015; Dist. Atty. Marion Weatherford 2015; Clerk Rena Kennedy 2015; Justice of the Peace Cris Patnode 2015; Sheriff Gary Bettencourt 2015; Surv. Bob Baggett 2015; Treas. Danelle Wetherell 2015; Assess. Dave Messenger 2017

Grant County

County Seat: Courthouse, 201 S Humbolt St., Suite 290, Canyon City 97820
Phone: 541-575-1675 (General); 541-575-1438 (Court Administrator)
Fax: 541-575-2248
E-mail: percyb@grantcounty-or.gov
Web: www.gcoregonlive2.com
Established: Oct. 14, 1864

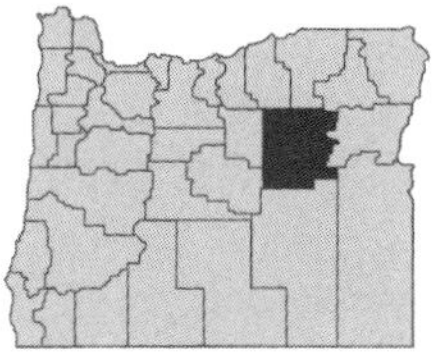

Elev. at Canyon City: 3,194'
Area: 4,528 sq. mi.
Average Temp.:
January 30.7°
July 68.4°
Assessed Value: $494,906,289
Real Market Value: $1,248,059,900
Annual Precipitation: 14.28"
Economy: Forest products, agriculture, hunting, livestock and recreation
Points of Interest: John Day Fossil Beds National Monument, Veteran's Memorial, Kam Wah Chung Museum, Joaquin Miller Cabin, Grant County Historical Museum, Sacred Totem Pole, Grant County Historical Mural, Dewitt Museum, Depot Park, Sumpter Valley Railroad, Strawberry Mountain Wilderness and North Fork John Day River Wilderness

Grant County was created in 1864 from Wasco and Umatilla Counties and was named for General Ulysses S. Grant. It shares boundaries with more counties (eight) than any other county in Oregon.

Grant County contains the headwaters of the John Day River, which has more miles of Wild and Scenic designation than any other river in the United States. More than 60 percent of the land in the county is in public ownership.

County Officials: Commissioners—Boyd Britton (R) 2015, Chris Labhart (R) 2017, Judge Scott Myers (R) 2019; Dist. Atty. Ryan Joslin 2015; Assess. Lane Burton 2017; Clerk Brenda Percy 2015; Justice of the Peace Kathleen Stinnett 2019; Sheriff Glenn Palmer 2017; Surv. Mike Springer 2017; Treas. Kathy Smith 2017

Harney County

County Seat: Courthouse, 450 N Buena Vista Ave., Burns 97720
Phone: 541-573-6641 (General); 541-573-5207 (Court Administrator)
Fax: 541-573-8370
E-mail: clerk@co.harney.or.us
Web: www.co.harney.or.us
Established: Feb. 25, 1889

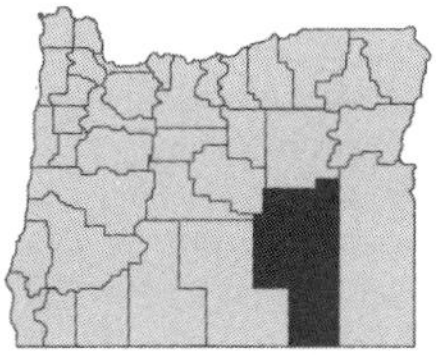

Elev. at Burns: 4,118'
Area: 10,228 sq. mi.
Average Temp.:
January 27.5°
July 69.4°
Assessed Value: $482,879,278
Real Market Value: $1,267,124,347
Annual Precipitation: 10.13"
Economy: Forest products, manufacturing, livestock and agriculture
Points of Interest: Steens Mountain, Malheur National Wildlife Refuge, Alvord Desert, Alvord Hot Springs, Squaw Butte Experimental Station, "P" Ranch Round Barn, Frenchglen, Wild Horse Corrals, Delintment Lake, Yellowjacket Lake

In 1826, Peter Skene Ogden became the first white man to explore this area when he led a fur brigade for the Hudson's Bay Company. In 1889, Harney, the largest county in Oregon, was carved out of Grant County and named for Major General William S. Harney, commander of the Department of Oregon, U.S. Army, from 1858–59. Harney was instrumental in opening areas of Eastern Oregon for settlement.

A fierce political battle, with armed night riders who spirited county records from Harney to Burns, ended with Burns as the county seat in 1890. The courthouse was constructed five years later. Burns' first newspaper was established in 1884, and its first church in 1887.

Harney County shares the largest Ponderosa pine forest in the nation with Grant County and has more than 100,000 beef cattle on its vast ranges. Its abundance of game, campsites, excellent fishing and bird watching have stimulated fast-growing recreational activities.

County Officials: Commissioners—Judge Steven E. Grasty 2019, Dan Nichols 2017, Peter Runnels 2015; Dist. Atty. Tim Colahan 2017; Assess. Ted Tiller 2015; Clerk Derrin (Dag) Robinson 2017; Justice of the Peace Donna Thomas 2019; Sheriff David Glerup 2017; Surv. Kenny Delano; Treas. Ellen (Nellie) Franklin 2015

Hood River County

County Seat: 601 State St., Hood River 97031-2093

Phone: 541-386-3970 (General); 541-386-3535 (Court Administrator)

Fax: 541-387-6864

E-mail: brian.beebe@admin.co.hood-river.or.us

Web: www.co.hood-river.or.us

Established: June 23, 1908

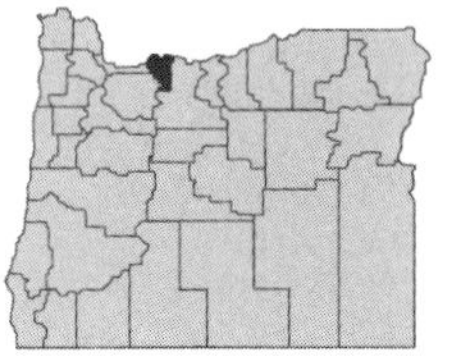

Elev. at Hood River: 154'

Area: 533 sq. mi.

Average Temp.: January 33.6° July 72°

Assessed Value: $1,894,013,143

Real Market Value: $3,497,686,474

Annual Precipitation: 30.85"

Economy: Agriculture, food processing, forest products and recreation

Points of Interest: Bridge of the Gods, Cloud Cap Inn, Mt. Hood Recreation Area, Mt. Hood Meadows Ski Resort, Lost Lake, Panorama Point, Hood River Valley at blossom time

The first white settlers in Hood River County filed a donation land claim in 1854. The first school was built in 1863, and a road from The Dalles was completed in 1867. By 1880, there were 17 families living in the valley. Hood River County was created in 1908 from Wasco County.

Agriculture, timber, lumber and recreation are the major sources of revenue and industry. Fruit grown in the fertile valley is of such exceptional quality that the county leads the world in Anjou pear production. There are more than 14,000 acres of commercial orchards growing pears, apples, cherries and peaches. Hood River County also has two ports and two boat basins, with one serving local barge traffic, a steel boat manufacturing firm and Mid-Columbia yachting interests. Windsurfing on the Columbia River is a popular sport and attracts windsurfers from all over the world.

County Officials: Commissioners—Bob Benton 2015, Karen Joplin 2015, Maui Meyer 2017, Les Perkins 2017, Ron Rivers, Chair 2019; Dist. Atty. John Sewell 2017; Assess./Clerk Brian Beebe; Justice of the Peace Cindy Mitchell 2015; Sheriff Matt English 2017; Surv. Randy Johnston; Treas. Sandra Borowy; Co. Admin. David Meriwether

Jackson County

County Seat: Courthouse, 10 S Oakdale Ave., Medford 97501

Phone: 541-774-6029 (General); 541-776-7171 (Court Administrator - Justice Bldg., 100 S Oakdale Ave., Medford 97501)

Fax: 541-774-6455

E-mail: walkercd@jacksoncounty.org

Web: www.co.jackson.or.us

Established: Jan. 12, 1852

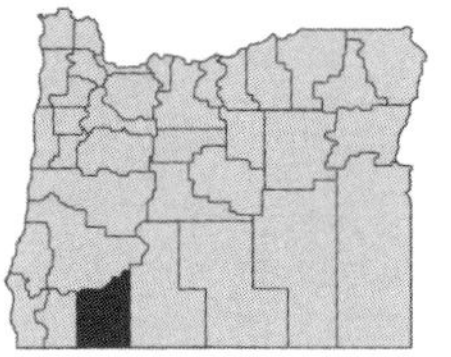

Elev. at Medford: 1,382'

Area: 2,801 sq. mi.

Average Temp.: January 37.6° July 72.5°

Assessed Value: $16,373,155,857

Real Market Value: $20,963,859,574

Annual Precipitation: 19.84"

Economy: Medical, retail, tourism, agriculture, manufacturing and forest products

Points of Interest: Mt. Ashland Ski Resort, Historic Jacksonville, Oregon Shakespeare Festival, Peter Britt Music Festival, Southern Oregon University, pear orchards, Howard Prairie Lake, Emigrant Lake, Hyatt Lake, Fish Lake, Rogue River, Lithia Park, Lost Creek Dam, Butte Creek Mill, Crater Lake Highway

Named for President Andrew Jackson, Jackson County was formed in 1852 from Lane County and the unorganized area south of Douglas and Umpqua Counties. It included lands which now lie in Coos, Curry, Josephine, Klamath and Lake Counties. The discovery of gold near Jacksonville in 1852 and completion of a wagon road, which joined the county with California to the south and Douglas County to the north, brought many pioneers.

County Officials: Commissioners—Doug Breidenthal (R) 2017, John Rachor (R) 2015, Don Skundrick (R) 2015; Dist. Atty. Beth Heckert 2017; Assess. Josh Gibson 2017; Clerk Chris Walker 2015; Justice of the Peace Joe Charter 2017; Sheriff Michael Winters 2015; Surv. Scott Fein 2017; Finance Director/Treas. Shannon Bell; Co. Admin. Danny Jordan

Jefferson County

County Seat: 66 SE D St., Madras 97741
Phone: 541-475-4451 (General); 541-475-3317 (Court Administrator)
Fax: 541-325-5018
E-mail: Kathy.Marston@co.jefferson.or.us
Web: www.co.jefferson.or.us
Established: Dec. 12, 1914

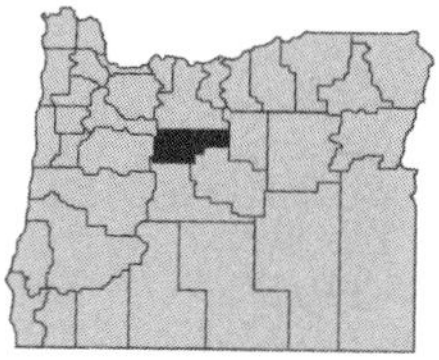

Elev. at Madras: 2,242'
Area: 1,791 sq. mi.
Average Temp.: January 37.4° July 70.1°
Assessed Value: $1,428,714,661
Real Market Value: $2,321,745,390
Annual Precipitation: 10.2"
Economy: Agriculture, forest products and recreation
Points of Interest: Mt. Jefferson, Warm Springs Indian Reservation, Metolius River, Black Butte, Suttle Lake, Blue Lake, Santiam Summit, Lake Billy Chinook behind Round Butte Dam, Haystack Reservoir, Priday Agate Beds

Jefferson County was established in 1914 from a portion of Crook County. It was named for Mount Jefferson on its western boundary. The county owes much of its agricultural prosperity to the railroad, which arrived in 1911, and to the development of irrigation projects in the late 1930s. The railroad, which links Madras with the Columbia River, was completed after constant feuds and battles between two lines working on opposite sides of the Deschutes River.

Vegetable, grass and flower seeds, garlic, mint and sugar beets are cultivated on some 60,000 irrigated acres. Jefferson County also has vast acreages of rangelands and a healthy industrial base related to forest products. The Warm Springs Forest Products Industry, a multi-million dollar complex owned by the Confederated Tribes of the Warm Springs Reservation—partially located in the northwestern corner of the county—is the single biggest industry. With 300 days of sunshine and a low yearly rainfall, fishing, hunting, camping, boating, water-skiing and rock hunting are popular recreations.

County Officials: Commissioners—Mike Ahern (D) 2015, Wayne Fording (R) 2017, John Hatfield (R) 2015; Dist. Atty. Steven Lariche 2017; Assess. Jean McCloskey 2017; Clerk Kathleen Marston (R) 2015; Sheriff Jim Adkins (R) 2015; Surv. Gary L. DeJarnatt 2017; Treas. Deena Goss (R) 2017

Josephine County

County Seat: Courthouse, 500 NW 6th St., Grants Pass 97526; Mailing Address: PO Box 69, Grants Pass 97526
Phone: 541-474-5243 (General); 541-476-2309 (Court Administrator)
Fax: 541-474-5246
E-mail: clerk@co.josephine.or.us
Web: www.co.josephine.or.us
Established: Jan. 22, 1856

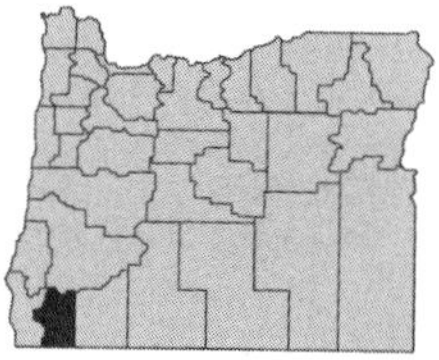

Elev. at Grants Pass: 948'
Area: 1,641 sq. mi.
Average Temp.: January 39.9° July 71.6°
Assessed Value: $6,267,269,432
Real Market Value: $7,275,733,739
Annual Precipitation: 32.31"
Economy: Tourism, recreation, forest products, electronics and software
Points of Interest: Oregon Caves National Monument, Wolf Creek Tavern, Sunny Valley Covered Bridge and Interpretive Center, Hellgate Canyon-Rogue River, Grants Pass Historic District, Growers Market, Kalmiopsis Wilderness, Rogue Community College, Barnstormers Theater, Rogue Music Theater

Josephine County, named for Virginia "Josephine" Rollins, the first white woman to make this county her home, was established in 1856 out of the western portion of Jackson County. The county seat was originally located in Sailor Diggings (later, Waldo), but in July of 1857 was relocated to Kerbyville, situated on the main route between the port of Crescent City, California and the gold fields.

The discovery of rich placers at Sailor Diggings in 1852 and the resulting gold rush brought the first settlers to this region. Several U.S. Army forts were maintained in the county and many engagements during the Rogue River Indian War (1855–1858) took place within its boundaries. In 1886, the county seat was finally relocated to Grants Pass, a new town on the railroad that was completed through Oregon that same year. Grants Pass is now the departure point for most Rogue River scenic waterway guided fishing and boat trips. The Illinois River, one of the Rogue's tributaries, has also been designated a scenic waterway.

County Officials: Commissioners—Simon Hare 2015; Keith Heck 2017, Cherryl Walker 2017, Dist. Atty. Stephen D. Campbell 2017; Assess. Connie Roach 2017; Clerk Art Harvey 2017; Sheriff Gil Gilbertson 2015; Surv. Peter D. Allen 2017; Treas. Eve Arce 2017

Klamath County

County Seat: 305 Main St., Klamath Falls 97601-6391
Phone: 541-883-5134 (General); 541-883-5503 (Court Administrator)
Fax: 541-885-6757
E-mail: lsmith@co.klamath.or.us
Web: www.klamathcounty.org
Established: Oct. 17, 1882
Elev. at Klamath Falls: 4,105'
Area: 6,135 sq. mi.
Average Temp.: January 29.8° July 68.0°

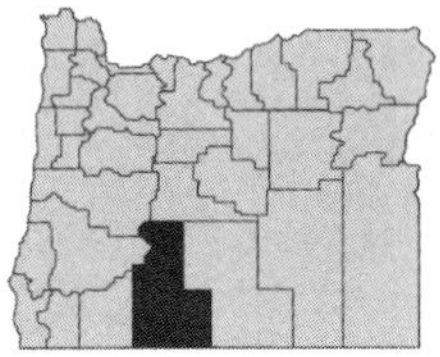

Assessed Value: $5,236,276,297
Real Market Value: $7,790,983,264
Annual Precipitation: 14.31"
Economy: Forest products, agriculture, geothermal energy, tourism and recreation
Points of Interest: Crater Lake National Park, Collier Memorial State Park and Logging Museum, Klamath Lake (largest lake in Oregon), seven National Wildlife Refuges, Oregon Institute of Technology (OIT), Klamath County Museum, Favell Museum of Western Art, Ross Ragland Performing Arts Theatre

The Klamath or "Clamitte" Tribe, for which Klamath County was named, has had a presence for 10,000 years. White settlement began in 1846 along the Applegate Immigrant Trail, which precipitated clashes between the two cultures and led to the Modoc Indian War of 1872. The Oregon Legislature created Klamath County by dividing Lake County in 1882. Linkville was named county seat and its name was changed to Klamath Falls in 1893.

Klamath County's present-day position as a great lumber, agriculture and distribution center was assured in the early 1900s with the coming of the railroad and the start of one of the most successful of all federal reclamation projects—the Klamath Project, which drained much of the 128 square mile Lower Klamath Lake to provide 188,000 acres of irrigable land.

Natural geothermal hot wells provide heat for many homes, businesses and the OIT campus. The full potential of this energy resource continues to be studied. Klamath is recognized for its scenic beauty, outdoor recreation, abundant waterfowl and diverse landscape.

County Officials: Commissioners—James J. Bellet (R) 2017, Dennis Linthicum (R) 2015, Tom Mallams (R) 2017; Dist. Atty. vacant; Assess. Leonard Hill 2017; Clerk Linda Smith 2015; Justice of the Peace Karen Oakes 2017; Sheriff Frank Skrah 2017; Surv. Mike Markus 2017; Treas. Jason Link 2017

Lake County

County Seat: Courthouse, 513 Center St., Lakeview 97630
Phone: 541-947-6006 (General); 541-947-6051 (Court Administrator)
Fax: 541-947-6015
Web: www.lakecountyor.org
Established: October 24, 1874
Elev. at Lakeview: 4,800'
Area: 8,359 sq. mi.
Average Temp.: January 28.4° July 67.0°

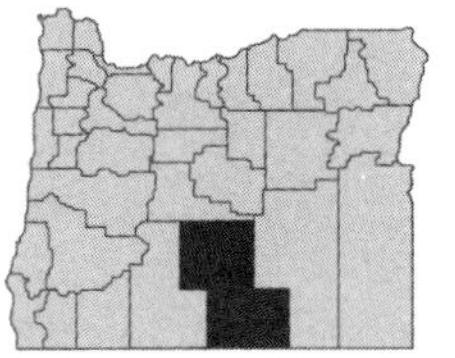

Assessed Value: $974,419,878
Real Market Value: $13,478,290
Annual Precipitation: 15.80"
Economy: Livestock, forest products, agriculture, recreation
Points of Interest: Hart Mountain Antelope Refuge, Fort Rock and Fort Rock Homestead Village Museum, Abert Lake and Rim, Goose Lake, Hunter's Hot Springs, Old Perpetual Geyser, Schminck Memorial Museum and Lake County Museum, Lake County Round-Up Museum, Warner Canyon Ski Area, Gearhart Wilderness, Lost Forest, Crack-in-the-Ground, Sheldon National Wildlife Refuge, Summer Lake Hot Springs, Hole-in-the-Ground, sunstones (Oregon's state gemstone) near Plush, Warner Wetlands, Summer Lake Wildlife Area

Lake County was created from Jackson and Wasco Counties by the 1874 Legislature. It then included the present Klamath County and all of the present Lake County except Warner Valley. In 1882, Klamath was removed and, in 1885, the Warner area from Grant County was added.

Linkville, now Klamath Falls, was the first county seat. M. Bullard gave 20 acres as the Lakeview townsite. In the 1875 election, the county seat was moved to Lakeview. The Hart Mountain Antelope Refuge is a 270,000 acre wildlife haven for antelope, mule deer, bighorn sheep and upland birds. A number of migratory waterfowl flyways converge on Goose Lake, south of Lakeview, the Warner Wetlands near Plush and the Summer Lake Wildlife area. Lakeview has been deemed the hang gliding capital of the West.

County Officials: Commissioners—Ken Kestner (R) 2015, Dan Shoun (D) 2015, Bradley Winters (R) 2017; Dist. Atty. Ulys Stapleton 2017; Assess. Larry Reeder 2015; Clerk Stacie Geaney 2017; Sheriff Phil McDonald 2015; Surv. Darryl Anderson 2015; Treas. Ann Crumrine 2017

Lane County

County Seat: Courthouse, 125 E 8th Ave., Eugene 97401
Phone: 541-682-4203 (General); 541-682-4166 (Court Administrator)
Fax: 541-682-4616
Web: www.lanecounty.org
Established: Jan. 28, 1851

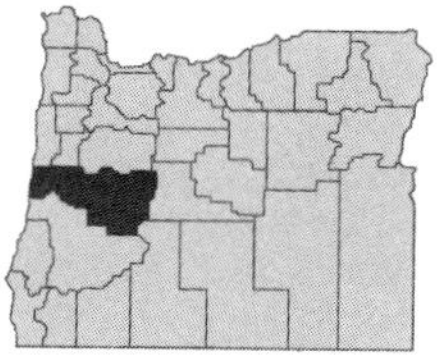

Elev. at Eugene: 422'
Area: 4,620 sq. mi.
Average Temp.:
January 40°
July 70°
Assessed Value: $27,224,318,409
Real Market Value: $43,038,475,753
Annual Precipitation: 46"
Economy: Agriculture, higher education, high technology, forest products, recreation, recreational vehicle manufacturing and tourism
Points of Interest: Twenty historic covered bridges, Bohemia Mines, coastal sand dunes, Darlingtonia Botanical Wayside, Fern Ridge Reservoir, Heceta Head Lighthouse, Hendricks Park Rhododendron Garden, hot springs, Hult Center for the Performing Arts, Lane Community College, Lane ESD Planetarium, Martin Rapids whitewater, McKenzie Pass, Mt. Pisgah Arboretum, Old Town Florence, Pac-12 sports events, Proxy Falls, sea lion caves, University of Oregon, vineyards and wineries, Waldo Lake, Washburne State Park tide pools, Willamette Pass ski area

Lane County was named for General Joseph Lane, a rugged frontier hero who was Oregon's first territorial governor. Pioneers traveling the Oregon Trail in the late 1840s came to Lane County mainly to farm. The county's first district court met under a large oak tree until a clerk's office could be built in 1852. A few years later, the first courthouse opened in what is now downtown Eugene. With the building of the railroads, the market for timber opened in the 1880s. Today, wood products are still an important part of the economy in addition to high-technology manufacturing and tourism. Lane County government operates under a home rule charter approved by voters in 1962.

Although 90 percent of Lane County is forest land, Eugene and Springfield comprise the second largest urban area in Oregon.

County Officials: Commissioners—Jay Bozievich 2015, Pat Farr 2017, Sid Leiken 2015, Peter Sorenson 2017, Faye Stewart 2015; Dist. Atty. Alex Gardner 2017; Assess. Anette Spickard 2015; Clerk Cheryl Betschart; Justice of the Peace Cindy Cable 2015; Sheriff Tom Turner 2017; Surv. Mike Jackson; Co. Admin. Liane Richardson

Lincoln County

County Seat: Courthouse, 225 W Olive St., Rm. 201, Newport 97365
Phone: 541-265-6611 (General); 541-265-4236 (Court Administrator)
Fax: 541-265-4950
E-mail: rbovett@co.lincoln.or.us
Web: www.co.lincoln.or.us
Established: Feb. 20, 1893

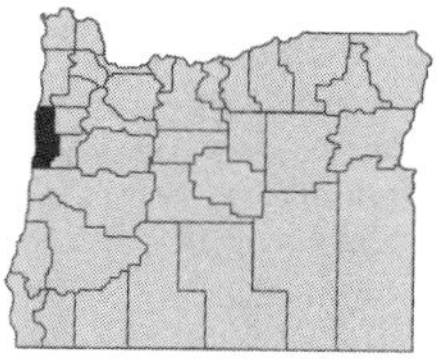

Elev. at Newport: 134'
Area: 992 sq. mi.
Average Temp.:
January 44.4°
July 57.6°
Assessed Value: $6,690,813,000
Real Market Value: $9,494,084,570
Annual Precipitation: 71.93"
Economy: Tourism, government, services and retail, forest products and fishing
Points of Interest: Agate Beach, Alsea Bay Interpretive Center, Beverly Beach State Park, Boiler Bay, Cape Perpetua Visitors' Center, Cascade Head, Connie Hansen Garden Conservancy, Devils Lake, Lincoln County Historical Museum, Newport Performing and Visual Arts Centers, OSU Hatfield Marine Science Center and Interpretive Center, Oregon Coast Aquarium, Otter Crest Viewpoint, Seal Rock Park, South Beach State Park, Yaquina Arts Center, Yaquina Bay State Park and Lighthouse, Yaquina Head Outstanding Natural Area

With miles of beach and coastline, Lincoln County is one of the most popular visitor destinations on the Oregon Coast. Named for President Abraham Lincoln, Lincoln County was created by the Oregon Legislature in 1893. Lincoln County has a very temperate climate and a short, but productive, growing season.

Depoe Bay is known as "the whale watching capital of the world." Lincoln City offers more than 2,000 hotel, motel and bed and breakfast rooms and resorts, as well as the Siletz Tribe's Chinook Winds Casino. Newport, known as Oregon's oceanography research center, features numerous interpretive centers and the Oregon Coast Aquarium, along with a large fishing fleet and working bay front. Siletz is the home of the Administration Center and reservation of the Confederated Tribes of Siletz Indians of Oregon. Toledo is known as Lincoln County's industrial center. Waldport features the Alsea Bay Interpretive Center. Yachats is known as the "Gem of the Oregon Coast."

County Officials: Commissioners—Bill Hall (D) 2017, Don Lindly (D) 2015, Terry Thompson (D) 2015; Dist. Atty. Robert Bovett 2017; Assess. Rob Thomas 2015; Clerk Dana Jenkins 2015; Sheriff Dennis Dotson 2017; Surv. John Waffenschmidt 2017; Treas. Linda Pilson 2017

Linn County

County Seat: Courthouse, 300 SW 4th Ave., Albany 97321

Phone: 541-967-3825 (General); 541-967-3802 (Court Administrator)

Fax: 541-926-8226

E-mail: sdruckenmiller@co.linn.or.us

Web: www.co.linn.or.us

Established: Dec. 28, 1847

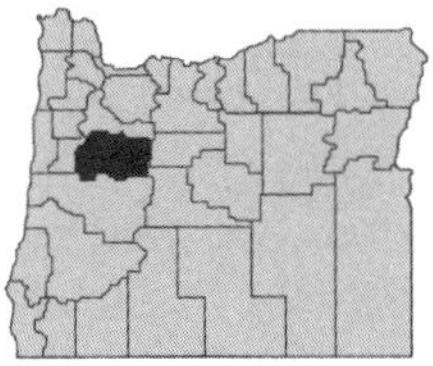

Elev. at Albany: 210'

Area: 2,297 sq. mi.

Average Temp.:
January 39.0°
July 65.6°

Assessed Value: $8,147,244,638

Real Market Value: $10,572,478,266

Annual Precipitation: 42.55"

Economy: Agriculture, forest products, rare metals, manufacturing and recreation

Points of Interest: Willamette and Santiam Rivers; Foster, Green Peter and Detroit Reservoirs; Cascade Mountain range with Mt. Jefferson, Hoodoo Ski Bowl and the Pacific Crest Trail, covered bridges, Fair and Expo Center, Brownsville Museum and Albany historic districts

Linn County was created in 1847, and named for U.S. Senator Lewis F. Linn of Missouri, who was the author of the Donation Land Act, which provided free land to settlers in the West. Linn County is in the center of the Willamette Valley, with the Willamette River as its western boundary and the crest of the Cascades as its eastern boundary. The climate and soil conditions provide one of Oregon's most diversified agriculture areas, allowing a wide variety of specialty crops and leading the nation in the production of common and perennial ryegrass. Linn County is also home to major producers of rare and primary metals, processed food, manufactured homes and motor homes as well as the traditional logging and wood products industries.

Recreational opportunities are extensive and include hiking, climbing and skiing, picnicking and camping in county and state parks, boating, water skiing and fishing on lakes and rivers, petrified wood and agate beds, covered bridges and historic districts and events.

County Officials: Commissioners—John K. Lindsey (R) 2015, Roger Nyquist (R) 2017, William Tucker (R) 2017; Dist. Atty. Douglas Marteeny 2017; Assess. Dave Swartzlender 2017; Clerk Steven Druckenmiller 2015; Justice of the Peace Jad Lemhouse 2015; Sheriff Tim Mueller 2015; Surv. Charles Gibbs 2017; Treas. Michelle Hawkins 2017; Co. Admin. Ralph Wyatt

Malheur County

County Seat: 251 B St. W, Vale 97918

Phone: 541-473-5151 (General); 541-473-5171 (Court Administrator)

Fax: 541-473-5523

E-mail: ddelong@malheur.co.org

Web: www.malheurco.org

Established: Feb. 17, 1887

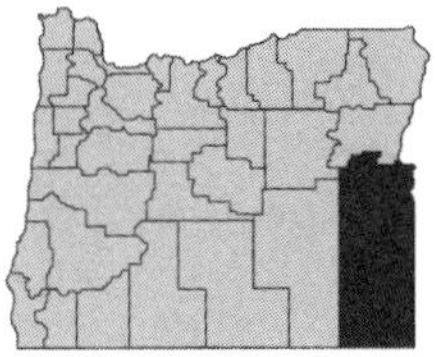

Elev. at Vale: 2,243'

Area: 9,926 sq. mi.

Average Temp.:
January 28.7°
July 75.6°

Assessed Value: $1,853,186,194

Real Market Value: $2,921,575,560

Annual Precipitation: 9.64"

Economy: Agriculture, livestock, food processing and recreation

Points of Interest: Oregon Trail, Keeney Pass, Owyhee Lake, Succor Creek State Park, Leslie Gulch Canyon, Jordan Craters, grave of trapper John Baptiste Charbonneau, Nyssa Agricultural Museum, Vale Oregon Trail Murals, Jordan Valley Basque Pelota Court, the Four Rivers Cultural Center

Malheur County was created in 1887 from Baker County. Malheur County derives its name from the "Riviere au Malheur" or "Unfortunate River" (later changed to "Malheur River"), named by French trappers whose property and furs were stolen from their river encampment.

Malheur County is a place filled with fascinating history, diverse landscape and friendly people. The landscape is enchanting and provides for a wide variety of excellent recreation such as hunting, fishing, hiking, rock climbing, rock hounding, boating and water skiing. The county is 94 percent rangeland. Basques, primarily shepherds, settled in Jordan Valley in the 1890s. Irrigated fields in the county's northeast corner, known as Western Treasure Valley, are the center of intensive and diversified farming.

County Officials: Commissioners—Donald Hodge (R) 2015, Judge Dan Joyce (R) 2015, Lawrence (Larry) P. Wilson (R) 2017; Dist. Atty. Dan Norris 2017; Assess. Dave Ingram 2017; Clerk Deborah DeLong 2015; Justice of the Peace Margaret (Margie) Mahony 2019; Sheriff Brian E. Wolfe 2017; Surv. Tom Edwards; Treas. Jennifer Forsyth 2015; Co. Admin. and CIO Lorinda DuBois

Marion County

County Seat: 100 High St. NE, Salem 97301
Phone: 503-588-5225 (General); 503-588-5105 (Court Administrator)
Fax: 503-373-4408
E-mail: clerksoffice@co.marion.or.us
Web: www.co.marion.or.us
Established: July 5, 1843

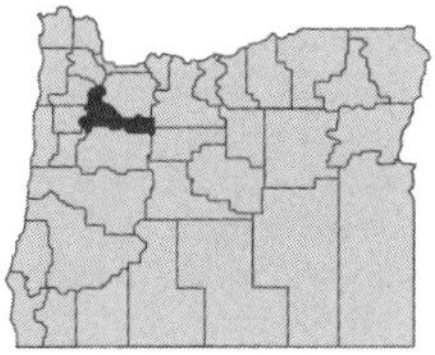

Elev. at Salem: 154'
Area: 1,194 sq. mi.
Average Temp.: January 39.3° July 66.3°
Assessed Value: $20,218,793,942
Real Market Value: $32,586,520,234
Annual Precipitation: 40.35"
Economy: Government, agriculture, food processing, forest products, manufacturing, education and tourism
Points of Interest: State Capitol, Champoeg State Park, Silver Falls State Park, The Oregon Garden, Wheatland Ferry, Buena Vista Ferry, Detroit Dam and Santiam River, Breitenbush Hot Springs, Mt. Angel Abbey, food processing plants, Willamette University, Chemeketa Community College, Mission Mill Museum Village, Bush House, Deepwood House and the Gilbert House Children's Museum

Marion County, then called Champooick, was created by the Provisional Government in 1843, 16 years before Oregon gained statehood. In 1849, the name was changed to Marion in honor of General Francis Marion.

The county, located in the heart of the Willamette Valley, has the Willamette River as its western boundary and the Cascade Range on the east. Salem, the county seat, is one of the valley's oldest cities. Among its public buildings are the Marion County Courthouse, State Capitol, Capitol Mall buildings and Salem Civic Center. The county was presided over by the Marion County Court until January 1, 1963, when the court was abolished and replaced by a Board of Commissioners.

County Officials: Commissioners—Sam Brentano (R) 2017, Janet Carlson (R) 2015, Patricia Milne (R) 2015; Dist. Atty. Walter Beglau 2015; Assess. Tom Rohlfing 2017; Clerk Bill Burgess 2017; Justices of the Peace Steven R. Summers 2015, Janice D. Zyrynoff 2017; Sheriff Jason Myers 2015; Surv. Mark Riggins; Treas. Laurie Steele 2015; Co. Admin. John Lattimer

Morrow County

County Seat: Courthouse, 100 S Court St., Heppner 97836; PO Box 788, Heppner 97836
Phone: 541-676-5604 (General); 541-676-5264 (Court Administrator)
Fax: 541-676-9876
E-mail: bchilders@co.morrow.or.us
Web: http://morrowcountyoregon.com
Established: Feb. 16, 1885

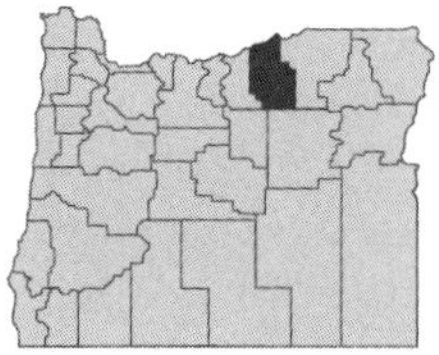

Elev. at Heppner: 1,955'
Area: 2,049 sq. mi.
Average Temp.: January 33.1° July 69.0°
Assessed Value: $1,572,094,739
Real Market Value: $2,137,135,582
Annual Precipitation: 12.5"
Economy: Agriculture, food processing, dairies, utilities, forest products, livestock and recreation
Points of Interest: Columbia River, coal-fired generating plant, Blue Mountains, Umatilla National Forest, Oregon Trail, Blue Mountain Scenic Byway, Morrow County Museum, Port of Morrow and the Lewis and Clark Route

Morrow County, created from Umatilla County in 1885, is located east of the Cascades in north-central Oregon. It was named for J. L. Morrow, an early resident. Morrow County contains more than one million acres of gently rolling plains and broad plateaus. This rich agricultural land can be roughly divided into three occupational zones—increasing amounts of irrigation farming in the north, vast fields of wheat yielding to cattle ranches in the center, and timber products in the south. With the advent of center pivot irrigation technology, Morrow County became one of Oregon's fastest growing areas in terms of population, personal income, and agricultural and industrial development. The Port of Morrow, second largest in the state in terms of tonnage, serves as a gateway to the Pacific Northwest and Pacific Rim markets.

County Officials: Commissioners—Ken Grieb (R) 2015, Leann Rea (D) 2017, Judge Terry Tallman (R) 2017; Dist. Atty. Justin Nelson 2015; Assess. Greg Sweek 2017; Clerk Bobbi Childers 2017; Justice of the Peace Annetta Spicer 2015; Sheriff Kenneth Matlack 2017; Surv. Stephen Haddock 2017; Treas. Gayle Gutierrez 2017

Multnomah County

County Seat: 501 SE Hawthorne Blvd., Portland 97214
Phone: 503-823-4000 (General); 503-988-3957 (Court Administrator)
Web: http://web.multco.us/
Established: Dec. 22, 1854

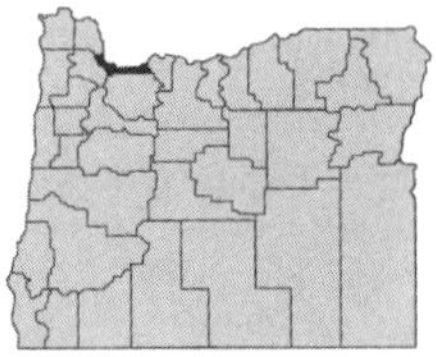

Elev. at Portland: 77'
Area: 465 sq. mi.
Average Temp.:
January 38.9°
July 67.7°
Assessed Value: $64,001,093,024
Real Market Value: $117,198,491,832
Annual Precipitation: 37.39"
Economy: Manufacturing, transportation, wholesale and retail trade, and tourism
Points of Interest: Oregon History Center, Oregon Museum of Science and Industry, Oregon Zoo, Portland Art Museum, Washington Park, Rose Test Gardens, Japanese Gardens, Columbia River Gorge, Multnomah Falls, Blue Lake Park, Oxbow Park, Pittock Mansion, Port of Portland, Memorial Coliseum, Oregon Convention Center, Rose Garden Arena

Lewis and Clark made note of "Multnomah" the tribal village on Sauvie Island in 1805 and applied that name to all tribal people of the area. The name is derived from "nematlnomaq," probably meaning "downriver." Multnomah County was created from parts of Washington and Clackamas Counties by the Territorial Legislature in 1854, five years before Oregon became a state, because citizens found it inconvenient to travel to Hillsboro to conduct county business.

The county is both the smallest in size and largest in population in Oregon. Over 50 percent of its people live in Portland, a busy metropolis dominated by rivers and greenery. The remaining area includes picturesque rural land, from pastoral farms on Sauvie Island to the rugged Columbia River Gorge and the western slopes of Mt. Hood.

County Officials: Commissioners—Jeff Cogen, Chair 2015; Deborah Kafoury 2017, Diane McKeel 2017, Judy Shiprack 2017, Loretta Smith 2015; Dist. Atty. Rodney Underhill 2017; Assess. Randy Walruff; Recorder Cindy Swick; Sheriff Dan Staton 2015; Surv. James Clayton; Treas/CFO Mark Campbell; Auditor Steve March 2015; CIO Joanne Fuller

Polk County

County Seat: Courthouse, 850 Main St., Dallas 97338
Phone: 503-623-8173 (General); 503-623-3154 (Court Administrator)
Fax: 503-623-0896
E-mail: unger.valerie@co.polk.or.us
Web: www.co.polk.or.us
Established: Dec. 22, 1845

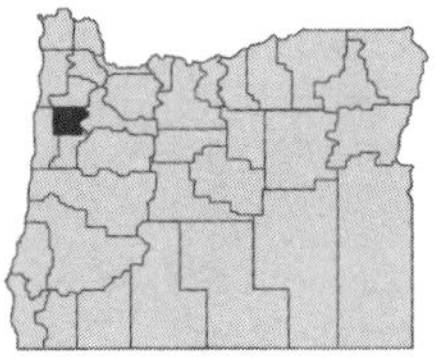

Elev. at Dallas: 325'
Area: 745 sq. mi.
Average Temp.:
January 39.1°
July 65.6°
Assessed Value: $4,826,035,276
Real Market Value: $6,690,073,438
Annual Precipitation: 51.66"
Economy: Agriculture, forest products, manufacturing, electronics and education
Points of Interest: Western Oregon University, covered bridges, historic courthouse, Brunk House, Baskett Slough Wildlife Refuge, mountain scenery, wineries, National Historic Trail, Confederated Tribes of Grand Ronde Headquarters and Spirit Mountain Casino

Polk County was created from the original Yamhill district in 1845 by the Provisional Legislature. It was named for then President James Knox Polk. The first county seat was at Cynthia Ann. City officials later changed its name to Dallas, after Vice-President George M. Dallas, and moved the community about a mile to improve its water supply.

The first courthouse was at Cynthia Ann. A second courthouse burned in 1898, and was replaced with the present building built with sandstone quarried three miles west of Dallas. A three-story office annex was completed in 1966. Polk County Human Services was consolidated in the newly acquired Academy Building in 1989.

Traveling back roads in Polk County will reveal many attractions, from covered bridges and pleasant parks to vineyards, wineries, and bed and breakfast lodgings spotting the surrounding hills. Many roads meander through beautiful fertile valleys from the Willamette River to the timbered foothills of the Coast Range. Polk County was the primary destination of early wagon trains which took the southern route to Oregon. Cities located in Polk County include Dallas, Independence, Monmouth, Falls City and portions of Salem and Willamina.

County Officials: Commissioners—Mike Ainsworth, Chair 2015, Craig Pope 2015, Jennifer Wheeler 2017; Dist. Atty. Aaron Felton 2017; Assess. Douglas P. Schmidt 2017; Clerk Valerie Unger 2017; Sheriff Robert Wolfe 2015; Surv. Eric Berry; Treas. Linda Fox 2017; Co. Admin. Greg P. Hansen

Sherman County

County Seat: Courthouse, 500 Court St., Moro 97039
Phone: 541-565-3606 (Clerk); 541-565-3650 (Court Clerk)
Fax: 541-565-3771
E-mail: jeninem@co.sherman.or.us
Web: www.sherman-county.com
Established:
Feb. 25, 1889

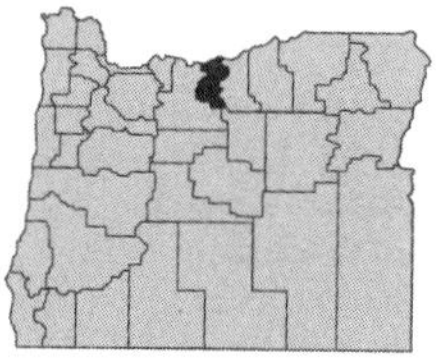

Elev. at Moro:
1,807'
Area: 831 sq. mi.
Average Temp.:
January 30.7°
July 67.9°
Assessed Value:
$404,337,621
Real Market Value: $1,742,682,182
Annual Precipitation: 9.15"
Economy: Tourism, wind energy, wheat, barley and cattle
Points of Interest: Historic county courthouse, Sherman County Museum, Gordon Ridge, John Day Dam, Sherar's Grade, Deschutes State Park, LePage Park, Giles French Park, Sherman County Fairgrounds and recreational vehicle Park

Sherman County, created in 1889 from the northeast corner of Wasco County, was named for General William Tecumseh Sherman. It was separated from Wasco County as much for its unique geological setting as for the settlers' desire to have their own political process. The rolling hills are bordered by the deep canyons of the John Day River to the east, the Columbia River to the north, and the Deschutes River and Buck Hollow to the west and south.

The county was settled in the 1870s by stockmen. By 1881, the homesteaders arrived, permanently changing the area by plowing and fencing the land. Since then, the county has been a wheat-growing area with miles of waving grain on rolling hills of wind-blown glacial silt. The total absence of timber in the county exemplifies the true meaning of the "wide open spaces of the West." Its pastoral landscape has spectacular views of canyons and rivers with mountains silhouetted in the distance. Recreation abounds on the rivers, from the famous and scenic fly-fishing and whitewater rafting stream of the Deschutes to water-skiing, wind-surfing, boating, fishing and rafting on the John Day and Columbia Rivers. Sherman County is one of Oregon's leaders in soil and water conservation.

County Officials: Commissioners—Steve Burnet (R) 2015, Mike Smith (R) 2017, Judge Gary Thompson 2019; Dist. Atty. Wade McLeod 2015; Assess. Richard Stradley 2017; Clerk Jenine McDermid 2017; Justice of the Peace Ron McDermid 2017; Sheriff Brad Lohrey 2017; Surv. Daryl Ingebo; Treas. Marnene Benson-Wood 2015

Tillamook County

County Seat: Courthouse, 201 Laurel Ave., Tillamook 97141
Phone: 503-842-2034 (General); 503-842-2596, ext. 124 (Court Administrator)
Fax: 503-842-2721
E-mail: toneil@co.tillamook.or.us
Web: www.co.tillamook.or.us
Established:
Dec. 15, 1853

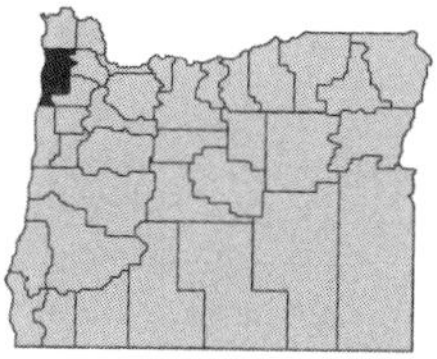

Elev. at Tillamook:
22'
Area: 1,125 sq. mi.
Average Temp.:
January 42.2°
July 58.2°
Assessed Value:
$4,134,296,384
Real Market Value: $5,467,447,447
Annual Precipitation: 90.90"
Economy: Agriculture, forest products, fishing and recreation
Points of Interest: Neah-Kah-Nie Mountain; Tillamook, Nehalem, Netarts and Nestucca Bays; Oswald West State Park, Nehalem Bay State Park, Bob Straub State Park, Cape Lookout State Park; Pioneer Museum, Blue Heron Cheese Factory, Tillamook Cheese Factory, Naval Air Station Museum, Haystack Rock at Cape Kiwanda, Whalen Island State Park

Tillamook County was formed in 1853 from Yamhill and Clatsop Counties. The name Tillamook comes from the Tillamook (or Killamook) Tribe.

Dairy farms dominate the county's fertile valley. It is the home of the world-famous Tillamook Cheese Factory. The reforested, 355,000 acre "Tillamook Burn" area continues to mature. Commercial thinning will become increasingly evident. With 75 miles of scenic coastline, four bays and nine rivers, Tillamook County offers the finest deep-sea and stream fishing, charter and dory boats, clamming, crabbing, beachcombing and hiking. Its forests also furnish excellent hunting.

County Officials: Commissioners—Bill Baertlein 2017, Tim Josi 2015, Mark Labhart 2017; Dist. Atty. William Porter 2015; Assess. Denise Vandecoevering 2017; Clerk Tassi O'Neil 2017; Justice of the Peace Joel Stevens 2017; Sheriff Andy Long 2017; Surv. Dan McNutt 2017; Treas. Debbie Clark 2017

Umatilla County

County Seat: Courthouse, 216 SE 4th St., Pendleton 97801
Phone: 541-276-7111 (General); 541-278-0341, Pendleton, 541-667-3020, Hermiston (Court Administrators)
Fax: 541-278-5463
E-mail: pattic@co.umatilla.or.us
Web: www.co.umatilla.or.us
Established: Sept. 27, 1862
Elev. at Pendleton: 1,069'
Area: 3,231 sq. mi.
Average Temp.: January 31.9° July 73.6°
Assessed Value: $4,730,751,626
Real Market Value: $6,187,672,233
Annual Precipitation: 12.97"

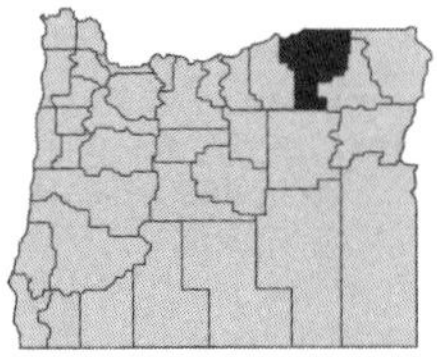

Economy: Agriculture, food processing, forest products, tourism, manufacturing, recreation, aggregate production and wind power generation
Points of Interest: Pendleton Round-Up, Pendleton Woolen Mills, Old Town Pendleton, County Historical Society, Pendleton Underground, McNary Dam and Recreation Area, Echo Museum and Historic Area, Hat Rock, Battle Mountain and Emigrant Springs State Parks, Weston Historic District, Frazier Farmstead Museum in Milton-Freewater, North Fork Umatilla Wilderness Area, Tollgate-Spout Springs Recreation Area, Courthouse Clock Tower, Stateline Wind Project, Confederated Tribes of the Umatilla Indian Reservation's Wildhorse Casino and Tamastslikt Cultural Center

Umatilla County traces its creation in 1862 to the regional gold rushes, which spawned the riverport of Umatilla City and brought stockraisers to the lush grasslands.

Although Lewis and Clark and the Oregon Trail pioneers passed through Umatilla County, it did not bloom until the arrival of the railroad in 1881 and the development of dryland wheat farming.

Water in the form of irrigation has been key to economic diversification and growth, most recently in the Hermiston area, where the desert now yields lush watermelons and other products. Tourism is also increasingly important to Umatilla County where "Let-er-Buck" is heard by Pendleton Round-Up crowds.

County Officials: Commissioners—Bill Elfering 2017, Larry Givens 2015, William S. Hansell 2015; Dist. Atty. Daniel R. Primus 2017; Assess. Paul Chalmers; Rec. Mgr. Jean Hemphill; Sheriff Terry Rowan 2017; Surv. Dave Krumbein; Financial Mgr. Robert Pahl; Admin. Serv. Dir. Dan Lonai

Union County

County Seat: Union County Commissioners, 1106 K Ave., La Grande 97850
Phone: 541-963-1001 (General); 541-962-9500, ext. 232 (Court Administrator)
Fax: 541-963-1079
E-mail: rchurch@union-county.org
Web: www.union-county.org
Established: Oct. 14, 1864
Elev. at La Grande: 2,788'
Area: 2,038 sq. mi.
Average Temp.: January 30.9° July 70.4°
Assessed Value: $1,582,852,956
Real Market Value: $3,198,450,880
Annual Precipitation: 18.79"

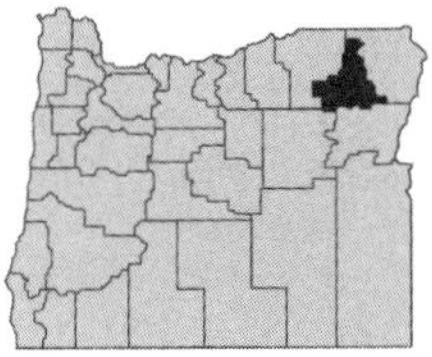

Economy: Agriculture, forest products, education and government
Points of Interest: Meacham and Tollgate winter sports areas, Grande Ronde Valley, Eastern Oregon University (La Grande)

Union County was created in 1864 and named for the town of Union, which had been established two years before and named by its founders for patriotic reasons during the Civil War. The county comprised a part of the northern portion of Baker County and, in 1899, Union County gave up its eastern portion to Wallowa County.

The Grande Ronde Valley in Union County is nearly table flat and is covered with the rich silt of an old lake bed. Highly diversified, with a 160-day growing season and an annual rainfall of twenty inches, the valley boasts of never having had a general crop failure. The county's 1,092 farms average 473 acres a unit.

Union County's front door opens to the rugged Wallowa Mountains. Its back door faces the Blue Mountains, which attract hikers, skiers and hunters.

County Officials: Commissioners—Mark Davidson (R) 2017, William D. Rosholt (R) 2015, Steve McClure (R) 2015; Dist. Atty. Timothy Thompson 2017; Assess. Linda Hill 2017; Clerk Robin Church 2017; Sheriff Boyd Rasmussen 2017; Surv. Rick Robinson 2017; Treas. Donna Marshall 2017; Co. Admin. and Chief Info. Officer Shelley Burgess

Wallowa County

County Seat: Courthouse, 101 S River St., Enterprise 97828
Phone: 541-426-4543 ext. 15 (General); 541-426-4991 (Court Administrator)
Fax: 541-426-0582
E-mail: wcboc@co.wallowa.or.us
Web: www.co.wallowa.or.us
Established: Feb. 11, 1887
Elev. at Enterprise: 3,757'
Area: 3,153 sq. mi.
Average Temp.: January 24.2° July 63.0°

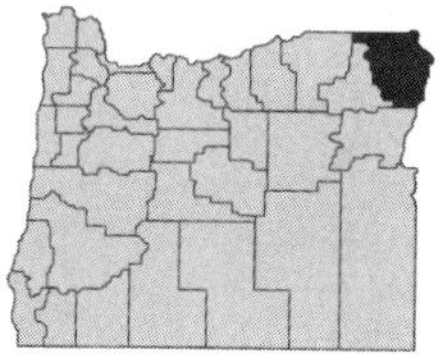

Assessed Value: $663,578,549
Real Market Value: $1,573,337,950
Annual Precipitation: 13.08"
Economy: Agriculture, art, livestock, forest products and recreation
Points of Interest: Wallowa Lake, art galleries, Mt. Howard gondola, Eagle Cap Wilderness, Hells Canyon National Recreation Area, Minam, Wallowa and Grande Ronde Rivers

This rather isolated area was claimed by the Chief Joseph band of the Nez Perce as its hunting and fishing grounds. The Nez Perce used the word "wallowa" to designate a tripod of poles used to support fish nets. In 1871, the first white settlers came to Wallowa County crossing the mountains in search of livestock feed in the Wallowa Valley. The area had been part of Union County since 1864, but it was carved from that county in 1887 by a legislative act.

Wallowa County is a land of rugged mountains, gentle valleys and deep canyons. Peaks in the Wallowa Mountains soar to almost 10,000 feet in elevation and the Snake River dips to about 1,000 feet above sea level. Hells Canyon, carved by the Snake, is the nation's deepest gorge averaging 5,500 feet from rim to river.

The scenery in the county is spectacular and serves as a magnet for tourists. Unrivaled opportunities for outdoor recreation create the county's reputation as a visitors' paradise. Permanent residents enjoy the same recreation opportunities, adding to a high quality of life supported by traditional farm and forest industries, as well as art and tourism.

County Officials: Commissioners—Paul Castilleja (R) 2015, Mike Hayward, Chair (R) 2017, Susan Roberts (R) 2017; Dist. Atty. Mona K. Williams 2015; Assess. Gay Fregulia 2017; Clerk Dana Roberts 2015; Sheriff Steve Rogers 2017; Surv. Richard Shaver; Treas. Shonelle Dutcher-Pryse 2017

Wasco County

County Seat: Courthouse, 511 Washington St., The Dalles 97058
Phone: 541-506-2500 (General); 541-506-2700 (Court Administrator)
Fax: 541-506-2531
E-mail: countyclerk@co.wasco.or.us
Web: www.co.wasco.or.us
Established: Jan. 11, 1854
Elev. at The Dalles: 98'
Area: 2,396 sq. mi.
Average Temp.: January 33.4° July 73.1°

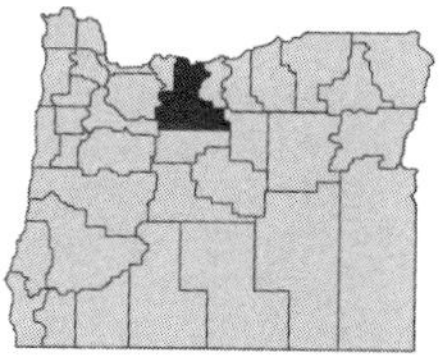

Assessed Value: $1,853,554,229
Real Market Value: $2,654,524,149
Annual Precipitation: 14.9"
Economy: Agriculture, forest products, manufacturing, electric power, aluminum and transportation
Points of Interest: Columbia and Deschutes Rivers, Fort Dalles Museum, Pulpit Rock, The Dalles Dam, Celilo Converter Station, Confederated Tribes of the Warm Springs Reservation and Kah-Nee-Ta Resort, Mt. Hood, Sorosis Park, original Wasco County Courthouse, St. Peter's Landmark and the Columbia River Gorge Discovery Center

When the Territorial Legislature created Wasco County in 1854 from parts of Clackamas, Lane, Linn and Marion Counties, it embraced all of Oregon east of the Cascade Range, most of Idaho and parts of Montana and Wyoming. It was named for the Wasco (or Wascopam) Tribe.

Wasco's county seat is The Dalles. Now the trading hub of north-central Oregon, The Dalles gained earlier fame as the town at the end of the Oregon Trail. Thousands of years before that, humans scratched pictographs on rocks overlooking the Columbia River in this area. Later, tribes gathered for generations near Celilo Falls to trade and fish. The county's tribal heritage continues in evidence today. Kah-Nee-Ta, a popular Oregon resort, is located on the Confederated Tribes of the Warm Springs Reservation in southern Wasco County.

County Officials: Commissioners—Scott Hege 2015, Steve Kramer 2017, Rod Runyon, Chair, 2015; Dist. Atty. Eric Nisley 2017; Assess. Tim Lynn 2017; Clerk Linda Brown 2017; Sheriff Rick Eiesland 2017; Surv. Dan Boldt; Treas. Chad Krause 2017

Washington County

County Seat: 155 N 1st Ave., Suite 300, Hillsboro 97124
Phone: 503-846-8611 (General); 503-846-8888 (Court Administrator)
Fax: 503-846-4545
E-mail: elections@co.washington.or.us
Web: www.co.washington.or.us
Established: July 5, 1843

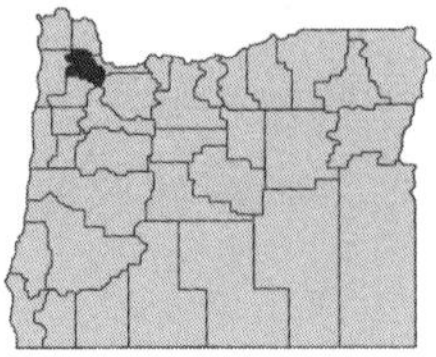

Elev. at Hillsboro: 196'
Area: 727 sq. mi.
Average Temp.: January 39.9° July 66.6°
Assessed Value: $49,355,659,075
Real Market Value: $67,614,912,187
Annual Precipitation: 37.71"
Economy: Agriculture, horticulture, forest products, food processing, high tech, sports equipment and apparel
Points of Interest: Tualatin Valley orchards and vineyards, Pacific University, Wilson River and Sunset Highways, Hagg Lake, Old Scotch Church

The original four counties created by the Provisional Government of Oregon were: Twality, Clackamas, Yamhill and Champoick. Twality was changed to Washington in honor of President George Washington by the Territorial Legislature on September 3, 1849. The actual organization of Washington County government followed several years later.

Now one of the state's fastest developing areas, the fertile Tualatin Valley was once filled with beaver and was a favorite hunting ground for Hudson's Bay Company trappers. The first white settlers arrived around 1840, lured by rich soil. Despite its rapid urbanization, the valley still contains prime agricultural land. Many small towns rich in history dot the area. Pacific University, founded as Tualatin Academy in 1849, is one of the oldest colleges in the West. Washington County operates under a home rule charter approved by voters in 1962. The Northwest's largest enclosed shopping center, Washington Square, is located south of Beaverton.

County Officials: Commissioners—Andy Duyck, Chair 2015, Greg Malinowski 2015, Roy Rogers 2017, Dick Schouten 2017, Bob Terry 2015; Dist. Atty. Robert Hermann 2015; Assess./Clerk Richard Hobernicht; Justice of the Peace James Shartel 2015; Sheriff Pat Garrett 2017; Surv. James Elam; Auditor John Hutzler, 2015; Co. Admin. Robert Davis; Chief Info. Officer Phillip Bransford

Wheeler County

County Seat: Courthouse, 701 Adams St., Fossil 97830
Phone: 541-763-2400 (General); 541-763-2541 (Court Administrator)
Fax: 541-763-2026
E-mail: bsitton@co.wheeler.or.us
Web: www.wheelercounty-oregon.com
Established: Feb. 17, 1899

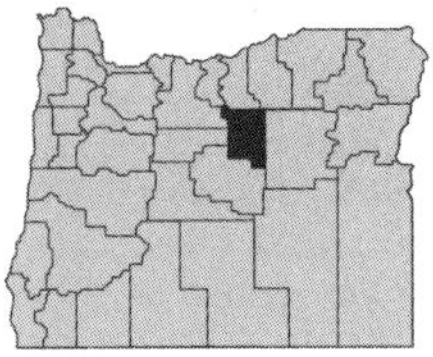

Elev. at Fossil: 2,654'
Area: 1,813 sq. mi.
Average Temp.: January 35° July 66°
Assessed Value: $121,074,005
Real Market Value: $886,328,122
Annual Precipitation: 14.66"
Economy: Livestock and tourism
Points of Interest: Painted Hills, John Day Fossil Beds, John Day River

Wheeler County was formed by the Oregon Legislature in 1899 from parts of Grant, Gilliam and Crook Counties and was named for Henry H. Wheeler, who operated the first mail stage line from The Dalles to Canyon City. The new county consisted of 1,656 square miles with an estimated 46 townships, a population of 1,600 and taxable property worth one million dollars.

Wheeler County is as rugged and uneven as any Oregon county, with the terrain varying widely from sagebrush, juniper and rim rock to stands of pine and fir. Portions of two national forests lie within its boundaries with forest lands covering nearly one-third of the county. The area is probably best known as one of the most outstanding depositories of prehistoric fossils on the North American continent.

County Officials: Commissioners—H. John Asher 2017, Judge Jeanne E. Burch 2017, Chris Perry 2017; Dist. Atty. Daniel Ousley 2017; Assess. Donald R. Cossitt 2015; Clerk Barbara Sitton 2017; Justices of the Peace Linda Keys 2017, Robin Ordway 2015; Sheriff Chris Humphreys 2017; Surv. Robert Bagett 2017; Treas. Nancy L. Misener 2015

Yamhill County

County Seat: Courthouse, 535 NE 5th St., McMinnville 97128
Phone: 503-434-7501 (General); 503-434-7530 (Court Administrator)
Fax: 503-434-7553
Web: www.co.yamhill.or.us
Established: July 5, 1843
Elev. at McMinnville: 157'
Area: 718 sq. mi.
Average Temp.: January 39.0° July 65.0°

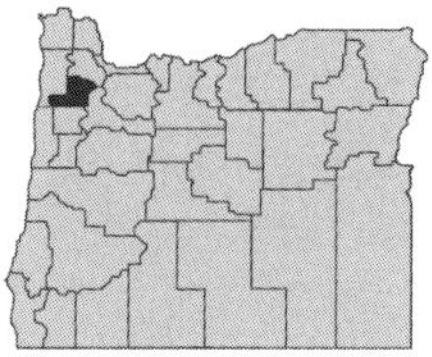

Assessed Value: $7,031,962,167
Real Market Value: $8,911,055,976
Annual Precipitation: 43.6"
Economy: Agriculture, wine production, steel manufacturing, forest products, dental instruments and aircraft servicing
Points of Interest: Linfield College, George Fox University, Herbert Hoover House, military blockhouse, Yamhill County Historical Museum, Wheatland Ferry, Captain Michael Smith Evergreen Aviation and Space Museum, Rogers Landing

Yamhill County was created in 1843 as one of Oregon's original four districts. Its present boundaries were established in 1860. The county was named after the Yamhelas, members of the Kalapuya Tribe, who lived along the Yamhill River in the western Willamette Valley.

Today, agriculture is still the county's primary industry. Nursery and greenhouse crops; fruits, nuts, berries; and hay, silage, field and grass seeds are major agricultural products. Yamhill County ranks sixth out of Oregon's 36 counties in annual market value of its agricultural production. Yamhill County is also the heart of Oregon's wine industry. Thirty-six wineries represent the largest concentration of wineries in any county and produce the greatest number of award-winning wines in the state. A third of the county is covered with commercial timber. The mainstay of the western valley area is logging and timber products. Nonseasonal industries include a steel rolling mill, electronic and dental equipment manufacturing, an international airline and helicopter company, and a newsprint mill.

County Officials: Commissioners—Kathy George Chair (R) 2015, Allen Springer (D) 2017, Mary Stern 2015; Dist. Atty. Bradley Berry 2017; Assess. Scott Maytubby 2017; Clerk Brian Van Bergen 2017; Sheriff Jack Crabtree 2015; Surv. Dan Linscheid 2015; Treas. Michael Green 2017

Regional Governments

The Oregon Regional Councils Association (ORCA), formed in 1984 under ORS Chapter 190, promotes cooperation between levels of government.

The multi-jurisdictional councils are voluntary associations cooperating on issues and problems which cross city, county and, in some cases, state boundaries. The association provides a forum for exchanging and discussing common issues.

Central Oregon Intergovernmental Council

Contact: Tom Moore, Executive Director
Address: 334 NE Hawthorne Ave., Bend 97701
Phone: 541-548-8163
Fax: 541-923-3416
Web: www.coic.org

Lane Council of Governments

Contact: Brenda Wilson, Executive Director
Address: 859 Willamette St., Suite 500, Eugene 97401
Phone: 541-682-4283
Fax: 541-682-4099
Web: www.lcog.org

Mid-Columbia Council of Governments

Contact: John Arens, Executive Director
Address: 1113 Kelly Ave., The Dalles 97058
Phone: 541-298-4101
Fax: 541-298-2084
Web: www.mccog.com

Mid-Willamette Valley Council of Governments

Contact: Nancy Boyer, Executive Director
Address: 100 High St. SE, Salem 97301
Phone: 503-588-6177
Fax: 503-588-6094
Web: www.mwvcog.org

Northwest Senior and Disability Services

Contact: Melinda Compton, Exec. Director (Program)
Rodney Schroeder, Exec. Director (Operations)
Address: 3410 Cherry Ave. NE, Salem 97303
Phone: 503-304-3400; Toll-free: 1-800-469-8772
Fax: 503-304-3434
Web: www.nwsds.org

Oregon Cascades West Council of Governments

Contact: Cynthia Solie, Executive Director
Address: 1400 Queen Ave. SE, Suite 201, Albany 97322
Phone: 541-967-8720
Fax: 541-967-6123
Web: www.ocwcog.org

Rogue Valley Council of Governments

Contact: Michael Cavallaro, Executive Director
Address: 155 N 1st St., PO Box 3275, Central Point 97502
Phone: 541-664-6674
Fax: 541-664-7927
Web: www.rvcog.org

Metro

Contact: Tom Hughes, Council President
Address: Metro Regional Center, 600 NE Grand Ave., Portland 97232-2736
Phone: 503-797-1700
Fax: 503-797-1799
Web: www.oregonmetro.gov

Councilors: Tom Hughes 2014, District 1: Shirley Craddick 2014, District 2: Carlotta Collette 2014, District 3: Craig Dirksen 2016, District 4: Kathryn Harrington 2014, District 5: Sam Chase 2016, District 6: Bob Stacey 2016. Auditor: Suzanne Flynn 2014. The council president and auditor are elected regionally. The remaining six councilors are elected by district. All serve four-year terms. The auditor reviews Metro's operations.

Metro serves nearly 1.5 million people in 467 square miles covering the urban portions of Clackamas, Multnomah and Washington Counties in northwestern Oregon. There are 25 cities in Metro's service area, including Beaverton, Gresham, Hillsboro, Lake Oswego, Milwaukie, Oregon City and Portland.

Metro has primary responsibility for regional land-use and transportation planning and is required to address other issues of "metropolitan concern" that cross jurisdictional boundaries. This grant of authority clearly underscores Metro's commitment to maintain and enhance the livability of the region.

The Metro Council is the only regional governing body in the United States directly elected by the region's voters. The council appoints a chief operating officer to carry out council policies and manage Metro operations. The COO oversees approximately 750 full-time and 1,000 part-time employees, from economists to park rangers and from cartographers to zoo keepers.

History

Metro was formed in 1979 when voters approved the merger of the Columbia Region Association of Governments, which had land-use and transportation planning responsibilities, with the Metropolitan Service District, which provided regional services including solid waste management and operation of a metropolitan zoo. An elected council and executive officer governed the new Metropolitan Service District that operated with its former authority and that of the council of governments. A 1992 charter gave Metro the nation's only elected regional government organized under a home-rule charter approved by voters. The charter was amended in 2000, esblishing the regionally elected office of council president and replacing the elected executive officer with the appointed COO.

In 1980, Metro became responsible for regional solid waste disposal when it took over operation of the one existing publicly owned regional landfill and began construction of a transfer station. In November 1986, voters approved general obligation bond funding for the Oregon Convention Center, built and operated by Metro. In January 1990, Metro assumed management responsibility for the Portland Center for the Performing Arts, Portland Civic Stadium and Portland Memorial Coliseum (although the City of Portland later renegotiated the management of Civic Stadium — now JELD-WEN Field — and Memorial Coliseum through new agreements with private operators). In 1994, Metro assumed management responsibility for the Multnomah County parks system and the Portland Expo Center. Ownership of these facilities was transferred to Metro on July 1, 1996.

In May 1995, voters authorized $135.6 million in general obligation bonds to acquire and protect a regional system of natural areas, parks and streams. In 2006, voters approved another $227.4 million bond measure to continue this work.

In 1996, voters approved a $28.8 million measure to make improvements to the Oregon Zoo, followed by another bond measure in 2008 that authorized $125 million to improve outdated facilities and make the zoo more sustainable.

Funding

About half of Metro's operating revenues come from user fees related to solid waste disposal and waste prevention and from admission fees from Metro's visitor venues. Other revenues include grants, property taxes collected primarily for debt service on voter-approved bond measures, and excise taxes paid on Metro facilities, services and construction activity within the region.

Services

Regional land use and transportation planning and development: The 2040 Growth Concept is the region's long-range plan. It guides urban growth boundary management, efficient use of land, protection of farms, forests and natural areas, a balanced transportation system, a healthy economy supporting the creation of new jobs, and diverse housing options.

Urban growth boundary management: Under Oregon law, Metro manages a single urban growth boundary for the greater Portland metropolitan region. The UGB protects farms and forests outside the boundary, promotes vibrant communities inside the boundary, helps local governments plan the location of public structures, and promotes efficient use of urban land, public facilities and services. Every five years, state law requires the Metro Council to analyze whether the UGB can accommodate the population and employment growth forecast for the next 20 years and, if necessary, to expand the boundary to meet regional needs.

Data Resource Center: Metro offers state-of-the-art mapping, analysis and forecasting tools that are used for everything from locating businesses to planning new transportation projects. The region's local governments rely on and contribute to this data center, eliminating duplication between governments.

Solid waste management and recycling: Metro develops the region's solid waste management plan and manages the disposal of the region's garbage. Metro owns and operates two solid waste and recycling transfer stations and two hazardous waste facilities, and it runs a recycling information hotline. Metro has recycled more than 1 million gallons of latex paint since 1992, saving natural resources and landfill space.

Protecting natural areas: Metro's natural areas program has protected more than 10,000 acres across the Portland metropolitan area. Today, Metro owns and manages a total of 16,000 acres of publicly owned parks and natural areas, more than a third of the region's total. Metro's system of regional parks and natural areas includes Smith and Bybee Lakes Wildlife Area, a 2,000-acre freshwater wetland in North Portland; Oxbow Regional Park, a 1,200-acre forested natural area on the Sandy River east of Gresham, and Graham Oaks Natural Area, a 250-acre area of restored oak woodlands in Wilsonville.

Venues for public gatherings and entertainment: Metro operates the region's public assembly facilities — the Oregon Convention Center, Portland Center for the Performing Arts, and Portland Expo Center – as well as the Oregon Zoo. These venues host hundreds of events each year, drawing millions of people. The Oregon Convention Center generates more than $400 million a year in economic benefit. The zoo has the highest annual attendance of all paid-admissions visitor facilities in Oregon.

Port Districts of Oregon

Port of Alsea, Estab. 1910

Address: 365-A Port St., PO Box 1060, Waldport 97394
Phone: 541-563-3872
Fax: 541-563-8538
Web: www.portofalsea.com

Commissioners: Rob Bishop, Suzanne Groshong, John Johnson, Jan Powers, Joe Smolen; Port Mgr. Maggie Rivers. Meets 3rd Wednesday of the month.

Port of Arlington, Estab. 1933

Address: 100 Island Pkwy., PO Box 279, Arlington 97812
Phone: 541-454-2868
E-mail: portofarlington@gorge.net

Commissioners: Duane Johnson, Dewey Kennedy, Laura Pryor, Timothy Wetherell; Ron Wilson; Exec. Sec. Denise Ball. Meets 2nd Tuesday of the month.

Port of Astoria, Estab. 1914

Address: 10 Pier One Bldg., Ste. 308, (mail to: 10 Pier One, Ste., 103), Astoria 97103
Phone: 503-741-3300
Fax: 503-741-3345
Web: www.portofastoria.com

Commissioners: Jack Bland, Dan Hess, Floyd Holcom, Bill Hunsinger, Larry Pfund; CEO Hank Bynaker. Meets 3rd Tuesday of the month.

Port of Bandon, Estab. 1913

Address: PO Box 206, Bandon 97411
Phone: 541-347-3206
Fax: 541-347-4645
Web: www.portofbandon.com

Commissioners: Wayne Butler, Rick Goche, Donny Goddard, Robert S. Miller III, Reg Pullen; Port Mgr. Gina Dearth; Harbor Master Robert Dearth. Meets 4th Thursday of the month 5:00 p.m.

Port of Brookings Harbor, Estab. 1956

Address: PO Box 848, Brookings 97415
Phone: 541-469-2218
Fax: 541-469-0672
Web: www.port-brookings-harbor.com

Commissioners: Roy Davis, Ted Freeman, Sue Gold, Jim Relaford, Mike Manning, Interim; Exec. Dir. Ted Fitzgerald. Meets 3rd Tuesday of the month.

Port of Cascade Locks, Estab. 1937

Address: PO Box 307, Cascade Locks 97014
Phone: 541-374-8619
Fax: 541-374-8428
Web: www.portofcascadelocks.org

Commissioners: Joeinne Caldwell, Brenda Cramblett, Jesse Groves, Donna Mohr, Samantha Verschuren; Port Mgr. Chuck Daughtry. Meets 1st and 3rd Thursdays of the month.

Port of Coos Bay, Estab. 1909

Address: PO Box 1215, Coos Bay 97420
Phone: 541-267-7678
Fax: 541-269-1475
Web: www.portofcoosbay.com

Commissioners: Jerry Hampel, David Kronsteiner, R. Brady Scott; CEO David Koch. Meets 3rd Thursday of the month.

Port of Garibaldi, Estab. 1910

Address: PO Box 10, Garibaldi 97118
Phone: 503-322-3292
Fax: 503-322-0029
Web: www.portofgaribaldi.org

Commissioners: Kelly Barnett, Robert Browning, Valerie Folkema, John Luquette, David May; Port Mgr. Kevin Greenwood. Meets 2nd Wednesday of the month.

Port of Gold Beach, Estab. 1955

Address: PO Box 1126, Gold Beach 97444
Phone: 541-247-6269
Fax: 541-247-6268
Web: www.portofgoldbeach.com

Commissioners: Lawrence Johnson, Bill McNair, Larry Prestininzi, Charles Riddle, Milt Walker; Port Mgr. Debbie Collins. Meets 3rd Thursday of the month.

Port of Hood River, Estab. 1933

Address: 1000 E Port Marina Dr., Hood River 97031
Phone: 541-386-1645
Fax: 541-386-1395
Web: www.portofhoodriver.com

Commissioners: Jon Davies, Fred Duckwall, Richard McBride, Brian Shortt, Hoby Streich; Exec. Dir. Michael McElwee. Meets 1st and 3rd Tuesdays of the month at 5:00 p.m.

Port of Morrow, Estab. 1958

Address: PO Box 200, Boardman 97818
Phone: 541-481-7678
Fax: 541-481-2679
Web: www.portofmorrow.com

Commissioners: Jerry Healy, Larry Lindsay, Marv Padberg, Don Russell, Joe Taylor; Gen. Mgr. Gary Neal. Meets 2nd Wednesday of the month.

Port of Nehalem, Estab. 1909

Address: 36155 9th St., Rm. 10, PO Box 476, Nehalem 97131-0476
Phone: 503-368-7212
Fax: 503-368-7234
E-mail: portofnehalem@nehalemtel.net

Commissioners: Don Cameron, Rick R. Dart, Deslee Kahrs, Lindy Scovell, Dale Stockton; Adm. Sec. Betty L. Conrad. Meets 4th Wednesday of the month; 3rd Wednesday in November and December.

Port of Newport, Estab. 1910

Address: 600 SE Bay Blvd., Newport 97365
Phone: 541-265-7758
Fax: 541-265-4235
Web: www.portofnewport.com

Commissioners: JoAnn Barton, Walter Chuck, Dean Fleck, David Jincks, Don Mathews; Gen. Mgr. Don Mann. Meets 4th Tuesday of the month.

Port of Port Orford, Estab. 1919

Address: PO Box 490, Port Orford 97465
Phone: 541-332-7121
Fax: 541-332-7121
Web: www.portofportorford.com

Commissioners: Phil Colzzi, Robert Mielenz, Sam Scaffo, Dianne Schofield, Brett Webb; Port Mgr. Gary Anderson. Meets 3rd Tuesday of the month.

Port of Portland, Estab. 1891

Address: 7200 NE Airport Wy., PO Box 3529, Portland 97218
Phone: 503-415-6000; 1-800-547-8411
Web: www.portofportland.com

Commissioners: Peter Bragdon, Jim Carter, Tom Chamberlain, Steven H. Corey, Diana Daggett, Bruce C. Holte, Linda Pearce, Paul Rosenbaum; Exec. Dir. Bill Wyatt. Meets 2nd Wednesday of the month.

Port of St. Helens, Estab. 1941

Address: 100 E St., PO Box 190, Columbia City 97018
Phone: 503-397-2888
Fax: 503-397-6924
Web: www.portsh.org

Commissioners: Mike Avent, Vice President Colleen DeShazer, Chris Iverson, Pres. Robert Keyser, Terry Luttrell; Exec. Dir. Patrick Trapp. Meets 2nd and 4th Wednesdays of the month.

Port of Siuslaw, Estab. 1909

Address: 100 Harbor St., PO Box 1220, Florence 97439
Phone: 541-997-3426
Fax: 541-997-9407
Web: www.portofsiuslaw.com

Commissioners: John Buchanan, William "Bill" Fleenor, Joshua Green, John Scott, Robert Thorp; Port Mgr. Robert Forsythe. Meets 3rd Wednesday of the month.

Port of The Dalles, Estab. 1933

Address: 3636 Klindt Dr., The Dalles 97058
Phone: 541-298-4148
Fax: 541-298-2136
Web: www.portofthedalles.com

Commissioners: Mike Courtney, David Griffith, Kristi McCavic, Bob McFadden, Greg Weast; Exec. Dir. Andrea Klaas. Meets 2nd Wednesday of the month.

Port of Tillamook Bay, Estab. 1953

Address: 4000 Blimp Blvd., Tillamook 97141
Phone: 503-842-2413
Fax: 503-842-3680
Web: www.potb.org

Commissioners: Bill Bartlein, Georgine Beveridge, Carolyn Decker, Bob Olsen, Jim Young; General Mgr. Michele Bradley. Meets 3rd Tuesday of the month.

Port of Toledo, Estab. 1910

Address: 496 NE Hwy. 20, Unit #1, PO Box 428 Toledo 97391-9720
Phone: 541-336-5207
Fax: 541-336-5160
Web: www.portoftoledo.org

Commissioners: Chuck Gerttula, Rick Graff, Gregg Harrison, Michael Kriz, Penny Ryerson; Port Mgr. Bud Shuemake. Meets 3rd Tuesday of the month.

Port of Umatilla, Estab. 1940

Address: PO Box 879, Umatilla 97882
Phone: 541-922-3224
Fax: 541-922-5609
Web: www.portofumatilla.com

Commissioners: Kurt Bendixsen, Tim Mabry, Marjorie Roff, Jerry Simpson, John Turner; Gen. Mgr. Kim Puzey. Meets Tuesday after 1st Wednesday of the month.

Port of Umpqua, Estab. 1913

Address: 1877 Winchester Ave., PO Box 388, Reedsport 97467
Phone: 541-271-2232
Fax: 541-271-2747
Web: www.portofumpqua.net

Commissioners: Barry Nelson, Steve Reese, Jessica Terra, Donna Train, Keith Tymchuk; Port Mgr. Charmaine Vitek. Meets 3rd Wednesday of the month.

Special Service Districts

Contact: Frank Stratton, Executive Director
Address: Special Districts Association of Oregon, PO Box 12613, Salem 97309-0613
Phone: 503-371-8667; Toll-free: 1-800-285-5461
Fax: 503-371-4781
Web: www.sdao.com

ORS 198.010 and 198.335 authorize these 28 types of districts: water control, irrigation, ports, regional air quality control authorities, fire, hospital, mass transit, sanitary districts and authorities, people's utility, domestic water supply districts and authorities, cemetery, park and recreation, metropolitan service, special road, road assessment, highway lighting, health, vector control, water improvement, weather modification, geothermal heating, transportation, county service, chemical control, weed control, emergency communications, diking, and soil and water conservation districts.

Special Districts are financed through property taxes, fees for services, or a combination thereof. Most special districts are directed by a governing body elected by the voters.

Formed in 1979, the Special Districts Association of Oregon (SDAO) provides support services to member districts throughout the state in the areas of research and technical assistance, legislative representation, training programs, insurance services, information and reference materials, financing services, and employee benefits programs.

Transit Districts

Basin Transit Service Transportation District

Contact: Ernest Palmer, General Manager
Address: 1130 Adams St., Klamath Falls 97601
Phone: 541-883-2877
Fax: 541-884-6287
Web: http://www.basintransit.com

Grant County Transportation District

Contact: Jim Sanders, Chair
Address: PO Box 126, John Day 97845
Phone: 541-575-2370
Fax: 541-575-2721

Hood River County Transportation District

Contact: Dan Schwanz, Executive Director
Address: 224 Wasco Loop, PO Box 1147, Hood River 97031
Phone: 541-386-4202
Fax: 541-386-1228
Web: http://community.gorge.net/hrctd/

Lane Transit District

Contact: Ron Kilcoyne, General Manager
Address: PO Box 7070, Springfield 97475
Phone: 541-682-6100
Fax: 541-682-6111
Web: www.ltd.org/

Lincoln County Transit

Contact: Cynda Bruce, General Manager
Address: 410 NE Harney St., Newport 97365
Phone: 541-265-4900
Fax: 541-574-1296
Web: www.co.lincoln.or.us/transit/index.html

Rogue Valley Transportation District

Contact: Julie A. Brown, General Manager
Address: 3200 Crater Lake Ave., Medford 97504
Phone: 541-779-5821
Fax: 541-773-2877
Web: www.rvtd.org/

Salem Area Mass Transit District

Contact: Allan Pollock, General Manager
Address: 925 Commercial St. SE, Suite 100, Salem 97302
Phone: 503-588-2424
Fax: 503-566-3933
Web: www.cherriots.org/

South Clackamas Transportation District

Contact: Shirley Lyons, Manager
Address: PO Box 517, Molalla 97038
Phone: 503-632-7000
Fax: 503-632-5214
Web: www.southclackamastransportation.com/

Sunset Empire Transportation District

Contact: Jay Flint, Executive Director
Address: 465 NE Skipanon Dr., Warrenton 97146
Phone: 503-861-7433
Fax: 503-861-4299
Web: www.ridethebus.org/

Tillamook County Transportation District

Contact: Doug Pilant, General Manager
Address: 3600 Third St., Tillamook 97141
Phone: 503-815-8283
Fax: 503-815-2834

Tri-County Metropolitan Transportation District of Oregon (TriMet)

Contact: Neil McFarlane, General Manager
Address: 4012 SE 17th Ave., Portland 97202
Phone: 503-962-7505
Fax: 503-962-6451
Web: www.trimet.org/

Elections and Records

The "Over the Top" Doughboy statue by John Paulding honors 75,000 Americans who died in France during WWI. It is located in Veterans' Heritage Park in Salem—Oregon State Archives Scenic Photograph marPICT0002

The "Oregon System"—procedures for initiative, referendum and recall—gained Oregon national recognition for the degree of citizen involvement in the processes of self-government. Most recently, vote-by-mail has drawn national attention to Oregon. This detailed history of elections in Oregon illustrates the tangible results of participation in our government.

Voting and Voter Registration

Source: Office of the Secretary of State, Elections Division
Address: 255 Capitol St. NE, Suite 501, Salem 97310
Phone: 503-986-1518
Web: www.oregonvotes.gov

Elections in Oregon

All regular elections in Oregon are held on one of four days each year, except in cases of emergency. The election days are:

- the second Tuesday in March,
- the third Tuesday in May,
- the third Tuesday in September, and
- the first Tuesday after the first Monday in November.

Elections are conducted by mail. Voters who are registered as of the 21st day before an election are mailed a ballot to vote and return by election day. The use of vote-by-mail was first approved on a limited basis by the Legislature in 1981 and was made a permanent feature of some elections in 1987.

In 1998, Oregon voters amended state law to require that the primary and general elections in May and November of even-numbered years also be conducted through vote-by-mail. Beginning in 2000, primary and general elections have been conducted by mail. In 2007, the Legislature provided that all elections will be conducted by mail. At the primary election, voters who are registered in the major political parties, currently the Democratic and Republican parties, nominate candidates to run in the general election. All voters may vote on nonpartisan contests, such as judicial elections, which are also held at the primary election. Most statewide ballot measures are on the general election ballot.

Registering to Vote

Registration by mail was authorized by the 1975 Legislature and is now the method most people use to register to vote in Oregon. Forms are located in most banks and public buildings, in every county elections office and in many state agencies. Forms also can be obtained from the Office of the Secretary of State, Elections Division, 255 Capitol St. NE, Suite 501, Salem 97310.

Date of Election	**Deadline to Register***
March 12, 2013	February 19, 2013
May 21, 2013	April 30, 2013
September 17, 2013	August 27, 2013
November 5, 2013	October 15, 2013

*A voter registration card received in an elections office after the deadline date meets the registration deadline if it has a timely, valid postmark.

The federal Help America Vote Act of 2002 provided new, nationwide voter registration requirements for voting in federal elections.

To register to vote, a person must be a resident of Oregon and be able to answer "yes" to the following questions on the voter registration card:

- "Are you a citizen of the United States of America?" and
- "Are you at least 17 years of age?"

If you are 17 years of age, you will not receive a ballot until an election occurs on or after your 18th birthday. The 2007 Legislature passed HB 2910 to allow an otherwise qualified person, who is at least 17 years of age, to register to vote.

New laws require that people must provide identifying information to register to vote. A person registering to vote is asked to provide identification only if they are a new registrant in the state. Identification is not required for updates. As of January 1, 2006, individuals must provide a current, valid Oregon Driver and Motor Vehicles (DMV) Driver License or identification (ID) card. If the individual does not have a current, valid Oregon DMV Driver License/ID, the last four digits of the individual's Social Security number must be provided. If the individual has neither a current, valid Oregon DMV Driver License/ID nor a Social Security number, the individual must affirm this and, if they are registering by mail, must provide a copy of one of the following:

- valid photo identification,
- paycheck stub,
- utility bill,
- bank statement,
- government document or
- proof of eligibility under the Uniformed and Overseas Citizens Absentee Voting Act or the Voting Accessibility for the Elderly and Handicapped Act.

If identification is not provided at the time of registration, it will be requested by election officials in order for the person to vote at the next federal election.

Oregon residents who are not U.S. citizens by the deadline to register to vote, but who will be citizens by election day, should contact their county elections office for information about how to register to vote.

Persons who become residents of Oregon after the deadline to register for a U.S. presidential election may be eligible to vote for U.S. president and vice president. Contact your county elections office for more information.

Important! Persons registered to vote in other states may not transfer their voter registration to Oregon. To register to vote in Oregon, a person must complete either an Oregon voter registration card or a Federal Postcard Application, which is available in most states.

How to Maintain a Current Voter Registration

Registered voters must notify their county elections office in writing if:

- their residence or mailing address changes,
- their name changes or
- they wish to change political party affiliation.

A voter may notify county elections officials of changes to the above by sending a new voter registration card to the appropriate county.

A voter may update voter registration information as late as election day and vote in that election.

If a voter has moved from one county in Oregon to another, the voter should fill out a voter registration card and send it to the new county elections office. If the voter registration card is sent after the 21st day before an election, the voter should call the county elections official to find out how to receive a ballot for that election.

Voting Absentee

Absentee ballots are mailed to military and other out-of-state voters in advance of the regular mailing of ballots. Voters should contact their local elections office to obtain an absentee ballot.

Voters' Pamphlets

For each primary and general election and for most special elections, the Elections Division produces and distributes to every household one or more pamphlets containing information about candidates and measures that will appear on the ballot at the election. Many county elections offices also produce pamphlets that contain information about local candidates and measures.

2014 Filing Deadlines

- The candidate filing period for the May 20, 2014 primary election begins on September 12, 2013 and ends on March 11, 2014. The deadline for filing *Voters' Pamphlet* material with the state Elections Division is March 13, 2014.
- The candidate filing period for the November 4, 2014 general election begins on June 4, 2014 and ends on August 26, 2014. The deadline for filing *Voters' Pamphlet* material with the state Elections Division is August 26, 2014.

Recent Election History

2012 Special Election

Election Date: January 31, 2012

Source: *Abstracts of Votes,* available from the Office of the Secretary of State, Elections Division, 255 Capitol St. NE, Suite 501, Salem 97310

Web: www.oregonvotes.gov

Key: *Elected; D = Democratic Party; L = Libertarian Party; P = Progressive Party; R = Republican Party

United States Representative

1st Congressional District

	Total
Bonamici, Suzanne—D*	113,404
Cornilles, Rob—R	83,396
Foster. James—L	6,618
Reynolds, Steve—P	6,798
Miscellaneous	547

2012 Primary Election

Election Date: May 15, 2012

Source: *Abstracts of Votes,* available from the Office of the Secretary of State, Elections Division, 255 Capitol St. NE, Suite 501, Salem 97310

Web: www.oregonvotes.gov

Key: *Nominated; **Elected; WI = Write In

United States President

Democrat	**Total**
Obama, Barack*	309,358
Miscellaneous	16,998
Republican	
Gingrich, Newt	15,451
Paul, Ron	36,810
Romney, Mitt*	204,176
Santorum, Rick	27,042
Miscellaneous	4,476

United States Representative

1st Congressional District

Democrat	**Total**
Bonamici, Suzanne*	57,146
Miscellaneous	608
Republican	
Michaels, Lisa	14,274
Morgan, Delinda*	18,996
Miscellaneous	447

2nd Congressional District

Democrat	**Total**
Segers, Joyce B.*	31,157
Sweeney, John	8,825
Miscellaneous	751
Republican	
Walden, Greg*	77,498
Miscellaneous	581

3rd Congressional District

Democrat	**Total**
Blumenauer, Earl*	84,628
Miscellaneous	969
Republican	
Green, Ronald*	14,844
Lopez, Delia	8,237
Miscellaneous	424

4th Congressional District

Democrat	Total
DeFazio, Peter A.*	69,864
Robinson, Matthew L.	7,665
Miscellaneous	212
Republican	
Robinson, Art*	50,090
Miscellaneous	1,414

5th Congressional District

Democrat	Total
Schrader, Kurt*	51,652
Miscellaneous	805
Republican	
Thompson, Fred*	33,448
Bowerman, Karen	16,174
Miscellaneous	320

Secretary of State

Democrat	Total
Brown, Kate*	284,470
Wells, Paul Damian	26,177
Miscellaneous	1,510
Republican	
Buehler, Knute*	199,179
Miscellaneous	4,558

State Treasurer

Democrat	Total
Wheeler, Ted*	272,278
Miscellaneous	1,365
Republican	
Cox, Thomas B. (WI)*	12,885
Miscellaneous	11,337

Attorney General

Democrat	Total
Holton, Dwight	110,891
Rosenblum, Ellen*	202,935
Miscellaneous	657
Republican	
Buchal, James L. (WI)*	12,816
Miscellaneous	12,622

Judge of the Supreme Court

Nonpartisan — Total

Position 2

Brewer, Dave**	439,042
Miscellaneous	3,857

Position 3

Baldwin, Richard C.*	165,687
Cook, Nena*	196,161
Sercombe, Timothy J.	162,033
Miscellaneous	2,772

Position 6

Linder, Virginia L.**	415,738
Miscellaneous	5,107

Judge of the Court of Appeals

Nonpartisan — Total

Position 5

Haselton, Rick**	408,689
Miscellaneous	3,886

Position 6

Arlow, Allan J.	103,844
Egan, James C.*	226,518
Volpert, Tim*	166,079
Miscellaneous	2,614

Position 8

Nakamoto, Lynn R.**	422,598
Miscellaneous	3,857

Position 9

Hadlock, Erika**	417,733
Miscellaneous	3,775

Position 10

Armstrong, Rex**	406,111
Miscellaneous	3,782

Judge of the Circuit Court

Nonpartisan — Total

1st District—Position 5

Gerking, Timothy**	23,775
Miscellaneous	123

1st District—Position 9

Grensky, Ron**	25,794
Miscellaneous	218

2nd District—Position 1

Rasmussen, Karsten H.**	39,457
Miscellaneous	332

2nd District—Position 10

Mooney, Josephine**	37,832
Miscellaneous	286

2nd District—Position 13

Carlson, Cynthia D.**	37,873
Miscellaneous	298

2nd District—Position 14

Vogt, Debra K.**	39,083
Miscellaneous	343

3rd District—Position 1

Rhoades, Jamese**	28,398
Miscellaneous	279

3rd District—Position 3

Norblad, Albin W.**	29,443
Miscellaneous	440

3rd District—Position 7

Graves, Dennis J.**	28,698
Miscellaneous	259

3rd District—Position 11

Bennett, Channing	16,373
Abar, Donald D.**	18,012
Miscellaneous	155

4th District—Position 3

Hodson, Jerry B.**	71,044
Miscellaneous	1,033

4th District—Position 4

Nelson, Adrienne**	74,220
Miscellaneous	963

4th District—Position 7

LaBarre, Jerome**	71,278
Miscellaneous	1,132

4th District—Position 8

Bergstrom, Eric J.**	71,663
Miscellaneous	992

4th District—Position 12

Wilson, Janice R.**	72,187
Miscellaneous	966

4th District—Position 16

Svetkey, Susan M.**	72,734
Miscellaneous	912

4th District—Position 23

Jones, Edward**	70,810
Miscellaneous	994

4th District—Position 28

Matarazzo, Judith Hudson**	71,389
Miscellaneous	939

4th District—Position 29

Villa-Smith, Kathryn**	70,773
Miscellaneous	925

4th District—Position 31

Albrecht, Cheryl**	71,608
Miscellaneous	919

4th District—Position 32

Wyatt, Merri Souther**	71,357
Miscellaneous	1,033

4th District—Position 35

Kurshner, Paula J.**	71,359
Miscellaneous	1,009

4th District—Position 37

Roberts, Leslie**	70,710
Miscellaneous	1,129

5th District—Position 1

Jones, Jeffrey S.**	40,999
Miscellaneous	287

5th District—Position 3

Shepley, Wm. Bruce	22,967
Wetzel, Mike**	28,104
Miscellaneous	175

5th District—Position 8

Maurer, Steven L.**	40,018
Miscellaneous	339

5th District—Position 11

Norby, Susie L.**	41,482
Miscellaneous	361

6th District—Position 5

Brauer, Christopher R.**	8,950
Miscellaneous	86

8th District—Position 1

Baxter, Gregory L.**	3,389
Miscellaneous	32

9th District—Position 1

Sullivan, Patricia**	4,880
Miscellaneous	68

11th District—Position 1

Brady, Alta Jean**	20,499
Miscellaneous	173

11th District—Position 2

Bagley, Beth*	9,815
Balyeat, Andrew C.*	7,356
Brenneman, Aaron	3,500
Spear, Jr., Thomas M.	4,195
Miscellaneous	51

12th District—Position 1

Avera, Sally**	6,861
Butterfield, Stan	6,337
Miscellaneous	27

14th District—Position 1

Hull, Thomas M.**	14,176
Miscellaneous	212

14th District—Position 2

Walker, Victory D.**	4,669
Wolke, Pat**	14,420
Miscellaneous	94

15th District—Position 3

Margolis, Jesse C.**	13,880
Miscellaneous	148

15th District—Position 5

Bechtold, Paula M.**	14,578
Miscellaneous	160

16th District—Position 5

Ambrosini, George**	18,062
Miscellaneous	204

17th District—Position 2

Sanders, Paulette E.**	7,222
Miscellaneous	72

17th District—Position 3

Branford, Thomas O.**	7,302
Miscellaneous	61

18th District—Position 3

Matyas, Cindee S.**	6,633
Miscellaneous	98

20th District—Position 3

Letourneau, Donald R.**	43,381
Miscellaneous	371

20th District—Position 6

Bailey, D. Charles**	43,043
Miscellaneous	335

20th District—Position 12

Cobb, Rita Batz**	44,964
Miscellaneous	312

20th District—Position 13

Fun, Jim**	43,344
Miscellaneous	316

23rd District—Position 3

Murphy, Daniel R.**	11,507
Miscellaneous	100

23rd District—Position 4

Novotny, DeAnn L.**	11,263
Miscellaneous	87

25th District—Position 2

Stone, Ronald W.**	13,008
Miscellaneous	118

2012 General Election

Election Date: November 6, 2012

Source: *Abstracts of Votes,* available from the Office of the Secretary of State, Elections Division, 255 Capitol St. NE, Suite 501, Salem 97310

Web: www.oregonvotes.gov

Key: *Elected; WI = Write In
C = Constitution Party
D = Democratic Party
L = Libertarian Party
P = Progressive Party
PG = Pacific Green Party
R = Republican Party

United States President

	Total
Anderson, Ross C. (Rocky)—P	3,384
Christensen, Will—C	4,432
Johnson, Gary—L	24,089
Obama, Barack—D*	970,488
Romney, Mitt—R	754,175
Stein, Jill—PG	19,427
Miscellaneous	13,275

United States Representative

1st Congressional District

	Total
Bonamici, Suzanne—D*	197,845
Ekstrom, Bob—C	8,918
Morgan, Delinda—R	109,699
Reynolds, Steven—P	15,009
Miscellaneous	509

2nd Congressional District

	Total
Segers, Joyce B.—D	96,741
Tabor, Joe—L	7,025
Walden, Greg—R*	228,043
Miscellaneous	446

3rd Congressional District

	Total
Blumenauer, Earl—D*	264,979
Broadnax, Woodrow—PG	13,159
Cline, Michael—L	6,640
Green, Ronald—R	70,325
Miscellaneous	772

4th Congressional District

	Total
DeFazio, Peter A.—D*	212,866
Huntting, Chuck—L	6,205
Robinson, Art—R	140,549
Miscellaneous	468

5th Congressional District

	Total
Baldwin, Raymond—C	3,600
Lugo, Christina Jean—PG	7,516
Schrader, Kurt—D*	177,229
Thompson, Fred—R	139,223
Miscellaneous	402

Secretary of State

	Total
Brown, Kate—D*	863,656
Buehler, Knute—R	727,607
Knight, Bruce Alexander—L	24,273
Wolfe, Robert—P	21,783
Woolley, Seth—PG	44,235
Miscellaneous	2,561

State Treasurer

	Total
Cox, Tom—R	609,989
Mahler, John F.—L	30,002
Marsh, Michael Paul—C	15,415
Wheeler, Ted—D*	955,213
Whitten, Cameron—P	38,762
Miscellaneous	2,181

Attorney General

	Total
Buchal, James L.—R	639,363
Henry, Chris—P	28,187
Leuenberger, James E.—C	45,451
Rosenblum, Ellen—D*	917,627
Miscellaneous	2,975

Commissioner of the Bureau of Labor and Industries

Nonpartisan	**Total**
Avakian, Brad*	681,987
Starr, Bruce	606,735
Miscellaneous	9,616

Judge of the Supreme Court

Nonpartisan	Total
Position 3	
Baldwin, Richard C.*	641,605
Cook, Nena	606,689
Miscellaneous	9,148

Judge of the Court of Appeals

Nonpartisan	Total
Position 6	
Egan, James C.*	688,939
Volpert, Tim	489,022
Miscellaneous	8,846

Judge of the Circuit Court

Nonpartisan	Total
1st District—Position 7	
Bloom, Benjamin M.*	37,863
Orr, David	34,577
Miscellaneous	195
2nd District—Position 7	
McAlpin, Jay (WI)*	21,152
Miscellaneous	18,133
2nd District—Position 8	
Love, Valeri L.*	76,141
Miscellaneous	1,552
2nd District—Position 12	
Conover, R. Curtis*	71,480
Miscellaneous	1,365
3rd District—Position 5	
Day, Vance D.*	74,640
Miscellaneous	1,151
3rd District—Position 8	
Leith, David E.*	70,448
Miscellaneous	1,063
3rd District—Position 10	
Partridge, Lindsay*	72,287
Miscellaneous	993
3rd District—Position 12	
Geyer, Courtland*	72,329
Miscellaneous	962
6th District—Position 1	
Hampton, Lynn W.*	13,173
Lieuallen, Jon	10,708
Miscellaneous	34
6th District—Position 4	
Temple. Eva J.*	17,298
Miscellaneous	175
7th District—Position 1	
Olson, John A.*	12,937
Miscellaneous	190
9th District—Position 2	
Hung, Lung S.*	6,957
Zanotelli, Brian	2,020
Miscellaneous	10
10th District—Position 1	
Dretke, Brian C.*	9,545
Miscellaneous	148
11th District—Position 2	
Bagley, Beth*	32,959
Balyeat, Andy	27,733
Miscellaneous	179
11th District—Position 3	
DeHoog, Roger J.*	38,564
Miscellaneous	544
12th District—Position 3	
Hill, Norman R.*	19,849
Tipton, Gerald R.	6,304
Miscellaneous	117
20th District—Position 9	
Garcia, Oscar*	125,861
Miscellaneous	2,210
20th District—Position 11	
Factora Wipper, Janelle*	117,188
Miscellaneous	2,073
22nd District—Position 1	
Hillman, Annette C.*	10,386
Miscellaneous	168

Elections and Records

Voter Participation 1982–2012

***Presidential election year**

Primary Election

Year	Registered Voters	Voted	Percent
1982	1,437,693	669,529	46.6
1984*	1,457,067	767,565	52.7
1986	1,458,300	693,821	47.6
1988*	1,366,294	753,112	55.1
1990	1,437,462	660,990	46.0

Year	Registered Voters	Voted	Percent
1992*	1,543,353	758,459	49.1
1994	1,730,562	661,717	38.2
1996*	1,851,499	698,990	37.8
1998	1,906,677	665,340	34.9
2000*	1,808,080	927,351	51.3
2002	1,839,072	858,524	46.6
2004*	1,862,919	864,833	46.4
2006	1,965,939	758,393	38.6
2008*	2,008,957	1,170,526	58.3
2010	2,033,951	846,515	41.6
2012*	2,021,263	787,847	38.9

General Election

Year	Registered Voters	Voted	Percent
1982	1,516,589	1,063,913	70.2
1984*	1,608,693	1,265,824	78.7
1986	1,502,244	1,088,140	72.4
1988*	1,528,478	1,235,199	80.8
1990	1,476,500	1,133,125	76.7
1992*	1,775,416	1,498,959	84.4
1994	1,832,774	1,254,265	68.4
1996*	1,962,155	1,399,180	71.3
1998	1,965,981	1,160,400	59.0
2000*	1,954,006	1,559,215	79.8
2002	1,872,615	1,293,756	69.1
2004*	2,141,243	1,851,593	86.5
2006	1,976,669	1,399,650	70.8
2008*	2,153,914	1,845,251	85.7
2010	2,068,798	1,487,210	71.9
2012*	2,199,360	1,820,507	82.8

Voter Registration by County—November 6, 2012

County	Democrat	Republican	*Nonaffiliated	**Other	Total
Baker	2,600	4,735	2,196	636	10,167
Benton	22,497	14,331	12,133	3,338	52,229
Clackamas	86,498	79,442	48,709	14,792	229,441
Clatsop	8,907	6,325	5,019	1,437	21,688
Columbia	11,889	8,758	6,496	1,906	29,049
Coos	13,097	12,355	7,033	2,434	34,919
Crook	3,326	5,632	2,431	901	12,290
Curry	4,339	5,702	2,707	1,110	13,858
Deschutes	31,118	36,777	21,334	8,107	97,336
Douglas	18,770	27,685	11,701	4,426	62,582
Gilliam	351	574	236	79	1,240
Grant	1,084	2,332	826	259	4,501
Harney	996	2,269	838	189	4,292
Hood River	4,918	3,111	2,877	751	11,657
Jackson	40,343	45,299	25,138	9,238	120,018
Jefferson	3,193	4,006	2,073	770	10,042
Josephine	14,551	21,817	11,170	4,318	51,856
Klamath	8,841	16,945	6,564	2,327	34,677
Lake	939	2,364	680	262	4,245
Lane	93,325	58,887	46,969	15,757	214,938
Lincoln	11,727	7,445	6,514	1,917	27,603
Linn	20,417	24,681	13,844	4,417	63,359
Malheur	2,840	6,208	2,891	553	12,492
Marion	54,132	55,913	31,588	9,775	151,408
Morrow	1,405	2,023	1,174	332	4,934
Multnomah	237,218	69,624	107,259	32,139	446,240

County	Democrat	Republican	*Nonaffiliated	**Other	Total
Polk	15,004	16,942	9,105	2,573	43,624
Sherman	348	598	222	52	1,220
Tillamook	6,012	4,912	3,135	938	14,997
Umatilla	9,113	13,411	8,207	2,380	33,111
Union	4,241	7,190	3,181	1,038	15,650
Wallowa	1,279	2,536	823	229	4,867
Wasco	5,089	4,540	3,083	843	13,555
Washington	114,613	89,150	71,102	17,571	292,436
Wheeler	280	432	194	50	956
Yamhill	17,061	19,907	11,297	3,548	51,813
Totals	**872,361**	**684,858**	**490,749**	**151,392**	**2,199,360**

*A "Nonaffiliated" voter is one who has chosen not to be a member of any political party and has indicated this on his or her voter registration card.

**"Other" includes all voters registered with minor political parties.

Oregon Election History

Voter Registration for General Elections 1950–2012

Year	Democrat	Republican	Other	Total
1950	378,357	361,158	11,755	751,270
1952	416,589	421,681	13,246	851,516
1954	402,283	404,694	12,562	819,539
1956	451,179	413,659	13,114	877,952
1958	447,198	395,089	12,759	855,046
1960	480,588	405,195	14,833	900,616
1962	473,561	395,351	14,778	883,690
1964	511,973	402,336	18,152	932,461
1966	518,228	412,586	19,011	949,825
1968	530,074	420,943	20,834	971,851
1970	521,662	410,693	23,104	955,459
1972	673,710	473,907	50,059	1,197,676
1974	652,414	439,667	50,992	1,143,073
1976	794,218	497,297	128,631	1,420,146
1978	808,182	511,621	163,536	1,482,339
1980	784,129	564,771	220,322	1,569,222
1982	751,100	551,718	213,771	1,516,589
1984	792,208	594,387	222,098	1,608,693
1986	728,177	587,154	186,913	1,502,244
1988	737,489	590,648	200,341	1,528,478
1990	692,100	570,933	213,467	1,476,500
1992	792,551	642,206	340,659	1,775,416
1994	786,990	665,956	379,828	1,832,774
1996	805,286	714,548	442,321	1,962,155
1998	791,970	704,593	469,418	1,965,981
2000	769,195	699,179	485,632	1,954,006
2002	729,460	680,444	462,711	1,872,615
2004	829,193	761,715	550,335	2,141,243
2006	767,562	706,365	502,742	1,976,669
2008	929,741	695,677	528,496	2,153,914
2010	863,322	664,123	541,353	2,068,798
2012	872,361	684,858	642,141	2,199,360

Votes Cast in Oregon for United States President 1860–2012

Key: *Elected; **Received highest vote in Oregon but lost election nationwide

Year	Candidate	Party	Votes
1860	John Bell	Constitutional Union	212
	John C. Breckenridge	Democrat	5,074
	Stephen Douglas	Douglas Democrat	4,131
	Abraham Lincoln*	Republican	5,344

Year	Candidate	Party	Votes
1864	Abraham Lincoln*	Republican	9,888
	George McClellan	Democrat	8,457
1868	U.S. Grant*	Republican	10,961
	Horatio Seymour**	Democrat	11,125
1872	U.S. Grant*	Republican	11,818
	Horace Greeley	Democrat-Liberal Republicans	7,742
	Charles O'Connor	National Labor Reformers	587
1876	Peter Cooper	Greenback	510
	Rutherford B. Hayes*	Republican	15,214
	Samuel Tilden	Democrat	14,157
1880	James A. Garfield*	Republican	20,619
	Winfield Hancock	Democrat	19,955
	James B. Weaver	Greenback Labor	249
1884	James G. Blaine**	Republican	26,860
	General B.F. Butler	Greenback Labor (Workingman)	726
	Grover Cleveland*	Democrat	24,604
	John P. St. John	Prohibition	492
1888	Grover Cleveland	Democrat	26,522
	Robert H. Cowdrey	United Labor	363
	Clinton B. Fisk	Prohibition	1,677
	Benjamin Harrison*	Republican	33,291
1892	John Bidwell	Prohibition	2,281
	Grover Cleveland*	Democrat	14,243
	Benjamin Harrison**	Republican	35,002
	James B. Weaver[1]	Populist	26,965
1896	William J. Bryan	Democrat, People's Party and Silver Republican	46,739
	Joshua Levering	Prohibition	919
	William McKinley*	Republican	48,779
	John M. Palmer	National (Gold) Democrat	977
1900	Wharton Barker	Regular People's	275
	William J. Bryan	Democrat People's	33,385
	Eugene V. Debs	Social-Democrats	1,494
	William McKinley*	Republican	46,526
	John G. Woolley	Prohibition	2,536
1904	Eugene V. Debs	Socialist	7,619
	Alton Parker	Democrat	17,327
	Theodore Roosevelt*	Republican	60,455
	Silas C. Swallow	Prohibition	3,806
	Thomas E. Watson	People's	753
1908	William J. Bryan	Democrat	38,049
	Eugene W. Chafin	Prohibition	2,682
	Eugene V. Debs	Socialist	7,339
	Thomas L. Hisgen	Independence	289
	William H. Taft*	Republican	62,530
1912	Eugene W. Chafin	Prohibition	4,360
	Eugene V. Debs	Socialist	13,343
	Theodore Roosevelt	Progressive	37,600
	William H. Taft	Republican	34,673
	Woodrow Wilson*	Democrat	47,064
1916	Allan L. Benson	Socialist	9,711
	J. Frank Hanley	Prohibition	4,729
	Charles Evans Hughes**	Republican	126,813
	John M. Parker[2]	Progressive	310
	Woodrow Wilson*	Democrat	120,087
1920	James M. Cox	Democrat	80,019
	William W. Cox	Industrial Labor	1,515
	Eugene V. Debs	Socialist	9,801
	Warren G. Harding*	Republican	143,592
	Aaron S. Watkins	Prohibition	3,595

Year	Candidate	Party	Votes
1924	Calvin Coolidge*	Republican	142,579
	John W. Davis	Democrat	67,589
	Frank T. Johns	Socialist Labor	917
	Robert M. LaFollette	Independent	68,403
1928	William Z. Foster	Independent	1,094
	Herbert Hoover*	Republican	205,341
	Verne L. Reynolds	Socialist Labor	1,564
	Alfred E. Smith	Democrat	109,223
	Norman Thomas	Socialist Principles-Independent	2,720
1932	William Z. Foster	Communist	1,681
	Herbert Hoover	Republican	136,019
	Verne L. Reynolds	Socialist Labor	1,730
	Franklin D. Roosevelt*	Democrat	213,871
	Norman Thomas	Socialist	15,450
1936	John W. Aiken	Socialist Labor	500
	Alfred M. Landon	Republican	122,706
	William Lemke	Independent	21,831
	Franklin D. Roosevelt*	Democrat	266,733
	Norman Thomas	Independent	2,143
1940	John W. Aiken	Socialist Labor	2,487
	Franklin D. Roosevelt*	Democrat	258,415
	Wendell L. Willkie	Republican	219,555
1944	Thomas E. Dewey	Republican	225,365
	Franklin D. Roosevelt*	Democrat	248,635
	Norman Thomas	Independent	3,785
	Claude A. Watson	Independent	2,362
1948	Thomas E. Dewey**	Republican	260,904
	Norman Thomas	Independent	5,051
	Harry S. Truman*	Democrat	243,147
	Henry A. Wallace	Progressive	14,978
1952	Dwight D. Eisenhower*	Republican	420,815
	Vincent Hallinan	Independent	3,665
	Adlai Stevenson	Democrat	270,579
1956	Dwight D. Eisenhower*	Republican	406,393
	Adlai Stevenson	Democrat	329,204
1960	John F. Kennedy*	Democrat	367,402
	Richard M. Nixon**	Republican	408,060
1964	Barry M. Goldwater	Republican	282,779
	Lyndon B. Johnson*	Democrat	501,017
1968	Hubert H. Humphrey	Democrat	358,866
	Richard M. Nixon*	Republican	408,433
	George C. Wallace	Independent	49,683
1972	George S. McGovern	Democrat	392,760
	Richard M. Nixon*	Republican	486,686
	John G. Schmitz	Independent	46,211
1976	Jimmy Carter*	Democrat	490,407
	Gerald Ford**	Republican	492,120
	Eugene J. McCarthy	Independent	40,207
1980	John Anderson	Independent	112,389
	Jimmy Carter	Democrat	456,890
	Ed Clark	Libertarian	25,838
	Barry Commoner	Independent	13,642
	Ronald Reagan*	Republican	571,044
1984	Walter F. Mondale	Democrat	536,479
	Ronald Reagan*	Republican	685,700
1988	George Bush*	Republican	560,126
	Michael S. Dukakis**	Democrat	616,206
	Lenora B. Fulani	Independent	6,487
	Ron Paul	Libertarian	14,811

1992	George Bush	Republican	475,757
	Bill Clinton*	Democrat	621,314
	Lenora Fulani	New Alliance Party	3,030
	Andre Marrou	Libertarian	4,277
	Ross Perot	Independent Initiative Party of Oregon	354,091
1996	Harry Browne	Libertarian	8,903
	Bill Clinton*	Democrat	649,641
	Bob Dole	Republican	538,152
	John Hagelin	Natural Law	2,798
	Mary Cal Hollis	Socialist	1,922
	Ralph Nader	Pacific	49,415
	Ross Perot	Reform	121,221
	Howard Phillips	U.S. Taxpayers	3,379
2000	Harry Browne	Libertarian	7,447
	Patrick J. Buchanan	Independent	7,063
	George W. Bush*	Republican	713,577
	Al Gore**	Democrat	720,342
	John Hagelin	Reform	2,574
	Ralph Nader	Pacific Green	77,357
	Howard Phillips	Constitution	2,189
2004	Michael Badnarik	Libertarian	7,260
	George W. Bush*	Republican	866,831
	David Cobb	Pacific Green	5,315
	John F. Kerry**	Democrat	943,163
	Michael Anthony Peroutka	Constitution	5,257
2008	Baldwin, Chuck	Constitution	7,693
	Barr, Bob	Libertarian	7,635
	McCain, John	Republican	738,475
	McKinney, Cynthia	Pacific Green	4,543
	Nader, Ralph	Peace	18,614
	Obama, Barack*	Democrat	1,037,291
2012	Anderson, Ross C. (Rocky)	Progressive	3,384
	Christensen, Will	Constitution	4,432
	Johnson, Gary	Libertarian	24,089
	Obama, Barack*	Democrat	970,488
	Romney, Mitt	Republican	754,175
	Stein, Jill	Pacific Green	19,427

[1]One Weaver elector was endorsed by the Democrats and elected as a Fusionist, receiving 35,811 votes.
[2]Vice-presidential candidate

Initiative, Referendum and Recall

In 1902, Oregon voters overwhelmingly approved a legislatively referred ballot measure that created Oregon's initiative and referendum process. In 1904, voters enacted the direct primary and, in 1908, Oregon's Constitution was amended to allow for recall of public officials. These were the culmination of efforts by the Direct Legislation League, a group of political activists that progressive leader William S. U'Ren founded in 1898.

This system of empowering the people to propose new laws or change the Constitution of Oregon through a general election ballot measure became nationally known as "the Oregon System."

Initiative: Registered voters may place on the ballot any issue that amends the Oregon Constitution or changes the Oregon Revised Statutes (ORS).

Referendum: Registered voters may attempt to reject any bill passed by the Legislature by placing a referendum on the ballot.

Referral: The Legislature may refer any bill it passes to voters for approval. It must do so for any amendment to the Oregon Constitution.

Since 1902, the people have passed 122 of the 359 initiative measures placed on the ballot and 23 of the 64 referenda on the ballot. During the same period, the Legislature has referred 428 measures to the people, of which 253 have passed.

Both houses of the Legislature must vote to refer a statute or constitutional amendment for popular vote. Such referrals cannot be vetoed by the governor.

To place an initiative or referendum on the ballot, supporters must obtain a specified number of signatures from registered voters. The number required is determined by a fixed percentage of the votes cast for all candidates for governor at the general election preceding the filing of the petition. In the 2010 General Election, 1,453,548 votes were cast for governor. Therefore:

- Referendum petitions require four percent, or 58,142 signatures.
- Initiative petitions for statutory enactments require six percent, or 87,213 signatures.
- Initiative petitions for constitutional amendments require eight percent, or 116,284 signatures.

The original constitutional amendment, passed in 1902, provided that a fixed percentage of the votes cast for justice of the Supreme Court would determine the number of signatures required to place an initiative or referendum on the ballot. Both a statutory enactment and a constitutional amendment required eight percent of the votes cast, while a referendum required five percent of the votes cast. In 1954, the people amended the Oregon Constitution to increase the required number of signatures to 10 percent for a constitutional amendment. In 1968, a vote of the people established the current requirements.

Prior to 1954, measures on the ballot were not numbered. They are listed below in order of appearance on the ballot. The 2001 Legislature amended state law to require that ballot measure numbers not repeat in any subsequent election. Numbers assigned for each election begin with the next number after the last number assigned in the previous election.

Key: *Adopted; L = Referred by the Legislature; I = Submitted by initiative petition; R = Referendum by petition; (Also, see footnotes on p. 314.)

Election Date/Measure Number/Ballot Title	Yes	No
June 2, 1902		
1. Limits Uses Initiative and Referendum—L[1]	*62,024	5,668
June 6, 1904		
1. Office of State Printer—L[1]	*45,334	14,031
2. Direct Primary Nominating Convention Law—I[2]	*56,205	16,354
3. Local Option Liquor Law—I[2]	*43,316	40,198
June 4, 1906		
1. Shall act appropriating money maintaining Insane Asylum, Penitentiary, Deaf-Mute, Blind School, University, Agricultural College, and Normal Schools be approved—R	*43,918	26,758
2. Equal Suffrage Constitutional Amendment—I[1]	36,902	47,075
3. Amendment to local option law giving anti-prohibitionists and prohibitionists equal privileges—I[2]	35,297	45,144
4. Law to abolish tolls on the Mount Hood and Barlow Road and providing for its ownership by the State—I[2]	31,525	44,527
5. Constitutional amendment providing method of amending constitution and applying the referendum to all laws affecting constitutional conventions and amendments—I[1]	*47,661	18,751
6. Constitutional amendment giving cities and towns exclusive power to enact and amend their charters—I[1]	*52,567	19,852
7. Constitutional amendment to allow the state printing, binding, and Printers' compensation to be regulated by law at any time—I[1]	*63,749	9,571
8. Constitutional amendment for the initiative and referendum on local, special and municipal laws and parts of laws—I[1]	*47,678	16,735
9. Bill for a law prohibiting free passes and discrimination by railroad companies and other public service corporations—I[2]	*57,281	16,779
10. An act requiring sleeping car companies, refrigerator car companies and oil companies to pay an annual license upon gross earnings—I[2]	*69,635	6,441
11. An act requiring express companies, telegraph companies and telephone companies to pay an annual license upon gross earnings—I[2]	*70,872	6,360
June 1, 1908		
1. To Increase Compensation of Legislators from $120 to $400 Per Session—L[1]	19,691	68,892
2. Permitting Location of State Institutions at Places Other than the State Capitol—L[1]	*41,975	40,868

Elections and Records

Election Date/Measure Number/Ballot Title	Yes	No
3. Reorganization System of Courts and Increasing the Number of Supreme Judges from Three to Five—L[1]	30,243	50,591
4. Changing Date of General Elections from June to November—L[1]	*65,728	18,590
5. Giving Sheriffs Control of County Prisoners—R	*60,443	30,033
6. Requiring Railroads to Give Public Officials Free Passes—R	28,856	59,406
7. Appropriating $100,000 for Building Armories—R	33,507	54,848
8. Increasing Annual Appropriation for University of Oregon from $47,500 to $125,000—R	*44,115	40,535
9. Equal Suffrage—I[1]	36,858	58,670
10. Fishery Law Proposed by Fishwheel Operators—I[2]	*46,582	40,720
11. Giving Cities Control of Liquor Selling, Poolrooms, Theaters, etc., subject to local option law—I[1]	39,442	52,346
12. Modified Form of Single Tax Amendment—I[1]	32,066	60,871
13. Recall Power on Public Officials—I[1]	*58,381	31,002
14. Instructing Legislature to Vote for People's Choice for United States Senator—I[2]	*69,668	21,162
15. Authorizing Proportional Representation Law—I[1]	*48,868	34,128
16. Corrupt Practices Act Governing Elections—I[2]	*54,042	31,301
17. Fishery Law Proposed by Gillnet Operators—I[2]	*56,130	30,280
18. Requiring Indictment To Be By Grand Jury—I[1]	*52,214	28,487
19. Creating Hood River County—I[2]	*43,948	26,778
November 8, 1910		
1. Permitting Female Taxpayers to Vote—I[1]	35,270	59,065
2. Establishing Branch Insane Asylum in Eastern Oregon—L[2]	*50,134	41,504
3. Calling Convention to Revise State Constitution—L[2]	23,143	59,974
4. Providing Separate Districts for Election of Each State Senator and Representative—L[1]	24,000	54,252
5. Repealing Requirements That All Taxes Shall Be Equal and Uniform—L[1]	37,619	40,172
6. Permitting Organized Districts to Vote Bonds for Construction of Railroads by Such Districts—L[1]	32,884	46,070
7. Authorizing Collection of State and County Taxes on Separate Classes of Property—L[1]	31,629	41,692
8. Requiring Baker County to Pay $1,000 a Year to Circuit Judge in Addition to His State Salary—R	13,161	71,503
9. Creating Nesmith County From Parts of Lane and Douglas—I[2]	22,866	60,951
10. To Establish a State Normal School at Monmouth—I[2]	*50,191	40,044
11. Creating Otis County From Parts of Harney, Malheur and Grant—I[2]	17,426	62,016
12. Annexing Part of Clackamas County to Multnomah—I[2]	16,250	69,002
13. Creating Williams County From Parts of Lane and Douglas—I[2]	14,508	64,090
14. Permitting People of Each County to Regulate Taxation for County Purposes and Abolishing Poll Taxes—I[1]	*44,171	42,127
15. Giving Cities and Towns Exclusive Power to Regulate Liquor Traffic Within Their Limits—I[1]	*53,321	50,779
16. For Protection of Laborers in Hazardous Employment, Fixing Employers' Liability, etc.—I[2]	*56,258	33,943
17. Creating Orchard County From Part of Umatilla—I[2]	15,664	62,712
18. Creating Clark County From Part of Grant—I[2]	15,613	61,704
19. To Establish State Normal School at Weston—I[2]	40,898	46,201
20. To Annex Part of Washington County to Multnomah—I[2]	14,047	68,221
21. To Establish State Normal School at Ashland—I[2]	38,473	48,655
22. Prohibiting Liquor Traffic—I[1]	43,540	61,221
23. Prohibiting the Sale of Liquors and Regulating Shipments of Same, and Providing for Search for Liquor—I[2]	42,651	63,564
24. Creating Board to Draft Employers' Liability Law for Submission to Legislature—I[2]	32,224	51,719
25. Prohibiting Taking of Fish in Rogue River Except With Hook and Line—I[2]	*49,712	33,397
26. Creating Deschutes County Out of Part of Crook—I[2]	17,592	60,486
27. Bill for General Law Under Which New Counties May Be Created or Boundaries Changed—I[2]	37,129	42,327

Election Date/Measure Number/Ballot Title	Yes	No
28. Permitting Counties to Vote Bonds for Permanent Road Improvement—I[1]	*51,275	32,906
29. Permitting Voters in Direct Primaries to Express Choice for President and Vice President, to Select Delegates to National Convention and Nominate Candidates for Presidential Electors—I[2]	*43,353	41,624
30. Creating Board of People's Inspectors of Government, Providing for Reports of Board in Official State Gazette to be Mailed to All Registered Voters Bi-monthly—I[2]	29,955	52,538
31. Extending Initiative and Referendum, Making Term of Members of Legislature Six Years, Increasing Salaries, Requiring Proportional Representation in Legislature, Election of President of Senate and Speaker of House Outside of Members, etc.—I[1]	37,031	44,366
32. Permitting Three-Fourths Verdict in Civil Cases—I[1]	*44,538	39,399
November 5, 1912		
1. Equal Suffrage Amendment—I[1]	*61,265	57,104
2. Creating Office of Lieutenant Governor—L[1]	50,562	61,644
3. Divorce of Local and State Taxation—L[1]	51,582	56,671
4. Permitting Different Tax Rates on Classes of Property—L[1]	52,045	54,483
5. Repeal of County Tax Option—L[1]	*63,881	47,150
6. Majority Rule on Constitutional Amendments—L[1]	32,934	70,325
7. Double Liability on Bank Stockholders—L[1]	*82,981	21,738
8. Statewide Public Utilities Regulation—R	*65,985	40,956
9. Creating Cascade County—I[2]	26,463	71,239
10. Millage Tax for University and Agricultural College—I[2]	48,701	57,279
11. Majority Rule on Initiated Laws—I[1]	35,721	68,861
12. County Bond and Road Construction Act—Grange Bill—I[2]	49,699	56,713
13. Creating State Highway Department—Grange Bill—I[2]	23,872	83,846
14. Changing Date State Printer Bill Becomes Effective—I[2]	34,793	69,542
15. Creating Office of Hotel Inspector—I[2]	16,910	91,995
16. Eight-hour Day on Public Works—I[2]	*64,508	48,078
17. Blue Sky Law—I[2]	48,765	57,293
18. Relating to Employment of State Prisoners—I[2]	*73,800	37,492
19. Relating to Employment of County and City Prisoners—I[2]	*71,367	37,731
20. State Road Bonding Act—I[2]	30,897	75,590
21. Limiting State Road Indebtedness—I[1]	*59,452	43,447
22. County Bonding Act—I[2]	43,611	60,210
23. Limiting County Road Indebtedness—I[1]	*57,258	43,858
24. Providing Method for Consolidating Cities and Creating New Counties—I[2]	40,199	56,992
25. Income Tax Amendment—I[1]	52,702	52,948
26. Tax Exemption on Household Effects—I[2]	*60,357	51,826
27. Tax Exemption on Moneys and Credits—I[2]	42,491	66,540
28. Revising Inheritance Tax Laws—I[2]	38,609	63,839
29. Freight Rates Act—I[2]	*58,306	45,534
30. County Road Bonding Act—I[1]	38,568	63,481
31. Abolishing Senate; Proxy Voting; U'Ren Constitution—I[1]	31,020	71,183
32. Statewide Single Tax with Graduated Tax Provision—I[1]	31,534	82,015
33. Abolishing Capital Punishment—I[2]	41,951	64,578
34. Prohibits Boycotts and Pickets—I[2]	49,826	60,560
35. Prohibits Use of Public Streets, Parks and Grounds in Cities over 5,000 Without Permit—I[2]	48,987	62,532
36. Appropriation for University of Oregon—R	29,437	78,985
37. Appropriation for University of Oregon—R	27,310	79,376
November 4, 1913 (Special Referendum Election)		
1. State University Building Repair Fund—R	*56,659	40,600
2. University of Oregon New Building Appropriation—R	*53,569	43,014
3. Sterilization Act—R	41,767	53,319
4. County Attorney Act—R	*54,179	38,159
5. Workmen's Compensation Act—R	*67,814	28,608

Election Date/Measure Number/Ballot Title	Yes	No
November 3, 1914		
1. Requiring Voters to be Citizens of the United States—L[1]	*164,879	39,847
2. Creating Office of Lieutenant Governor—L[1]	52,040	143,804
3. Permitting Certain City and County Boundaries to be Made Identical, and Governments Consolidated—L[1]	77,392	103,194
4. Permitting State to Create an Indebtedness Not to Exceed Two Percent of Assessed Valuation for Irrigation and Power Projects and Development of Untilled Lands—L[1]	49,759	135,550
5. Omitting Requirement that "All Taxation Shall Be Equal And Uniform"—L[1]	59,206	116,490
6. Changing Existing Rule of Uniformity and Equality of Taxation—Authorizing Classification of Property for Taxation Purposes—L[1]	52,362	122,704
7. To Establish State Normal School at Ashland—L[2]	84,041	109,643
8. Enabling Incorporated Municipalities to Surrender Charters and To Be Merged in Adjoining City or Town—L[1]	*96,116	77,671
9. To Establish State Normal School at Weston—L[2]	87,450	105,345
10. Providing Compensation for Members of Legislature at Five Dollars Per Day—L[1]	41,087	146,278
11. Universal Constitutional Eight Hour Day Amendment—I[1]	49,360	167,888
12. Eight-hour Day and Room-Ventilation Law for Female Workers—I[2]	88,480	120,296
13. Nonpartisan Judiciary Bill Prohibiting Party Nominations for Judicial Officers—I[2]	74,323	107,263
14. $1,500 Tax Exemption Amendment—I[1]	65,495	136,193
15. Public Docks and Water Frontage Amendment—I[1]	67,128	114,564
16. Municipal Wharves and Docks Bill—I[2]	67,110	111,113
17. Prohibition Constitutional Amendment—I[1]	*136,842	100,362
18. Abolishing Death Penalty—I[1]	*100,552	100,395
19. Specific Personal Graduated Extra-tax Amendment of Article IX, Oregon Constitution—I[1]	59,186	124,943
20. Consolidating Corporation and Insurance Departments—I[2]	55,469	120,154
21. Dentistry Bill—I[2]	92,722	110,404
22. County Officers Term Amendment—I[1]	82,841	107,039
23. A Tax Code Commission Bill—I[2]	34,436	143,468
24. Abolishing Desert Land Board and Reorganizing Certain State Offices—I[2]	32,701	143,366
25. Proportional Representation Amendment to Oregon Constitution—I[1]	39,740	137,116
26. State Senate Constitutional Amendment—I[1]	62,376	123,429
27. Department of Industry and Public Works Amendment—I[1]	57,859	126,201
28. Primary Delegate Election Bill—I[2]	25,058	153,638
29. Equal Assessment and Taxation and $300 Exemption Amendment—I[1]	43,280	140,507
November 7, 1916		
1. Single Item Veto Amendment—L[1]	*141,773	53,207
2. Ship Tax Exemption Amendment—L[1]	*119,652	65,410
3. Negro and Mulatto Suffrage Amendment—L[1]	100,027	100,701
4. Full Rental Value Land Tax and Homemakers' Loan Fund Amendment—I[1]	43,390	154,980
5. For Pendleton Normal School and Ratifying Location Certain State Institutions—I[1]	96,829	109,523
6. Anti-compulsory Vaccination Bill—I[2]	99,745	100,119
7. Bill Repealing and Abolishing the Sunday Closing Law—I[2]	*125,836	93,076
8. Permitting Manufacture and Regulating Sale 4 Percent Malt Liquors—I[1]	85,973	140,599
9. Prohibition Amendment Forbidding Importation of Intoxicating Liquors for Beverage Purposes—I[1]	*114,932	109,671
10. Rural Credits Amendment—I[1]	*107,488	83,887
11. State-wide Tax and Indebtedness Limitation Amendment—I[1]	*99,536	84,031
June 4, 1917 (Special Election)		
1. Authorizing Ports to Create Limited Indebtedness to Encourage Water Transportation—L[1]	*67,445	54,864
2. Limiting Number of Bills Introduced and Increasing Pay of Legislators—L[1]	22,276	103,238

Election Date/Measure Number/Ballot Title	Yes	No
3. Declaration Against Implied Repeal of Constitutional Provisions by Amendments Thereto—L[1]	37,187	72,445
4. Uniform Tax Classification Amendment—L[1]	*62,118	53,245
5. Requiring Election City, Town and State Officers at Same Time—L[1]	*83,630	42,296
6. Four Hundred Thousand Dollar Tax Levy for a New Penitentiary—L[2]	46,666	86,165
7. Six Million Dollar State Road Bond Issue and Highway Bill—L[2]	*77,316	63,803
November 5, 1918		
1. Establishing and Maintaining Southern and Eastern Oregon Normal Schools—L[1]	49,935	66,070
2. Establishing Dependent, Delinquent and Defective Children's Home, Appropriating Money Therefor—L[2]	43,441	65,299
3. Prohibiting Seine and Setnet Fishing in Rogue River and Tributaries—R	45,511	50,227
4. Closing the Willamette River to Commercial Fishing South of Oswego—R	*55,555	40,908
5. Delinquent Tax Notice Bill—I[2]	*66,652	41,594
6. Fixing Compensation for Publication of Legal Notice—I[2]	*50,073	41,816
7. Authorizing Increase in Amount of Levy of State Taxes for Year 1919 (submitted by state tax commission under chapter 150, Laws 1917)	41,364	56,974
June 3, 1919 (Special Election)		
1. Six Percent County Indebtedness for Permanent Roads Amendment—L[1]	*49,728	33,561
2. Industrial and Reconstruction Hospital Amendment—L[1]	38,204	40,707
3. State Bond Payment of Irrigation and Drainage District Bond Interest—L[1]	*43,010	35,948
4. Five Million Dollar Reconstruction Bonding Amendment—L[1]	39,130	40,580
5. Lieutenant Governor Constitutional Amendment—L[1]	32,653	46,861
6. The Roosevelt Coast Military Highway Bill—L[2]	*56,966	29,159
7. Reconstruction Bonding Bill—L[2]	37,294	42,792
8. Soldiers', Sailors' and Marines' Educational Financial Aid Bill—L[2]	*49,158	33,513
9. Market Roads Tax Bill—L[2]	*53,191	28,039
May 21, 1920 (Special Election)		
1. Extending Eminent Domain Over Roads and Ways—L[1]	*100,256	35,655
2. Limitation of 4 Percent State Indebtedness for Permanent Roads—L[1]	*93,392	46,084
3. Restoring Capital Punishment—L[1]	*81,756	64,589
4. Crook and Curry Counties Bonding Amendment—L[1]	*72,378	36,699
5. Successor to Governor—L[1]	*78,241	56,946
6. Higher Educational Tax Act—L[2]	*102,722	46,577
7. Soldiers', Sailors' and Marines' Educational Aid Revenue Bill—L[2]	*91,294	50,482
8. State Elementary School Fund Tax—L[2]	*110,263	39,593
9. Blind School Tax Measure—L[2]	*115,337	30,739
November 2, 1920		
1. Compulsory Voting and Registration Amendment—L[1]	61,258	131,603
2. Constitutional Amendment Regulating Legislative Sessions and the Payment of Legislators—L[1]	80,342	85,524
3. Oleomargarine Bills—R	67,101	119,126
4. Single Tax Constitutional Amendment—I[1]	37,283	147,426
5. Fixing Term of Certain County Officers—I[1]	*97,854	80,983
6. Port of Portland Dock Commission Consolidation—I[2]	80,493	84,830
7. Anti-compulsory Vaccination Amendment—I[1]	63,018	127,570
8. Constitutional Amendment Fixing Legal Rate of Interest in Oregon—I[1]	28,976	158,673
9. Roosevelt Bird Refuge—I[2]	78,961	107,383
10. Divided Legislative Session Constitutional Amendment—I[1]	57,791	101,179
11. State Market Commission Act—I[2]	51,605	119,464
June 7, 1921 (Special Election)		
1. Legislative Regulation and Compensation Amendment—L[1]	42,924	72,596
2. World War Veterans' State Aid Fund, Constitutional Amendment—L[1]	*88,219	37,866
3. Emergency Clause Veto Constitutional Amendment—L[1]	*62,621	45,537
4. Hygiene Marriage Examination and License Bill—L[2]	56,858	65,793
5. Women Jurors and Revised Jury Law—L[2]	*59,882	59,265

Election Date/Measure Number/Ballot Title	Yes	No
November 7, 1922		
1. Amendment Permitting Linn County Tax Levy to Pay Outstanding Warrants—L	*89,177	57,049
2. Amendment Permitting Linn and Benton Counties to Pay Outstanding Warrants—L[1]	*86,547	53,844
3. Single Tax Amendment—I[1]	39,231	132,021
4. 1925 Exposition Tax Amendment—I[2]	82,837	95,587
5. Income Tax Amendment—I[2]	54,803	112,197
6. Compulsory Education Bill—I[2]	*115,506	103,685
November 6, 1923 (Special Election)		
1. Income Tax Act—L[2]	*58,647	58,131
November 4, 1924		
1. Voters' Literacy Amendment—L[1]	*184,031	48,645
2. Public Use and Welfare Amendment—L[1]	*134,071	65,133
3. Bonus Amendment—L[1]	*131,199	92,446
4. Oleomargarine Condensed Milk Bill—R	91,597	157,324
5. Naturopath Bill—I[2]	75,159	122,839
6. Workmen's Compulsory Compensation Law for Hazardous Occupations—I[1]	73,270	151,862
7. Income Tax Repeal—I[2]	*123,799	111,055
November 2, 1926		
1. Klamath County Bonding Amendment—L[1]	*81,954	68,128
2. Six Percent Limitation Amendment—L[1]	54,624	99,125
3. Repeal of Free Negro and Mulatto Section of the Constitution—L[1]	*108,332	64,954
4. Amendment Prohibiting Inheritance and Income Taxes—L[1]	59,442	121,973
5. The Seaside Normal School Act—L[2]	47,878	124,811
6. The Eastern Oregon State Normal School Act—L[2]	*101,327	80,084
7. The Recall Amendment—L[1]	*100,324	61,307
8 Curry County Bonding or Tax Levy Amendment—L[1]	*78,823	61,472
9. Amendment Relating to Elections to Fill Vacancies in Public Offices—L[1]	*100,397	54,474
10. Klamath and Clackamas County Bonding Amendment—L[1]	*75,229	61,718
11. The Eastern Oregon Tuberculosis Hospital Act—L[2]	*131,296	48,490
12. Cigarette and Tobacco Tax Bill—R	62,254	123,208
13. Motor Bus and Truck Bill—R	*99,746	78,685
14. Act Appropriating Ten Percent of Self-sustaining Boards' Receipts—R	46,389	97,460
15. Income Tax Bill With Property Tax Offset—I[2]	50,199	122,512
16. Bus and Truck Operating License Bill—I[2]	76,164	94,533
17. Fish Wheel, Trap, Seine and Gillnet Bill—I[2]	*102,119	73,086
18. Income Tax Bill—I[2]	83,991	93,997
19. Oregon Water and Power Board Development Measure—I[1]	35,313	147,092
20. Amendment Fixing Salaries of County Officers of Umatilla County—L[2]	1,988	2,646
21. To Provide Salaries for Certain Officials of Clackamas County—L[2]	2,826	6,199
June 28, 1927 (Special Election)		
1. Repeal of Negro, Chinaman and Mulatto Suffrage Section of Constitution—L[1]	*69,373	41,887
2. Portland School District Tax Levy Amendment—L[1]	46,784	55,817
3. Criminal Information Amendment—L[1]	*64,956	38,774
4. Legislators' Pay Amendment—L[1]	28,380	81,215
5. Voters' Registration Amendment—L[1]	*55,802	49,682
6. State and County Officers, Salary Amendment—L[1]	46,999	61,838
7. City and County Consolidation Amendment—L[1]	41,309	57,613
8. Veterans' Memorial and Armory Amendment—L[1]	25,180	80,476
9. State Tax Limitation Amendment—L[1]	19,393	84,697
10. Income Tax Bill—L[2]	48,745	67,039
11. Property Assessment and Taxation Enforcement Bill—L[2]	31,957	70,871
12. Nestucca Bay Fish Closing Bill—R	*53,684	47,552
November 6, 1928		
1. Five Cent Gasoline Tax Bill—I[1]	71,824	198,798
2. Bill for Reduction of Motor Vehicle License Fees—I[1]	98,248	174,219
3. Income Tax Bill—I[2]	118,696	132,961

Election Date/Measure Number/Ballot Title	Yes	No
4. Limiting Power of Legislature Over Laws Approved by the People—I^1	108,230	124,200
5. Deschutes River Water and Fish Bill—I^2	78,317	157,398
6. Rogue River Water and Fish Bill—I^2	79,028	156,009
7. Umpqua River Water and Fish Bill—I^2	76,108	154,345
8. McKenzie River Water and Fish Bill—I^2	77,974	153,418
November 4, 1930		
1. Repeal of State Payment of Irrigation and Drainage District Interest—L^1	*96,061	74,892
2. State Cabinet Form of Government Constitutional Amendment—L^1	51,248	135,412
3. Bonus Loan Constitutional Amendment—L^1	92,602	101,785
4. Motor Vehicle License Tax Constitutional Amendment—L^1	71,557	115,480
5. Motor Vehicle License Tax Constitutional Amendment—L^1	63,683	111,441
6. Constitutional Amendment for Filling Vacancies in the Legislature—L^1	*85,836	76,455
7. Legislators' Compensation Constitutional Amendment—L^1	70,937	108,070
8. Two Additional Circuit Judges Bill—R	39,770	137,549
9. Income Tax Bill—R	*105,189	95,207
10. Anti-cigarette Constitutional Amendment—I^1	54,231	156,265
11. Rogue River Fishing Constitutional Amendment—I^1	96,596	99,490
12. Lieutenant Governor Constitutional Amendment—I^1	92,707	95,277
13. People's Water and Power Utility Districts Constitutional Amendment—I^1	*117,776	84,778
November 8, 1932		
1. Taxpayer Voting Qualification Amendment—L^1	*189,321	124,160
2. Amendment Authorizing Criminal Trials Without Juries by Consent of Accused—L^1	*191,042	111,872
3. Six Percent Tax Limitation Amendment—L^1	*149,833	121,852
4. Oleomargarine Tax Bill—R	131,273	200,496
5. Bill Prohibiting Commercial Fishing on the Rogue River—R	127,445	180,527
6. Higher Education Appropriation Bill—R	58,076	237,218
7. Bill to Repeal State Prohibition Law of Oregon—I^2	*206,619	138,775
8. The Freight Truck and Bus Bill—I^2	151,790	180,609
9. Bill Moving University, Normal and Law Schools, Establishing Junior Colleges—I^2	47,275	292,486
10. Tax and Debt Control Constitutional Amendment—I^1	99,171	162,552
11. Tax Supervising and Conservation Bill—I^2	117,940	154,206
12. Personal Income Tax Law Amendment—I^2	144,502	162,468
13. State Water Power and Hydroelectric Constitutional Amendment—I^1	*168,937	130,494
July 21, 1933 (Special Election)		
1. An Amendment to the Constitution of the United States of America—L^0	*136,713	72,854
2. Soldiers and Sailors Bonus Limitation Amendment—L^1	*113,267	75,476
3. County Manager Form of Government Constitutional Amendment—L^1	66,425	117,148
4. Prosecution by Information and Grand Jury Modification Amendment—L^1	67,192	110,755
5. Debt and Taxation Limitations for Municipal Corporations Constitutional Amendment—L^1	82,996	91,671
6. State Power Fund Bonds—L^2	73,756	106,153
7. Sales Tax Bill—L^2	45,603	167,512
8. Repeal of Oregon Prohibition Constitutional Amendment—L^1	*143,044	72,745
9. Oleomargarine Tax Bill—R	66,880	144,542
May 18, 1934 (Special Election)		
1. County Indebtedness and Funding Bond Constitutional Amendment—L^1	83,424	96,629
2. Criminal Trial Without Jury and Non-unanimous Verdict Constitutional Amendment—L^1	*117,446	83,430
3. Bill Authorizing a State Tuberculosis Hospital in Multnomah County—L^2	*104,459	98,815
4. Bill Authorizing a State Insane Hospital in Multnomah County—L^2	92,575	108,816
5. School Relief Sales Tax Bill—R	64,677	156,182
November 6, 1934		
1. Grange Power Bill—R	124,518	139,283
2. Limitations of Taxes on Taxable Property Constitutional Amendment—I^1	100,565	161,644

Election Date/Measure Number/Ballot Title	Yes	No
3. Healing Arts Constitutional Amendment—I[1]	70,626	191,836
January 31, 1936 (Special Election)		
1. Bill Changing Primary Elections to September With Other Resulting Changes—L[2]	61,270	155,922
2. Compensation of Members of the Legislature Constitutional Amendment—L[1]	28,661	184,332
3. Sales Tax Bill—L[2]	32,106	187,319
4. Bill Authorizing Student Activity Fees in State Higher Educational Institutions—R	50,971	163,191
November 3, 1936		
1. Bill Amending Old Age Assistance Act of 1935—R	174,293	179,236
2. Amendment Forbidding Prevention or Regulation of Certain Advertising If Truthful—I[1]	100,141	222,897
3. Tax Limitation Constitutional Amendment for School Districts Having 100,000 Population—I[1]	112,546	203,693
4. Noncompulsory Military Training Bill—I[2]	131,917	214,246
5. Amendment Limiting and Reducing Permissible Taxes on Tangible Property—I[1]	79,604	241,042
6. State Power Bill—I[2]	131,489	208,179
7. State Hydroelectric Temporary Administrative Board Constitutional Amendment—I[1]	100,356	208,741
8. State Bank Bill—I[2]	82,869	250,777
November 8, 1938		
1. Governor's 20-day Bill Consideration Amendment—L[1]	*233,384	93,752
2. Amendment Repealing the Double Liability of Stockholders in Banking Corporations—L[1]	133,525	165,797
3. Legislators Compensation Constitutional Amendments—L[1]	149,356	169,131
4. Bill Requiring Marriage License Applicants Medically Examined; Physically and Mentally—L[2]	*277,099	66,484
5. Slot Machines Seizure by Sheriffs and Destruction on Court Order—R	*204,561	126,580
6. Prohibiting Slot Machines, Pin-ball, Dart and Other Similar Games—R	*197,912	129,043
7. Townsend Plan Bill—I[3]	*183,781	149,711
8. Citizens' Retirement Annuity Bill; Levying Transactions Tax to Provide Fund—I[2]	112,172	219,557
9. Bill Regulating Picketing and Boycotting by Labor Groups and Organizations—I[2]	*197,771	148,460
10. Water Purification and Prevention of Pollution Bill—I[2]	*247,685	75,295
11. Bill Regulating Sale of Alcoholic Liquor for Beverage Purposes—I[2]	118,282	222,221
12. Constitutional Amendment Legalizing Certain Lotteries and Other Forms of Gambling—I[1]	141,792	180,329
November 5, 1940		
1. Amendment Removing Office Time Limit of State Secretary and Treasurer—L[1]	163,942	213,797
2. Amendment Making Three Years' Average People's Voted Levies, Tax Base—L[1]	129,699	183,488
3. Amendment Repealing the Double Liability of Stockholders of State Banks—L[1]	157,891	191,290
4. Legislators' Compensation Constitutional Amendment—L[1]	186,830	188,031
5. Bill Changing the Primary Nominating Elections from May to September—R	156,421	221,203
6. Bill to Further Regulate Sale and Use of Alcoholic Liquor—R	158,004	235,128
7. Bill Repealing Present Liquor Law; Authorizing Private Sale, Licensed, Taxed—I[2]	90,681	309,183
8. Amendment Legalizing Certain Gambling and Gaming Devices and Certain Lotteries—I[1]	150,157	258,010
9. Bill to Repeal the Oregon Milk Control Law—I[2]	201,983	213,838
November 3, 1942		
1. Legislators' Compensation Constitutional Amendment—L[1]	*129,318	109,898
2. Rural Credits Loan Fund Repeal Amendment—L[1]	*101,425	88,857

Election Date/Measure Number/Ballot Title	Yes	No
3. Amendment Specifying Exclusive Uses of Gasoline and Motor Vehicle Taxes—L[1]	*125,990	86,332
4. Amendment Authorizing Regulation by Law of Voting Privilege Forfeiture—L[1]	101,508	103,404
5. Cigarette Tax Bill—R	110,643	127,366
6. Bill Restricting and Prohibiting Net Fishing Coastal Streams and Bays—R	97,212	137,177
7. Bill Distributing Surplus Funds to School Districts, Reducing Taxes Therein—I[2]	*136,321	92,623
November 7, 1944		
1. Amendment To Provide Alternative Means for Securing Bank Deposits—L[1]	*228,744	115,745
2. Amendment Authorizing Change to Managerial Form of County Government—L[1]	*175,716	154,504
3. Amendment Authorizing "Oregon War Veterans' Fund," Providing Tax Therefor—L[1]	*190,520	178,581
4. Amendment to Authorize Legislative Regulation of Voting Privilege Forfeiture—L[1]	*183,855	156,219
5. Bill Providing Educational Aid to Certain Veterans World War II—L[2]	*238,350	135,317
6. Bill Imposing Tax on Retail Sales of Tangible Personal Property—L[2]	96,697	269,276
7. Burke Bill; Only State Selling Liquor over 14 Hundredths Alcohol—R	*228,853	180,158
8. Constitutional Amendment Increasing State Tax Fund for Public School Support—I[1]	177,153	186,976
9. Constitutional Amendment Providing Monthly Annuities From a Gross Income Tax—I[1]	180,691	219,981
June 22, 1945 (Special Election)		
1. Bill Authorizing Tax Levy for State Building Fund—L[2]	*78,269	49,565
2. Bill Authorizing Cigarette Tax to Support Public Schools—L[2]	60,321	67,542
November 5, 1946		
1. Constitutional Amendment Providing for Succession to Office of Governor—L[1]	*221,547	70,322
2. Bill Authorizing Tax for Construction and Equipment of State Armories—L[2]	75,693	219,006
3. Bill Establishing Rural School Districts and School Boards—L[2]	*155,733	134,673
4. Bill Authorizing Chinamen to Hold Real Estate and Mining Claims—L[1]	*161,865	133,111
5. Amendment Permitting Legislative Bills to be Read by Title Only—L[1]	*145,248	113,279
6. Constitutional Amendment Increasing Number of Senators to Thirty-one—L[1]	88,717	185,247
7. Bill Regulating Fishing in Coastal Streams and Inland Waters—R	*196,195	101,398
8. To Create State Old-age and Disability Pension Fund—I[2]	86,374	244,960
9. To Create Basic School Support Fund by Annual Tax Levy—I[2]	*157,904	151,765
October 7, 1947 (Special Election)		
1. Bill Taxing Retail Sales for School, Welfare and Governmental Purposes—L[2]	67,514	180,333
2. Cigarette Tax Bill—R	103,794	140,876
November 2, 1948		
1. Constitutional Six Percent Tax Limitation Amendment—L[1]	150,032	268,155
2. Constitutional Amendment Authorizing Indebtedness for State Forestation—L[1]	*211,912	209,317
3. Bill Authorizing State Boys' Camp Near Timber, Oregon—L[2]	*227,638	219,196
4. Bill Amending Licensing and Acquisition Provisions for Hydroelectric Commission Act—R	173,004	242,100
5. Constitutional Amendment Fixing Qualifications of Voters in School Elections—I[1]	*284,776	164,025
6. Oregon Old Age Pension Act—I[2]	*313,212	172,531
7. Bill Increasing Personal Income Tax Exemptions—I[2]	*405,842	63,373
8. Oregon Liquor Dispensing Licensing Act—I[2]	210,108	273,621
9. World War II Veterans' Bonus Amendment—I[1]	198,283	265,805

Election Date/Measure Number/Ballot Title	Yes	No
10. Prohibiting Salmon Fishing in Columbia River With Fixed Appliances—I[2]	*273,140	184,834
11. Question of Authorizing Additional State Tax, to be Offset by Income Tax Funds—R	143,856	256,167
November 7, 1950		
1. Constitutional Amendment Fixing Legislators' Annual Compensation—L[1]	*243,518	205,361
2. Constitutional Amendment Lending State Tax Credit for Higher Education Buildings—L[1]	*256,895	192,573
3. Constitutional Amendment Augmenting "Oregon War Veterans' Fund"—L[1]	*268,171	183,724
4. Increasing Basic School Support Fund by Annual Tax Levy—L[2]	*234,394	231,856
5. Needy Aged Persons Public Assistance Act—R	*310,143	158,939
6. Providing Uniform Standard Time in Oregon—R	*277,633	195,319
7. World War II Veterans' Compensation Fund—I[1]	*239,553	216,958
8. Constitutional Amendment for Legislative Representation Reapportionment—I[1]	190,992	215,302
9. Making Sale of Promotively Advertised Alcoholic Beverage Unlawful—I[2]	113,524	378,732
November 4, 1952		
1. Amendment Making Superintendent of Public Instruction Appointive—L[1]	282,882	326,199
2. World War Veterans' State Aid Sinking Fund Repeal—L[1]	*454,898	147,128
3. Act Authorizing Domiciliary State Hospital for Aged Mentally Ill—L[2]	*480,479	153,402
4. Amendment Legal Voters of Taxing Unit Establish Tax Base—L[1]	*355,136	210,373
5. Amendment to Augment Oregon War Veterans' Fund—L[1]	*465,605	132,363
6. Amendment Creating Legislative Assembly Emergency Committee—L[1]	*364,539	194,492
7. Amendment Fixing Elective Terms of State Senators and Representatives—L[1]	*483,356	103,357
8. Amendatory Act Title Subject Amendment—L[1]	*315,071	191,087
9. Act Limiting State Property Tax—L[2]	*318,948	272,145
10. Motor Carrier Highway Transportation Tax Act—R	*409,588	230,241
11. School District Reorganization Act—R	295,700	301,974
12. Cigarette Stamp Tax Revenue Act—R	233,226	413,137
13. Establishing United States Standard Time in Oregon—I[2]	*399,981	256,981
14. Constitutional Amendment Prohibiting Lotteries, Bookmaking, Pari-mutuel Betting on Animal Racing—I[1]	230,097	411,884
15. Constitutional Amendment Authorizing Alcoholic Liquor Sale by Individual Glass—I[1]	*369,127	285,446
16. Constitutional Amendment Providing Equitable Taxing Method for Use of Highways—I[1]	135,468	484,730
17. Milk Production and Marketing Act Bill—I[2]	313,629	337,750
18. Constitutional Legislative Senator and Representative Apportionment Enforcement Amendment—I[1]	*357,550	194,292
November 2, 1954		
1. Salaries of State Legislators—L[1]	216,545	296,008
2. Subdividing Counties for Electing State Legislators—L[1]	*268,337	208,077
3. Mental Hospital In or Near Portland—L[2]	*397,625	128,685
4. Constitutional Amendments—How Proposed by People—L[1]	*251,078	230,770
5. State Property Tax—L[1]	208,419	264,569
6. Establishing Daylight Saving Time—I[2]	252,305	300,007
7. Prohibiting Certain Fishing in Coastal Streams—I[2]	232,775	278,805
8. Repealing Milk Control Law—I[2]	*293,745	247,591
November 6, 1956		
1. State Tax Laws—Immediate Effect Authorized—L[1]	175,932	487,550
2. Authorizing State Acceptance of Certain Gifts—L[1]	*498,633	153,033
3. Salaries of Certain State Officers—L[1]	*390,338	263,155
4. Qualifications for County Coroner and Surveyor—L[1]	*455,485	182,550
5. Salaries of State Legislators—L[1]	320,741	338,365
6. Cigarette Tax—R	280,055	414,613

Election Date/Measure Number/Ballot Title	Yes	No
7. Prohibiting Certain Fishing in Coastal Streams—I[2]	*401,882	259,309
November 4, 1958		
1. Fixing State Boundaries—L[1]	*399,396	114,318
2. Increasing Funds for War Veterans' Loans—L[1]	232,246	318,685
3. Salaries of State Legislators—L[1]	236,000	316,437
4. Capital Punishment Bill—L[1]	264,434	276,487
5. Financing Urban Redevelopment Projects—L[1]	221,330	268,716
6. Modifying County Debt Limitation—L[1]	*252,347	224,426
7. Special Grand Jury Bill—L[1]	*357,792	136,745
8. Authorizes Different Use of State Institution—L[1]	*303,282	193,177
9. Temporary Appointment and Assignment of Judges—L[1]	*373,466	125,898
10. State Power Development—L[1]	218,662	291,210
11. County Home Rule Amendment—L[1]	*311,516	157,023
12. Authorizing Discontinuing Certain State Tuberculosis Hospitals—L[1]	*319,790	195,945
13. Persons Eligible to Serve in Legislature—I[1]	*320,751	201,700
May 20, 1960		
1. Salaries of State Legislators—L[1]	250,456	281,542
November 8, 1960		
1. Fixing Commencement of Legislators' Term—L[1]	*579,022	92,187
2. Daylight Saving Time—L[2]	357,499	393,652
3. Financing Urban Redevelopment Projects—L[1]	*335,792	312,187
4. Permitting Prosecution by Information or Indictment—L[1]	306,190	340,197
5. Authorizing Legislature to Propose Revised Constitution—L[1]	*358,367	289,895
6. State Bonds for Higher Education Facilities—L[1]	*467,557	233,759
7. Voter Qualification Amendment—L[1]	*508,108	183,977
8. Authorizing Bonds for State Building Program—L[1]	232,250	433,515
9. Compulsory Retirement for Judges—L[1]	*578,471	123,283
10. Elective Offices: When to Become Vacant—L[1]	*486,019	169,865
11. Financing Improvements in Home Rule Counties—L[1]	*399,210	222,736
12. Continuity of Government in Enemy Attack—L[1]	*578,266	88,995
13. War Veterans' Bonding and Loan Amendment—L[1]	*415,931	266,630
14. Personal Income Tax Bill—R	115,610	570,025
15. Billboard Control Measure—I[2]	261,735	475,290
May 18, 1962		
1. Six Percent Limitation Amendment—L[1]	141,728	262,140
2. Salaries of State Legislators—L[1]	*241,171	178,749
November 6, 1962		
1. Reorganize State Militia—L[1]	*312,680	234,440
2. Forest Rehabilitation Debt Limit Amendment—L[1]	*323,799	199,174
3. Permanent Road Debt Limit Amendment—L[1]	*319,956	200,236
4. Power Development Debt Limit Amendment—L[1]	*298,255	208,755
5. State Courts Creation and Jurisdiction—L[1]	*307,855	193,487
6. Daylight Saving Time—L[2]	*388,154	229,661
7. Constitutional Six Percent Limitation Amendment—L[1]	*270,637	219,509
8. Legislative Apportionment Constitutional Amendment—I[1]	197,322	325,182
9. Repeals School District Reorganization Law—I[2]	206,540	320,917
October 15, 1963 (Special Election)		
1. Personal and Corporation Income Tax Bill—R	103,737	362,845
May 15, 1964		
1. Authorizing Bonds for Education Building Program—L[1]	*327,220	252,372
November 3, 1964		
1. Capital Punishment Bill—L[1]	*455,654	302,105
2. Leasing Property for State Use—L[1]	*477,031	238,241
3. Amending State Workmen's Compensation Law—I[2]	205,182	549,414
4. Prohibiting Commercial Fishing for Salmon, Steelhead—I[2]	221,797	534,731
May 24, 1966		
1. Cigarette Tax Bill—L[2]	*310,743	181,957
2. Superintendent of Public Instruction Constitutional Amendment—L[1]	197,096	267,319

Election Date/Measure Number/Ballot Title	Yes	No
November 8, 1966		
1. Public Transportation System Employes Constitutional Amendment—L[1]	*468,103	123,964
2. State Bonds for Educational Facilities—L[1]	237,282	332,983
May 28, 1968		
1. Common School Fund Constitutional Amendment—L[1]	*372,915	226,191
2. Constitutional Amendment Changing Initiative — Referendum Requirements—L[1]	*321,731	244,750
3. Higher Education and Community College Bonds—L[1]	*353,383	261,014
November 5, 1968		
1. Constitutional Amendment Broadening Veterans Loan Eligibility—L[1]	*651,250	96,065
2. Constitutional Amendment for Removal of Judges—L[1]	*690,989	56,973
3. Empowering Legislature to Extend Ocean Boundaries—L[1]	*588,166	143,768
4. Constitutional Amendment Broadening County Debt Limitation—L[1]	331,617	348,866
5. Government Consolidation City-County Over 300,000—L[1]	*393,789	278,483
6. Bond Issue to Acquire Ocean Beaches—I[1]	315,175	464,140
7. Constitutional Amendment Changing Property Tax Limitation—I[1]	276,451	503,443
June 3, 1969 (Special Election)		
1. Property Tax Relief and Sales Tax—L[1]	65,077	504,274
May 26, 1970		
1. Capital Construction Bonds for State Government—L[1]	190,257	300,126
2. Repeals "White Foreigner" Section of Constitution—L[1]	*326,374	168,464
3. Revised Constitution for Oregon—L[1]	182,074	322,682
4. Pollution Control Bonds—L[1]	*292,234	213,835
5. Lowers Oregon Voting Age to 19—L[1]	202,018	336,527
6. Local School Property Tax Equalization Measure—L[1]	180,602	323,189
November 3, 1970		
1. Constitutional Amendment Concerning Convening of Legislature—L[1]	261,428	340,104
2. Automatic Adoption, Federal Income Tax Amendments—L[1]	*342,138	269,467
3. Constitutional Amendment Concerning County Debt Limitation—L[1]	283,659	294,186
4. Investing Funds Donated to Higher Education—L[1]	*332,188	268,588
5. Veterans' Loan Amendment—L[1]	*481,031	133,564
6. Limits Term of Defeated Incumbents—L[1]	*436,897	158,409
7. Constitutional Amendment Authorizing Education Bonds—L[1]	269,372	318,651
8. Allows Penal Institutions Anywhere in Oregon—L[1]	*352,771	260,100
9. Scenic Waterways Bill—I[2]	*406,315	214,243
10. New Property Tax Bases for Schools—I[1]	223,735	405,437
11. Restricts Governmental Powers Over Rural Property—I[1]	272,765	342,503
January 18, 1972 (Special Election)		
1. Increases Cigarette Tax—R	*245,717	236,937
May 23, 1972		
1. Eliminates Literacy Requirement; Lowers Voting Age—L[1]	327,231	349,746
2. Repeals Requirement for Decennial State Census—L[1]	*420,568	206,436
3. Allows Legislators to Call Special Sessions—L[1]	241,371	391,698
4. Capital Construction Bonds for State Government—L[1]	232,391	364,323
5. Irrigation and Water Development Bonds—L[1]	233,175	374,295
6. Enabling County-City Vehicle Registration Tax—R	120,027	491,551
November 7, 1972		
1. Eliminates Location Requirements for State Institutions—L[1]	*594,080	232,948
2. Qualifications for Sheriff Set By Legislature—L[1]	*572,619	281,720
3. Amends County Purchase and Lease Limitations—L[1]	329,669	462,932
4. Changes State Constitution Provision Regarding Religion—L[1]	336,382	519,196
5. Minimum Jury Size of Six Members—L[1]	*591,191	265,636
6. Broadens Eligibility for Veterans' Loans—L[1]	*736,802	133,139
7. Repeals Governor's Retirement Act—I[2]	*571,959	292,561
8. Changes Succession to Office of Governor—I[1]	*697,297	151,174
9. Prohibits Property Tax for School Operations—I[1]	342,885	558,136
May 1, 1973 (Special Election)		
1. Property Tax Limitation; School Tax Revision—L[2]	253,682	358,219

Election Date/Measure Number/Ballot Title	Yes	No
May 28, 1974		
1. Income, Corporate Tax, School Support Increase—L[2]	136,851	410,733
2. Highway Fund Use for Mass Transit—L[1]	190,899	369,038
3. New School District Tax Base Limitation—L[1]	166,363	371,897
4. Authorizes Bonds for Water Development Fund—L[1]	198,563	328,221
5. Increases Veterans' Loan Bonding Authority—L[1]	*381,559	164,953
6. Permits Legislature to Call Special Session—L[1]	246,525	298,373
November 5, 1974		
1. Liquor Licenses for Public Passenger Carriers—L[1]	353,357	384,521
2. Opens All Legislative Deliberations to Public—L[1]	*546,255	165,778
3. Revises Constitutional Requirements for Grand Juries—L[1]	*437,557	246,902
4. Governor Vacancy Successor Age Requirement Eliminated—L[1]	*381,593	331,756
5. The measure designated as Number 5 by the 1973 Legislature was moved to the May 28, 1974 primary election by the 1974 special session. On the advice of the Attorney General, this measure number was left blank.		
6. Permits Establishing Qualifications for County Assessors—L[1]	*552,737	146,364
7. Tax Base Includes Revenue Sharing Money—L[1]	322,023	329,858
8. Revises School District Election Voting Requirements—L[1]	337,565	378,071
9. Permits State Employes to be Legislators—L[1]	218,846	476,547
10. Revises Oregon Voter Qualification Requirements—L[1]	*362,731	355,506
11. Right to Jury in Civil Cases—L[1]	*480,631	216,853
12. Community Development Fund Bonds—L[1]	277,723	376,747
13. Obscenity and Sexual Conduct Bill—R	*393,743	352,958
14. Public Officials' Financial Ethics and Reporting. This measure was also referred to all 36 counties, with 30 voting yes and 6 voting no; and all cities with governing bodies, with 153 voting yes and 90 voting no.—L[2]	*498,002	177,946
15. Prohibits Purchase or Sale of Steelhead—I[2]	*458,417	274,182
May 25, 1976		
1. Expands Veterans' Home-Farm Loan Eligibility—L[1]	*549,553	158,997
2. Discipline of Judges—L[1]	*639,977	59,774
3. Housing Bonds—L[1]	*315,588	362,414
4. Authorizes Vehicle Tax Mass Transit Use—L[1]	170,331	531,219
November 2, 1976		
1. Validates Inadvertently Superseded Statutory Amendments—L[1]	*607,325	247,843
2. Allows Changing City, County Election Days—L[1]	376,489	536,967
3. Lowers Minimum Age for Legislative Service—L[1]	285,777	679,517
4. Repeals Emergency Succession Provision—L[1]	*507,308	368,646
5. Permits Legislature to Call Special Session—L[1]	*549,126	377,354
6. Allows Charitable, Fraternal, Religious Organizations Bingo—L[1]	*682,252	281,696
7. Partial Public Funding of Election Campaigns—L[2]	263,738	659,327
8. Increases Motor Fuel, Ton-Mile Taxes—R	465,143	505,124
9. Regulates Nuclear Power Plant Construction Approval—I[2]	423,008	584,845
10. Repeals Land Use Planning Coordination Statutes—I[2]	402,608	536,502
11. Prohibits Adding Fluorides to Water Systems—I[2]	419,567	555,981
12. Repeals Intergovernmental Cooperation, Planning District Statutes—I[2]	333,933	525,868
May 17, 1977 (Special Election)		
1. School Operating Levy Measure—L[1]	112,570	252,061
2. Authorizes Additional Veterans' Fund Uses—L[1]	*200,270	158,436
3. Increases Veterans' Loan Bonding Authority—L[1]	*250,783	106,953
November 8, 1977 (Special Election)		
1. Water Development Loan Fund Created—L[1]	*124,484	118,953
2. Development of Nonnuclear Energy Resources—L[1]	105,219	137,693
May 23, 1978		
1. Home Rule County Initiative-Referendum Requirements—L[1]	*306,506	156,623
2. Open Meetings Rules for Legislature—L[1]	*435,338	80,176
3. Housing for Low Income Elderly—L[1]	*291,778	250,810
4. Domestic Water Fund Created—L[1]	148,822	351,843

Elections and Records

Election Date/Measure Number/Ballot Title	Yes	No
5. Highway Repair Priority, Gas Tax Increase—L[2]	190,301	365,170
6. Reorganizes Metropolitan Service District, Abolishes CRAG—L[2,4]	*110,600	91,090
November 7, 1978		
1. Appellate Judge Selection, Running on Record—L[1]	358,504	449,132
2. Authorizes Senate Confirmation of Governor's Appointments—L[1]	*468,458	349,604
3. Vehicle and Fee Increase Referendum—R	208,722	673,802
4. Shortens Formation Procedures for People's Utility Districts—I[2]	375,587	471,027
5. Authorizes, Regulates Practice of Denture Technology—I[2]	*704,480	201,463
6. Limitations on Ad Valorem Property Taxes—I[1]	424,029	453,741
7. Prohibits State Expenditures, Programs or Services for Abortion—I[1]	431,577	461,542
8. Requires Death Penalty for Murder under Specified Conditions—I[2]	*573,707	318,610
9. Limitations on Public Utility Rate Base—I[2]	*589,361	267,132
10. Land Use Planning, Zoning Constitutional Amendment—I[1]	334,523	515,138
11. Reduces Property Tax Payable by Homeowner and Renter—L[1]	383,532	467,765
12. Support of Constitutional Amendment (Federal) Requires Balance Budget—L[5]	*641,862	134,758
May 20, 1980		
1. Constitutional Amendment Limits Uses of Gasoline and Highway User Taxes—L[1]	*451,695	257,230
2. Amends Liquor by the Drink Constitutional Provision—L[1]	325,030	384,346
3. State Bonds for Small Scale Local Energy Project Loan Fund—L[1]	*394,466	278,125
4. Veterans' Home and Farm Loan Eligibility Changes—L[1]	*574,148	130,452
5. Continues Tax Reduction Program—L[2]	*636,565	64,979
6. Definition of Multifamily Low Income Elderly Housing—L[1]	*536,002	138,675
November 4, 1980		
1. Repeal of Constitutional Provision Requiring Elected Superintendent of Public Instruction—L[1]	291,142	820,892
2. Guarantees Mentally Handicapped Voting Rights, Unless Adjudged Incompetent to Vote—L[1]	*678,573	455,020
3. Dedicates Oil, Natural Gas Taxes to Common School Fund—L[1]	*594,520	500,586
4. Increases Gas Tax from Seven to Nine Cents per Gallon—L[2]	298,421	849,745
5. Forbids Use, Sale of Snare, Leghold Traps for Most Purposes—I[2]	425,890	728,173
6. Constitutional Real Property Tax Limit Preserving 85% Districts' 1977 Revenue—I[1]	416,029	711,617
7. Nuclear Plant Licensing Requires Voter Approval, Waste Disposal Facility Existence—I[2]	*608,412	535,049
8. State Bonds for Fund to Finance Correctional Facilities—L[1]	523,955	551,383
May 18, 1982		
1. Use of State Bond Proceeds to Finance Municipal Water Projects—L[1]	*333,656	267,137
2. Multifamily Housing for Elderly and Disabled Persons—L[1]	*389,820	229,049
3. State Bonds for Fund to Finance Corrections Facilities—L[1]	281,548	333,476
4. Raises Taxes on Commercial Vehicles, Motor Vehicles Fuels for Roads—L[2]	308,574	323,268
5. Governor to Appoint Chief Justice of Oregon Supreme Court—L[2]	159,811	453,415
November 2, 1982		
1. Increases Tax Base When New Property Construction Increases District's Value—L[1]	219,034	768,150
2. Lengthens Governor's Time for Postsession Veto or Approval of Bills—L[1]	385,672	604,864
3. Constitutional Real Property Tax Limit Preserving 85% Districts' 1979 Revenue—I[1]	504,836	515,626
4. Permits Self-Service Dispensing of Motor Vehicle Fuel at Retail—I[2]	440,824	597,970
5. People of Oregon Urge Mutual Freeze on Nuclear Weapons Development—I[3]	*623,089	387,907
6. Ends State's Land Use Planning Powers, Retains Local Planning—I[2]	461,271	565,056
May 15, 1984		
1. State May Borrow and Lend Money for Public Works Projects—L[1]	332,175	365,571
2. Increases Fees for Licensing and Registration of Motor Vehicles—L[2]	234,060	487,457

Election Date/Measure Number/Ballot Title	Yes	No
November 6, 1984		
1. Changes Minimum Requirements for Recall of Public Officers—L[1]	*664,464	470,139
2. Constitutional Real Property Tax Limit—I[1]	599,424	616,252
3. Creates Citizens' Utility Board to Represent Interests of Utility Consumers—I[2]	*637,968	556,826
4. Constitutional Amendment Establishes State Lottery, Commission; Profits for Economic Development—I[1]	*794,441	412,341
5. Statutory Provisions for State Operated Lottery if Constitutionally Authorized—I[2]	*786,933	399,231
6. Exempts Death Sentences from Constitutional Guarantees Against Cruel, Vindictive Punishments—I[1]	*653,009	521,687
7. Requires by Statute Death or Mandatory Imprisonment for Aggravated Murder—I[2]	*893,818	295,988
8. Revises Numerous Criminal Laws Concerning Police Powers, Trials, Evidence, Sentencing—I[2]	552,410	597,964
9. Adds Requirements for Disposing Wastes Containing Naturally Occurring Radioactive Isotopes—I[2]	*655,973	524,214
September 17, 1985 (Special Election)		
1. Amends Constitution. Approves Limited 5% Sales Tax for Local Education—L[1]	189,733	664,365
May 20, 1986		
1. Constitutional Amendment: Bans Income Tax on Social Security Benefits—L[1]	*534,476	118,766
2. Constitutional Amendment: Effect on Merger of Taxing Units on Tax Base—L[1]	*333,277	230,886
3. Constitutional Amendment: Verification of Signatures on Initiative and Referendum Petitions—L[1]	*460,148	132,101
4. Requires Special Election for U.S. Senator Vacancy, Removes Constitutional Provision—L[1]	*343,005	269,305
5. Constitutional Amendment: $96 Million Bonds for State-County Prison Buildings—L[1]	300,674	330,429
November 4, 1986		
1. Deletes Constitutional Requirement that Secretary of State Live in Salem—L[1]	*771,959	265,999
2. Constitutional Amendment Revising Legislative District Reapportionment Procedures After Federal Census—L[1]	*637,410	291,355
3. Constitutional Amendment Allows Charitable, Fraternal, Religious Organizations to Conduct Raffles—L[1]	*736,739	302,957
4. Replaces Public Utility Commissioner with Three Member Public Utility Commission—L[2]	*724,577	297,973
5. Legalizes Private Possession and Growing of Marijuana for Personal Use—I[2]	279,479	781,922
6. Constitutional Amendment Prohibits State Funding Abortions. Exception: Prevent Mother's Death—I[1]	477,920	580,163
7. Constitutional 5% Sales Tax, Funds Schools, Reduces Property Tax—I[1]	234,804	816,369
8. Prohibits Mandatory Local Measured Telephone Service Except Mobile Phone Service—I[2]	*802,099	201,918
9. Amends Constitution. Limits Property Tax Rates and Assessed Value Increases—I[1]	449,548	584,396
10. Revises Many Criminal Laws Concerning Victims' Rights, Evidence, Sentencing, Parole—I[2]	*774,766	251,509
11. Homeowner's, Renter's Property Tax Relief Program; Sales Tax Limitation Measure—I[1]	381,727	639,034
12. State Income Tax Changes, Increased Revenue to Property Tax Relief—I[2]	299,551	720,034
13. Constitutional Amendment: Twenty Day Pre-election Voter Registration Cutoff—I[1]	*693,460	343,450
14. Prohibits Nuclear Power Plant Operation Until Permanent Waste Site Licensed—I[2]	375,241	674,641

Election Date/Measure Number/Ballot Title	Yes	No
15. Supersedes "Radioactive Waste" Definition; Changes Energy Facility Payment Procedure—I[2]	424,099	558,741
16. Phases Out Nuclear Weapons Manufactured With Tax Credits, Civil Penalty—I[2]	400,119	590,971
May 19, 1987 (Special Election)		
1. State Role In Selection of High-Level Nuclear Waste Repository Site—L[2]	*299,581	100,854
2. Continues Existing Levies To Prevent School Closures: Tax Base Elections—L[1]	*223,417	178,839
May 17, 1988		
1. Authorizes Water Development Fund Loans for Fish Protection, Watershed Restoration—L[1]	*485,629	191,008
2. Protective Headgear for Motorcycle Operators and Passengers and Moped Riders—L[2]	*486,401	224,655
November 8, 1988		
1. Extends Governor's Veto Deadline After Legislature Adjourns; Requires Prior Announcement—L[1]	*615,012	520,939
2. Common School Fund Investments; Using Income for State Lands Management—L[1]	*621,894	510,694
3. Requires the Use of Safety Belts—L[2]	528,324	684,747
4. Requires Full Sentences Without Parole, Probation for Certain Repeat Felonies—I[2]	*947,805	252,985
5. Finances Intercollegiate Athletic Fund by Increasing Malt Beverage, Cigarette Taxes—I[2]	449,797	759,360
6. Indoor Clean Air Law Revisions Banning Public Smoking—I[2]	430,147	737,779
7. Oregon Scenic Waterway System—I[2]	*663,604	516,998
8. Revokes Ban on Sexual Orientation Discrimination in State Executive Branch—I[2]	*626,751	561,355
May 16, 1989 (Special Election)		
1. Establishes New Tax Base Limits on Schools—L[1]	183,818	263,283
June 27, 1989 (Special Election)		
1. Removes Constitutional Limitation on Use of Property Forfeited To State—L[1]	*340,506	141,649
2. Prohibits Selling/Exporting Timber from State Lands Unless Oregon Processed—L[1]	*446,151	48,558
May 15, 1990		
1. Permits Using Local Vehicle Taxes for Transit if Voters Approve—L[1]	294,099	324,458
2. Amends Constitution; Allows Pollution Control Bond Use for Related Activities—L[1]	*352,922	248,123
3. Amends State Constitution; Requires Annual Legislative Sessions of Limited Duration—L[1]	294,664	299,831
4. Amends Laws on Organization of International Port of Coos Bay—L[2]	4,234	4,745
5A. Advisory Vote: Changing the School Finance System—L[5]	*462,090	140,747
5B. Advisory Vote: Income Tax Increase Reducing Homeowner School Property Taxes—L[5]	177,964	408,842
5C. Advisory Vote: Income Tax Increase Eliminating Homeowner School Property Taxes—L[5]	128,642	449,725
5D. Advisory Vote: Sales Tax Reducing School Property Taxes—L[5]	202,367	385,820
5E. Advisory Vote: Sales Tax Eliminating School Property Taxes—L[5]	222,611	374,466
November 6, 1990		
1. Grants Metropolitan Service District Electors Right to Home Rule—L[1]	*510,947	491,170
2. Constitutional Amendment Allows Merged School Districts to Combine Tax Bases—L[1]	*680,463	354,288
3. Repeals Tax Exemption, Grants Additional Benefit Payments for PERS Retirees—R	406,372	617,586
4. Prohibits Trojan Operation Until Nuclear Waste, Cost, Earthquake Standards Met—I[2]	446,795	660,992
5. State Constitutional Limit on Property Taxes for Schools, Government Operations—I[1]	*574,833	522,022

Election Date/Measure Number/Ballot Title	Yes	No
6. Product Packaging Must Meet Recycling Standards or Receive Hardship Waiver—I[2]	467,418	636,804
7. Six-County Work in Lieu of Welfare Benefits Pilot Program—I[2]	*624,744	452,853
8. Amends Oregon Constitution to Prohibit Abortion With Three Exceptions—I[1]	355,963	747,599
9. Requires the Use of Safety Belts—I[2]	*598,460	512,872
10. Doctor Must Give Parent Notice Before Minor's Abortion—I[2]	530,851	577,806
11. School Choice System, Tax Credit for Education Outside Public Schools—I[1]	351,977	741,863
May 19, 1992		
1. Amends Constitution: Future Fuel Taxes May Go to Police—L[1]	244,173	451,715
November 3, 1992		
1. Bonds May be Issued for State Parks—L[1]	653,062	786,017
2. Future Fuel Taxes May Go to Parks—L[1]	399,259	1,039,322
3. Limits Terms for Legislature, Statewide Offices, Congressional Offices—I[1]	*1,003,706	439,694
4. Bans Operation of Triple Truck-Trailer Combinations on Oregon Highways—I[2]	567,467	896,778
5. Closes Trojan Until Nuclear Waste, Cost, Earthquake, Health Conditions Met—I[2]	585,051	874,636
6. Bans Trojan Power Operation Unless Earthquake, Waste Storage Conditions Met—I[2]	619,329	830,850
7. Raises Tax Limit on Certain Property; Residential Renters' Tax Relief—I[1]	362,621	1,077,206
8. Restricts Lower Columbia Fish Harvests to Most Selective Means Available—I[2]	576,633	828,096
9. Government Cannot Facilitate, Must Discourage Homosexuality, Other "Behaviors"—I[1]	638,527	828,290
June 29, 1993 (Special Election)		
1. Allows Voter Approval of Urban Renewal Bond Repayment Outside Limit—L[1]	180,070	482,714
November 9, 1993 (Special Election)		
1. Should We Pass A 5% Sales Tax for Public Schools with these Restrictions?—L[1]	240,991	721,930
May 17, 1994		
2. Allows New Motor Vehicle Fuel Revenues for Dedicated Purposes—L[1]	158,028	446,665
November 8, 1994		
3. Amends Constitution: Changes Deadline for Filling Vacancies at General Election—L[1]	*776,197	382,126
4. Amends Constitution: Creates Vacancy if State Legislator Convicted of Felony—L[1]	*1,055,111	145,499
5. Amends Constitution: Bars New or Increased Taxes without Voter Approval—I[1]	543,302	671,025
6. Amends Constitution: Candidates May Use Only Contributions from District Residents—I[1]	*628,180	555,019
7. Amends Constitution: Guarantees Equal Protection: Lists Prohibited Grounds of Discrimination—I[1]	512,980	671,021
8. Amends Constitution: Public Employees Pay Part of Salary for Pension—I[1]	*611,760	610,776
9. Adopts Contribution and Spending Limits, Other Campaign Finance Law Changes—I[2]	*851,014	324,224
10. Amends Constitution: Legislature Cannot Reduce Voter-Approved Sentence Without 2/3 Vote—I[1]	*763,507	415,678
11. Mandatory Sentences for Listed Felonies; Covers Persons 15 and Up—I[2]	*788,695	412,816
12. Repeals Prevailing Rate Wage Requirement for Workers on Public Works—I[2]	450,553	731,146
13. Amends Constitution: Governments Cannot Approve, Create Classifications Based on, Homosexuality—I[1]	592,746	630,628

Election Date/Measure Number/Ballot Title	Yes	No
14. Amends Chemical Process Mining Laws: Adds Requirements, Prohibitions, Standards, Fees—I[1]	500,005	679,936
15. Amends Constitution: State Must Maintain Funding for Schools, Community Colleges—I[1]	438,018	760,853
16. Allows Terminally Ill Adults to Obtain Prescription for Lethal Drugs—I[2]	*627,980	596,018
17. Amends Constitution: Requires State Prison Inmates to Work Full Time—I[1]	*859,896	350,541
18. Bans Hunting Bears with Bait, Hunting Bears, Cougars with Dogs—I[2]	*629,527	586,026
19. Amends Constitution: No Free Speech Protection for Obscenity, Child Pornography—I[1]	549,754	652,139
20. Amends Constitution: "Equal Tax" on Trade Replaces Current Taxes—I[1]	284,195	898,416
May 16, 1995 (Special Election)		
21. Dedication of Lottery Funds to Education—L[1]	*671,027	99,728
22. Inhabitancy in State Legislative Districts—L[1]	*709,931	45,311
May 21, 1996		
23. Amends Constitution: Increases Minimum Value in Controversy Required to Obtain Jury Trial—L[1]	*466,580	177,218
24. Amends Constitution: Initiative Petition Signatures Must Be Collected From Each Congressional District—L[1]	279,399	360,592
25. Amends Constitution: Requires 3/5 Majority in Legislature to Pass Revenue-Raising Bills—L[1]	*349,918	289,930
November 5, 1996		
26. Amends Constitution: Changes the Principles that Govern Laws for Punishment of Crime—L[1]	*878,677	440,283
27. Amends Constitution: Grants Legislature New Power Over Both New, Existing Administrative Rules—L[1]	349,050	938,819
28. Amends Constitution: Repeals Certain Residency Requirements for State Veterans' Loans—L[1]	*708,341	593,136
29. Amends Constitution: Governor's Appointees Must Vacate Office If Successor Not Timely Confirmed—L[1]	335,057	958,947
30. Amends Constitution: State Must Pay Local Governments Costs of State-Mandated Programs—L[1]	*731,127	566,168
31. Amends Constitution: Obscenity May Receive No Greater Protection Than Under Federal Constitution—L[1]	630,980	706,974
32. Authorizes Bonds for Portland Region Light Rail, Transportation Projects Elsewhere—R[2]	622,764	704,970
33. Amends Constitution: Limits Legislative Change to Statutes Passed by Voters—I[1]	638,824	652,811
34. Wildlife Management Exclusive to Commission; Repeals 1994 Bear/Cougar Initiative—I[2]	570,803	762,979
35. Restricts Bases for Providers to Receive Pay for Health Care—I[2]	441,108	807,987
36. Increases Minimum Hourly Wage to $6.50 Over Three Years—I[2]	*769,725	584,303
37. Broadens Types of Beverage Containers Requiring Deposit and Refund Value—I[2]	540,645	818,336
38. Prohibits Livestock in Certain Polluted Waters or on Adjacent Lands—I[2]	479,921	852,661
39. Amends Constitution: Government, Private Entities Cannot Discriminate Among Health Care Provider Categories—I[1]	569,037	726,824
40. Amends Constitution: Gives Crime Victims Rights, Expands Admissible Evidence, Limits Pretrial Release—I[1]	*778,574	544,301
41. Amends Constitution: States How Public Employee Earnings Must Be Expressed—I[1]	446,115	838,088
42. Amends Constitution: Requires Testing of Public School Students; Public Report—I[1]	460,553	857,878
43. Amends Collective Bargaining Law for Public Safety Employees—I[2]	547,131	707,586
44. Increases, Adds Cigarette and Tobacco Taxes; Changes Tax Revenue Distribution—I[2]	*759,048	598,543
45. Amends Constitution: Raises Public Employees' Normal Retirement Age; Reduces Benefits—I[1]	458,238	866,461

Election Date/Measure Number/Ballot Title	Yes	No
46. Amends Constitution: Counts Non-Voters As "No" Votes on Tax Measures—I[1]	158,555	1,180,148
47. Amends Constitution: Reduces and Limits Property Taxes; Limits Local Revenues, Replacement Fees—I[1]	*704,554	642,613
48. Amends Constitution: Instructs State, Federal Legislators to Vote for Congressional Term Limits—I[1,3]	624,771	671,095
May 20, 1997 (Special Election)		
49. Amends Constitution: Restricts Inmate Lawsuits; Allows Interstate Shipment of Prison Made Products—L[1]	*699,813	70,940
50. Amends Constitution: Limits Assessed Value of Property for Tax Purposes; Limits Property Tax Rates—L[1]	*429,943	341,781
November 4, 1997 (Special Election)		
51. Repeals Law Allowing Terminally Ill Adults To Obtain Lethal Prescription—L[2]	445,830	666,275
52. Authorizes State Lottery Bond Program To Finance Public School Projects—L[2]	*805,742	293,425
May 19, 1998		
53. Amends Constitution: Eliminates Voter Turnout Requirement For Passing Certain Property Tax Measures—L[1]	303,539	319,871
November 3, 1998		
54. Amends Constitution: Authorizes State To Guarantee Bonded Indebtedness Of Certain Education Districts—L[1]	*569,982	474,727
55. Amends Constitution: Permits State To Guarantee Earnings On Prepaid Tuition Trust Fund—L[1]	456,464	579,251
56. Expands Notice To Landowners Regarding Changes To Land Use Laws—L[2]	*874,547	212,737
57. Makes Possession Of Limited Amount Of Marijuana Class C Misdemeanor—R[2]	371,967	736,968
58. Requires Issuing Copy Of Original Oregon Birth Certificate to Adoptees—I[2]	*621,832	462,084
59. Amends Constitution: Prohibits Using Public Resources To Collect Money For Political Purposes—I[1]	539,757	561,952
60. Requires Vote By Mail In Biennial Primary, General Elections—I[2]	*757,204	334,021
61. Vote Not Tallied By Court Order		
62. Amends Constitution: Requires Campaign Finance Disclosures; Regulates Signature Gathering; Guarantees Contribution Methods—I[1]	*721,448	347,112
63. Amends Constitution: Measures Proposing Supermajority Voting Requirements Require Same Supermajority For Passage—I[1]	*566,064	457,762
64. Prohibits Many Present Timber Harvest Practices, Imposes More Restrictive Regulations—I[2]	215,491	897,535
65. Amends Constitution: Creates Process For Requiring Legislature To Review Administrative Rules—I[1]	483,811	533,948
66. Amends Constitution: Dedicates Some Lottery Funding To Parks, Beaches; Habitat, Watershed Protection—I[1]	*742,038	362,247
67. Allows Medical Use Of Marijuana Within Limits; Establishes Permit System—I[2]	*611,190	508,263
November 2, 1999 (Special Election)		
68. Amends Constitution: Allows Protecting Business, Certain Government Programs From Prison Work Programs—L[1]	*406,526	289,407
69. Amends Constitution: Grants Victims Constitutional Rights In Criminal Prosecutions, Juvenile Court Delinquency Proceedings—L[1]	*406,393	292,419
70. Amends Constitution: Gives Public, Through Prosecutor, Right To Demand Jury Trial In Criminal Cases—L[1]	289,783	407,429
71. Amends Constitution: Limits Pretrial Release Of Accused Person To Protect Victims, Public—L[1]	*404,404	292,696
72. Amends Constitution: Allows Murder Conviction By 11 To 1 Jury Verdict—L[1]	316,351	382,685
73. Amends Constitution: Limits Immunity From Criminal Prosecution Of Person Ordered To Testify About His Or Her Conduct—L[1]	320,160	369,843

Election Date/Measure Number/Ballot Title	Yes	No
74. Amends Constitution: Requires Terms Of Imprisonment Announced In Court Be Fully Served, With Exceptions—L[1]	*368,899	325,078
75. Amends Constitution: Persons Convicted Of Certain Crimes Cannot Serve On Grand Juries, Criminal Trial Juries—L[1]	*399,671	292,445
76. Amends Constitution: Requires Light, Heavy Motor Vehicle Classes Proportionately Share Highway Costs—L[1]	*372,613	314,351
May 16, 2000		
77. Amends Constitution: Makes Certain Local Taxing Districts' Temporary Property Tax Authority Permanent—L[1]	336,253	432,541
78. Amends Constitution: Lengthens Period For Verifying Signatures On Initiative And Referendum Petitions—L[1]	*528,129	327,440
79. Amends Constitution: Increases Signatures Required To Place Initiative Amending Constitution On Ballot—L[1]	356,912	505,081
80. Amends Constitution: Authorizes Using Fuel Tax, Vehicle Fees For Increasing Highway Policing—L[1]	310,640	559,941
81. Amends Constitution: Allows Legislature To Limit Recovery Of Damages In Civil Actions—L[1]	219,009	650,348
82. Repeals Truck Weight-Mile Tax; Establishes And Increases Fuel Taxes—R[2]	109,741	767,329
November 7, 2000		
83. Amends Constitution: Authorizes New Standards, Priorities For Veterans' Loans; Expands Qualified Recipients—L[1]	*1,084,870	365,203
84. Amends Constitution: State Must Continue Paying Local Governments For State-Mandated Programs—L[1]	*1,211,384	222,723
85. Amends Constitution: Modifies Population, Minimum Area Requirements For Formation Of New Counties—L[1]	634,307	767,366
86. Amends Constitution: Requires Refunding General Fund Revenues Exceeding State Estimates To Taxpayers—L[1]	*898,793	550,304
87. Amends Constitution: Allows Regulation Of Location Of Sexually Oriented Businesses Through Zoning—L[1]	694,410	771,901
88. Increases Maximum Deductible In Oregon For Federal Income Taxes Paid—L[2]	*739,270	724,097
89. Dedicates Tobacco Settlement Proceeds To Specified Health, Housing, Transportation Programs—L[2]	622,814	828,117
90. Authorizes Rates Giving Utilities Return On Investments In Retired Property—R[2]	158,810	1,208,545
91. Amends Constitution: Makes Federal Income Taxes Fully Deductible On Oregon Tax Returns—I[1]	661,342	814,885
92. Amends Constitution: Prohibits Payroll Deductions For Political Purposes Without Specific Written Authorization—I[1]	656,250	815,338
93. Amends Constitution: Voters Must Approve Most Taxes, Fees; Requires Certain Approval Percentage—I[1]	581,186	865,091
94. Repeals Mandatory Minimum Sentences For Certain Felonies, Requires Resentencing—I[2]	387,068	1,073,275
95. Amends Constitution: Student Learning Determines Teacher Pay; Qualifications, Not Seniority, Determine Retention—I[1]	514,926	962,250
96. Amends Constitution: Prohibits Making Initiative Process Harder, Except Through Initiative; Applies Retroactively—I[1]	527,613	866,588
97. Bans Body-Gripping Animal Traps, Some Poisons; Restricts Fur Commerce—I[2]	606,939	867,219
98. Amends Constitution: Prohibits Using Public Resources For Political Purposes; Limits Payroll Deductions—I[1]	678,024	776,489
99. Amends Constitution: Creates Commission Ensuring Quality Home Care Services For Elderly, Disabled—I[1]	*911,217	539,414
1. Amends Constitution: Legislature Must Fund School Quality Goals Adequately; Report; Establish Grants—I[1]	*940,223	477,461
2. Amends Constitution: Creates Process For Requiring Legislature To Review Administrative Rules—I[1]	605,575	779,190
3. Amends Constitution: Requires Conviction Before Forfeiture; Restricts Proceeds Usage; Requires Reporting, Penalty—I[1]	*952,792	465,081

Election Date/Measure Number/Ballot Title	Yes	No
4. Dedicates Tobacco-Settlement Proceeds; Earnings Fund Low-Income Health Care—I[2]	650,850	789,543
5. Expands Circumstances Requiring Background Checks Before Transfer Of Firearm—I[2]	*921,926	569,996
6. Provides Public Funding To Candidates Who Limit Spending, Private Contributions—I[2]	586,910	838,011
7. The Secretary of State has been enjoined from canvassing the votes for this measure—I[1]		
8. Amends Constitution: Limits State Appropriations To Percentage Of State's Prior Personal Income—I[1]	608,090	789,699
9. Prohibits Public School Instruction Encouraging, Promoting, Sanctioning Homosexual, Bisexual Behaviors—I[2]	702,572	788,691
May 21, 2002		
10. Amends Constitution: Allows Public Universities to Receive Equity in Private Companies as Compensation for Publicly Created Technology—L[1]	*608,640	177,004
11. Amends Constitution: Authorizes Less Expensive General Obligation Bond financing for OHSU Medical Research and other Capital Costs—L[1]	*589,869	190,226
12. Removed from Ballot		
13. Amends Constitution: Authorizes Using Education Fund Principal in Specified Circumstances; Transfers $220 Million to School Fund—L[1]	376,605	411,923
September 17, 2002 (Special Election, see Note below)		
19. Amends Constitution: Authorizes Using Education Stability Fund Principal in Specified Circumstances; Transfers $150 Million to State School Fund; Creates School Capital Matching Subaccount in Stability Fund—L[1]	*496,815	306,440
20. Increases Cigarette Tax; Uses Revenue for Health Plan, Other Programs—L[2]	*522,613	289,119
November 5, 2002		
14. Amends Constitution: Removes Historical Racial References in Obsolete Sections of Constitution—L[1]	*867,901	352,027
15. Amends Constitution: Authorizes State to Issue General Obligation Bonds for Seismic Rehabilitation of Public Education Buildings—L[1]	*671,640	535,638
16. Amends Constitution: Authorizes State to Issue General Obligation Bonds for Seismic Rehabilitation of Emergency Services Buildings—L[1]	*669,451	530,587
17. Amends Constitution: Reduces Minimum Age Requirement to Serve as State Legislator from 21 Years to 18 Years—L[1]	341,717	910,331
18. Amends Constitution: Allows Certain Tax Districts to Establish Permanent Property Tax Rates and Divide into Tax Zones—L[1]	450,444	704,116
Note: An early Special Election was held for Measures 19 and 20 (see above)		
21. Amends Constitution: Revises Procedure for Filling Judicial Vacancies, Electing Judges; Allows Vote for "None of the Above"—I[1]	526,450	668,256
22. Amends Constitution: Requires Supreme Court Judges and Court of Appeals Judges to be Elected by District—I[1]	595,936	610,063
23. Creates Health Care Finance Plan for Medically Necessary Services; Creates Additional Income, Payroll Taxes—I[2]	265,310	969,537
24. Allows Licensed Denturists to Install Partial Dentures; Authorizes Cooperative Dentist-Denturist Business Ventures—I[2]	*907,979	286,492
25. Increases Minimum Wage to $6.90 in 2003; Increases for Inflation in Future Years—I[2]	*645,016	611,658
26. Amends Constitution: Prohibits Payment, Receipt of Payment Based on the Number of Initiative, Referendum Petition Signatures Obtained—I[1]	*921,606	301,415
27. Requires Labeling of Genetically-Engineered Foods Sold or Distributed in or from Oregon—I[2]	371,851	886,806
January 28, 2003 (Special Election)		
28. Temporarily Increases Income Tax Rates—L[2]	575,846	676,312
September 16, 2003 (Special Election)		
29. Amends Constitution: Authorizes State of Oregon to Incur General Obligation Debt for Savings on Pension Liabilities—L[1]	*360,209	291,778

Election Date/Measure Number/Ballot Title	Yes	No
February 3, 2004 (Special Election)		
30. Enacts Temporary Personal Income Tax Surcharge; Increases, Changes Corporate, Other Taxes; Avoids Specific Budget Cuts—R[2]	481,315	691,462
November 2, 2004		
31. Amends Constitution: Authorizes Law Permitting Postponement of Election for Particular Public Office When Nominee for Office Dies—L[1]	*1,122,852	588,502
32. Amends Constitution: Deletes Reference to Mobile Homes from Provision Dealing with Taxes and Fees on Motor Vehicles—L[1]	*1,048,090	661,576
33. Amends Medical Marijuana Act: Requires Marijuana Dispensaries for Supplying Patients/Caregivers; Raises Patients' Possession Limit—I[2]	764,015	1,021,814
34. Requires Balancing Timber Production, Resource Conservation/Preservation in Managing State Forests; Specifically Addresses Two Forests—I[2]	659,467	1,060,496
35. Amends Constitution: Limits Noneconomic Damages (Defined) Recoverable for Patient Injuries Caused by Healthcare Provider's Negligence or Recklessness—I[1]	869,054	896,857
36. Amends Constitution: Only Marriage Between One Man and One Woman Is Valid or Legally Recognized as Marriage—I[1]	*1,028,546	787,556
37. Governments Must Pay Owners, or Forgo Enforcement, when Certain Land Use Restrictions Reduce Property Value—I[2]	*1,054,589	685,079
38. Abolishes SAIF; State Must Reinsure, Satisfy SAIF's Obligations; Dedicates Proceeds, Potential Surplus to Public Purposes—I[2]	670,935	1,037,722
November 7, 2006		
39. Prohibits Public Body from Condemning Private Real Property If Intends to Convey to Private Party—I[2]	*881,820	431,844
40. Amends Constitution: Requires Oregon Supreme Court Judges and Court of Appeals Judges To Be Elected by District—I[1]	576,153	749,404
41. Allows Income Tax Deduction Equal to Federal Exemptions Deduction to Substitute for State Exemption Credit—I[2]	483,443	818,452
42. Prohibits Insurance Companies from Using Credit Score or "Credit Worthiness" in Calculating Rates or Premiums—I[2]	479,935	876,075
43. Requires 48-Hour Notice to Unemancipated Minor's Parent Before Providing Abortion; Authorizes Lawsuits, Physician Discipline—I[2]	616,876	746,606
44. Allows Any Oregon Resident Without Prescription Drug Coverage to Participate in Oregon Prescription Drug Program—I[2]	*1,049,594	296,649
45. Amends Constitution: Limits State Legislators: Six Years as Representative, Eight Years as Senator, Fourteen Years in Legislature—I[1]	555,016	788,895
46. Amends Constitution: Allows Laws Regulating Election Contributions, Expenditures Adopted by Initiative or 3/4 of Both Legislative Houses—I[1]	520,342	770,251
47. Revises Campaign Finance Laws: Limits or Prohibits Contributions and Expenditures; Adds Disclosure, New Reporting Requirements—I[2]	*694,918	615,256
48. Amends Constitution: Limits Biennial Percentage Increase in State Spending to Percentage Increase in State Population, Plus Inflation—I[1]	379,971	923,629
November 6, 2007 (Special Election)		
49. Modifies Measure 37: Clarifies Right to Build Homes; Limits Large Developments; Protects Farms, Forests, Groundwater—L[2]	*718,023	437,351
50. Amends Constitution: Dedicates Funds to Provide Health Care for Children, Fund Tobacco Prevention, Through Increased Tobacco Tax—L[1]	472,063	686,470
May 20, 2008		
51. Amends Constitution: Enables Crime Victims to Enforce Existing Constitutional Rights in Prosecutions, Delinquency Proceedings; Authorizes Implementing Legislation—L[1]	*744,195	249,143
52. Amends Constitution: Enables Crime Victims to Enforce Existing Constitutional Rights in Prosecutions, Delinquency Proceedings; Authorizes Implementing Legislation—L[1]	*738,092	247,738
53. Amends Constitution: Modifies Provisions Governing Civil Forfeitures Related to Crimes; Permits Use of Proceeds by Law Enforcement—L[1]	*490,158	489,477
November 4, 2008		
54. Amends Constitution: Standardizes Voting Eligibility for School Board Elections with Other State and Local Elections—L[1]	*1,194,173	450,979

Election Date/Measure Number/Ballot Title	Yes	No
55. Amends Constitution: Changes Operative Date of Redistricting Plans; Allows Affected Legislators to Finish Term in Original District—L[1]	*1,251,478	364,993
56. Amends Constitution: Provides that May and November Property Tax Elections are Decided by Majority of Voters Voting—L[1]	*959,118	735,500
57. Increases Sentences for Drug Trafficking, Theft Against Elderly and Specified Repeat Property and Identity Theft Crimes; Requires Addiction Treatment for Certain Offenders—L[2]	*1,058,955	665,942
58. Prohibits Teaching Public School Student in Language Other Than English for More Than Two Years—I[2]	756,903	977,696
59. Creates an Unlimited Deduction for Federal Income Taxes on Individual Taxpayers' Oregon Income-Tax Returns—I[2]	615,894	1,084,422
60. Teacher "Classroom Performance," Not Seniority, Determines Pay Raises; "Most Qualified" Teachers Retained, Regardless of Seniority—I[2]	673,296	1,070,682
61. Creates Mandatory Minimum Prison Sentences for Certain Theft, Identity Theft, Forgery, Drug, and Burglary Crimes—I[2]	848,901	887,165
62. Amends Constitution: Allocates 15% of Lottery Proceeds to Public Safety Fund for Crime Prevention, Investigation, Prosecution—I[2]	674,428	1,035,756
63. Exempts Specified Property Owners From Building Permit Requirements for Improvements Valued At/Under 35,000 Dollars—I[2]	784,376	928,721
64. Penalizes Person, Entity for Using Funds Collected with "Public Resource" (Defined) for "Political Purpose"—I[2]	835,563	854,327
65. Changes General Election Nomination Processes for Major/Minor Party, Independent Candidates for Most Partisan Offices—I[2]	553,640	1,070,580
January 26, 2010 (Special Election)		
66. Raises tax on household income at and above $250,000 (and $125,000 for individual filers). Reduces income taxes on unemployment benefits in 2009. Provides funds currently budgeted for education, health care, public safety, other services—R[2]	*692,687	583,707
67. Raises $10 corporate minimum tax, business minimum tax, corporate profits tax. Provides funds currently budgeted for education, health care, public safety, other services—R[2]	*682,720	591,188
May 18, 2010		
68. Revises Constitution: Allows State To Issue Bonds To Match Voter Approved School District Bonds For School Capital Costs—L[1]	*498,073	267,052
69. Amends Constitution: Continues And Modernizes Authority For Lowest Cost Borrowing For Community Colleges And Public Universities—L[1]	*546,649	216,157
November 2, 2010		
70. Amends Constitution: Expands availability of home ownership loans for Oregon veterans through Oregon War Veterans' Fund—L[1]	*1,180,933	217,679
71. Amends Constitution: Requires legislature to meet annually; limits length of legislative sessions; provides exceptions—L[1]	*919,040	435,776
72. Amends Constitution: Authorizes exception to $50,000 state borrowing limit for state's real and personal property projects—L[1]	*774,582	536,204
73. Requires increased minimum sentences for certain repeated sex crimes, incarceration for repeated driving under influence—I[2]	*802,388	608,317
74. Establishes medical marijuana supply system and assistance and research programs; allows limited selling of marijuana—I[2]	627,016	791,186
75. Authorizes Multnomah County casino; casino to contribute monthly revenue percentage to state for specified purposes—I[2]	448,162	959,342
76. Amends Constitution: Continues lottery funding for parks, beaches, wildlife habitat, watershed protection beyond 2014; modifies funding process—I[1]	*972,825	432,552
November 6, 2012		
77. Amends Constitution: Governor may declare "catastrophic disaster" (defined); requires legislative session; authorizes suspending specified constitutional spending restrictions—L[1]	*957,646	673,468
78. Amends Constitution: Changes constitutional language describing governmental system of separation of powers; makes grammatical and spelling changes—L[1]	*1,165,963	458,509

Election Date/Measure Number/Ballot Title	Yes	No
79. Amends Constitution: Prohibits real estate transfer taxes, fees, other assessments, except those operative on December 31, 2009—I[1]	*976,587	679,710
80. Allows personal marijuana, hemp cultivation/use without license; commission to regulate commercial marijuana cultivation/sale—I[2]	810,538	923,071
81. Prohibits commercial non-tribal fishing with gillnets in Oregon "inland waters," allows use of seine nets—I[2]	567,996	1,072,614
82. Amends Constitution: Authorizes establishment of privately-owned casinos; mandates percentage of revenues payable to dedicated state fund—I[1]	485,240	1,226,331
83. Authorizes privately-owned Wood Village casino; mandates percentage of revenues payable to dedicated state fund—I[2]	500,123	1,207,508
84. Phases out existing inheritance taxes on large estates, and all taxes on intra-family property transfers—I[2]	776,143	912,541
85. Amends Constitution: Allocates corporate income/excise tax "kicker" refund to additionally fund K through 12 public education—I[1]	*1,007,122	672,586

[0]Repeal of federal prohibition amendment

[1]Constitutional amendment

[2]Statutory enactment

[3]Required communication to federal officials on behalf of people of Oregon

[4]Tri-county measure voted on in Clackamas, Multnomah and Washington Counties

[5]Advisory vote for legislators' information

Earliest Authorities in Oregon

Pacific Fur Company*

Fort Astoria

Name	Term of Service	By What Authority/Remarks
McDougall, Duncan	Mar. 22, 1811–Feb. 15, 1812 Aug. 4, 1812–Aug. 20, 1813 Aug. 26, 1813–Oct. 16, 1813	Acting agent and partner; served in absence of Wilson Price Hunt by agreement with partners
Hunt, Wilson Price	Feb. 15, 1812–Aug. 4, 1812 Aug. 20, 1813–Aug. 26, 1813	Agent and partner by Articles of Agreement, June 23, 1810, Article 21

*Sold to John George McTavish and John Stuart, partners of the North West Company, Oct. 16, 1813; sale confirmed by Wilson Price Hunt, agent, March 10, 1814

North West Company

Headquarters, Columbia District, Fort George (Astoria)

McTavish, John George	Oct. 16, 1813–Dec. 1, 1813	Acting governor and partner
McDonald, John (of Garth)	Dec. 1, 1813–Apr. 4, 1814	Governor and partner, Alexander Henry, trader
McTavish, Donald	Apr. 23, 1814–May 22, 1814	Governor and partner; with Alexander Henry, drowned in the Columbia River
Keith, James	May 22, 1814–June 7, 1816	Acting governor and partner

Chief of the Coast	Term of Service	Chief of the Interior
Keith, James	June 7, 1816–Mar. 21, 1821	McKenzie, Donald

Hudson's Bay Company*

Headquarters, Columbia District, Fort George (Astoria) 1821–1825; Fort Vancouver, 1825–1846

Chief Factor	Term of Service	Junior Chief Factor
McMillan, James	Spring, 1821–Fall, 1821	Cameron, John Dougald
Cameron, John Dougald	Fall, 1821–Spring, 1824	Kennedy, Alexander
Kennedy, Alexander	Spring, 1824–Mar. 18, 1825	McLoughlin, John
McLoughlin, John	Mar. 18, 1825–May 31, 1845	None appointed

*Appointments in 1821 by agreement with North West Company; and 1822–1825 by council of Northern Department, Sir George Simpson, Governor

Oregon (Walamet) Mission of the Methodist Episcopal Church

Mission Bottom 1834–1841; Chemeketa (Salem) 1841–1847

Name	Term of Service	Position
Lee, Jason	Oct. 6, 1834–Mar. 26, 1838	Appointed superintendent upon recommendation of the Board of Managers of the Missionary Society
Leslie, David	Mar. 26, 1838–May 27, 1840	Acting superintendent in absence of Lee
Lee, Jason	May 27, 1840–Dec. 25, 1843	Superintendent
Leslie, David	Dec. 25, 1843–June 1, 1844	Acting superintendent in absence of Lee
Gary, George	June 1, 1844–July 18, 1847	Appointed superintendent; instructed to dissolve the mission properties

Provisional Government Executive Committee

Name	Term of Service	By What Authority/Remarks
Hill, David; Beers, Alanson; Gale, Joseph	July 5, 1843–May 25, 1844	Elected by meeting of inhabitants of the Oregon Territory
Stewart, P.G.; Russell Osborn; Bailey, W.J.	May 25, 1844–July 14, 1845	By vote of the people

Governors of Oregon

Under Provisional Government

Name/Political Party[1]	Term of Service	By What Authority/Remarks
Abernethy, George	July 14, 1845–Mar. 3, 1849	By people at 1845 general election; reelected 1848

Under Territorial Government

Name/Political Party	Term of Service	By What Authority/Remarks
Lane, Joseph—D	Mar. 3, 1849–June 18, 1850	Appointed by President Polk; resigned
Prichette, Kintzing—D	June 18, 1850–Aug. 18, 1850	Acting governor, was secretary
Gaines, John P.—W	Aug. 18, 1850–May 16, 1853	Appointed by President Taylor
Lane, Joseph—D	May 16, 1853–May 19, 1853	Appointed by President Pierce; resigned
Curry, George L.—D	May 19, 1853–Dec. 2, 1853	Acting governor, was secretary
Davis, John W.—D	Dec. 2, 1853–Aug. 1, 1854	Appointed by President Pierce; resigned
Curry, George L.—D	Aug. 1, 1854–Mar. 3, 1859	Acting governor, was secretary; appointed by President Pierce, Nov. 1, 1854

Under State Government

Name/Political Party	Term of Service	By What Authority/Remarks
Whiteaker, John—D	Mar. 3, 1859–Sept. 10, 1862	Elected 1858
Gibbs, A.C.—R	Sept. 10, 1862–Sept. 12, 1866	Elected 1862
Woods, George L.—R	Sept. 12, 1866–Sept. 14, 1870	Elected 1866
Grover, LaFayette—D	Sept. 14, 1870–Feb. 1, 1877	Elected 1870; reelected 1874; resigned
Chadwick, Stephen F.—D	Feb. 1, 1877–Sept. 11, 1878	Was secretary of state
Thayer, W.W.—D	Sept. 11, 1878–Sept. 13, 1882	Elected 1878
Moody, Z.F.—R	Sept. 13, 1882–Jan. 12, 1887	Elected 1882
Pennoyer, Sylvester—DP	Jan. 12, 1887–Jan. 14, 1895	Elected 1886; reelected 1890
Lord, William Paine—R	Jan. 14, 1895–Jan. 9, 1899	Elected 1894
Geer, T.T.—R	Jan. 9, 1899–Jan. 14, 1903	Elected 1898
Chamberlain, George E.—D	Jan. 15, 1903–Feb. 28, 1909	Elected 1902; reelected 1906; resigned
Benson, Frank W.—R	Mar. 1, 1909–June 17, 1910	Was secretary of state; resigned
Bowerman, Jay[2]—R	June 17, 1910–Jan. 8, 1911	Was president of Senate
West, Oswald—D	Jan. 11, 1911–Jan. 12, 1915	Elected 1910
Withycombe, James—R	Jan. 12, 1915–Mar. 3, 1919	Elected 1914; reelected 1918; died in office

Name/Political Party	Term of Service	By What Authority/Remarks
Olcott, Ben W.—R	Mar. 3, 1919–Jan. 8, 1923	Was secretary of state
Pierce, Walter M.—D	Jan. 8, 1923–Jan. 10, 1927	Elected 1922
Patterson, I.L.—R	Jan. 10, 1927–Dec. 21, 1929	Elected 1926; died in office
Norblad, A.W.[3]—R	Dec. 22, 1929–Jan. 12, 1931	Was president of Senate
Meier, Julius L.—I	Jan. 12, 1931–Jan. 14, 1935	Elected 1930
Martin, Charles H.—D	Jan. 14, 1935–Jan. 9, 1939	Elected 1934
Sprague, Charles A.—R	Jan. 9, 1939–Jan. 11, 1943	Elected 1938
Snell, Earl—R	Jan. 11, 1943–Oct. 28, 1947	Elected 1942; reelected 1946; died in office
Hall, John H.[4]—R	Oct. 30, 1947–Jan. 10, 1949	Was speaker of House
McKay, Douglas—R	Jan. 10, 1949–Dec. 27, 1952	Elected 1948; reelected 1950; resigned
Patterson, Paul L.—R	Dec. 27, 1952–Jan. 31, 1956	Was president of Senate; elected 1954; died in office
Smith, Elmo—R	Feb. 1, 1956–Jan. 14, 1957	Was president of Senate
Holmes, Robert D.—D	Jan. 14, 1957–Jan. 12, 1959	Elected 1956
Hatfield, Mark O.—R	Jan. 12, 1959–Jan. 9, 1967	Elected 1958; reelected 1962
McCall, Tom—R	Jan. 9, 1967–Jan 13, 1975	Elected 1966; reelected 1970
Straub, Robert W.—D	Jan. 13, 1975–Jan. 8, 1979	Elected 1974
Atiyeh, Victor G.—R	Jan. 8, 1979–Jan. 12, 1987	Elected 1978; reelected 1982
Goldschmidt, Neil—D	Jan. 12, 1987–Jan. 14, 1991	Elected 1986
Roberts, Barbara—D	Jan. 14, 1991–Jan. 9, 1995	Elected 1990
Kitzhaber, John—D	Jan. 9, 1995–Jan. 13, 2003	Elected 1994; reelected 1998
Kulongoski, Theodore R.—D	Jan. 13, 2003–Jan. 10, 2011	Elected 2002; reelected 2006
Kitzhaber, John—D	Jan. 10, 2011–	Elected 2010

[1]D = Democrat; R = Republican; DP = Democrat People's; I = Independent; W = Whig

[2]Jay Bowerman became governor when Frank Benson, who was serving as both governor and secretary of state, became incapacitated. Benson resigned as governor but continued as secretary of state until his death.

[3]In 1920, the Constitution was changed to allow the president of the Senate to succeed as governor.

[4]A plane crash on October 28, 1947 killed Governor Earl Snell, Secretary of State Robert S. Farrell Jr., President of the Senate Marshall E. Cornett and the pilot, Cliff Hogue. John H. Hall, Speaker of the House and next in line of succession, automatically became governor. Earl Newbry was appointed by John H. Hall to the position of secretary of state.

Secretaries of State of Oregon

Under Provisional Government

Name/Political Party	Term of Service	By What Authority/Remarks
LeBreton, George W.	Feb. 18, 1841–Mar. 4, 1844	Elected by meeting of inhabitants of the Willamette Valley to office of clerk of courts and public recorder, thus served as first secretary; reelected 1843; died in office
Johnson, Overton	Mar. 4, 1844–May 25, 1844	Appointed clerk and recorder
Long, Dr. John E.	May 25, 1844–June 21, 1846	Elected clerk and recorder by people at first 1844 general election; reelected 1845 general election; reelected 1845 by Legislature; drowned
Prigg, Frederick	June 26, 1846–Sept. 16, 1848	Appointed secretary to succeed Long; elected 1846 by Legislature; resigned
Holderness, Samuel M.	Sept. 19, 1848–Mar. 10, 1849	Appointed to succeed Prigg; elected 1848 by Legislature

Under Territorial Government

Magruder, Theophilus	Mar. 10, 1849–Apr. 9, 1849	Elected by Legislature
Prichette, Kintzing—D	Apr. 9, 1849–Sept. 18, 1850	Appointed by President Polk

Name/Political Party	Term of Service	By What Authority/Remarks
Hamilton, Gen. E.D.—W	Sept. 18, 1850–May 14, 1853	Appointed by President Taylor
Curry, George L.—D	May 14, 1853–Jan. 27, 1855	Appointed by President Pierce
Harding, Benjamin—D	Jan. 27, 1855–Mar. 3, 1859	Appointed by President Pierce

Under State Government

Name/Political Party	Term of Service	By What Authority/Remarks
Heath, Lucien—D	Mar. 3, 1859–Sept. 8, 1862	Elected 1858
May, Samuel E.—R	Sept. 8, 1862–Sept. 10, 1870	Elected 1862; reelected 1866
Chadwick, Stephen F.[1]—D	Sept. 10, 1870–Sept. 2, 1878	Elected 1870; reelected 1874
Earhart, R.P.—R	Sept. 2, 1878–Jan. 10, 1887	Elected 1878; reelected 1882
McBride, George W.—R	Jan. 10, 1887–Jan. 14, 1895	Elected 1886; reelected 1890
Kincaid, Harrison R.—R	Jan. 14, 1895–Jan. 9, 1899	Elected 1894
Dunbar, Frank I.—R	Jan. 9, 1899–Jan. 14, 1907	Elected 1898; reelected 1902
Benson, Frank W.[2]—R	Jan. 15, 1907–Apr. 14, 1911	Elected 1906; reelected 1910; died in office
Olcott, Ben W.[3]—R	Apr. 17, 1911–May 28, 1920	Appointed by Governor West; elected 1912; reelected 1916; resigned
Kozer, Sam A.—R	May 28, 1920–Sept. 24, 1928	Appointed by Governor Olcott; elected 1920; reelected 1924; resigned
Hoss, Hal E.—R	Sept. 24, 1928–Feb. 6, 1934	Appointed by Governor Patterson; elected 1928; reelected 1932; died in office
Stadelman, P.J.—R	Feb. 9, 1934–Jan. 7, 1935	Appointed by Governor Meier
Snell, Earl—R	Jan. 7, 1935–Jan. 4, 1943	Elected 1934; reelected 1938
Farrell, Robert S., Jr.—R	Jan. 4, 1943–Oct. 28, 1947	Elected 1942; reelected 1946; died in office
Newbry, Earl T.—R	Nov. 3, 1947–Jan. 7, 1957	Appointed by Governor Hall; elected 1948; reelected 1952
Hatfield, Mark O.—R	Jan. 7, 1957–Jan. 12, 1959	Elected 1956; resigned
Appling, Howell, Jr.—R	Jan. 12, 1959–Jan. 4, 1965	Appointed by Governor Hatfield; elected 1960
McCall, Tom—R	Jan. 4, 1965–Jan. 9, 1967	Elected 1964; resigned
Myers, Clay—R	Jan. 9, 1967–Jan. 3, 1977	Appointed by Governor McCall; elected 1968; reelected 1972
Paulus, Norma—R	Jan. 3, 1977–Jan. 7, 1985	Elected 1976; reelected 1980
Roberts, Barbara—D	Jan. 7, 1985–Jan. 14, 1991	Elected 1984; reelected 1988; resigned
Keisling, Phil—D	Jan. 14, 1991–Nov. 8, 1999	Appointed by Governor Roberts; elected 1992; reelected 1996; resigned
Bradbury, Bill—D	Nov. 8, 1999–Jan. 5, 2009	Appointed by Governor Kitzhaber; elected 2000; reelected 2004
Brown, Kate—D	Jan. 5, 2009–	Elected 2008; reelected 2012

[1]When Stephen Chadwick succeeded L.F. Grover as governor in 1877, he did not resign as secretary of state. He signed documents and proclamations twice—as governor and as secretary of state—until September 1878.

[2]Frank Benson served as both secretary of state and governor. See Footnote 2 under Governors of Oregon.

[3]When James Withycombe died in office on March 3, 1919, Ben W. Olcott succeeded him as governor. However, Governor Olcott did not resign or appoint a new secretary of state until May 28, 1920.

Treasurers of Oregon

Under Provisional Government

Name/Political Party	Term of Service	By What Authority/Remarks
Gray, W.H.	Mar. 1, 1843–July 5, 1843	Elected by meeting of citizens of the Willamette Valley

Name/Political Party	Term of Service	By What Authority/Remarks
Willson, W.H.	July 5, 1843–May 14, 1844	Elected by meeting of the inhabitants of the Willamette settlements
Foster, Phillip	July 2, 1844–July 7, 1845	Elected by people at first 1844 general election
Ermatinger, Francis	July 7, 1845–Mar. 3, 1846	Elected by people at 1845 general election; reelected 1845 by Legislature; resigned
Couch, John H.	Mar. 4, 1846–Sept. 27, 1847	Appointed to succeed Ermatinger; elected by Legislature 1846; resigned
Kilbourn, William K.	Oct. 11, 1847–Sept. 28, 1849	Appointed to succeed Couch; elected by Legislature 1849

Under Territorial Government

Taylor, James	Sept. 28, 1849–Feb. 8, 1851	Elected by Legislature
Rice, L.A.	Feb. 8, 1851–Sept. 22, 1851	Elected by Legislature; resigned
Buck, William W.	Sept. 27, 1851–Dec. 16, 1851	Appointed to succeed Rice
Boon, John D.—D	Dec. 16, 1851–Mar. 1, 1855	Elected by Legislature
Lane, Nat H.—D	Mar. 1, 1855–Jan. 10, 1856	Elected by Legislature
Boon, John D.—D	Jan. 10, 1856–Mar. 3, 1859	Elected by Legislature

Under State Government

Boon, John D.—D	Mar. 3, 1859–Sept. 8, 1862	Elected 1858
Cooke, E.N.—R	Sept. 8, 1862–Sept. 12, 1870	Elected 1862; reelected 1866
Fleischner, L.—D	Sept. 12, 1870–Sept. 14, 1874	Elected 1870
Brown, A.H.—D	Sept. 14, 1874–Sept. 9, 1878	Elected 1874
Hirsch, E.—R	Sept. 9, 1878–Jan. 10, 1887	Elected 1878; reelected 1882
Webb, G.W.—D	Jan. 10, 1887–Jan. 12, 1891	Elected 1886
Metschan, Phil—R	Jan. 12, 1891–Jan. 9, 1899	Elected 1890; reelected 1894
Moore, Charles S.—R	Jan. 9, 1899–Jan. 14, 1907	Elected 1898; reelected 1902
Steel, George A.—R	Jan. 15, 1907–Jan. 3, 1911	Elected 1906
Kay, Thomas B.—R	Jan. 4, 1911–Jan. 6, 1919	Elected 1910; reelected 1914
Hoff, O.P.—R	Jan. 6, 1919–Mar. 18, 1924	Elected 1918; reelected 1922; died in office
Myers, Jefferson—D	Mar. 18, 1924–Jan. 4, 1925	Appointed by Governor Pierce
Kay, Thomas B.—R	Jan. 4, 1925–April 29, 1931	Elected 1924; reelected 1928; died in office
Holman, Rufus C.—R	May 1, 1931–Dec. 27, 1938	Appointed by Governor Meier; elected 1932; reelected 1936; resigned
Pearson, Walter E.—D	Dec. 27, 1938–Jan. 6, 1941	Appointed by Governor Martin
Scott, Leslie M.—R	Jan. 6, 1941–Jan. 3, 1949	Elected 1940; reelected 1944
Pearson, Walter J.—D	Jan. 3, 1949–Jan. 5, 1953	Elected 1948
Unander, Sig—R	Jan. 5, 1953–Dec. 31, 1959	Elected 1952; reelected 1956; resigned
Belton, Howard C.—R	Jan. 4, 1960–Jan. 4, 1965	Appointed by Governor Hatfield; elected 1960
Straub, Robert—D	Jan. 4, 1965–Jan. 1, 1973	Elected 1964; reelected 1968
Redden, James A.—D	Jan. 1, 1973–Jan. 3, 1977	Elected 1972
Myers, Clay—R	Jan. 3, 1977–Apr. 1, 1984	Elected 1976; reelected 1980; resigned
Rutherford, Bill—R	Apr. 1, 1984–July 9, 1987	Appointed by Governor Atiyeh; elected 1984; resigned
Meeker, Tony—R	July 9, 1987–Jan. 4, 1993	Appointed by Governor Goldschmidt; elected 1988
Hill, Jim—D	Jan. 4, 1993–Jan. 1, 2001	Elected 1992; reelected 1996
Edwards, Randall—D	Jan. 1, 2001–Jan. 5, 2009	Elected 2000; reelected 2004
Westlund, Ben—D	Jan. 5, 2009–Mar. 7, 2010	Elected 2008; died in office
Ted Wheeler—D	Mar. 11, 2010–	Appointed by Governor Kulongoski; elected 2010; reelected 2012

Oregon Supreme Court Justices[1]

Under Provisional Government

Name	Term of Service	By What Authority/Remarks
Babcock, Dr. Ira L.	Feb. 18, 1841–May 1, 1843	Supreme judge with probate powers elected at meeting of inhabitants of the Willamette Valley
Wilson, W.E.	No record of service	Supreme judge with probate powers; elected at meeting of inhabitants of the Willamette Settlements, May 2, 1843
Russell, Osborn	Oct. 2, 1843–May 14, 1844	Supreme judge and probate judge; appointed by the Executive Committee
Babcock, Dr. Ira L.	June 27, 1844–Nov. 11, 1844	Presiding judge, Circuit Court; elected at first general election May 1844; resigned
Nesmith, James W.	Dec. 25, 1844–Aug. 9, 1845	Presiding judge, Circuit Court; appointed by Executive Committee; elected by people 1845
Ford, Nathaniel	Declined service	Supreme judge; elected by Legislature Aug. 9, 1845; declined to serve
Burnett, Peter H.	Sept. 6, 1845–Dec. 29, 1846	Supreme judge; elected by Legislature; declined appointment to Supreme Court 1848
Thornton, J. Quinn	Feb. 20, 1847–Nov. 9, 1847	Supreme judge; appointed by Governor Abernethy; resigned
Lancaster, Columbia	Nov. 30, 1847–Apr. 9, 1849	Supreme judge; appointed by Governor Abernethy
Lovejoy, A.L.	No record of service	Supreme judge; elected by Legislature Feb. 16, 1849

Under Territorial[2] and State Government[3]

Name	Term of Service	By What Authority/Remarks
Bryant, William P.	1848–1850	Appointed 1848; resigned 1850; chief justice 1848–1850
Pratt, Orville C.	1848–1852	Appointed 1848; term ended 1852
Nelson, Thomas	1850–1853	Appointed 1850 to succeed Bryant; term ended 1853; chief justice 1850–1853
Strong, William	1850–1853	Appointed 1850 to succeed Burnett; term ended 1853
Williams, George H.	1853–1858	Appointed 1853, 1857; resigned 1858; chief justice 1853–1858
Olney, Cyrus	1853–1858	Appointed 1853, 1857; resigned 1858
Deady, Matthew P.	1853–1859	Appointed 1853, 1857; elected 1858; resigned 1859
McFadden, Obadiah B.	1853–1854	Appointed 1853; term ended 1854
Boise, Reuben P.	1858–1870, 1876–1880	Appointed 1858 to succeed Olney; elected 1859; reelected 1864; term ended 1870; elected 1876; term ended 1878; appointed 1878; term ended 1880; chief justice 1862–1864, 1867–1870
Wait, Aaron E.	1859–1862	Elected 1858; resigned May 1, 1862; chief justice 1859–1862
Stratton, Riley E.	1859–1866	Elected 1858, 1864; died Dec. 26, 1866
Prim, Paine Page	1859–1880	Appointed 1859 to succeed Deady; elected 1860; reelected 1866, 1872; term ended 1878; appointed 1878; term ended 1880; chief justice 1864–1866, 1870–1872, 1876–1878
Page, William W.	1862	Appointed May 1862 to succeed Wait; term ended Sept. 1862
Shattuck, Erasmus D.	1862–1867, 1874–1878	Elected 1862; resigned Dec. 1867; elected 1874; term ended 1878; chief justice 1866–1867

Elections and Records

Name	Term of Service	By What Authority/Remarks
Wilson, Joseph G.	1862–1870	New appointment Oct. 17, 1862; elected 1864; resigned May 1870
Skinner, Alonzo A.	1866–1867	Appointed 1866 to succeed Stratton; term ended 1867
Upton, William W.	1867–1874	Appointed Dec. 1867 to succeed Shattuck; elected 1868; term ended 1874; chief justice 1872–1874
Kelsay, John	1868–1870	Elected 1868 to succeed Stratton; term ended 1870
Whitten, Benoni	1870	Appointed May 1870 to succeed Wilson; term ended Sept. 1870
McArthur, Lewis L.	1870–1878	Elected 1870; reelected 1876; term ended 1878
Thayer, Andrew J.	1870–1873	Elected 1870; died Apr. 26, 1873
Bonham, Benjamin F.	1870–1876	Elected 1870; term ended 1876; chief justice 1874–1876
Moser, Lafayette F.	1873–1874	Appointed May 1873 to succeed A.J. Thayer; term ended 1874
Burnett, John	1874–1876	Elected 1874; term ended 1876
Watson, James F.	1876–1878	Elected 1876; term ended 1878
Kelly, James K.	1878–1880	Appointed 1878; term ended 1880; chief justice 1878–1880
Lord, William P.	1880–1894	Elected 1880; reelected 1882, 1888; term ended 1894; chief justice 1880–1882, 1886–1888, 1892–1894
Watson, Edward B.	1880–1884	Elected 1880; term ended 1884; chief justice 1882–1884
Waldo, John B.	1880–1886	Elected 1880; term ended 1886; chief justice 1884–1886
Thayer, William W.	1884–1890	Elected 1884; term ended 1890; chief justice 1888–1890
Strahan, Reuben S.	1886–1892	Elected 1886; term ended 1892; chief justice 1890–1892
Bean, Robert S.	1890–1909	Elected 1890; reelected 1896, 1902, 1908; resigned May 1, 1909; chief justice 1894–1896, 1900–1902, 1905–1909
Moore, Frank A.	1892–1918	Elected 1892; reelected 1898, 1904, 1910, 1916; died Sept. 25, 1918; chief justice 1896–1898, 1902–1905, 1909–1911, 1915–1917
Wolverton, Charles E.	1894–1905	Elected 1894, 1900; resigned Dec. 4, 1905; chief justice 1898–1900, 1905
Hailey, Thomas G.	1905–1907	Appointed Dec. 5, 1905 to succeed Wolverton; term ended Jan. 15, 1907
Eakin, Robert	1907–1917	Elected 1906, 1912; resigned Jan. 8, 1917; chief justice 1911–1913
King, William R.	1909–1911	Appointed Feb. 12, 1909; term ended Jan. 1, 1911
Slater, Woodson T.	1909–1911	Appointed Feb. 12, 1909; term ended Jan. 1, 1911
McBride, Thomas A.	1909–1930	Appointed May 1, 1909 to succeed Robert S. Bean; elected 1914; reelected 1920, 1926; died Sept. 9, 1930; chief justice 1913–1915, 1917–1921, 1923–1927
Bean, Henry J.	1911–1941	Elected 1910; reelected 1914, 1920, 1926, 1932, 1938; died May 8, 1941; chief justice 1931–1933, 1937–1939
Burnett, George H.	1911–1927	Elected 1910; reelected 1916, 1922; died Sept. 10, 1927; chief justice 1921–1923, 1927
McNary, Charles L.	1913–1915	Appointed June 3, 1913; term ended Jan. 4, 1915
Ramsey, William M.	1913–1915	Appointed June 3, 1913; term ended Jan. 4, 1915
Benson, Henry L.	1915–1921	Elected 1914; reelected 1920; died Oct. 16, 1921
Harris, Lawrence T.	1915–1924	Elected 1914; reelected 1920; resigned Jan. 15, 1924

Name	Term of Service	By What Authority/Remarks
McCamant, Wallace	1917–1918	Appointed Jan. 8, 1917 to succeed Eakin; resigned June 4, 1918
Johns, Charles A.	1918–1921	Appointed June 4, 1918 to succeed McCamant; elected 1918; resigned Oct. 7, 1921
Olson, Conrad P.	1918–1919	Appointed Sept. 27, 1918 to succeed Moore; term ended Jan. 7, 1919
Bennett, Alfred S.	1919–1920	Elected 1918; resigned Oct. 5, 1920
Brown, George M.	1920–1933	Appointed Oct. 14, 1920 to succeed Bennett; elected 1920; reelected 1926; term ended 1933
McCourt, John	1921–1924	Appointed Oct. 8, 1921 to succeed Johns; elected 1922; died Sept. 12, 1924
Rand, John L.	1921–1942	Appointed Oct. 18, 1921 to succeed Benson; elected 1922; reelected 1928, 1934, 1940; died Nov. 19, 1942; chief justice 1927–1929, 1933–1935, 1939–1941
Coshow, Oliver P.	1924–1931	Appointed Jan. 15, 1924 to succeed Harris; elected 1924; term ended 1931; chief justice 1929–1931
Pipes, Martin L.	1924	Appointed Sept. 1924 to succeed McCourt; term ended Dec. 31, 1924
Belt, Harry H.	1925–1950	Elected 1924; reelected 1930, 1936, 1942, 1948; died Aug. 6, 1950; chief justice 1945–1947
Rossman, George	1927–1965	Appointed Sept. 13, 1927 to succeed George H. Burnett; elected 1928; reelected 1934, 1940, 1946, 1952, 1958; term ended 1965; chief justice 1947–1949
Kelly, Percy R.	1930–1949	Appointed Sept. 24, 1930 to succeed McBride; elected 1930; reelected 1936, 1942, 1948; died June 14, 1949; chief justice 1941–1943
Campbell, James U.	1931–1937	Elected 1930; reelected 1936; died July 16, 1937; chief justice 1935–1937
Bailey, John O.	1933–1950	Elected 1932; reelected 1938, 1944; resigned Nov. 15, 1950; chief justice 1943–1945
Lusk, Hall S.	1937–1960	Appointed July 22, 1937 to succeed Campbell; elected 1938; reelected 1944, 1950, 1956; resigned Mar. 15, 1960; 1961–1968 recalled to temporary active service 1961 through 1968; chief justice 1949–1951
Brand, James T.	1941–1958	Appointed May 14, 1941 to succeed Henry J. Bean; elected 1942; reelected 1948, 1954; resigned June 30, 1958; chief justice 1951–1953
Hay, Arthur D.	1942–1952	Appointed Nov. 28, 1942 to succeed Rand; elected 1944; reelected 1950; died Dec. 19, 1952
Page, E.M.	1949–1950	Appointed July 8, 1949 to succeed Percy R. Kelly; resigned Jan. 18, 1950
Latourette, Earl C.	1950–1956	Appointed Jan. 19, 1950 to succeed E.M. Page; elected 1950; died Aug. 18, 1956; chief justice 1953–1955
Warner, Harold J.	1950–1963	Appointed Sept. 5, 1950 to succeed Belt; elected 1950; reelected 1956; term ended 1963; chief justice 1955–1957
Tooze, Walter L.	1950–1956	Appointed Nov. 16, 1950 to succeed Bailey; elected 1950; reelected 1956; died Dec. 21, 1956
Perry, William C.	1952–1970	Appointed Dec. 26, 1952 to succeed Hay; elected 1954; reelected 1960, 1966; resigned June 1, 1970; chief justice 1957–1959, 1967–1970
McAllister, William M.	1956–1976	Appointed Aug. 24, 1956 to succeed Latourette; elected 1956; reelected 1962, 1968, 1974; resigned Dec. 31, 1976; chief justice 1959–1967

Name	Term of Service	By What Authority/Remarks
Kester, Randall B.	1957–1958	Appointed Jan. 3, 1957 to succeed Tooze; resigned Mar. 1, 1958
Sloan, Gordon	1958–1970	Appointed Mar. 1, 1958 to succeed Kester; elected 1958; reelected 1964; resigned Oct. 1, 1970
O'Connell, Kenneth J.	1958–1977	Appointed July 1, 1958 to succeed Brand; elected 1958; reelected 1964, 1970; term ended 1977; chief justice 1970–1976
Goodwin, Alfred T.	1960–1969	Appointed Mar. 18, 1960 to succeed Lusk; elected 1960; reelected 1966; resigned Dec. 19, 1969
Denecke, Arno H.	1963–1982	Elected 1962; reelected 1968, 1974, 1980; resigned June 30, 1982; chief justice 1976–1982
Holman, Ralph M.	1965–1980	Elected 1964; reelected 1970, 1976; resigned Jan. 20, 1980
Tongue, Thomas H.	1969–1982	Appointed Dec. 29, 1969 to succeed Goodwin; elected 1970; reelected 1976; resigned Feb. 7, 1982
Howell, Edward H.	1970–1980	Appointed June 1, 1970 to succeed Perry; elected 1970; reelected 1976; resigned Nov. 30, 1980
Bryson, Dean F.	1970–1979	Elected 1970; appointed Oct. 23, 1970 (before elective term began) to succeed Sloan; reelected 1976; resigned April 1, 1979
Lent, Berkeley	1977–1988	Elected 1976; reelected 1982; resigned Sept. 30, 1988; chief justice 1982–1983
Linde, Hans	1977–1990	Appointed Jan. 3, 1977 to succeed McAllister; elected 1978; reelected 1984; resigned Jan. 31, 1990
Peterson, Edwin J.	1979 –1993	Appointed May 15, 1979 to succeed Bryson; elected 1980; reelected 1986, 1992; resigned Dec. 31, 1993; chief justice 1983–1991
Tanzer, Jacob	1980–1982	Appointed Jan. 21, 1980 to succeed Holman; elected 1980; resigned Dec. 31, 1982
Campbell, J.R.	1980–1988	Appointed Dec. 1, 1980 to succeed Howell; elected 1982; resigned Dec. 31, 1988
Roberts, Betty	1982–1986	Appointed Feb. 8, 1982 to succeed Tongue; elected 1982; resigned Feb. 7, 1986
Carson, Wallace P., Jr.	1982–2006	Appointed July 14, 1982 to succeed Denecke; elected 1982; reelected 1988, 1994, 2000; chief justice 1991–2005; resigned Dec. 31, 2006
Jones, Robert E.	1983–1990	Appointed Dec. 16, 1982 to succeed Tanzer; elected 1984; resigned April 30, 1990
Gillette, W. Michael	1986–2011	Appointed Feb. 10, 1986 to succeed Roberts; elected 1986; reelected 1992, 1998, 2004
Van Hoomissen, George	1988–2001	Elected May 17, 1988 to succeed Lent; reelected 1994; resigned Dec. 31, 2000
Fadeley, Edward N.	1988–1998	Elected Nov. 8, 1988 to succeed Campbell; reelected 1994; resigned Jan. 31, 1998
Unis, Richard	1990–1996	Appointed Feb. 1, 1990 to succeed Linde; elected 1990; resigned June 30, 1996
Graber, Susan P.[4]	1990–1998	Appointed May 2, 1990 and Jan. 7, 1991 to succeed Jones; elected 1992; resigned April 1, 1998
Durham, Robert D.	1994–2013	Appointed Jan. 4, 1994 to succeed Peterson; elected 1994; reelected 2000, 2006
Kulongoski, Ted	1997–2001	Elected May, 1996; resigned June 14, 2001
Leeson, Susan M.	1998–2003	Appointed Feb. 26, 1998 to succeed Fadeley; elected 1998; resigned Jan. 31, 2003
Riggs, R. William	1998–2006	Appointed Sept. 8, 1998 to succeed Graber; elected 1998; reelected 2004, resigned Sept. 30, 2006
De Muniz, Paul J.	2001–2013	Elected Nov. 7, 2000 to succeed Van Hoomissen; reelected 2006; chief justice 2006–2012

Name	Term of Service	By What Authority/Remarks
Balmer, Thomas A.	2001–	Appointed Sept. 20, 2001 to succeed Kulongoski; elected 2002; reelected 2008; chief justice 2012 to date
Kistler, Rives	2003–	Appointed Aug. 15, 2003 to succeed Leeson; elected 2004; reelected 2010
Walters, Martha Lee	2006–	Appointed Oct. 1, 2006 to succeed Riggs; elected 2008
Linder, Virginia L.	2007–	Elected Nov. 7, 2006 to succeed Carson; reelected 2012
Landau, Jack L.	2011–	Elected 2010 to succeed Gillette
Brewer, Dave	2013–	Elected 2012 to succeed De Muniz
Baldwin, Richard C.	2013–	Elected 2012 to succeed Durham

[1]Unless otherwise noted, justices took office in the year in which elected until 1905. Since then, terms have started on the first Monday in January and continued until the first Monday six years hence or until a successor has been sworn in, if later.

[2]Appointments under territorial government were made by the president of the United States.

[3]From 1859 to 1862, there were four Supreme Court justices. In 1862, a fifth justice was added. The justices at that time also rode circuit. In 1878, the Supreme Court and Circuit Court were separated; the Supreme Court then had three justices. In 1910, the number increased to five. The final increase to the present seven occurred in 1913.

[4]When Justice Jones resigned, he had already filed to run for another term and his name appeared on the ballot at the 1990 primary election. Because he was elected for another term, which began January 7, 1991, he had to resign from his new term, and Justice Graber was appointed again at that time.

Judges of the Oregon Court of Appeals

The Oregon Court of Appeals was established July 1, 1969 with five members, expanded to six members October 5, 1973 and to ten members September 1, 1977.

Name	Term of Service	By What Authority/Remarks
Langtry, Virgil	1969–1976	Appointed July 1, 1969; elected 1970; resigned Sept. 15, 1976
Foley, Robert H.	1969–1976	Appointed July 1, 1969; elected 1970; resigned Aug. 16, 1976
Schwab, Herbert M.	1969–1980	Appointed July 1, 1969; elected 1970; reelected 1976; resigned Dec. 31, 1980; chief judge 1969–1980
Fort, William S.	1969–1977	Appointed July 1, 1969; elected 1970; term ended 1977
Branchfield, Edward H.	1969–1971	Appointed July 1, 1969; term ended 1971
Thornton, Robert Y.	1971–1983	Elected 1970; reelected 1976; term ended 1983
Tanzer, Jacob	1973–1975, 1976–1980	Appointed to new seat Oct. 5, 1973; term ended Jan. 6, 1975; elected 1976; appointed Aug. 16, 1976 (before elective term began) to succeed Foley; resigned Jan. 21, 1980
Lee, Jason	1975–1980	Elected 1974; died Feb. 19, 1980
Johnson, Lee	1977–1978	Elected 1976; resigned Dec. 18, 1978
Richardson, William L.	1976–1997	Elected 1976; appointed Oct. 15, 1976 (before elective term began) to succeed Langtry; reelected 1982, 1988, 1994; chief judge 1993–1997; resigned June 30, 1997
Buttler, John H.	1977–1992	Appointed to new seat Sept. 1, 1977; elected 1978; reelected 1984, 1990; resigned Dec. 31, 1992
Joseph, George M.	1977–1992	Appointed to new seat Sept. 1, 1977; elected 1978; reelected 1984, 1990; resigned Dec. 31, 1992; chief judge 1981–1992
Gillette, W. Michael	1977–1986	Appointed to new seat Sept. 1, 1977; elected 1978; reelected 1984; resigned Feb. 10, 1986
Roberts, Betty	1977–1982	Appointed to new seat Sept. 1, 1977; elected 1978; resigned Feb. 8, 1982
Campbell, J.R.	1979–1980	Appointed Mar. 19, 1979 to succeed Johnson; elected 1980; resigned Nov. 30, 1980

Name	Term of Service	By What Authority/Remarks
Warden, John C.	1980–1988	Appointed Feb. 19, 1980 to succeed Tanzer; term ended Jan. 5, 1981; appointed Jan. 6, 1981 to succeed Schwab; elected 1982; resigned Dec. 30, 1988
Warren, Edward H.	1980–1999	Appointed Mar. 10, 1980 to succeed Lee; elected 1980; reelected 1986, 1992, 1998; resigned 1999
Van Hoomissen, George A.	1981–1988	Elected 1980; reelected 1986; resigned Sept. 30, 1988
Young, Thomas F.	1981–1988	Appointed Jan. 5, 1981 to succeed Campbell; elected 1982; died Jan. 3, 1988
Rossman, Kurt C.	1982–1994	Appointed Mar. 2, 1982 to succeed Roberts; elected 1982; reelected 1988; resigned Dec. 31, 1994
Newman, Jonathan	1983–1991	Elected 1982; reelected 1988; resigned Aug. 31, 1991
Deits, Mary J.	1986–2004	Appointed Feb. 28, 1986 to succeed Gillette; elected 1986; reelected 1992, 1998; chief judge 1997–2004; resigned Oct. 31, 2004
Riggs, R. William	1988–1998	Appointed Oct. 24, 1988 to fill Van Hoomissen position; elected 1988 to succeed Warden; reelected 1994; resigned Sept. 8, 1998
Graber, Susan P.	1988–1990	Appointed Feb. 11, 1988 to succeed Young; elected 1988; resigned May 2, 1990
Edmonds, Walter I., Jr.	1989–2009	Appointed Jan. 1, 1989 to succeed Van Hoomissen; elected 1990; reelected 1996, 2002, 2008; retired Dec. 31, 2009
De Muniz, Paul J.	1990–2000	Appointed May 11, 1990 to succeed Graber; elected 1990; reelected 1996; resigned Dec. 29, 2000
Durham, Robert D.	1991–1994	Appointed Nov. 14, 1991 to succeed Newman; elected 1992; resigned Jan. 4, 1994
Landau, Jack L.	1993–2011	Appointed Dec. 15, 1992 to succeed Joseph; elected 1994; reelected 2000, 2006; resigned Jan. 3, 2011
Leeson, Susan M.	1993–1998	Appointed Dec. 15, 1992 to succeed Buttler; elected 1994; resigned Feb. 26, 1998
Haselton, Rick	1994–	Appointed Mar. 4, 1994 to succeed Durham; elected 1994; reelected 2000, 2006, 2012
Armstrong, Rex	1995–	Elected 1994; reelected 2000, 2006, 2012
Linder, Virginia L.	1997–2007	Appointed Sept. 24, 1997 to succeed Richardson; elected 1998; reelected 2004; resigned Jan. 2, 2007
Wollheim, Robert D.	1998–	Appointed Feb. 27, 1998 to succeed Leeson; elected 1998; reelected 2004, 2010
Brewer, Dave	1999–2012	Appointed Jan. 14, 1999 to succeed Warren; elected 2000; reelected 2006; chief judge 2004–2012
Kistler, Rives	1999–2003	Appointed Jan. 14, 1999 to succeed Riggs; elected 2000; resigned Aug. 14, 2003
Schuman, David	2001–	Appointed March 19, 2001 to succeed De Muniz; elected 2002; reelected 2008
Ortega, Darleen	2003–	Appointed Oct. 13, 2003 to succeed Kistler; elected 2004; reelected 2010
Rosenblum, Ellen F.	2007–2011	Elected 2006; retired May 1, 2011
Sercombe, Timothy	2007–	Appointed March 26, 2007 to succeed Linder; elected 2008
Duncan, Rebecca	2010–	Appointed Jan. 7, 2010 to succeed Edmonds; elected 2010
Nakamoto, Lynn R.	2011–	Appointed Dec. 7, 2010 to succeed Landau; elected 2012
Hadlock, Erika	2011–	Appointed July 7, 2011 to succeed Rosenblum; elected 2012
Egan, James C.	2013–	Elected 2012

Judges of the Oregon Tax Court

The Oregon Tax Court was established January 1, 1962.

Name	Term of Service	By What Authority/Remarks
Gunnar, Peter M.	1962–1965	Appointed by Governor Hatfield Jan. 1, 1962; elected 1962; resigned Feb. 18, 1965
Howell, Edward H.	1965–1970	Appointed by Governor Hatfield Feb. 19, 1965; elected 1966; resigned May 31, 1970
Roberts, Carlisle B.	1970–1983	Appointed by Governor McCall June 1, 1970; elected 1970; reelected 1976; term ended 1983
Stewart, Samuel B.	1983–1985	Elected 1982; died Feb. 25, 1985
Byers, Carl N.	1985–2001	Appointed by Governor Atiyeh Mar. 6, 1985; elected 1986; reelected 1992, 1998; retired 2001
Breithaupt, Henry C.	2001–	Appointed by Governor Kitzhaber June 29, 2001 to succeed Byers; elected 2002; reelected 2008

Attorneys General of Oregon

Name/Political Party	Term of Service	By What Authority/Remarks
Chamberlain, George E.—D	May 20, 1891–Jan. 14, 1895	Appointed by Governor Pennoyer; elected June 1892
Idleman, Cicero M.—R	Jan. 14, 1895–Jan. 9, 1899	Elected 1894
Blackburn, D.R.N.—R	Jan. 9, 1899–Jan. 12, 1903	Elected 1898
Crawford, Andrew M.—R	Jan. 13, 1903–Jan. 3, 1915	Elected 1902; reelected 1906, 1910
Brown, George M.—R	Jan. 4, 1915–Oct. 14, 1920	Elected 1914; reelected 1918; resigned
Van Winkle, Isaac H.—R	Oct. 14, 1920–Dec. 14, 1943	Appointed by Governor Olcott; elected 1920; reelected 1924, 1928, 1932, 1936, 1940; died in office
Neuner, George—R	Dec. 21, 1943–Jan. 5, 1953	Appointed by Governor Snell; elected 1944; reelected 1948
Thornton, Robert Y.—D	Jan. 5, 1953–May 20, 1969	Elected 1952; reelected 1956, 1960, 1964
Johnson, Lee—R	May 20, 1969–Jan. 3, 1977	Elected 1968; reelected 1972
Redden, James—D	Jan. 3, 1977–Mar. 24, 1980	Elected 1976
Brown, James M.—D	Mar. 24, 1980–Jan. 4, 1981	Appointed by Governor Atiyeh
Frohnmayer, David B.—R	Jan. 5, 1981–Dec. 31, 1991	Elected 1980; reelected 1984, 1988; resigned 1991
Crookham, Charles S.—R	Jan. 2, 1992–Jan. 3, 1993	Appointed by Governor Roberts
Kulongoski, Ted—D	Jan. 4, 1993–Jan. 4, 1997	Elected 1992
Myers, Hardy—D	Jan. 6, 1997–Jan. 5, 2009	Elected 1996; reelected 2000, 2004
Kroger, John R.—D	Jan. 5, 2009–June 29, 2012	Elected 2008; resigned 2012
Rosenblum, Ellen—D	June 29, 2012–	Appointed by Governor Kitzaber; elected 2012

Commissioners, Labor and Industries[1]

Name/Political Party	Term of Service	By What Authority/Remarks
Hoff, O.P.—R	June 2, 1903–Jan. 6, 1919	Appointed by Governor Chamberlain; elected 1906; reelected 1910, 1914
Gram, C.H.—R	Jan. 6, 1919–Jan. 4, 1943	Elected 1918; reelected 1922, 1926, 1930, 1934, 1938
Kimsey, W.E.—R	Jan. 4, 1943–Jan. 3, 1955	Elected 1942; reelected 1946, 1950
Nilsen, Norman O.—D	Jan. 3, 1955–Jan. 6, 1975	Elected 1954; reelected 1958, 1962, 1966, 1970
Stevenson, Bill—D	Jan. 6, 1975–Jan. 1, 1979	Elected 1974
Roberts, Mary Wendy—D.	Jan. 1, 1979–Jan 2, 1995	Elected 1978; reelected 1982, 1986, 1990
Roberts, Jack—R	Jan. 2, 1995–Jan. 6, 2003	Elected 1994; reelected 1998
Gardner, Dan[2]	Jan. 6, 2003–April 7, 2008	Elected 2002; reelected 2006; resigned 2008

Name/Political Party	Term of Service	By What Authority/Remarks
Avakian, Brad	Apr. 8, 2008–	Appointed by Governor Kulongoski; elected 2008; reelected 2012

[1]This position, originally called Labor Commissioner, was changed to Commissioner of the Bureau of Labor Statistics and Inspector of Factories and Workshops in 1918. In 1930, the name changed to Commissioner of the Bureau of Labor. The 1979 Legislature changed the name to Commissioner of Labor and Industries.

[2]The 1995 Legislature made this position nonpartisan, and the 1998 election was the first for this position after the change.

Superintendents of Public Instruction[1]

Name/Political Party	Term of Service	By What Authority/Remarks
Simpson, Sylvester C.—D	Jan. 29, 1873–Sept. 14, 1874	Appointed by Governor Grover
Rowland, L.L.—R	Sept. 14, 1874–Sept. 9, 1878	Elected 1874
Powell, J.L.—R	Sept. 9, 1878–Sept. 11, 1882	Elected 1878
McElroy, E.B.—R	Sept. 11, 1882–Jan. 14, 1895	Elected 1882; reelected 1886, 1890
Irwin, G.M.—R	Jan. 14, 1895–Jan. 9, 1899	Elected 1894
Ackerman, J.H.—R	Jan. 9, 1899–Jan. 3, 1911	Elected 1898; reelected 1902, 1906
Alderman, L.R.—R	Jan. 4, 1911–Jan. 28, 1913	Elected 1910; resigned
Churchill, J.A.—R	July 1, 1913–June 1, 1926	Appointed by Governor West; elected 1914; reelected 1918, 1922; resigned
Turner, R.R.—D	June 1, 1926–Jan. 3, 1927	Appointed by Governor Pierce
Howard, Charles A.—R	Jan. 3, 1927–Sept. 1, 1937	Elected 1926; reelected 1930, 1934; resigned
Putnam, Rex—D	Sept. 1, 1937–Jan. 31, 1961	Appointed by Governor Martin; elected 1938; reelected 1942, 1946, 1950, 1954, 1958; resigned
Minear, Leon P.	Feb. 1, 1961–Mar. 31, 1968	Appointed by Governor Hatfield; elected 1966; resigned
Fasold, Jesse V.	Apr. 8, 1968–June 30, 1968	Appointed by Governor McCall; resigned
Parnell, Dale	July 1, 1968–Mar. 31, 1974	Appointed by Governor McCall; elected 1968; reelected 1970; resigned
Fasold, Jesse V.	Apr. 1, 1974–Jan. 6, 1975	Appointed by Governor McCall
Duncan, Verne A.	Jan. 6, 1975–Nov. 15, 1989	Elected 1974; reelected 1978, 1982, 1986; resigned 1989
Erickson, John	Dec. 18, 1989–Sept. 30, 1990	Appointed by Governor Goldschmidt; resigned
Paulus, Norma	Oct. 1, 1990–Jan. 4, 1999	Elected 1990; appointed by Governor Goldschmidt (before elective term began); reelected 1994
Bunn, Stan	Jan. 4, 1999–Jan. 6, 2003	Elected 1998
Castillo, Susan[2]	Jan. 6, 2003–June 29, 2012	Elected 2002; reelected 2006, 2010; resigned 2012

[1]From 1942 to 1961, this office was filled by election on nonpartisan ballot. In 1961, the state Legislature passed a statute making the office appointive by the State Board of Education. The Supreme Court declared this unconstitutional in 1965, and a constitutional amendment to place the method of selection in the hands of the state Legislature was defeated in 1966. Another attempt to repeal the constitutional provision requiring election was defeated in 1980.

[2]In 2011, Senate Bill 552 created a new statutory provision naming the governor as Superintendent of Public Instruction. Susan Castillo served until her 2012 resignation as the last elected superintendent.

Presidents of the Senate

Session	Name/Political Party	City	County
1860	Elkins, Luther—D		Linn
1862	Bowlby, Wilson—R		Washington
1864	Mitchell, J.H.—R	Portland	Multnomah
1865[1]	Mitchell, J.H.—R	Portland	Multnomah

Session	Name/Political Party	City	County
1866	Cornelius, T.R.—R		Washington
1868	Burch, B.F.—D		Polk
1870	Fay, James D.—D		Jackson
1872	Fay, James D.—D		Jackson
1874	Cochran, R.B.—D		Lane
1876	Whiteaker, John—D		Lane
1878	Whiteaker, John—D		Lane
1880	Hirsch, Sol—R	Portland	Multnomah
1882	McConnell, W.J.—R		Yamhill
1885[2]	Waldo, William—R	Salem	Marion
1887	Carson, John C.—R	Portland	Multnomah
1889	Simon, Joseph—R	Portland	Multnomah
1891	Simon, Joseph—R	Portland	Multnomah
1893	Fulton, C.W.—R	Astoria	Clatsop
1895	Simon, Joseph—R	Portland	Multnomah
1897	Simon, Joseph—R	Portland	Multnomah
1898[1]	Simon, Joseph—R	Portland	Multnomah
1899	Taylor, T.C.—R	Pendleton	Umatilla
1901	Fulton, C.W.—R	Astoria	Clatsop
1903[2]	Brownell, George C.—R	Oregon City	Clackamas
1905	Kuykendall, W.—R	Eugene	Lane
1907	Haines, E.W.—R	Forest Grove	Washington
1909[2]	Bowerman, Jay—R	Condon	Gilliam
1911	Selling, Ben—R	Portland	Multnomah
1913	Malarkey, Dan J.—R	Portland	Multnomah
1915	Thompson, W. Lair—R	Lakeview	Lake
1917	Moser, Gus C.—R	Portland	Multnomah
1919	Vinton, W.T.—R	McMinnville	Yamhill
1920[1]	Vinton, W.T.—R	McMinnville	Yamhill
1921[2]	Ritner, Roy W.—R	Pendleton	Umatilla
1923	Upton, Jay—R	Prineville	Crook
1925	Moser, Gus C.—R	Portland	Multnomah
1927	Corbett, Henry L.—R	Portland	Multnomah
1929	Norblad, A.W.—R	Astoria	Clatsop
1931	Marks, Willard L.—R	Albany	Linn
1933[3]	Kiddle, Fred E.—R	Island City	Union
1935[2]	Corbett, Henry L.—R	Portland	Multnomah
1937	Franciscovich, F.M.—R	Astoria	Clatsop
1939	Duncan, Robert M.—R	Burns	Harney
1941	Walker, Dean H.—R	Independence	Polk
1943	Steiwer, W.H.—R	Fossil	Wheeler
1945	Belton, Howard C.—R	Canby	Clackamas
1947	Cornett, Marshall E.—R	Klamath Falls	Klamath
1949	Walsh, William E.—R	Coos Bay	Coos
1951	Patterson, Paul L.—R	Hillsboro	Washington
1953	Marsh, Eugene E.—R	McMinnville	Yamhill
1955	Smith, Elmo—R	John Day	Grant
1957[2]	Overhulse, Boyd R.—D	Madras	Jefferson
1959	Pearson, Walter J.—D	Portland	Multnomah
1961	Boivin, Harry D.—D	Klamath Falls	Klamath
1963[2]	Musa, Ben—D	The Dalles	Wasco
1965[2]	Boivin, Harry D.—D	Klamath Falls	Klamath
1967[2]	Potts, E.D.—D	Grants Pass	Josephine
1969	Potts, E.D.—D	Grants Pass	Josephine
1971[2]	Burns, John D.—D	Portland	Multnomah
1973	Boe, Jason—D	Reedsport	Douglas
1974[1]	Boe, Jason—D	Reedsport	Douglas
1975	Boe, Jason—D	Reedsport	Douglas
1977	Boe, Jason—D	Reedsport	Douglas
1978[1]	Boe, Jason—D	Reedsport	Douglas
1979	Boe, Jason—D	Reedsport	Douglas

Session	Name/Political Party	City	County
1980[1]	Boe, Jason—D	Reedsport	Douglas
1981[4]	Heard, Fred W.—D	Klamath Falls	Klamath
1983[3]	Fadeley, Edward N.—D	Eugene	Lane
1985	Kitzhaber, M.D., John A.—D	Roseburg	Douglas
1987	Kitzhaber, M.D., John A.—D	Roseburg	Douglas
1989[2]	Kitzhaber, M.D., John A.—D	Roseburg	Douglas
1991	Kitzhaber, M.D., John A.—D	Roseburg	Douglas
1993	Bradbury, Bill—D	Bandon	Coos
1995[2]	Smith, Gordon H.—R	Pendleton	Umatilla
1997	Adams, Brady—R	Grants Pass	Josephine
1999	Adams, Brady—R	Grants Pass	Josephine
2001[5]	Derfler, Gene—R	Salem	Marion
2003	Courtney, Peter—D	Salem	Marion
2005	Courtney, Peter—D	Salem	Marion
2007	Courtney, Peter—D	Salem	Marion
2009	Courtney, Peter—D	Salem	Marion
2011	Courtney, Peter—D	Salem	Marion
2013	Courtney, Peter—D	Salem	Marion

[1]Special session
[2]Regular and special session
[3]Regular and two special sessions
[4]Regular and four special sessions
[5]Regular and five special sessions

Speakers of the House of Representatives

Session	Name/Political Party	City	County
1860	Harding, B.F.—D		Marion
1862	Palmer, Joel—R		Yamhill
1864	Moores, I.R.—R		Marion
1865[1]	Moores, I.R.—R		Marion
1866	Chenoweth, F.A.—R		Benton
1868	Whiteaker, John J.—D		Lane
1870	Hayden, Benjamin—D		Polk
1872	Mallory, Rufus—R		Marion
1874	Drain, J.C.—D		Douglas
1876	Weatherford, J.K.—D	Albany	Linn
1878	Thompson, J.M.—D		Lane
1880	Moody, Z.F.—R	The Dalles	Wasco
1882	McBride, George W.—R		Columbia
1885[2]	Keady, W.P.—R	Corvallis	Benton
1887	Gregg, J.T.—R	Salem	Marion
1889	Smith, E.L.—R	Hood River	Hood River
1891	Geer, T.T.—R	Macleay	Marion
1893	Keady, W.P.—R	Portland	Multnomah
1895	Moores, C.B.—R	Salem	Marion
1897[4]	House failed to organize		
1898[1]	Carter, E.V.—R	Ashland	Jackson
1899	Carter, E.V.—R	Ashland	Jackson
1901	Reeder, L.B.—R	Pendleton	Umatilla
1903[2]	Harris, L.T.—R	Eugene	Lane
1905	Mills, A.L.—R	Portland	Multnomah
1907	Davey, Frank—R	Salem	Marion
1909[2]	McArthur, C.N.—R	Portland	Multnomah
1911	Rusk, John P.—R	Joseph	Wallowa
1913	McArthur, C.N.—R	Portland	Multnomah
1915	Selling, Ben—R	Portland	Multnomah
1917	Stanfield, R.N.—R	Stanfield	Umatilla
1919	Jones, Seymour—R	Salem	Marion
1920[1]	Jones, Seymour—R	Salem	Marion
1921[2]	Bean, Louis E.—R	Eugene	Lane

Session	Name/Political Party	City	County
1923	Kubli, K.K.—R	Portland	Multnomah
1925	Burdick, Denton G.—R	Redmond	Deschutes
1927	Carkin, John H.—R	Medford	Jackson
1929	Hamilton, R.S.—R	Bend	Deschutes
1931	Lonergan, Frank J.—R	Portland	Multnomah
1933[3]	Snell, Earl W.—R	Arlington	Gilliam
1935	Cooter, John E.—D	Toledo	Lincoln
1935[1]	Latourette, Howard—D	Portland	Multnomah
1937	Boivin, Harry D.—D	Klamath Falls	Klamath
1939	Fatland, Ernest R.—R	Condon	Gilliam
1941	Farrell, Robert S., Jr.—R	Portland	Multnomah
1943	McAllister, William M.—R	Medford	Jackson
1945	Marsh, Eugene E.—R	McMinnville	Yamhill
1947	Hall, John H.—R	Portland	Multnomah
1949	Van Dyke, Frank J.—R	Medford	Jackson
1951	Steelhammer, John F.—R	Salem	Marion
1953	Wilhelm, Rudie, Jr.—R	Portland	Multnomah
1955	Geary, Edward A.—R	Klamath Falls	Klamath
1957[2]	Dooley, Pat—D	Portland	Multnomah
1959	Duncan, Robert B.—D	Medford	Jackson
1961	Duncan, Robert B.—D	Medford	Jackson
1963[2]	Barton, Clarence—D	Coquille	Coos
1965[2]	Montgomery, F.F.—R	Eugene	Lane
1967[2]	Montgomery, F.F.—R	Eugene	Lane
1969	Smith, Robert F.—R	Burns	Harney
1971[2]	Smith, Robert F.—R	Burns	Harney
1973	Eymann, Richard O.—D	Springfield	Lane
1974[1]	Eymann, Richard O.—D	Springfield	Lane
1975	Lang, Philip D.—D	Portland	Multnomah
1977	Lang, Philip D.—D	Portland	Multnomah
1978[1]	Lang, Philip D.—D	Portland	Multnomah
1979	Myers, Hardy—D	Portland	Multnomah
1980[1]	Myers, Hardy—D	Portland	Multnomah
1981[5]	Myers, Hardy—D	Portland	Multnomah
1983[3]	Kerans, Grattan—D	Eugene	Lane
1985	Katz, Vera—D	Portland	Multnomah
1987	Katz, Vera—D	Portland	Multnomah
1989[2]	Katz, Vera—D	Portland	Multnomah
1991	Campbell, Larry—R	Eugene	Lane
1993	Campbell, Larry—R	Eugene	Lane
1995[2]	Clarno, Bev—R	Bend	Deschutes
1997	Lundquist, Lynn—R	Powell Butte	Deschutes
1999	Snodgrass, Lynn—R	Boring	Clackamas
2001[6]	Simmons, Mark—R	Elgin	Union
2003	Minnis, Karen—R	Wood Village	Multnomah
2005	Minnis, Karen—R	Wood Village	Multnomah
2007	Merkley, Jeff—D	Portland	Multnomah
2009	Hunt, Dave—D	Gladstone	Clackamas
2011	Hanna, Bruce (co-speaker)—R	Roseburg	Douglas, Lane
2011	Roblan, Arnie (co-speaker)—D	Coos Bay	Coos, Douglas, Lane
2013	Kotek, Tina—D	Portland	Multnomah

[1]Special session

[2]Regular and special session

[3]Regular and two special sessions

[4]E.J. Davis was elected speaker by less than a quorum. Subsequently, Henry L. Benson was elected speaker by less than a quorum. The Supreme Court revised an 1871 decision and ordered the secretary of state to audit claims and draw warrants for all claims which the Legislature, through its enactments, permitted and directed, either expressly or by implication.

[5]Regular and four special sessions

[6]Regular and five special sessions

U.S. Senators from Oregon

First Position[2]

Name/Political Party	Term of Service[1]	By What Authority/Remarks
Smith, Delazon[3]—D	Feb. 14–Mar. 3, 1859	Elected by Legislature 1858
Baker, Edward[4]—R	Dec. 5, 1860–Oct. 21, 1861	Elected by Legislature 1860; died in office
Stark, Benjamin—D	Oct. 29, 1861–Sept. 11, 1862	Appointed by Governor Whiteaker to succeed Baker
Harding, Benjamin F.—D	Sept. 11, 1862–1865	Elected by Legislature to succeed Baker
Williams, George H.—R	1865–1871	Elected by Legislature 1864
Kelly, James K.—D	1871–1877	Elected by Legislature 1870
Grover, LaFayette—D	1877–1883	Elected by Legislature 1876
Dolph, Joseph N.—R	1883–1895	Elected by Legislature 1882; reelected 1889
McBride, George W.—R	1895–1901	Elected by Legislature 1895
Mitchell, John H.—R	1901–1905	Elected by Legislature 1901; died in office Dec. 8, 1905
Gearin, John M.—D	Dec. 12, 1905–Jan. 23, 1907	Appointed by Governor Chamberlain to succeed Mitchell
Mulkey, Fred W.—R	Jan. 23–Mar. 2, 1907	Selected by general election 1906 for short term; elected by Legislature to serve remaining term of Mitchell and Gearin
Bourne, Jonathan, Jr.—R	1907–1913	Selected by general election1906; elected by Legislature 1907
Lane, Harry—D	1913–May 23, 1917	Selected by general election 1912; elected by Legislature 1913; died in office
McNary, Charles L.—R	May 29, 1917–Nov. 5, 1918	Appointed by Governor Withycombe to succeed Lane
Mulkey, Fred W.—R	Nov. 5–Dec. 17, 1918	Elected 1918 for short term; resigned to permit reappointment of McNary
McNary, Charles L.—R	Dec. 17, 1918–Feb. 24, 1944	Appointed 1918 for unexpired short term; elected 1918; reelected 1924, 1930, 1936, 1942; died in office
Cordon, Guy—R	Mar. 4, 1944–1955	Appointed by Governor Snell to succeed McNary; elected 1944; reelected 1948
Neuberger, Richard L.—D	1955–Mar. 9, 1960	Elected 1954; died in office
Lusk, Hall S.—D	Mar. 16, 1960–Nov. 8, 1960	Appointed by Governor Hatfield to succeed Neuberger
Neuberger, Maurine—D	Nov. 8, 1960–1967	Elected 1960 for short and full terms
Hatfield, Mark O.—R	1967–1997	Elected 1966; reelected 1972, 1978, 1984, 1990
Smith, Gordon H.—R	1997–2009	Elected 1996; reelected 2002
Merkley, Jeff—D	2009–	Elected 2008

Second Position[2]

Name/Political Party	Term of Service[1]	By What Authority/Remarks
Lane, Joseph—D	Feb. 14, 1859–1861	Elected by Legislature 1858
Nesmith, James W.—D	1861–1867	Elected by Legislature 1860
Corbett, Henry W.—R	1867–1873	Elected by Legislature 1866
Mitchell, John H.—R	1873–1879	Elected by Legislature 1872
Slater, James H.—D	1879–1885	Elected by Legislature 1878
Mitchell, John H.—R	1885–1897	Elected by Legislature 1885; reelected 1891
Corbett, Henry W.—R[5]	March, 1897	Appointed by Governor Lord, not seated

Name/Political Party	Term of Service[1]	By What Authority/Remarks
Simon, Joseph—R	Oct. 6, 1898–1903	Elected by Legislature to fill vacancy
Fulton, Charles W.—R	1903–1909	Elected by Legislature 1903
Chamberlain, George E.—D[6]	1909–1921	Selected by general election 1908; elected by Legislature; reelected by people 1914
Stanfield, Robert N.—R	1921–1927	Elected 1920
Steiwer, Frederick—R	1927–Feb. 1, 1938	Elected 1926; reelected 1932; resigned
Reames, Alfred Evan—D	Feb. 1–Nov. 9, 1938	Appointed by Governor Martin to succeed Steiwer
Barry, Alex G.—R	Nov. 9, 1938–1939	Elected 1938 for short term
Holman, Rufus C.—R	1939–1945	Elected 1938
Morse, Wayne[7]—D	1945–1969	Elected 1944; reelected 1950, 1956, 1962
Packwood, Robert—R	1969–1995	Elected 1968; reelected 1974, 1980, 1986, 1992; resigned 1995
Wyden, Ron[8]—D	1996–	Elected 1996; reelected 1998, 2004, 2010

[1]Unless otherwise noted, normal terms of office began on the fourth day of March and ended on the third day of March until 1933 when terms were changed to begin and end on the third day of January, unless a different date was set by Congress.

[2]Delazon Smith and Joseph Lane drew lots in 1859 for the short and long term senate seats. Smith won the short term of only 17 days expiring March 3, 1859 (designated first position). Lane won the long term expiring March 3, 1861 (designated second position).

[3]When the Legislature first met after statehood in May 1859, Smith was defeated for reelection, and no successor was named. Consequently, Oregon had only one U.S. senator from March 3, 1859 until Baker was elected October 1, 1860.

[4]Senator Edward Baker was killed in the Battle of Balls Bluff, Virginia while serving as a colonel in the Civil War, the only U.S. senator to serve in military action while a senator. His statue, cast of horatio stone and marble, stands 6 ft. 5 in. tall in the Capitol rotunda in Washington, D.C.

[5]When the Legislature failed to elect a successor to Mitchell, Governor Lord appointed Henry Corbett. After conflict, however, the U.S. Senate decided the governor did not have this authority and refused to seat Corbett. Therefore, Oregon was represented by only one U.S. senator from March 4, 1897 to October 6, 1898.

[6]Direct election of U.S. senators resulted from Oregon's ratification of Article XVII of the U.S. Constitution on January 23, 1913 (effective May 31, 1913). Oregon initiated a direct primary for selecting candidates in 1904.

[7]Wayne Morse was elected as a Republican in 1944 and reelected as a Republican in 1950. He changed to Independent in 1952 and to Democrat in 1955. He was reelected as a Democrat in 1956 and 1962.

[8]Elected to fill the unexpired term of Robert Packwood due to Senator Packwood's resignation. The elections, both primary and general, to fill Senator Packwood's seat were conducted by mail. The special primary and general elections were the first statewide vote-by-mail elections to fill a federal office in United States history.

U.S. Representatives from Oregon

Name/Political Party	Term of Service[1]	By What Authority/Remarks
Thurston, Samuel R.—D	June 6, 1849–Apr. 9, 1851	Territorial Delegate elected 1849; died at sea returning home from first session
Lane, Joseph—D	June 2, 1851–Feb. 14, 1859	Territorial Delegate elected 1851; reelected 1853, 1855, 1857
Grover, LaFayette—D	Feb. 15–Mar. 3, 1859	First Representative at large, elected 1858 for short term
Stout, Lansing—D	1859–1861	Elected 1858
Shiel, George K.—D	1861–1863	Elected 1860
McBride, John R.—R	1863–1865	Elected 1862
Henderson, J.H.D.—R	1865–1867	Elected 1864

Name/Political Party	Term of Service[1]	By What Authority/Remarks
Mallory, Rufus—R	1867–1869	Elected 1866
Smith, Joseph S.—D	1869–1871	Elected 1868
Slater, James H.—D	1871–1873	Elected 1870
Wilson, Joseph G.—R	1873	Elected 1872; died in July, 1873 before qualifying
Nesmith, James W.—D	1873–1875	Elected 1873
La Dow, George A.—D	1875	Elected 1874; died Mar. 4, 1875 before qualifying
Lane, Lafayette—D	Oct. 25, 1875–1877	Elected 1875
Williams, Richard—R	1877–1879	Elected 1876
Whiteaker, John—D	1879–1881	Elected 1878
George, Melvin C.—R	1881–1885	Elected 1880; reelected 1882
Hermann, Binger—R	1885–1893	Elected 1884; reelected 1886, 1888, 1890

1st District

Name/Political Party	Term of Service	By What Authority/Remarks
Hermann, Binger—R	1893–1897	Elected 1892; reelected 1894
Tongue, Thomas H.—R	1897–Jan. 11, 1903	Elected 1896; reelected 1898, 1900, 1902; died in office
Hermann, Binger—R	June 1, 1903–1907	Elected 1903 to succeed Tongue; reelected 1904
Hawley, Willis C.—R	1907–1933	Elected 1906; reelected 1908, 1910, 1912, 1914, 1916, 1918, 1920, 1922, 1924, 1926, 1928, 1930
Mott, James W.—R	1933–Nov. 12, 1945	Elected 1932; reelected 1934, 1936, 1938, 1940, 1942, 1944; died in office
Norblad, A. Walter, Jr.—R	Jan. 11, 1946–Sept. 20, 1964	Elected 1945 to succeed Mott; reelected 1946, 1948, 1950, 1952, 1954, 1956, 1958, 1960, 1962; died in office
Wyatt, Wendell—R	Nov. 3, 1964–1975	Elected 1964 to succeed Norblad; reelected 1966, 1968, 1970, 1972
AuCoin, Les—D	1975–1993	Elected 1974; reelected 1976, 1978, 1980, 1982, 1984, 1986, 1988, 1990
Furse, Elizabeth—D	1993–1999	Elected 1992; reelected 1994, 1996
Wu, David—D	1999–2011	Elected 1998; reelected 2000, 2002, 2004, 2006, 2008, 2010; resigned 2011
Bonamici, Suzanne—D[2]	2012–	Elected 2012; reelected 2012

2nd District

Name/Political Party	Term of Service	By What Authority/Remarks
Ellis, William R.—R	1893–1899	Elected 1892; reelected 1894, 1896
Moody, Malcolm A.—R	1899–1903	Elected 1898; reelected 1900
Williamson, John N.—R	1903–1907	Elected 1902; reelected 1904
Ellis, William R.—R	1907–1911	Elected 1906; reelected 1908
Lafferty, Abraham W.—R.	1911–1913	Elected 1910
Sinnott, N.J.—R	1913–May 31, 1928	Elected 1912; reelected 1914, 1916, 1918, 1920, 1922, 1924, 1926; resigned
Butler, Robert R.—R	Nov. 6, 1928–Jan. 7, 1933	Elected 1928 to succeed Sinnott; reelected 1930; died in office
Pierce, Walter M.—D	1933–1943	Elected 1932; reelected 1934, 1936, 1938, 1940
Stockman, Lowell—R	1943–1953	Elected 1942; reelected 1944, 1946, 1948, 1950
Coon, Samuel H.—R	1953–1957	Elected 1952; reelected 1954
Ullman, Albert C.—D	1957–1981	Elected 1956; reelected 1958, 1960, 1962, 1964, 1966, 1968, 1970, 1972, 1974, 1976,1978

Name/Political Party	Term of Service[1]	By What Authority/Remarks
Smith, Denny—R	1981–1983	Elected 1980
Smith, Robert F.—R	1983–1995	Elected 1982; reelected 1984, 1986, 1988, 1990, 1992
Cooley, Wes—R	1995–1997	Elected 1994
Smith, Robert F.—R	1997–1999	Elected 1996
Walden, Greg—R	1999–	Elected 1998; reelected 2000, 2002, 2004, 2006, 2008, 2010, 2012

3rd District

Name/Political Party	Term of Service	By What Authority/Remarks
Lafferty, Abraham W.—R	1913–1915	Elected 1912
McArthur, Clifton N.—R	1915–1923	Elected 1914; reelected 1916, 1918, 1920
Watkins, Elton—D	1923–1925	Elected 1922
Crumpacker, Maurice E.—R	1925–July 25, 1927	Elected 1924; reelected 1926; died in office
Korell, Franklin F.—R	Oct. 18, 1927–1931	Elected 1927; reelected 1928
Martin, Charles H.—D	1931–1935	Elected 1930; reelected 1932
Ekwall, William A.—R	1935–1937	Elected 1934
Honeyman, Nan Wood—D	1937–1939	Elected 1936
Angell, Homer D.—R	1939–1955	Elected 1938; reelected 1940, 1942, 1944, 1946, 1948, 1950, 1952
Green, Edith S.—D	1955–1975	Elected 1954; reelected 1956, 1958, 1960, 1962, 1964, 1966, 1968, 1970, 1972
Duncan, Robert B.—D	1975–1981	Elected 1974; reelected 1976, 1978
Wyden, Ron—D	1981–1996	Elected 1980; reelected 1982, 1984, 1986, 1988, 1990, 1992, 1994
Blumenauer, Earl—D[3]	1996–	Elected 1996; reelected 1998, 2000, 2002, 2004, 2006, 2008, 2010, 2012

4th District

Name/Political Party	Term of Service	By What Authority/Remarks
Ellsworth, Harris—R	1943–1957	Elected 1942; reelected 1944, 1946, 1948, 1950, 1952, 1954
Porter, Charles O.—D	1957–1961	Elected 1956; reelected 1958
Durno, Edwin R.—R	1961–1963	Elected 1960
Duncan, Robert B.—D	1963–1967	Elected 1962; reelected 1964
Dellenback, John—R	1967–1975	Elected 1966; reelected 1968, 1970, 1972
Weaver, James—D	1975–1987	Elected 1974; reelected 1976, 1978, 1980, 1982, 1984
DeFazio, Peter A.—D	1987–	Elected 1986; reelected 1988, 1990, 1992, 1994, 1996, 1998, 2000, 2002, 2004, 2006, 2008, 2010, 2012

5th District

Name/Political Party	Term of Service	By What Authority/Remarks
Smith, Denny—R	1983–1991	Elected 1982; reelected 1984, 1986, 1988
Kopetski, Mike	1991–1995	Elected 1990; reelected 1992
Bunn, Jim—R	1995–1997	Elected 1994
Hooley, Darlene—D	1997–2009	Elected 1996; reelected 1998, 2000, 2002, 2004, 2006, 2008
Schrader, Kurt—D	2009–	Elected 2008, 2010, 2012

[1]Unless otherwise noted, normal terms of office began on the fourth day of March and ended on the third day of March until 1933 when terms were changed to begin and end on the third day of January, unless a different date was set by Congress.

[2]Elected in the January 31, 2012, Special Election to finish the unexpired term of Representative David Wu.

[3]Elected in 1996 to finish the unexpired term of Representative Ron Wyden. Reelected to a full term at the November 5, 1996, General Election.

The Smith Rock State Park "Monkey Face" rock formation—Oregon State Archives Scenic Photograph desDB166

The splendor of Oregon began well before it became a territory o a state. Historian Stephen Dow Beckham's finely executed histor introduces the reader to the physical and geological changes tha created the land we know as Oregon. He escorts us through the time when the Northwest was occupied by the first tribal people and th events that have occurred since Lewis and Clark spread word of th Columbia River and the Pacific Northwest to the rest of the nation.

Oregon History

Written by Stephen Dow Beckham
Pamplin Professor of History
Lewis & Clark College

An Inhabited Land

Nature marked time. Spring followed winter, passed into summer, merged into fall and, inevitably, gave birth to another winter. The progression was endless and predictable. Water was a consistent ingredient. The steady rain and mist fed the coast and western valleys, nourishing lush forests and grasslands. Salmon surged up the streams, filling the water from bank to bank in a cycle of birth and dying. The fish, exhausted after their journey and spawning, were dragged back downstream by the current. Bears and eagles watched and feasted, while the smolts stirred from the gravel to slip unnoticed down the rivers to the sea and renew the endless process.

Beyond the Cascade Mountains in the vast, arid stretches of central and eastern Oregon, the rainfall was less but life was nevertheless abundant. Aromatic sagebrush, hardy juniper, the sunny faces of balsam root, and tufts of lomatium gave form and color to the landscape. In the fall, countless birds passed across the sky winging their way southward on their annual migration. Geese, ducks, pelicans, and sandhill cranes settled down to search for seeds, feed on brine shrimp in the alkaline lakes, or gain energy for their push to their winter rookeries. Nature constructed elaborate stage sets in the mountains, as tamarack, vine maple, big-leaf maple and alder shed their chlorophyll and transformed from green to red, gold and brown. The turning of the leaves, like the migration of birds and of salmon, steelhead, sturgeon and smelt, marked the change of seasons. Winter brought quiet. Life slowed and snow blanketed part of the land. Living things battened down and endured. Then, as always in nature, the process started over again.

The inevitable exceptions to these predictable events were dramatic and often inexplicable. From time to time, the Cascade peaks shuddered and erupted with uncommon fury, releasing ash flows, watery floods of muddy debris, plumes of smoke, and slowly oozing lava. Occasionally, a rupture appeared in the earth and, as in ancient times when the great basalt flows spread like taffy, layer upon layer, to form the Columbia Plateau, lavas poured out on the surface. They diverted rivers and formed a jumbled landscape, almost fortified in appearance, before ceasing their advance and cooling. Sometimes the earth simply shook and, with great drama, rose or fell. These massive quakes plunged forests surrounding wetlands into estuaries or the sea; they unleashed landslides that sometimes dammed rivers. The earthquakes, driven by the thrust of the Pacific Plate under the continent, changed the face of the land.

Humans witnessed these things.

For at least 10,000 years, and ,perhaps, for another 5,000 to 10,000 years before that, they were in Oregon. Their names for themselves, their languages and their lifeways are unknown, but they were here. Evidence of their presence is subtle but certain. In central and eastern Oregon, where discovery of prehistory is easier because the vegetation is sparse and artifacts are more likely to be preserved in dry rock shelters, archaeologists have found numerous traces. The record, while incomplete, is compelling.

Humans hunted the megafauna of the Late Pleistocene. Massive creatures, far larger than any alive today, lived during the Wisconsin Ice Age, which began to end about 15,000 years ago. Mammoths, mastodons, horses and camels lived contemporaneously with Oregon's first human inhabitants. Scattered in the sands of the High Desert are a mix of camel bones and pieces of fluted projectile points. Big-game hunters using the atlatl—a spear-throwing device that gave them greater leverage and improved both distance and velocity—killed the big-game animals that were yet in the land. Whether hunting hastened the animals' passing or whether environmental conditions drove them to extinction is not clear, but the animals and humans were neighbors in Oregon ten or more millennia ago.

The story of prehistory in Oregon has unfolded steadily since the advent of archaeological investigations mounted in the 1870s by Paul Schumacher and A.W. Chase along the coast. While the early researchers were primarily relic collectors, Dr. Luther S. Cressman of the University of Oregon helped in the 1930s to develop the discipline of systematic scientific research verifying the deep time frame of people's presence in Oregon. Cressman's primary contributions unfolded at Fort Rock Cave, a deep rock shelter that, 10,000 years ago, was home to people living on an island in a vast inland lake in south-central Oregon. Cressman and his students investigated several sites, testing and excavating, but leaving portions of each location. How fortunate was that discipline, for following World War II and the development of radiocarbon dating, Cressman returned to Fort Rock to open new units of the site and established that, more than 10,000 years ago the region had been occupied by humans.

Oregon's archaeological record grows fuller each year. It documents more than ten millennia of human habitation and successive adaptations to changing environmental conditions. At the end of the 18th century, Oregon possessed several distinctive lifeways. These, for the convenience of description, have been described in geographical terms as Coast, Plateau and Great Basin. While this lumping violates some of the integrity of distinctive cultural practices, it helps clarify the complex human adaptations to distinctive biotic regions of the state.

Northwest Coast

The people of the shoreline and western Oregon valleys, in general, shared lifeways common with native people residing along the North Pacific from Cape Mendocino to southeast Alaska. From the Clatsop at the mouth of the Columbia to the Chetco at the California border and from the Clackamas near the falls of the Willamette to the Takelma and Shasta of the Rogue River Valley—these people shared a common setting: a wet, temperate region, heavily forested, connected by rivers running into the sea. Their environment provided the essentials of life: cedar to frame and cover their houses, materials for clothing and dugout canoes, salmon and other fish as primary subsistence, and a bounty of game, roots and berries to supplement their diet.

For these people life was predictable and generally easy. They had to work hard to secure and maintain supplies of firewood, repair their fishing traps, weirs, and nets, and engage in extensive gathering activities, but for them, nature was generous. Shoreline residents harvested vast quantities of mollusks and crustaceans from the intertidal zones. Valley natives dug camas and wapato, gathered and processed acorns, hunted deer and elk and worked a bit harder to survive. Annually, they set fire to the meadows, opening and shaping the landscapes of the Willamette, Umpqua, and Rogue River valleys. Burning stimulated nutritious browse for deer, assisted women in the harvest of tarweed seeds, stimulated the regeneration of berries and maintained an open understory, which undoubtedly enhanced the security of settlements.

Oregon natives of the western part of the state possessed sufficient time and wealth to develop special arts. The Chinookans of the Columbia River carved handsome, high-prowed canoes with animal effigies on their bows and erected remarkable wooden spirit figures at vigil and grave sites. The Tututni and Chetco of the south coast bartered for raw materials and made massive obsidian wealth-display blades; wove intricately decorated basketry with geometric designs of beargrass, maidenhair fern, and wild hazel bark; and sent their young people off on spirit quests to sacred sites atop mountain peaks or promontories overlooking the sea. The Coquille, Coos, Lower Umpqua, Siuslaw, Alsea, and Tillamook occupied estuaries that carry their names. A dozen bands from the Tualatin to the Santiam and Yoncalla lived in the Willamette Valley and northern Umpqua Valley. South of them resided the Upper Umpqua, Cow Creek, Shasta Costa, Takelma, and Shasta. Western Oregon people had connections of trade and commerce reaching into northern California and to coastal Washington and British Columbia. They were involved in the flow of dentalium shells, elk hide armor, slaves, and surplus foods. Their lifeways echoed the strong traditions of art, ceremony, social class distinction and emphasis on wealth that ran for hundreds of miles along the North Pacific Coast.

Columbia Plateau

Living east of the Cascades, the people of Oregon's interior nevertheless had access to unparalleled riverine resources. The Columbia and its tributaries—Deschutes, John Day, Umatilla, Snake, Grande Ronde, and Owyhee—were filled with fish. For at least 10,000 years, Celilo Falls, the place where the Columbia dropped over a series of basalt ledges and surged almost on its side through Five Mile Rapids, was their major fishery. So vast were the harvests of fish, the tribes that gathered at Celilo controlled one of the greatest, longest-operating trade centers in the American West. The commerce of Celilo was varied. Arriving from the coast were sleek dugout canoes, paddles, cattail matting, prized shells, and special foodstuffs such as smelt. From the south came war captives to be bartered into slavery, obsidian from more than twenty quarry sites destined for the hands of craftsmen in Washington and British Columbia (where none of this vital projectile material existed naturally), and, just prior to Euro-American contact, herds of horses. From the east came carefully preserved beargrass for basketry, buffalo hides and saddles and, again, just before the arrival of American explorers, remarkable trade goods—glass beads, weapons, metal-tipped tools, and cotton and woolen cloth and clothing.

The Plateau people occupied a challenging environment. Summers were hot and windy; winters were cold and windy. The lodges to shelter human activities thus varied from pole-frame, mat-covered summer encampments to semisubterranean pit houses, framed with a cone of rafters covered with brush and earth to provide a refuge from the icy cold, snow, and darkness of winter. In spite of its harshness, the region abounded in life. Following annual ceremonies, the women harvested the roots of wild celeries, balsams, and lomatiums. They picked huckleberries in the nearby mountains and gathered nutritious moss. The men ran down deer in the snow to secure not only meat but hides to tan for clothing and moccasins. They dipped, clubbed, netted, and speared salmon and wind-dried them in curing sheds along the river.

Oregon's Plateau tribes included the Wasco, Wishram, Warm Springs (or Tenino), John Day, Cayuse, Umatilla, and Nez Perce. They lived from the Cascade Mountains to the Wallowas, from the margins of the rivers to summer camps at high elevations. Their seasonal round responded to the rhythms of nature and took them from fishing camps to berry-picking sites and hunting camps high in the mountains. With the onset of winter, they returned to lower elevations and their permanent villages along the margins of the principal streams.

Great Basin

The high desert region is majestic and harsh. It is an unforgiving landscape where, at times, life is a scramble. For the Northern Paiute, Western Shoshoni, Bannock, Klamath and Modoc, survival demanded unremitting labor and almost constant movement. While the Klamath and Modoc possessed staple foods such as suckers, trout, wocus (water lily seed) and huckleberries, the tribes to the east had a more marginal existence. Their resilience in coping with high elevation, extreme temperatures, arid conditions and isolation spoke to their time-tested survival skills in a challenging environment. The Klamath Basin peoples actually lived at a point of transition between Plateau, Basin, Coast and California lifeways, whereas the Northern Paiute, who held vast stretches of central and southeastern Oregon, were more closely tied to the basin environment.

Oregon's Great Basin peoples engaged in a seasonal round that often required 200 or more miles of travel per year. In winter, they resided on the margins of lakes and rivers, seeking the lowest elevation and most moderate temperatures in harsh conditions. Their homes included rock shelters as well as lodges covered with brush and tule mats. In winters, confinement and the months of the long moons encouraged storytelling and necessitated tapping the food resources carefully stored in the previous seasons. When spring became summer, these people were on the move. They hunted waterfowl, antelope, and deer; gathered roots, berries, seeds and nuts; fished; and traveled. They moved to higher and higher elevations following food sources, until the aspen leaves turned to bright gold, telling them it was time to leave the high country and return to the winter encampments.

The peoples of the Great Basin traveled in extended family groups but sometimes gathered as bands for communal hunts. Women and children fanned out through the countryside and, moving slowly toward a ravine and making great noise, drove all creatures before them. Far down the trace, etched eons ago by erosion through basalt, the men stretched fiber nets. Here they clubbed frightened rabbits or, when lucky, killed deer and antelope with bow and arrow. Paddling carefully in the predawn cold onto the waters of the lakes in the middle of the High Desert, the men silently stretched nets between poles and, with a great noise, spooked the unsuspecting water birds. The birds rose to flee in the mist, only to become entangled in the mesh of netting, which the men then collapsed into the water, harvesting a bountiful supply of food for their families.

Great Basin residents practiced a mixed economy. They hunted, fished, trapped, dug, and picked food resources. They moved with the seasons in an almost continuous quest for subsistence. They covered a vast, open country, leaving their petroglyphs at sacred sites, caching foods, camping in rock shelters used by the ancient inhabitants of the region. Their finely developed survival skills enabled them to endure and prosper in a land that held them, at times, at the edge of existence.

The first inhabitants occupied three distinct biotic provinces or geographical areas. Their adaptation and mastery of the environment reached from the margins of the fog-shrouded and wet Pacific shoreline to the arid reaches of sagebrush and bunchgrass of the interior. Their subsistence activities took them from sea level to tree line in the Wallowas and on Steens Mountain. They were at home in the desert and in the grasslands of the Columbia Plateau. In the fall, they set fire to the meadows to keep open the western Oregon valleys as well as to maintain the bald headlands along the Oregon coast. At the south-facing bases of the headlands, they often erected their plank houses facing into the sun. They plied the rivers with dugout canoes; they hunted for ducks and geese on the lakes with balsa rafts made of dried tules.

The first inhabitants knew this land. They gave it names. They explained its features in their oral histories, through experienced storytellers reciting the stories. They told of the myth age when only animals and no humans were in the land. They recounted tales of transition, when animals and humans interacted on a personal basis, a time when humans were not quite fully formed. They told of the historic past, of things remembered and partly remembered. They did this with gesture, eye contact, voice modulation, and sometimes by musical interlude wherein they or someone in the crowd sang a song relevant to the story. Their techniques varied. The Tillamook, for example, repeated stories line-by-line as they listened to the teller, thereby memorizing over a period of years the stories and history of their tribe. The challenge to the storyteller was thus to deliver with talent and stay true to the story elements, yet build the drama and unleash creativity.

The first inhabitants held a rich land. Its resources far exceeded their needs and their wants. They lived fully. While there is some evidence of migration and population dynamics, those tales of prehistory are lost in the mists of time. What is known is that Oregon was fully occupied by the 18th century. people of more than 30 different languages lived throughout the state. They knew and loved the land. It was their home.

Some Came By Sea

The first moment of contact was not recorded. Possibly, it occurred when a Manila Galleon made a landfall somewhere along the Oregon Coast. How the viewers must have wondered when, looking out to sea, they saw a great ship, propelled by billowing sails, not paddles, scudding to the wind and laboring through the waves. The prospect for such an encounter unfolded in 1565 when the Spanish, after several years of probing for a route, finally found a means to send a vessel northeast from the Philippines to catch the great Japanese Current for a sweeping circular transit of the North Pacific. While normally the galleons—one per year for 250 years—did not make a landfall until south of Cape Mendocino in northern California, some did so farther north.

The *San Francisco Xavier,* one of 30 vessels that failed to arrive in Acapulco or any of the other destination ports along the west coast of New Spain (Mexico), likely wrecked in 1707 on the Nehalem sand spit near the base of Neahkahnie Mountain. Tillamook tribal tales of strangers in their midst, discoveries of large chunks of beeswax and a lidded silver vase, and legends of buried treasure hint that a wayward galleon may have crashed into the shore. A thousand-ton vessel, it was probably laden with silk, porcelain, altar pieces reworked in Asia from gold and silver shipped from Central America, pepper, cloves, and other luxury items—each stored in cargo space allotted to the merchants who controlled the monopoly of the galleon trade.

Spanish voyages in the North Pacific were part of the nation's efforts to seek colonies, mission fields, and wealth. As early as 1543, Bartolome Ferrelo, a surviving captain of the ill-fated expedition under Juan Cabrillo, may have sailed as far north as the Oregon-California border. He and his shipmates sought the fabled Straits of Anian—a passage through the continent. Cape Ferrelo on the south coast bears his name. Some also believe that Francis Drake sojourned on the *Golden Hind* in 1579 in coastal Oregon. Having raided Spanish ports and stolen immense wealth in his voyage northward from Cape Horn, Drake was hiding out before crossing the Pacific and rounding the world to return to England. Although his anchorage is claimed at sites in California, heralded in a marker at Cape Arago, and said to have been at Whale Cove, no one has produced conclusive evidence of his visit to Oregon. Sebastian Vizcaino, sailing for Spain in 1603, possibly sighted and named Cape Sebastian north of the California border. The promontory marked his northernmost exploration along the Pacific shoreline.

Then came silence. As had been the case for thousands of years, Oregon was wholly an indigenous people's land. The mid-1700s, however, unleashed forces that would forever change native dominion in the American West. The forces were in part intellectual. Europe had engaged in a Renaissance, a rekindling of energies and rediscovery of classical learning. Emerging nation-states took pride in commerce, art, and education. The turning point, however, was the Enlightenment. By the early 18th century, several nations had philosophical societies whose members hungered for knowledge and who sought natural laws or evidence for what governed the universe. They became eager students of the world. Carl Linne, a Swede, developed systems to classify all living things as plants or animals, seeking to order the descriptions and terminologies. Luke Howard, an Englishman, developed a nomenclature for clouds. Isaac Newton provided mathematical evidence on the working of gravity and descriptions of optics. The quest for knowledge, developing collections of "curiosities," and, in time, exploring unknown lands took on national significance.

The reaching out of Russians to the Aleutians and into Alaska between 1728 and 1769 shocked the Spanish. Following the discoveries of Vitus Bering, Russian fur seekers swept into the region, destroying Aleut villages, enslaving the natives, and securing riches by shipping furs to the Asian and European markets. A cardinal principle of Spain, exercised since the 1520s, was to create protective borderlands to insulate her wealthiest colonies from foreign predators. By the 1760s, officials in New Spain were gravely worried that the Russians, somewhere to the north, might fall upon their outlying colonies in Baja California, Pimeria Alta (Arizona), or New Mexico. Viceroy Antonio de Bucareli in 1769 thus dispatched Gaspar de Portola by sea and Juan Batista de Anza by land with priests, soldiers, and families of workers to establish a new borderland—Alta California. Within two decades, these Spanish colonists had a chain of missions, presidios, and pueblos extending from San Diego to San Francisco Bay.

When the Russians did not appear, the Spanish reached out again. In 1775, the viceroy ordered the first of a series of maritime expeditions to explore the coastline northward. The voyages of Juan Perez, Bruno Hezeta, and Bodega y Quadra gave more form to the European understanding of the coast. Working under wretched conditions, sailing against the current and suffering from ill health and spoiled water, the mariners nevertheless began an important era in exploration.

The British came next. In 1778, Captain James Cook, aboard *H.M.S. Resolution,* made a landfall on the central Oregon coast. He commemorated the day by naming the headland Cape Foulweather. A famed mariner who had twice before explored the Pacific, Cook was sent to find the Northwest Passage, a mythical sea route through the continent. He could not find what did not exist, but Cook sailed north to the Arctic Ocean and charted much of the outer coast. The Spanish responded immediately and dispatched Ignacio de Arteaga and Bodega y Quadra in 1779 to explore parts of coastal Alaska. In the 1780s, the French expedition under Comte de

Laperouse and the Spanish expedition under Alessandro Malaspina sailed the shore to chart, collect specimens of natural history and native culture, and assess the prospects of new colonies.

Significant in discerning the features of coastal Oregon were the labors of independent mariners, dispatched not by their governments but by investors who sought wealth through the fur trade. Cook's men discovered when they reached China in 1779 that a sea otter pelt purchased for a broken file or a few brass buttons brought a thousand-fold return when bartered to the merchants of the Pearl River delta. Captain John Meares of England and Captain Robert Gray of Boston both sailed the coast of Oregon in 1788–89 and traded with natives who paddled out to sea in their canoes or who, in Gray's trade at Tillamook Bay, dared to barter with the foreigners who sailed across the bar and dropped anchor near their villages.

On a second voyage to the coast in 1792, Gray decided to risk a perilous crossing, the unknown bar of the Columbia River. Although the river had been discerned by Hezeta and tentatively designated Rio San Roque, no mariner had entered it. Gray did. He and his men sailed through the breakers and over the shoals, passing the base of Cape Disappointment, named in frustration by Meares on a previous voyage, and dropped anchor in the broad estuary of the great river. Gray named it Columbia in honor of his ship, the *Columbia Rediviva*. A few weeks later, Gray encountered the exploring party headed by Captain George Vancouver, another British expedition in search of the Northwest Passage. Gray told Vancouver of his "discovery" of the Columbia, a watershed known and occupied by thousands of people for at least 10,000 years. Vancouver could not resist. He dispatched Lieutenant William Broughton aboard the *Chatham* into the Columbia to chart its course. Broughton and his crew used two whaleboats to conduct reconnaissance as far east as the entrance to the Columbia Gorge, noting depths of the channel and tribal villages along the shore, persuaded, at last, that the river did not pass through the continent.

By the end of the 18th century, an estimated 300 vessels from a dozen different countries had sailed to the Northwest Coast. Some of these had passed along the shores of Oregon. The logs of James Cook, John Meares, Robert Gray, John Boit and Robert Haswell, as well as eight diaries of George Vancouver's shipmates recorded first impressions of the land and its people. "They were of a middling size with mild pleasing features & nowise sullen or distrustful in their behaviour," wrote Dr. Archibald Menzies in 1792 when describing the Quah-to-mah Tribe near Cape Blanco.

The mariners named headlands, charted offshore rocks, explored some of the estuaries, notably the Columbia and Puget Sound, and obtained useful knowledge. The narratives of Cook and Vancouver were published shortly after their journeys. They whetted the appetite of others who wanted to know more about these lands. The collections of bows, arrows, baskets and plants secured by Vancouver's expedition went into the holdings of the British Museum. What had been unknown was now better understood. The currents of the Enlightenment had swept halfway round the world and touched the Oregon Country.

Land-based Fur Trade and Exploration

The mariners who sailed the coast or ran their vessels tentatively into the estuaries and harbors of Oregon initiated inexorable forces of change. They introduced trade goods that swept in swift current through the traditional cultures of the native peoples, altering forever their clothing, technology, and means of subsistence. They introduced diseases such as smallpox, measles, and fevers; in time these pathogens decimated the Indian population. However, an event that would have even greater consequence was the November, 1805, arrival at the mouth of the Columbia River of a weary, but eager, exploring party under the command of Meriwether Lewis and William Clark.

Dispatched in 1804 by President Thomas Jefferson, this military expedition, financed at public expense and underwritten in part by the American Philosophical Society, was the American nation's belated commitment to the Enlightenment. Ostensibly, the party was to explore the newly acquired Louisiana Territory. Jefferson, however, wanted to find a water route, so far as practical, for the transit of commerce across North America. An avid student of nature and civilization, he laid out detailed instructions for the explorers to observe the flora, fauna, geology, climate and tribal culture. They were to map the land, take temperatures of hot springs, note locations of major geographical features, record tribal vocabularies and open diplomatic relations between the tribes and the United States.

The scripting of the expedition could not have been more perfect. The cast of characters included two stalwart leaders, young Army recruits, French-Canadian hunters, a Shoshoni woman—Sacagawea—and her infant son—Baptiste Charbonneau—York, an African-American slave of William Clark's, and a shaggy Newfoundland dog. The success of the Corps of Discovery in carrying out its multiple missions gave it luster while heightening interest in western lands and in government-financed exploration.

Lewis and Clark accomplished their mission with verve. They crossed the Rockies, entered the Bitterroot Valley of Montana, followed the Nez Perce Trail west of Lolo Pass and, then, embarked by dugouts to descend the Clearwater, Snake and Columbia Rivers. They camped on the north and south banks of the Columbia, portaged at Celilo

Falls, passed through the Gorge and established their winter quarters at Fort Clatsop on the Oregon shore near the river's mouth. During the rain-soaked winter of 1805–06, they wrote their journals, boiled salt from seawater on the nearby beach of the Pacific, recorded cultural information from the Clatsop and Chinook people, drew numerous maps, and hoped a trading vessel might carry some of their treasured notes safely to the president. None appeared. The following spring, the party departed for home, paddling against the swift current until it reached the mouth of the Umatilla River. Having bartered for horses sufficient to carry the party and its supplies, the men set out overland to retrace their steps across the mountains and plains.

News of the Lewis and Clark Expedition enlivened interest in distant frontiers. Already, fur seekers were pushing up the Missouri, Arkansas and Red rivers. The descriptions of swift streams and ponds filled with beaver, mink, otter and marten in the mountains persuaded several investors to send men with traps and trade goods to exploit those resources. John Colter, a member of the Corps of Discovery, turned around before reaching St. Louis and signed on with a fur trapping party headed for the Yellowstone country. The rush for furs had taken on a new life. This time Americans were major players.

Jefferson turned over the journals of the leaders to Nicholas Biddle, who edited them in an abridged two-volume edition, *The Journals of Lewis & Clark* (1814). So popular were their accounts of adventure that an eager public literally read the books to pieces.

Lewis and Clark had created a remarkable legacy. They had dramatically enhanced the geographical understanding of a far-flung part of North America. They collected 178 plant specimens—140 in the Oregon Country. They made notes upon or brought home specimens of 122 species and subspecies of animals—65 west of the Continental Divide. They expanded a nation's horizon and understanding in noteworthy ways.

The stirrings of change picked up momentum in 1808 when Simon Fraser and other employees of the North West Company, a fur-trading enterprise based in Montreal, crossed the Rockies and descended a mighty stream—the Fraser—to the Pacific Ocean. David Thompson, a skilled cartographer also in the employ of the North West Company, came next. He and his party crossed the Rockies and descended the Columbia. When he reached the ocean in 1811, he found an American fur trade post on the south shore. The Pacific Fur Company had already established a toehold, the first permanent Euro-American settlement in the region, at Astoria.

The new post on the lower Columbia River fulfilled the speculative dream of John Jacob Astor. An emigrant from Germany who prospered as a middleman in the fur trade and investor in New York real estate, Astor had listened keenly to reports of the Lewis and Clark Expedition. One of America's first millionaires, Astor thought big. His vision was to establish a post near the ocean shore in the Pacific Northwest. Land-based trappers and traders would secure furs for his rich trade in Canton. His warehouses on the lower Pearl River would exchange otter pelts for silks and porcelains for the American market. His sailing vessels would supply both his Columbia River post and the Russian American Company in Alaska. These ambitions led Astor to found the American Fur Company for the Rocky Mountain region in 1808, the Pacific Fur Company for the Columbia watershed in 1810, and the South West Company in 1811.

To attain his goals in Oregon, Astor planned a two-prong approach. He outfitted the *Tonquin,* a ship under Captain Jonathan Thorn, with trade goods, tools and everything needed to sustain his new fort on the Columbia. Sailing in September, 1810, the *Tonquin* arrived in March, 1811, at the Columbia River. Astor also ordered Wilson Price Hunt to lead an overland party, which departed from St. Louis in September, 1810, for an arduous and nearly fatal winter crossing of the continent. Ultimately, in spite of drownings at the mouth of the Columbia and terrible privations for the overland party, the Astorians began clearing the dense spruce forest to erect their fort. "The buildings consisted of apartments for the proprietors and clerks, with a capacious dining-hall for both, extensive warehouses for the trading goods and furs, a provision store, a trading shop, smith's forge, carpenter's workshop," noted Ross Cox. All was enclosed by a log stockade with two bastions in which the Astorians mounted six-pound cannon.

Although the Pacific Fur Company's outpost appeared substantial when David Thompson arrived at its doorstep in 1812, its tenure proved fragile. The *Tonquin* was blown up and sank on a trading voyage north along the coast. Supplies were infrequent. The men at Astoria were driven by starvation to establish Willamette Post in the lower Willamette Valley to relieve some of the pressure on stores at the river's mouth. The connections with China were infrequent. When the partners-in-the-field at Astoria learned of the outbreak of the War of 1812, they rightly feared a British naval vessel might enter the river and seize their post. Thus, in 1813, they sold out to the North West Company. The sale ended Astor's dreams for the Pacific Fur Company. His investment, however, proved highly consequential for the United States.

The Treaty of Ghent (1814) provided in the peace terms ending the war with Great Britain that all conditions would revert to "status ante bellum." The Americans subsequently interpreted this clause to mean that the American claim to the Oregon

Country—enhanced by the construction of the fort at Astoria—remained unextinguished. To buttress this prospect, the U.S. Navy dispatched Captain James Biddle on the U.S.S. *Ontario* to the Columbia River. In 1818, Biddle declared American possession of both shores of the estuary. John B. Prevost, an American special agent, arrived later that year and symbolically reasserted his nation's interest by raising The Stars and Stripes on the flagpole at Fort George, the post purchased and named by the North West Company for King George III of England.

During the 1810s, the competition between the North West Company and the Hudson's Bay Company, the older, larger rival for control of the fur trade, erupted into bloodshed in the Red River Valley in Canada. Determined to end the conflict and to bring stability to the frontier, the British parliament, in 1821, forcibly merged the companies. One firm survived—the Hudson's Bay Company, founded in 1670. This British corporation took over the interests of the North West Company in the Oregon Country. For the next 25 years, the Hudson's Bay Company helped shape the destiny of the region.

The Hudson's Bay Company had a single concern: profit. To satisfy investors interested in return on their money, the directors in London named George Simpson to superintend the field operations. Simpson, in turn, named Dr. John McLoughlin, a former North West Company employee, to serve as Chief Factor in the watershed of the Columbia River. The directions of Simpson and steady hand of McLoughlin proved highly significant in the history of Oregon. Collectively, they agreed on a simple, effective set of policies: peace with the tribes, fair prices for furs secured through trade and self-sufficiency for the posts in the region.

The Oregon Country was so distant that the company workers in the region had to provide for their own subsistence. Vessels could bring in tools and trade goods, but they could not provide food to sustain the nearly 600 men working for the company and their families. Simpson and McLoughlin thus developed the post system. Fort Vancouver, founded in 1822 near the confluence of the Willamette and Columbia rivers, was the hub. The spokes of connection reached to Fort George at the mouth of the Columbia, Fort Umpqua in southwestern Oregon, Fort Boise on the western Snake Plain in Idaho, and to Fort Nisqually, Fort Okanogan, and Fort Walla Walla in Washington. A series of more distant forts in British Columbia and southeast Alaska completed the system. Post traders were encouraged to plant vegetables, lay out orchards and raise livestock. These stations tested the region's agricultural potentials. They found considerable promise in their ventures.

Simpson and McLoughlin also instituted the brigade system. In addition to the posts where nearby tribes bartered furs for trade goods, the company outfitted brigades of 20 to 50 or more employees who, with their Indian wives and children, went into the field to trap and trade for months. Brigade leaders in Oregon included John Work, Michel LaFramboise, Alexander Roderick McLeod, and Peter Skene Ogden. The brigades penetrated the far reaches of the state. McLeod, for example, explored the Oregon coast south to the Rogue River in the 1820s. Work led brigades back and forth via the Willamette, Umpqua and Rogue Valleys to the Sacramento Valley of California. Ogden mounted five brigades to the upper Snake River. His mission, defined by Simpson, was to eradicate the fur-bearing animals of the region. The plan of ecological disruption mounted by the company was to create an area so devoid of furs that Americans crossing the Rockies would become discouraged and turn back. The Hudson's Bay Company largely succeeded in all these objectives.

Simpson and McLoughlin also launched other initiatives. They established a coastal maritime trade. The *Beaver,* a steam-powered sidewheeler, brought manufactured items to native villages along the shore north to Alaska. They opened retail stores in San Francisco and Honolulu and offered lumber cut at the company mill on the north bank of the Columbia as well as salted salmon from Pillar Rock and Cascades fisheries on the river. They established the Puget Sound Agricultural Company with farms at Nisqually and Cowlitz Landings.

The legacies of the Hudson's Bay Company were many. Its employees fished for salmon, felled the towering firs, manufactured lumber, grew bountiful gardens, raised cereal crops, tended horses on the plateau and cows on the meadows west of the Cascades, and trapped and traded for furs. The brigade leaders mapped much of the land; their diaries, closely held by the company, contained valuable geographical information. The company had great impact on the tribes. It spread manufactured goods, hastened cultural change and introduced new diseases. Most of the firm's employees—including natives from Hawaii and Polynesia—married native women creating a mixed-blood population. Their children had connections with both local and foreign worlds and often grew up bilingual. The company spread the Chinook Jargon far and wide. This trade vocabulary of nearly 1,000 words was founded on the Chinookan language of the Columbia River. It became the primary means of communication across tribal lines and with Euro-Americans throughout the region.

The success of the Hudson's Bay Company in the Pacific Northwest did not pass unnoticed. In the 1820s, Hall Jackson Kelley, an ardent, visionary schoolteacher in Massachusetts, began promoting American colonization of the region. Kelley printed circulars and pamphlets that raved about the region's potentials. He talked about the "spontaneous growth of the soil" and the "fruits of laborious industry," which would make Americans rich if they would settle in Oregon. Nathaniel Jarvis Wyeth, a wealthy Boston ice merchant, responded and, when Kelley's colony failed to develop, he formed the Pacific Trading Company, a joint-stock venture, to develop Oregon.

Wyeth's plans echoed those of John Jacob Astor. In 1832, he set out with uniformed associates to cross the continent and locate forts in the Oregon Country. His plan was to supply his land-based traders from western stations and ship furs and salmon to Asia. Desertions reduced his party to 11. John McLoughlin played the good host and extended the hospitality of Fort Vancouver to the American but did little to encourage his enterprise. In 1834, Wyeth returned to Oregon. He traveled with companions overland, driving wagons across the Great Plains and to South Pass, the subsequent route of the Oregon Trail. His party built Fort Hall on the upper Snake and erected Fort William on Sauvie Island at the mouth of the Willamette. Wyeth then set out to trap for furs in the Deschutes watershed. His diary documented his lonely, fruitless efforts to wrest a fortune from the fur-bearing animals of central Oregon. Wyeth's competitors were too powerful. The American Fur Company commanded the trade in the Rockies; the Hudson's Bay Company had a firm grip on the Pacific Northwest. Wyeth's supply ship arrived late and carried out a cargo of poorly preserved salmon. In 1836, he gave up. His business, which showed so much promise, had foundered on the realities of competition and demanding conditions in Oregon.

A fascinating legacy from the fur trade era was how its operators played host to wandering naturalists. David Douglas was singular among these. A Scotsman in the employ of the Royal Horticultural Society of London, Douglas came to Oregon in 1825–27 and 1830–32 to collect plants of potential uses in European landscapes as well as to obtain herbarium specimens to enlarge the understanding of botany. Douglas was ardent in his assignment. In 1826, he traveled alone into the South Umpqua watershed of southwestern Oregon in a quest for the sugar pine trees that produced the handsome seeds he had viewed at Fort Vancouver. His diaries documented his explorations; his name became popularly attached to *Pseudotsuga menziesii,* the famed Douglas Fir. In 1834, Thomas Nuttall, of Harvard University's Arnold Arboretum, and naturalist John Kirk Townsend accompanied Wyeth on his second overland journey. Townsend's *Narrative of Travels Beyond the Rocky Mountains* (1839) gave a positive account of the American West. The duplicates of his bird and mammal skins he sold to John James Audubon. These specimens added to scientific understanding and were rendered into lifelike images by the famed painter in his books on North American birds and the quadrupeds.

By the early 1840s, the fur trade was in decline. Changes in fashion had significantly reduced the interest in men's top hats made of hair stripped from beaver pelts. Extermination of fur-bearing animals in vast parts of the American West was another factor. Furs were neither abundant nor cheap. The days of the fur trade were ending, but the legacy of the enterprise was large. The fur trade had opened primary routes of travel, altered tribal lifeways, filled in geographical information and produced an important literature about Oregon. The Astorians—Ross Cox, Alexander Ross, Gabriel Franchere, Robert Stuart and Peter Corney—all produced books in the 19th century describing Oregon. More significant, however, were the companion volumes penned by Washington Irving. His works, *Astoria or Anecdotes of an Enterprise Beyond the Rocky Mountains* (1836) and *Adventures of Captain Bonneville* (1837), were read by an eager public. Irving described the temperate climate and abundant resources of Oregon, portraying the land as a place of adventure and possible prosperity.

Federal Interests

The government of the United States maintained special interests in Oregon. It founded its claims on the "doctrine of the right of discovery." Although Robert Gray was a mariner for a private fur-trading company, he sailed under a sea letter issued by President George Washington. His crossing of the bar of the Columbia initiated the U.S. claim to having "discovered" Oregon. The Lewis and Clark Expedition was a military expedition financed and directed by the government. Fort Clatsop, though occupied less than five months in 1805–06, was deemed an American outpost. So, too, the Pacific Fur Company's Fort Astoria was an American venture, and the United States through the actions of Captain Biddle and John Prevost asserted national interests in 1818, pursuant to the terms of the Treaty of Ghent.

In 1818, the United States and Great Britain met in diplomatic conference to try to resolve their interests in the Oregon Country. The negotiators, at loggerheads over the extension of the 49th parallel to the Pacific, reached a compromise. In the Convention of 1818, they agreed to shared spheres of interest in the Columbia watershed, deferring the question of sovereignty for the time being.

The Americans were not idle. In the 1819 Adams-Onis Treaty, whereby Spain ceded Florida to the United States, American negotiators secured all of the Spanish "discovery rights" north of the 42nd parallel—the northern boundary of California. In 1824, the United States negotiated an agreement permitting trade for ten years in Alaska and fixing Russia's southern boundary at 50° 40'. Slowly, steadily, the United States had narrowed the field among the nations vying for control of the Oregon Country. Great Britain, the United States and the indigenous people remained as competitors. In 1827, the two countries agreed to extend indefinitely their earlier agreement that each had a sphere of interest in the region. The new condition added to the convention was that either nation might give notice and demand a resolution of the issue within one year.

American "discovery rights" gained Supreme Court sanction when, in 1823, Chief Justice John Marshall ruled in a matter involving former tribal lands. Marshall opined in *Johnson v. McIntosh* that because natives were wanderers over the face of the earth, their rights were impaired and subordinate to the "discovery rights" of Europeans. While tribes retained an occupancy right, title was not vested in them. The Marshall ruling became a convenient justification to dispossess hundreds of tribes of their homelands.

President Andrew Jackson, an expansionist with interests in the West, attempted in 1835 to purchase the harbor of San Francisco for $500,000 from Mexico. The following year he dispatched the brig *Loriot* to the West Coast. Lieutenant William A. Slacum carried a presidential commission to examine Puget Sound, the Columbia estuary, and San Francisco Bay, assess those anchorages for strategic value, and examine the frontier economy of the region. Slacum's report, printed in the *United States Congressional Serial Set,* made a strong case for American acquisition of all three harbors.

Jackson next endorsed, and Congress funded, the multifaceted U.S. Exploring Expedition. Under the command of Lieutenant Charles Wilkes, this Navy party included five vessels, more than 300 seamen, and a corps of talented scientists, artists and officers. After exploring the coasts of South America, Australia and Hawaii, the expedition, in 1841, sailed to Puget Sound and the Columbia River. Overland parties traveled south via the Cowlitz to Fort Vancouver, east through the Gorge to Fort Walla Walla, and south through the Willamette Valley to Sutter's Fort on the Sacramento River. James Dwight Dana collected fossils at Saddle Mountain at the mouth of the Columbia; Titian Ramsay Peale sketched the Umpqua Mountains; Horatio Hale compiled tribal vocabularies; and Charles Wilkes penned a fact-filled description of western Oregon.

In 1845, the narrative and scientific reports of the Wilkes Expedition, as it was popularly called, began to appear. Volumes four and five contained candid information about Oregon. Wilkes described the Willamette Valley and its "advantages for raising crops, pasturage of stock, and the facilities of settlers becoming rich." He wrote: "The salmon-fishery may be classed as one of the great sources of wealth, for it affords a large amount of food at a very low price, and of the very best quality. . . ." The sixth volume of reports, an atlas, included numerous charts of Puget Sound and the Columbia River useful for mariners. Over the next dozen years, specialists wrote scientific assessments of the flora and fauna collected by the expedition and published 14 oversized folios of hand-colored illustrations of the specimens. The knowledge about Oregon had increased dramatically and was based on sound authority.

While the Wilkes party was on the high seas headed to the Pacific Northwest, Robert Greenhow, librarian to the Department of State, compiled his *Memoir, Historical and Political, on the Northwest Coast of North America* (1840). Senator Lewis Linn of Missouri had the report printed for the Select Committee on Oregon Territory and requested the immediate publication of an additional 2,500 copies for the Senate to distribute. Greenhow presented a history of exploration, covered the diplomacy of sovereignty issues, discussed the fur trade and argued that Oregon was a region "lying entirely within the undisputed limits of the Republic." Therein he revealed his agenda. Greenhow's memoir was a brief to make the case for American sovereignty over the Pacific Northwest.

Thomas Hart Benton, senator from Missouri and, for more than 20 years, a champion of American expansion, in 1842, secured congressional funding for his son-in-law, John Charles Fremont, to explore west to South Pass. The following year, Fremont, a member of the U.S. Topographical Engineers, set out again, guided by Kit Carson, to follow overland emigrants across the Oregon Trail. Fremont kept a diary and collected minerals, plants and zoological specimens. Charles Preuss, his cartographer, prepared eight detailed strip maps showing the route of the trail to Fort Walla Walla. In the map margins were notations on fords, grazing sites, camping locations, and the availability of firewood. Fremont's wife, Jessie, turned her husband's diaries into flowing prose. Published by the Government Printing Office in large numbers, the Fremont narratives and Preuss maps became a major publicity piece for Oregon and a virtual travelers' guide to the trail.

In early 1846, Lieutenant Neil M. Howison sailed to Oregon on the *Shark* to carry out another reconnaissance. Delayed by the wreck of the ship on the Columbia bar, Howison sojourned for five months and examined the land, interviewed residents, visited tribal villages and reflected on what he saw. He noted that the influence of Dr. John McLoughlin had "done more than any other man toward the rapid development of the resources of the country." Howison described wolves, grizzly bears, elk and the thriving condition of cattle and sheep. "I can think of nothing vegetable in nature," he commented, "that Oregon will not produce." His report was ultimately issued in the *United States Con-*

gressional Serial Set in 1848. It was another candid assessment of Oregon by an objective observer.

During the period 1792 to 1846, the U.S. government thus aided and abetted American interest in Oregon. The nation's leaders, both public and private, took actions to help buttress claims to Oregon through discovery, diplomacy, exercise of will, and the persuasive historical research of Robert Greenhow. The explorations of Lewis and Clark, Slacum, the Wilkes expedition, John Fremont and Neil M. Howison generated maps, reports and collections of specimens. These were analyzed and published. The evidence was growing about the prospects of the Pacific Northwest and Oregon, in particular.

Souls to Save

The first three decades of the 19th century were a time of intense religious fervor in America. The Second Great Awakening, kindled by the exhortations of Rev. Timothy Dwight, swept across the land. Camp meetings, revivals, sectarian controversies, the founding of home and foreign mission societies, building of seminaries to educate the ministry, and publication of books, tracts, hymns, and translations of the scriptures into native languages were all part of the religious commitment. Shakers gathered in celibate communities. Mormon converts followed the teachings of Joseph Smith, Jr. Revivals sweeping over the country produced conversions and, in some, anticipation of the return of Christ to Earth.

In 1832, the *Christian Advocate and Journal* carried a feature story about four Indians from the interior of the Pacific Northwest who had arrived in St. Louis. Although they may have come to confer with William Clark, the explorer and then superintendent of tribal affairs in the Louisiana Territory, the press interpreted their visit as a cry from heathens seeking the white man's book of God. This news proved electrifying to a population eager to promote evangelical Christianity. With the alleged request from the "savages of Oregon" for the word of God, mission societies were ready to send workers to the field to reap souls.

Rev. Jason Lee was first to respond. In 1833, the Methodist Episcopal Church authorized Lee, his nephew, Daniel Lee, and three lay assistants to go to Oregon. With mission board underwriting and a determination to preach to the tribes people, this party embraced its calling and joined Nathaniel Wyeth in 1834 on his second overland trek to the Columbia estuary. Thus Nuttall and Townsend, with interests in natural history; Wyeth, who hoped to compete with the Hudson's Bay Company; and a cadre of missionaries joined forces to traverse the continent.

Although the initial request for missionaries had presumably come from the Nez Perces or Flatheads in the interior, Lee conferred with McLoughlin on a likely location for a mission west of the Cascades. He selected Mission Bottom on the southwest side of French Prairie in the northern Willamette Valley. Proximity to Fort Vancouver, the proven agricultural potential of the area, the nearby population of retired fur trappers, and the isolation of any site east of the mountains weighed heavily in Lee's decision.

The Methodists tried hard. They built a station, fenced and tilled fields, opened a school, and ministered to the Kalapuyans, whose villages had been ravaged by a horrendous fever starting in 1829. By the mid-1830s, as many as 70 percent had perished. Lee and his associates thus coped with orphans, solitary survivors of families or entire villages and the aged. To cope with the challenges, Lee ambitiously planned to increase his crew of workers. He sent back positive reports, and in 1838, returned to the East to seek money and recruits. He raised an estimated $100,000 and brought 32 adults and 18 of their children to Oregon in 1839. The expanded staff opened a mission on the Clatsop Plains, another among the Clackamas people at Oregon City, a third at The Dalles, and yet another at the southern end of Puget Sound. In spite of their efforts, the Methodist laborers were not good linguists nor effective missionaries. The converts were few. Dr. Elijah White, a recruit, fired off criticisms to the mission board, which suspended Lee and closed the operations in 1843.

The Methodists, though converting few Indians, had tested the potentials of Oregon and succeeded in raising cereal crops, vegetables and livestock. Their families prospered. They staked out land claims, including one which encroached on Dr. McLoughlin's milling site at Willamette Falls. Writing home about what they found, they gave good reports of Oregon. These Americans helped set the stage for overland emigration.

In the 1820s, the American Board of Commissioners for Foreign Missions (ABCFM) had sent workers among the Cherokee, Creek, Choctaw and other tribes. An ecumenical project drawing on the resources of the Congregational, Presbyterian, and Dutch Reformed denominations, the ABCFM also responded to the alleged request of Oregon Indians for missionaries. In 1835, Rev. Samuel Parker and Rev. Marcus Whitman traveled west to survey prospects. Although Whitman turned back at Green River in the Rocky Mountains, Parker continued to Oregon, explored widely and, after returning home by sea via Hawaii, published *Journal of an Exploring Tour Beyond the Rocky Mountains* (1838). Whitman had seen enough to persuade him to devote his energies to the natives of the Pacific Northwest.

In 1836, Whitman, his new wife Narcissa, Rev. Henry H. Spalding and his wife Eliza, set out for Oregon. Both women kept diaries, leaving a fascinating chronicle of the journey of the first white women across the continent. Jane Barnes, a barmaid from Portsmouth, England, had lived for a few months at Astoria during the tenure of the North West Company, but she had traveled by sea. The transit of two missionary women overland was duly noted by residents of the American frontier interested in lands in Oregon.

After visiting Fort Vancouver and obtaining supplies from the Hudson's Bay Company, the Whitmans settled at Waiilatpu, "the place of the rye grass," on the margins of the Walla Walla River near the base of the Blue Mountains. Their mission was to the Cayuse, Umatilla, and Nez Perce people. The Spaldings selected a site at Lapwai, Idaho on the lower Clearwater River in Nez Perce country. For the next 11 years these missionaries and their associates who founded other stations on the Columbia Plateau wrestled with survival, mastering native languages and trying to convert the tribal people. An issue facing all was whether or not it was essential to transform Indians into sedentary farmers dressed like white people as a precondition to conversion to Christianity. The Indians found little attraction in the hard labor of farming, were reluctant to give up their traditional fisheries and hunting, and seemed generally disinterested in the whites' teachings. When Whitman whipped them for disobedience, he fell in their esteem. Conversions were few; troubles accumulated.

In 1838, Fathers Francois N. Blanchet and Modest Demers set out with a Hudson's Bay Company brigade from Red River. They crossed overland through Canada and descended the Columbia to found Catholic missions in the region. The Anglican ministry of Rev. Herbert Beaver at Fort Vancouver in 1836–38 was short-lived and controversial. The fur trappers, many of them nominally Catholic or possessing Catholic ancestors, were receptive to Blanchet and Demers, who moved swiftly, marrying couples, baptizing Indian wives and children, and recording an impressive tally in their sacramental ledgers. They established missions at Fort Vancouver, Cowlitz Prairie, and French Prairie.

Where the protestants had only marginal success in gaining converts, the Catholics prospered. There were several reasons. They did not insist on a change in lifeways as a condition for baptism. They wore vestments, burned incense, rang handbells, recited a ritualistic mass and generated a sense of mystery and interest in their services. They were single men governed by vows of chastity and steadfast purpose of ministry to their flock. They were bound by a commitment to poverty and not engaged in staking land claims or contesting McLoughlin for a mill site. They had a distant but consistent base of support through the Catholic Church. They had already established connections to the native peoples because women from almost every tribe or band in the Pacific Northwest had married Catholic men. They were skilled linguists and were willing to undergo years of patient work to master the native languages.

In 1834 and 1835, a group of retired fur trappers, most of them French-Canadians living on French Prairie, had petitioned the Bishop of Red River in Canada for a priest. In 1836, they had built a log chapel. Blanchet and Demers thus found a receptive audience when they established the St. Paul Mission in October, 1839. The parishioners erected a meeting hall and lodgings for the priests in 1841. The grandly named St. Joseph's College, a school funded in part by a bequest from a French philanthropist, opened in 1843 with 30 boys and three instructors. Nuns arrived in 1844 to establish Saint Marie de Willamette, a girls' school. Parishioners between 1844 and 1846 kilned bricks and erected the St. Paul Church.

Missions further accelerated changes in the lives of Oregon tribes. Many tribes, particularly in western Oregon, were imprinted by the itinerant priests and carried for generations a commitment to Catholicism. This was especially the case among the Kalapuyans and Upper Chinookans. Adrian Croquet, a Belgian priest, ministered to them on the Grand Ronde Reservation from 1860 to 1898. Catholic Oblate missions of St. Ann, St. Rose of the Cayouse, Walla Walla, St. Anthony, and Frenchtown likewise led to conversions among the Confederated Tribes of the Umatilla.

The protestants largely failed in their missionary efforts but left an impact in other ways. They proved that Euro-American families could thrive in the Oregon Country. They grew vegetables and fruit and raised livestock. They wrote reports and lectured in the East about the prospects of the region. They spoke of its mild climate, fertile soil, towering forests, abundant fish and wild game. They helped set the stage for the opening of the Oregon Trail.

Overland to Oregon

Some said there was a contagion in the land and called it the "Oregon Fever." It caused dreams, persuaded men and women to give up all that was familiar, risk their lives and fortunes, and set out for the far shores of the Pacific. The overland emigrations of the mid-nineteenth century were one of the epochal events of human history. Seldom had so many people traveled so far by land to seek a new beginning.

The motives for moving to Oregon were clear. Tens of thousands of Americans residing along the frontier from Minnesota to Texas were land speculators. Many had moved before, to buy a new farm, erect a home and barn, clear and fence fields and sell their "improvements." They were poised to do so again, particularly when senators Lewis Linn and Thomas Hart Benton of Missouri repeatedly introduced bills in Congress calling for grants of up to 1,000 free acres for those who would settle in

Oregon. Land speculation ran in their veins. Even when the bills did not pass, thousands were ready to take the risk and hope, in time, Congress would reward their labors.

Oregon had a good press founded on careful observations and scientific authority. The reports of Lewis and Clark, the Astorians, the narratives of John B. Wyeth (1833), Samuel Parker (1838), William Slacum (1838), John Kirk Townsend (1839), Lieutenant John C. Fremont (1845), Lieutenant Charles Wilkes (1846), and Lieutenant Neil Howison (1848) described a rich land with attractive potentials. Letters from missionaries to newspapers and magazines, sermons and lectures delivered during fund-raising in the East, summary reports such as that by Robert Greenhow (1840)—all laid before the public the region's prospects. The pull factors attracting emigration to Oregon were land, timber, salmon, a climate favorable for agriculture, sites for water power and a peaceful environment. Relations with natives had remained positive and stable throughout the fur-trade era.

On the other end, several push factors motivated frontier residents to consider relocating. The late 1830s and early 1840s were a period of calamitous flooding along the Missouri, Mississippi, and Ohio Rivers. Many who had foolishly built on the floodplains watched their cabins, barns, and split-rail fences wash away in freshets and waited anxiously for weeks as floodwaters drowned their fields and ruined their crops. The Panic of 1837 plunged the country toward depression. Bank failures, currency problems, poor credit, and the inability to pay off loans beset millions. Many hungered for a chance to walk away from their losses and heartaches for a new beginning. Recurrent fevers, particularly malaria, beset many who lived on the frontier. Oregon had a good reputation for health; though thousands of indigenous people perished in the 1830s, most Euro-Americans remained well.

So the stage was set: Oregon's allure was strong, and the pressure to move out pushed many. A small emigration of about 100 people in 1842 followed Dr. Elijah White westward. The following spring, nearly a thousand emigrants gathered along the Missouri frontier to wait until the prairies were dry enough to permit travel. They had loaded their wagons with dried fruit and vegetables, flour, bran, cornmeal, beans, bacon, ham and kegs of vinegar. They brought weapons, clothing, tools, blankets and quilts and a few treasured possessions. Most carried light tinware for eating, a reflector oven for baking biscuits, a spider for holding the coffee pot and a frying pan. Musicians put in a violin, accordion or Jew's harp. All else they sold or gave away to family and friends. Those who brought too much were compelled to abandon their possessions along the trail.

No one had ever seen anything like it before. The waves of emigrants grew. More than 3,000 traveled overland to Oregon in 1845; by 1850, an estimated 9,000 had crossed the trail to the Pacific Northwest. They knew their journey was a rite of passage. For the first time in their lives, and for many the only time, they penned daily entries in diaries. Their trip was epochal. They were part of history and wanted to record their participation in it.

The overland journey exacted many tolls. For some it was death on the trail. In many respects, the Oregon Trail became one continuous, linear cemetery. Along its course lay the remains of men, women, and children who died of cholera, measles, dysentery, drownings and accidents. Guns misfired; wagons overturned; cattle bolted; clothing caught on fire—the calamities that befell those on a four- to six-month camping trip were many. In spite of the hardships of 1,950 miles of trail between St. Joseph, Missouri, and Oregon City, Oregon, the trip was a great adventure. Vast herds of buffalo, visits by tribal people wanting to trade, the distant Wind River Mountains, basalt flows and canyons along the Snake, and the succession of sunrises and sunsets were all part of the experience. Boys found swimming holes. Women and girls did their best to create a semblance of home by cooking creatively and maintaining norms of domesticity. The men went hunting and fishing, bartered with one another for horses and gear, and carved or marked their names in axle grease on prominent rocks near the trail.

The overland journey was often the migration of an extended family. Parents, children, and grandparents made up the parties. Sometimes several brothers, their families, their sisters and their families, and young hired hands from the neighborhood constituted the group. If one family migrated in 1846, three related families might migrate in 1847 to join them in Oregon. The Applegate family, immigrants of 1843 to Polk County and settlers by 1848 of the Umpqua Valley, were illustrative. Three brothers, their wives, and 39 children constituted this clan. The families took adjoining land claims near Yoncalla. The connections of kinship and friendship were part of the social fabric that knit frontier Oregon in the mid-nineteenth century.

The primary Oregon Trail ran from Fort Hall to Fort Boise in Idaho, then via Burnt River to the Grande Ronde Valley. It crossed the Blue Mountains and the Columbia Plateau, running up to 20 miles south of the river almost to The Dalles. Travelers then made a perilous trip by canoe, bateau, or log raft through the Columbia Gorge to western Oregon. By 1846, they had another option, transit of the Barlow Road, a rugged, rock-filled trace through the forests across the Cascade Mountains to Oregon City.

In 1845, Stephen H. L. Meek led nearly a thousand emigrants with their 200 wagons and livestock east from the Snake River onto Oregon's high desert. The shortcut he proposed over the Cascades proved a terrible trail. Eventually, the wagon train had to work its way through the Deschutes River watershed to regain the old trail at The Dalles. That same year Samuel Barlow, Joel Palmer, William Rector and others blazed a trace around the southern slopes of Mount Hood. They were compelled to abandon their wagons in the mountains, but the following year workmen opened the Barlow Road, a final overland segment of the Oregon Trail. Thousands traveled its course and paid the toll until 1919, when it passed to the State of Oregon. In 1846, explorers from the Willamette Valley opened the Applegate Trail. This route cut southwest from Fort Hall, crossed the deserts of northern Nevada, passed through the Klamath Basin and Rogue River Valley, and then entered the Willamette Valley from the south. Many who settled in southwestern Oregon in the 1850s and 1860s were emigrants on the Applegate Trail.

The Oregon Trail pioneers were creatures of habit. They carried their attitudes, prejudices and ideas as part of their baggage. They were imitators rather than innovators. They attempted, as best they could remember, to recreate the governmental and social institutions they had left behind. They founded schools and academies and erected Federal, Greek Revival and Gothic Revival buildings to house them—just like at home. Although they saw themselves as stalwart, brave and independent, they were actually a highly dependent people, demanding righteously that the federal government give them land, survey their claims, guard them from Indians, erect lighthouses, establish postal routes and construct wagon roads. They saw themselves as makers of history but seldom perceived they were locked into the historical fabric of which they were merely threads.

The "Oregon Question" and Provisional Government

Oregon was a prize lusted for by two partisans. In 1845, President James K. Polk informed Great Britain he wanted resolution of the issue of sovereignty in the Pacific Northwest. In the agreement reached in 1828, the nations had one year in which to resolve the long-simmering "Oregon Question." Polk was an avowed expansionist. A Democrat, he sought the presidency in 1844 on a simple platform: the annexation of Texas and the occupation of Oregon. The Tyler administration took care of acquiring Texas before Polk was sworn into office, but he persisted in an aggressive agenda of American expansion. Polk campaigned under the popular slogan "54-40 or fight," a contention that the southern boundary of Russian America was the northern boundary of Oregon. He pressed through diplomatic channels and used his inaugural address to assert American rights to all of Oregon. His ambitions far exceeded the area of American activity.

Resolution came on June 15, 1846, in the Oregon Treaty. Polk was already in pursuit of a greater prize—California—and had helped engineer a declaration of war against Mexico by massing troops along the Texas border until they were attacked by Mexican soldiers. Oregon became a sidebar in the unfolding story of the Mexican War. While Congress was willing to plunge the country into a war against its neighbor to the south, it was opposed to entering a conflict with Great Britain. That nation, beset with internal disputes over Corn Law reform, was likewise eager to reach a settlement. Thus, in 1846, the two countries agreed to extend the boundary on the 49th parallel westward from the crest of the Rockies to the primary channel between Vancouver Island and the continent. British citizens and the Hudson's Bay Company retained trading and navigational rights in the Columbia River, though the United States subsequently terminated those privileges in 1859.

By 1846, the arguments of the United States to claim the Oregon Country were founded on more than "discovery rights." Several thousand Americans had settled in the region. Every year, the arrival of new emigrants tipped the scale against the Hudson's Bay Company. The Americans had also established a Provisional Government. Its genesis came with the death in 1841 of Ewing Young. A former mountain man who had built up cattle herds in the Chehalem Valley and owned more than $3,000 in promissory notes from his neighbors, Young died without heirs. Residents gathered after his funeral to discuss what to do with his property. They agreed to name a committee to draft a civil code. Father Blanchet served as chair. When they assembled four months later, Blanchet reported his committee had not met. Disagreements between French-Canadians and Americans about the form of self-government and its powers had created an impasse.

The arrival of overland emigrants in 1842, and the increase of retired fur trappers who settled in the Willamette Valley with their mixed-blood families complicated matters. Old settlers and new arrivals worried about their land claims. They wondered what might happen if Congress passed Linn's bills granting lands to Americans who settled in Oregon. Wild animals brought to a head the decisions for a government. Grizzlies, black bears, cougars, and wolves ranged freely in the Willamette Valley. Their destruction of livestock gave cause in the spring of 1843 for a "Wolf Meeting." A second Wolf Meeting led to the decision to create a system of government. On May 2, 1843, at Champoeg, Joseph Meek posed the critical question: "Who's for a divide? All for the report of the committee and organization follow me," he shouted. By a close vote, perhaps 52 to 50, those wanting the government prevailed.

What was the significance of the Provisional Government? In spite of claims that the vote in the spring of 1843 on French Prairie sealed the fate of American sovereignty to the Oregon Country, there is no evidence that the Polk administration weighed the action. What was important and known to the decision-makers across the continent was that an American colony had developed on the shores of the far Pacific Ocean. The Provisional Government informed the Polk administration of its existence. It passed memorials in 1843 and 1845 seeking congressional attention to the needs of Americans in Oregon. The memorial of June 28, 1845, petitioned for naval yards, mail service, land grants, military protection and territorial status. On December 8, 1845, Thomas Hart Benton presented the document to the Senate. These endorsements and his election were all the expansionist President Polk needed in an era when many felt it was America's manifest destiny to spread from sea to sea. Whitman's ride across the continent in 1838 and the events at Champoeg—the lore of Oregon history—did not tip the scales. The United States had embarked on a grand scheme of territorial growth. Oregon was only part of the plan.

The Oregon Provisional Government played an important role in creating order on a frontier. For more than two decades, the Hudson's Bay Company held and exercised civil authority and control of the fur trade, while maintaining peace in dealing with tribes. Its power did not extend to American settlers and ended in 1846 with the Oregon Treaty. The Provisional Government filled the void. It provided for laws governing land claims, instituted taxation, formed counties, created the offices of governor and legislators, and set up a court system. Popularly elected representatives hammered out these decisions between 1843 and 1845. The proposals were often revised, for newly arrived emigrants increased the electorate and brought their experience and men with political ambitions. The Provisional Government was in constant flux, but George Abernethy, a former lay worker for the Methodist Mission, continued as governor.

J. Henry Brown collected the correspondence and decisions made in Oregon City and published them as *Brown's Political History of Oregon* (1892). He dedicated his documentary volume to the "intrepid men and women" who helped lay the foundation of the Pacific states and "builded better than they knew." The legislature patterned many of its laws on those of the Iowa Territory, including weights and measures, criminal codes, and vagrancy. In 1843, the legislature put bounties on wolves, panthers, bears, and lynxes. Cash payments for the skin of the head with ears of these animals soon decimated their population and led to the extinction of several species in Oregon. The Law of Land Claims permitted individuals to file on as much as a square mile, but only one claim at a time, and restricted filings on key town sites or water-power locations.

The Provisional Legislature banned permanent residency of free African-Americans and mulattoes. Any reaching age 18 had two years to leave the Oregon Country, as did anyone held in slavery. The initial penalty for failure to leave was not less than 20 nor more than 39 lashes. In 1844, the legislature amended the law to put violators out to low bid for public labor and removal. The law, though never enforced, confirmed the racial prejudice of the frontier generation moving into the Willamette Valley.

Cayuse Indian War

Cold winds swept across the Columbia Plateau. In November, 1847, they heralded the onset of the winter of discontent. Too long had the Cayuse tribe suffered from new diseases and the failed ministrations of Dr. Marcus Whitman. In their culture, a shaman or curer who failed was subject to death. This doctor, a strapping, determined white man had come into their lands uninvited. The mission he and his wife established worked like a magnet to draw emigrants. Each year, the wagon trains descended the Blue Mountains and, like the grasshoppers that swept across the countryside, they heralded discomforting changes. Smallpox, measles, fevers, death and mourning came in their wake.

On November 29, 1847, a band of Cayuse men, fed by fear and resentment, fell upon the missionary station. In a matter of hours, they murdered Marcus and Narcissa Whitman and a dozen others. Two more died subsequently of exposure and 47, many orphaned children of emigrants, were taken captive. The Spaldings fled Lapwai and skirted the Cayuse homeland in their dash to safety. Panic swept through the Willamette settlements. Initially, the settlers thought the tribes of the Columbia Plateau might drive through the Gorge and attempt to murder them, too.

The Provisional Legislature faced its greatest test. While Peter Skene Ogden of the Hudson's Bay Company was rushing east with 16 men to try to ransom the hostages, Governor Abernethy called for "immediate and prompt action." The legislature authorized raising companies of volunteers to go to war against the Cayuse Tribe. It entrusted command to Colonel Cornelius Gilliam and named a committee to negotiate with the Hudson's Bay Company for loans of arms, ammunition, and supplies to mount the campaign. The government wrestled with two approaches: one, to send peace commissioners to try to persuade the Cayuse to turn over the perpetrators; or, two, to wage a war of retribution. In short order, it did both. Governor Abernethy appointed a peace commission—Joel Palmer, Henry A. G. Lee, and Robert Newell. Gilliam, who did not approve of the commission, set out in January, 1848 with more than 500 volunteers.

History

The Cayuse War became, at times, a war of nerves. The peace commissioners tried to end hostilities and get the Cayuse to turn over the killers of those at the Whitman station. Gilliam and his forces, eager for action, provoked conflicts with both friendly and hostile Cayuse. In March, having persuaded the Cayuse to surrender five men, the military brought them to Oregon City. They were charged, tried, and hanged in 1850. The guilt of the five men and the jurisdiction of the court were not fully established. Controversy swirled for decades after this trial—the first culminating in capital punishment following legal proceedings in the Oregon Territory.

Territorial Government

The Oregon Country lay in limbo following the 1846 treaty with Great Britain. Congress had not acted and was diverted by both the Mexican War and the slavery question. The tragedy at the Whitman Mission demanded action. In December, 1847, the Provisional Legislature drafted another memorial to lay again before Congress its "situation and wants." The petition discussed the deaths at Waiilatpu, lack of revenue laws and uneasiness about land claims. Should Congress act, the memorial pointed out that "the present citizens of this country have strong claims upon the patronage of the General Government" for any appointments. Joseph Meek with nine compatriots carried the petition east in the early spring of 1848.

Much was at stake. If Congress created the Oregon Territory, the region would fall under the mantle of federal authority and funding. The residents of the region might expect, at last, action on the free land proposals and a host of benefits from the creation of a vital infrastructure to enhance security, improve commerce, and ease communication problems. On August 14, 1848, President Polk signed the Organic Act creating the Oregon Territory. Uncle Sam could now begin his labors in the Pacific Northwest in earnest.

Joseph Lane, a Mexican War hero and resident of Indiana, was appointed governor. He set out overland for Oregon City, where he was inaugurated on March 3, 1849, proclaiming the sprawling region under the administration of the United States. The event was of singular consequence. Territorial status brought not only a governor but also three judges, an attorney, and a marshal—all federal appointees. Oregonians who were male, 21 years or older, and citizens of the United States had the franchise and could elect a territorial legislature. Its laws, however, were subject to veto by Congress, and the legislature had limited power to incur debt. The residents could elect a delegate to speak for their interests before Congress. Samuel R. Thurston, the first named, lacked the power to vote, but he could advocate territorial interests.

The Organic Act extended the Northwest Ordinance of 1787 to the region. This legislation of the Continental Congress articulated the philosophy for development of new territories in the Ohio and upper Mississippi Valleys. It prohibited slavery, provided land grants for support of public schools, and affirmed "utmost good faith" in dealing with tribes. The ordinance and its inclusion in the Organic Act thus recognized aboriginal land title throughout the region. It voided the land laws of the Provisional Government, except for the claims to 640 acres of the various missions to the tribes. Oregon's act granted two square miles of land per township to fund schools.

Land remained foremost in the minds of the Oregonians. Thurston knew the anxiety and jockeying for claims. Thousands had risked their lives and futures on the prospect of getting free farms in Oregon. On September 29, 1850, Congress passed what became known as the Oregon Donation Land Act, establishing the system of land survey prior to deeding properties. By 1851, John P. Preston, surveyor-general, and his crews had established the Willamette Meridian running north and south between Canada and California and begun survey of the east and west Baseline. The coordinates met at Willamette Stone Park in the west hills above Portland. The system left an indelible imprint. From the beginning of time, nature, had etched the land in gentle contours. Henceforth straight lines, section corners and a massive grid system—followed by roads, timber harvests and fields—imprinted the landscape. The beauty of the system was that it was regular. It gave every parcel of land a unique address based on its distance from the primary coordinates.

Congress also established the General Land Office, the first of which opened in Oregon City and was followed, in time, by branches in The Dalles, La Grande, and Roseburg. Seekers of Donation Lands—ultimately 7,437 successful claimants in Oregon—could register their claims and await the surveys of the townships and their particular claims. Once the surveys were completed, they could obtain title, subdivide and sell. Speculation was built into the fabric of the act, particularly because it permitted both men and women to acquire up to 320 acres—a square mile for married couples. This was far more land than any farmer might till or manage.

Territorial status brought highly significant investments in Oregon. The U.S. Coast Survey dispatched William Pope McArthur and the vessel *Ewing* to begin charting the coastline. Over the next several years, the Coast Survey examined the shoreline and the estuaries. It produced charts with depth readings, noted dangerous rocks, and gave form to the shore. Its reports included handsome engravings of coastal headlands as mariners saw them from sea.

Dr. Elijah White had served since 1843 as Indian agent in Oregon. His appointment was strange in that he worked on federal salary when American sovereignty was not established. In 1849, Joseph Lane began duties both as governor and ex-officio superintendent of Indian affairs. He was succeeded by Anson Dart of Wisconsin and next by Joel Palmer, negotiator of several of the region's ratified treaties. The superintendents named Indian agents to serve at The Dalles, Clatsop Plains, Willamette Valley, Umpqua Valley, Rogue River Valley and Port Orford.

Important federal services that came with territorial status included opening of postal routes and offices, federal courts and customs houses. John Shively, an 1843 emigrant, was appointed as Oregon's first postmaster in 1847 in Astoria. Postal routes created vital communication links along a frontier. Congress established customs districts with agents at Port Orford, Umpqua River and Astoria. In later years, it opened offices for the Yaquina District and Portland. Federal officials were charged with collecting duties and recording statistical information on the ebb and flow of commerce. Their reports showed the rise of agriculture and industry, particularly the impact of the markets produced by the California Gold Rush for Oregon crops and lumber. Court officials had charge of dispute resolution. With three districts, they had a wide geographical reach and traveled a circuit to adjudicate complaints.

Using executive authority, U.S. presidents in the 1850s began withdrawing land from public entry to set aside sites for federal projects, including reservations for lighthouses, forts, and tribes. Several instances of the withdrawals proved unwise. In the case of lighthouses, some sites were too high above the sea or too remote from supplies to permit economical construction of stations. Most forts, though constructed, were of limited utility and were soon abandoned. The Coast (or Siletz) Reservation and the Grand Ronde Reservation, however, were two instances where presidential withdrawals helped shape both indigenous history and settlement patterns. The large Siletz Reservation was dismembered in 1865 and 1875 and again after 1892. The tribal tenure, though diminishing, slowed pioneer settlement along much of the central coast.

Territorial status meant the arrival of the U.S. Army. Congress appropriated $76,500 in 1846 to establish garrisons along the Oregon Trail, but the project was diverted by the Mexican War. In 1849, the Mounted Riflemen finally headed west under the command of Major Osborne Cross. Their assignment was to build and staff forts to preclude further difficulties with the tribes. When the Riflemen's heavy wagons bogged down on the southern slopes of Mount Hood, the soldiers dug pits and cached many of their supplies at a place later known as Government Camp. They then pushed on to occupy temporary quarters at Oregon City and Astoria. During the 1850s, the U.S. Army established Fort Orford (1851), Fort Dalles (1852), Fort Lane (1853), Fort Cascades (1855) on the north bank of the Columbia in the Gorge, Fort Umpqua, Fort Yamhill and Fort Hoskins (all 1856). Construction created jobs for carpenters, brick masons and laundresses. Soldiers brought payrolls flowing into the local economy as well as a sense of security from the tribes.

The Army provided another important service. Its engineers were authorized by Congress to survey and construct the Scottsburg-Myrtle Creek and Myrtle Creek-Camp Stuart military wagon roads. These routes connected in 1853–55 to carry freight and travelers from the head of tidewater on the Umpqua River to the mining districts in the Rogue River Valley and northern California. The Army also dispatched Lieutenant George Derby to survey a road over the Coast Range between Astoria and Salem. Although opened by axemen, the route drew only limited use. Derby, in 1855, surveyed and supervised construction of the Fort Vancouver-Fort Cascades Military Portage Road into the Columbia Gorge. Uncle Sam's engineers, soldiers and laborers helped create primary travel corridors to remote parts of the territory. As college graduates, the military officers also recorded weather data, collected fossils, pickled zoological specimens, wrote down tribal word lists and sent interesting materials and communications to the Smithsonian Institution. These labors contributed to further understanding about the region.

While the federal government annually considered projects in the Oregon Territory, the legislature wrestled with local issues. These included frustration with the repeated appointment of nonresidents of the region to key positions; political fighting among Whigs, Democrats and Know-Nothings; and the outbreak of warfare with the tribes. Residents of Puget Sound and the Walla Walla district were especially restive with a government located in Oregon City or, after 1851, in Salem. Congress addressed this matter and on March 2, 1853, President Millard Fillmore signed legislation creating the Washington Territory. This action gave final definition to Oregon's geography.

Another important consequence of territorial status was the extension of the Pacific Railroad Surveys into Oregon in 1855–56. Funded by Congress and staffed by the Topographical Engineers, this project sought five alternative routes across the continent to connect the Mississippi Valley with the Pacific Ocean. Additionally, the surveyors examined possibilities for north-south connections between the rail lines. Lieutenants Robert Stockton Williamson and Henry L. Abbot directed the surveys through the Willamette and Rogue River Valleys and along the eastern flank of the Cascade Mountains. Their handsome reports, accompanied by geological observations by Dr. John Strong Newberry, included hand-colored plates showing the countryside, botanical, zoological, and paleontological collections, and profiles of possible grades for railroad routes.

Territorial government catapulted the residents of Oregon into the nexus of federal authority. Although cheerfully independent, Oregonians embraced territorial status with expectation. They had frustration about political cronies named to top government posts, but they gained important services and facilities funded at national expense.

Spread of Settlement

Euro-American settlement in Oregon spread rapidly. Retired mountain men settled in French Prairie, Tualatin Plains and the Chehalem Valley. By 1843, overland emigrants had crossed to the west bank of the Willamette to stake claims along Rickreall and Salt Creeks. By 1845, they were at the lower reaches of the Santiam and Mary's Rivers. Settlers reached the southern end of the Willamette Valley in 1848, and, within a year, were pouring over the hills into the Umpqua Valley. Parties coming by sea settled in 1851 at the mouth of the Umpqua River and at Port Orford on the south coast. Others, restless with their sandy claims on the Clatsop Plains, braved the Indian trail across Neahkahnie Mountain to establish a colony on Tillamook Bay.

The field notes of the land surveyors and their township maps of the 1850s work like a time machine to reveal settlement patterns. Sometimes they noted tribal villages, often located at the confluences of stream courses or at the base of south-facing slopes to catch the rays of sunlight. They charted a network of trails transforming into wagon roads with ferries at river crossings. They showed house locations confirming that many settlers, savvy about flooding in mid-America, built their claim cabins far back from the riverbanks and often positioned them facing fields, the back door to the forest and its generous supplies of firewood. They documented the prairie condition of the western Oregon valleys, the consequence of tribal fire ecology.

The Bureau of the Census in 1850 recorded 11,873 Oregonians: 4,671 females and 7,202 males—a gender disparity of 40 to 60 percent. In towns, nearly 70 percent of the residents were men. "At Astoria, Milton City, and Portland," wrote demographer William Bowen, "they outnumbered women more than three to one." Bowen also found the imprint of kinship as an integrating force in frontier Oregon. "The neighborhood was one of the most basic associations of rural frontier life," he said, "a union of persons with similar backgrounds in small, fairly homogeneous communities, each slightly different from the rest." This meant that closely knit neighborhoods were quick to meet individual needs, prone to exclude outsiders (especially minorities, foreigners and single men), but open to individuals who married into families and thereby joined the community. Bowen thus concluded that Oregon had two societies in the 1850s: a rural frontier dominated by extended families or clans and an urban frontier "drawing its members disproportionately from the ranks of unmarried men from the Northeast or abroad."

Urban development and farm improvements were driven by the California Gold Rush. A number of Oregonians headed south for the diggings in 1848 and many more did so in 1849. The men plowed and planted crops, departed for the mines, and left the women and children to weed, combat birds and varmints, water the vegetables and mind the claim. Hundreds returned in the fall for harvest, their saddlebags heavy with leather pouches of gold dust and nuggets. Most discovered that the boom in California created a lucrative market for wheat, apples, vegetables, oysters, shingles, piling and lumber. The influx of 100,000 new residents and statehood for California in 1850 became an important stimulus and force of stability in the Oregon economy.

Opportunities beckoned. Captain Asa Mead Simpson of Brunswick, Maine, grasped some. Six months in the Sierras convinced him in 1849 that there were better ways to find fortune in the West. He opened lumberyards in Stockton, Sacramento and San Francisco. In the early 1850s, he laid the foundations of a commercial empire stretching from Monterey Bay to Puget Sound. He shipped steam engines and saws for mills at Port Orford, Coos Bay, Umpqua River, Astoria and Gray's Harbor in the Washington Territory. With his partner, Captain George Flavel, he constructed and operated steam tugs to provide bar pilot service for his vessels and those of others. Simpson ran his enterprises for 64 years. His crews built more than 50 ships at his yards on the southern Oregon coast at North Bend.

Aaron Meier, a Jewish emigrant from Germany, worked his way north in the mid-1850s from the Sierra gold fields to new mines in the Rogue River Valley. He carried needles, thread, buttons and bolts of cloth in his traveling dry goods business. He worked hard, saved, and, in 1857, opened a small retail store in Portland, then a town of 1,300 residents. The city's boom during the 1860s with opening of new mining fields in the interior and the flow of capital through the emerging city gave him the chance to expand his business. In time, Sigmund Frank, his son-in-law, joined him. Meier & Frank Department Store was on its way to becoming one of the nation's largest retail outlets.

In 1852, Abigail Scott Duniway arrived in Oregon after her mother and a brother died during the overland crossing. Abigail married young and with her husband, Ben Duniway, selected a donation claim near Lafayette in Yamhill County. Then misfortune struck. Ben signed a note, using the farm as collateral. They lost the farm and Ben, injured in a farming accident, was an invalid for the rest of his life. Having a young family and no options, Abigail assumed full responsibilities. She taught school, made hats, ran a boarding house and aspired to be somebody. By 1859, she had started to define her future. She wrote *Captain Gray's Company,* a novel based on her Oregon Trail diary. Having found her voice, in later years she became a nationally known suffrage advocate and for 16 years was editor and publisher of *The New Northwest,* a weekly newspaper.

Joel Palmer visited Oregon in 1845 and helped open the Barlow Road. He was much impressed with what he saw and described it in *Journal of Travels Over the Rocky Mountains* (1847). He emigrated with his family from Indiana in 1847, and platted Dayton on his farm at the falls of the Yamhill River. Palmer's opportunities came in public service. He served as commissary-general and a peace commissioner in the Cayuse War and, in 1853, was appointed superintendent of Indian affairs. Over the next 24 months, he negotiated ten treaties, eight of which were ratified. A humane man, he nevertheless implemented a program of dramatic reduction of tribal domain but tried to provide reservations close to aboriginal areas and sought to preserve peace.

Matthew Paul Deady, a lawyer from Ohio, began teaching school in 1849 in Yamhill County. He soon returned to the practice of law, was elected to the Territorial Legislature, and, in 1853, was named judge of the territorial supreme court. Deady served in the constitutional convention, as federal district judge, drafter of civil and criminal codes, compiler of Oregon laws, and a founder of the University of Oregon. His diary, published long after his death as *Pharisee Among Philistines* (1975), confirmed his biting intellect and close observations of society.

Simpson, Meier, Duniway, Palmer and Deady were representative of the newcomers. Thousands aspired to make something of themselves. Oregon was a great platform for dreaming dreams and improving one's lot. A number rose to the surface early, finding their callings in business, public service, literature and social reform. Thousands of others engaged in hard work, some laboring in quiet desperation and others for a modest improvement in condition.

By the early 1860s, settlement moved in new directions. Some overland emigrants had stopped at The Dalles. The community emerged by 1850 as a primary outfitting point on the western Columbia Plateau and grew steadily. By 1862, settlers were claiming lands in the Grande Ronde and Powder River Valleys, along the John Day, in the Crooked River and Ochoco region of central Oregon, and in the Klamath Basin. The children of Oregon Trail pioneers were engaged in eastward migration. Precluded by high land prices or multiple heirs in large families from owning farms in western Oregon, they took surplus livestock and headed over the Cascades to the lush meadows along the margins of the region's streams and lakes. Members of the Riddle family, who settled in 1851 in the South Umpqua Valley, were pioneer settlers in the Harney Basin. James and Elizabeth Foster in 1872 moved their large family to Summer Lake. Foster's parents had emigrated through central Oregon in 1845 in the party led by Stephen H. L. Meek. Thousands of others followed this pattern.

Oregon remained a rural, small-town region in the 19th century. The Donation Land Act, by allowing claims from 160 to 320 acres per person, effectively dispersed the population. A number of townsites became ghost towns. Randolph, Waldo, Dardanelles, Elizabethtown and Sailor's Diggings in the mines of southern Oregon vanished when the gold was gone. Cincinnati, Champoeg, Multnomah City, Peoria and Lancaster were once thriving communities along the Willamette. Auburn, Greenhorn, Granite and Bourne for a time served the mining populations of northeastern Oregon. Floods, fires, playing out of mineral deposits and changing travel patterns pushed them into oblivion.

Some communities naturally attracted growth. Ashland at the base of the Siskiyous in the Bear Creek Valley, Roseburg in the Umpqua Valley, Marshfield on upper Coos Bay, Prineville on the Crooked River, Pendleton at the base of the Blue Mountains and Baker City near the mines in the Blue Mountains became crossroads communities. For many towns, the key to success was to capture county government. Promoters vied for such locations, for they guaranteed a flow of people recording deeds, appearing in court, securing contracts or coping with society's needs. County government was as important as a good mill site, coal mine, or wagon road crossing in helping to anchor a community.

Indian Wars

Camas lilies bloomed in such profusion that meadows looked like lakes amid the forests. The tarweed seeds ripened and the women set the fires. Armed with beaters and funnel-shaped baskets, they began the annual cycle of gathering. Acorns ripened, matured, and fell from the oaks. Their flour, when leached of tannic acid, provided a nutritious gruel or bread when baked on flat stones near the fires. Salmon surged up the rivers. Eels clung to the rocks as they ascended the rapids. Deer and elk browsed on the nutritious plants in the foothills. Flecks of gold glistened in the crystal-clear water of the streambeds.

This was the setting when, during the winter of 1851–52, packers on the trail to California discovered the placer mines of southwestern Oregon. Within weeks, a reckless population, most of them hardened miners from California, surged over the Siskiyous or stepped off the gangplanks of ships putting in at Crescent City, Port Orford, Umpqua City or Scottsburg. The rush was on. It meant quick riches for those who found the right pothole in bedrock filled with nuggets or the fortunate miners whose riffle boxes captured the fine particles of gold that glistened in the black sand. For the tribes of the Rogue River country, it meant that all they had known and their very lives were at stake.

The causes of conflict erupted everywhere. The Donation Land Act became law in 1850. Years passed before treaties, negotiated in 1853 and 1854, were ratified. Some, such as those of Anson Dart or the Willamette Valley Treaty Commission of 1851, never gained Senate approval. In spite of the promises of superintendents of Indian Affairs, Dart and Palmer, the white people poured in. Dispossession ruled. The miners drove the Takelma, Shasta, Chetco, Shasta Costa, Mikonotunne, Tututni, Galice Creeks and Cow Creeks from their villages. Located on old stream terraces, these villages were prime locations for placer deposits.

The hungry newcomers hunted the game, decimating the deer and elk populations. The Territorial Legislature in 1854 prohibited sale of ammunition or guns to Indians, deepening their disadvantage. The miners and residents of Jacksonville, Canyonville, Kerbyville and Gold Beach liked bacon and ham. They let hogs run wild, catching them in baited traps. The hogs ate the acorns, a primary subsistence food for the tribes.

Mining debris poured down the Illinois, Rogue, South Coquille and South Umpqua Rivers. The salmon runs diminished; the eels died. Crayfish, fresh water mussels and trout choked on the flood of mud. Starvation threatened. The claimants of Donation Lands fenced their fields with split-rail fences and built log cabins. They worked with a will to stop tribal field burning. The tribal women found it impossible to harvest tarweed seeds and the blackberries that formerly regenerated with the annual fires did not grow back. The settlers turned under the fields of camas lilies, and their cattle and horses grazed off the blue-flowering plants.

The mining districts—whether in the Rogue River country or the Blue Mountains of northeastern Oregon—caused major ecological disruption. The rush for quick wealth through mineral exploitation unraveled nature's ways and long-established human subsistence activities. Then came the "exterminators"—unprincipled men who believed that "the only good Indian was a dead Indian." They formed volunteer companies and perpetrated massacres against the Chetco tribe in 1853, the Lower Coquille Tribe in 1854, and in wanton aggression against Takelma people camped near the Table Rock Reservation in 1855.

Frederick M. Smith, sub-Indian agent at Port Orford, in 1854 addressed the attacks on the tribes in his district. They were ravaged by hunger, dispossession of their villages, onset of new and fatal diseases, and overt murders. Reporting the massacre of the Lower Coquille Tribe, he wrote: *"Bold, brave, courageous men!* to attack a friendly and defenceless tribe; *to burn, roast, and shoot sixteen of their number, and all on suspicion* that they were about to rise and drive from their country *three hundred white men!"* Smith's lament, the mourning cries of the Indian women, the death rituals of rubbing the hair with pitch and the inexorable course of hunger, attack and death precipitated the conflicts known as the Rogue River Wars. The troubles seethed between 1852 and 1856. Finally, the U.S. Army had sufficient forces to mount a campaign in 1855–56 to destroy the tribes' ability to resist.

Vanquished by the combined operations of the Oregon Volunteers and Army regulars, the tribes of the Rogue and Umpqua Valleys and the southwestern Oregon coast were then removed to the Siletz and Grand Ronde reservations. Forced marches through winter snows or over the rocky headlands and through the sand dunes of coastal Oregon became trails of tears for hundreds driven to the distant reservations. Other survivors were herded aboard the *Columbia,* a sidewheel steamer, which removed them from Port Orford to the Columbia and lower Willamette River area. Then, they had to walk the muddy trail to the reservations.

The myth of independence was shattered by the actions of Oregon's frontier residents. For their "services rendered" in the conflicts of 1853, the volunteers billed the federal government for $107,287, and they were the primary cause of the hostilities. When the conflicts ended in 1856, they worked for years to gain settlement. Finally, in 1890, Congress passed the Oregon Indian Depredation Claims Act. Aged pioneers filed affidavits to claim reimbursement for lost pillows, ricks of hay, rail fences and beans and bacon during the conflicts of the 1850s. A dependent generation's elders once again tapped the federal treasury for support.

Troubles with the tribes erupted anew in the 1850s on the Columbia Plateau. In 1855, Superintendent Joel Palmer and Governor Isaac I. Stevens of Washington Territory summoned the tribes of the eastern plateau to the Walla Walla Treaty Council. In a matter of days, they hammered out agreements, ceding lands but reserving others with the Nez Perce, Cayuse, Umatilla, and Yakima. Subsequently, Palmer met the Wasco, Wishram and Warm Springs (or Tenino) at The Dalles and entered into a treaty with them. All of these agreements were noteworthy for enumerating rights. The tribes, who had engaged in traditional subsistence activities from time immemorial, reserved rights to fish "at usual and accustomed grounds and stations," to erect fish-processing sheds for drying their catch, and to hunt, gather and graze livestock on unenclosed lands.

While Congress was considering the treaties, the Bureau of Indian Affairs began urging the tribes to remove to their new reservations and take up an agrarian lifestyle. Few wanted to engage in such backbreaking labor or give up fishing, hunting and gathering. The pressure was on. Immigrants arrived every fall and settlement spread east from The Dalles. Pioneer cabins lined the shores of the Gorge, threatening to disrupt the tribal fisheries. Then came gold discoveries on the Fraser and Thompson Rivers in British Columbia and in the Colville district on the north-central plateau. The influx of miners led to an eruption of troubles and, in time, to the Yakima Indian War of 1855–58. The forces of the U.S. Army, supplemented by companies of Oregon Volunteers, defeated the hostile bands.

The 1850s were a wrenching time of transition. Steadily, tribal numbers diminished, their food sources destroyed and their lands appropriated. These were terrible times for the region's native people.

Statehood

Issues far from Oregon shaped affairs along the Pacific Coast in the 1850s. Sectional tensions heightened during the bumbling presidencies of Millard Fillmore, Franklin Pierce and James Buchanan. The Compromise of 1850 gained a little time, but its concessions satisfied neither pro-slavery extremists in the South nor abolitionists in the North. The nation was on its course to the Civil War. Harriet Beecher Stowe's novel, *Uncle Tom's Cabin,* enraged slaveowners as it swept across the country in a powerful indictment of the "peculiar institution." Formation of the Republican Party in 1854, troubles in "Bleeding Kansas" in 1856, the Dred Scott decision in 1857, and John Brown's raid on the federal arsenal at Harper's Ferry in 1858 confirmed the divisions and tensions. The Republicans had drawn the line—no further expansion of slavery. They nominated John C. Fremont, a popular western explorer, for the presidency. Although Fremont lost, within four years their candidate, Abraham Lincoln, was headed to Washington, D.C., as the 16th president. Passions were high. Then came secession and war.

Three parties vied for political control in Oregon. The Democrats were an odd lot, including northerners opposed to slavery and southern diehards who supported an institution barred by the Organic Act of 1848. The Whigs held political patronage in the early 1850s but watched their party disintegrate nationally. The Know-Nothings were opposed to the political clique that had managed territorial government in Salem. These divisions confirmed the heavy hold of old persuasions and attitudes—the intellectual baggage carried by the immigrants.

Without enabling legislation from Congress, Oregonians voted in June 1857 to hold a constitutional convention. The delegates assembled in Salem during the summer and drafted a governing document. It was modeled on those of Iowa, Indiana, and Michigan. The constitution limited public debt and placed tight controls on banks and corporations. An agricultural people, the convention delegates argued, had little use for frivolous expenditures or unnecessary institutions. In the fall voters faced three questions. Did they approve the constitution? They voted yes. Did they want slavery? They voted 7,727 no and 2,645 yes. Did they want freed African-Americans to live in Oregon? They voted eight to one against permitting their residency.

The actions in 1857 were predictable. Oregonians hungered for control of their own government and an end to the patronage appointments produced by shifting administrations in Washington, D.C. They also affirmed they did not want slavery in Oregon. The question of driving free African-Americans from the new state revealed resoundingly racist attitudes. They did not see freed slaves, Indians or women standing equally before the law. In this Oregonians differed little from Thomas Jefferson. Architect of the Declaration of Independence and its gracefully worded affirmations of natural rights, Jefferson was a slave-owner all his adult life. He could not rise to the noble philosophy of personal freedom he articulated in the 1770s. Oregonians in 1857 appeared to have drunk from the same well.

In June, 1858, residents of the territory elected officials as defined by their new constitution. For months the fate of Oregon statehood floated on shifting political coalitions distrustful of changing the fragile balance of power in Congress. It was known Oregon would be a free state, yet its newly elected senators—Joseph Lane and Delazon Smith—were proslavery Democrats. Finally Congress acted and on February 14, 1859, President Buchanan signed the bill. Oregon joined the federal union.

Civil War in Oregon

The plunge to Civil War exploded on April 12, 1861, in the bombardment of Fort Sumter in Charleston Harbor. When it became apparent the conflict would not be short, the Army began removing regular soldiers from the District of Oregon. Because of the responsibility to guard the reservations and maintain a military presence, especially in central and eastern Oregon where gold discoveries generated a rapid influx of miners and settlers, federal and state officials scrambled to find replacement troops. The Department of the Pacific raised recruits and dispatched companies of California Volunteers to Fort Yamhill, Fort Hoskins and Siletz Blockhouse. The Army abandoned Fort Umpqua in 1862. The First Oregon Volunteer Cavalry and the First Washington Territory Infantry went to central Oregon. During the Civil War, Oregon raised six companies of cavalry. Known officially as the First Oregon Cavalry, they served until June, 1865.

Secessionist sympathizers surfaced in Oregon. The Knights of the Golden Circle, an anti-Union group, reportedly plotted the seizure of Fort Vancouver, military headquarters on the Columbia River. They did not act. When pro-Confederate partisans raised their flag in Jacksonville, they faced opposition and backed down. The Long Tom Rebellion was perhaps the most noteworthy outbreak of secessionist feeling. Emboldened by the assassination of President Lincoln, Philip Henry Mulkey walked the streets of Eugene on May 6, 1865, shouting: "Hurrah for Jeff Davis, and damn the man that won't!" The First Oregon Volunteer Infantry arrested Mulkey, who promptly grabbed a glass of water and toasted Jeff Davis, the Confederate president. A pro-Union mob, wanting to lynch Mulkey, broke down the jail door. Mulkey slashed one of the men with a hidden knife. Mulkey's supporters from the Long Tom district were ready to fight, but the infantry slipped Mulkey out of town under an armed guard, loaded him on a steamboat, and sent him off to three months in jail at Fort Vancouver. Mulkey sued for $10,000 for false arrest. After 14 court appearances over a two-year period, he settled for $200.

For many of the soldiers, the Civil War in Oregon was a monotonous, numbing assignment. In their monthly post returns, officers recorded desertions, suicides and bouts in the brig because of drunkenness and misbehavior. The tribes were quiet on the Siletz and Grand Ronde Reservations. The rain was predictable and depressing. "Nothing transpired of importance," recorded Royal A. Bensell, a soldier at Fort Yamhill. Too many days brought that refrain in his Civil War diary.

East of the Cascades the troops had active engagement. Gold discoveries at Canyon City and other diggings on the headwaters of the John Day River and in the Powder River country on the eastern slopes of the Blue Mountains had drawn thousands of miners. The Northern Paiute, disrupted in their seasonal round and tempted by the easy pickings of clothing, food, and horses, embarked on raids and conflicts that demanded military intervention. The Oregon Volunteer Infantry and Cavalry established Camp Watson (1864) after placing troops at temporary stations: Dahlgren, Currey, Gibbs, Henderson and Maury. The forces engaged in lengthy and often fruitless explorations searching for the elusive Indians.

Realizing that the problems east of the Cascades were of long duration, the U.S. Army established Fort Klamath (1863), Camp Warner (1866), and Fort Harney (1867). During the summer of 1864, Captains John M. Drake, George B. Curry and Lieutenant-Colonel Charles Drew led troops on sweeps through southeastern Oregon, northern Nevada and southwestern Idaho. They had little success in finding the "enemy." "These tribes can be gathered upon a reservation, controlled, subsisted for a short time, and afterwards be made to subsist themselves," commented the superintendent of Indian affairs, "for one-tenth the cost of supporting military forces in pursuit of them." In time, that happened. The Klamath Reservation and the short-lived Malheur Reservation included various bands of Northern Paiute. The Civil War in Oregon mostly involved guarding reservations or pursuing native people who were masters of escape in their own homelands.

Uncle Sam's Handiwork

Statehood meant that Oregonians had two senators and a representative to make their case in Congress. The congressional delegation delivered. Some argued it was critical to open communications across the new state. The Republican Party was not of a mind to continue projects wholly in the control and labor of federal employees. Its philosophy was to throw as much action as possible into the private sector. Thus, between 1865 and 1869 Congress liberally awarded land grants to the State of Oregon to pass on to companies constructing "military wagon roads." Theoretically, the routes were to link strategic locations suitable for use by troops during emergencies.

The new roads were the Oregon Central, Corvallis-Yaquina Bay, Willamette Valley and Cascade Mountain, The Dalles-Boise and the Coos Bay. Two provided routes from Willamette Valley points in Albany and Springfield eastward to Boise. A third connected The Dalles via the John Day watershed to Boise. Two ran toward the coast: one from Albany to Yaquina City and another from Roseburg to Coos Bay. Under the terms of the grants, as soon as a company had completed a stretch of road, it could apply to the governor for certification of its success. The governor or his designated official would visit the route. If the road was deemed suitable for wagon use, the company then received three square miles of land for every mile of road. The tally for the five roads ran into millions of acres.

Land-grant wagon roads were founded on speculation and fraud. None of the companies had the experience, capital or leadership to build satisfactory routes through such challenging terrain. They cleared and carved out traces, leaving many streams unbridged and routes subject to slides and frequent closures. The Oregon Central Military Wagon Road Company was unblushing in its scam. When its surveyors reached the Cascade summit, rather than heading east toward Boise, they swept south through the upper Deschutes and into the Klamath Reservation, cutting a swath of checkerboard lands out of the lush meadows along the Williamson and Sprague Rivers. They moved on toward Goose Lake into Guano Valley, then over the southern slopes of Steens Mountain into the Pueblo Valley before turning northeasterly toward Boise. Their meandering route captured tens of thousands of acres of prime grazing land, dismembered the Klamath Reservation and ensured a much larger grant than if they had surveyed a route directly toward Idaho.

Wagon road companies locked up land for years. The General Land Office held hundreds of thousands of acres of unclaimed grants. As long as the company or its successor purchasers did not take title, they did not have to pay taxes. The longer they waited, the greater the appreciation of value in timber, minerals or grazing. By avoiding paying taxes and letting land values increase, the companies—or those who bought them to speculate in the grants—calculated a better return. Further, the companies did not maintain the roads yet dared to demand tolls from travelers. Lamentations of local residents who lived in the alternate sections along the routes finally compelled Congress to investigate and the courts to take back the remaining portions of the grants.

Among the loudest critics of the wagon road companies were land seekers. In the Homestead Act (1862), Congress gave the land-hungry an unparalleled opportunity. For a modest filing fee, five years of residency and claim improvements, homesteaders could receive as much as 160 acres of the public domain for free. Congress became increasingly generous in giving away federal lands. It passed bounty land acts for veterans of wars, the Desert Land Act (1877), Enlarged Homestead Act (1909), and Stock Raising Homestead Act (1916). Shrewd speculators might accumulate hundreds of acres by working the system. Between 1850 and 1940, millions of acres in Oregon passed from public to private ownership through the land distribution acts promoted by developers of the American West.

Congressional action shaped Oregon in other areas. The coast was a dangerous place where strong winds buffeted the shore. Narrow channels led over fluctuating bars into the estuaries. The headlands were remote, hulking forms on the eastern landscape. Mariners desperately needed services. The bar of the Columbia gained a reputation as the "graveyard of the Pacific." Boats foundered, grounded and smashed on rocky headlands, taking hundreds of lives. The U.S. Coast Survey continued to chart the estuaries and compile information in the *Coast Pilot,* an annual publication with data on landmarks, rocks, buoys and anchorages. The U.S. Light-House Board was called upon to provide more assistance.

On a case-by-case basis, Congress appropriated funds for design and construction of important facilities. These included lighthouses: Cape Arago (1866), Cape Blanco (1870), Yaquina Bay (1872), Cape Foulweather (1873), Point Adams (1875), Tillamook Rock (1881), Warrior Rock (1888) at the mouth of the Willamette River, Cape Meares (1890), Umpqua River, Heceta Head, Coquille River (all 1894), and Desdemona Sands (1905). The goal was to create a system of stations with interlocking lights. On a clear night at sea, a mariner might expect to sight at any point a distinctive beacon on shore to pinpoint the location. Fog signals powered by steam engines blasted warnings from a number of the stations to tell captains to drop anchor or beat a retreat until the mists cleared.

In 1892, an appropriation of $60,000 funded construction of *Columbia River Lightship No. 50.* Anchored off the treacherous bar of the Columbia, the lightship had a lonely crew of eight who, for decades, kept watch, maintained kerosene lights, and fed coal into boilers to power a massive fog signal. Their wave-tossed perch with booming horn drew hardy men who, like those at remote lighthouses, endured modest pay and isolation.

Congress also funded construction of stations and staffing for the U.S. Life-Saving Service. The first station opened in 1878 at the Cape Arago Lighthouse near the entrance to Coos Bay. Numerous shipwrecks and loss of life associated with the export of coal and lumber from the harbor brought federal action. The small building had a surfboat and one oarsman. Launching the craft and rowing to a vessel in distress depended upon volunteers. By the end of the 19th century, the U.S. Life-Saving Service had stations at Warrenton, Tillamook Bay, Yaquina Bay, Coos Bay and the Umpqua and Coquille Rivers. Each had crew quarters, a boat house and a practice mast for breeches-buoy drill. In the early 20th century, the USLSS erected stations at Port Orford and Siuslaw River.

In the 1870s, the U.S. Geological Survey (USGS) began work in Oregon. John Evans, U.S. Geologist for the Oregon Territory, had mounted initial surveys of mining areas in 1855–56. In the final three decades of the 19th century, the agency inaugurated studies of mining districts to assess coal and gold deposits. Its skilled cartographers also commenced topographic mapping in conjunction with the National Geodetic Survey. These maps, revised at 20-to-30 year intervals in the 20th century, gave form to the land. They provided vital information on roads, settlements, and terrain. In the 1890s, the USGS performed a remarkable service. Its employees mounted the first comprehensive assessment of forests in the state. They estimated standing volumes of hardwoods and softwoods, mapped areas ravaged by forest fires, photographed the terrain and published technical reports on forest conditions and grazing impacts.

By 1856, the Bureau of Indian Affairs had embarked on its mission to attempt to transform tribes into the mainstream culture in one generation. It founded its work upon an agrarian economy regardless of the terrain, elevation or traditional subsistence patterns of the tribes. Oregon's reservations were Siletz, Grand Ronde, Warm Springs, Umatilla, Klamath and Malheur. The tribes retained but a fraction of their aboriginal lands. The Nez Perce, whose 1855 treaty reserved their tribal lands in northeastern Oregon, were beset by trespassers who, in 1877, provoked the Nez Perce War and the exodus of Chief Joseph's band. This band orchestrated a brilliant retreat through the Pacific Northwest, for months eluding the U.S. Army. When they finally surrendered, the government confined them first in Oklahoma and, after 1885, on the Colville Reservation in Washington.

Indian agents, subagents, farmers, teachers, and doctors—all in the employ of the federal government—mounted the programs. They created farms and insisted, in spite of the weather, that tribes raise wheat in the boggy soil along the Oregon coast. Hundreds died in this ill-fated experiment. They also attempted to compel the Klamath and Warm Springs tribes to become farmers. The setting for their farms was amenable to gathering root crops or berries, but not to cereal or vegetable crop production. Terrible hardship ensued.

In 1879, Lt. Melville C. Wilkinson of the U.S. Army opened the Indian Training School in Forest Grove, on four acres of land rented from Pacific University. $5,000 was provided to start the school. Wilkinson, with the help of eight Puyallup Indian boys began construction on the buildings in 1880. The initial class of students consisted of fourteen boys and four girls. All the students came from the State of Washington, seventeen of them from the Puyallup Reservation on the Puget Sound and one boy from the Nisqually Reservation. These students were taught blacksmithing, shoemaking, carpentering, wagon making, girl's industries and advancement in studies. The local community did not support expansion of the campus. So Henry J. Minthorn, the second superintendent of the school, considered three sites for a new school. Newberg offered 100 acres of heavily timbered land, Forest Grove offered 23 acres with a pasture parcel of 75 acres approximately four miles away from the main site, and Salem offered 171 partially cleared, sparsely timbered land north of town. He chose the Salem site since it was close to the State Capital and had the most acreage, and in 1885, moved the school, changing its name to Chemawa Indian School.

In 1887, the General Allotment Act launched a major assault on tribalism. The law, extended over the next few years to Oregon reservations, provided for dividing up the tribal estate into individual allotments of 80 to 160 acres. The plan was for each Indian to receive a tract, farm it, transform in lifeways, master English and, after the passage of 25 years, gain certification as "competent." He then became a citizen of the United States, received title to the allotment, and could pay taxes on the land! The program fostered a dramatic loss in tribal lands and created a nightmare of checkerboard ownerships within reservations.

The Army Corps of Engineers was also on duty in 19th century Oregon. Its employees mounted river navigability studies on the Columbia, Umpqua and Willamette, and planned dredging and jetty projects at several estuaries. These men charted the rivers, designed improvements and, with federal appropriations, oversaw blasting of rocks and reefs. Between 1878 and 1896, the Corps of Engineers supervised the region's most expensive "pork barrel" project—construction of the massive bypass canal and locks at the Cascades of the Columbia. The Corps also constructed the Yamhill River Locks (1900) and, starting in 1888, initiated jetty projects at Coquille River, Coos Bay, Siuslaw River, Yaquina Bay and Columbia River. By 1920, the Corps of Engineers had spent $4.7 million on river and harbor projects; local contributions added nearly a fifth more when required by legislation. The flow of federal dollars was an immense benefit to Oregonians, for the state did not have the resources to fund such large-scale projects.

Uncle Sam delivered. Federal projects included land grants for wagon roads, homesteads, and war veterans. Congress paid for soldiers to fight Indians, personnel to manage reservations, funds to build and staff lighthouses and lifesaving stations, operation of postal routes, post offices, the federal court system, customs houses, the General Land Office, mapping and mineral assessments by the U.S. Geological Survey, and updating of navigational information by the U.S. Coast Survey. Uncle Sam was a key player in a state populated by farmers, stockraisers, fishers, miners, loggers, sawmill workers and small-town business people.

Minorities

The welcome mat was not out. Oregon's early generations defined opportunity narrowly. The land and resources were the domain of men and women of Caucasian background; others need not apply. Even when the Donation Land Act provided that women qualified for claims, brothers and brothers-in-law tried to wrest claims away from widows. Entreaties of women for fairer treatment finally led to passage of the Married Women's Property Act in 1866, the right to vote in school elections in 1878, and admission to the bar in 1886. Women were a minority in Oregon. The frontier demography, especially in mining districts and rural areas, remained predominantly male for decades. Women's efforts to gain the general franchise were repeatedly rebuffed and not realized until the 20th century.

African-Americans were unequivocally not wanted. Some, nevertheless, persisted quietly and settled in the state. The Census of 1850 reported either 54 or 56 African-Americans in the entire Pacific Northwest. The Census of 1860 identified

124 blacks and mulattoes, a tiny fraction of the more than 52,000 residents enumerated. Those who settled in Oregon took risks, but they had known prejudice and discrimination far worse in other parts of the country. Sometimes, however, racial episodes erupted. These occurred sporadically in several parts of the state over a period of 70 years. By 1890, for example, the African-American population of Coos County was 36. Most worked for the local railroad or at the Beaver Hill and Libby coal mines. Recruited in West Virginia, they had migrated across the country and walked through the Coast Range from Roseburg to the lower Coquille River, only to find that they and their families were expected to live in leaking boxcars. The men had to work in the deep shafts reaching below sea level for 90 cents per day. When they complained, they were accused of fomenting labor strife and compelled to leave.

Alonzo Tucker was an African-American who worked as a bootblack and operator of a gym in Marshfield. In 1902, dubious charges of rape were leveled against him by a white woman. When a mob of 200 armed men marched on the jail, the marshal lost control of Tucker, who hid beneath a dock. He was twice shot the next morning and then hanged from the Fourth Street Bridge by a mob that had grown to more than 300. The coroner's inquest found no fault; the victim, the report said, had died of loss of blood from a gunshot wound. No indictments were brought. The local newspaper observed that the lynch mob was "quiet and orderly" and that the vigilante proceeding was no "unnecessary disturbance of the peace." In 1907, the Marshfield School Board instituted segregated education, alleging that the four African-American students "will materially retard the progress of the five hundred white children."

Not all African-Americans faced treatments like those in turn-of-the-century Coos County. Some found steady employment with the railroads, both on construction crews and on Pullman cars. Others opened restaurants, barber shops, beauty shops, and saloons. In 1903, McCants Stewart passed the Oregon bar exam and began legal practice. Dr. J. A. Merriam entered medical practice in Portland in that decade. A number entered the ministry and labored at the pulpit, in choirs and in social halls to influence the spirituality of their families, friends, and neighbors. Outreach came in many forms. The Colored Benevolent Association of Portland, founded in 1867, fraternal lodges, baseball teams and women's clubs were other means for African-Americans to help their communities.

Chinese-Americans

Poverty, warfare, overpopulation and ambition racked the peoples of the Pearl River Delta in the mid-19th century. Foreigners carved out enclaves in Macao, Hong Kong and Canton, bribed their way into the Chinese economy by importing opium and siphoned off a rich trade in luxury items. Many Chinese aspired to a better life and Gum San—Gold Mountain—beckoned. Tales of gold discoveries along the Pacific Coast proved irresistible. Thousands of men responded. Their plan was simple—go to Gum San, work hard every day, store up gold and return to purchase land and hold position in Chinese society.

As the gold rush drifted northward into Oregon, the Chinese followed the discoveries. They were relegated to the worked-over placers, barred from some districts altogether, and compelled to pay a head tax because of race. They worked, paid and endured. By the 1870s, for example, Chinese males constituted nearly half the population of Grant County. They lived frugally and labored hard. They moved tons of rock to get to pay dirt in crevices and potholes in the upper John Day diggings. They ran restaurants, laundries, herbal pharmacies and gambling dens.

Because of their distinctive dress, language, religion and difference from the surrounding culture, the Chinese were treated brutally. The editor of the *Grant County News* on October 15, 1885, observed: "To every one it is apparent that the Chinese are a curse and a blight to this county, not only financially, but socially and morally. . . . What the Chinaman wears, he brings from China, and what he eats (except rats and lizards), he brings across the ocean, and thus American trade or production reaps no benefit from his presence." The presence of tongs—kinship and social organizations—and Chinese determination to carry wealth home fostered intense discrimination. Murders, assaults, segregation, intimidation, special taxation and opposition confronted the Chinese at every turn.

What did they do? They persevered and many achieved their goals. They found employment in railroad construction. Chinese laborers provided much of the backbreaking toil to make the cuts for the Oregon & California Railroad as it inched southward through the Umpqua Mountains to the Rogue River Valley or on the line of the Oregon Railway & Navigation Company as it stretched eastward in 1880–82 through the Columbia Gorge. Willing to endure cannery work, Chinese men by the 1870s had acquired a near monopoly of work in canneries from Astoria to The Dalles. They gutted the fish, operated the steam pressure cookers, fastened the labels, and prepared tons of cases for shipment to a world market. They labored at nearly 40 canneries lining the shores of the Columbia for low wages and compulsory residency in company dormitories.

The Chinese congregated in Chinatown in Portland or, when their seasonal work diminished, traveled to communities in San Francisco, Seattle, or Vancouver, British Columbia. Anti-Chinese bigotry grew in the 1880s. Chinese were driven out of several communities—Oregon City, Albina and

Mount Tabor. In 1887, vigilantes murdered ten or twelve Chinese miners in Hells Canyon on the Oregon-Idaho border. The Chinese Exclusion Act then cut off immigration, leaving nearly 9,000 Chinese men in Oregon with little prospect of bringing a bride from home or paying for passage of family members. The downward spiral began. Each year, Oregon had fewer residents of Chinese ancestry. Those who had resources returned home. Others, like Doc Hay and Lung On, remained, running an herbal drug store and car dealership in John Day. Bert Why operated a grocery store in North Bend. Most of the men who stayed remained single and lived lonely lives in Gum San.

Japanese-Americans

Jobs and land lured Japanese immigrants by the last decade of the 19th century. Overpopulation and limited opportunity at home, the favorable publicity of labor recruiters and adventure drew Japanese to Oregon. They found places to work and live. Many men hired on as laborers to build railroads. Tadashichi Tanaka, Shinzaburo Ban and Shintaro Takaki were all involved in 1891 in recruiting rail workers. The men helped build the Union Pacific, Southern Pacific, feeder lines and logging railroads.

Japanese immigrant families settled in the Treasure Valley near Ontario, Hood River Valley, and at Gresham. The prospect of gaining a few acres, planting a garden, setting out an orchard, and producing high-quality vegetables and fruits drew husbands, wives, and children to work together to establish a substantial hold in a new land. Others settled on Second, Third and Fourth streets in Northwest Portland, where they became shopkeepers. Some men worked in sawmills, but at risk. In 1925, for example, a woman in Toledo on Yaquina Bay sparked a nasty attack on Japanese families. Threats of violence and bricks thrown through windows drove 25 Japanese men, women and children from the town, and earned Rosemary Shenk a court appearance.

Other Newcomers

Oregon, by the end of the 19th century, in spite of exclusionist attitudes and wars fought against Indians by the pioneer generation, had a changing complexion. Jewish merchants operated mercantile stores, enriched cultural life through their love of music and literature and founded synagogues. Japanese and Chinese workers took some of the worst but necessary jobs. They helped build the state's vital transportation links. They canned fish, raised fruit and ran small businesses. African-Americans dominated the Pullman services, mined coal and grew steadily in numbers. Oregon was not a comfortable place for minorities, but negative treatment was also dished out to "dumb Swedes," "beer-drinking Germans" and Irish and Italian Catholics. Many Oregonians wore their fears of those who were different on their shirtsleeves.

Emerging Economies

Natural resources drove economic development. A popular song said: "There'll be apples on each branch in Oregon; there'll be valleys filled with golden grain. There'll be cattle on each ranch in Oregon; and there'll be plenty of sun and rain." Farming, stockraising, mining, fishing and logging became mainstays. Land became the target. The trick was to find, coax, extricate and harvest everything useful the state had to offer, provided it was possible to get it to market.

Farmers took their oxen with plows and harrows into the prairies of the Rogue, Umpqua and Willamette valleys to turn the sod and sow crops. They raised wheat, oats, barley, corn and potatoes. Swampy lands at Cipole, Gaston and Lake Labish produced fabulous onions. In time, experimentation led to specialty crops: hops for making malt in the brewing business, flax for linen manufacturing, hemp for paper and rope, and grapes for wine. Oregon farmers, by the 1880s, went wild for prunes. Thousands of acres of hillside lands were opened and groomed as orchards. Investors erected prune dryers and flooded the world market with more prunes than could be consumed. Some directed their energies next into filberts, walnuts, turkey raising and hog production. The agricultural potentials of western Oregon were varied.

Stockraising attracted a number of investors. Dairy farmers began their workday before sunrise and were still milking cows after sunset. Their cows grazed on the meadows surrounding Tillamook Bay, Nestucca, Salmon River, Coos Bay, Coquille River and in the Willamette Valley. The sprawling hinterlands of Oregon—two-thirds of the state laying beyond the Cascades—became cattle, sheep and horse country in the 19th century. The dramatic rise of livestock production occurred between 1862 and 1882. It responded to the presence of hungry men in the mines of the Blue Mountains, transcontinental railroad connections in Nevada with boxcars and refrigerator cars to haul meat to major cities, woolen mills demanding material for their spindles, and land amenable to pastoral labors. Pete French, Ben Snipes, David Shirk, John S. Devine, W. B. Todhunter, Dr. Bernard Daly, and others became barons of the ranges. By strategically gaining control of springs, streambanks, and lake margins, they were able to run their vast herds on the public domain without competition. David Shirk's herds ranged up and down Guano Valley. Devine and Todhunter ran the Whitehorse Ranch in the Pueblo Valley. Pete French, whose kingdom lay at the base of Steens Mountain, was gunned down by an angry homesteader in 1897. The jury trying the alleged murderer ruled that French had died of "natural causes"—a bullet in the head. There was no conviction.

Smaller producers also came into Trans-Cascadia. Some tended herds of sheep—as many as 5,000 in a flock—in lonely labor. The work entailed months driving the sheep to summer range at high elevation, backbreaking days of shearing and wrestling wool bales onto wagons, and marking and doctoring the critters. Sheep and cattle raisers did not mix. Angry words sometimes led to gunshots that felled livestock and nearly plunged Central Oregon partisans into a cycle of sheep and cattle wars. Basque and Mexican shepherds brought their skills to Jordan Valley, Catlow Valley and Treasure Valley. Some filed on homesteads. Donato Uvernaga and Simon Acordagoitia, Basques who settled on the Owyhee, hand-dug canals and built a hulking waterwheel. The steady current lifted metal buckets of life-giving water from the river to nourish the fields these immigrants cleared of sagebrush deep in the canyons below the Mahogany Mountains.

Mining shifted rapidly from placer deposits to lode claims. In that transition, the mining moved from an individual to a corporate enterprise, for shared capital and risk were usually necessary to open adits, erect a shaft house, install a stamp mill or flotation table and hire the crews necessary to operate a mine. Cooks and flunkies produced the grub served in the mess hall. Miners rode the ore buckets or climbed rickety ladders into the mine. The company engineer or mine manager directed the flow of ore through the processing plants. Oregon's 19th century ventures included gold mines in the Bohemia District of the Western Cascades, Siskiyous and Blue Mountains. Much of the gold and silver produced in Oregon and farther east in Idaho flowed through Portland, stimulating the development of the state's largest city. Between 1864 and 1870, for example, $29.8 million in mineral wealth passed through Portland. Between 1852 and 1964, Oregon produced an estimated $136 million in gold and silver. Approximately 73 percent came from the mines of Baker and Grant Counties.

Quicksilver mines tapped deposits in Lane and Douglas Counties. Brave miners engaged in the risky business of smelting the ores to fill flasks of mercury at London, Nonpareil, Milltown Hill and other small communities that grew up at the mine portals. In the 1880s, Will Q. Brown opened nickel deposits at Riddle in the South Umpqua Valley. Over the next 90 years, this mine produced more than $1 billion in nickel, generating an important payroll for Douglas County.

The need for fuel for steam engines drove Oregon's coal mining industry. Steam schooners, locomotives, donkey engines and mill equipment depended on cheap, plentiful coal. The mines at Coos Bay opened in 1853, and, for nearly a century, the coal fields of the lower Coquille River and Coos Bay fired Oregon industry and helped heat San Francisco. The Beaver Hill Mine, one of the largest on the coast, had shafts reaching nearly 1,100 feet below sea level. The Coos Bay, Roseburg & Eastern Railroad moved coal from the mines to the bunkers at Coos Bay where it was loaded on steamers that would take it to distant markets.

Salmon annually filled the rivers. Some say the runs were so thick that it was possible to walk dryshod across the streams! Robert Deniston Hume grasped the potential. His brothers were pioneer cannery operators on the Sacramento and, starting in 1867, on the Columbia River. In 1876, Hume settled at the mouth of the Rogue River. By bravado and cunning, he carved out such an empire that, in time, he was referred to as a "pygmy monopolist." Hume gained ownership of both banks of the river from the Pacific upstream to the head of tidewater. This holding made it impossible for any competitor to land a boat or draw nets filled with fish without trespassing on his land. In time, Hume constructed a company town—Wedderburn—where he ran a cannery, store, race track and cold storage plant. His vessels, the *Alexander Duncan, Berwick,* and *Mary D. Hume,* transported his catch to markets. Hume became a pioneer in the hatchery business when, in 1877, he began experimenting with raising fish on Indian Creek, near the mouth of the Rogue River.

Canneries at Coos Bay, Umpqua River, Kernville and the Nestucca River processed the runs on the coastal streams. Canneries lined the banks of the Columbia between The Dalles and the sea. Samuel Elmore, Ben Young, Frank Warren and Frank Seufert were major players in the salmon canning business. The trick was to move quickly when new technology gave advantage. Laborers caught the fish in traps, seine nets, set nets and at fishwheels whose paddles scooping with the current, pulled salmon, sturgeon, eels and steelhead from the river and dumped them into fish boxes headed for a cannery.

Transportation systems were central to the future of most investments and profits in Oregon enterprise. Packet service and schooners carried passengers and freight along the coast. Sternwheelers picked up and delivered milk on the estuaries and carried commerce and passengers on most of the larger streams. Steamboats plied the Willamette, transforming landings into sites for warehouses, grist mills and small towns. Steamboats traversed Upper Klamath Lake and Goose Lake, taking children to school and tourists or shoppers to specific destinations. Investors constructed steamboats above the Cascades for water travel on the Columbia east to The Dalles and also on the upper river above Celilo Falls with connections to the mouth of the Snake and on to Lewiston, Idaho.

Packing companies and teamsters responded to the needs of mining communities and residents of distant communities. Outfitted with mules and horses, they carried the food, clothing and tools demanded by the miners in Canyon City, Auburn and Baker City or the farmers along Crooked River and Ochoco Creek. Teamsters like Henry H. Wheeler braved blizzards in winter and scorching heat in summer to carry mail, passengers and freight across the Columbia Plateau and into the mountains of eastern Oregon.

Railroads heralded the most significant advances in transportation. Between 1855 and 1862, Joseph Ruckel and Harrison Olmstead laid the foundation. They hired men, secured a right-of-way, and constructed roadbed and trestles for a horse-drawn cart to travel their "railway" along the Oregon shore at the Cascade Rapids of the Columbia. They were locked in bitter competition with Bradford & Company, competitors on the north bank. Pressing against both firms was the Oregon Steam Navigation Company which had developed in the 1850s a significant hold on steamboat service on the lower Willamette and Columbia Rivers. In 1860, Jacob Kamm, John C. Ainsworth and other investors in the OSN Company incorporated, and, in rapid steps bought out the Bradfords, Ruckel, and Olmstead. Holding the critical sea-level portages through the Columbia Gorge, they were ready to craft a major transportation system. Within months, they accomplished their goal.

The OSN Company, one of the state's first large corporations, developed an intricate system of steamboats, portage railroads and freight lines that gave it a hold on much of the commerce of the Pacific Northwest. It also built Oregon's first railroad. In 1862, as word of rich mines in the interior hit the front pages of newspapers, Ainsworth was in San Francisco purchasing rails and a small locomotive, the Oregon Pony, for shipment to the Gorge. Within a few months, workers transformed the old cart-rail system of Ruckel and Olmstead into Oregon's first railroad line—a five-mile route from Tanner Creek to the head of the Cascades. Other crews had taken on the bigger task of building a railroad for 14 miles from The Dalles to Celilo. Although its investors sold a major interest to the Northern Pacific in 1872, they bought back the shares following the Panic of 1873. They finally sold out in 1880. Those who held stock in the OSN Company were worth millions. Their daring and commitment had played a major role in helping anchor Portland as a hub of commerce and trade in the Pacific Northwest.

Railroads provided critical links to Oregon towns. In many instances they created towns. In 1880, Henry Villard headed a group of investors who bought out the OSN Company. Their firm, the Oregon Railway & Navigation Company, built a railroad along the south bank of the Columbia east to the Umatilla River. In 1883, having gained control of the Northern Pacific, Villard created Oregon's first transcontinental link with the OR&N. His Oregon Short Line Railroad ran southeast over the Blue Mountains to Huntington and in 1884 joined a connection into Idaho to the Union Pacific. This provided a second transcontinental connection for the state.

Construction of the Oregon & California Railroad, a north-south line to run from Portland to the Sacramento Valley, was a long-desired goal but its completion proved frustrating. Driven by a fabulous land grant of nearly five million acres from Congress, rival companies vied for the right to construct the route. Ben Holladay, operator of the Overland Mail and the Pacific Mail Steamship Company, ultimately prevailed. He formed the Oregon & California Railroad Company, sold bonds and began building. The line reached Roseburg in 1872, and then stopped. Bad times in national finances were part of the problem. Poor potentials for returns on exceedingly expensive construction into the Rogue River Valley and over the Siskiyou Mountains were another. Construction resumed in 1882, and ultimately linked the line into the Southern Pacific system in California.

The primary lines of the OR&N to the interior and the O&C through the western Oregon valleys encouraged logging, lumber manufacturing, export of wool and livestock, and sale of fruit, cereal crops, and other agricultural commodities to a vastly expanded market. The primary lines also encouraged two generations of smaller operators such as T. Egenton Hogg to dream of connecting units or even of new transcontinental linkages. Hogg managed in the 1880s to build a line from salt water at Yaquina City over the Coast Range and east via the Santiam as far as Detroit. The route of his Oregon Pacific Railroad appeared on maps in the 1890s, but it never reached the Deschutes or the Harney Basin, where speculators laid out towns in anticipation of its arrival.

The pieces were mostly in place by the latter 19th century for the state to sustain steady growth. Oregon had a resource-dependent economy driven by exploitation of fish, timber, minerals and agricultural lands. The state had steamboats, stage lines, pack teams, and railroads to serve residents of small towns as well as emerging cities. Oregon's population grew steadily. At statehood in 1859, Oregon had 52,465 residents. The figure more than tripled to 174,768 in 1880, and reached 413,536 in 1900.

Troubled Times

Discontents stirred in the hearts and minds of Oregonians in the last three decades of the 19th century. Life left some feeling cheated. Hard work did not bring sufficient wages or sale of farm commodities to secure a decent living. Many jobs took place in the midst of danger in poorly lighted sawmills, dust-filled coal mines, slippery canneries,or woolen mills with whirling spindles. Loggers confronted falling trees, flying cables, surging freshets and wretched living conditions in the camps where they lived. Clerks were underpaid and labored six days a week in monotonous jobs where they had neither health nor retirement plans and little prospect for advancement. Women attended academies, public schools, normal schools, colleges and universities, but male Oregonians refused to grant them the right to vote. Too many, it seemed, coped with alcoholic husbands who plundered the egg and butter money for a few more coins to spend on "demon liquor."

The disenchanted found inspiration for reconstructing their world. Ideologies beckoned alluringly and became part of an interesting mix of forces that set the stage for significant changes in Oregon. They ranged from arguments for women's suffrage to the pleas of the Christian Women's Temperance Union to control, if not suspend, the manufacture and sale of alcoholic beverages. The ideologies ran from economic and social theories to racist and bigoted attacks on minorities and immigrants. Many suggested political action might solve a state's or a nation's problems in a time of increasing industrialization.

California journalist Henry George promoted a simple solution to destitution. He argued in *Progress and Poverty* (1879) that the United States could eradicate poverty by implementing a tax of 100 percent on the "unearned increment," the inflationary value of real estate. The redistribution of the "single tax," he said, could meet need and solve societal problems. Tens of thousands read his book and became "single taxers."

Edward Bellamy's *Looking Backward* (1887) intrigued others. Bellamy used a shallow plot line about a man who fell into a mesmeric trance in 1887—a time of labor strife, urban pollution, slums and poverty—and who awakened in 2000. He found a reconstructed American society and economy with abundant prosperity and peace. All had changed through the miracle of "nationalism." In Bellamy's world the solution was government ownership of all means of production, transportation, housing and basic utilities.

Hard rock miners listened to the speakers from the Knights of Labor and the Western Federation of Miners. Many were not happy with their lot. Coal miners on Oregon's southwest coast endured low wages, explosions, and horrendous working conditions. Men extracting quicksilver in Douglas County slowly poisoned themselves tending the furnaces to produce flasks of mercury. Gold miners labored hundreds of feet below ground in the quartz deposits of the Bohemia Mining District in the Western Cascades and in mine shafts in the Blue and Wallowa Mountains of eastern Oregon. They were inspired by the prospect of forming unions and joining with fellow miners to wrest better pay and safer working conditions from the companies for which they labored.

Thousands of farmers turned first to the Patrons of Husbandry, joining Granges, engaging in the rituals of the organization, and pressing the legislature to meet the needs of agrarians. Others joined the Northwestern Alliance, a nonpartisan organization of farmers who hoped for reform. Alliance members and Grangers lobbied for collection and publication of agricultural statistics, strengthening of education at Oregon Agricultural College in Corvallis, development of experimental farms to test crops, breeds of livestock, and the impact of fertilizer and chemical sprays. And not a few heard about Mary Elizabeth Lease of Kansas, who told farmers in America's heartland that they should "raise less corn and more hell!"

Many agrarians embraced the People's Party. In 1892, its platform attempted to create an agenda to meet their needs. The populists endorsed limits on immigration, government ownership of railroads, telegraph and telephone, free coinage of silver to stimulate western mining, secret ballot, direct election of senators, and the subtreasury system whereby the government would buy unsold farm commodities, hold them, and then unload the products on the world market. Farmers would receive subtreasury notes—backed by the government—when they deposited potatoes, wheat, barley or apples at the federal warehouse—and could pay off their loans. William Hope Harvey's *Coin's Financial School* (1892) made the case for expanding the amount of money in circulation. Professor Coin argued that if the federal government would purchase and coin all available silver, the nation's economy could be corrected, farmers could pay off the mortgages for steam tractors and combines, and prosperity would return.

As these ideas swept through the newspapers, out of the mouths of speakers, and through books, they found believers. In 1890, Oregon had 2,555 men employed in logging and log transportation, 1,962 working in sawmills, 2,756 engaged in fishing or the oyster harvest, 2,308 mining, and 17,316 working as agricultural laborers. Tens of thousands more Oregonians lived on family farms. Men rode the range to tend cattle, sheep and horses, while women preserved food and cooked huge meals at roundup and shearing times. The farm population—owners and hired laborers—endured continuous work, dark nights, isolation, taxes on their lands, and uncertainty.

In 1889, many of the discontented met in Salem to form the Union Party. The meeting drew Prohibition advocates, members of the Knights of Labor, and the interest of Democrat Sylvester Pennoyer, seeking another term as governor. This was the atmosphere of social and political discontent that brought Oregonians to the People's Party. Hundreds turned out for rallies to meet General James B. Weaver, populist candidate for president. Abigail Scott Duniway, continuing her unrelenting campaign for women's suffrage, in 1892 introduced Mary Elizabeth Lease, the "Kansas Pythoness" and populist stump speaker, to an eager audience in Portland. Duniway's 1894 speech to an estimated 2,800 strikers inspired some to call her the "Patrick Henry of the Northwest" and led her brother, editor of *The Oregonian,* to refuse to print the text of her address.

While the Republicans and Democrats continued their hold on the majority of state offices, they found populists among their ranks in the legislature. Oregon Democrats got the reform message in the 1890s. Historian Dorothy O. Johansen quoted the saying "Scratch a Western Democrat and you find a Populist," an apt assessment of the Democrats' embrace of free silver, banking reform, income tax, and reform in government.

Oregon government needed change. Oregon Senator John Hipple Mitchell, a slippery man when it came to wives and influence peddling, reportedly said: "Ben Holladay's politics are my politics and what Ben Holladay wants I want." Holladay's hold on regional transportation systems and Mitchell's retainer as legal counsel for both the Oregon & California Railroad and the Northern Pacific left little doubt about the senator's loyalties. He may have been elected by the legislature, but he appeared to be in the pocket of special interests.

Frustrated Oregonians also turned to the pathetic performance of the builders of the state's military wagon roads. The grants locked up hundreds of thousands of acres in checkerboard sections on both margins of the traces and, by the 1890s, many of the holdings had passed to out-of-state owners. The grant for the Coos Bay Wagon Road—105,120 acres—passed quickly into the hands of speculators little interested in the road or its operation. For a time, Californians Leland Stanford, Mark Hopkins, Charles Crocker and Collis P. Huntington owned much of the grant. Other portions went to the Southern Oregon Improvement Company, a pool of investors in Boston and New Bedford, Massachusetts. Edward Martin of San Francisco formed the Eastern Oregon Land Company when he secured 450,000 acres of the land grant for The Dalles-Boise Military Wagon Road.

By not taking title to the grants, the owners avoided taxation, yet no settler could homestead or purchase the land from the General Land Office. A few Oregonians perpetrated unblushing frauds in the scramble for properties under the Swamp Lands Act. Ostensibly the law encouraged reclamation and irrigation. It created, however, a situation where unscrupulous public officials conspired with speculators to gain ownership of tidelands, lush lake margins and even dry ground. Plunderers also took advantage of the 1887 decision of the legislature to sell school lands, sections 16 and 36, in each township. Had the lands or revenues gone into a school fund, the endowment could have financed public education in Oregon in perpetuity.

In the 1890s, neither the ideologues nor the political activists carried the day. Society, business and political affairs continued much as usual. The times of discontent, however, set the stage for change. Ideas circulated that posed the prospect for deep-seated reform. All that was needed was some principled leadership, public indignation with the corruption, and the will to try something new.

The Oregon System

William U'Ren was a quiet, contemplative man. Little in his countenance or demeanor betrayed the inner fire that drove his determination to change public participation in Oregon government. A single-tax advocate, U'Ren moved on to embrace the ideas of James W. Sullivan, author of *Direct Legislation by the Citizenship Through the Initiative and Referendum* (1892). If U'Ren could empower common citizens, he could wage war on vested interests, corruption, and the tensions that set classes against each other. U'Ren jettisoned the single tax, embraced Sullivan's philosophy, converted to populism, and in 1897, gained a seat in the legislature as a candidate of the People's Party. U'Ren was in a position to cut a deal because populists held 13 critical votes to swing power in the legislature.

The time for dealing was at hand. Senator John H. Mitchell, despised by many, came out firmly for the Republican platform and the gold standard. Jonathan Bourne, Jr., a Republican and silver mine owner, saw a chance to dump Mitchell, provided he could win populist votes. U'Ren set the price: initiative, referendum, voter registration, and an elections procedure law. Bourne bought the package but had to play a cat-and-mouse game in what was known as the "Holdup of '97." Bourne, U'Ren, and others forged a coalition and blocked the House from organizing. The Committee on Credentials declined to report, the anti-Mitchell representatives refused to take their oaths of office, and the Mitchell forces could not elect him, lacking a quorum in the House. U'Ren and Bourne pushed through each of the promised measures. By a cumbersome process, the legislature twice approved a constitutional amendment and, after ratification by a resounding public vote in 1902, Oregonians instituted the initiative and referendum, having amended the state constitution for the first time since 1859.

The combination of voter commitment to enact long-needed laws and the ability to do so with the initiative helped propel Oregon to national attention as a state leading in progressivism. The largely nonpartisan Oregon System, as it was heralded, addressed the accumulated social evils that had grown in numbers and complexity. The means were at hand to make government more efficient, honest, and responsive to human need.

Oregonians tallied important enactments: Direct Primary Law (1904), extension of initiative and referendum to local laws, city home rule, indictment by grand jury, taxes on telephone, telegraph, and railroad companies (all 1906), a recall amendment to the State Constitution, the Corrupt Practices Act (both 1908), three-fourths verdict in civil cases, and employers' liability act (both 1910), women's suffrage, prohibition on private employment of convict labor, eight-hour day on public works (all 1912), presidential preference primary (1913), Prohibition, and an eight-hour day and room ventilation for women workers (both 1914). Other laws abolished capital punishment, the infamous Oregon Boot, a heavy manacle attached to legs of prisoners, and required publication of the *Oregon Blue Book*.

The Oregon Land Fraud trials captured local and national interest. Francis Heney, special federal prosecutor, brought to justice 33 who had pillaged the federal lands, state school lands and the timbered resources of the Siletz Indian Reservation. The kingpin of the Oregon Land Fraud Ring, Stephen A. D. Puter, penned in his prison cell *Looters of the Public Domain* (1908), a tell-all book with portraits of his co-conspirators and copies of documents confirming their criminal acts. Heney's prosecutions cleaned out many of the personnel of the General Land Office; twice indicted, but failed to convict, Binger Hermann, an Oregonian and former commissioner of the General Land Office in Washington, D.C.; and obtained prison sentences for Senator John H. Mitchell and Congressman John N. Williamson.

Oregon governors George E. Chamberlain, who served from 1903 to 1909, and Oswald West, who served from 1911 to 1915, were in office during the era of progressivism and each, in a nonpartisan manner, helped facilitate the Oregon System. To persuade the legislature that he intended for progressive reform to prevail, in 1911, West vetoed 63 bills. When good legislation failed, he saw that it surfaced as initiative measures. As a consequence, Oregonians gained a workers' compensation act, banking laws, and a Public Utility Commission. By executive order in 1913, West declared that Oregon beaches were public highways and set the precedent for the much-litigated but protected right of public access to the entire state shoreline. He gave full authority to his secretary, Fern Hobbs, and sent her with members of the National Guard to Copperfield, a notorious boom town on the railroad in Baker County. With a declaration of martial law on January 1, 1914, she closed all saloons and houses of prostitution. She left the guardsmen to monitor the situation. West never minced words. In his reminiscences he wrote about Oregon's land fraud ring: "These looters of the public domain—working with crooked federal and state officials—through rascality and fraud, gained title to thousands of acres of valuable, publicly-owned timber lands, and at minimum prices." West pounded them, even when penning his recollections in 1950.

Progressivism touched Oregon in another way. In 1907, Congress considered a crucial agricultural appropriations bill. Powerful lobbyists for timber companies persuaded Senator Charles Fulton from Astoria to attach to it an amendment rescinding presidential authority to create any more forest reserves in the Pacific Northwest under the Forest Reserve Act of 1891. In less than ten days, Gifford Pinchot, new head of the U.S. Forest Service, and President Theodore Roosevelt poured over maps and identified millions of acres of critical forests. Roosevelt exercised the last hours of his executive authority and created the "Midnight Reserves." Oregon's national forests multiplied severalfold by the stroke of a pen and the willpower of two conservationists.

The Oregon System was the creative response to a mix of ideologies and discontents. It broke the power of many special interests and old political coalitions. It became a model for the rest of the country and was emulated in dozens of states and cities drawing inspiration from the power of a determined citizenry.

Mixed Blessings

Progressivism waned with the onset of World War I. Oregonians and other Americans began to tire of crusades. The entry into the Great War tested the resolution to continue problem-solving. Peace and commitment to its maintenance were casualties of both the war and the postwar world.

Industrial strife mounted when worker expectations remained unrealized as prosperity increased after 1900. Alienated, fearful and distrustful of the establishment, some workers gravitated toward the Socialist Party and militant labor unions. The West Coast Shingle Weaver's Union as chartered by the American Federation of Labor and the International Union of Shingle Weavers, Sawmill Workers and Woodsmen sought recruits. The Industrial Workers of the World grew by the thousands when disgruntled loggers and mill workers enlisted in its ranks. Known to most by its initials, IWW, the union was perceived by management as the "I Won't Work" contingent. Free speech fights, confrontations, strikes, and demands for better working conditions and higher wages became the tense legacy of workers and management on the eve of World War I.

Illustrative of the tensions were the vigilante actions of the businessmen of Bandon. In 1913, enraged by the publication of *Social Justice*, they seized its editor and publisher. Dr. Bailey K. Leach had used his newspaper to denounce vigilantism, the Boy Scouts of America as a paramilitary organization, and perceived thought control in the public library, which refused to accession Socialist literature. A mob grabbed Dr. Leach, placed a noose around his neck and "deported" him from Bandon. Beaten and left barefoot on the North Spit at Coos Bay, having been compelled to kneel and kiss the American flag, he walked through the sand dunes and up the Umpqua River to the office of Governor Oswald West to complain of his treatment. An investigation mounted by the State Supreme Court led to the disbarment of an attorney in Marshfield. Leach was lucky. When IWW organizer Wesley Everest was deported in similar fashion from Coos Bay, he went to Centralia, Washington, to promote the union. In 1919, he was seized by a mob, castrated, and hanged from a railroad bridge. No one was charged with Everest's murder. To many, the rousing hymn of the IWW, "Hallelujah, I'm a Bum," justified violations of civil liberties and the law.

To counter the growth of labor unions and the Socialist Party, the federal government took control of spruce production in western Oregon and Washington. Deemed an essential material for airplane manufacturing, spruce became the assignment of the U.S. Army's Spruce Production Division. It assumed responsibilities for logging, lumbering, and filling orders. In 1917, General Brice P. Disque took command of troops who erected mills at Coquille and Toledo, Oregon and Vancouver and Port Gamble, Washington. The Spruce Division produced 54 million board feet of airplane wing beams in Oregon and left a modern electrical sawmill and extensive railroad network in Lincoln County, which, in time, passed into private ownership.

The federal government also created the Loyal Legion of Loggers and Lumbermen. Ostensibly an employer-employee union, the 4-Ls recruited thousands of workers who pledged not to strike and to help the nation in its production of war materials. The Emergency Fleet Corporation, a federal agency, contracted with yards to turn out vessels for the war effort. Shipbuilders in Portland, Astoria, Tillamook and Marshfield produced steel and wooden-hull vessels for the EFC. Fort Stevens at Warrenton took on new life since its primary construction during the Civil War and Spanish-American War. Troops drilled and trained on its parade grounds; some departed with other Oregonians for service on the battlefields of Europe.

World War I was a mixed blessing for Oregon. Initially, it stimulated the economy with the production of war materials, foodstuffs, and ships, but it set the stage for the collapse of shipbuilding and the falloff of lumber production in the 1920s. Everywhere were signs of trouble: few housing starts, instability in banking, speculation in the stock market and migration. More than 50,000 people left Oregon following World War I. Opportunities beckoned elsewhere.

In a sense, Oregon made their transit possible. Between 1911 and 1922, state, county, and local funds helped build the Columbia River Highway. The Columbia Gorge section, designed by Samuel Lancaster, an engineer brought in from Tennessee, ran eastward with gentle grades and sensitive integration with the environment to open access to scenic waterfalls, hiking trails, and spectacular vistas between Portland and The Dalles. Modern construction techniques, including steel-reinforced poured-concrete bridges, created the region's first paved highway. In 1913, Oregon created the State Highway Commission. Four years later, it expanded its membership and the legislature began steady appropriations to "Get Oregon Out of the Mud." The "good roads" campaign took on real life in 1919 when Oregon enacted a gasoline tax. The first state in the country to pay for roads through a gas tax, Oregon embraced the automobile age and began construction of the Pacific Highway. From its crossing at the Interstate Bridge across the Willamette, the route ran south via the Willamette, Umpqua, and Rogue Valleys to California. Paved in concrete, its gentle course ran through productive farmlands, crossed rivers on major bridges, wended its way up the slopes of the Siskiyous and confirmed Oregon's commitment to good roads.

Road construction led to legislation in 1921, promoted by Governor Ben Olcott, to authorize the State Highway Commission to acquire rights-of-way for scenic conservation and roadside forest preserves. In 1922, the state accepted the gift of Sarah Helmick State Park in Polk County. These actions received legislative direction in 1925 with authorization to acquire lands for park purposes for waysides and natural areas. Governor I. L. Patterson, in 1929, named the first State Park Commission, which worked closely with Samuel H. Boardman, the state parks engineer, for building a land base of state-owned park properties.

Although highway construction helped one sector of the economy, the advent of automobile traffic sounded the death knell for steamboats on the rivers and, in time, Oregon's electrical railroad system. The Oregon Electric Railway operated daily trains over 122 miles of track by 1912 between Portland and Eugene. A "No Soot-No Cinders" route, the commuter line also ran west to Forest Grove. The Southern Pacific's Red Electric began connections in 1914. It ran from Portland to Corvallis via Lake Oswego and Newberg. A branch line swung west to Hillsboro, Forest Grove and McMinnville. For a time, travelers had the choice of ten departures from Portland and at least two from McMinnville. The efficiency of the electrics and the interurban lines was eclipsed by cars and buses. The 1920s were a time of transition. Smells of draft animals and the clacking sound of horseshoes mixed with the swift movement of electrical railroads and gasoline-driven cars and trucks. In time, the familiar

"Galloping Goose," the solitary passenger-mail car that ran on many of Oregon's short lines, disappeared. Residents of Friend, Shaniko, Prairie City, Cherry Grove, Bull Run, and other small towns would have to travel by road, not rail.

Wartime stress, emphasis on patriotism, distrust of German-Americans, eugenics campaigns championed by Dr. Bethenia Owens-Adair, and anti-Catholic bigotry created fertile ground in Oregon for the rise of the American Protective Association, Federation of Patriotic Societies, and the Ku Klux Klan. With a combined membership estimated at more than 64,000 Oregonians, these organizations fed on the fear and distrust of residents in a period of social flux and uncertainty. Although minorities were few in number, racism and bigotry were imported ideas. They came with newcomers from other parts of the country and grew in soil that already nurtured suspicion and tendencies to vigilante action. Chapters of the Ku Klux Klan formed in Tillamook, Medford, Eugene and Portland, as well as many other towns. Robed Klansmen paraded in the streets, ignited crosses on hillsides, nailed American flags to the doors of Catholic schools, and intimidated African-Americans.

The Klan, FOPS, and Scottish Rite Masons sponsored a bill, passed in 1922 in the general election, to compel all children to attend public schools. The overtly anti-Catholic measure threatened to close all parochial schools and military academies. The state Supreme Court ruled the law unconstitutional in 1924, and the U.S. Supreme Court concurred in 1925. The Ku Klux Klan found a strange champion in the Oregon legislature. Kaspar K. Kubli, speaker of the House of Representatives, happened to possess winning initials and became a rallying point for efforts to drive through the Alien Property Act of 1923. The law prohibited Japanese from purchasing or leasing land in Oregon. The legislature also passed a law forbidding wearing of sectarian clothing, namely priestly vestments or nuns' habits, in classrooms.

A number of historians have written about the flaws of the 1920s and the nation's serious engagement with public-sanctioned bigotry. While some of the laws were overt, many more went on quietly but consistently. Oregon's indigenous people, who became citizens of the United States in 1924, were forbidden to purchase alcohol, though some applied for a special card that certified their entitlement to drink. Oregon realtors declined to sell homes in certain areas to minorities. Oregon developers wrote into deeds restrictive covenants that prohibited holding ducks and geese and sale of the house and land to anyone of Chinese or Japanese ancestry. Large neighborhoods of Portland—Garthwick, Dunthorpe, Eastmoreland, Westmoreland—and Lake Oswego were kept "white" for decades by subtle but effective discrimination.

One of the hard-fought agendas of the 1920s was the encouragement of public power. In 1930, Oregonians approved the creation of public utility districts. The action shook some of the well-established utility companies, for they now faced the prospect that if their rates and actions were out of line with public interest, voters could set up their own company, and vie for hydropower rights on a stream or build a sawdust-fired electrical plant and offer service to consumers.

The 1920s were a period of rapid adjustment from wartime preparedness and boom to an uneven and deteriorating economy. Oregon moved from progressivism to the rise of selfish interests and secret societies that threatened liberties and promoted bigotry. Yet, in spite of following strange paths, the state laid the foundation of a fine highway system, state parks, and competitive rates for electrical power.

The Great Depression

On October 29, 1929, a calamity rocked the United States. Within hours the stock market, buoyed by speculation and unreasonable expectations, plunged into the abyss of "Black Tuesday." The onset of the Great Depression meant little to tens of thousands of Oregonians. They were already living in depressed circumstances, trying to make a go of arid homesteads, stump farms, or underpaid jobs in sawmills. Those who had savings, however, felt the debacle acutely. Banks went bankrupt. In spite of handsome buildings and facades of stability, white marble counters, brass grills at the teller cages, and hulking vaults, their resources were vulnerable and they fell by the droves, wiping out the accumulated resources of depositors. Bank failures led to foreclosures on homes, farms, and businesses and contributed to the general malaise that had seized the country.

In spite of his reputation as a humanitarian, President Herbert Hoover, a sometime Oregonian who had grown up in Newberg, wrestled unsuccessfully with checking the economic free-fall. Hoover was trapped both by his political philosophy and by problems so complex that no one really had a viable solution for them.

So, in 1933, the nation turned to a pragmatist—Franklin Delano Roosevelt—who also did not have solutions but who had promised to try to remedy the Great Depression through bold actions. Roosevelt began deliberately in March. He declared a national "bank holiday," closing all financial institutions across the country so that federal inspectors could examine their books. If a bank reopened, it would do so because the government found it sound. It could be trusted. If a bank's affairs were beyond redemption, it remained closed. Roosevelt also spoke to all Americans—including hundreds of thousands of Oregonians who, since 1921, had purchased radios. In a series of "fireside chats" broadcast from the White House, he waged a campaign to build confidence. He promoted the reform, relief, and recovery agendas of the New Deal.

While few believe the Democrat programs of the 1930s effectively turned around the Great Depression, they were of immense consequence to Oregon. Through deficit spending and passing on payment obligations to succeeding generations, Congress authorized programs that helped change the face of Oregon. The Beer Act of March, 1933 set the stage for repeal of Prohibition and permitted hop-raisers and brewers like Blitz-Weinhard to resume production. Far more significant, however, was the creation that same month of the Civilian Conservation Corps. Intended to provide unemployment relief for several million young Americans, the CCC developed projects in public land states like Oregon. The CCC established base camps and spike camps in most of the national forests and began a remarkable program of construction. The workers cut trails; built roads; constructed bridges; built campgrounds with handsome log facilities for cooking, eating, and public meetings; laid telephone wires; constructed drift fences to manage cattle; built log corrals; enclosed springs; dammed creeks to create small reservoirs; constructed guard stations and ranger stations; and carried the materials board-by-board to lofty peaks for fire lookouts. From Hells Canyon to the Chetco River and from the Oriana Corral on the Fremont National Forest to the campground at Eagle Creek in the Columbia Gorge, the CCC made enduring, handsome improvements on federal lands.

Similarly, the Works Projects Administration drew unemployed architects, stone masons, painters, weavers, metal workers, plumbers, and artisans into special Oregon projects. The WPA built Timberline Lodge, a dramatic recreation hotel, on the southern slopes of Mount Hood. WPA artisans created towering murals, iron gates, and furniture for the new library on the campus of the University of Oregon. WPA laborers erected post offices, customs buildings, and federal buildings from Burns to Tillamook. Not since Andrew Carnegie's matching-funds projects for public libraries in the 1910s had Oregon seen such a profusion of public structures.

The Public Works Administration and the Public Buildings Administration worked with the WPA in other ways to transform Oregon. Projects included a city hall in Canby, a dramatic capitol and state library in Salem, an armory in Klamath Falls, a high school in Corvallis, a dormitory at the State School for the Blind, a sewage disposal plant in Medford, and five stunning bridges spanning major estuaries on the Oregon coast. The bridges, completed in 1936, cost $5.4 million. In the midst of the Great Depression, Oregon embarked on grading and paving Highway 101 to forge another important transportation link.

The WPA also employed teachers, lawyers, and architects. It mounted the Oregon Folklore Project, the Oregon Writers' Program and the Inventory of the County Archives of Oregon. These workers published *Oregon: End of the Trail* (1940), *Mount Hood: A Guide* (1940), the annual *Oregon Almanac: A Handbook of Fact and Fancy, Oregon Oddities*—a magazine used in public schools—and 14 of a projected 35 descriptive guides to records in county courthouses. Each of the guides included an overview of county history based upon a review of the archives. In many instances, these were the first historical assessments of Oregon counties. Working almost in tandem with the WPA were drafters, historians and photographers engaged in the Historic American Buildings Survey. They compiled information, including measured drawings, on nearly a hundred significant structures in Oregon.

The New Deal had a grassroots impact in Oregon. This was most dramatically confirmed when, in 1935, Congress funded construction of a project that Roosevelt had promised during his 1932 campaign swing through the state. Bonneville Dam, one of the great engineering marvels of the early 20th century, was to span the Columbia River at the western end of the Gorge. Its massive reservoir would back up waters to The Dalles. Its locks would lift ships and barges for easy transit to the grain elevators of the western plateau. Its turbines would generate massive amounts of electricity to power industry and diversify the region's economy. Above all, construction of the dam would provide employment for 4,000 laborers and the multiplier effect would generate thousands more jobs to feed, house and provide services to these workers and their families. Because navigation was a critical element with the building of the locks, the Army Corps of Engineers secured project supervision. Initial estimates for the dam, lock, powerhouse and federal townsites for management personnel ran to $81 million.

As the dam neared completion, the Bonneville Power Administration in 1937 took over responsibility for construction of transmission lines and marketing of power to utility companies, public utility districts, and industrial users such as aluminum plants in Troutdale and The Dalles. In 1941, the BPA hired Woody Guthrie to compose and sing songs celebrating power development on the Columbia River. Guthrie's 17 songs included the popular "Roll On, Columbia." Its lyrics touted the New Deal achievements:

"At Bonneville now there are ships in the locks,
The waters have risen and cleared all the rocks,
Shiploads of plenty will steam past the docks,
So roll on, Columbia, roll on."

The New Deal touched the lives of Oregonians in other ways. The Taylor Grazing Act in 1934 changed the free-for-all of livestock using the public domain. Henry Gerber and local ranchers in the Langell Valley of Klamath County were acutely aware of the need to allocate grazing rights. The Bonanza Grazing Unit, headed by Gerber, was the first organized in the United States under the Taylor Act. In time, the law brought 152 million acres under the U.S. Grazing Service and called for local boards of landowners to allocate the animal units per month allowed in national forests or on lands administered by the General Land Office. In 1946, Congress merged the land office and the grazing service to create the Bureau of Land Management.

The Soil Conservation Service, created in 1936, provided counsel and assistance to farmers faced with erosion by wind and water on the Columbia Plateau. The Production Credit Association worked with farmers to scale down mortgage payments by extending the length of their loans. The Federal Housing Administration, set up in 1934, provided low-interest loans to try to encourage home construction. The Bankhead-Jones Act of 1937 provided federal dollars to buy out impoverished homesteaders and transform the lands into federal holdings. The National Grasslands between Madras and Prineville was a product of the Bankhead-Jones Act. The Rural Electrification Administration worked with private utilities and public utility districts to extend lines to remote areas. By the late 1930s, thousands of rural Oregonians for the first time had electrical service and would be able to use a radio, refrigerator, vacuum cleaner, electric stove, washing machine and lights.

The Great Depression took a toll on Oregon but created a setting for massive improvement of infrastructure. Roads, bridges, buildings, dams, locks, powerhouses, electrical transmission lines, recreation facilities and range management were an impressive tally of accomplishments. While many Oregonians were driven into a subsistence lifestyle of "making do" with homemade clothing, a garden and austerity, the federal projects had infused confidence, generated payrolls, and laid the foundations for new industries and much wider use of public lands in the state.

World War II

The attack on Pearl Harbor on December 7, 1941, pulled the United States out of neutrality and plunged the nation again into world war. Because Oregon lay along the nation's Pacific Coast, it was considered in the war zone. The consequences were almost immediate. To create a wartime mentality as well as to prepare against attack, residents of coastal communities faced nightly blackouts. Block wardens monitored compliance. Shades and blankets covered windows and many painted over the upper half of their car headlamps. Volunteers joined the Ground Observer Corps to log the make and identity of airplanes. Soldiers maintained coastal patrols, supplementing Coast Guard personnel in their watch of the sea. Jeeps ran along the beaches to isolated dugouts where foot patrols with dogs stood duty.

War preparedness had begun in the late 1930s with scrap drives. Schoolchildren competed to see who could tally the heaviest pile of metal. The occasional school that located an old logging railroad locomotive surged to top honors. With the declaration of war, Oregonians confronted rationing of tires, gasoline, meat, sugar, and clothing. For those who lived far from town, rationing necessitated careful trip planning.

Executive Order 9066 of February 19, 1942, fell heavily on the Japanese-American population of Oregon. Although most were American citizens and many had sons, brothers, and fathers who had enlisted or were drafted into military service, the families of Japanese background living west of the Cascades in Oregon were placed under curfew and ordered to report to evacuation centers, preliminaries to removal to distant relocation camps. Over 120,000 Japanese-Americans from Oregon, Washington, and California endured relocation. Japanese-Americans in Hawaii—more fully in the war zone—were exempted from relocation. Those who were removed, lost homes, crops, farm animals, property, bank accounts and personal possessions.

The war gripped the United States and Oregonians. Dozens of towns erected permanent billboards that carried the names of citizens killed in defense of their country. Oregon had 2,826 wartime deaths and over 5,000 wounded. Tensions rose when a Japanese submarine surfaced off the mouth of the Columbia River and on June 21, 1942, fired 17 shells at Fort Stevens. Concern rose again on September 9 of the same year, when a small airplane, launched by a catapult from the deck of a Japanese submarine off Brookings, carried Nubuo Fujita and Shoji Okuda over the Siskiyou National Forest to drop incendiary bombs on Mount Emily. Oregon suffered civilian casualties on May 5, 1945, when participants in a church picnic near Bly poked an incendiary balloon that had floated across the Pacific. The device, intended to set forest fires, exploded and killed the minister's wife and five children.

A wartime economy helped pull Oregon out of the Great Depression. Federal expenditures mounted dramatically. The investment included facilities, construction salaries, and assembling of large numbers of personnel who needed housing, food, clothing and other services. The U.S. Army built Camp Adair north of Corvallis and Camp Abbott on the upper Deschutes River south of Bend. These troop-training facilities served thousands of recruits. Camp Adair even included a fake Japanese village where soldiers practiced assaults should they reach the main islands of Japan. The Umatilla Army Depot near Hermiston became a sprawling repository for munitions in hundreds of semisubterranean silos. The Army also constructed hangars and airfields at Portland, Astoria, Newport, North Bend and Floras Lake. The U.S. Navy built the Tongue Point Naval Station at Astoria, and at the Tillamook Naval Air Station, erected two of the largest wood-frame buildings in the world. Blimps, stationed at Blimperon 33, moved out of these massive hangars and glided up and down the coast to patrol for enemy ships and submarines.

The electricity from Bonneville, dubbed by some in 1939 as the "dam of doubt," moved through the BPA grid to aluminum plants from Longview to Spokane. Inexpensive electricity heated the smelters to process bauxite into rolls of aluminum, which moved by rail to the Boeing manufacturing plants on Puget Sound. There was no doubt about the dramatic rise of employment where nearly 50,000 workers by 1944 were able to produce 16 airplanes every 24 hours. In Portland and nearby Vancouver, Henry J. Kaiser's shipyards employed an estimated 100,000 workers. Men and women worked side by side to build "Baby Flattops" and "Liberty Ships." By 1945, some 150,000 workers were engaged in 85 shipyards in Oregon and Washington.

Jobs in aluminum plants, shipyards, military bases, and lumber production for the war effort created a surge of migration. During World War II, an estimated 194,000 people moved into the state. For the first time, Oregon's African-American population grew substantially—in Portland increasing from 2,565 in 1940 to 25,000 in 1944. Drawn by jobs, steady salaries, and the area's reputation as a decent place to live, newcomers coped with inflated rents, shantytowns, camps, and trailer parks. In 1942, Edgar Kaiser met some of the housing problem by building Vanport on the south bank of the Columbia. With 35,000 residents, the community became Oregon's second largest town until destroyed in May, 1948, by breaking levees during a major flood. Public housing projects, dubbed "cardboard palaces" by some, met short-term needs and, in some instances, were used for years or were transformed into student housing on college campuses.

When World War II ended, Oregon was a different place. The economy was good, even when labor disputes erupted with the West Coast Longshoremen's Union. The federal projects of the 1930s created an extensive infrastructure for the use and enjoyment of national forests and the public domain. Many Oregonians had disposable income and savings. The future beckoned far more brightly than during the drab years of the Great Depression or the uncertainties of World War II.

Rapid Developments

Postwar Oregon prospered. Although housing was short, residents made do. The GI Bill provided funding for a generation eager for higher education but blocked from the opportunity because of the Great Depression and World War II. College enrollments swelled as returning veterans and recent high school graduates settled down to earn degrees and pursue civilian careers. The state's college campuses grew in response to the increasing numbers of students. The legislature appropriated funds for new facilities at La Grande, Monmouth, Eugene, Klamath Falls and Corvallis. From its beginnings at Vanport College, Portland State University emerged as a new urban campus in the state's largest city. In addition, the state's private colleges and universities likewise grew in enrollments and transformed from their sectarian origins to independent liberal arts institutions.

Savings that had accumulated during the war, low-interest FHA loans, and dramatic population growth in California fueled a booming logging and lumbering economy. Between 1945 and 1990, the state became a national leader in manufacture of forest products. For decades, Coos Bay held the title as the world's largest lumber shipping port. Oregon sawmills' wigwam burners belching smoke and sawdust cinders and heavily laden log trucks were icons for a thriving industry.

The infrastructure of roads, guard stations and ranger stations—a legacy of labors by the CCC—improved forest access. The shift from custodial care of the national forests to full-scale harvest of timber was the most dramatic factor in the growth of logging and lumber manufacturing. Court rulings to take back the O&C Railroad grant in 1915 brought 2.3 million acres and an estimated 50 billion board feet of timber to federal control. In 1919, recapture of the Coos Bay Wagon Road grant brought back another 96,000 acres of virgin forest and 2.5 billion board feet of timber. The Stanfield Act of 1926 set a formula for the revenues, later revised in 1937 and 1953 by Congress. The final distribution called for 50 percent of the timber receipts from O&C and Coos Bay Wagon Road lands to go to western Oregon counties, 25 percent to the federal treasury, and 25 percent to the U.S. Forest Service or the BLM for reforestation. The demand for lumber and the vested interest of Oregon counties in securing income from the sale of trees from federally managed forests helped drive the boom in this segment of Oregon's economy.

Logging and lumbering enterprises were highly competitive. Small operators, known as gyppos, struggled to hold together their businesses while they moved from contract to contract, cutting logs, running small mills, and seizing a share of the market. Some, like Kenneth Ford of Roseburg Lumber Company, persevered and became major figures in the industry. Many more ran small operations, employed several dozen workers, and, when fortunes changed, closed out their operations. Outside capital flowed into Oregon after 1945. Weyerhaeuser Corporation, Menasha Corporation, Evans Products, and Georgia-Pacific were among several firms with national connections that turned to old timber holdings or purchased unlogged forests from Oregon companies. These larger firms embraced new technologies and products, developing plywood and particleboard in addition to dimensional lumber. They created cost savings through greater efficiencies and research and development.

While some enterprises were thriving, others struggled. The salmon catch and pack in Oregon canneries peaked in the 1890s and headed steadily downward. Efforts to check the trend, especially in the Columbia River, led to construction of the state's Central Hatchery in 1909 at Bonneville and in 1926 to abolition of fishwheels. The hulking fishwheels, turned by the river's current, had scooped up tons of fish. While horse-drawn seine nets and mesh fishtraps at the river's mouth may have taken a greater toll on the salmon, the fishwheels were a visible symbol of overharvest. After 1950, Oregon's fish canneries steadily diminished; the last closed in 1979. The great silvery horde of fish no longer filled the streams. Conservation of remaining stocks dictated sharp restrictions on commercial and sport fishing.

Dam construction, an enduring commitment of federal investment in Oregon, moved steadily forward. It took a tremendous toll on anadromous fish, but so did logging, urbanization, and agricultural activities. During the 1950s and 1960s, the Army Corps of Engineers had oversight of massive new projects—The Dalles, John Day and McNary Dams on the main stem of the Columbia, several more dams upstream, and Oxbow and Brownlee Dams on the Snake River along Oregon's eastern border. Federal projects also checked the Willamette. Pre-1940 Corps projects had included Fern Ridge, Cottage Grove, and Dorena Reservoirs. Postwar construction, financed by multimillion-dollar congressional appropriations, built Detroit, Big Cliff, Green Peter, and Foster Dams on the Santiam forks; Lookout Point, Dexter, and Hills Creek Dams on the Middle Fork of the Willamette; Cougar and Blue River Dams in the McKenzie watershed; and Fall Creek Dam near Eugene. By 1960, these facilities had largely tamed the Willamette River, checking floodwaters and generating electricity.

Federal improvements touched Oregon in other significant ways. Beginning in the 1870s, renewing in the 1890s, and proceeding regularly through the 20th century, Congress made appropriations in the 1899 Rivers and Harbors Act for major construction in Oregon. Projects included jetties at the mouths of the Columbia, Yaquina, Coquille, and Coos Bay. Congress also funded the Celilo Canal and Locks, (1906–16), a complicated transportation system blasted through basalt to provide ship passage around Five Mile Rapids and Celilo Falls into the upper Columbia River. Congress regularly renewed or funded start-up projects that dredged channels, removed rocks, and led to construction of new jetties on most of Oregon's coastal estuaries. Singularly significant in the postwar era was the Interstate Highway Act of 1956. Billions of federal dollars began flowing back to the states, allowing construction in Oregon of nonstop freeways—I-5 running north and south through western Oregon valleys between Washington and California and I-84 running east and west from Portland to Boise, Idaho. These projects created not only payrolls but significant contributions to the state's economy through efficient shipment of commodities.

Postwar changes swept through Oregon agriculture. While cattle-raising and wheat production remained mainstays in eastern Oregon, specialized crops of alfalfa, sugar beets, and potatoes drew a number of farmers to focus their energies on lands watered by turn-of-the-century reclamation projects. Farmers in the Treasure Valley near Ontario, the upper Deschutes watershed, and the Klamath Basin tapped irrigation water to embark on these ventures. On Oregon's southwestern coast, cranberry production, founded in 1887, became important as Ocean Spray diversified its product line to include ruby-red juice fortified by Oregon cranberries. Walnuts, filberts and turkeys created income for farmers in Yamhill and Washington Counties. Pear, peach, apple, and cherry production prospered in the Hood River and Rogue River Valleys. Slowly, but steadily, grass seed and nursery products grew in acreage in the Willamette Valley. Rose bushes, irises, grafted fruit trees, and ornamental shrubs grew in the valley's fertile soils. Workers dug, baled, and shipped these specialty products to national markets. Venturesome investors cleared old prune orchards and forested hillsides, planted vineyards, and constructed wineries. A new industry found a good market for Oregon wines.

Tourism emerged as a major industry. Oregon's scenic beauty of mountains, forests, deserts and Pacific shoreline proved an irresistible attraction. Good roads, one of the largest state park systems in the country, restaurants, and hotels and motels facilitated the annual surge of visitors. Millions traveled Highway 101, exploring the cheese factory at Tillamook, gift shops in Lincoln City, and the Sea Lion Caves. They toured sawmills at North Bend, rode a mail boat on the Rogue River, or purchased salt water taffy, carved myrtlewood, seashells, and cranberry candy. Others flocked to the Shakespearean plays in Ashland, marveled at Crater Lake, went bow-and-arrow hunting for deer at Hart Mountain, skied at Mount Bachelor, stayed overnight at Timberline Lodge, took a jetboat into Hells Canyon, or visited the John Day Fossil Beds National Monument. Those who came to visit bought meals, lodging and keepsakes. They added to the state's prosperity.

Postwar Oregon was a troubled time for the state's Native Americans. Douglas O. McKay, former governor, had been appointed as Secretary of the Interior in the Eisenhower Cabinet. Believing strongly in economy in government and seeing the Bureau of Indian Affairs as an anachronism of inefficiency, McKay joined others in pressing to sever ties with tribes. House Concurrent Resolution 108 in 1952 stated that it was the sense of Congress that the federal government should set indigenous people free. Between 1954 and 1960, Congress terminated all government-to-government relationships with the Klamath and every tribe and band west of the Cascades in Oregon. The program required sale of reservation lands, issuance of deeds for individual trust lands, and curtailment of all BIA and Indian Health Service benefits. Then the momentum waned. Thousands of Oregon's native peoples had fallen into limbo as "terminated Indians." Finally in 1977, Senator Mark O. Hatfield introduced legislation to amend the situation for the Confederated Tribes of the Siletz. On a case-by-case basis, the terminated tribes sought and won, by 1989, the restoration of their federal relations. The road back was, for some, a frustrating journey of years of waiting, petitioning, and documenting their ongoing tribal life.

Elements of boom and bust coursed through Oregon in the years between 1945 and 1990. Booming conditions drove new construction and business prosperity in many small towns. Tens of thousands of new residents moved into the state. Yet, not all was well in Oregon. The measures were visible: diminishing runs of fish, a vast checkerboard of clearcuts on the sides of mountains, a Willamette River so fetid that only the foolhardy dared to swim in it, spread of cheat grass and Russian olive, and other invading species like shad, bass, and squawfish. It was time to consider the consequences of rapid development.

Taking Stock

In 1962, Thomas Lawson McCall, a journalist, caught the state's attention with a television documentary, *"Pollution in Paradise."* In his clipped, forceful narration and with compelling photography, McCall showed what had happened to the Willamette River. Sewage, industrial wastes, garbage, abandoned docks and warehouses, tires, and hulks of automobiles befouled a once pristine, fish-filled stream. Between 1850 and 1920, the Willamette had served as western Oregon's artery of commerce and transportation. Use had bred abuse and, almost without seeing it, Oregonians had transformed the stream into an open sewer.

Tom McCall was elected governor in 1966. Stressing an eleventh commandment, "Thou shalt not pollute," McCall, a Republican, forged a broad-based coalition to address the consequences of rapid development, growing population, and ecological changes in the state. McCall's ideas were not always popular and his commentary sometimes appeared quirky. His approach, however, was earnest and, for a majority, compelling. During his eight years in office, he and like-minded leaders—Stafford Hansell, a hogfarmer from Boardman, L. B. Day, a labor leader from Salem, and others—began a process of moving Oregonians from outright "ownership" of land to "stewardship."

The tally of accomplishments during the McCall years included creation of the Department of Environmental Quality (1969), extensive research and solution to Willamette Valley fieldburning, blocking of shipment of additional tons of nerve gas to the Umatilla Army Depot, creation of the Willamette Greenway—a 170-mile-long corridor of easements and park properties, the Bottle Bill (1971) requiring deposits on returnable beverage containers, and Senate Bill 100. This much-debated bill created the Land Conservation and Development Commission (1973). The LCDC moved every county and incorporated town into a system of statewide land-use planning. Hearings on draft goals and guidelines drew thousands of participants to meetings. Volunteers and staff hammered out a system for evaluating, in light of the statewide guidelines, comprehensive land-use plans required of all government entities. Repeatedly, critics tried to overturn the LCDC. Each time a majority of voters sustained the system. Oregonians had started to come to terms with the realities of growth and the responsibilities inherent in sustaining livability.

The 1990s were a sobering decade for dozens of small towns and for the thousands involved in logging and lumbering. The boom ended in the forest products industry. Shrill voices decried the Endangered Species Act of 1973 and charged that spotted owls and marbled murrelets were not worth jobs and payrolls. The reality was that Oregon had not attained sustained yield in management of forests and that overharvest, similar to overfishing, forced adjustment. Sawmills closed. Towns like Powers, West Fir, Oakridge, Swiss Home, Hines, Valsetz and Vernonia were shaken by the closures and departure of residents. Most communities adjusted. Some Oregonians, however, wrestled with difficulty when they discovered that the national forests and lands administered by the Bureau of Land Management—acreage on the other side of their fence—belonged to all the people of the United States, not the locals, and that interest groups thousands of miles away had a valid voice in crafting land policy and use of public resources.

The 1990s was also a decade of diversification in Oregon's economy. High-tech industries came of age. From modest beginnings in a garage in 1948, Howard Vollum and Jack Murdock built Tektronix, an electronics company, into one of the nation's largest companies by the mid-1980s. Oregon's reputation as a decent place to live with willing workers encouraged several corporations—among them Hewlett-Packard, Intel and Wacker Siltronics—to construct fabrication plants and manufacture computer components. These billion-dollar facilities contributed to a thriving urban Oregon economy. While many rural Oregonians struggled with survival, many urban Oregonians found good jobs in new industries. Phil Knight and Bill Bowerman, longtime track coach at the University of Oregon, transformed the tennis shoe into a styled, engineered icon of the "fitness generation." Their Nike Corporation grew by the 1990s into a major manufacturer and retailer of sports and casual clothing. Its distinctive "swoosh" logo appeared on the outfits of professional athletes, amateurs, and even great-grandmothers who found ease and comfort wearing nonlacing tennis shoes or fleece jogging outfits.

In 1984, residents of the state approved a lottery. It grew rapidly in popularity as new games and promotions increased player options. Gambling profits proved irresistible to legislators who appropriated them to meet costs of basic social services and education. In 1992, the Cow Creek Band of the Umpqua Tribe negotiated the first gaming compact with the governor under the Indian Gaming Regulatory Act. Within five years, the tribe was the second largest employer in Douglas County, operating a casino, restaurants, hotel, truck stop and other businesses at Canyonville. Other tribes followed. In 1998, Spirit Mountain Casino, owned by the Confederated Tribes of the Grand Ronde community, surpassed Multnomah Falls as the most visited traveler destination in Oregon.

Oregon had not solved all its problems. Adequate financing for education at all levels eluded legislators, governors, teachers' unions and students. Salmon recovery plans, at times, seemed more abundant than fish. Tribes, federal and state agencies, sport and commercial fishing organizations, and fish biologists all wrestled with finding ways to save remaining runs and rebuilding those that teetered on the edge of extinction. Poverty continued to grip Oregonians. Thousands of new residents—many of them Hispanics who had found hard jobs and tough living conditions in following the harvests and working in the state's nursery business—tried to make do.

A willingness to embrace new ventures has persisted in Oregon. In 1990, Measure 5 placed severe limitations on property taxes to support schools and government. In 1993, Oregonians were first in the nation to hold a vote-by-mail election. The following year they approved a Death With Dignity Act, permitting doctor-assisted suicide. In 1998, Oregon raised the minimum wage to the highest in the nation, easing for the hourly worker some of the struggle for existence but threatening enterprises operating on a shoestring. Oregonians refused to approve a sales tax, but continued to pay high property taxes and income taxes.

Such is the course of Oregon history. A majestic territory of immense potentials drew newcomers in the 1840s. In less than a decade, they wrested control from the tribes, changed the face of the land with surveys and property ownership, and engaged in ambitious exploitation of the state's resources. When it finally became evident that nature's plenty could not continue to yield in profusion, Oregonians embraced new models for doing things.

The state's history has stories of triumph and tragedy, hope and perseverance, and taking risks. The Oregon System became a national model for improving government in the 20th century. Oregon has served as a great testing ground for federal projects which have provided a medley of benefits—electricity, navigation, irrigation, timber harvests, tourist facilities, and jobs. Oregon has led the nation in environmental legislation and commitment to working for quality of life for all of its citizens. For generations, Oregonians have celebrated the special words in their state song: "Hail to thee, Land of Promise, My Oregon." Oregon's promise is strong and therein lies the state's future.

Chronological History of Oregon

Oregon's history contains many more significant dates than space will permit, but this list should prove helpful to those embarking on a study of the state.

Oregon Country 1543–1847

1543—Bartolome Ferrelo possibly reaches southwest coast

1565—Manila Galleon trade opens across North Pacific

1579—Sir Francis Drake allegedly visits Oregon

1603—Sebastian Vizcaino possibly sights Cape Sebastian

1707—*San Francisco Xavier* probably wrecks at Nehalem

1765—First use of word "Ouragon" in Maj. Robert Rogers' petition to explore American West

1774—Capt. Juan Perez sails to Northwest Coast for Spain

1775—Capt. Bruno Hezeta sees mouth of Columbia and names it Rio San Roque

1775–1780—First smallpox outbreak among Oregon's indigenous people

1778—Capt. James Cook makes landfall at Cape Foulweather and discovers fur wealth of Northwest Coast

1779—Jonathan Carver's book refers to the "River Oregon"

1788—Capt. Robert Gray trades with tribes in Tillamook Bay

Marius Lopius, African with Gray, probably murdered at Tillamook

1792—Capt. Robert Gray enters and names the Columbia River

Capt. George Vancouver expedition charts Columbia estuary

1801–1802—Second smallpox outbreak among Oregon's Tribes

1803—Louisiana Purchase extends United States to Rocky Mountains

1804—President Thomas Jefferson dispatches Lewis and Clark Expedition

1805—Lewis and Clark Expedition explores lower Snake and Columbia Rivers and establishes Fort Clatsop

1806—Lewis and Clark Expedition returns to the United States

1811—Pacific Fur Company establishes Fort Astoria

David Thompson descends Columbia River from Canada

1812—Overland Astorians discover South Pass in Wyoming, later route of Oregon Trail

1813—North West Company purchases Fort Astoria and names it Fort George

1814—Treaty of Ghent resolves the War of 1812

First English woman, Jane Barnes, visits Fort George

First domestic livestock imported by sea from California

1817—William Cullen Bryant refers to "Oregon" in poem *Thanatopsis*

1818—North West Company establishes Fort Nez Perces

James Biddle and John Prevost assert United States interests in Oregon

United States and Great Britain agree to "joint occupancy" of Oregon

1819—Adams-Onis Treaty cedes Spain's discovery rights north of 42 degrees to the U.S.

1821—Hudson's Bay Company subsumes North West Company

1824—U.S. and Russia agree to 50 degrees as southern boundary of Russian interests

Dr. John McLoughlin begins long tenure as Chief Factor for Hudson's Bay Company

1825—Workmen build Fort Vancouver on Columbia River

David Douglas begins botanical collecting

1827—U.S. and Great Britain agree to indefinite "joint occupancy"

First sawmill begins cutting lumber near Fort Vancouver

1828—Jedediah Smith's party travels overland from California but Indians murder 15 men on the Umpqua River

First grist mill starts making flour at Fort Vancouver

1829—Dr. John McLoughlin establishes claim at Willamette Falls, later Oregon City

1830—Fever pandemic begins calamitous death toll of tribes

1832—Newspapers report four Indians from Pacific Northwest in St. Louis seeking missionaries

Nathaniel Wyeth enters Oregon fur trade

Capt. B. L. E. Bonneville arrives overland to trap and trade for furs on Columbia Plateau

Hudson's Bay Company establishes Fort Umpqua at Elkton

1833—First school opens at Fort Vancouver

First lumber exports by Hudson's Bay Company to China

1834—Jason Lee's party establishes Methodist Mission near Wheatland

John K. Townsend and Thomas Nuttall collect natural history specimens

1836—First steamship *Beaver* begins service for Hudson's Bay Company on the Columbia River

Lt. William Slacum mounts reconnaissance of western Oregon

Whitman-Spalding mission party, including Narcissa Whitman and Eliza Spalding, arrives overland via Oregon Trail

Washington Irving publishes *Astoria*

1838—Willamette Cattle Company drives livestock overland from California

Priests Blanchet and Demers arrive overland from Canada

1839—Catholics establish mission at St. Paul

First book, a Nez Perce language primer, printed at Lapwai, Idaho

1841—Lt. Charles Wilkes mounts reconnaissance with U.S. Exploring Expedition

Ewing Young's death leads to public meetings

First Catholic boys' school founded at St. Paul

First ship, *Star of Oregon,* built by settlers

1842—Methodist missionaries found the Oregon Institute in Salem, an antecedent to Willamette University

First brick building, a house, erected by George Gay in Polk County

1843—First large migration of over 900 immigrants arrives via Oregon Trail

Lt. John C. Fremont mounts reconnaissance of Oregon Trail

"Wolf Meetings" lead to Provisional Government

Oregonians submit petition to Senate seeking U.S. jurisdiction

1844—First plat surveyed for a town at Oregon City

First Catholic girls' school founded at St. Paul

1845—Meek Cut-off opens as alleged short-cut to Oregon Trail

Estimated 3,000 overland immigrants arrive

Oregonians petition Congress for federal services

First Provisional governor, George Abernethy, elected

Francis Pettygrove and A. L. Lovejoy name Portland and commence plat of city

1846—Lt. Neil Howison mounts reconnaissance of western Oregon

Barlow Road opens as toll route

Applegate Trail opens as alternative to Oregon Trail

Oregon Treaty affirms U.S. sovereignty to Pacific Northwest

First newspaper, *Oregon Spectator,* founded in Oregon City

1847—Cayuse Tribe attacks Whitman Mission

Oregon Volunteers engage in Cayuse Indian War

First postmaster, John Shively, named at Astoria

First English book, a *"Blue Back Speller,"* printed in Oregon City

The Oregon Territory 1848–58

1848—Joseph Meek carries petition east seeking federal "patronage"

Organic Act creates Oregon Territory

James Marshall discovers gold in California

First U.S. Customs Service office opens in Astoria

1849—First territorial governor, Joseph Lane, assumes duties

First Mounted Riflemen of U.S. Army arrive overland

First "Beaver" gold coins minted in Oregon City

1850—Congress passes Oregon Donation Land Act

First capital punishment—five Cayuse are hanged in Oregon City

Investors start printing *The Oregonian* in Portland

U.S. Census enumerates 11,873 Oregonians

1851—John Preston initiates cadastral land survey system

First General Land Office opens in Oregon City

Willamette Valley Treaty Commission negotiates treaties

Teamsters discover gold in Rogue River Valley

Anson Dart convenes Tansy Point Treaty Council at mouth of Columbia

First U.S. Army post, Fort Orford, built at Port Orford

U.S. Coast Survey begins charting shoreline

1852—U.S. Army establishes Fort Dalles on Oregon Trail

Congress names Salem capital of Oregon Territory

1853—Territorial legislature adopts Oregon law code

U.S. Army establishes Fort Lane in Rogue River Valley

Territorial legislature publishes *Oregon Archives*

Congress funds Scottsburg-Myrtle Creek Wagon Road

Cow Creek and Rogue River Tribes negotiate treaties with U.S.

Oregon Institute becomes Willamette University

Congress carves Washington Territory out of Oregon Territory

First coal exports begin on southwest Oregon coast

1854—Volunteers massacre Coquille Indians

Legislature prohibits sale of arms and ammunition to tribes

Legislature prohibits sale of ardent spirits to tribes

Legislature bars testimony of "Negroes, mulattoes, and Indians, or persons one half or more of Indian blood" in proceedings involving a white person

1855—Pacific Railroad Surveys examine potential routes

Umatilla and Nez Perce tribes sign treaties at Walla Walla Treaty Council, reserving land and rights to food resources

Warm Springs tribes sign treaty reserving land and rights to food resources

Rogue River Indian War commences

Yakima Indian War commences

President James Buchanan creates Siletz Reservation

Territorial capitol burns in Salem

1856—U.S. Army establishes Forts Umpqua, Hoskins, and Yamhill

President James Buchanan creates Grand Ronde Reservation

U.S. Army orders closure of settlement east of Cascades because of warfare with tribes

1857—Constitutional Convention meets in Salem

Draft constitution bars African-Americans from residency

Aaron Meier founds Meier & Frank Department Store

1858—First election selects state officials

State of Oregon 1859–Present

1859—Congress grants Oregon statehood on February 14

First bank established by Ladd & Tilton in Portland

First elected governor of state, John Whiteaker, inaugurated

1860—U.S. Census enumerates 52,465 residents

Oregon Steam Navigation Company commences service

First daily stage operates between Portland and Sacramento

1861—First Oregon State Fair held at Oregon City

1862—Congress passes Homestead Act

First Oregon Cavalry raises six companies

Gold rush commences to Blue Mountains

First portage railroad completed at Cascades

1863—U.S. Army establishes Fort Klamath

1864—Telegraph line connects Portland-Sacramento

U.S. Army establishes Camp Watson

Treaty creates Klamath Reservation

Popular vote approves Salem as state capital

1865—Long Tom Rebellion confirms pro-southern sympathies

Congress authorizes Oregon Central Military Wagon Road

1866—First lighthouse, Cape Arago, illuminates light signal

U.S. Army establishes Camp Warner

Married Women's Property Act protects women's rights

Congress authorizes Corvallis-Yaquina Bay Military Wagon Road

Congress authorizes Willamette Valley-Cascade Mountain Military Wagon Road

1867—U.S. Army establishes Fort Harney

Congress authorizes The Dalles-Boise Military Wagon Road

1868—Oregon State Agricultural College (OSU) opens

1869—Direct export of wheat to Europe begins

Congress authorizes Coos Bay Military Wagon Road

1870—U.S. Census enumerates 90,923 residents

Abigail Scott Duniway launches suffrage campaign

1872—Oregon & California Railroad completes line to Roseburg

Modoc Indian War commences

1873—Oregon Patrons of Husbandry (Grange) forms chapters

Modoc Indians face trial and execution at Fort Klamath

Oregon Pioneer Association forms

1875—First U.S. Life-Saving Service station opens near Coos Bay

1876—University of Oregon opens

Robert D. Hume builds salmon cannery on Rogue River

1877—Nez Perce Indian War involves Chief Joseph's band

Congress passes Desert Land Act

1878—High schools authorized for districts with 1,000 students

Bannock-Paiute Indian War sweeps into southeastern Oregon

Women gain right to vote in school elections

1879—BIA Indian Training School opens in Forest Grove

1880—U.S. Census enumerates 174,768 residents

O.R.&N. Company begins railroad through Gorge

1881—BIA Chemawa School opens near Salem

1882—Normal schools open in Monmouth, Ashland and Drain to train teachers

1883—O.R.&N. Company railroad reaches Umatilla providing transcontinental links

1884—Oregon Short Line railroad extends to Huntington

1886—Oregon Supreme Court admitted Mary Gysin Leonard to the state bar as Oregon's first female lawyer

Chief Joseph's Nez Perce band locates on Colville Reservation

1887—Thugs murder ten Chinese miners in Hells Canyon

General Allotment Act assaults tribal lands on reservations

Cranberry harvests commence

1888—First Agricultural Experiment Station opens at Corvallis

1890—Congress passes Oregon Indian Depredation Claims Act

U.S. Census enumerates 313,767 residents

Chinese Consolidated Benevolent Association founded

1891—Congress passes Forest Reserve Act

1892—Congress authorizes Columbia River Lightship No. 50

Portland Art Association forms

1894—Mazama Club forms to promote outdoor adventure

1896—Workmen complete Cascade Locks

1897—Holdup of '97 blocks state legislature

1898—Oregon Historical Society receives charter

1900—Workmen complete Yamhill River Locks

U.S. Census enumerates 413,536 residents

1902—Crater Lake National Park opens

Congress passes Federal Reclamation Act

Voters amend Constitution for Initiative and Referendum

1903—Heppner Flood kills 225 people

First *Voters' Pamphlet* published

1904—Direct primary law passes
First African-American, George Hardin, named officer in Portland Police Bureau

1905—Lewis & Clark Centennial Exposition celebrates history
Klamath Irrigation Project commences
Oregon land fraud trials pursue wrongdoers
U.S. Forest Service begins work in national forests

1906—City home rule law approved
Indictment by grand jury law approved
Taxes begin on telephone, telegraph, and railroads
First meeting of Association of Oregon Counties

1907—President Theodore Roosevelt creates "Midnight Reserves" setting aside millions of acres of national forests

1908—Constitution amended for Recall provision
Corrupt Practices Act approved
First woman, Lola Baldwin, named head of Women's Division, Portland Police

1909—State's Central Fish Hatchery opens at Bonneville
Oregon Caves National Monument created
Pendleton Round-Up begins
Congress passes Enlarged Homestead Act

1910—U.S. Census enumerates 672,765 residents
Three-fourths verdict in civil cases approved
Employers' Liability Act approved

1911—Oregon Department of Forestry created
Columbia Gorge River Highway construction begins
Oregon Trunk Railroad completes line to Bend

1912—Women's suffrage approved
Prohibition of private convict labor approved
Eight-hour day on public works approved

1913—Oregon Highway Commission established
Presidential preference primary law approved
Gov. Oswald West declares beaches open to public

1914—Death penalty abolished
Prohibition approved
Eight-hour day approved for women
Congress revests O & C Railroad land grant
Legislature requires publication of *Oregon Blue Book*

1916—Workmen complete Celilo Locks and Canal
Congress passes Stock-Raising Homestead Act

1917—U.S. Army Spruce Production Division begins logging

1918—Influenza pandemic kills hundreds
Emergency Fleet Corporation contracts for ships
Oregonians enlist to serve in World War I

1919—First gasoline tax in U.S. authorized to fund highways
Congress revests Coos Bay Wagon Road land grant

1920—Death penalty reinstated
Oregon League of Women Voters founded
U.S. Census enumerates 783,389 residents

1921—Ku Klux Klan organizes chapters

1922—First state park accepted by Oregon Highway Commission and named for Sarah Helmick
Compulsory School Act approved
First African-American woman, Beatrice Cannady, admitted to Oregon Bar
Japanese American Citizens' League founded

1923—Alien Land Law approved
Prohibition of sectarian garb in schools approved
Alien Business Restriction Law approved

1924—Compulsory School Act held unconstitutional
Congress extends citizenship to American Indians
Clarke-McNary Act aids federal-state forest fire protection

1925—State parks and waysides authorized
League of Oregon Cities founded

1926—Fishwheels abolished
Astor Column completed
Exclusion of African-Americans clause removed from constitution

1929—State Park Commission created

1930—Vale Irrigation Project begins water delivery
U.S. Census enumerates 953,786 residents
First woman, Mary Jane Spurlin, appointed judge in Oregon to Multnomah County District Court

1933—Tillamook Burn destroys 240,000 acres of forest
Civilian Conservation Corps and Works Projects Administration start projects

1934—First grazing district under Taylor Grazing Act forms at Bonanza

1935—Congress authorizes Bonneville Dam
Fire destroys State Capitol

1936—Bandon Fire destroys town and kills 11 residents
Workmen complete five major bridges on Highway 101
First woman, Nan Wood Honeyman, elected from Oregon to U.S. House of Representatives

1937—President F. D. Roosevelt dedicates Timberline Lodge
Gas chamber built for capital punishments
Oregon Shakespeare Festival forms in Ashland
Congress creates Bonneville Power Administration
Bankhead-Jones Act authorizes buy out of homesteaders

1938—544 Report for Willamette flood control approved

Bonneville Dam completed

1939—Tillamook Burn destroys 190,000 acres of forest

State capitol completed in Salem

1940—U.S. Census enumerates 1,089,684 residents

1941—Oregonians enlist to serve in World War II

1942—Executive Order 9066 authorizes removal of Japanese-Americans to internment camps

Japanese submarine shells Fort Stevens

Japanese airplane firebombs Siskiyou National Forest

U.S. Army builds Camp Adair and Camp Abbott

U.S. Navy builds Tillamook and Tongue Point Naval Air Stations

Vanport founded to house wartime workers

1945—Six Oregonians die in explosion of Japanese incendiary balloon

Tillamook Burn destroys 180,000 acres of forest

Supplement to 1923 Alien Land Law passes

1946—Portland State University (PSU) founded

Rural School Law encourages consolidation of districts

1947—Plane crash kills Governor Snell, Secretary of State Farrell, and others

1948—Flood destroys Vanport in hours

Vollum and Murdock found Tektronix

1949—State Department of Forestry begins replanting Tillamook Burn

Fair Labor Practices Commission established

State Supreme Court invalidates 1923 and 1945 Alien Land acts

First woman, Dorothy McCullough Lee, elected Portland mayor

1950—U.S. Census enumerates 1,521,341 residents

1952—Constitution amended to provide for equal representation in state legislature

1954—Congress terminates Western Oregon Indian tribes

1956—Congress authorizes Interstate freeway system

Congress terminates Klamath Indian Tribe

1960—Census enumerates 1,768,687 residents

Congress passes Multiple Use-Sustained Yield Act for management of national forests

First female U.S. Senator from Oregon, Maurine Neuberger, elected

1962—Columbus Day Storm causes major damage in Western Oregon

1964—Death penalty abolished

1966—Workmen complete Astoria-Megler Bridge spanning Columbia estuary

I-5 affords non-stop driving through Oregon

1969—Department of Environmental Quality created

Federal District Court in *Sohappy v. Smith* affirms tribal treaty fishing rights in Columbia River

1970—U.S. Census enumerates 2,091,000 residents

1971—Bottle Bill approved

Congress confirms Burns Paiute Reservation

1973—Land Conservation and Development Commission created

Public Meetings Law approved

Public Records Law approved

Tillamook State Forest created

Congress approves Endangered Species Act

1974—Congress creates John Day Fossil Beds National Monument

Oregon Health Sciences University forms out of mergers

Governor Tom McCall sets odd/even gasoline refueling days

1975—Congress creates Hells Canyon National Recreation Area

1976—First woman, Norma Paulus, elected secretary of state

First Oregon nuclear power plant, Trojan, built north of St. Helens

1977—Aerosol sprays banned by law

Congress restores Confederated Tribes of Siletz

First woman, Betty Roberts, appointed to Oregon Court of Appeals

1978—Death penalty reinstated

1979—Federal District Court in *Kimball v. Callahan* affirms Klamath Indian hunting and fishing rights within former reservation

1980—U.S. Census enumerates 2,633,000 residents

Congress creates new Siletz Reservation

Mt. St. Helens eruption disrupts ship traffic on Columbia River

1981—Bhagwan Shree Rajneesh establishes Rajneeshpuram in Antelope

1982—Congress restores Cow Creek Band of Umpqua Tribe

First woman, Betty Roberts, appointed justice of Oregon Supreme Court

1983—Congress restores Confederated Tribes of Grand Ronde Indian Community

1984—Congress restores Confederated Tribes of Coos, Lower Umpqua, and Siuslaw

First Oregon lottery ratified by voters

1985—Bhagwan Shree Rajneesh deported and fined $400,000

First woman, Vera Katz, selected speaker of Oregon House

1986—Congress restores Klamath Tribe

Metropolitan Area Express (MAX) begins light-rail service in Portland

1988—Congress creates new Grand Ronde Reservation

Congress approves Civil Liberties Act paying $20,000 to each surviving interned Japanese-American

1989—Congress restores Coquille Tribe

First Sports Action Lottery in U.S. sells tickets

1990—U.S. Census enumerates 2,842,000 residents

Ballot Measure 5 limits property taxes to support schools and government

U.S. Department of Fish and Wildlife lists Northern Spotted Owl as endangered

First woman, Barbara Roberts, elected governor

1992—First African-American, James A. Hill, Jr., elected to state office

First gaming compact signed with Cow Creek and Umpqua Tribe for casino

1993—First statewide vote-by-mail election held in U.S.

1994—First Death With Dignity Act approved permitting doctor-assisted suicide

1996—First vote-by-mail election for federal office held

1998—Metropolitan Area Express (MAX) extends light-rail service 18 miles west from Portland

1999—U.S. Department of Fish and Wildlife lists several salmon species from Columbia and Willamette Rivers as endangered

2000—U.S. Census enumerates 3,421,399 residents

2001—Metropolitan Area Express (MAX) extends light-rail service to Portland Airport

2002—Susan Castillo first Hispanic woman elected to statewide office

Near record forest fire season leaves 1,000,000 acres burned

2003—Oregon begins 10-year plan to fix deteriorating bridges

2004—Trojan, Oregon's only nuclear power plant decommissioned

L. L. Stub Stewart State Park opens, Oregon's first new state park campground in more than 30 years

2005—Oregon State Quarter released with design featuring Crater Lake

2006—Trojan, Oregon's decommissioned nuclear power plant imploded

2007—Oregon's constitution 150 years old

Sandy River's Marmot Dam, built in 1912, removed

2008—New Carissa, freighter that ran aground on Coos Bay beach in 1999, dismantled and removed

2009—Oregon celebrates its sesquicentennial on February 14, 2009

Oregon unemployment rate tops 12% amid recession

Portland Timbers became Major League Soccer's eighteenth team on March 20, 2009

2010—Governor's panel predicts 10 years of state budget deficits

2012—Oregon legislature began annual sessions, with the even-numbered years having a month-long session in February

Act of Congress Admitting Oregon into the Union

Preamble

Whereas the people of Oregon have framed, ratified and adopted a constitution of state government which is republican in form, and in conformity with the Constitution of the United States and have applied for admission into the Union on an equal footing with the other states; therefore —

1. Admission of State—Boundaries

That Oregon be, and she is hereby, received into the Union on an equal footing with the other states in all respects whatever, with the following boundaries: In order that the boundaries of the state may be known and established, it is hereby ordained and declared that the State of Oregon shall be bounded as follows, to wit: Beginning one marine league at sea, due west from the point where the forty-second parallel of north latitude intersects the same, thence northerly, at the same distance from the line of the coast lying west and opposite the state, including all islands within the jurisdiction of the United States, to a point due west and opposite the middle of the north ship channel of the Columbia River; thence easterly, to and up the middle channel of said river, and, where it is divided by islands, up the middle and widest channel thereof, to a point near Fort Walla Walla, where the forty-sixth parallel of north latitude crosses said river, thence east, on said parallel, to the middle of the main channel of the Shoshone or Snake River; thence up the middle of the main channel of said river, to the mouth of the Owyhee River; thence due south, to the parallel of latitude forty-two degrees north; thence west, along said parallel, to the place of beginning, including jurisdiction in civil and criminal cases upon the Columbia River and Snake River, concurrently with states and territories of which those rivers form a boundary in common with this state.

2. Concurrent Jurisdiction on Columbia & Other Rivers—Navigable Waters to be Common Highways

The said State of Oregon shall have concurrent jurisdiction on the Columbia and all other rivers and waters bordering on the said State of Oregon, so far as the same shall form a common boundary

History

to said state, and any other state or states now or hereafter to be formed or bounded by the same; and said rivers and waters, and all the navigable waters of said state, shall be common highways and forever free, as well as to the inhabitants of said state as to all other citizens of the United States, without any tax, duty & impost, or toll thereof.

3. Representation in Congress

Until the next census and apportionment of representatives, the State of Oregon shall be entitled to one representative in the Congress of the United States.

4. Propositions Submitted to People of State

The following propositions be and the same are hereby offered to the said people of Oregon for their free acceptance or rejection, which, if accepted, shall be obligatory on the United States and upon the said State of Oregon, to wit:

School Lands

First, that sections numbered sixteen and thirty-six in every township of public lands in said state, and where either of said sections, or any part thereof, has been sold or otherwise disposed of, other lands equivalent thereto, and as contiguous as may be, shall be granted to said state for the use of schools.

University Lands

Second, the seventy-two sections of land shall be set apart and reserved for the use and support of a state university, to be selected by the Governor of said state, subject to the approval of the Commissioner of the General Land Office, and to be appropriated and applied in such manner as the legislature of said state may prescribe for the purpose aforesaid, but for no other purpose.

Lands For Public Buildings

Third, that ten entire sections of land, to be selected by the Governor of said state, in legal subdivisions, shall be granted to said state for the purpose of completing the public buildings, or for the erection of others at the seat of government, under the direction of the legislature thereof.

Salt Springs & Contiguous Lands

Fourth, that all salt springs within said state, not exceeding twelve in number, with six sections of land adjoining, or as contiguous as may be to each, shall be granted to said state for its use, the same to be selected by the Governor thereof within one year after the admission of said state, and when so selected, to be used or disposed of on such terms, conditions and regulations as the legislature shall direct; provided, that no salt spring or land, the right whereof is now vested in any individual or individuals, or which may be hereafter confirmed or adjudged to any individual or individuals, shall by this article be granted to said state.

Percentage on Land Sales

Fifth, that 5 per centum of the net proceeds of sales of all public lands lying within said state which shall be sold by Congress after the admission of said state into the Union, after deducting all the expenses incident to the same, shall be paid to said state, for the purpose of making public roads and internal improvements, as the legislature shall direct; provided, that the foregoing propositions, hereinbefore offered, are on the condition that the people of Oregon shall provide by an ordinance, irrevocable without the consent of the United States, that said state shall never interfere with the primary disposal of the soil within the same by the United States, or with any regulations Congress may find necessary for securing the title in said soil to bona fide purchasers thereof; and that in no case shall nonresident proprietors be taxed higher than residents.

Conditions on Which Propositions Are Offered

Sixth, and that the state shall never tax the lands or the property of the United States in said state; provided, however, that in case any of the lands herein granted to the State of Oregon have heretofore been confirmed to the Territory of Oregon for the purposes specified in this act, the amount so confirmed shall be deducted from the quantity specified in this act.

5. Residue of Territory

Until Congress shall otherwise direct, the residue of the Territory of Oregon shall be and is hereby incorporated into and made a part of the Territory of Washington.

Approved February 14, 1859.

Proposition of Congress accepted by the Legislative Assembly of the State of Oregon on June 3, 1859.

Constitution

An old truck on a farm near Enterprise—Oregon State Archives Scenic Photograph walDB0575

The Oregon Constitution has been the foundation of government in Oregon since 1859. Oregonians have amended it repeatedly, and, since 1902, citizens have been able to place amendments on the statewide ballot by means of the initiative process. This section contains the full text of the Oregon Constitution.

CONSTITUTION OF OREGON
2011 EDITION

The Oregon Constitution was framed by a convention of 60 delegates chosen by the people. The convention met on the third Monday in August 1857 and adjourned on September 18 of the same year. On November 9, 1857, the Constitution was approved by the vote of the people of the Oregon Territory. The Act of Congress admitting Oregon into the Union was approved February 14, 1859, and, on that date, the Constitution went into effect.

The Constitution is here published as it is in effect following the approval of amendments on May 18, 2010, and November 2, 2010. The text of the original signed copy of the Constitution is filed in the Office of the Secretary of State and is retained unless it has been repealed or superseded by amendment. Where the original text has been amended or where a new provision has been added to the original Constitution, the source of the amendment or addition is indicated in the source note immediately following the text of the amended or new provision. Notations also have been made setting out the history of repealed sections.

Unless otherwise specifically noted, the leadlines for the sections have been supplied by Legislative Counsel.

PREAMBLE

We the people of the State of Oregon to the end that Justice be established, order maintained, and liberty perpetuated, do ordain this Constitution. —

ARTICLE I
BILL OF RIGHTS

Section 1. Natural rights inherent in people. We declare that all men, when they form a social compact are equal in right: that all power is inherent in the people, and all free governments are founded on their authority, and instituted for their peace, safety, and happiness; and they have at all times a right to alter, reform, or abolish the government in such manner as they may think proper. —

Section 2. Freedom of worship. All men shall be secure in the Natural right, to worship Almighty God according to the dictates of their own consciences. —

Section 3. Freedom of religious opinion. No law shall in any case whatever control the free exercise, and enjoyment of religeous [sic] opinions, or interfere with the rights of conscience. —

Section 4. No religious qualification for office. No religious test shall be required as a qualification for any office of trust or profit. —

Section 5. No money to be appropriated for religion. No money shall be drawn from the Treasury for the benefit of any religeous [sic], or theological institution, nor shall any money be appropriated for the payment of any religeous [sic] services in either house of the Legislative Assembly. —

Section 6. No religious test for witnesses or jurors. No person shall be rendered incompetent as a witness, or juror in consequence of his opinions on matters of religeon [sic]; nor be questioned in any Court of Justice touching his religeous [sic] belief to affect the weight of his testimony. —

Section 7. Manner of administering oath or affirmation. The mode of administering an oath, or affirmation shall be such as may be most consistent with, and binding upon the conscience of the person to whom such oath or affirmation may be administered. —

Section 8. Freedom of speech and press. No law shall be passed restraining the free expression of opinion, or restricting the right to speak, write, or print freely on any subject whatever; but every person shall be responsible for the abuse of this right. —

Section 9. Unreasonable searches or seizures. No law shall violate the right of the people to be secure in their persons, houses, papers, and effects, against unreasonable search, or seizure; and no warrant shall issue but upon probable cause, supported by oath, or affirmation, and particularly describing the place to be searched, and the person or thing to be seized. —

Section 10. Administration of justice. No court shall be secret, but justice shall be administered, openly and without purchase, completely and without delay, and every man shall have remedy by due course of law for injury done him in his person, property, or reputation. —

Section 11. Rights of Accused in Criminal Prosecution. In all criminal prosecutions, the accused shall have the right to public trial by an impartial jury in the county in which the offense shall have been committed; to be heard by himself and counsel; to demand the nature and cause of the accusation against him, and to have a copy thereof; to meet the witnesses face to face, and to have compulsory process for obtaining witnesses in his favor; provided, however, that any accused person, in other than capital cases, and with the consent of the trial judge, may elect to waive trial by jury and consent to be tried by the judge of the court alone, such election to be in writing; provided, however, that in the circuit court ten members of the jury may render a verdict of guilty or not guilty, save and except a verdict of guilty of first degree murder, which shall be found only by a unanimous verdict, and not otherwise; provided further, that the existing laws and constitutional provisions relative to criminal prosecutions shall be continued and remain in effect as to all prosecutions for crimes committed before the taking effect of this amendment. [Constitution of 1859; Amendment proposed by S.J.R. 4, 1931, and adopted by the people Nov. 8, 1932; Amendment proposed by S.J.R. 4, 1931 (2d s.s.), and adopted by the people May 18, 1934]

Note: The leadline to section 11 was a part of the measure submitted to the people by S.J.R. 4, 1931.

Section 12. Double jeopardy; compulsory self-incrimination. No person shall be put in jeopardy twice for the same offence [sic], nor be compelled in any criminal prosecution to testify against himself. —

Constitution

Section 13. Treatment of arrested or confined persons. No person arrested, or confined in jail, shall be treated with unnecessary rigor. —

Section 14. Bailable offenses. Offences [sic], except murder, and treason, shall be bailable by sufficient sureties. Murder or treason, shall not be bailable, when the proof is evident, or the presumption strong. —

Section 15. Foundation principles of criminal law. Laws for the punishment of crime shall be founded on these principles: protection of society, personal responsibility, accountability for one's actions and reformation. [Constitution of 1859; Amendment proposed by S.J.R. 32, 1995, and adopted by the people Nov. 5, 1996]

Section 16. Excessive bail and fines; cruel and unusual punishments; power of jury in criminal case. Excessive bail shall not be required, nor excessive fines imposed. Cruel and unusual punishments shall not be inflicted, but all penalties shall be proportioned to the offense.—In all criminal cases whatever, the jury shall have the right to determine the law, and the facts under the direction of the Court as to the law, and the right of new trial, as in civil cases. —

Section 17. Jury trial in civil cases. In all civil cases the right of Trial by Jury shall remain inviolate. —

Section 18. Private property or services taken for public use. Private property shall not be taken for public use, nor the particular services of any man be demanded, without just compensation; nor except in the case of the state, without such compensation first assessed and tendered; provided, that the use of all roads, ways and waterways necessary to promote the transportation of the raw products of mine or farm or forest or water for beneficial use or drainage is necessary to the development and welfare of the state and is declared a public use. [Constitution of 1859; Amendment proposed by S.J.R. 17, 1919, and adopted by the people May 21, 1920; Amendment proposed by S.J.R. 8, 1923, and adopted by the people Nov. 4, 1924]

Section 19. Imprisonment for debt. There shall be no imprisonment for debt, except in case of fraud or absconding debtors. —

Section 20. Equality of privileges and immunities of citizens. No law shall be passed granting to any citizen or class of citizens privileges, or immunities, which, upon the same terms, shall not equally belong to all citizens. —

Section 21. Ex-post facto laws; laws impairing contracts; laws depending on authorization in order to take effect; laws submitted to electors. No *ex-post facto* law, or law impairing the obligation of contracts shall ever be passed, nor shall any law be passed, the taking effect of which shall be made to depend upon any authority, except as provided in this Constitution; provided, that laws locating the Capitol of the State, locating County Seats, and submitting town, and corporate acts, and other local, and Special laws may take effect, or not, upon a vote of the electors interested. —

Section 22. Suspension of operation of laws. The operation of the laws shall never be suspended, except by the Authority of the Legislative Assembly.

Section 23. Habeas corpus. The privilege of the writ of habeas corpus shall not be suspended unless in case of rebellion, or invasion the public safety require it. —

Section 24. Treason. Treason against the State shall consist only in levying war against it, or adhering to its enemies, giving them aid or comfort. — No person shall be convicted of treason unless on the testimony of two witnesses to the same overt act, or confession in open Court. —

Section 25. Corruption of blood or forfeiture of estate. No conviction shall work corruption of blood, or forfeiture of estate. —

Section 26. Assemblages of people; instruction of representatives; application to legislature. No law shall be passed restraining any of the inhabitants of the State from assembling together in a peaceable manner to consult for their common good; nor from instructing their Representatives; nor from applying to the Legislature for redress of greviances [sic]. —

Section 27. Right to bear arms; military subordinate to civil power. The people shall have the right to bear arms for the defence [sic] of themselves, and the State, but the Military shall be kept in strict subordination to the civil power[.] —

Section 28. Quartering soldiers. No soldier shall, in time of peace, be quartered in any house, without the consent of the owner, nor in time of war, except in the manner prescribed by law. —

Section 29. Titles of nobility; hereditary distinctions. No law shall be passed granting any title of Nobility, or conferring hereditary distinctions. —

Section 30. Emigration. No law shall be passed prohibiting emigration from the State. —

Section 31. Rights of aliens; immigration to state.:RF8. [Constitution of 1859; repeal proposed by H.J.R. 16, 1969, and adopted by the people May 26, 1970]

Section 32. Taxes and duties; uniformity of taxation. No tax or duty shall be imposed without the consent of the people or their representatives in the Legislative Assembly; and all taxation shall be uniform on the same class of subjects within the territorial limits of the authority levying the tax. [Constitution of 1859; Amendment proposed by H.J.R. 16, 1917, and adopted by the people June 4, 1917]

Section 33. Enumeration of rights not exclusive. This enumeration of rights, and privileges shall not be construed to impair or deny others retained by the people. —

Section 34. Slavery or involuntary servitude. There shall be neither slavery, nor involuntary servitude in the State, otherwise than as a punishment for crime, whereof the party shall have been duly convicted.— [Added to Bill of Rights as unnumbered section by vote of the people at time of adoption of the Oregon Constitution in accordance with section 4 of Article XVIII thereof]

Section 35. Restrictions on rights of certain persons.:RF8. [Added to Bill of Rights as unnumbered section by vote of the people at time of adoption of the Oregon Constitution in accordance with Section 4 of Article XVIII thereof; Repeal proposed by H.J.R. 8, 1925, and adopted by the people Nov. 2, 1926]

Section 36. Liquor prohibition.:RF8. [Created through initiative petition filed July 1, 1914, and adopted by the people Nov. 3, 1914; Repeal proposed by initiative petition filed March 20, 1933, and adopted by the people July 21, 1933]

Section 36. Capital punishment abolished.:RF8. [Created through initiative petition filed July 2, 1914, and adopted by the people Nov. 3, 1914; Repeal proposed by S.J.R. 8, 1920 (s.s.), and adopted by the people May 21, 1920, as Const. Art. I, §38]

Note: RF8. At the general election in 1914 two sections, each designated as section 36, were created and added to the Constitution by separate initiative petitions. One of these sections was the prohibition section and the other abolished capital punishment.

Section 36a. Prohibition of importation of liquors.:RF8. [Created through initiative petition filed July 6, 1916, and adopted by the people Nov. 7, 1916; Repeal proposed by initiative petition filed March 20, 1933, and adopted by the people July 21, 1933]

Section 37. Penalty for murder in first degree.:RF8. [Created through S.J.R. 8, 1920, and adopted by the people May 21, 1920; Repeal proposed by S.J.R. 3, 1963, and adopted by the people Nov. 3, 1964]

Section 38. Laws abrogated by amendment abolishing death penalty revived.:RF8. [Created through S.J.R. 8, 1920, and adopted by the people May 21, 1920; Repeal proposed by S.J.R. 3, 1963, and adopted by the people Nov. 3, 1964]

Section 39. Sale of liquor by individual glass. The State shall have power to license private clubs, fraternal organizations, veterans' organizations, railroad corporations operating interstate trains and commercial establishments where food is cooked and served, for the purpose of selling alcoholic liquor by the individual glass at retail, for consumption on the premises, including mixed drinks and cocktails, compounded or mixed on the premises only. The Legislative Assembly shall provide in such detail as it shall deem advisable for carrying out and administering the provisions of this amendment and shall provide adequate safeguards to carry out the original intent and purpose of the Oregon Liquor Control Act, including the promotion of temperance in the use and consumption of alcoholic beverages, encourage the use and consumption of lighter beverages and aid in the establishment of Oregon industry. This power is subject to the following:

(1) The provisions of this amendment shall take effect and be in operation sixty (60) days after the approval and adoption by the people of Oregon; provided, however, the right of a local option election exists in the counties and in any incorporated city or town containing a population of at least five hundred (500). The Legislative Assembly shall prescribe a means and a procedure by which the voters of any county or incorporated city or town as limited above in any county, may through a local option election determine whether to prohibit or permit such power, and such procedure shall specifically include that whenever fifteen per cent (15%) of the registered voters of any county in the state or of any incorporated city or town as limited above, in any county in the state, shall file a petition requesting an election in this matter, the question shall be voted upon at the next regular November biennial election, provided said petition is filed not less than sixty (60) days before the day of election.

(2) Legislation relating to this matter shall operate uniformly throughout the state and all individuals shall be treated equally; and all provisions shall be liberally construed for the accomplishment of these purposes. [Created through initiative petition filed July 2, 1952, and adopted by the people Nov. 4, 1952]

Section 40. Penalty for aggravated murder. Notwithstanding sections 15 and 16 of this Article, the penalty for aggravated murder as defined by law shall be death upon unanimous affirmative jury findings as provided by law and otherwise shall be life imprisonment with minimum sentence as provided by law. [Created through initiative petition filed July 6, 1983, and adopted by the people Nov. 6, 1984]

Section 41. Work and training for corrections institution inmates; work programs; limitations; duties of corrections director. (1) Whereas the people of the state of Oregon find and declare that inmates who are confined in corrections institutions should work as hard as the taxpayers who provide for their upkeep; and whereas the people also find and declare that inmates confined within corrections institutions must be fully engaged in productive activity if they are to successfully re-enter society with practical skills and a viable work ethic; now, therefore, the people declare:

(2) All inmates of state corrections institutions shall be actively engaged full-time in work or on-the-job training. The work or on-the-job training programs shall be established and overseen by the corrections director, who shall ensure that such programs are cost-effective and are designed to develop inmate motivation, work capabilities and cooperation. Such programs may include boot camp prison programs. Education may be provided to inmates as part of work or on-the-job training so long as each inmate is engaged at least half-time in hands-on training or work activity.

(3) Each inmate shall begin full-time work or on-the-job training immediately upon admission to a corrections institution, allowing for a short time for administrative intake and processing. The specific quantity of hours per day to be spent in work or on-the-job training shall be determined by the corrections director, but the overall time spent in work or training shall be full-time. However, no inmate has a legally enforceable right to a job or to otherwise participate in work, on-the-job training or educational programs or to compensation for work or labor performed while an inmate of any state, county or city corrections facility or institution. The corrections director may reduce or exempt participation in work or training programs by those inmates deemed by corrections officials as physically or mentally disabled, or as too dangerous to society to engage in such programs.

(4) There shall be sufficient work and training programs to ensure that every eligible inmate is productively involved in one or more programs. Where an inmate is drug and alcohol addicted so as to prevent the inmate from effectively participating in work or training programs, corrections officials shall provide appropriate drug or alcohol treatment.

(5) The intent of the people is that taxpayer-supported institutions and programs shall be free to benefit from inmate work. Prison work programs shall be designed and carried out so as to achieve savings in government operations, so as to achieve a net profit in private sector activities or so as to benefit the community.

(6) The provisions of this section are mandatory for all state corrections institutions. The provisions of this section are permissive for county or city corrections facilities. No law, ordinance or charter shall prevent or restrict a county or city governing body from implementing all or part of the provisions of this section. Compensation, if any, shall be determined and established by the governing body of the county or city which chooses to engage in prison work programs, and the governing body may choose to adopt any power or exemption allowed in this section.

(7) The corrections director shall contact public and private enterprises in this state and seek proposals to use inmate work. The corrections director may: (a) install and equip plants in any state corrections institution, or any other location, for the employment or training of any of the inmates therein; or (b) purchase, acquire, install,

maintain and operate materials, machinery and appliances necessary to the conduct and operation of such plants. The corrections director shall use every effort to enter into contracts or agreements with private business concerns or government agencies to accomplish the production or marketing of products or services produced or performed by inmates. The corrections director may carry out the director's powers and duties under this section by delegation to others.

(8) Compensation, if any, for inmates who engage in prison work programs shall be determined and established by the corrections director. Such compensation shall not be subject to existing public or private sector minimum or prevailing wage laws, except where required to comply with federal law. Inmate compensation from enterprises entering into agreements with the state shall be exempt from unemployment compensation taxes to the extent allowed under federal law. Inmate injury or disease attributable to any inmate work shall be covered by a corrections system inmate injury fund rather than the workers compensation law. Except as otherwise required by federal law to permit transportation in interstate commerce of goods, wares or merchandise manufactured, produced or mined, wholly or in part by inmates or except as otherwise required by state law, any compensation earned through prison work programs shall only be used for the following purposes:

(a) Reimbursement for all or a portion of the costs of the inmate's rehabilitation, housing, health care, and living costs;

(b) Restitution or compensation to the victims of the particular inmate's crime;

(c) Restitution or compensation to the victims of crime generally through a fund designed for that purpose;

(d) Financial support for immediate family of the inmate outside the corrections institution; and

(e) Payment of fines, court costs, and applicable taxes.

(9) All income generated from prison work programs shall be kept separate from general fund accounts and shall only be used for implementing, maintaining and developing prison work programs. Prison industry work programs shall be exempt from statutory competitive bid and purchase requirements. Expenditures for prison work programs shall be exempt from the legislative appropriations process to the extent the programs rely on income sources other than state taxes and fees. Where state taxes or fees are the source of capital or operating expenditures, the appropriations shall be made by the legislative assembly. The state programs shall be run in a businesslike fashion and shall be subject to regulation by the corrections director. Expenditures from income generated by state prison work programs must be approved by the corrections director. Agreements with private enterprise as to state prison work programs must be approved by the corrections director. The corrections director shall make all state records available for public scrutiny and the records shall be subject to audit by the Secretary of State.

(10) Prison work products or services shall be available to any public agency and to any private enterprise of any state, any nation or any American Indian or Alaskan Native tribe without restriction imposed by any state or local law, ordinance or regulation as to competition with other public or private sector enterprises. The products and services of corrections work programs shall be provided on such terms as are set by the corrections director. To the extent determined possible by the corrections director, the corrections director shall avoid establishing or expanding for-profit prison work programs that produce goods or services offered for sale in the private sector if the establishment or expansion would displace or significantly reduce preexisting private enterprise. To the extent determined possible by the corrections director, the corrections director shall avoid establishing or expanding prison work programs if the establishment or expansion would displace or significantly reduce government or nonprofit programs that employ persons with developmental disabilities. However, the decision to establish, maintain, expand, reduce or terminate any prison work program remains in the sole discretion of the corrections director.

(11) Inmate work shall be used as much as possible to help operate the corrections institutions themselves, to support other government operations and to support community charitable organizations. This work includes, but is not limited to, institutional food production; maintenance and repair of buildings, grounds, and equipment; office support services, including printing; prison clothing production and maintenance; prison medical services; training other inmates; agricultural and forestry work, especially in parks and public forest lands; and environmental clean-up projects. Every state agency shall cooperate with the corrections director in establishing inmate work programs.

(12) As used throughout this section, unless the context requires otherwise: "full-time" means the equivalent of at least forty hours per seven day week, specifically including time spent by inmates as required by the Department of Corrections, while the inmate is participating in work or on-the-job training, to provide for the safety and security of the public, correctional staff and inmates; "corrections director" means the person in charge of the state corrections system.

(13) This section is self-implementing and supersedes all existing inconsistent statutes. This section shall become effective April 1, 1995. If any part of this section or its application to any person or circumstance is held to be invalid for any reason, then the remaining parts or applications to any persons or circumstances shall not be affected but shall remain in full force and effect. [Created through initiative petition filed Jan. 12, 1994, and adopted by the people Nov. 8, 1994; Amendment proposed by H.J.R. 2, 1997, and adopted by the people May 20, 1997; Amendment proposed by H.J.R. 82, 1999, and adopted by the people Nov. 2, 1999]

Note: RF8. Added to Article I as unnumbered section by initiative petition (Measure No. 17, 1994) adopted by the people Nov. 8, 1994.

Note: RF8. An initiative petition (Measure No. 40, 1996) proposed adding a new section relating to crime victims' rights to the Oregon Constitution. That section, appearing as section 42 of Article I in previous editions of this Constitution, was declared void for not being enacted in compliance with section 1, Article XVII of this Constitution. See Armatta v. Kitzhaber, 327 Or. 250, 959 P.2d 49 (1998).

Section 42. Rights of victim in criminal prosecutions and juvenile court delinquency proceedings. (1) To preserve and protect the right of crime victims to justice, to ensure crime victims a meaningful role in the criminal and juvenile justice systems, to accord crime victims due dignity and respect and to ensure that criminal and juvenile court delinquency proceedings are conducted to seek the truth as to the defendant's innocence or guilt, and also to ensure that a fair balance is struck between the rights of crime victims and the rights of criminal defendants in the course and conduct of criminal and juvenile court delinquency proceedings, the following rights are hereby granted to victims in all prosecutions for crimes and in juvenile court delinquency proceedings:

(a) The right to be present at and, upon specific request, to be informed in advance of any critical stage of the proceedings held in open court when the defendant will be present, and to be heard at the pretrial release hearing and the sentencing or juvenile court delinquency disposition;

(b) The right, upon request, to obtain information about the conviction, sentence, imprisonment, criminal history and future release from physical custody of the criminal defendant or convicted criminal and equivalent information regarding the alleged youth offender or youth offender;

(c) The right to refuse an interview, deposition or other discovery request by the criminal defendant or other person acting on behalf of the criminal defendant provided, however, that nothing in this paragraph shall restrict any other constitutional right of the defendant to discovery against the state;

(d) The right to receive prompt restitution from the convicted criminal who caused the victim's loss or injury;

(e) The right to have a copy of a transcript of any court proceeding in open court, if one is otherwise prepared;

(f) The right to be consulted, upon request, regarding plea negotiations involving any violent felony; and

(g) The right to be informed of these rights as soon as practicable.

(2) This section applies to all criminal and juvenile court delinquency proceedings pending or commenced on or after the effective date of this section. Nothing in this section reduces a criminal defendant's rights under the Constitution of the United States. Except as otherwise specifically provided, this section supersedes any conflicting section of this Constitution. Nothing in this section is intended to create any cause of action for compensation or damages nor may this section be used to invalidate an accusatory instrument, conviction or adjudication or otherwise terminate any criminal or juvenile delinquency proceedings at any point after the case is commenced or on appeal. Except as otherwise provided in subsections (3) and (4) of this section, nothing in this section may be used to invalidate a ruling of a court or to suspend any criminal or juvenile delinquency proceedings at any point after the case is commenced.

(3)(a) Every victim described in paragraph (c) of subsection (6) of this section shall have remedy by due course of law for violation of a right established in this section.

(b) A victim may assert a claim for a right established in this section in a pending case, by a mandamus proceeding if no case is pending or as otherwise provided by law.

(c) The Legislative Assembly may provide by law for further effectuation of the provisions of this subsection, including authorization for expedited and interlocutory consideration of claims for relief and the establishment of reasonable limitations on the time allowed for bringing such claims.

(d) No claim for a right established in this section shall suspend a criminal or juvenile delinquency proceeding if such a suspension would violate a right of a criminal defendant guaranteed by this Constitution or the Constitution of the United States.

(4) Upon the victim's request, the prosecuting attorney, in the attorney's discretion, may assert and enforce a right established in this section.

(5) Upon the filing by the prosecuting attorney of an affidavit setting forth cause, a court shall suspend the rights established in this section in any case involving organized crime or victims who are minors.

(6) As used in this section:

(a) "Convicted criminal" includes a youth offender in juvenile court delinquency proceedings.

(b) "Criminal defendant" includes an alleged youth offender in juvenile court delinquency proceedings.

(c) "Victim" means any person determined by the prosecuting attorney or the court to have suffered direct financial, psychological or physical harm as a result of a crime and, in the case of a victim who is a minor, the legal guardian of the minor.

(d) "Violent felony" means a felony in which there was actual or threatened serious physical injury to a victim or a felony sexual offense.

(7) In the event that no person has been determined to be a victim of the crime, the people of Oregon, represented by the prosecuting attorney, are considered to be the victims. In no event is it intended that the criminal defendant be considered the victim. [Created through H.J.R. 87, 1999, and adopted by the people Nov. 2, 1999; Amendment proposed by H.J.R. 49, 2007, and adopted by the people May 20, 2008]

Note: RF8. The effective date of House Joint Resolutions 87, 89, 90 and 94, compiled as sections 42, 43, 44 and 45, Article I, is Dec. 2, 1999.

Note: RF8. Sections 42, 43, 44 and 45, were added to Article I as unnumbered sections by the amendments proposed by House Joint Resolutions 87, 89, 90 and 94, 1999, and adopted by the people Nov. 2, 1999.

Section 43. Rights of victim and public to protection from accused person during criminal proceedings; denial of pretrial release. (1) To ensure that a fair balance is struck between the rights of crime victims and the rights of criminal defendants in the course and conduct of criminal proceedings, the following rights are hereby granted to victims in all prosecutions for crimes:

(a) The right to be reasonably protected from the criminal defendant or the convicted criminal throughout the criminal justice process and from the alleged youth offender or youth offender throughout the juvenile delinquency proceedings.

(b) The right to have decisions by the court regarding the pretrial release of a criminal defendant based upon the principle of reasonable protection of the victim and the public, as well as the likelihood that the criminal defendant will appear for trial. Murder, aggravated murder and treason shall not be bailable when the proof is evident or the presumption strong that the person is guilty. Other violent felonies shall not be bailable when a court has determined there is probable cause to believe the criminal defendant committed the crime, and the court finds, by clear and convincing evidence, that there is danger of physical injury or sexual victimization to the victim or members of the public by the criminal defendant while on release.

(2) This section applies to proceedings pending or commenced on or after the effective date of this section. Nothing in this section abridges any right of the criminal defendant guaranteed by the Constitution of the United States, including the rights to be represented by counsel, have counsel appointed if indigent, testify, present witnesses, cross-examine witnesses or present information at the release hearing. Nothing in this section creates any cause of action for compensation or damages nor may this section be used to invalidate an accusatory instrument, conviction or adjudication or otherwise terminate any criminal or juvenile delinquency proceeding at any point after the case is commenced or on appeal. Except as otherwise provided in paragraph (b) of subsection (4) of this section and in subsection (5) of this section, nothing in this section may be used to invalidate a ruling of a court or to suspend any criminal or juvenile delinquency proceedings at any point after the case is commenced. Except as otherwise specifically provided, this section supersedes any conflicting section of this Constitution.

(3) As used in this section:

(a) "Victim" means any person determined by the prosecuting attorney or the court to have suffered direct financial, psychological or physical harm as a result of a crime and, in the case of a victim who is a minor, the legal guardian of the minor.

(b) "Violent felony" means a felony in which there was actual or threatened serious physical injury to a victim or a felony sexual offense.

(4)(a) The prosecuting attorney is the party authorized to assert the rights of the public established by this section.

(b) Upon the victim's request, the prosecuting attorney, in the attorney's discretion, may assert and enforce a right established in this section.

(5)(a) Every victim described in paragraph (a) of subsection (3) of this section shall have remedy by due course of law for violation of a right established in this section.

(b) A victim may assert a claim for a right established in this section in a pending case, by a mandamus proceeding if no case is pending or as otherwise provided by law.

(c) The Legislative Assembly may provide by law for further effectuation of the provisions of this subsection, including authorization for expedited and interlocutory consideration of claims for relief and the establishment of reasonable limitations on the time allowed for bringing such claims.

(d) No claim for a right established in this section shall suspend a criminal or juvenile delinquency proceeding if such a suspension would violate a right of a criminal defendant or alleged youth offender guaranteed by this Constitution or the Constitution of the United States.

(6) In the event that no person has been determined to be a victim of the crime, the people of Oregon, represented by the prosecuting attorney, are considered to be the victims. In no event is it intended that the criminal defendant be considered the victim. [Created through H.J.R. 90, 1999, and adopted by the people Nov. 2, 1999; Amendment proposed by H.J.R. 50, 2007, and adopted by the people May 20, 2008]

Note: RF8. See notes under section 42 of this Article.

Section 44. Term of imprisonment imposed by court to be fully served; exceptions. (1)(a) A term of imprisonment imposed by a judge in open court may not be set aside or otherwise not carried out, except as authorized by the sentencing court or through the subsequent exercise of:

(A) The power of the Governor to grant reprieves, commutations and pardons; or

(B) Judicial authority to grant appellate or post-conviction relief.

(b) No law shall limit a court's authority to sentence a criminal defendant consecutively for crimes against different victims.

(2) This section applies to all offenses committed on or after the effective date of this section. Nothing in this section reduces a criminal defendant's rights under the Constitution of the United States. Except as otherwise specifically provided, this section supersedes any conflicting section of this Constitution. Nothing in this section creates any cause of action for compensation or damages nor may this section be used to invalidate an accusatory instrument, ruling of a court, conviction or adjudication or otherwise suspend or terminate any criminal or juvenile delinquency proceedings at any point after the case is commenced or on appeal.

(3) As used in this section, "victim" means any person determined by the prosecuting attorney to have suffered direct financial, psychological or physical harm as a result of a crime and, in the case of a victim who is a minor, the legal guardian of the minor. In the event no person has been determined to be a victim of the crime, the people of Oregon, represented by the prosecuting attorney, are considered to be the victims. In no event is it intended that the criminal defendant be considered the victim. [Created through H.J.R. 94, 1999, and adopted by the people Nov. 2, 1999]

Note: RF8. See notes under section 42 of this Article.

Section 45. Person convicted of certain crimes not eligible to serve as juror on grand jury or trial jury in criminal case. (1) In all grand juries and in all prosecutions for crimes tried to a jury, the jury shall be composed of persons who have not been convicted:

(a) Of a felony or served a felony sentence within the 15 years immediately preceding the date the persons are required to report for jury duty; or

(b) Of a misdemeanor involving violence or dishonesty or served a sentence for a misdemeanor involving violence or dishonesty within the five years immediately preceding the date the persons are required to report for jury duty.

(2) This section applies to all criminal proceedings pending or commenced on or after the effective date of this section, except a criminal proceeding in which a jury has been impaneled and sworn on the effective date of this section. Nothing in this section reduces a criminal defendant's rights under the Constitution of the United States. Except as otherwise specifically provided, this section supersedes any conflicting section of this Constitution. Nothing in this section is intended to create any cause of action for compensation or damages nor may this section be used to disqualify a jury, invalidate an accusatory instrument, ruling of a court, conviction or adjudication or otherwise suspend or terminate any criminal proceeding at any point after a jury is impaneled and sworn or on appeal. [Created through H.J.R. 89, 1999, and adopted by the people Nov. 2, 1999]

Note: RF8. See notes under section 42 of this Article.

ARTICLE II
SUFFRAGE AND ELECTIONS

Section 1. Elections free. All elections shall be free and equal. —

Section 2. Qualifications of electors. (1) Every citizen of the United States is entitled to vote in all elections not otherwise provided for by this Constitution if such citizen:

(a) Is 18 years of age or older;

(b) Has resided in this state during the six months immediately preceding the election, except that provision may be made by law to permit a person who has resided in this state less than 30 days immediately preceding the election, but who is otherwise qualified under this subsection, to vote in the election for candidates for nomination or election for President or Vice President of the United States or elector of President and Vice President of the United States; and

(c) Is registered not less than 20 calendar days immediately preceding any election in the manner provided by law.

(2) Provision may be made by law to require that persons who vote upon questions of levying special taxes or issuing public bonds shall be taxpayers. [Constitution of 1859; Amendment proposed by initiative petition filed Dec. 20, 1910, and adopted by the people Nov. 5, 1912; Amendment proposed by S.J.R. 6, 1913, and adopted by the people Nov. 3, 1914; Amendment proposed by S.J.R. 6, 1923, and adopted by the people Nov. 4, 1924; Amendment proposed by H.J.R. 7, 1927, and adopted by the people June 28, 1927; Amendment proposed by H.J.R. 5, 1931, and adopted by the people Nov. 8, 1932; Amendment proposed by H.J.R. 26, 1959, and adopted by the people Nov. 8, 1960; Amendment proposed by H.J.R. 41, 1973, and adopted by the people Nov. 5, 1974; Amendment proposed by initiative petition filed July 20, 1986, and adopted by the people Nov. 4, 1986; Amendment proposed by H.J.R. 4, 2007, and adopted by the people Nov. 4, 2008]

Note: RF8. The leadline to section 2 was a part of the measure submitted to the people by initiative petition (Measure No. 13, 1986) and adopted by the people Nov. 4, 1986.

Section 3. Rights of certain electors. A person suffering from a mental handicap is entitled to the full rights of an elector, if otherwise qualified, unless the person has been adjudicated incompetent to vote as provided by law. The privilege of an elector, upon conviction of any crime which is punishable by imprisonment in the penitentiary, shall be forfeited, unless otherwise provided by law. [Constitution of 1859; Amendment proposed by S.J.R. 9, 1943, and adopted by the people Nov. 7, 1944; Amendment proposed by S.J.R. 26, 1979, and adopted by the people Nov. 4, 1980]

Section 4. Residence. For the purpose of voting, no person shall be deemed to have gained, or lost a residence, by reason of his presence, or absence while employed in the service of the United States, or of this State; nor while engaged in the navigation of the waters of this State, or of the United States, or of the high seas; nor while a student of any Seminary of Learning; nor while kept at any alms house, or other assylum [sic], at public expence [sic]; nor while confined in any public prison. —

Section 5. Soldiers, seamen and marines; residence; right to vote. No soldier, seaman, or marine in the Army, or Navy of the United States, or of their allies, shall be deemed to have acquired a residence in the state, in consequence of having been stationed within the same; nor shall any such soldier, seaman, or marine have the right to vote. —

Section 6. Right of suffrage for certain persons.:RF8. [Constitution of 1859; Repeal proposed by H.J.R. 4, 1927, and adopted by the people June 28, 1927]

Section 7. Bribery at elections. Every person shall be disqualified from holding office, during the term for which he may have been elected, who shall have given, or offered a bribe, threat, or reward to procure his election. —

Section 8. Regulation of elections. The Legislative Assembly shall enact laws to support the privilege of free suffrage, prescribing the manner of regulating, and conducting elections, and prohibiting under adequate penalties, all undue influence therein, from power, bribery, tumult, and other improper conduct. —

Section 9. Penalty for dueling. Every person who shall give, or accept a challenge to fight a duel, or who shall knowingly carry to another person such challenge, or who shall agree to go out of the State to fight a duel, shall be ineligible to any office of trust, or profit. —

Section 10. Lucrative offices; holding other offices forbidden. No person holding a lucrative office, or appointment under the United States, or under this State, shall be eligible to a seat in the Legislative Assembly; nor shall any person hold more than one lucrative office at the same time, except as in this Constition [sic] expressly permitted; Provided, that Officers in the Militia, to which there is attached no annual salary, and the Office of Post Master, where the compensation does not exceed One Hundred Dollars per annum, shall not be deemed lucrative. —

Section 11. When collector or holder of public moneys ineligible to office. No person who may hereafter be a collector, or holder of public moneys, shall be eligible to any office of trust or profit, until he shall have accounted for, and paid over according to law, all sums for which he may be liable. —

Section 12. Temporary appointments to office. In all cases, in which it is provided that an office shall not be filled by the same person, more than a certain number of years continuously, an appointment *pro tempore* shall not be reckoned a part of that term. —

Section 13. Privileges of electors. In all cases, except treason, felony, and breach of the peace, electors shall be free from arrest in going to elections, during their attendance there, and in returning from the same; and no elector shall be obliged to do duty in the Militia on any day of election, except in time of war, or public danger. —

Section 14. Time of holding elections and assuming duties of office. The regular general biennial election in Oregon for the year A. D. 1910 and thereafter shall be held on the first Tuesday after the first Monday in November. All officers except the Governor, elected for a six year term in 1904 or for a four year term in 1906 or for a two year term in 1908 shall continue to hold their respective offices until the first Monday in January, 1911; and all officers, except the Governor elected at any regular general biennial election after the adoption of this amendment shall assume the duties of their respective offices on the first Monday in January following such election. All laws pertaining to the nomination of candidates, registration of voters and all other things incident to the holding of the regular biennial election shall be enforced and be effected the same number of days before the first Tuesday after the first Monday in November that they have heretofore been before the first Monday in June biennially, except as may hereafter be provided by law. [Constitution of 1859; Amendment proposed by H.J.R. 7, 1907, and adopted by the people June 1, 1908]

Section 14a. Time of holding elections in incorporated cities and towns. Incorporated cities and towns shall hold their nominating and regular elections for their several elective officers at the same time that the primary and general biennial elections for State and county officers are held, and the election precincts and officers shall be the same for all elections held at the same time. All provisions of the charters and ordinances of incorporated cities and towns pertaining to the holding of elections shall continue in full force and effect except so far as they relate to the time of holding such elections. Every officer who, at the time of the adoption of this amendment, is the duly qualified incumbent of an elective office of an incorporated city or town shall hold his office for the term for which he was elected and until his successor is elected and qualified. The Legislature, and cities and towns, shall enact such supplementary legislation as may be necessary to carry the provisions of this amendment into effect. [Created through H.J.R. 22, 1917, and adopted by the people June 4, 1917]

Section 15. Method of voting in legislature. In all elections by the Legislative Assembly, or by either branch thereof, votes shall be given openly or viva voce, and not by ballot, forever; and in all elections by the people, votes shall be given openly, or viva voce, until the Legislative Assembly shall otherwise direct. —

Section 16. Election by plurality; proportional representation. In all elections authorized by this constitution until otherwise provided by law, the person or persons receiving the highest number of votes shall be declared elected, but provision may be made by law for elections by equal proportional representation of all the voters for every office which is filled by the election of two or more persons whose official duties, rights and powers are equal and concurrent. Every qualified elector resident in his precinct and registered as may be required by law, may vote for one person under the title for each office. Provision may be made by law for the voter's direct or indirect expression of his first, second or additional choices among the candidates for any office. For an office which is filled by the election of one person it may be required by law that the person elected shall be the final choice of a majority of the electors voting for candidates for that office. These principles may be applied by law to nominations by political parties and organizations. [Constitution of 1859; Amendment proposed by initiative petition filed Jan. 29, 1908, and adopted by the people June 1, 1908]

Section 17. Place of voting. All qualified electors shall vote in the election precinct in the County where they may reside, for County Officers, and in any County in the State for State Officers, or in any County of a Congressional District in which such electors may reside, for Members of Congress. —

Section 18. Recall; meaning of words "the legislative assembly shall provide." (1) Every public officer in Oregon is subject, as herein provided, to recall by the electors of the state or of the electoral district from which the public officer is elected.

(2) Fifteen per cent, but not more, of the number of electors who voted for Governor in the officer's electoral district at the most recent election at which a candidate for Governor was elected to a full term, may be required to file their petition demanding the officer's recall by the people.

(3) They shall set forth in the petition the reasons for the demand.

(4) If the public officer offers to resign, the resignation shall be accepted and take effect on the day it is offered, and the vacancy shall be filled as may be provided by law. If the public officer does not resign within five days after the petition is filed, a special election shall be ordered to be held within 35 days in the electoral district to determine whether the people will recall the officer.

(5) On the ballot at the election shall be printed in not more than 200 words the reasons for demanding the recall of the officer as set forth in the recall petition, and, in not more than 200 words, the officer's justification of the officer's course in office. The officer shall continue to perform the duties of office until the result of the special election is officially declared. If an officer is recalled from any public office the vacancy shall be filled immediately in the manner provided by law for filling a vacancy in that office arising from any other cause.

(6) The recall petition shall be filed with the officer with whom a petition for nomination to such office should be filed, and the same officer shall order the special election when it is required. No such petition shall be circulated against any officer until the officer has actually held the office six months, save and except that it may be filed against a senator or representative in the legislative assembly at any time after five days from the beginning of the first session after the election of the senator or representative.

(7) After one such petition and special election, no further recall petition shall be filed against the same officer during the term for which the officer was elected unless such further petitioners first pay into the public treasury which has paid such special election expenses, the whole amount of its expenses for the preceding special election.

(8) Such additional legislation as may aid the operation of this section shall be provided by the legislative assembly, including provision for payment by the public treasury of the reasonable special election campaign expenses of such officer. But the words, "the legislative

assembly shall provide," or any similar or equivalent words in this constitution or any amendment thereto, shall not be construed to grant to the legislative assembly any exclusive power of lawmaking nor in any way to limit the initiative and referendum powers reserved by the people. [Created through initiative petition filed Jan. 29, 1908, and adopted by the people June 1, 1908; Amendment proposed by S.J.R. 16, 1925, and adopted by the people Nov. 2, 1926; Amendment proposed by H.J.R. 1, 1983, and adopted by the people Nov. 6, 1984]

Note: RF8. "Recall." constituted the leadline to section 18 and was a part of the measure submitted to the people by S.J.R. 16, 1925.

Note: RF8. An initiative petition (Measure No. 3, 1992) proposed adding new sections relating to term limits to the Oregon Constitution. Those sections, appearing as sections 19, 20 and 21 of Article II in previous editions of this Constitution, were declared void for not being enacted in compliance with section 1, Article XVII of this Constitution. See Lehman v. Bradbury, 333 Or. 231, 37 P.3d 989 (2002).

Section 22. Political campaign contribution limitations. Section (1) For purposes of campaigning for an elected public office, a candidate may use or direct only contributions which originate from individuals who at the time of their donation were residents of the electoral district of the public office sought by the candidate, unless the contribution consists of volunteer time, information provided to the candidate, or funding provided by federal, state, or local government for purposes of campaigning for an elected public office.

Section (2) Where more than ten percent (10%) of a candidate's total campaign funding is in violation of Section (1), and the candidate is subsequently elected, the elected official shall forfeit the office and shall not hold a subsequent elected public office for a period equal to twice the tenure of the office sought. Where more than ten percent (10%) of a candidate's total campaign funding is in violation of Section (1) and the candidate is not elected, the unelected candidate shall not hold a subsequent elected public office for a period equal to twice the tenure of the office sought.

Section (3) A qualified donor (an individual who is a resident within the electoral district of the office sought by the candidate) shall not contribute to a candidate's campaign any restricted contributions of Section (1) received from an unqualified donor for the purpose of contributing to a candidate's campaign for elected public office. An unqualified donor (an entity which is not an individual and who is not a resident of the electoral district of the office sought by the candidate) shall not give any restricted contributions of Section (1) to a qualified donor for the purpose of contributing to a candidate's campaign for elected public office.

Section (4) A violation of Section (3) shall be an unclassified felony. [Created through initiative petition filed Jan. 25, 1993, and adopted by the people Nov. 8, 1994]

Note: RF8. An initiative petition (Measure No. 6, 1994) adopted by the people Nov. 8, 1994, proposed a constitutional amendment as an unnumbered section. Section 22 sections (1), (2), (3) and (4) were designated in the proposed amendment as "SECTION 1.," "SECTION 2.," "SECTION 3." and "SECTION 4.," respectively.

Section 23. Approval by more than majority required for certain measures submitted to people. (1) Any measure that includes any proposed requirement for more than a majority of votes cast by the electorate to approve any change in law or government action shall become effective only if approved by at least the same percentage of voters specified in the proposed voting requirement.

(2) For the purposes of this section, "measure" includes all initiatives and all measures referred to the voters by the Legislative Assembly.

(3) The requirements of this section apply to all measures presented to the voters at the November 3, 1998 election and thereafter.

(4) The purpose of this section is to prevent greater-than-majority voting requirements from being imposed by only a majority of the voters. [Created through initiative petition filed Jan. 15, 1998, and adopted by the people Nov. 3, 1998]

Note: RF8. Added as unnumbered section to the Constitution but not to any Article therein by initiative petition (Measure No. 63, 1998) adopted by the people Nov. 3, 1998.

Note: RF8. An initiative petition (Measure No. 62, 1998) proposed adding new sections and a subsection relating to political campaigns to the Oregon Constitution. Those sections, appearing as sections 24 to 32 of Article II and sections 1 (6), 1b and 1c of Article IV in previous editions of this Constitution, were declared void for not being enacted in compliance with section 1, Article XVII of this Constitution. See Swett v. Bradbury, 333 Or. 597, 43 P.3d 1094 (2002).

Section 24. Death of candidate prior to election. When any vacancy occurs in the nomination of a candidate for elective public office in this state, and the vacancy is due to the death of the candidate, the Legislative Assembly may provide by law that:

(1) The regularly scheduled election for that public office may be postponed;

(2) The public office may be filled at a subsequent election; and

(3) Votes cast for candidates for the public office at the regularly scheduled election may not be considered. [Created through S.J.R. 19, 2003, and adopted by the people Nov. 2, 2004]

ARTICLE III
DISTRIBUTION OF POWERS

Section 1. Separation of powers. The powers of the Government shall be divided into three seperate [sic] departments, the Legislative, the Executive, including the administrative, and the Judicial; and no person charged with official duties under one of these departments, shall exercise any of the functions of another, except as in this Constitution expressly provided. —

Section 2. Budgetary control over executive and administrative officers and agencies. The Legislative Assembly shall have power to establish an agency to exercise budgetary control over all executive and administrative state officers, departments, boards, commissions and agencies of the State Government. [Created through S.J.R. 24, 1951, and adopted by the people Nov. 4, 1952]

Note: RF8. Section 2 was designated as "Sec. 1" by S.J.R. 24, 1951, and adopted by the people Nov. 4, 1952.

Section 3. Joint legislative committee to allocate emergency fund appropriations and to authorize expenditures beyond budgetary limits. (1) The Legislative Assembly is authorized to establish by law a joint committee composed of members of both houses of the Legislative Assembly, the membership to be as fixed by law, which committee may exercise, during the interim between sessions of the Legislative Assembly, such of the following powers as may be conferred upon it by law:

(a) Where an emergency exists, to allocate to any state agency, out of any emergency fund that may be appropriated to the committee for that purpose, additional funds beyond the amount appropriated to the agency by the Legislative Assembly, or funds to carry on an activity required by law for which an appropriation was not made.

(b) Where an emergency exists, to authorize any state agency to expend, from funds dedicated or continuously appropriated for the uses and purposes of the agency, sums in excess of the amount of the budget of the agency as approved in accordance with law.

(c) In the case of a new activity coming into existence at such a time as to preclude the possibility of submitting a budget to the Legislative Assembly for approval, to approve, or revise and approve, a budget of the money appropriated for such new activity.

(d) Where an emergency exists, to revise or amend the budgets of state agencies to the extent of authorizing transfers between expenditure classifications within the budget of an agency.

(2) The Legislative Assembly shall prescribe by law what shall constitute an emergency for the purposes of this section.

(3) As used in this section, "state agency" means any elected or appointed officer, board, commission, department, institution, branch or other agency of the state government.

(4) The term of members of the joint committee established pursuant to this section shall run from the adjournment of one odd-numbered year regular session to the organization of the next odd-numbered year regular session. No member of a committee shall cease to be such member solely by reason of the expiration of his term of office as a member of the Legislative Assembly. [Created through S.J.R. 24, 1951, and adopted by the people Nov. 4, 1952; Amendment proposed by S.J.R. 41, 2010, and adopted by the people Nov. 2, 2010]

Note: RF8. Section 3 was designated as "Sec. 2" by S.J.R. 24, 1951, and adopted by the people Nov. 4, 1952.

Section 4. Senate confirmation of executive appointments. (1) The Legislative Assembly in the manner provided by law may require that all appointments and reappointments to state public office made by the Governor shall be subject to confirmation by the Senate.

(2) The appointee shall not be eligible to serve until confirmed in the manner required by law and if not confirmed in that manner, shall not be eligible to serve in the public office.

(3) In addition to appointive offices, the provisions of this section shall apply to any state elective office when the Governor is authorized by law or this Constitution to fill any vacancy therein, except the office of judge of any court, United States Senator or Representative and a district, county or precinct office. [Created through S.J.R. 20, 1977, and adopted by the people Nov. 7, 1978]

ARTICLE IV
LEGISLATIVE DEPARTMENT

Section 1. Legislative power; initiative and referendum. (1) The legislative power of the state, except for the initiative and referendum powers reserved to the people, is vested in a Legislative Assembly, consisting of a Senate and a House of Representatives.

(2)(a) The people reserve to themselves the initiative power, which is to propose laws and amendments to the Constitution and enact or reject them at an election independently of the Legislative Assembly.

(b) An initiative law may be proposed only by a petition signed by a number of qualified voters equal to six percent of the total number of votes cast for all candidates for Governor at the election at which a Governor was elected for a term of four years next preceding the filing of the petition.

(c) An initiative amendment to the Constitution may be proposed only by a petition signed by a number of qualified voters equal to eight percent of the total number of votes cast for all candidates for Governor at the election at which a Governor was elected for a term of four years next preceding the filing of the petition.

(d) An initiative petition shall include the full text of the proposed law or amendment to the Constitution. A proposed law or amendment to the Constitution shall embrace one subject only and matters properly connected therewith.

(e) An initiative petition shall be filed not less than four months before the election at which the proposed law or amendment to the Constitution is to be voted upon.

(3)(a) The people reserve to themselves the referendum power, which is to approve or reject at an election any Act, or part thereof, of the Legislative Assembly that does not become effective earlier than 90 days after the end of the session at which the Act is passed.

(b) A referendum on an Act or part thereof may be ordered by a petition signed by a number of qualified voters equal to four percent of the total number of votes cast for all candidates for Governor at the election at which a Governor was elected for a term of four years next preceding the filing of the petition. A referendum petition shall be filed not more than 90 days after the end of the session at which the Act is passed.

(c) A referendum on an Act may be ordered by the Legislative Assembly by law. Notwithstanding section 15b, Article V of this Constitution, bills ordering a referendum and bills on which a referendum is ordered are not subject to veto by the Governor.

(4)(a) Petitions or orders for the initiative or referendum shall be filed with the Secretary of State. The Legislative Assembly shall provide by law for the manner in which the Secretary of State shall determine whether a petition contains the required number of signatures of qualified voters. The Secretary of State shall complete the verification process within the 30-day period after the last day on which the petition may be filed as provided in paragraph (e) of subsection (2) or paragraph (b) of subsection (3) of this section.

(b) Initiative and referendum measures shall be submitted to the people as provided in this section and by law not inconsistent therewith.

(c) All elections on initiative and referendum measures shall be held at the regular general elections, unless otherwise ordered by the Legislative Assembly.

(d) Notwithstanding section 1, Article XVII of this Constitution, an initiative or referendum measure becomes effective 30 days after the day on which it is enacted or approved by a majority of the votes cast thereon. A referendum ordered by petition on a part of an Act does not delay the remainder of the Act from becoming effective.

(5) The initiative and referendum powers reserved to the people by subsections (2) and (3) of this section are further reserved to the qualified voters of each municipality and district as to all local, special and municipal legislation of every character in or for their municipality or district. The manner of exercising those powers shall be provided by general laws, but cities may provide the manner of exercising those powers as to their municipal legislation. In a city, not more than 15 percent of the qualified voters may be required to propose legislation by the initiative, and not more than 10 percent of the qualified voters may be required to order a referendum on legislation. [Created through H.J.R. 16, 1967, and adopted by the people May 28, 1968 (this section adopted in lieu of former sections 1 and 1a of this Article); Amendment proposed by S.J.R. 27, 1985, and adopted by the people May 20, 1986; Amendment proposed by S.J.R. 3, 1999, and adopted by the people May 16, 2000]

Note: RF8. An initiative petition (Measure No. 62, 1998) proposed adding new sections and a subsection relating to political campaigns to the Oregon Constitution. Those sections, appearing as sections 24 to 32 of Article II and sections 1 (6), 1b and 1c of Article IV in previous editions of this Constitution, were declared void for not being enacted in compliance with section 1, Article XVII of this Constitution. See Swett v. Bradbury, 333 Or. 597, 43 P.3d 1094 (2002).

Section 1. Legislative authority vested in assembly; initiative and referendum; style of bills.:RF8. [Constitution of 1859; Amendment proposed by H.J.R. 1, 1901, and adopted by the people June 2, 1902; Amendment proposed by S.J.R. 6, 1953, and adopted by the people Nov. 2, 1954; Repeal proposed by H.J.R. 16, 1967, and adopted by the people May 28, 1968 (present section 1 of this Article adopted in lieu of this section)]

Section 1a. Initiative and referendum on parts of laws and on local, special and municipal laws.:RF8. [Created through initiative petition filed Feb. 3, 1906, and adopted by the people June 4, 1906; Repeal proposed by H.J.R. 16, 1967, and adopted by the people May 28, 1968 (present section 1 of this Article adopted in lieu of this section)]

Note: RF8. Section 1b as submitted to the people was preceded by the following::PAR8.To protect the integrity of initiative and referendum petitions, the People of Oregon add the following provisions to the Constitution of the State of Oregon:

Section 1b. Payment for signatures. It shall be unlawful to pay or receive money or other thing of value based on the number of signatures obtained on an initiative or referendum petition. Nothing herein prohibits payment for signature gathering which is not based, either directly or indirectly, on the number of signatures obtained. [Created through initiative petition filed Nov. 7, 2001, and adopted by the people Nov. 5, 2002]

Note: RF8. Added as unnumbered section to the Constitution but not to any Article therein by initiative petition (Measure No. 26, 2002) adopted by the people Nov. 5, 2002.

Section 1d. Effective date of amendment to section 1, Article IV, by S.J.R. 3, 1999.:RF8. [Created through S.J.R. 3, 1999, and adopted by the people May 16, 2000; Repealed Dec. 31, 2002, as specified in text of section adopted by the people May 16, 2000]

Section 2. Number of Senators and Representatives. The Senate shall consist of sixteen, and the House of Representatives of thirty four members, which number shall not be increased until the year Eighteen Hundred and Sixty, after which time the Legislative Assembly may increase the number of Senators and Representatives, always keeping as near as may be the same ratio as to the number of Senators, and Representatives: Provided that the Senate shall never exceed thirty and the House of Representatives sixty members. —

Section 3. How Senators and Representatives chosen; filling vacancies; qualifications. (1) The senators and representatives shall be chosen by the electors of the respective counties or districts or subdistricts within a county or district into which the state may from time to time be divided by law.

(2)(a) If a vacancy occurs in the office of senator or representative from any county or district or subdistrict, the vacancy shall be filled as may be provided by law.

(b) Except as provided in paragraph (c) of this subsection, a person who is appointed to fill a vacancy in the office of senator or representative must be an inhabitant of the district the person is appointed to represent for at least one year next preceding the date of the appointment.

(c) For purposes of an appointment occurring during the period beginning on January 1 of the year a reapportionment becomes operative under section 6 of this Article, the person must have been an inhabitant of the district for one year next preceding the date of the appointment or from January 1 of the year the reapportionment becomes operative to the date of the appoint-

Constitution

ment, whichever is less. [Constitution of 1859; Amendment proposed by S.J.R. 20, 1929, and adopted by the people Nov. 4, 1930; Amendment proposed by H.J.R. 20, 1953, and adopted by the people Nov. 2, 1954; Amendment proposed by S.J.R. 14, 1995, and adopted by the people May 16, 1995; Amendment proposed by H.J.R. 31, 2007, and adopted by the people Nov. 4, 2008]

Section 3a. Applicability of qualifications for appointment to legislative vacancy.:RF8. [Section 3a was designated section 1b, which was created by S.J.R. 14, 1995, and adopted by the people May 16, 1995; Repealed Dec. 31, 1999, as specified in text of section adopted by the people May 16, 1995]

Section 4. Term of office of legislators; classification of Senators. (1) The Senators shall be elected for the term of four years, and Representatives for the term of two years. The term of each Senator and Representative shall commence on the second Monday in January following his election, and shall continue for the full period of four years or two years, as the case may be, unless a different commencing day for such terms shall have been appointed by law.

(2) The Senators shall continue to be divided into two classes, in accordance with the division by lot provided for under the former provisions of this Constitution, so that one-half, as nearly as possible, of the number of Senators shall be elected biennially.

(3) Any Senator or Representative whose term, under the former provisions of this section, would have expired on the first Monday in January 1961, shall continue in office until the second Monday in January 1961. [Constitution of 1859; Amendment proposed by S.J.R. 23, 1951, and adopted by the people Nov. 4, 1952; Amendment proposed by S.J.R. 28, 1959, and adopted by the people Nov. 8, 1960]

Section 5. Census.:RF8. [Constitution of 1859; Repeal proposed by H.J.R. 16, 1971, and adopted by the people May 23, 1972]

Section 6. Apportionment of Senators and Representatives.:RF8. [Constitution of 1859; Amendment proposed by initiative petition filed July 3, 1952, and adopted by the people Nov. 4, 1952; Repeal proposed by H.J.R. 6, 1985, and adopted by the people Nov. 4, 1986 (present section 6 of this Article adopted in lieu of this section)]

Section 6. Apportionment of Senators and Representatives; operative date. (1) At the odd-numbered year regular session of the Legislative Assembly next following an enumeration of the inhabitants by the United States Government, the number of Senators and Representatives shall be fixed by law and apportioned among legislative districts according to population. A senatorial district shall consist of two representative districts. Any Senator whose term continues through the next odd-numbered year regular legislative session after the operative date of the reapportionment shall be specifically assigned to a senatorial district. The ratio of Senators and Representatives, respectively, to population shall be determined by dividing the total population of the state by the number of Senators and by the number of Representatives. A reapportionment by the Legislative Assembly becomes operative as described in subsection (6) of this section.

(2) This subsection governs judicial review and correction of a reapportionment enacted by the Legislative Assembly.

(a) Original jurisdiction is vested in the Supreme Court, upon the petition of any elector of the state filed with the Supreme Court on or before August 1 of the year in which the Legislative Assembly enacts a reapportionment, to review any reapportionment so enacted.

(b) If the Supreme Court determines that the reapportionment thus reviewed complies with subsection (1) of this section and all law applicable thereto, it shall dismiss the petition by written opinion on or before September 1 of the same year and the reapportionment becomes operative as described in subsection (6) of this section.

(c) If the Supreme Court determines that the reapportionment does not comply with subsection (1) of this section and all law applicable thereto, the reapportionment shall be void. In its written opinion, the Supreme Court shall specify with particularity wherein the reapportionment fails to comply. The opinion shall further direct the Secretary of State to draft a reapportionment of the Senators and Representatives in accordance with the provisions of subsection (1) of this section and all law applicable thereto. The Supreme Court shall file its order with the Secretary of State on or before September 15. The Secretary of State shall conduct a hearing on the reapportionment at which the public may submit evidence, views and argument. The Secretary of State shall cause a transcription of the hearing to be prepared which, with the evidence, shall become part of the record. The Secretary of State shall file the corrected reapportionment with the Supreme Court on or before November 1 of the same year.

(d) On or before November 15, the Supreme Court shall review the corrected reapportionment to assure its compliance with subsection (1) of this section and all law applicable thereto and may further correct the reapportionment if the court considers correction to be necessary.

(e) The corrected reapportionment becomes operative as described in subsection (6) of this section.

(3) This subsection governs enactment, judicial review and correction of a reapportionment if the Legislative Assembly fails to enact any reapportionment by July 1 of the year of the odd-numbered year regular session of the Legislative Assembly next following an enumeration of the inhabitants by the United States Government.

(a) The Secretary of State shall make a reapportionment of the Senators and Representatives in accordance with the provisions of subsection (1) of this section and all law applicable thereto. The Secretary of State shall conduct a hearing on the reapportionment at which the public may submit evidence, views and argument. The Secretary of State shall cause a transcription of the hearing to be prepared which, with the evidence, shall become part of the record. The reapportionment so made shall be filed with the Supreme Court by August 15 of the same year. The reapportionment becomes operative as described in subsection (6) of this section.

(b) Original jurisdiction is vested in the Supreme Court upon the petition of any elector of the state filed with the Supreme Court on or before September 15 of the same year to review any reapportionment and the record made by the Secretary of State.

(c) If the Supreme Court determines that the reapportionment thus reviewed complies with subsection (1) of this section and all law applicable thereto, it shall dismiss the petition by written opinion on or before October 15 of the same year and the reapportionment becomes operative as described in subsection (6) of this section.

(d) If the Supreme Court determines that the reapportionment does not comply with subsection (1) of this section and all law applicable thereto, the reapportionment shall be void. The Supreme Court shall return the reapportionment by November 1 to the Secretary of State accompanied by a written opinion specifying with particularity wherein the reapportionment fails to comply. The opinion shall further direct the Secretary of State to correct the reapportionment in those particulars, and in no others, and file the corrected reapportionment with the Supreme Court on or before December 1 of the same year.

(e) On or before December 15, the Supreme Court shall review the corrected reapportionment to assure its compliance with subsection (1) of this section and all law applicable thereto and may further correct the reapportionment if the court considers correction to be necessary.

(f) The reapportionment becomes operative as described in subsection (6) of this section.

(4) Any reapportionment that becomes operative as provided in this section is a law of the state except for purposes of initiative and referendum.

(5) Notwithstanding section 18, Article II of this Constitution, after the convening of the next odd-numbered year regular legislative session following the reapportionment, a Senator whose term continues through that legislative session is subject to recall by the electors of the district to which the Senator is assigned and not by the electors of the district existing before the latest reapportionment. The number of signatures required on the recall petition is 15 percent of the total votes cast for all candidates for Governor at the most recent election at which a candidate for Governor was elected to a full term in the two representative districts comprising the senatorial district to which the Senator was assigned.

(6)(a) Except as provided in paragraph (b) of this subsection, a reapportionment made under this section becomes operative on the second Monday in January of the next odd-numbered year after the applicable deadline for making a final reapportionment under this section.(b) For purposes of electing Senators and Representatives to the next term of office that commences after the applicable deadline for making a final reapportionment under this section, a reapportionment made under this section becomes operative on January 1 of the calendar year next following the applicable deadline for making a final reapportionment under this section. [Created through H.J.R. 6, 1985, and adopted by the people Nov. 4, 1986 (this section adopted in lieu of former section 6 of this Article); Amendment proposed by H.J.R. 31, 2007, and adopted by the people Nov. 4, 2008; Amendment proposed by S.J.R. 41, 2010, and adopted by the people Nov. 2, 2010]

Section 7. Senatorial districts; senatorial and representative subdistricts. A senatorial district, when more than one county shall constitute the same, shall be composed of contiguous counties, and no county shall be divided in creating such senatorial districts. Senatorial or representative districts comprising not more than one county may be divided into subdistricts from time to time by law. Subdistricts shall be composed of contiguous territory within the district; and the ratios to population of senators or representatives, as the case may be, elected from the subdistricts, shall be substantially equal within the district. [Constitution of 1859; Amendment proposed by H.J.R. 20, 1953, and adopted by the people Nov. 2, 1954]

Section 8. Qualification of Senators and Representatives; effect of felony conviction. (1)(a) Except as provided in paragraph (b) of this subsection, a person may not be a Senator or Representative if the person at the time of election:

(A) Is not a citizen of the United States; and

(B) Has not been for one year next preceding the election an inhabitant of the district from which the Senator or Representative may be chosen.

(b) For purposes of the general election next following the applicable deadline for making a final apportionment under section 6 of this Article, the person must have been an inhabitant of the district from January 1 of the year following the applicable deadline for making the final reapportionment to the date of the election.

(2) Senators and Representatives shall be at least twenty one years of age.

(3) A person may not be a Senator or Representative if the person has been convicted of a felony during:

(a) The term of office of the person as a Senator or Representative; or

(b) The period beginning on the date of the election at which the person was elected to the office of Senator or Representative and ending on the first day of the term of office to which the person was elected.

(4) A person is not eligible to be elected as a Senator or Representative if that person has been convicted of a felony and has not completed the sentence received for the conviction prior to the date that person would take office if elected. As used in this subsection, "sentence received for the conviction" includes a term of imprisonment, any period of probation or post-prison supervision and payment of a monetary obligation imposed as all or part of a sentence.

(5) Notwithstanding sections 11 and 15, Article IV of this Constitution:

(a) The office of a Senator or Representative convicted of a felony during the term to which the Senator or Representative was elected or appointed shall become vacant on the date the Senator or Representative is convicted.

(b) A person elected to the office of Senator or Representative and convicted of a felony during the period beginning on the date of the election and ending on the first day of the term of office to which the person was elected shall be ineligible to take office and the office shall become vacant on the first day of the next term of office.

(6) Subject to subsection (4) of this section, a person who is ineligible to be a Senator or Representative under subsection (3) of this section may:

(a) Be a Senator or Representative after the expiration of the term of office during which the person is ineligible; and

(b) Be a candidate for the office of Senator or Representative prior to the expiration of the term of office during which the person is ineligible.

(7)(a) Except as provided in paragraph (b) of this subsection, a person may not be a Senator or Representative if the person at all times during the term of office of the person as a Senator or Representative is not an inhabitant of the district from which the Senator or Representative may be chosen or which the Senator or Representative has been appointed to represent. A person does not lose status as an inhabitant of a district if the person is absent from the district for purposes of business of the Legislative Assembly.

(b) Following the applicable deadline for making a final apportionment under section 6 of this Article, until the expiration of the term of office of the person, a person may be an inhabitant of any district. [Constitution of 1859; Amendment proposed by H.J.R. 6, 1985, and adopted by the people Nov. 4, 1986; Amendment proposed by S.J.R. 33, 1993, and adopted by the people Nov. 8, 1994; Amendment proposed by S.J.R. 14, 1995, and adopted by the people May 16, 1995; Amendment proposed by H.J.R. 31, 2007, and adopted by the people Nov. 4, 2008]

Section 8a. Applicability of qualification for legislative office.:RF8. [Created by S.J.R. 14, 1995, and adopted by the people May 16, 1995; Repealed Dec. 31, 1999, as specified in text of section adopted by the people May 16, 1995]

Section 9. Legislators free from arrest and not subject to civil process in certain cases; words uttered in debate. Senators and Representatives in all cases, except for treason, felony, or breaches of the peace, shall be privileged from arrest during the session of the Legislative Assembly, and in going to and returning from the same; and shall not be subject to any civil process during the session of the Legislative Assembly, nor during the fifteen days next before the commencement thereof: Nor shall a member for words uttered in debate in either house, be questioned in any other place. —

Section 10. Annual regular sessions of the Legislative Assembly; organizational session; extension of regular sessions. (1) The Legislative Assembly shall hold annual sessions at the Capitol of the State. Each session must begin on the day designated by law as the first day of the session. Except as provided in subsection (3) of this section:

(a) A session beginning in an odd-numbered year may not exceed 160 calendar days in duration; and

(b) A session beginning in an even-numbered year may not exceed 35 calendar days in duration.

(2) The Legislative Assembly may hold an organizational session that is not subject to the limits of subsection (1) of this section for the purposes of introducing measures and performing the duties and effecting the organization described in sections 11 and 12 of this Article. The Legislative Assembly may not undertake final consideration of a measure or reconsideration of a measure following a gubernatorial veto when convened in an organizational session.

(3) A regular session, as described in subsection (1) of this section, may be extended for a period of five calendar days by the affirmative vote of two-thirds of the members of each house. A session may be extended more than once. An extension must begin on the first calendar day after the end of the immediately preceding session or extension except that if the first calendar day is a Sunday, the extension may begin on the next Monday. [Constitution of 1859; Amendment proposed by S.J.R. 41, 2010, and adopted by the people Nov. 2, 2010]

Section 10a. Emergency sessions of the Legislative Assembly. In the event of an emergency the Legislative Assembly shall be convened by the presiding officers of both Houses at the Capitol of the State at times other than required by section 10 of this Article upon the written request of the majority of the members of each House to commence within five days after receipt of the minimum requisite number of requests. [Created through H.J.R. 28, 1975, and adopted by the people Nov. 2, 1976]

Section 11. Legislative officers; rules of proceedings; adjournments. Each house when assembled, shall choose its own officers, judge of the election, qualifications, and returns of its own members; determine its own rules of proceeding, and sit upon its own adjournments; but neither house shall without the concurrence of the other, adjourn for more than three days, nor to any other place than that in which it may be sitting. —

Section 12. Quorum; failure to effect organization. Two thirds of each house shall constitute a quorum to do business, but a smaller number may meet; adjourn from day to day, and compel the attendance of absent members. A quorum being in attendance, if either house fail to effect an organization within the first five days thereafter, the members of the house so failing shall be entitled to no compensation from the end of the said five days until an organization shall have been effected. —

Section 13. Journal; when yeas and nays to be entered. Each house shall keep a journal of its proceedings.—The yeas and nays on any question, shall at the request of any two members, be entered, together with the names of the members demanding the same, on the journal; provided that on a motion to adjourn it shall require one tenth of the members present to order the yeas, and nays.

Section 14. Deliberations to be open; rules to implement requirement. The deliberations of each house, of committees of each house or joint committees and of committees of the whole, shall be open. Each house shall adopt rules to implement the requirement of this section and the houses jointly shall adopt rules to implement the requirements of this section in any joint activity that the two houses may undertake. [Constitution of 1859; Amendment proposed by S.J.R. 36, 1973, and adopted by the people Nov. 5, 1974; Amendment proposed by H.J.R. 29, 1977, and adopted by the people May 23, 1978]

Section 15. Punishment and expulsion of members. Either house may punish its members for disorderly behavior, and may with the concurrence of two thirds, expel a member; but not a second time for the same cause. —

Section 16. Punishment of nonmembers. Either house, during its session, may punish by imprisonment, any person, not a member, who shall have been guilty of disrespect to the house by disorderly or contemptious [sic] behavior in its presence, but such imprisonment shall not at any time, exceed twenty [sic] twenty four hours. —

Section 17. General powers of Legislative Assembly. Each house shall have all powers necessary for a branch of the Legislative Department, of a free, and independant [sic] State. —

Section 18. Where bills to originate. Bills may originate in either house, but may be amended, or rejected in the other; except that bills for raising revenue shall originate in the House of Representatives. —

Section 19. Reading of bills; vote on final passage. Every bill shall be read by title only on three several days, in each house, unless in case of emergency two-thirds of the house where such bill may be pending shall, by a vote of yeas and nays, deem it expedient to dispense with this rule; provided, however, on its final passage such bill shall be read section by section unless such requirement be suspended by a vote of two-thirds of the house where such bill may be pending, and the vote on the final passage of every bill or joint resolution shall be taken by yeas and nays. [Constitution of 1859; Amendment proposed by S.J.R. 15, 1945, and adopted by the people Nov. 5, 1946]

Section 20. Subject and title of Act. Every Act shall embrace but one subject, and matters properly connected therewith, which subject shall be expressed in the title. But if any subject shall be embraced in an Act which shall not be expressed in the title, such Act shall be void only as to so much thereof as shall not be expressed in the title.

This section shall not be construed to prevent the inclusion in an amendatory Act, under a proper title, of matters otherwise germane to the same general subject, although the title or titles of the original Act or Acts may not have been sufficiently broad to have permitted such matter to have been so included in such original Act or Acts, or any of them. [Constitution of 1859; Amendment proposed by S.J.R. 41, 1951, and adopted by the people Nov. 4, 1952]

Section 21. Acts to be plainly worded. Every act, and joint resolution shall be plainly worded, avoiding as far as practicable the use of technical terms. —

Section 22. Mode of revision and amendment. No act shall ever be revised, or amended by mere reference to its title, but the act revised, or section amended shall be set forth, and published at full length. However, if, at any session of the Legislative Assembly, there are enacted two or more acts amending the same section, each of the acts shall be given effect to the extent that the amendments do not conflict in purpose. If the amendments conflict in purpose, the act last signed by the Governor shall control. [Constitution of 1859; Amendment proposed by S.J.R. 28, 1975, and adopted by the people Nov. 2, 1976]

Section 23. Certain local and special laws prohibited. The Legislative Assembly, shall not pass special or local laws, in any of the following enumerated cases, that is to say: —

Regulating the jurisdiction, and duties of justices of the peace, and of constables;

For the punishment of Crimes, and Misdemeanors;

Regulating the practice in Courts of Justice;

Providing for changing the venue in civil, and Criminal cases;

Granting divorces;

Changing the names of persons;

For laying, opening, and working on highways, and for the election, or appointment of supervisors;

Vacating roads, Town plats, Streets, Alleys, and Public squares;

Summoning and empanneling [sic] grand, and petit jurors;

For the assessment and collection of Taxes, for State, County, Township, or road purposes;

Providing for supporting Common schools, and for the preservation of school funds;

In relation to interest on money;

Providing for opening, and conducting the elections of State, County, and Township officers, and designating the places of voting;

Providing for the sale of real estate, belonging to minors, or other persons laboring under legal disabilities, by executors, administrators, guardians, or trustees. —

Section 24. Suit against state. Provision may be made by general law, for bringing suit against the State, as to all liabilities originating after, or existing at the time of the adoption of this Constitution; but no special act authorizeing [sic] such suit to be brought, or making compensation to any person claiming damages against the State, shall ever be passed. —

Section 25. Majority necessary to pass bills and resolutions; special requirements for bills raising revenue; signatures of presiding officers required. (1) Except as otherwise provided in subsection (2) of this section, a majority of all the members elected to each House shall be necessary to pass every bill or Joint resolution.

(2) Three-fifths of all members elected to each House shall be necessary to pass bills for raising revenue.

(3) All bills, and Joint resolutions passed, shall be signed by the presiding officers of the respective houses. [Constitution of 1859; Amendment proposed by H.J.R. 14, 1995, and adopted by the people May 21, 1996]

Section 26. Protest by member. Any member of either house, shall have the right to protest, and have his protest, with his reasons for dissent, entered on the journal.:B1ART. —

Section 27. All statutes public laws; exceptions. Every Statute shall be a public law, unless otherwise declared in the Statute itself. —

Section 28. When Act takes effect. No act shall take effect, until ninety days from the end of the session at which the same shall have been passed, except in case of emergency; which emergency shall be declared in the preamble, or in the body of the law. —

Section 29. Compensation of members. The members of the Legislative Assembly shall receive for their services a salary to be established and paid in the same manner as the salaries of other elected state officers and employes. [Constitution of 1859; Amendment proposed by S.J.R. 3, 1941, and adopted by the people Nov. 3, 1942; Amendment proposed by H.J.R. 5, 1949, and adopted by the people Nov. 7, 1950; Amendment proposed by H.J.R. 8, 1961, and adopted by the people May 18, 1962]

Section 30. Members not eligible to other offices. No Senator or Representative shall, during the time for which he may have been elected, be eligible to any office the election to which is vested in the Legislative Assembly; nor shall be appointed to any civil office of profit which shall have been created, or the emoluments of which shall have been increased during such term; but this latter provision shall not be construed to apply to any officer elective by the people. —

Section 31. Oath of members. The members of the Legislative Assembly shall before they enter on the duties of their respective offices, take and subscribe the following oath or affirmation; — I do solemnly swear (or affirm as the case may be) that I will support the Constitution of the United States, and the Constitution of the State of Oregon, and that I will faithfully discharge the duties of Senator (or Representative as the case may be) according to the best of my Ability, And such oath may be administered by the Govenor [sic], Secretary of State, or a judge of the Supreme Court. —

Section 32. Income tax defined by federal law; review of tax laws required. Notwithstanding any other provision of this Constitution, the Legislative Assembly, in any law imposing a tax or taxes on, in respect to or measured by income, may define the income on, in respect to or by which such tax or taxes are imposed or measured, by reference to any provision of the laws of the United States as the same may be or become effective at any time or from time to time, and may prescribe exceptions or modifications to any such provisions. At each regular session the Legislative Assembly shall, and at any special session may, provide for a review of the Oregon laws imposing a tax upon or measured by income, but no such laws shall be amended or repealed except by a legislative Act. [Created through H.J.R. 3, 1969, and adopted by the people Nov. 3, 1970]

Section 33. Reduction of criminal sentences approved by initiative or referendum process. Notwithstanding the provisions of section 25 of this Article, a two-thirds vote of all the members elected to each house shall be necessary to pass a bill that reduces a criminal sentence approved by the people under section 1 of this Article. [Created through initiative petition filed Nov. 16, 1993, and adopted by the people Nov. 8, 1994]

ARTICLE V
EXECUTIVE DEPARTMENT

Section 1. Governor as chief executive; term of office; period of eligibility. The cheif [sic] executive power of the State, shall be vested in a Governor, who shall hold his office for the term of four years; and no person shall be eligible to such office more than Eight, in any period of twelve years. —

Section 2. Qualifications of Governor. No person except a citizen of the United States, shall be eligible to the Office of Governor, nor shall any person be eligible to that office who shall not have attained the age of thirty years, and who shall not have been three years next preceding his election, a resident within this State. The minimum age requirement of this section does not apply to a person who succeeds to the office of Governor under section 8a of this Article. [Constitution of 1859; Amendment proposed by H.J.R. 52, 1973, and adopted by the people Nov. 5, 1974]

Section 3. Who not eligible. No member of Congress, or person holding any office under the United States, or under this State, or under any other power, shall fill the Office of Governor, except as may be otherwise provided in this Constitution. —

Section 4. Election of Governor. The Governor shall be elected by the qualified Electors of the State at the times, and places of choosing members of the Legislative Assembly; and the returns of every Election for Governor, shall be sealed up, and transmitted to the Secretary of State; directed to the Speaker of the House of Representatives, who shall open, and publish them in the presence of both houses of the Legislative Assembly. —

Section 5. Greatest number of votes decisive; election by legislature in case of tie. The person having the highest number of votes for Governor, shall be elected; but in case two or more persons shall have an equal and the highest number of votes for Governor, the two houses of the Legislative Assembly at the next regular session thereof, shall forthwith by joint vote, proceed to elect one of the said persons Governor. —

Section 6. Contested elections. Contested Elections for Governor shall be determined by the Legislative Assembly in such manner as may be prescribed by law. —

Section 7. Term of office. The official term of the Governor shall be four years; and shall commence at such times as may be prescribed by this constitution, or prescribed by law. —

Section 8. Vacancy in office of Governor.:RF8. [Constitution of 1859; Amendment proposed by S.J.R. 10, 1920 (s.s.), and adopted by the people May 21, 1920; Amendment proposed by S.J.R. 8, 1945, and adopted by the people Nov. 5, 1946; Repeal proposed by initiative petition filed July 7, 1972, and adopted by the people Nov. 7, 1972 (present section 8a of this Article adopted in lieu of this section)]

Section 8a. Vacancy in office of Governor. In case of the removal from office of the Governor, or of his death, resignation, or disability to discharge the duties of his office as prescribed by law, the Secretary of State; or if there be none, or in case of his removal from office, death, resignation, or disability to discharge the duties of his office as prescribed by law, then the State Treasurer; or if there be none, or in case of his removal from office, death, resignation, or disability to discharge the duties of his office as prescribed by law, then the President of the Senate; or if there be none, or in case of his removal from office, death, resignation, or disability to discharge the duties of his office as prescribed by law, then the Speaker of the House of Representatives, shall become Governor until the disability be removed, or a Governor be elected at the next general biennial election. The Governor elected to fill the vacancy shall hold office for the unexpired term of the outgoing Governor. The Secretary of State or the State Treasurer shall appoint a person to fill his office until the election of a Governor, at which time the office so filled by appointment shall be filled by election; or, in the event of a disability of the Governor, to be Acting Secretary of State or Acting State Treasurer until the disability be removed. The person so appointed shall not be eligible to succeed to the office of Governor by automatic succession under this section during the term of his appointment. [Created through initiative petition filed July 7, 1972, and adopted by the people Nov. 7, 1972 (this section adopted in lieu of former section 8 of this Article)]

Section 9. Governor as commander in chief of state military forces. The Governor shall be commander in cheif [sic] of the military, and naval forces of this State, and may call out such forces to execute the laws, to suppress insurection [sic], or to repel invasion. —

Section 10. Governor to see laws executed. He shall take care that the Laws be faithfully executed. —

Section 11. Recommendations to legislature. He shall from time to time give to the Legislative Assembly information touching the condition of the State, and reccommend [sic] such measures as he shall judge to be expedient[.] —

Section 12. Governor may convene legislature. He may on extraordinary occasions convene the Legislative Assembly by proclamation, and shall state to both houses when assembled, the purpose for which they shall have been convened. —

Section 13. Transaction of governmental business. He shall transact all necessary business with the officers of government, and may require information in writing from the offices of the Administrative, and Military Departments upon any subject relating to the duties of their respective offices. —

Section 14. Reprieves, commutations and pardons; remission of fines and forfeitures. He shall have power to grant reprieves, commutations, and pardons, after conviction, for all offences [sic] except treason, subject to such regulations as may be provided by law. Upon conviction for treason he shall have power to suspend the execution of the sentence until the case shall be reported to the Legislative Assembly, at its next meeting, when the Legislative Assembly shall either grant a pardon, commute the sentence, direct the execution of the sentence, or grant a farther [sic] reprieve.

He shall have power to remit fines, and forfeitures, under such regulations as may be prescribed by law; and shall report to the Legislative Assembly at its next meeting each case of reprieve, commutation, or pardon granted, and the reasons for granting the same; and also the names of all persons in whose favor remission of fines, and forfeitures shall have been made, and the several amounts remitted[.] —

Section 15.:RF8. [This section of the Constitution of 1859 was redesignated as section 15b by the amendment proposed by S.J.R. 12, 1915, and adopted by the people Nov. 7, 1916]

Section 15a. Single item and emergency clause veto. The Governor shall have power to veto single items in appropriation bills, and any provision in new bills declaring an emergency, without thereby affecting any other provision of such bill. [Created through S.J.R. 12, 1915, and adopted by the people Nov. 7, 1916; Amendment proposed by S.J.R. 13, 1921, and adopted by the people June 7, 1921]

Section 15b. Legislative enactments; approval by Governor; notice of intention to disapprove; disapproval and reconsideration by legislature; failure of Governor to return bill. (1) Every bill which shall have passed the Legislative Assembly shall, before it becomes a law, be presented to the Governor; if the Governor approve, the Governor shall sign it; but if not, the Governor shall return it with written objections to that house in which it shall have originated, which house shall enter the objections at large upon the journal and proceed to reconsider it.

(2) If, after such reconsideration, two-thirds of the members present shall agree to pass the bill, it shall be sent, together with the objections, to the other house, by which it shall likewise be reconsidered, and, if approved by two-thirds of the members present, it shall become a law. But in all such cases, the votes of both houses shall be determined by yeas and nays, and the names of the members voting for or against the bill shall be entered on the journal of each house respectively.

(3) If any bill shall not be returned by the Governor within five days (Saturdays and Sundays excepted) after it shall have been presented to the Governor, it shall be a law without signature, unless the general adjournment shall prevent its return, in which case it shall be a law, unless the Governor within thirty days next after the adjournment (Saturdays and Sundays excepted) shall file such bill, with written objections thereto, in the office of the Secretary of State, who shall lay the same before the Legislative Assembly at its next session in like manner as if it had been returned by the Governor.

(4) Before filing a bill after adjournment with written objections, the Governor must announce publicly the possible intention to do so at least five days before filing the bill with written objections. However, nothing in this subsection requires the Governor to file any bill with objections because of the announcement. [Created through S.J.R. 12, 1915, and adopted by the people Nov. 7, 1916; Amendment proposed by H.J.R. 9, 1937, and adopted by the people Nov. 8, 1938; Amendment proposed by S.J.R. 4, 1987, and adopted by the people Nov. 8, 1988]

Note: RF8. See note at section 15, Article V.

Section 16. Governor to Fill Vacancies by Appointment. When during a recess of the legislative assembly a vacancy occurs in any office, the appointment to which is vested in the legislative assembly, or when at any time a vacancy occurs in any other state office, or in the office of judge of any court, the governor shall fill such vacancy by appointment, which shall expire when a successor has been elected and qualified. When any vacancy occurs in any elective office of the state or of any district or county thereof, the vacancy shall be filled at the next general election, provided such vacancy occurs more than sixty-one (61) days prior to such general election. [Constitution of 1859; Amendment proposed by H.J.R. 5, 1925, and adopted by the people Nov. 2, 1926; Amendment proposed by H.J.R. 30, 1985, and adopted by the people May 20, 1986; Amendment proposed by S.J.R. 4, 1993, and adopted by the people Nov. 8, 1994]

Note: RF8. The leadline to section 16 was a part of the measure submitted to the people by H.J.R. 5, 1925.

Section 17. Governor to issue writs of election to fill vacancies in legislature. He shall issue writs of Election to fill such vacancies as may have occured [sic] in the Legislative Assembly.

Section 18. Commissions. All commissions shall issue in the name of the State; shall be signed by the Govenor [sic], sealed with the seal of the State, and attested by the Secretary of State. —

ARTICLE VI
ADMINISTRATIVE DEPARTMENT

Section 1. Election of Secretary and Treasurer of state; terms of office; period of eligibility. There shall be elected by the qualified electors of the State, at the times and places of choosing Members of the Legislative Assembly, a Secretary, and Treasurer of State, who shall

Constitution

severally hold their offices for the term of four years; but no person shall be eligible to either of said offices more than Eight in any period of Twelve years. —

Section 2. Duties of Secretary of State. The Secretary of State shall keep a fair record of the official acts of the Legislative Assembly, and Executive Department of the State; and shall when required lay the same, and all matters relative thereto before either branch of the Legislative Assembly. He shall be by virtue of his office, Auditor of public Accounts, and shall perform such other duties as shall be assigned him by law. —

Section 3. Seal of state. There shall be a seal of State, kept by the Secretary of State for official purposes, which shall be called "The seal of the State of Oregon".—

Section 4. Powers and duties of Treasurer. The powers, and duties of the Treasurer of State shall be such as may be prescribed by law. —

Section 5. Offices and records of executive officers. The Governor, Secretary of State, and Treasurer of State shall severally keep the public records, books and papers at the seat of government in any manner relating to their respective offices. [Constitution of 1859; Amendment proposed by S.J.R. 13, 1985, and adopted by the people Nov. 4, 1986]

Section 6. County Officers: There shall be elected in each county by the qualified electors thereof at the time of holding general elections, a county clerk, treasurer and sheriff who shall severally hold their offices for the term of four years. [Constitution of 1859; Amendment proposed by initiative petition filed June 9, 1920, and adopted by the people Nov. 2, 1920; Amendment proposed by H.J.R. 7, 1955, and adopted by the people Nov. 6, 1956]

Note: RF8. The leadline to section 6 was a part of the measure proposed by initiative petition filed June 9, 1920, and adopted by the people Nov. 2, 1920.

Section 7. Other officers. Such other county, township, precinct, and City officers as may be necessary, shall be elected, or appointed in such manner as may be prescribed by law. —

Section 8. County officers' qualifications; location of offices of county and city officers; duties of such officers. Every county officer shall be an elector of the county, and the county assessor, county sheriff, county coroner and county surveyor shall possess such other qualifications as may be prescribed by law. All county and city officers shall keep their respective offices at such places therein, and perform such duties, as may be prescribed by law. [Constitution of 1859; Amendment proposed by H.J.R. 7, 1955, and adopted by the people Nov. 6, 1956; Amendment proposed by H.J.R. 42, 1971, and adopted by the people Nov. 7, 1972; Amendment proposed by H.J.R. 22, 1973, and adopted by the people Nov. 5, 1974]

Section 9. Vacancies in county, township, precinct and city offices. Vacancies in County, Township, precinct and City offices shall be filled in such manner as may be prescribed by law. —

Section 9a. County manager form of government.:RF8. [Created through H.J.R. 3, 1943, and adopted by the people Nov. 7, 1944; Repeal proposed by H.J.R. 22, 1957, and adopted by the people Nov. 4, 1958]

Section 10. County home rule under county charter. The Legislative Assembly shall provide by law a method whereby the legal voters of any county, by majority vote of such voters voting thereon at any legally called election, may adopt, amend, revise or repeal a county charter. A county charter may provide for the exercise by the county of authority over matters of county concern. Local improvements shall be financed only by taxes, assessments or charges imposed on benefited property, unless otherwise provided by law or charter. A county charter shall prescribe the organization of the county government and shall provide directly, or by its authority, for the number, election or appointment, qualifications, tenure, compensation, powers and duties of such officers as the county deems necessary. Such officers shall among them exercise all the powers and perform all the duties, as distributed by the county charter or by its authority, now or hereafter, by the Constitution or laws of this state, granted to or imposed upon any county officer. Except as expressly provided by general law, a county charter shall not affect the selection, tenure, compensation, powers or duties prescribed by law for judges in their judicial capacity, for justices of the peace or for district attorneys. The initiative and referendum powers reserved to the people by this Constitution hereby are further reserved to the legal voters of every county relative to the adoption, amendment, revision or repeal of a county charter and to legislation passed by counties which have adopted such a charter; and no county shall require that referendum petitions be filed less than 90 days after the provisions of the charter or the legislation proposed for referral is adopted by the county governing body. To be circulated, referendum or initiative petitions shall set forth in full the charter or legislative provisions proposed for adoption or referral. Referendum petitions shall not be required to include a ballot title to be circulated. In a county a number of signatures of qualified voters equal to but not greater than four percent of the total number of all votes cast in the county for all candidates for Governor at the election at which a Governor was elected for a term of four years next preceding the filing of the petition shall be required for a petition to order a referendum on county legislation or a part thereof. A number of signatures equal to but not greater than six percent of the total number of votes cast in the county for all candidates for Governor at the election at which a Governor was elected for a term of four years next preceding the filing of the petition shall be required for a petition to propose an initiative ordinance. A number of signatures equal to but not greater than eight percent of the total number of votes cast in the county for all candidates for Governor at the election at which a Governor was elected for a term of four years next preceding the filing of the petition shall be required for a petition to propose a charter amendment. [Created through H.J.R. 22, 1957, and adopted by the people Nov. 4, 1958; Amendment proposed by S.J.R. 48, 1959, and adopted by the people Nov. 8, 1960; Amendment proposed by H.J.R. 21, 1977, and adopted by the people May 23, 1978]

ARTICLE VII (Amended)
THE JUDICIAL DEPARTMENT

4. Supreme Court; terms; statements of decisions of court
5. Juries; indictment; information; verdict in civil cases
6. Incompetency or malfeasance of public officer
7. Oath of office of Judges of Supreme Court
8. Removal, suspension or censure of judges
9. Juries of less than 12 jurors

Section 1. Courts; election of judges; term of office; compensation. The judicial power of the state shall be vested in one supreme court and in such other courts as may from time to time be created by law. The judges of the supreme and other courts shall be elected by the legal voters of the state or of their respective districts for a term of six years, and shall receive such compensation as may be provided by law, which compensation shall not be diminished during the term for which they are elected. [Created through initiative petition filed July 7, 1910, and adopted by the people Nov. 8, 1910]

Section 1a. Retirement of judges; recall to temporary active service. Notwithstanding the provisions of section 1, Article VII (Amended) of this Constitution, a judge of any court shall retire from judicial office at the end of the calendar year in which he attains the age of 75 years. The Legislative Assembly or the people may by law:

(1) Fix a lesser age for mandatory retirement not earlier than the end of the calendar year in which the judge attains the age of 70 years;

(2) Provide for recalling retired judges to temporary active service on the court from which they are retired; and

(3) Authorize or require the retirement of judges for physical or mental disability or any other cause rendering judges incapable of performing their judicial duties.

This section shall not affect the term to which any judge shall have been elected or appointed prior to or at the time of approval and ratification of this section. [Created through S.J.R. 3, 1959, and adopted by the people Nov. 8, 1960]

Section 2. Amendment's effect on courts, jurisdiction and judicial system; Supreme Court's original jurisdiction. The courts, jurisdiction, and judicial system of Oregon, except so far as expressly changed by this amendment, shall remain as at present constituted until otherwise provided by law. But the supreme court may, in its own discretion, take original jurisdiction in mandamus, quo warranto and habeas corpus proceedings. [Created through initiative petition filed July 7, 1910, and adopted by the people Nov. 8, 1910]

Section 2a. Temporary appointment and assignment of judges. The Legislative Assembly or the people may by law empower the Supreme Court to:

(1) Appoint retired judges of the Supreme Court or judges of courts inferior to the Supreme Court as temporary members of the Supreme Court.

(2) Appoint members of the bar as judges pro tempore of courts inferior to the Supreme Court.

(3) Assign judges of courts inferior to the Supreme Court to serve temporarily outside the district for which they were elected.

A judge or member of the bar so appointed or assigned shall while serving have all the judicial powers and duties of a regularly elected judge of the court to which he is assigned or appointed. [Created through S.J.R. 30, 1957, and adopted by the people Nov. 4, 1958]

Section 2b. Inferior courts may be affected in certain respects by special or local laws. Notwithstanding the provisions of section 23, Article IV of this Constitution, laws creating courts inferior to the Supreme Court or prescribing and defining the jurisdiction of such courts or the manner in which such jurisdiction may be exercised, may be made applicable:

(1) To all judicial districts or other subdivisions of this state; or

(2) To designated classes of judicial districts or other subdivisions; or

(3) To particular judicial districts or other subdivisions. [Created through S.J.R. 34, 1961, and adopted by the people Nov. 6, 1962]

Section 3. Jury trial; re-examination of issues by appellate court; record on appeal to Supreme Court; affirmance notwithstanding error; determination of case by Supreme Court. In actions at law, where the value in controversy shall exceed $750, the right of trial by jury shall be preserved, and no fact tried by a jury shall be otherwise re-examined in any court of this state, unless the court can affirmatively say there is no evidence to support the verdict. Until otherwise provided by law, upon appeal of any case to the supreme court, either party may have attached to the bill of exceptions the whole testimony, the instructions of the court to the jury, and any other matter material to the decision of the appeal. If the supreme court shall be of opinion, after consideration of all the matters thus submitted, that the judgment of the court appealed from was such as should have been rendered in the case, such judgment shall be affirmed, notwithstanding any error committed during the trial; or if, in any respect, the judgment appealed from should be changed, and the supreme court shall be of opinion that it can determine what judgment should have been entered in the court below, it shall direct such judgment to be entered in the same manner and with like effect as decrees are now entered in equity cases on appeal to the supreme court. Provided, that nothing in this section shall be construed to authorize the supreme court to find the defendant in a criminal case guilty of an offense for which a greater penalty is provided than that of which the accused was convicted in the lower court. [Created through initiative petition filed July 7, 1910, and adopted by the people Nov. 8, 1910; Amendment proposed by H.J.R. 71, 1973, and adopted by the people Nov. 5, 1974; Amendment proposed by H.J.R. 47, 1995, and adopted by the people May 21, 1996]

Section 4. Supreme Court; terms; statements of decisions of court. The terms of the supreme court shall be appointed by law; but there shall be one term at the seat of government annually. At the close of each term the judges shall file with the secretary of state concise written statements of the decisions made at that term. [Created through initiative petition filed July 7, 1910, and adopted by the people Nov. 8, 1910]

Section 5. Juries; indictment; information.:RF8. [Created through initiative petition filed July 7, 1910, and adopted by the people Nov. 8, 1910; Amendment proposed by S.J.R. 23, 1957, and adopted by the people Nov. 4, 1958; Repeal proposed by S.J.R. 1, 1973, and adopted by the people Nov. 5, 1974 (present section 5 of this Article adopted in lieu of this section)]

Section 5. Juries; indictment; information; verdict in civil cases. (1) The Legislative Assembly shall provide by law for:

(a) Selecting juries and qualifications of jurors;

(b) Drawing and summoning grand jurors from the regular jury list at any time, separate from the panel of petit jurors;

(c) Empaneling more than one grand jury in a county; and

(d) The sitting of a grand jury during vacation as well as session of the court.

(2) A grand jury shall consist of seven jurors chosen by lot from the whole number of jurors in attendance at the court, five of whom must concur to find an indictment.

(3) Except as provided in subsections (4) and (5) of this section, a person shall be charged in a circuit court with the commission of any crime punishable as a felony only on indictment by a grand jury.

(4) The district attorney may charge a person on an information filed in circuit court of a crime punishable as a felony if the person appears before the judge of the circuit court and knowingly waives indictment.

(5) The district attorney may charge a person on an information filed in circuit court if, after a preliminary hearing before a magistrate, the person has been held to answer upon a showing of probable cause that a crime punishable as a felony has been committed and that the person has committed it, or if the person knowingly waives preliminary hearing.

(6) An information shall be substantially in the form provided by law for an indictment. The district attorney may file an amended indictment or information whenever, by ruling of the court, an indictment or information is held to be defective in form.

(7) In civil cases three-fourths of the jury may render a verdict. [Created through S.J.R. 1, 1973, and adopted by the people Nov. 5, 1974 (this section adopted in lieu of former section 5 of this Article)]

Section 6. Incompetency or malfeasance of public officer. Public officers shall not be impeached; but incompetency, corruption, malfeasance or delinquency in office may be tried in the same manner as criminal offenses, and judgment may be given of dismissal from office, and such further punishment as may have been prescribed by law. [Created through initiative petition filed July 7, 1910, and adopted by the people Nov. 8, 1910]

Section 7. Oath of office of Judges of Supreme Court. Every judge of the supreme court, before entering upon the duties of his office, shall take and subscribe, and transmit to the secretary of state, the following oath:

"I, __________:HR8., do solemnly swear (or affirm) that I will support the constitution of the United States, and the constitution of the State of Oregon, and that I will faithfully and impartially discharge the duties of a judge of the supreme court of this state, according to the best of my ability, and that I will not accept any other office, except judicial offices, during the term for which I have been elected." [Created through initiative petition filed July 7, 1910, and adopted by the people Nov. 8, 1910]

Section 8. Removal, suspension or censure of judges. (1) In the manner provided by law, and notwithstanding section 1 of this Article, a judge of any court may be removed or suspended from his judicial office by the Supreme Court, or censured by the Supreme Court, for:

(a) Conviction in a court of this or any other state, or of the United States, of a crime punishable as a felony or a crime involving moral turpitude; or

(b) Wilful misconduct in a judicial office where such misconduct bears a demonstrable relationship to the effective performance of judicial duties; or

(c) Wilful or persistent failure to perform judicial duties; or

(d) Generally incompetent performance of judicial duties; or

(e) Wilful violation of any rule of judicial conduct as shall be established by the Supreme Court; or

(f) Habitual drunkenness or illegal use of narcotic or dangerous drugs.

(2) Notwithstanding section 6 of this Article, the methods provided in this section, section 1a of this Article and in section 18, Article II of this Constitution, are the exclusive methods of the removal, suspension, or censure of a judge. [Created through S.J.R. 9, 1967, and adopted by the people Nov. 5, 1968; Amendment proposed by S.J.R. 48, 1975, and adopted by the people May 25, 1976]

Section 9. Juries of less than 12 jurors. Provision may be made by law for juries consisting of less than 12 but not less than six jurors. [Created through S.J.R. 17, 1971, and adopted by the people Nov. 7, 1972]

ARTICLE VII (Original)
THE JUDICIAL DEPARTMENT

Note: Original Article VII, compiled below, has been supplanted in part by amended Article VII and in part by statutes enacted by the Legislative Assembly. The provisions of original Article VII relating to courts, jurisdiction and the judicial system, by the terms of section 2 of amended Article VII, are given the status of a statute and are subject to change by statutes enacted by the Legislative Assembly, except so far as changed by amended Article VII.

Section 1. Courts in which judicial power vested. The Judicial power of the State shall be vested in a Suprume [sic] Court, Circuits [sic] Courts, and County Courts, which shall be Courts of Record having general jurisdiction, to be defined, limited, and regulated by law in accordance with this Constitution. — Justices of the Peace may also be invested with limited Judicial powers, and Municipal Courts may be created to administer the regulations of incorporated towns, and cities. —

Section 2. Supreme Court. The Supreme Court shall consist of Four Justices to be chosen in districts by the electors thereof, who shall be citizens of the United States, and who shall have resided in the State at least three years next preceding their election, and after their election to reside in their respective districts: The number of Justices, the Districts may be increased, but shall never exceed seven; and the boundaries of districts may be changed, but no Change of Districts, shall have the effect to remove a Judge from office, or require him to change his residence without his consent. [Constitution of 1859; Amendment proposed by S.J.R. 7, 2001, and adopted by the people Nov. 5, 2002]

Section 3. Terms of office of Judges. The Judges first chosen under this Constitution shall allot among themselves, their terms of office, so that the term of one of them shall expire in Two years, one in Four years, and Two in Six years, and thereafter, one or more shall be chosen every Two years to serve for the term of Six years. —

Section 4. Vacancy. Every vacancy in the office of Judge of the Supreme Court shall be filled by election for the remainder of the vacant term, unless it would expire at the next election, and until so filled, or when it would so expire, the Governor shall fill the vacancy by appointment. —

Section 5. Chief Justice. The Judge who has the shortest term to serve, or the oldest of several having such shortest term, and not holding by appointment shall be the Cheif [sic] Justice. —

Section 6. Jurisdiction. The Supreme Court shall have jurisdiction only to revise the final decisions of the Circuit Courts, and every cause shall be tried, and every decision shall be made by those Judges only, or a majority of them, who did not try the cause, or make the decision in the Circuit Court. —

Section 7. Term of Supreme Court; statements of decisions of court. The terms of the Supreme Court shall be appointed by Law; but there shall be one term at the seat of Government annually: —

And at the close of each term the Judges shall file with the Secretary of State, Concise written Statements of the decisions made at that term. —

Note: RF8. Section 7 is in substance the same as section 4 of amended Article VII.

Section 8. Circuit court. The Circuits [sic] Courts shall be held twice at least in each year in each County organized for judicial purposes, by one of the Justices of the Supreme Court at times to be appointed by law; and at such other times as may be appointed by the Judges severally in pursuance of law. —

Section 9. Jurisdiction of circuit courts. All judicial power, authority, and jurisdiction not vested by this Constitution, or by laws consistent therewith, exclusively in some other Court shall belong to the Circuit Courts, and they shall have appellate jurisdiction, and supervisory control over the County Courts, and all other inferior Courts, Officers, and tribunals. —

Section 10. Supreme and circuit judges; election in classes. The Legislative Assembly, may provide for the election of Supreme, and Circuit Judges, in distinct classes, one of which classes shall consist of three Justices of the Supreme Court, who shall not perform Circuit duty, and the other class shall consist of the necessary number of Circuit Judges, who shall hold full terms without allotment, and who shall take the same oath as the Supreme Judges. [Constitution of 1859; Amendment proposed by S.J.R. 7, 2001, and adopted by the people Nov. 5, 2002]

Section 11. County judges and terms of county courts. There shall be elected in each County for the term of Four years a County Judge, who shall hold the County Court at times to be regulated by law. —

Section 12. Jurisdiction of county courts; county commissioners. The County Court shall have the jurisdiction pertaining to Probate Courts, and boards of County Commissioners, and such other powers, and duties, and such civil Jurisdiction, not exceeding the amount or value of five hundred dollars, and such criminal jurisdiction not extending to death or imprisonment in the penitentiary, as may be prescribed by law.—But the Legislative Assembly may provide for the election of Two Commissioners to sit with the County Judge whilst transacting County business, in any, or all of the Counties, or may provide a seperate [sic] board for transacting such business. —

Section 13. Writs granted by county judge; habeas corpus proceedings. The County Judge may grant preliminary injuctions [sic], and such other writs as the Legislative Assembly may authorize him to grant, returnable to the Circuit Court, or otherwise as may be provided by law; and may hear, and decide questions arising upon habeas corpus; provided such decision be not against the authority, or proceedings of a Court, or Judge of equal, or higher jurisdiction. —

Section 14. Expenses of court in certain counties. The Counties having less than ten thousand inhabitants, shall be reimbursed wholly or in part for the salary, and expenses of the County Court by fees, percentage, & other equitable taxation, of the business done in said Court & in the office of the County Clerk. [Constitution of 1859; Amendment proposed by S.J.R. 7, 2001, and adopted by the people Nov. 5, 2002]

Section 15. County clerk; recorder. A County Clerk shall be elected in each County for the term of Two years, who shall keep all the public records, books, and papers of the County; record conveyances, and perform the duties of Clerk of the Circuit, and County Courts, and such other duties as may be prescribed by law: — But whenever the number of voters in any County shall exceed Twelve Hundred, the Legislative Assembly may authorize the election of one person as Clerk of the Circuit Court, one person as Clerk of the County Court, and one person Recorder of conveyances. —

Section 16. Sheriff. A sheriff shall be elected in each County for the term of Two years, who shall be the ministerial officer of the Circuit, and County Courts, and shall perform such other duties as may be prescribed by law. —

Section 17. Prosecuting attorneys. There shall be elected by districts comprised of one, or more counties, a sufficient number of prosecuting Attorneys, who shall be the law officers of the State, and of the counties within their respective districts, and shall perform such duties pertaining to the administration of Law, and general police as the Legislative Assembly may direct.—

Section 18. Verdict by Three-fourths Jury in Civil Cases; Jurors; Grand Jurors; Indictment May Be Amended, When.:RF8. [Constitution of 1859; Amendment proposed by initiative petition filed Jan. 30, 1908, and adopted by the people June 1, 1908; Amendment proposed by H.J.R. 14, 1927, and adopted by the people June 28, 1927; Repeal proposed by S.J.R. 23, 1957, and adopted by the people Nov. 4, 1958]

Section 19. Official delinquencies. Public Officers shall not be impeached, but incompetency, corruption, malfeasance, or delinquency in office may be tried in the same manner as criminal offences [sic], and judgment

Constitution

may be given of dismissal from Office, and such further punishment as may have been prescribed by law. —

Note: RF8. Section 19 is the same as section 6 of amended Article VII.

Section 20. Removal of Judges of Supreme Court and prosecuting attorneys from office. The Govenor [sic] may remove from Office a Judge of the Supreme Court, or Prosecuting Attorney upon the Joint resolution of the Legislative Assembly, in which Two Thirds of the members elected to each house shall concur, for incompetency, Corruption, malfeasance, or delinquency in office, or other sufficient cause stated in such resolution. —

Section 21. Oath of office of Supreme Court Judges. Every judge of the Supreme Court before entering upon the duties of his office shall take, subscribe, and transmit to the Secretary of State the following oath. — I :HR8. do solemnly swear (or affirm) that I will support the Constitution of the United States, and the constitution of the State of Oregon, and that I will faithfully, and impartially discharge the duties of a Judge of the Supreme, and Circuits [sic] Courts of said State according to the best of my ability, and that I will not accept any other office, except Judicial offices during the term for which I have been elected. —

ARTICLE VIII
EDUCATION AND SCHOOL LANDS

Section 1. Superintendent of Public Instruction. The Governor shall be superintendent of public instruction, and his powers, and duties in that capacity shall be such as may be prescribed by law; but after the term of five years from the adoption of this Constitution, it shall be competent for the Legislative Assembly to provide by law for the election of a superintendent, to provide for his compensation, and prescribe his powers and duties.:B1ART.

Section 2. Common School Fund. (1) The sources of the Common School Fund are:

(a) The proceeds of all lands granted to this state for educational purposes, except the lands granted to aid in the establishment of institutions of higher education under the Acts of February 14, 1859 (11 Stat. 383) and July 2, 1862 (12 Stat. 503).

(b) All the moneys and clear proceeds of all property which may accrue to the state by escheat.

(c) The proceeds of all gifts, devises and bequests, made by any person to the state for common school purposes.

(d) The proceeds of all property granted to the state, when the purposes of such grant shall not be stated.

(e) The proceeds of the five hundred thousand acres of land to which this state is entitled under the Act of September 4, 1841 (5 Stat. 455).

(f) The five percent of the net proceeds of the sales of public lands to which this state became entitled on her admission into the union.

(g) After providing for the cost of administration and any refunds or credits authorized by law, the proceeds from any tax or excise levied on, with respect to or measured by the extraction, production, storage, use, sale, distribution or receipt of oil or natural gas and the proceeds from any tax or excise levied on the ownership of oil or natural gas. However, the rate of such taxes shall not be greater than six percent of the market value of all oil and natural gas produced or salvaged from the earth or waters of this state as and when owned or produced. This paragraph does not include proceeds from any tax or excise as described in section 3, Article IX of this Constitution.

(2) All revenues derived from the sources mentioned in subsection (1) of this section shall become a part of the Common School Fund. The State Land Board may expend moneys in the Common School Fund to carry out its powers and duties under subsection (2) of section 5 of this Article. Unexpended moneys in the Common School Fund shall be invested as the Legislative Assembly shall provide by law and shall not be subject to the limitations of section 6, Article XI of this Constitution. The State Land Board may apply, as it considers appropriate, income derived from the investment of the Common School Fund to the operating expenses of the State Land Board in exercising its powers and duties under subsection (2) of section 5 of this Article. The remainder of the income derived from the investment of the Common School Fund shall be applied to the support of primary and secondary education as prescribed by law. [Constitution of 1859; Amendment proposed by H.J.R. 7, 1967, and adopted by the people May 28, 1968; Amendment proposed by H.J.R. 6, 1979, and adopted by the people Nov. 4, 1980; Amendment to subsection (2) proposed by S.J.R. 1, 1987, and adopted by the people Nov. 8, 1988; Amendment to paragraph (b) of subsection (1) proposed by H.J.R. 3, 1989, and adopted by the people June 27, 1989]

Section 3. System of common schools. The Legislative Assembly shall provide by law for the establishment of a uniform, and general system of Common schools. —

Section 4. Distribution of school fund income. Provision shall be made by law for the distribution of the income of the common school fund among the several Counties of this state in proportion to the number of children resident therein between the ages, four and twenty years. —

Section 5. State Land Board; land management. (1) The Governor, Secretary of State and State Treasurer shall constitute a State Land Board for the disposition and management of lands described in section 2 of this Article, and other lands owned by this state that are placed under their jurisdiction by law. Their powers and duties shall be prescribed by law.

(2) The board shall manage lands under its jurisdiction with the object of obtaining the greatest benefit for the people of this state, consistent with the conservation of this resource under sound techniques of land management. [Constitution of 1859; Amendment proposed by H.J.R. 7, 1967, and adopted by the people May 28, 1968]

Section 6. Qualifications of electors at school elections.:RF8. [Created through initiative petition filed June 25, 1948, and adopted by the people Nov. 2, 1948; Repeal proposed by H.J.R. 4, 2007, and adopted by the people Nov. 4, 2008]

Note: RF8. The leadline to section 6 was a part of the measure proposed by initiative petition filed June 25, 1948, and adopted by the people Nov. 2, 1948.

Section 7. Prohibition of sale of state timber unless timber processed in Oregon. (1) Notwithstanding subsection (2) of section 5 of this Article or any other provision of this Constitution, the State Land Board shall not authorize the sale or export of timber from lands described in section 2 of this Article unless such timber will be processed in Oregon. The limitation on sale or export in this subsection shall not apply to species, grades or quantities of timber which may be found by the State Land Board to be surplus to domestic needs.

(2) Notwithstanding any prior agreements or other provisions of law or this Constitution, the Legislative Assembly shall not authorize the sale or export of timber from state lands other than those described in section 2 of this Article unless such timber will be processed in Oregon. The limitation on sale or export in this subsection shall not apply to species, grades or quantities of timber which may be found by the State Forester to be surplus to domestic needs.

(3) This section first becomes operative when federal law is enacted allowing this state to exercise such authority or when a court or the Attorney General of this state determines that such authority lawfully may be exercised. [Created through S.J.R. 8, 1989, and adopted by the people June 27, 1989]

Section 8. Adequate and Equitable Funding. (1) The Legislative Assembly shall appropriate in each biennium a sum of money sufficient to ensure that the state's system of public education meets quality goals established by law, and publish a report that either demonstrates the appropriation is sufficient, or identifies the reasons for the insufficiency, its extent, and its impact on the ability of the state's system of public education to meet those goals.

(2) Consistent with such legal obligation as it may have to maintain substantial equity in state funding, the Legislative Assembly shall establish a system of Equalization Grants to eligible districts for each year in which the voters of such districts approve local option taxes as described in Article XI, section 11 (4)(a)(B) of this Constitution. The amount of such Grants and eligibility criteria shall be determined by the Legislative Assembly. [Created through initiative petition filed Oct. 22, 1999, and adopted by the people Nov. 7, 2000]

Note: RF8. Added to Article VIII as unnumbered section by initiative petition (Measure No. 1, 2000) adopted by the people Nov. 7, 2000.

Note: RF8. The leadline to section 8 was a part of the measure submitted to the people by Measure No. 1, 2000.

ARTICLE IX
FINANCE

Section 1. Assessment and taxation; uniform rules; uniformity of operation of laws. The Legislative Assembly shall, and the people through the initiative may, provide by law uniform rules of assessment and taxation. All taxes shall be levied and collected under general laws operating uniformly throughout the State. [Constitution of 1859; Amendment proposed by H.J.R. 16, 1917, and adopted by the people June 4, 1917]

Section 1a. Poll or head tax; declaration of emergency in tax laws. No poll or head tax shall be levied or collected in Oregon. The Legislative Assembly shall not declare an emergency in any act regulating taxation or exemption. [Created through initiative petition filed June 23, 1910, and adopted by the people Nov. 8, 1910; Amendment proposed by S.J.R. 10, 1911, and adopted by the people Nov. 5, 1912]

Section 1b. Ships exempt from taxation until 1935. All ships and vessels of fifty tons or more capacity engaged in either passenger or freight coasting or foreign trade, whose home ports of registration are in the State of Oregon, shall be and are hereby exempted from all taxes of every kind whatsoever, excepting taxes for State purposes, until the first day of January, 1935. [Created through S.J.R. 18, 1915, and adopted by the people Nov. 7, 1916]

Section 1c. Financing redevelopment and urban renewal projects. The Legislative Assembly may provide that the ad valorem taxes levied by any taxing unit, in which is located all or part of an area included in a redevelopment or urban renewal project, may be divided so that the taxes levied against any increase in the assessed value, as defined by law, of property in such area obtaining after the effective date of the ordinance or resolution approving the redevelopment or urban renewal plan for such area, shall be used to pay any indebtedness incurred for the redevelopment or urban renewal project. The legislature may enact such laws as may be necessary to carry out the purposes of this section. [Created through S.J.R. 32, 1959, and adopted by the people Nov. 8, 1960; Amendment proposed by H.J.R. 85, 1997, and adopted by the people May 20, 1997]

Section 2. Legislature to provide revenue to pay current state expenses and interest. The Legislative Assembly shall provide for raising revenue sufficiently to defray the expenses of the State for each fiscal year, and also a sufficient sum to pay the interest on the State debt, if there be any. —

Section 3. Laws imposing taxes; gasoline and motor vehicle taxes.:RF8. [Constitution of 1859; Amendment proposed by S.J.R. 11, 1941, and adopted by the people Nov. 3, 1942; Repeal proposed by S.J.R. 7, 1979, and adopted by the people May 20, 1980]

Section 3. Tax imposed only by law; statement of purpose. No tax shall be levied except in accordance with law. Every law imposing a tax shall state distinctly the purpose to which the revenue shall be applied. [Created through S.J.R. 7, 1979, and adopted by the people May 20, 1980 (this section and section 3a adopted in lieu of former section 3 of this Article)]

Section 3a. Use of revenue from taxes on motor vehicle use and fuel; legislative review of allocation of taxes between vehicle classes. (1) Except as provided in subsection (2) of this section, revenue from the following shall be used exclusively for the construction, reconstruction, improvement, repair, maintenance, operation and use of public highways, roads, streets and roadside rest areas in this state:

(a) Any tax levied on, with respect to, or measured by the storage, withdrawal, use, sale, distribution, importation or receipt of motor vehicle fuel or any other product used for the propulsion of motor vehicles; and

(b) Any tax or excise levied on the ownership, operation or use of motor vehicles.

(2) Revenues described in subsection (1) of this section:

(a) May also be used for the cost of administration and any refunds or credits authorized by law.

(b) May also be used for the retirement of bonds for which such revenues have been pledged.

(c) If from levies under paragraph (b) of subsection (1) of this section on campers, motor homes, travel trailers, snowmobiles, or like vehicles, may also be used for the acquisition, development, maintenance or care of parks or recreation areas.

(d) If from levies under paragraph (b) of subsection (1) of this section on vehicles used or held out for use for commercial purposes, may also be used for enforcement of commercial vehicle weight, size, load, conformation and equipment regulation.

(3) Revenues described in subsection (1) of this section that are generated by taxes or excises imposed by the state shall be generated in a manner that ensures that the share of revenues paid for the use of light vehicles, including cars, and the share of revenues paid for the use of heavy vehicles, including trucks, is fair and proportionate to the costs incurred for the highway system because of each class of vehicle. The Legislative Assembly shall provide for a biennial review and, if necessary, adjustment, of revenue sources to ensure fairness and proportionality. [Created through S.J.R. 7, 1979, and adopted by the people May 20, 1980 (this section and section 3 adopted in lieu of former section 3 of this Article); Amendment proposed by S.J.R. 44, 1999, and adopted by the people Nov. 2, 1999; Amendment proposed by S.J.R. 14, 2003, and adopted by the people Nov. 2, 2004]

Section 3b. Rate of levy on oil or natural gas; exception. Any tax or excise levied on, with respect to or measured by the extraction, production, storage, use, sale, distribution or receipt of oil or natural gas, or the ownership thereof, shall not be levied at a rate that is greater than six percent of the market value of all oil and natural gas produced or salvaged from the earth or waters of this state as and when owned or produced. This section does not apply to any tax or excise the proceeds of which are dedicated as described in sections 3 and 3a of this Article. [Created through H.J.R. 6, 1979, and adopted by the people Nov. 4, 1980]

Note: RF8. Section 3b was designated as "Section 3a" by H.J.R. 6, 1979, and adopted by the people Nov. 4, 1980.

Section 4. Appropriation necessary for withdrawal from treasury. No money shall be drawn from the treasury, but in pursuance of appropriations made by law. —

Section 5. Publication of accounts. An accurate statement of the receipts, and expenditures of the public money shall be published with the laws of each odd-numbered year regular session of the Legislative Assembly. [Constitution of 1859; Amendment proposed by S.J.R. 41, 2010, and adopted by the people Nov. 2, 2010]

Section 6. Deficiency of funds; tax levy to pay. Whenever the expenses, of any fiscal year, shall exceed the income, the Legislative Assembly shall provide for levying a tax, for the ensuing fiscal year, sufficient, with other sources of income, to pay the deficiency, as well as the estimated expense of the ensuing fiscal year. —

Section 7. Appropriation laws not to contain provisions on other subjects. Laws making appropriations, for the salaries of public officers, and other current expenses of the State, shall contain provisions upon no other subject. —

Section 8. Stationery for use of state. All stationary [sic] required for the use of the State shall be furnished by the lowest responsible bidder, under such regulations as may be prescribed by law. But no State Officer, or member of the Legislative Assembly shall be interested in any bid, or contract for furnishing such stationery. —

Section 9. Taxation of certain benefits prohibited. Benefits payable under the federal old age and survivors insurance program or benefits under section 3(a), 4(a) or 4(f) of the federal Railroad Retirement Act of 1974, as amended, or their successors, shall not be considered income for the purposes of any tax levied by the state or by a local government in this state. Such benefits shall not be used in computing the tax liability of any person under any such tax. Nothing in this section is intended to affect any benefits to which the beneficiary would otherwise be entitled. This section applies to tax periods beginning on or after January 1, 1986. [Created through H.J.R. 26, 1985, and adopted by the people May 20, 1986]

Section 10. Retirement plan contributions by governmental employees. (1) Notwithstanding any existing State or Federal laws, an employee of the State of Oregon or any political subdivision of the state who is a member of a retirement system or plan established by law, charter or ordinance, or who will receive a retirement benefit from a system or plan offered by the state or a political subdivision of the state, must contribute to the system or plan an amount equal to six percent of their salary or gross wage.

(2) On and after January 1, 1995, the state and political subdivisions of the state shall not thereafter contract or otherwise agree to make any payment or contribution to a retirement system or plan that would have the effect of relieving an employee, regardless of when that employee was employed, of the obligation imposed by subsection (1) of this section.

(3) On and after January 1, 1995, the state and political subdivisions of the state shall not thereafter contract or otherwise agree to increase any salary, benefit or other compensation payable to an employee for the purpose of offsetting or compensating an employee for the obligation imposed by subsection (1) of this section. [Created through initiative petition filed May 10, 1993, and adopted by the people Nov. 8, 1994]

Section 11. Retirement plan rate of return contract guarantee prohibited. (1) Neither the state nor any political subdivision of the state shall contract to guarantee any rate of interest or return on the funds in a retirement system or plan established by law, charter or ordinance for the benefit of an employee of the state or a political subdivision of the state. [Created through initiative petition filed May 10, 1993, and adopted by the people Nov. 8, 1994]

Section 12. Retirement not to be increased by unused sick leave. (1) Notwithstanding any existing Federal or State law, the retirement benefits of an employee of the state or any political subdivision of the state retiring on or after January 1, 1995, shall not in any way be increased as a result of or due to unused sick leave. [Created through initiative petition filed May 10, 1993, and adopted by the people Nov. 8, 1994]

Section 13. Retirement plan restriction severability. If any part of Sections 10, 11 or 12 of this Article is held to be unconstitutional under the Federal or State Constitution, the remaining parts shall not be affected and shall remain in full force and effect. [Created through initiative petition filed May 10, 1993, and adopted by the people Nov. 8, 1994]

Section 14. Revenue estimate; return of excess revenue to taxpayers; legislative increase in estimate. (1) As soon as is practicable after adjournment sine die of an odd-numbered year regular session of the Legislative Assembly, the Governor shall cause an estimate to be prepared of revenues that will be received by the General Fund for the biennium beginning July 1. The estimated revenues from corporate income and excise taxes shall be separately stated from the estimated revenues from other General Fund sources.

(2) As soon as is practicable after the end of the biennium, the Governor shall cause actual collections of revenues received by the General Fund for that biennium to be determined. The revenues received from corporate income and excise taxes shall be determined separately from the revenues received from other General Fund sources.

(3) If the revenues received by the General Fund from corporate income and excise taxes during the biennium exceed the amount estimated to be received from corporate income and excise taxes for the biennium, by two percent or more, the total amount of the excess shall be returned to corporate income and excise taxpayers.

(4) If the revenues received from General Fund revenue sources, exclusive of those described in subsection (3) of this section, during the biennium exceed the amount estimated to be received from such sources for the biennium, by two percent or more, the total amount of the excess shall be returned to personal income taxpayers.

(5) The Legislative Assembly may enact laws:

(a) Establishing a tax credit, refund payment or other mechanism by which the excess revenues are returned to taxpayers, and establishing administrative procedures connected therewith.

(b) Allowing the excess revenues to be reduced by administrative costs associated with returning the excess revenues.

(c) Permitting a taxpayer's share of the excess revenues not to be returned to the taxpayer if the taxpayer's share is less than a de minimis amount identified by the Legislative Assembly.

(d) Permitting a taxpayer's share of excess revenues to be offset by any liability of the taxpayer for which the state is authorized to undertake collection efforts.

(6)(a) Prior to the close of a biennium for which an estimate described in subsection (1) of this section has been made, the Legislative Assembly, by a two-thirds majority vote of all members elected to each House, may enact legislation declaring an emergency and increasing the amount of the estimate prepared pursuant to subsection (1) of this section.

(b) The prohibition against declaring an emergency in an act regulating taxation or exemption in section 1a, Article IX of this Constitution, does not apply to legislation enacted pursuant to this subsection.

(7) This section does not apply:

(a) If, for a biennium or any portion of a biennium, a state tax is not imposed on or measured by the income of individuals.

(b) To revenues derived from any minimum tax imposed on corporations for the privilege of carrying on or doing business in this state that is imposed as a fixed amount and that is nonapportioned (except for changes of accounting periods).

(c) To biennia beginning before July 1, 2001. [Created through H.J.R. 17, 1999, and adopted by the people Nov. 7, 2000; Amendment proposed by S.J.R. 41, 2010, and adopted by the people Nov. 2, 2010]

ARTICLE X
THE MILITIA

Section 1. State militia. The Legislative Assembly shall provide by law for the organization, maintenance and discipline of a state militia for the defense and protection of the State. [Constitution of 1859; Amendment proposed by H.J.R. 5, 1961, and adopted by the people Nov. 6, 1962]

Section 2. Persons exempt. Persons whose religious tenets, or conscientious scruples forbid them to bear arms shall not be compelled to do so. [Constitution of 1859; Amendment proposed by H.J.R. 5, 1961, and adopted by the people Nov. 6, 1962]

Section 3. Officers. The Governor, in his capacity as Commander-in-Chief of the military forces of the State, shall appoint and commission an Adjutant General. All other officers of the militia of the State shall be appointed and commissioned by the Governor upon the recommendation of the Adjutant General. [Constitution of 1859; Amendment proposed by H.J.R. 5, 1961, and adopted by the people Nov. 6, 1962]

Section 4. Staff officers; commissions.:RF8. [Constitution of 1859; Repeal proposed by H.J.R. 5, 1961, and adopted by the people Nov. 6, 1962]

Section 5. Legislature to make regulations for militia.:RF8. [Constitution of 1859; Repeal proposed by H.J.R. 5, 1961, and adopted by the people Nov. 6, 1962]

Section 6. Continuity of government in event of enemy attack.:RF8. [Created through H.J.R. 9, 1959, and adopted by the people Nov. 8, 1960; Repeal proposed by H.J.R. 24, 1975, and adopted by the people Nov. 2, 1976]

ARTICLE XI
CORPORATIONS AND INTERNAL IMPROVEMENTS

5. Restriction of municipal powers in Acts of incorporation
6. State not to be stockholder in company; exceptions
7. Credit of State Not to Be Loaned; Limitation Upon Power of Contracting Debts
8. State not to assume debts of counties, towns or other corporations
9. Limitations on powers of county or city to assist corporations
10. County debt limitation
11. Property tax limitations on assessed value and rate of tax; exceptions
11b. Property tax categories; limitation on categories; exceptions
11c. Limits in addition to other tax limits
11d. Effect of section 11b on exemptions and assessments
11e. Severability of sections 11b, 11c and 11d
11k. Limitation on applicability of section 11 (8) voting requirements to elections on measures held in May or November of any year
11L. Limitation on applicability of sections 11 and 11b on bonded indebtedness to finance capital costs
12. People's utility districts
13. Interests of employes when operation of transportation system assumed by public body
14. Metropolitan service district charter
15. Funding of programs imposed upon local governments; exceptions

Section 1. Prohibition of state banks. The Legislative Assembly shall not have the power to establish, or incorporate any bank or banking company, or monied [sic] institution whatever; nor shall any bank company, or instition [sic] exist in the State, with the privilege of making, issuing, or putting in circulation, any bill, check, certificate, prommisory [sic] note, or other paper, or the paper of any bank company, or person, to circulate as money. —

Note: RF8. The semicolon appearing in the signed Constitution after the word "whatever" in section 1 was not in the original draft reported to and adopted by the convention and is not part of the Constitution. State v. H.S. & L.A., 8 Or. 396, 401 (1880).

Section 2. Formation of corporations; municipal charters; intoxicating liquor regulation. Corporations may be formed under general laws, but shall not be created by the Legislative Assembly by special laws. The Legislative Assembly shall not enact, amend or repeal any charter or act of incorporation for any municipality, city or town. The legal voters of every city and town are hereby granted power to enact and amend their municipal charter, subject to the Constitution and criminal laws of the State of Oregon, and the exclusive power to license, regulate, control, or to suppress or prohibit, the sale of intoxicating liquors therein is vested in such municipality; but such municipality shall within its limits be subject to the provisions of the local option law of the State of Oregon. [Constitution of 1859; Amendment proposed by initiative petition filed Dec.13, 1905, and adopted by the people June 4, 1906; Amendment proposed by initiative petition filed June 23, 1910, and adopted by the people Nov. 8, 1910]

Section 2a. Merger of adjoining municipalities; county-city consolidation. (1) The Legislative Assembly, or the people by the Initiative, may enact a general law providing a method whereby an incorporated city or town or municipal corporation may surrender its charter and be merged into an adjoining city or town, provided a majority of the electors of each of the incorporated cities or towns or municipal corporations affected authorize the surrender or merger, as the case may be.

(2) In all counties having a city therein containing over 300,000 inhabitants, the county and city government thereof may be consolidated in such manner as may be provided by law with one set of officers. The consolidated county and city may be incorporated under general laws providing for incorporation for municipal purposes. The provisions of this Constitution applicable to cities, and also those applicable to counties, so far as not inconsistent or prohibited to cities, shall be applicable to such consolidated government. [Created through H.J.R. 10, 1913, and adopted by the people Nov. 3, 1914; Amendment proposed by S.J.R. 29, 1967, and adopted by the people Nov. 5, 1968]

Section 3. Liability of stockholders. The stockholders of all corporations and joint stock companies shall be liable for the indebtedness of said corporation to the amount of their stock subscribed and unpaid and no more, excepting that the stockholders of corporations or joint stock companies conducting the business of banking shall be individually liable equally and ratably and not one for another, for the benefit of the depositors of said bank, to the amount of their stock, at the par value thereof, in addition to the par value of such shares, unless such banking corporation shall have provided security through membership in the federal deposit insurance corporation or other instrumentality of the United States or otherwise for the benefit of the depositors of said bank equivalent in amount to such double liability of said stockholders. [Constitution of 1859; Amendment proposed by S.J.R. 13, 1911, and adopted by the people Nov. 5, 1912; Amendment proposed by H.J.R. 2, 1943, and adopted by the people Nov. 7, 1944]

Section 4. Compensation for property taken by corporation. No person's property shall be taken by any corporation under authority of law, without compensation being first made, or secured in such manner as may be prescribed by law.

Section 5. Restriction of municipal powers in Acts of incorporation. Acts of the Legislative Assembly, incorporating towns, and cities, shall restrict their powers of taxation, borrowing money, contracting debts, and loaning their credit. —

Section 6. State not to be stockholder in company; exceptions. (1) The state shall not subscribe to, or be interested in the stock of any company, association or corporation. However, as provided by law the state may hold and dispose of stock, including stock already received, that is donated or bequeathed; and may invest, in the stock of any company, association or corporation, any funds or moneys that:

(a) Are donated or bequeathed for higher education purposes;

(b) Are the proceeds from the disposition of stock that is donated or bequeathed for higher education purposes, including stock already received; or

(c) Are dividends paid with respect to stock that is donated or bequeathed for higher education purposes, including stock already received.

(2) Notwithstanding the limits contained in subsection (1) of this section, the state may hold and dispose of stock:

(a) Received in exchange for technology created in whole or in part by a public institution of post-secondary education; or

(b) Received prior to December 5, 2002, as a state asset invested in the creation or development of technology or resources within Oregon. [Constitution of 1859; Amendment proposed by H.J.R. 11, 1955, and adopted by the people Nov. 6, 1956; Amendment proposed by H.J.R. 27, 1969, and adopted by the people Nov. 3, 1970; Amendment proposed by S.J.R. 17, 2001, and adopted by the people May 21, 2002]

Section 7. Credit of State Not to Be Loaned; Limitation Upon Power of Contracting Debts. The Legislative Assembly shall not lend the credit of the state nor in any manner create any debt or liabilities which shall singly or in the aggregate with previous debts or liabilities exceed the sum of fifty thousand dollars, except in case of war or to repel invasion or suppress insurrection or to build and maintain permanent roads; and the Legislative Assembly shall not lend the credit of the state nor in any manner create any debts or liabilities to build and maintain permanent roads which shall singly or in the aggregate with previous debts or liabilities incurred for that purpose exceed one percent of the true cash value of all the property of the state taxed on an ad valorem basis; and every contract of indebtedness entered into or assumed by or on behalf of the state in violation of the provisions of this section shall be void and of no effect. This section does not apply to any agreement entered into pursuant to law by the state or any agency thereof for the lease of real property to the state or agency for any period not exceeding 20 years and for a public purpose. [Constitution of 1859; Amendment proposed by initiative petition filed July 2, 1912, and adopted by the people Nov. 5, 1912; Amendment proposed by H.J.R. 11, 1920 (s.s.), and adopted by the people May 21, 1920; Amendment proposed by S.J.R. 4, 1961, and adopted by the people Nov. 6, 1962; Amendment proposed by S.J.R. 19, 1963, and adopted by the people Nov. 3, 1964]

Note: RF8. The leadline to section 7 was a part of the measure submitted to the people by H.J.R. 11, 1920 (s.s.).

Section 8. State not to assume debts of counties, towns or other corporations. The State shall never assume the debts of any county, town, or other corporation whatever, unless such debts, shall have been created to repel invasion, suppress insurrection, or defend the State in war. —

Section 9. Limitations on powers of county or city to assist corporations. No county, city, town or other municipal corporation, by vote of its citizens, or otherwise, shall become a stockholder in any joint company, corporation or association, whatever, or raise money for, or loan its credit to, or in aid of, any such company, corporation or association. Provided, that any municipal corporation designated as a port under any general or special law of the state of Oregon, may be empowered by statute to raise money and expend the same in the form of a bonus to aid in establishing water transportation lines between such port and any other domestic or foreign port or ports, and to aid in establishing water transportation lines on the interior rivers of this state, or on the rivers between Washington and Oregon, or on the rivers of Washington and Idaho reached by navigation from Oregon's rivers; any debts of a municipality to raise money created for the aforesaid purpose shall be incurred only on approval of a majority of those voting on the question, and shall not, either singly or in the aggregate, with previous debts and liabilities incurred for that purpose, exceed one per cent of the assessed valuation of all property in the municipality. [Constitution of 1859; Amendment proposed by S.J.R. 13, 1917, and adopted by the people June 4, 1917]

Section 10. County debt limitation. No county shall create any debt or liabilities which shall singly or in the aggregate, with previous debts or liabilities, exceed the sum of $5,000; provided, however, counties may incur bonded indebtedness in excess of such $5,000 limitation to carry out purposes authorized by statute, such bonded indebtedness not to exceed limits fixed by statute. [Constitution of 1859; Amendment proposed by initiative petition filed July 7, 1910, and adopted by the people Nov. 8, 1910; Amendment proposed by initiative petition filed July 2, 1912, and adopted by the people Nov. 5, 1912; Amendment proposed by S.J.R. 11, 1919, and adopted by the people June 3, 1919; Amendment proposed by H.J.R. 7, 1920 (s.s.), and adopted by the people May 21, 1920; Amendment proposed by S.J.R. 1, 1921 (s.s.), and adopted by the people Nov. 7, 1922; Amendment proposed by S.J.R. 5, 1921 (s.s.), and adopted by the people Nov. 7, 1922; Amendment proposed by H.J.R. 3, 1925, and adopted by the people Nov. 2, 1926; Amendment proposed by S.J.R. 18, 1925, and adopted by the people Nov. 2, 1926; Amendment proposed by H.J.R. 19, 1925, and adopted by the people Nov. 2, 1926; Amendment proposed by H.J.R. 21, 1957, and adopted by the people Nov. 4, 1958]

Section 11. Tax and indebtedness limitation.:RF8. [Created through initiative petition filed July 6, 1916, and adopted by the people Nov. 7, 1916; Amendment proposed by H.J.R. 9, 1931, and adopted by the people Nov. 8, 1932; Amendment proposed by H.J.R. 9, 1951, and adopted by the people Nov. 4, 1952; Repeal proposed by S.J.R. 33, 1961, and adopted by the people Nov. 6, 1962 (second section 11 of this Article adopted in lieu of this section)]

Section 11. Tax base limitation.:RF8. [Created through S.J.R. 33, 1961, and adopted by the people Nov. 6, 1962 (this section adopted in lieu of first section 11 of this Article); Amendment proposed by H.J.R. 28, 1985, and adopted by the people May 20, 1986; Repeal proposed by H.J.R. 85, 1997, and adopted by the people May 20, 1997 (present section 11 of this Article adopted in lieu of this section and sections 11a, 11f, 11g, 11h, 11i and 11j of this Article)]

Section 11. Property tax limitations on assessed value and rate of tax; exceptions. (1)(a) For the tax year beginning July 1, 1997, each unit of property in this state shall have a maximum assessed value for ad valorem property tax purposes that does not exceed the property's real market value for the tax year beginning July 1, 1995, reduced by 10 percent.

(b) For tax years beginning after July 1, 1997, the property's maximum assessed value shall not increase by more than three percent from the previous tax year.

(c) Notwithstanding paragraph (a) or (b) of this subsection, property shall be valued at the ratio of average maximum assessed value to average real market value of property located in the area in which the property is located that is within the same property class, if on or after July 1, 1995:

(A) The property is new property or new improvements to property;

(B) The property is partitioned or subdivided;

(C) The property is rezoned and used consistently with the rezoning;

(D) The property is first taken into account as omitted property;

(E) The property becomes disqualified from exemption, partial exemption or special assessment; or

(F) A lot line adjustment is made with respect to the property, except that the total assessed value of all property affected by a lot line adjustment shall not exceed the total maximum assessed value of the affected property under paragraph (a) or (b) of this subsection.

(d) Property shall be valued under paragraph (c) of this subsection only for the first tax year in which the

Constitution

changes described in paragraph (c) of this subsection are taken into account following the effective date of this section. For each tax year thereafter, the limits described in paragraph (b) of this subsection apply.

(e) The Legislative Assembly shall enact laws that establish property classes and areas sufficient to make a determination under paragraph (c) of this subsection.

(f) Each property's assessed value shall not exceed the property's real market value.

(g) There shall not be a reappraisal of the real market value used in the tax year beginning July 1, 1995, for purposes of determining the property's maximum assessed value under paragraph (a) of this subsection.

(2) The maximum assessed value of property that is assessed under a partial exemption or special assessment law shall be determined by applying the percentage reduction of paragraph (a) and the limit of paragraph (b) of subsection (1) of this section, or if newly eligible for partial exemption or special assessment, using a ratio developed in a manner consistent with paragraph (c) of subsection (1) of this section to the property's partially exempt or specially assessed value in the manner provided by law. After disqualification from partial exemption or special assessment, any additional taxes authorized by law may be imposed, but in the aggregate may not exceed the amount that would have been imposed under this section had the property not been partially exempt or specially assessed for the years for which the additional taxes are being collected.

(3)(a)(A) The Legislative Assembly shall enact laws to reduce the amount of ad valorem property taxes imposed by local taxing districts in this state so that the total of all ad valorem property taxes imposed in this state for the tax year beginning July 1, 1997, is reduced by 17 percent from the total of all ad valorem property taxes that would have been imposed under repealed sections 11 and 11a of this Article (1995 Edition) and section 11b of this Article but not taking into account Ballot Measure 47 (1996), for the tax year beginning July 1, 1997.

(B) The ad valorem property taxes to be reduced under subparagraph (A) of this paragraph are those taxes that would have been imposed under repealed sections 11 or 11a of this Article (1995 Edition) or section 11b of this Article, as modified by subsection (11) of this section, other than taxes described in subsection (4), (5), (6) or (7) of this section, taxes imposed to pay bonded indebtedness described in section 11b of this Article, as modified by paragraph (d) of subsection (11) of this section, or taxes described in section 1c, Article IX of this Constitution.

(C) It shall be the policy of this state to distribute the reductions caused by this paragraph so as to reflect:

(i) The lesser of ad valorem property taxes imposed for the tax year beginning July 1, 1995, reduced by 10 percent, or ad valorem property taxes imposed for the tax year beginning July 1, 1994;

(ii) Growth in new value under subparagraph (A), (B), (C), (D) or (E) of paragraph (c) of subsection (1) of this section, as added to the assessment and tax rolls for the tax year beginning July 1, 1996, or July 1, 1997 (or, if applicable, for the tax year beginning July 1, 1995); and

(iii) Ad valorem property taxes authorized by voters to be imposed in tax years beginning on or after July 1, 1996, and imposed according to that authority for the tax year beginning July 1, 1997.

(D) It shall be the policy of this state and the local taxing districts of this state to prioritize public safety and public education in responding to the reductions caused by this paragraph while minimizing the loss of decision-making control of local taxing districts.

(E) If the total value for the tax year beginning July 1, 1997, of additions of value described in subparagraph (A), (B), (C), (D) or (E) of paragraph (c) of subsection (1) of this section that are added to the assessment and tax rolls for the tax year beginning July 1, 1996, or July 1, 1997, exceeds four percent of the total assessed value of property statewide for the tax year beginning July 1, 1997 (before taking into account the additions of value described in subparagraph (A), (B), (C), (D) or (E) of paragraph (c) of subsection (1) of this section), then any ad valorem property taxes attributable to the excess above four percent shall reduce the dollar amount of the reduction described in subparagraph (A) of this paragraph.

(b) For the tax year beginning July 1, 1997, the ad valorem property taxes that were reduced under paragraph (a) of this subsection shall be imposed on the assessed value of property in a local taxing district as provided by law, and the rate of the ad valorem property taxes imposed under this paragraph shall be the local taxing district's permanent limit on the rate of ad valorem property taxes imposed by the district for tax years beginning after July 1, 1997, except as provided in subsection (5) of this section.

(c)(A) A local taxing district that has not previously imposed ad valorem property taxes and that seeks to impose ad valorem property taxes shall establish a limit on the rate of ad valorem property tax to be imposed by the district. The rate limit established under this subparagraph shall be approved by a majority of voters voting on the question. The rate limit approved under this subparagraph shall serve as the district's permanent rate limit under paragraph (b) of this subsection.

(B) The voter participation requirements described in subsection (8) of this section apply to an election under this paragraph.

(d) If two or more local taxing districts seek to consolidate or merge, the limit on the rate of ad valorem property tax to be imposed by the consolidated or merged district shall be the rate that would produce the same tax revenue as the local taxing districts would have cumulatively produced in the year of consolidation or merger, if the consolidation or merger had not occurred.

(e)(A) If a local taxing district divides, the limit on the rate of ad valorem property tax to be imposed by each local taxing district after division shall be the same as the local taxing district's rate limit under paragraph (b) of this subsection prior to division.

(B) Notwithstanding subparagraph (A) of this paragraph, the limit determined under this paragraph shall not be greater than the rate that would have produced the same amount of ad valorem property tax revenue in the year of division, had the division not occurred.

(f) Rates of ad valorem property tax established under this subsection may be carried to a number of decimal places provided by law and rounded as provided by law.

(g) Urban renewal levies described in this subsection shall be imposed as provided in subsections (15) and (16) of this section and may not be imposed under this subsection.

(h) Ad valorem property taxes described in this subsection shall be subject to the limitations described in section 11b of this Article, as modified by subsection (11) of this section.

(4)(a)(A) A local taxing district other than a school district may impose a local option ad valorem property tax that exceeds the limitations imposed under this section by submitting the question of the levy to voters in the local taxing district and obtaining the approval of a majority of the voters voting on the question.

(B) The Legislative Assembly may enact laws permitting a school district to impose a local option ad valorem property tax as otherwise provided under this subsection.

(b) A levy imposed pursuant to legislation enacted under this subsection may be imposed for no more than five years, except that a levy for a capital project may be imposed for no more than the lesser of the expected useful life of the capital project or 10 years.

(c) The voter participation requirements described in subsection (8) of this section apply to an election held under this subsection.

(5)(a) Any portion of a local taxing district levy shall not be subject to reduction and limitation under paragraphs (a) and (b) of subsection (3) of this section if that portion of the levy is used to repay:

(A) Principal and interest for any bond issued before December 5, 1996, and secured by a pledge or explicit commitment of ad valorem property taxes or a covenant to levy or collect ad valorem property taxes;

(B) Principal and interest for any other formal, written borrowing of moneys executed before December 5, 1996, for which ad valorem property tax revenues have been pledged or explicitly committed, or that are secured by a covenant to levy or collect ad valorem property taxes;

(C) Principal and interest for any bond issued to refund an obligation described in subparagraph (A) or (B) of this paragraph; or

(D) Local government pension and disability plan obligations that commit ad valorem property taxes and to ad valorem property taxes imposed to fulfill those obligations.

(b)(A) A levy described in this subsection shall be imposed on assessed value as otherwise provided by law in an amount sufficient to repay the debt described in this subsection. Ad valorem property taxes may not be imposed under this subsection that repay the debt at an earlier date or on a different schedule than established in the agreement creating the debt.

(B) A levy described in this subsection shall be subject to the limitations imposed under section 11b of this Article, as modified by subsection (11) of this section.

(c)(A) As used in this subsection, "local government pension and disability plan obligations that commit ad valorem property taxes" is limited to contractual obligations for which the levy of ad valorem property taxes has been committed by a local government charter provision that was in effect on December 5, 1996, and, if in effect on December 5, 1996, as amended thereafter.

(B) The rates of ad valorem property taxes described in this paragraph may be adjusted so that the maximum allowable rate is capable of raising the revenue that the levy would have been authorized to raise if applied to property valued at real market value.

(C) Notwithstanding subparagraph (B) of this paragraph, ad valorem property taxes described in this paragraph shall be taken into account for purposes of the limitations in section 11b of this Article, as modified by subsection (11) of this section.

(D) If any proposed amendment to a charter described in subparagraph (A) of this paragraph permits the ad valorem property tax levy for local government pension and disability plan obligations to be increased, the amendment must be approved by voters in an election. The voter participation requirements described in subsection (8) of this section apply to an election under this subparagraph. No amendment to any charter described in this paragraph may cause ad valorem property taxes to exceed the limitations of section 11b of this Article, as amended by subsection (11) of this section.

(d) If the levy described in this subsection was a tax base or other permanent continuing levy, other than a levy imposed for the purpose described in subparagraph (D) of paragraph (a) of this subsection, prior to the effective date of this section, for the tax year following the repayment of debt described in this subsection the local taxing district's rate of ad valorem property tax established under paragraph (b) of subsection (3) of this section shall be increased to the rate that would have been in effect had the levy not been excepted from the reduction described in subsection (3) of this section. No adjustment shall be made to the rate of ad valorem property tax of local taxing districts other than the district imposing a levy under this subsection.

(e) If this subsection would apply to a levy described in paragraph (d) of this subsection, the local taxing district imposing the levy may elect out of the provisions of this subsection. The levy of a local taxing district making the election shall be included in the reduction and ad valorem property tax rate determination described in subsection (3) of this section.

(6)(a) The ad valorem property tax of a local taxing district, other than a city, county or school district, that is used to support a hospital facility shall not be subject to the reduction described in paragraph (a) of subsection (3) of this section. The entire ad valorem property tax imposed under this subsection for the tax year beginning July 1, 1997, shall be the local taxing district's permanent limit on the rate of ad valorem property taxes imposed by the district under paragraph (b) of subsection (3) of this section.

(b) Ad valorem property taxes described in this subsection shall be subject to the limitations imposed under section 11b of this Article, as modified by subsection (11) of this section.

(7) Notwithstanding any other existing or former provision of this Constitution, the following are validated, ratified, approved and confirmed:

(a) Any levy of ad valorem property taxes approved by a majority of voters voting on the question in an election held before December 5, 1996, if the election met the voter participation requirements described in subsection (8) of this section and the ad valorem property taxes were first imposed for the tax year beginning July 1, 1996, or July 1, 1997. A levy described in this paragraph shall not be subject to reduction under paragraph (a) of subsection (3) of this section but shall be taken into account in determining the local taxing district's permanent rate of ad valorem property tax under paragraph (b) of subsection (3) this section. This paragraph does not apply to levies

Constitution

described in subsection (5) of this section or to levies to pay bonded indebtedness described in section 11b of this Article, as modified by subsection (11) of this section.

(b) Any serial or one-year levy to replace an existing serial or one-year levy approved by a majority of the voters voting on the question at an election held after December 4, 1996, and to be first imposed for the tax year beginning July 1, 1997, if the rate or the amount of the levy approved is not greater than the rate or the amount of the levy replaced.

(c) Any levy of ad valorem property taxes approved by a majority of voters voting on the question in an election held on or after December 5, 1996, and before the effective date of this section if the election met the voter participation requirements described in subsection (8) of this section and the ad valorem property taxes were first imposed for the tax year beginning July 1, 1997. A levy described in this paragraph shall be treated as a local option ad valorem property tax under subsection (4) of this section. This paragraph does not apply to levies described in subsection (5) of this section or to levies to pay bonded indebtedness described in section 11b of this Article, as modified by subsection (11) of this section.

(8) An election described in subsection (3), (4), (5)(c)(D), (7)(a) or (c) or (11) of this section shall authorize the matter upon which the election is being held only if:

(a) At least 50 percent of registered voters eligible to vote in the election cast a ballot; or

(b) The election is a general election in an even-numbered year.

(9) The Legislative Assembly shall replace, from the state's General Fund, revenue lost by the public school system because of the limitations of this section. The amount of the replacement revenue shall not be less than the total replaced in fiscal year 1997-1998.

(10)(a) As used in this section:

(A) "Improvements" includes new construction, reconstruction, major additions, remodeling, renovation and rehabilitation, including installation, but does not include minor construction or ongoing maintenance and repair.

(B) "Ad valorem property tax" does not include taxes imposed to pay principal and interest on bonded indebtedness described in paragraph (d) of subsection (11) of this section.

(b) In calculating the addition to value for new property and improvements, the amount added shall be net of the value of retired property.

(11) For purposes of this section and for purposes of implementing the limits in section 11b of this Article in tax years beginning on or after July 1, 1997:

(a)(A) The real market value of property shall be the amount in cash that could reasonably be expected to be paid by an informed buyer to an informed seller, each acting without compulsion in an arm's length transaction occurring as of the assessment date for the tax year, as established by law.

(B) The Legislative Assembly shall enact laws to adjust the real market value of property to reflect a substantial casualty loss of value after the assessment date.

(b) The $5 (public school system) and $10 (other government) limits on property taxes per $1,000 of real market value described in subsection (1) of section 11b of this Article shall be determined on the basis of property taxes imposed in each geographic area taxed by the same local taxing districts.

(c)(A) All property taxes described in this section are subject to the limits described in paragraph (b) of this subsection, except for taxes described in paragraph (d) of this subsection.

(B) If property taxes exceed the limitations imposed under either category of local taxing district under paragraph (b) of this subsection:

(i) Any local option ad valorem property taxes imposed under this subsection shall be proportionally reduced by those local taxing districts within the category that is imposing local option ad valorem property taxes; and

(ii) After local option ad valorem property taxes have been eliminated, all other ad valorem property taxes shall be proportionally reduced by those taxing districts within the category, until the limits are no longer exceeded.

(C) The percentages used to make the proportional reductions under subparagraph (B) of this paragraph shall be calculated separately for each category.

(d) Bonded indebtedness, the taxes of which are not subject to limitation under this section or section 11b of this Article, consists of:

(A) Bonded indebtedness authorized by a provision of this Constitution;

(B) Bonded indebtedness issued on or before November 6, 1990; or

(C) Bonded indebtedness:

(i) Incurred for capital construction or capital improvements; and

(ii)(I) If issued after November 6, 1990, and approved prior to December 5, 1996, the issuance of which has been approved by a majority of voters voting on the question; or

(II) If approved by voters after December 5, 1996, the issuance of which has been approved by a majority of voters voting on the question in an election that is in compliance with the voter participation requirements in subsection (8) of this section.

(12) Bonded indebtedness described in subsection (11) of this section includes bonded indebtedness issued to refund bonded indebtedness described in subsection (11) of this section.

(13) As used in subsection (11) of this section, with respect to bonded indebtedness issued on or after December 5, 1996, "capital construction" and "capital improvements":

(a) Include public safety and law enforcement vehicles with a projected useful life of five years or more; and

(b) Do not include:

(A) Maintenance and repairs, the need for which could reasonably be anticipated.

(B) Supplies and equipment that are not intrinsic to the structure.

(14) Ad valorem property taxes imposed to pay principal and interest on bonded indebtedness described in section 11b of this Article, as modified by subsection (11) of this section, shall be imposed on the assessed value of the property determined under this section or, in the case of specially assessed property, as otherwise provided by law or as limited by this section, whichever is applicable.

(15) If ad valorem property taxes are divided as provided in section 1c, Article IX of this Constitution, in

order to fund a redevelopment or urban renewal project, then notwithstanding subsection (1) of this section, the ad valorem property taxes levied against the increase shall be used exclusively to pay any indebtedness incurred for the redevelopment or urban renewal project.

(16) The Legislative Assembly shall enact laws that allow collection of ad valorem property taxes sufficient to pay, when due, indebtedness incurred to carry out urban renewal plans existing on December 5, 1996. These collections shall cease when the indebtedness is paid. Unless excepted from limitation under section 11b of this Article, as modified by subsection (11) of this section, nothing in this subsection shall be construed to remove ad valorem property taxes levied against the increase from the dollar limits in paragraph (b) of subsection (11) of this section.

(17)(a) If, in an election on November 5, 1996, voters approved a new tax base for a local taxing district under repealed section 11 of this Article (1995 Edition) that was not to go into effect until the tax year beginning July 1, 1998, the local taxing district's permanent rate limit under subsection (3) of this section shall be recalculated for the tax year beginning on July 1, 1998, to reflect:

(A) Ad valorem property taxes that would have been imposed had repealed section 11 of this Article (1995 Edition) remained in effect; and

(B) Any other permanent continuing levies that would have been imposed under repealed section 11 of this Article (1995 Edition), as reduced by subsection (3) of this section.

(b) The rate limit determined under this subsection shall be the local taxing district's permanent rate limit for tax years beginning on or after July 1, 1999.

(18) Section 32, Article I, and section 1, Article IX of this Constitution, shall not apply to this section.

(19)(a) The Legislative Assembly shall by statute limit the ability of local taxing districts to impose new or additional fees, taxes, assessments or other charges for the purpose of using the proceeds as alternative sources of funding to make up for ad valorem property tax revenue reductions caused by the initial implementation of this section, unless the new or additional fee, tax, assessment or other charge is approved by voters.

(b) This subsection shall not apply to new or additional fees, taxes, assessments or other charges for a government product or service that a person:

(A) May legally obtain from a source other than government; and

(B) Is reasonably able to obtain from a source other than government.

(c) As used in this subsection, "new or additional fees, taxes, assessments or other charges" does not include moneys received by a local taxing district as:

(A) Rent or lease payments;

(B) Interest, dividends, royalties or other investment earnings;

(C) Fines, penalties and unitary assessments;

(D) Amounts charged to and paid by another unit of government for products, services or property; or

(E) Payments derived from a contract entered into by the local taxing district as a proprietary function of the local taxing district.

(d) This subsection does not apply to a local taxing district that derived less than 10 percent of the local taxing district's operating revenues from ad valorem property taxes, other than ad valorem property taxes imposed to pay bonded indebtedness, during the fiscal year ending June 30, 1996.

(e) An election under this subsection need not comply with the voter participation requirements described in subsection (8) of this section.

(20) If any provision of this section is determined to be unconstitutional or otherwise invalid, the remaining provisions shall continue in full force and effect. [Created through H.J.R. 85, 1997, and adopted by the people May 20, 1997 (this section adopted in lieu of former sections 11, 11a, 11f, 11g, 11h, 11i and 11j of this Article)]

Note: RF8. The effective date of House Joint Resolution 85, 1997, is June 19, 1997.

Section 11a. School district tax levy.:RF8. [Created through S.J.R. 3, 1987, and adopted by the people May 19, 1987; Repeal proposed by H.J.R. 85, 1997, and adopted by the people May 20, 1997 (present section 11 adopted in lieu of this section and sections 11, 11f, 11g, 11h, 11i and 11j of this Article)]

Section 11b. Property tax categories; limitation on categories; exceptions. (1) During and after the fiscal year 1991–92, taxes imposed upon any property shall be separated into two categories: One which dedicates revenues raised specifically to fund the public school system and one which dedicates revenues raised to fund government operations other than the public school system. The taxes in each category shall be limited as set forth in the table which follows and these limits shall apply whether the taxes imposed on property are calculated on the basis of the value of that property or on some other basis:

MAXIMUM ALLOWABLE TAXES
For Each $1000.00 of
Property's Real Market Value

Fiscal Year	School System	Other than Schools
1991–1992	$15.00	$10.00
1992–1993	$12.50	$10.00
1993–1994	$10.00	$10.00
1994–1995	$ 7.50	$10.00
1995–1996 and thereafter	$ 5.00	$10.00

Property tax revenues are deemed to be dedicated to funding the public school system if the revenues are to be used exclusively for educational services, including support services, provided by some unit of government, at any level from pre-kindergarten through post-graduate training.

(2) The following definitions shall apply to this section:

(a) "Real market value" is the minimum amount in cash which could reasonably be expected by an informed seller acting without compulsion, from an informed buyer acting without compulsion, in an "arms-length" transaction during the period for which the property is taxed.

(b) A "tax" is any charge imposed by a governmental unit upon property or upon a property owner as a direct consequence of ownership of that property except incurred charges and assessments for local improvements.

(c) "Incurred charges" include and are specifically limited to those charges by government which can be controlled or avoided by the property owner.

(A) because the charges are based on the quantity of the goods or services used and the owner has direct control over the quantity; or

(B) because the goods or services are provided only on the specific request of the property owner; or

(C) because the goods or services are provided by the governmental unit only after the individual property owner has failed to meet routine obligations of ownership and such action is deemed necessary to enforce regulations pertaining to health or safety.

Incurred charges shall not exceed the actual costs of providing the goods or services.

(d) A "local improvement" is a capital construction project undertaken by a governmental unit

(A) which provides a special benefit only to specific properties or rectifies a problem caused by specific properties, and

(B) the costs of which are assessed against those properties in a single assessment upon the completion of the project, and

(C) for which the payment of the assessment plus appropriate interest may be spread over a period of at least ten years.

The total of all assessments for a local improvement shall not exceed the actual costs incurred by the governmental unit in designing, constructing and financing the project.

(3) The limitations of subsection (1) of this section apply to all taxes imposed on property or property ownership except

(a) Taxes imposed to pay the principal and interest on bonded indebtedness authorized by a specific provision of this Constitution.

(b) Taxes imposed to pay the principal and interest on bonded indebtedness incurred or to be incurred for capital construction or improvements, provided the bonds are offered as general obligations of the issuing governmental unit and provided further that either the bonds were issued not later than November 6, 1990, or the question of the issuance of the specific bonds has been approved by the electors of the issuing governmental unit.

(4) In the event that taxes authorized by any provision of this Constitution to be imposed upon any property should exceed the limitation imposed on either category of taxing units defined in subsection (1) of this section, then, notwithstanding any other provision of this Constitution, the taxes imposed upon such property by the taxing units in that category shall be reduced evenly by the percentage necessary to meet the limitation for that category. The percentages used to reduce the taxes imposed shall be calculated separately for each category and may vary from property to property within the same taxing unit. The limitation imposed by this section shall not affect the tax base of a taxing unit.

(5) The Legislative Assembly shall replace from the State's general fund any revenue lost by the public school system because of the limitations of this section. The Legislative Assembly is authorized, however, to adopt laws which would limit the total of such replacement revenue plus the taxes imposed within the limitations of this section in any year to the corresponding total for the previous year plus 6 percent. This subsection applies only during fiscal years 1991-92 through 1995-96, inclusive. [Created through initiative petition filed May 8, 1990, and adopted by the people Nov. 6, 1990]

Section 11c. Limits in addition to other tax limits. The limits in section 11b of this Article are in addition to any limits imposed on individual taxing units by this Constitution. [Created through initiative petition filed May 8, 1990, and adopted by the people Nov. 6, 1990]

Section 11d. Effect of section 11b on exemptions and assessments. Nothing in sections 11b to 11e of this Article is intended to require or to prohibit the amendment of any current statute which partially or totally exempts certain classes of property or which prescribes special rules for assessing certain classes of property, unless such amendment is required or prohibited by the implementation of the limitations imposed by section 11b of this Article. [Created through initiative petition filed May 8, 1990, and adopted by the people Nov. 6, 1990]

Section 11e. Severability of sections 11b, 11c and 11d. If any portion, clause or phrase of sections 11b to 11e of this Article is for any reason held to be invalid or unconstitutional by a court of competent jurisdiction, the remaining portions, clauses and phrases shall not be affected but shall remain in full force and effect. [Created through initiative petition filed May 8, 1990, and adopted by the people Nov. 6, 1990]

Section 11f. School district tax levy following merger.:RF8. [Created through H.J.R. 14, 1989, and adopted by the people Nov. 6, 1990; Repeal proposed by H.J.R. 85, 1997, and adopted by the people May 20, 1997 (present section 11 adopted in lieu of this section and sections 11, 11a, 11g, 11h, 11i and 11j of this Article)]

Note: RF8. Section 11f was designated as "Section 11b" by H.J.R. 14, 1989, and adopted by the people Nov. 6, 1990.

Section 11g. Tax increase limitation; exceptions.:RF8. [Created through initiative petition filed Dec. 8, 1995, and adopted by the people Nov. 5, 1996; Repeal proposed by H.J.R. 85, 1997, and adopted by the people May 20, 1997 (present section 11 adopted in lieu of this section and sections 11, 11a, 11f, 11h, 11i and 11j of this Article)]

Section 11h. Voluntary contributions for support of schools or other public entities.:RF8. [Created through initiative petition filed Dec. 8, 1995, and adopted by the people Nov. 5, 1996; Repeal proposed by H.J.R. 85, 1997, and adopted by the people May 20, 1997 (present section 11 adopted in lieu of this section and sections 11, 11a, 11f, 11g, 11i and 11j of this Article)]

Section 11i. Legislation to implement limitation and contribution provisions.:RF8. [Created through initiative petition filed Dec. 8, 1995, and adopted by the people Nov. 5, 1996; Repeal proposed by H.J.R. 85, 1997, and adopted by the people May 20, 1997 (present section 11 adopted in lieu of this section and sections 11, 11a, 11f, 11g, 11h and 11j of this Article)]

Section 11j. Severability of sections 11g, 11h and 11i.:RF8. [Created through initiative petition filed Dec. 8, 1995, and adopted by the people Nov. 5, 1996; Repeal proposed by H.J.R. 85, 1997, and adopted by the people May 20, 1997 (present section 11 adopted in lieu of this section and sections 11, 11a, 11f, 11g, 11h and 11i of this Article)]

Section 11k. Limitation on applicability of section 11(8) voting requirements to elections on measures held in May or November of any year. Notwithstanding subsection (8) of section 11 of this Article, subsection (8) of section 11 of this Article does not apply to any measure voted on in an election held in May or November of any year. [Created through H.J.R. 15, 2007, and adopted by the people Nov. 4, 2008]

Section 11L. Limitation on applicability of sections 11 and 11b on bonded indebtedness to finance capital costs. (1) The limitations of sections 11 and 11b of this Article do not apply to bonded indebtedness incurred by local taxing districts if the bonded indebtedness was incurred on or after January 1, 2011, to finance capital costs as defined in subsection (5) of this section.

(2) Bonded indebtedness described in subsection (1) of this section includes bonded indebtedness issued to refund bonded indebtedness described in subsection (1) of this section.

(3) Notwithstanding subsection (1) of this section, subsection (8) of section 11 of this Article, as limited by section 11k of this Article, applies to measures that authorize bonded indebtedness described in subsection (1) of this section.

(4) The weighted average life of bonded indebtedness incurred on or after January 1, 2011, to finance capital costs may not exceed the weighted average life of the capital costs that are financed with that indebtedness.

(5)(a) As used in this section, "capital costs" means costs of land and of other assets having a useful life of more than one year, including costs associated with acquisition, construction, improvement, remodeling, furnishing, equipping, maintenance or repair.

(b) "Capital costs" does not include costs of routine maintenance or supplies. [Created through H.J.R. 13, 2009, and adopted by the people May 18, 2010]

Section 12. People's utility districts. Peoples' [sic] Utility Districts may be created of territory, contiguous or otherwise, within one or more counties, and may consist of an incorporated municipality, or municipalities, with or without unincorporated territory, for the purpose of supplying water for domestic and municipal purposes; for the development of water power and/or electric energy; and for the distribution, disposal and sale of water, water power and electric energy. Such districts shall be managed by boards of directors, consisting of five members, who shall be residents of such districts. Such districts shall have power:

(a) To call and hold elections within their respective districts.

(b) To levy taxes upon the taxable property of such districts.

(c) To issue, sell and assume evidences of indebtedness.

(d) To enter into contracts.

(e) To exercise the power of eminent domain.

(f) To acquire and hold real and other property necessary or incident to the business of such districts.

(g) To acquire, develop, and/or otherwise provide for a supply of water, water power and electric energy.

Such districts may sell, distribute and/or otherwise dispose of water, water power and electric energy within or without the territory of such districts.

The legislative assembly shall and the people may provide any legislation, that may be necessary, in addition to existing laws, to carry out the provisions of this section. [Created through initiative petition filed July 3, 1930, and adopted by the people Nov. 4, 1930]

Section 13. Interests of employes when operation of transportation system assumed by public body. Notwithstanding the provisions of section 20, Article I, section 10, Article VI, and sections 2 and 9, Article XI, of this Constitution, when any city, county, political subdivision, public agency or municipal corporation assumes responsibility for the operation of a public transportation system, the city, county, political subdivision, public agency or municipal corporation shall make fair and equitable arrangements to protect the interests of employes and retired employes affected. Such protective arrangements may include, without being limited to, such provisions as may be necessary for the preservation of rights, privileges and benefits (including continuation of pension rights and payment of benefits) under existing collective bargaining agreements, or otherwise. [Created through H.J.R. 13, 1965, and adopted by the people Nov. 8, 1966]

Section 14. Metropolitan service district charter. (1) The Legislative Assembly shall provide by law a method whereby the legal electors of any metropolitan service district organized under the laws of this state, by majority vote of such electors voting thereon at any legally called election, may adopt, amend, revise or repeal a district charter.

(2) A district charter shall prescribe the organization of the district government and shall provide directly, or by its authority, for the number, election or appointment, qualifications, tenure, compensation, powers and duties of such officers as the district considers necessary. Such officers shall among them exercise all the powers and perform all the duties, as granted to, imposed upon or distributed among district officers by the Constitution or laws of this state, by the district charter or by its authority.

(3) A district charter may provide for the exercise by ordinance of powers granted to the district by the Constitution or laws of this state.

(4) A metropolitan service district shall have jurisdiction over matters of metropolitan concern as set forth in the charter of the district.

(5) The initiative and referendum powers reserved to the people by this Constitution hereby are further reserved to the legal electors of a metropolitan service district relative to the adoption, amendment, revision or repeal of a district charter and district legislation enacted thereunder. Such powers shall be exercised in the manner provided for county measures under section 10, Article VI of this Constitution. [Created by S.J.R. 2, 1989, and adopted by the people Nov. 6, 1990]

Section 15. Funding of programs imposed upon local governments; exceptions. (1) Except as provided in subsection (7) of this section, when the Legislative Assembly or any state agency requires any local government to establish a new program or provide an increased level of service for an existing program, the State of Oregon shall appropriate and allocate to the local government moneys sufficient to pay the ongoing, usual and reasonable costs of performing the mandated service or activity.

(2) As used in this section:

(a) "Enterprise activity" means a program under which a local government sells products or services in competition with a nongovernment entity.

(b) "Local government" means a city, county, municipal corporation or municipal utility operated by a board or commission.

(c) "Program" means a program or project imposed by enactment of the Legislative Assembly or by rule or order of a state agency under which a local government must provide administrative, financial, social, health or other specified services to persons, government agencies or to the public generally.

(d) "Usual and reasonable costs" means those costs incurred by the affected local governments for a specific program using generally accepted methods of service delivery and administrative practice.

(3) A local government is not required to comply with any state law or administrative rule or order enacted or adopted after January 1, 1997, that requires the expenditure of money by the local government for a new program or increased level of service for an existing program until the state appropriates and allocates to the local government reimbursement for any costs incurred to carry out the law, rule or order and unless the Legislative Assembly provides, by appropriation, reimbursement in each succeeding year for such costs. However, a local government may refuse to comply with a state law or administrative rule or order under this subsection only if the amount appropriated and allocated to the local government by the Legislative Assembly for a program in a fiscal year:

(a) Is less than 95 percent of the usual and reasonable costs incurred by the local government in conducting the program at the same level of service in the preceding fiscal year; or

(b) Requires the local government to spend for the program, in addition to the amount appropriated and allocated by the Legislative Assembly, an amount that exceeds one-hundredth of one percent of the annual budget adopted by the governing body of the local government for that fiscal year.

(4) When a local government determines that a program is a program for which moneys are required to be appropriated and allocated under subsection (1) of this section, if the local government expended moneys to conduct the program and was not reimbursed under this section for the usual and reasonable costs of the program, the local government may submit the issue of reimbursement to nonbinding arbitration by a panel of three arbitrators. The panel shall consist of one representative from the Oregon Department of Administrative Services, the League of Oregon Cities and the Association of Oregon Counties. The panel shall determine whether the costs incurred by the local government are required to be reimbursed under this section and the amount of reimbursement. The decision of the arbitration panel is not binding upon the parties and may not be enforced by any court in this state.

(5) In any legal proceeding or arbitration proceeding under this section, the local government shall bear the burden of proving by a preponderance of the evidence that moneys appropriated by the Legislative Assembly are not sufficient to reimburse the local government for the usual and reasonable costs of a program.

(6) Except upon approval by three-fifths of the membership of each house of the Legislative Assembly, the Legislative Assembly shall not enact, amend or repeal any law if the anticipated effect of the action is to reduce the amount of state revenues derived from a specific state tax and distributed to local governments as an aggregate during the distribution period for such revenues immediately preceding January 1, 1997.

(7) This section shall not apply to:

(a) Any law that is approved by three-fifths of the membership of each house of the Legislative Assembly.

(b) Any costs resulting from a law creating or changing the definition of a crime or a law establishing sentences for conviction of a crime.

(c) An existing program as enacted by legislation prior to January 1, 1997, except for legislation withdrawing state funds for programs required prior to January 1, 1997, unless the program is made optional.

(d) A new program or an increased level of program services established pursuant to action of the Federal Government so long as the program or increased level of program services imposes costs on local governments that are no greater than the usual and reasonable costs to local governments resulting from compliance with the minimum program standards required under federal law or regulations.

(e) Any requirement imposed by the judicial branch of government.

(f) Legislation enacted or approved by electors in this state under the initiative and referendum powers reserved to the people under section 1, Article IV of this Constitution.

(g) Programs that are intended to inform citizens about the activities of local governments.

(8) When a local government is not required under subsection (3) of this section to comply with a state law or administrative rule or order relating to an enterprise activity, if a nongovernment entity competes with the local government by selling products or services that are similar to the products and services sold under the enterprise activity, the nongovernment entity is not required to comply with the state law or administrative rule or order relating to that enterprise activity.

(9) Nothing in this section shall give rise to a claim by a private person against the State of Oregon based on the establishment of a new program or an increased level of service for an existing program without sufficient appropriation and allocation of funds to pay the ongoing, usual and reasonable costs of performing the mandated service or activity.

(10) Subsection (4) of this section does not apply to a local government when the local government is voluntarily providing a program four years after the effective date of the enactment, rule or order that imposed the program.

(11) In lieu of appropriating and allocating funds under this section, the Legislative Assembly may identify and direct the imposition of a fee or charge to be used by a local government to recover the actual cost of the program. [Created through H.J.R. 2, 1995, and adopted by the people Nov. 5, 1996]

Section 15a. Subsequent vote for reaffirmation of section 15.:RF8. [Created through H.J.R. 2, 1995, and adopted by the people Nov. 5, 1996; Repeal proposed by S.J.R. 39, 1999, and adopted by the people Nov. 7, 2000]

ARTICLE XI-A
RURAL CREDITS

[Created through initiative petition filed July 6, 1916, and adopted by the people Nov. 7, 1916; Repeal proposed by S.J.R. 1, 1941, and adopted by the people Nov. 3, 1942]

ARTICLE XI-A
FARM AND HOME LOANS TO VETERANS

Section 1. State empowered to make farm and home loans to veterans; standards and priorities for loans. (1) Notwithstanding the limits contained in section 7, Article XI of this Constitution, the credit of the State of Oregon may be loaned and indebtedness incurred in an amount not to exceed eight percent of the true cash value of all the property in the state, for the purpose of creating a fund, to be known as the "Oregon War Veterans' Fund," to be advanced for the acquisition of farms and homes for the benefit of male and female residents of the State of Oregon who served in the Armed Forces of the United States. Secured repayment thereof shall be and is a prerequisite to the advancement of money from such fund, except that moneys in the Oregon War Veterans' Fund may also be appropriated to the Director of Veterans' Affairs to be expended, without security, for the following purposes:

(a) Aiding veterans' organizations in connection with their programs of service to veterans;

(b) Training service officers appointed by the counties to give aid as provided by law to veterans and their dependents;

(c) Aiding the counties in connection with programs of service to veterans;

(d) The duties of the Director of Veterans' Affairs as conservator of the estates of beneficiaries of the United States Veterans' Administration; and

(e) The duties of the Director of Veterans' Affairs in providing services to veterans, their dependents and survivors.

(2) The Director of Veterans' Affairs may establish standards and priorities with respect to the granting of loans from the Oregon War Veterans' Fund that, as determined by the director, best accomplish the purposes and promote the financial sustainability of the Oregon War Veterans' Fund, including, but not limited to, standards and priorities necessary to maintain the tax-exempt status of earnings from bonds issued under authority of this section and section 2 of this Article. [Created through H.J.R. 7, 1943, and adopted by the people Nov. 7, 1944; Amendment proposed by H.J.R. 1, 1949, and adopted by the people Nov. 7, 1950; Amendment proposed by H.J.R. 14, 1951, and adopted by the people Nov. 4, 1952; Amendment proposed by S.J.R. 14, 1959, and adopted by the people Nov. 8, 1960; Amendment proposed by H.J.R. 9, 1967, and adopted by the people Nov. 5, 1968; Amendment proposed by H.J.R. 33, 1969, and adopted by the people Nov. 3, 1970; Amendment proposed by H.J.R. 12, 1973, and adopted by the people May 28, 1974; Amendment proposed by H.J.R. 10, 1977, and adopted by the people May 17, 1977; Amendment proposed by S.J.R. 53, 1977, and adopted by the people May 17, 1977; Amendment proposed by S.J.R. 2, 1999, and adopted by the people Nov. 7, 2000; Amendment proposed by H.J.R. 7, 2009, and adopted by the people Nov. 2, 2010]

Section 2. Bonds. Bonds of the state of Oregon containing a direct promise on behalf of the state to pay the face value thereof, with the interest therein provided for, may be issued to an amount authorized by section 1 hereof for the purpose of creating said "Oregon War Veterans' Fund." Said bonds shall be a direct obligation of the state and shall be in such form and shall run for such periods of time and bear such rates of interest as provided by statute. [Created through H.J.R. 7, 1943, and adopted by the people Nov. 7, 1944; Amendment proposed by H.J.R. 1, 1949, and adopted by the people Nov. 7, 1950]

Section 3. Eligibility to receive loans. No person shall receive money from the Oregon War Veterans' Fund except the following:

(1) A person who:

(a) Resides in the State of Oregon at the time of applying for a loan from the fund;

(b) Is a veteran, as that term is defined by Oregon law;

(c) Served under honorable conditions on active duty in the Armed Forces of the United States; and

(d) Satisfies the requirements applicable to the funding source for the loan from the Oregon War Veterans' Fund.

(2)(a) The spouse of a person who is qualified to receive a loan under subsection (1) of this section but who has either been missing in action or a prisoner of war while on active duty in the Armed Forces of the United States even though the status of missing or being a prisoner occurred prior to completion of a minimum length of service or the person never resided in this state, provided the spouse resides in this state at the time of application for the loan.

(b) The surviving spouse of a person who was qualified to receive a loan under subsection (1) of this section but who died while on active duty in the Armed Forces of the United States even though the death occurred prior to completion of a minimum length of service or the person never resided in this state, provided the surviving spouse resides in this state at the time of application for the loan.

(c) The eligibility of a surviving spouse under this subsection shall terminate on the spouse's remarriage.

(3) As used in this section, "active duty" does not include attendance at a school under military orders, except schooling incident to an active enlistment or a regular tour of duty, or normal military training as a reserve officer or member of an organized reserve or National Guard unit. [Created through H.J.R. 7, 1943, and adopted by the people Nov. 7, 1944; Amendment proposed by H.J.R. 1, 1949, and adopted by the people Nov. 7, 1950; Amendment proposed by H.J.R. 14, 1951, and adopted by the people Nov. 4, 1952; Amendment proposed by S.J.R. 14, 1959, and adopted by the people Nov. 8, 1960; Amendment proposed by H.J.R. 9, 1967, and adopted by the people Nov. 5, 1968; Amendment proposed by S.J.R. 23, 1971, and adopted by the people Nov. 7, 1972; Amendment proposed by H.J.R. 23, 1975, and adopted by the people May 25, 1976; Amendment proposed by H.J.R. 23, 1979, and adopted by the people May 20, 1980; Amendment proposed by S.J.R. 3, 1995, and adopted by the people Nov. 5, 1996; Amendment proposed by S.J.R. 2, 1999, and adopted by the people Nov. 7, 2000; Amendment proposed by H.J.R. 7, 2009, and adopted by the people Nov. 2, 2010]

Section 4. Tax levy. There shall be levied each year, at the same time and in the same manner that other taxes are levied, a tax upon all property in the state of Oregon not exempt from taxation, not to exceed two (2) mills on each dollar valuation, to provide for the payment of principal and interest of the bonds authorized to be issued by this article. The two (2) mills additional tax herein provided for hereby is specifically authorized and said tax levy hereby authorized shall be in addition to all other taxes which may be levied according to law. [Created through H.J.R. 7, 1943, and adopted by the people Nov. 7, 1944; Amendment proposed by H.J.R. 85, 1997, and adopted by the people May 20, 1997]

Section 5. Repeal of conflicting constitutional provisions. The provisions of the constitution in conflict with this amendment hereby are repealed so far as they conflict herewith. [Created through H.J.R. 7, 1943, and adopted by the people Nov. 7, 1944]

Section 6. Refunding bonds. Refunding bonds may be issued and sold to refund any bonds issued under authority of sections 1 and 2 of this article. There may be issued and outstanding at any one time bonds aggregating the amount authorized by section 1 hereof, but at no time shall the total of all bonds outstanding, including refunding bonds, exceed the amount so authorized. [Created through H.J.R. 7, 1943, and adopted by the people Nov. 7, 1944]

ARTICLE XI-B
STATE PAYMENT OF IRRIGATION AND DRAINAGE DISTRICT INTEREST

[Created through H.J.R. 32, 1919, and adopted by the people June 3, 1919; Repeal proposed by H.J.R. 1, 1929, and adopted by the people Nov. 4, 1930]

ARTICLE XI-C
WORLD WAR VETERANS' STATE AID SINKING FUND

[Created through H.J.R. 12, 1921, and adopted by the people June 7, 1921; Amendment proposed by H.J.R. 7, 1923, and adopted by the people Nov. 4, 1924; Repeal proposed by S.J.R. 12, 1951, and adopted by the people Nov. 4, 1952]

ARTICLE XI-D
STATE POWER DEVELOPMENT

Sec. 1. State's rights, title and interest to water and water-power sites to be held in perpetuity
2. State's powers enumerated
3. Legislation to effectuate article
4. Construction of article

Section 1. State's rights, title and interest to water and water-power sites to be held in perpetuity. The rights, title and interest in and to all water for the development of water power and to water power sites, which the state of Oregon now owns or may hereafter acquire, shall be held by it in perpetuity. [Created through initiative petition filed July 7, 1932, and adopted by the people Nov. 8, 1932]

Section 2. State's powers enumerated. The state of Oregon is authorized and empowered:

(1) To control and/or develop the water power within the state;

(2) To lease water and water power sites for the development of water power;

(3) To control, use, transmit, distribute, sell and/or dispose of electric energy;

(4) To develop, separately or in conjunction with the United States, or in conjunction with the political subdivisions of this state, any water power within the state, and to acquire, construct, maintain and/or operate hydroelectric power plants, transmission and distribution lines;

(5) To develop, separately or in conjunction with the United States, with any state or states, or political subdivisions thereof, or with any political subdivision of this state, any water power in any interstate stream and to acquire, construct, maintain and/or operate hydroelectric power plants, transmission and distribution lines;

(6) To contract with the United States, with any state or states, or political subdivisions thereof, or with any political subdivision of this state, for the purchase or acquisition of water, water power and/or electric energy for use, transmission, distribution, sale and/or disposal thereof;

(7) To fix rates and charges for the use of water in the development of water power and for the sale and/or disposal of water power and/or electric energy;

(8) To loan the credit of the state, and to incur indebtedness to an amount not exceeding one and one-half percent of the true cash value of all the property in the state taxed on an ad valorem basis, for the purpose of providing funds with which to carry out the provisions of this article, notwithstanding any limitations elsewhere contained in this constitution;

(9) To do any and all things necessary or convenient to carry out the provisions of this article. [Created through initiative petition filed July 7, 1932, and adopted by the people Nov. 8, 1932; Amendment proposed by S.J.R. 6, 1961, and adopted by the people Nov. 6, 1962]

Section 3. Legislation to effectuate article. The legislative assembly shall, and the people may, provide any legislation that may be necessary in addition to existing laws, to carry out the provisions of this article; Provided, that any board or commission created, or empowered to administer the laws enacted to carry out the purposes of this article shall consist of three members and be elected without party affiliation or designation. [Created through initiative petition filed July 7, 1932, and adopted by the people Nov. 8, 1932]

Section 4. Construction of article. Nothing in this article shall be construed to affect in any way the laws, and the administration thereof, now existing or hereafter enacted, relating to the appropriation and use of water for beneficial purposes, other than for the development of water power. [Created through initiative petition filed July 7, 1932, and adopted by the people Nov. 8, 1932]

ARTICLE XI-E
STATE REFORESTATION

Section 1. State empowered to lend credit for forest rehabilitation and reforestation; bonds; taxation. The credit of the state may be loaned and indebtedness incurred in an amount which shall not exceed at any one time 3/16 of 1 percent of the true cash value of all the property in the state taxed on an ad valorem basis, to provide funds for forest rehabilitation and reforestation and for the acquisition, management, and development of lands for such purposes. So long as any such indebtedness shall remain outstanding, the funds derived from the sale, exchange, or use of said lands, and from the disposal of products therefrom, shall be applied only in the liquidation of such indebtedness. Bonds or other obligations issued pursuant hereto may be renewed or refunded. An ad valorem tax shall be levied annually upon all the property in the state of Oregon taxed on an ad valorem basis, in sufficient amount to provide for the payment of such indebtedness and the interest thereon. The legislative assembly may provide other revenues to supplement or replace the said tax levies. The legislature shall enact legislation to carry out the provisions hereof. This amendment shall supersede all constitutional provisions in conflict herewith. [Created through H.J.R. 24, 1947, and adopted by the people Nov. 2, 1948; Amendment proposed by S.J.R. 7, 1961, and adopted by the people Nov. 6, 1962; Amendment proposed by H.J.R. 85, 1997, and adopted by the people May 20, 1997]

ARTICLE XI-F(1)
HIGHER EDUCATION BUILDING PROJECTS

Section 1. State empowered to lend credit for higher education building projects. The credit of the state may be loaned and indebtedness incurred in an amount which shall not exceed at any one time three-fourths of one percent of the true cash value of all the taxable property in the state, as determined by law to provide funds with which to acquire, construct, improve, repair, equip and furnish buildings, structures, land and other projects, or parts thereof, that the legislative assembly determines will benefit higher education institutions or activities. [Created through H.J.R. 26, 1949, and adopted by the people Nov. 7, 1950; Amendment proposed by H.J.R. 12, 1959, and adopted by the people Nov. 8, 1960; Amendment proposed by H.J.R. 101, 2010, and adopted by the people May 18, 2010]

Section 2. Limitation on authorization to incur indebtedness. Indebtedness shall not be incurred to finance projects described in section 1 of this Article unless the constructing authority conservatively estimates that the constructing authority will have sufficient revenues to pay the indebtedness and operate the projects financed with the proceeds of the indebtedness. For purposes of this section, "revenues" includes all funds available to the constructing authority except amounts appropriated by the legislative assembly from the General Fund. [Created through H.J.R. 26, 1949, and adopted by the people Nov. 7, 1950; Amendment proposed by H.J.R. 101, 2010, and adopted by the people May 18, 2010]

Section 3. Sources of revenue. Ad valorem taxes shall be levied annually upon all the taxable property in the state of Oregon in sufficient amount, with the aforesaid revenues, to provide for the payment of such indebtedness and the interest thereon. The legislative assembly may provide other revenues to supplement or replace such tax levies. [Created through H.J.R. 26, 1949, and adopted by the people Nov. 7, 1950; Amendment proposed by H.J.R. 101, 2010, and adopted by the people May 18, 2010]

Section 4. Bonds. Bonds issued pursuant to this article shall be the direct general obligations of the state, and be in such form, run for such periods of time, and bear such rates of interest, as shall be provided by statute. Such bonds may be refunded with bonds of like obligation. Unless provided by statute, no bonds shall be issued pursuant to this article for the construction of buildings or other structures for higher education until after all of the aforesaid outstanding revenue bonds shall have been redeemed or refunded. [Created through H.J.R. 26, 1949, and adopted by the people Nov. 7, 1950]

Section 5. Legislation to effectuate Article. The legislative assembly shall enact legislation to carry out the provisions hereof. This article shall supersede all conflicting constitutional provisions. [Created through H.J.R. 26, 1949, and adopted by the people Nov. 7, 1950]

ARTICLE XI-F(2)
VETERANS' BONUS

Section 1. State empowered to lend credit to pay veterans' bonus; issuance of bonds. Notwithstanding the limitations contained in Section 7 of Article XI of the constitution, the credit of the State of Oregon may be loaned and indebtedness incurred to an amount not exceeding 5 percent of the assessed valuation of all the property in the state, for the purpose of creating a fund to be paid to residents of the State of Oregon who served in the armed forces of the United States between September 16, 1940, and June 30, 1946, and were honorably discharged from such service, which fund shall be known as the "World War II Veterans' Compensation Fund."

Bonds of the State of Oregon, containing a direct promise on behalf of the state to pay the face value thereof with the interest thereon provided for may be issued to an amount authorized in Section 1 hereof for the purpose of creating said World War II Veterans' Compensation Fund. Refunding bonds may be issued and sold to refund any bonds issued under authority of Section 1 hereof. There may be issued and outstanding at any one time bonds aggregating the amount authorized by Section 1, but at no time shall the total of all bonds outstanding, including refunding bonds, exceed the amount so authorized. Said bonds shall be a direct obligation of the State and shall be in such form and shall run for such periods of time and bear such rates of interest as shall be provided by statute. No person shall be eligible to receive money from said fund except the veterans as defined in Section 3 of this act [sic]. The legislature shall and the people may provide any additional legislation that may be necessary, in addition to existing laws, to carry out the provisions of this section. [Created through initiative petition filed June 30, 1950, and adopted by the people Nov. 7, 1950]

Section 2. Definitions. The following words, terms, and phrases, as used in this act [sic] shall have the following meaning unless the text otherwise requires:

(1) "Domestic service" means service within the continental limits of the United States, excluding Alaska, Hawaii, Canal Zone and Puerto Rico.

(2) "Foreign Service" means service in all other places, including sea duty.

(3) "Husband" means the unremarried husband, and "wife" means the unremarried wife.

(4) "Child or Children" means child or children of issue, child or children by adoption or child or children to whom the deceased person has stood in loco parentis for one year or more immediately preceding his death.

(5) "Parent or Parents" means natural parent or parents; parent or parents by adoption; or, person or persons, including stepparent or stepparents, who have stood in loco parentis to the deceased person for a period of one year or more immediately prior to entrance into the armed service of the United States.

(6) "Veterans" means any person who shall have served in active duty in the armed forces of the United States at any time between September 16, 1940, and June 30, 1946, both dates inclusive, and who, at the time of

commencing such service, was and had been a bona fide resident of the State of Oregon for at least one year immediately preceding the commencement of such service, and who shall have been separated from such service under honorable conditions, or who is still in such service, or who has been retired. [Created through initiative petition filed June 30, 1950, and adopted by the people Nov. 7, 1950]

Section 3. Amount of bonus. Every veteran who was in such service for a period of at least 90 days shall be entitled to receive compensation at the rate of Ten Dollars ($10.00) for each full month during which such veteran was in active domestic service and Fifteen Dollars ($15.00) for each full month during which such veteran was in active foreign service within said period of time. Any veteran who was serving on active duty in the armed forces between September 16, 1940, and June 30, 1946, whose services were terminated by reason of service-connected disabilities, and who, upon filing a claim for disabilities with the United States Veterans' Administration within three months after separation from the armed service, was rated not less than 50% disabled as a result of such claim, shall be deemed to have served sufficient time to entitle him or her to the maximum payment under this act [sic] and shall be so entitled. The maximum amount of compensation payable under this act [sic] shall be six hundred dollars ($600.00) and no such compensation shall be paid to any veteran who shall have received from another state a bonus or compensation because of such military service. [Created through initiative petition filed June 30, 1950, and adopted by the people Nov. 7, 1950]

Section 4. Survivors of certain deceased veterans entitled to maximum amount. The survivor or survivors, of the deceased veteran whose death was caused or contributed to by a service:HYP.connected disease or disability incurred in service under conditions other than dishonorable, shall be entitled, in the order of survivorship provided in this act [sic], to receive the maximum amount of said compensation irrespective of the amount such deceased would have been entitled to receive if living. [Created through initiative petition filed June 30, 1950, and adopted by the people Nov. 7, 1950]

Section 5. Certain persons not eligible. No compensation shall be paid under this act [sic] to any veteran who, during the period of service refused on conscientious, political or other grounds to subject himself to full military discipline and unqualified service, or to any veteran for any periods of time spent under penal confinement during the period of active duty, or for service in the merchant marine: Provided, however, that for the purposes of this act [sic], active service in the chaplain corps, or medical corps shall be deemed unqualified service under full military discipline. [Created through initiative petition filed June 30, 1950, and adopted by the people Nov. 7, 1950]

Section 6. Order of distribution among survivors. The survivor or survivors of any deceased veteran who would have been entitled to compensation under this act [sic], other than those mentioned in Section 4 of this act [sic], shall be entitled to receive the same amount of compensation as said deceased veteran would have received, if living, which shall be distributed as follows:

(1) To the husband or wife, as the case may be, the whole amount.

(2) If there be no husband or wife, to the child or children, equally; and

(3) If there be no husband or wife or child or children, to the parent or parents, equally. [Created through initiative petition filed June 30, 1950, and adopted by the people Nov. 7, 1950]

Section 7. Bonus not saleable or assignable; bonus free from creditors' claims and state taxes. No sale or assignment of any right or claim to compensation under this act [sic] shall be valid, no claims of creditors shall be enforcible against rights or claims to or payments of such compensation, and such compensation shall be exempt from all taxes imposed by the laws of this state. [Created through initiative petition filed June 30, 1950, and adopted by the people Nov. 7, 1950]

Section 8. Administration of article; rules and regulations. The director of Veterans' Affairs, State of Oregon, referred to herein as the "director" hereby is authorized and empowered, and it shall be his duty, to administer the provisions of this act [sic], and with the approval of the veterans advisory committee may make such rules and regulations as are deemed necessary to accomplish the purpose hereof. [Created through initiative petition filed June 30, 1950, and adopted by the people Nov. 7, 1950]

Section 9. Applications. All applications for certificates under this act [sic] shall be made within two years from the effective date hereof and upon forms to be supplied by the director. Said applications shall be duly verified by the claimant before a notary public or other person authorized to take acknowledgments, and shall set forth applicant's name, residence at the time of entry into the service, date and place of enlistment, induction or entry upon active federal service, beginning and ending dates of foreign service, date of discharge, retirement or release from active federal service, statement of time lost by reason of penal confinement during the period of active duty; together with the applicant's original discharge, or certificate in lieu of lost discharge, or certificate of service, or if the applicant has not been released at the time of application, a statement by competent military authority that the applicant during the period for which compensation is claimed did not refuse to subject himself to full military discipline and unqualified service, and that the applicant has not been separated from service under circumstances other than honorable. The director may require such further information to be included in such application as deemed necessary to enable him to determine the eligibility of the applicant. Such applications, together with satisfactory evidence of honorable service, shall be filed with the director. The director shall make such reasonable requirements for applicants as may be necessary to prevent fraud or the payment of compensation to persons not entitled thereto. [Created through initiative petition filed June 30, 1950, and adopted by the people Nov. 7, 1950]

Section 10. Furnishing forms; printing, office supplies and equipment; employes; payment of expenses. The director shall furnish free of charge, upon request, the necessary forms upon which applications may be made and may authorize the county clerks, Veterans organizations and other organizations, and notaries public willing to assist veterans without charge, to act for him in receiving application under this act [sic], and shall furnish such clerks, organizations and notaries public, with the proper forms for such purpose. The director hereby is authorized and directed with the approval of the veterans' advisory committee, to procure such printing, office supplies and equipment and to employ such persons as may be necessary in order to properly carry out the provisions of this act [sic], and all expense incurred by him in the administration thereof shall be paid out of the World War II Veterans' Compensation Fund, in the manner provided by law for payment of claims from other state funds. [Created through initiative petition filed June 30, 1950, and adopted by the people Nov. 7, 1950]

ARTICLE XI-G
HIGHER EDUCATION INSTITUTIONS AND ACTIVITIES; COMMUNITY COLLEGES

Section 1. State empowered to lend credit for financing higher education institutions and activities, and community colleges. (1) Notwithstanding the limitations contained in section 7, Article XI of this Constitution, and in addition to other exceptions from the limitations of such section, the credit of the state may be loaned and indebtedness incurred in an amount not to exceed at any time three-fourths of one percent of the true cash value of all taxable property in the state, as determined by law.

(2) Proceeds from any loan authorized or indebtedness incurred under this section shall be used to provide funds with which to acquire, construct, improve, repair, equip and furnish buildings, structures, land and other projects, or parts thereof, that the Legislative Assembly determines will benefit higher education institutions or activities or community colleges authorized by law to receive state aid.

(3) The amount of any indebtedness incurred under this section in any biennium shall be matched by an amount that is at least equal to the amount of the indebtedness. The matching amount must be used for the same or similar purposes as the proceeds of the indebtedness and may consist of moneys appropriated from the General Fund or any other moneys available to the constructing authority for such purposes. However, the matching amount may not consist of proceeds of indebtedness incurred by the state under any other Article of this Constitution. Any matching amount appropriated from the General Fund to meet the requirements of this subsection must be specifically designated therefor by the Legislative Assembly.

(4) Nothing in this section prevents the financing of projects, or parts thereof, by a combination of the moneys available under this section, under Article XI-F(1) of this Constitution, and from other lawful sources. [Created through H.J.R. 8, 1963 (s.s.), and adopted by the people May 15, 1964; Amendment proposed by H.J.R. 2, 1967 (s.s.), and adopted by the people May 28, 1968; Amendment proposed by H.J.R. 101, 2010, and adopted by the people May 18, 2010]

Section 2. Bonds. Bonds issued pursuant to this Article shall be the direct general obligations of the state and shall be in such form, run for such periods of time, and bear such rates of interest as the Legislative Assembly provides. Such bonds may be refunded with bonds of like obligation. [Created through H.J.R. 8, 1963 (s.s.), and adopted by the people May 15, 1964]

Section 3. Sources of revenue. Ad valorem taxes shall be levied annually upon the taxable property within the State of Oregon in sufficient amount to provide for the prompt payment of bonds issued pursuant to this Article and the interest thereon. The Legislative Assembly may provide other revenues to supplement or replace, in whole or in part, such tax levies. [Created through H.J.R. 8, 1963 (s.s.), and adopted by the people May 15, 1964]

ARTICLE XI-H
POLLUTION CONTROL

Section 1. State empowered to lend credit for financing pollution control facilities or related activities. In the manner provided by law and notwithstanding the limitations contained in sections 7 and 8, Article XI, of this Constitution, the credit of the State of Oregon may be loaned and indebtedness incurred in an amount not to exceed, at any one time, one percent of the true cash value of all taxable property in the state:

(1) To provide funds to be advanced, by contract, grant, loan or otherwise, to any municipal corporation, city, county or agency of the State of Oregon, or combinations thereof, for the purpose of planning, acquisition, construction, alteration or improvement of facilities for or activities related to, the collection, treatment, dilution and disposal of all forms of waste in or upon the air, water and lands of this state; and

(2) To provide funds for the acquisition, by purchase, loan or otherwise, of bonds, notes or other obligations of any municipal corporation, city, county or agency of the State of Oregon, or combinations thereof, issued or made for the purposes of subsection (1) of this section. [Created through H.J.R. 14, 1969, and adopted by the people May 26, 1970; Amendment proposed by S.J.R. 41, 1989, and adopted by the people May 22, 1990]

Section 2. Only facilities 70 percent self-supporting and self-liquidating authorized; exceptions. The facilities for which funds are advanced and for which bonds, notes or other obligations are issued or made and acquired pursuant to this Article shall be only such facilities as conservatively appear to the agency designated by law to make the determination to be not less than 70 percent self-supporting and self-liquidating from revenues, gifts, grants from the Federal Government, user charges, assessments and other fees. This section shall not apply to any activities for which funds are advanced and shall not apply to facilities for the collection, treatment, dilution, removal and disposal of hazardous substances. [Created through H.J.R. 14, 1969, and adopted by the people May 26, 1970; Amendment proposed by S.J.R. 41, 1989, and adopted by the people May 22, 1990]

Section 3. Authority of public bodies to receive funds. Notwithstanding the limitations contained in section 10, Article XI of this Constitution, municipal corporations, cities, counties, and agencies of the State of Oregon, or combinations thereof, may receive funds referred to in section 1 of this Article, by contract, grant, loan or otherwise and may also receive such funds through disposition to the state, by sale, loan or otherwise, of bonds, notes or other obligations issued or made for the purposes set forth in section 1 of this Article. [Created through H.J.R. 14, 1969, and adopted by the people May 26, 1970]

Section 4. Sources of revenue. Ad valorem taxes shall be levied annually upon all taxable property within the State of Oregon in sufficient amount to provide, together with the revenues, gifts, grants from the Federal Government, user charges, assessments and other fees referred to in section 2 of this Article for the payment of indebtedness incurred by the state and the interest thereon. The Legislative Assembly may provide other revenues to supplement or replace such tax levies. [Created through H.J.R. 14, 1969, and adopted by the people May 26, 1970]

Section 5. Bonds. Bonds issued pursuant to section 1 of this Article shall be the direct obligations of the state and shall be in such form, run for such periods of time, and bear such rates of interest, as shall be provided by law. Such bonds may be refunded with bonds of like obligation. [Created through H.J.R. 14, 1969, and adopted by the people May 26, 1970]

Section 6. Legislation to effectuate Article. The Legislative Assembly shall enact legislation to carry out the provisions of this Article. This Article shall supersede all conflicting constitutional provisions and shall supersede any conflicting provision of a county or city charter or act of incorporation. [Created through H.J.R. 14, 1969, and adopted by the people May 26, 1970]

ARTICLE XI-I(1)
WATER DEVELOPMENT PROJECTS

Section 1. State empowered to lend credit to establish Water Development Fund; eligibility; use. Notwithstanding the limits contained in sections 7 and 8, Article XI of this Constitution, the credit of the State of Oregon may be loaned and indebtedness incurred in an amount not to exceed one and one-half percent of the true cash value of all the property in the state for the purpose of creating a fund to be known as the Water Development Fund. The fund shall be used to provide financing for loans for residents of this state for construction of water development projects for irrigation, drainage, fish protection, watershed restoration and municipal uses and for the acquisition of easements and rights of way for water development projects authorized by law. Secured repayment thereof shall be and is a prerequisite to the advancement of money from such fund. As used in this section, "resident" includes both natural persons and any corporation or cooperative, either for profit or nonprofit, whose principal income is from farming in Oregon or municipal or quasi-municipal or other body subject to the laws of the State of Oregon. Not less than 50 percent of the potential amount available from the fund will be reserved for irrigation and drainage projects. For municipal use, only municipalities and communities with populations less than 30,000 are eligible for loans from the fund. [Created through S.J.R. 1, 1977, and adopted by the people Nov. 8, 1977; Amendment proposed by S.J.R. 6, 1981, and adopted by the people May 18, 1982; Amendment proposed by H.J.R. 45, 1987, and adopted by the people May 17, 1988]

Section 2. Bonds. Bonds of the State of Oregon containing a direct promise on behalf of the state to pay the face value thereof, with the interest therein provided for, may be issued to an amount authorized by section 1 of this Article for the purpose of creating such fund. The bonds shall be a direct obligation of the state and shall be in such form and shall run for such periods of time and bear such rates of interest as provided by statute. [Created through S.J.R. 1, 1977, and adopted by the people Nov. 8, 1977]

Section 3. Refunding bonds. Refunding bonds may be issued and sold to refund any bonds issued under authority of sections 1 and 2 of this Article. There may be issued and outstanding at any time bonds aggregating the amount authorized by section 1 of this Article but at no time shall the total of all bonds outstanding, including refunding bonds, exceed the amount so authorized. [Created through S.J.R. 1, 1977, and adopted by the people Nov. 8, 1977]

Section 4. Sources of revenue. Ad valorem taxes shall be levied annually upon all the taxable property in the State of Oregon in sufficient amount to provide for the payment of principal and interest of the bonds issued pursuant to this Article. The Legislative Assembly may provide other revenues to supplement or replace, in whole or in part, such tax levies. [Created through S.J.R. 1, 1977, and adopted by the people Nov. 8, 1977]

Section 5. Legislation to effectuate Article. The Legislative Assembly shall enact legislation to carry out the provisions of this Article. This Article supersedes any conflicting provision of a county or city charter or act of incorporation. [Created through S.J.R. 1, 1977, and adopted by the people Nov. 8, 1977]

ARTICLE XI-I(2)
MULTIFAMILY HOUSING FOR ELDERLY AND DISABLED

Section 1. State empowered to lend credit for multifamily housing for elderly and disabled persons. In the manner provided by law and notwithstanding the limitations contained in section 7, Article XI of this Constitution, the credit of the State of Oregon may be loaned and indebtedness incurred in an amount not to exceed, at any one time, one-half of one percent of the true cash value of all taxable property in the state to provide funds to be advanced, by contract, grant, loan or otherwise, for the purpose of providing additional financing for multifamily housing for the elderly and for disabled persons. Multifamily housing means a structure or facility designed to contain more than one living unit. Additional financing may be provided to the elderly to purchase ownership interest in the structure or facility. [Created through H.J.R. 61, 1977, and adopted by the people May 23, 1978; Amendment proposed by S.J.R. 34, 1979, and adopted by the people May 20, 1980; Amendment proposed by H.J.R. 1, 1981, and adopted by the people May 18, 1982]

Section 2. Sources of revenue. The bonds shall be payable from contract or loan proceeds; bond reserves; other funds available for these purposes; and, if necessary, state ad valorem taxes. [Created through H.J.R. 61, 1977, and adopted by the people May 23, 1978]

Section 3. Bonds. Bonds issued pursuant to section 1 of this Article shall be the direct obligations of the state and shall be in such form, run for such periods of time and bear such rates of interest as shall be provided by law. The bonds may be refunded with bonds of like obligation. [Created through H.J.R. 61, 1977, and adopted by the people May 23, 1978]

Section 4. Legislation to effectuate Article. The Legislative Assembly shall enact legislation to carry out the provisions of this Article. This Article shall supersede all conflicting constitutional provisions. [Created through H.J.R. 61, 1977, and adopted by the people May 23, 1978]

ARTICLE XI-J
SMALL SCALE LOCAL ENERGY LOANS

Section 1. State empowered to loan credit for small scale local energy loans; eligibility; use. Notwithstanding the limits contained in sections 7 and 8, Article XI of this Constitution, the credit of the State of Oregon may be loaned and indebtedness incurred in an amount not to exceed one-half of one percent of the true cash value of all the property in the state for the purpose of creating a fund to be known as the Small Scale Local Energy Project Loan Fund. The fund shall be used to provide financing for the development of small scale local energy projects. Secured repayment thereof shall be and is a prerequisite to the advancement of money from such fund. [Created through S.J.R. 24, 1979, and adopted by the people May 20, 1980]

Section 2. Bonds. Bonds of the State of Oregon containing a direct promise on behalf of the state to pay the face value thereof, with the interest therein provided for, may be issued to an amount authorized by section 1 of this Article for the purpose of creating such fund. The bonds shall be a direct obligation of the state and shall be in such form and shall run for such periods of time and bear such rates of interest as provided by statute. [Created through S.J.R. 24, 1979, and adopted by the people May 20, 1980]

Section 3. Refunding bonds. Refunding bonds may be issued and sold to refund any bonds issued under authority of sections 1 and 2 of this Article. There may be issued and outstanding at any time bonds aggregating the amount authorized by section 1 of this Article but at no time shall the total of all bonds outstanding including refunding bonds, exceed the amount so authorized. [Created through S.J.R. 24, 1979, and adopted by the people May 20, 1980]

Section 4. Sources of revenue. Ad valorem taxes shall be levied annually upon all the taxable property in the State of Oregon in sufficient amount to provide for the payment of principal and interest of the bonds issued pursuant to this Article. The Legislative Assembly may provide other revenues to supplement or replace, in whole or in part, such tax levies. [Created through S.J.R. 24, 1979, and adopted by the people May 20, 1980]

Section 5. Legislation to effectuate Article. The Legislative Assembly shall enact legislation to carry out the provisions of this Article. This Article supersedes any conflicting provision of a county or city charter or act of incorporation. [Created through S.J.R. 24, 1979, and adopted by the people May 20, 1980]

ARTICLE XI-K
GUARANTEE OF BONDED INDEBTEDNESS OF EDUCATION DISTRICTS

Section 1. State empowered to guarantee bonded indebtedness of education districts. To secure lower interest costs on the general obligation bonds of school districts, education service districts and community college districts, the State of Oregon may guarantee the general obligation bonded indebtedness of those districts as provided in sections 2 to 6 of this Article and laws enacted pursuant to this Article. [Created through H.J.R. 71, 1997, and adopted by the people Nov. 3, 1998]

Section 2. State empowered to lend credit for state guarantee of bonded indebtedness of education districts. In the manner provided by law and notwithstanding the limitations contained in sections 7 and 8, Article XI of this Constitution, the credit of the State of Oregon may be loaned and indebtedness incurred, in an amount not to exceed, at any one time, one-half of one percent of the true cash value of all taxable property in the state, to provide funds as necessary to satisfy the state guaranty of the bonded general obligation indebtedness of school districts, education service districts and community college districts that qualify, under procedures that shall be established by law, to issue general obligation bonds that are guaranteed by the full faith and credit of this state. The state may guarantee the general obligation debt of qualified school districts, education service districts and community college districts and may guarantee general obligation bonded indebtedness incurred to refund the school district, education service district or community college district general obligation bonded indebtedness. [Created through H.J.R. 71, 1997, and adopted by the people Nov. 3, 1998]

Section 3. Repayment by education districts. The Legislative Assembly may provide that reimbursement to the state shall be obtained from, but shall not be limited to, moneys that otherwise would be used for the support of the educational programs of the school district, the education service district or the community college district that incurred the bonded indebtedness with respect to which any payment under the state's guaranty is made. [Created through H.J.R. 71, 1997, and adopted by the people Nov. 3, 1998]

Section 4. Sources of revenue. The State of Oregon may issue bonds if and as necessary to provide funding to satisfy the state's guaranty obligations undertaken pursuant to this Article. In addition, notwithstanding anything to the contrary in Article VIII of this Constitution, the state may borrow available moneys from the Common School Fund if such borrowing is reasonably necessary to satisfy the state's guaranty obligations undertaken pursuant to this Article. The State of Oregon also may issue bonds if and as necessary to provide funding to repay the borrowed moneys, and any interest thereon, to the Common School Fund. The bonds shall be payable from any moneys reimbursed to the state under section 3 of this Article, from any moneys recoverable from the school district, the education service district or the community college district that incurred the bonded indebtedness with respect to which any payment under the state's guaranty is made, any other funds available for these purposes and, if necessary, from state ad valorem taxes. [Created through H.J.R. 71, 1997, and adopted by the people Nov. 3, 1998]

Section 5. Bonds. Bonds of the state issued pursuant to this Article shall be the direct obligations of the state and shall be in such form, run for such periods of time and bear such rates of interest as shall be provided by law. The bonds may be refunded with bonds of like obligation. [Created through H.J.R. 71, 1997, and adopted by the people Nov. 3, 1998]

Section 6. Legislation to effectuate Article. The Legislative Assembly shall enact legislation to carry out the provisions of this Article, including provisions that authorize the state's recovery, from any school district, education service district or community college district that incurred the bonded indebtedness with respect to which any payment under the state's guaranty is made, any amounts necessary to make the state whole. This Article shall supersede all conflicting constitutional provisions and shall supersede any conflicting provision of any law, ordinance or charter pertaining to any school district, education service district or community college district. [Created through H.J.R. 71, 1997, and adopted by the people Nov. 3, 1998]

ARTICLE XI-L
OREGON HEALTH AND SCIENCE UNIVERSITY

Sec. 1. State empowered to lend credit for financing capital costs of Oregon Health and Science University; bonds
2. Sources of repayment
3. Refunding bonds
4. Legislation to effectuate Article
5. Relationship to conflicting provisions of Constitution

Section 1. State empowered to lend credit for financing capital costs of Oregon Health and Science University; bonds. (1) In the manner provided by law and notwithstanding the limitations contained in section 7, Article XI of this Constitution, the credit of the State of Oregon may be loaned and indebtedness incurred, in an aggregate outstanding principal amount not to exceed, at any one time, one-half of one percent of the real market value of all property in the state, to provide funds to finance capital costs of Oregon Health and Science University. Bonds issued under this section may not be paid from ad valorem property taxes.

(2) Any indebtedness incurred under this section shall be in the form of general obligation bonds of the State of Oregon containing a direct promise on behalf of the State of Oregon to pay the principal, premium, if any, and interest on such bonds, in an aggregate outstanding principal amount not to exceed the amount authorized in subsection (1) of this section. The bonds shall be the direct obligation of the State of Oregon and shall be in such form, run for such period of time, have such terms and bear such rates of interest as may be provided by statute. The full faith and credit and taxing power of the State of Oregon shall be pledged to the payment of the principal, premium, if any, and interest on such bonds provided, however, that the ad valorem taxing power of the State of Oregon may not be pledged to the payment of such bonds.

(3) The proceeds from bonds issued under this section shall be used to finance capital costs of Oregon Health and Science University and costs of issuing bonds pursuant to this Article. Bonds issued under this section to finance capital costs of Oregon Health and Science University shall be issued in an aggregate principal amount that produces net proceeds for the university in an amount that does not exceed $200 million.

(4) The proceeds from bonds issued under this section may not be used to finance operating costs of Oregon Health and Science University.

(5) As used in this Article, "bonds" means bonds, notes or other financial obligations of the State of Oregon issued under this section. [Created through H.J.R. 19, 2001, and adopted by the people May 21, 2002]

Section 2. Sources of repayment. The principal, premium, if any, interest and any other amounts payable with respect to bonds issued under section 1 of this Article shall be repaid as determined by the Legislative Assembly from the following sources:

(1) Amounts appropriated for such purpose by the Legislative Assembly from the General Fund, including any taxes levied to pay the bonds other than ad valorem property taxes;

(2) Amounts allocated for such purpose by the Legislative Assembly from the proceeds of the State Lottery or from the Master Settlement Agreement entered into on November 23, 1998, by the State of Oregon and leading United States tobacco product manufacturers; and

(3) Amounts appropriated or allocated for such purpose by the Legislative Assembly from other sources of revenue. [Created through H.J.R. 19, 2001, and adopted by the people May 21, 2002]

Section 3. Refunding bonds. Bonds issued under section 1 of this Article may be refunded with bonds of like obligation. [Created through H.J.R. 19, 2001, and adopted by the people May 21, 2002]

Section 4. Legislation to effectuate Article. The Legislative Assembly may enact legislation to carry out the provisions of this Article. [Created through H.J.R. 19, 2001, and adopted by the people May 21, 2002]

Section 5. Relationship to conflicting provision of Constitution. This Article shall supersede all conflicting provisions of this constitution. [Created through H.J.R. 19, 2001, and adopted by the people May 21, 2002]

ARTICLE XI-M
SEISMIC REHABILITATION OF PUBLIC EDUCATION BUILDINGS

Sec. 1. State empowered to lend credit for seismic rehabilitation of public education buildings
2. Sources of repayment
3. Refunding bonds
4. Legislation to effectuate Article
5. Relationship to conflicting provisions of Constitution

Note: RF8. Article XI-M was designated as "Article XI-L" by S.J.R. 21, 2001, and adopted by the people Nov. 5, 2002.

Section 1. State empowered to lend credit for seismic rehabilitation of public education buildings; bonds. (1) In the manner provided by law and notwithstanding the limitations contained in section 7, Article XI of this Constitution, the credit of the State of Oregon may be loaned and indebtedness incurred, in an aggregate outstanding principal amount not to exceed, at any one time, one-fifth of one percent of the real market value of all property in the state, to provide funds for the planning and implementation of seismic rehabilitation of public education buildings, including surveying and conducting engineering evaluations of the need for seismic rehabilitation.

(2) Any indebtedness incurred under this section must be in the form of general obligation bonds of the State of Oregon containing a direct promise on behalf of the State of Oregon to pay the principal, premium, if any, interest and other amounts payable with respect to the bonds, in an aggregate outstanding principal amount not to exceed the amount authorized in subsection (1) of this section. The bonds are the direct obligation of the State of Oregon and must be in a form, run for a period of time, have terms and bear rates of interest as may be provided by statute. The full faith and credit and taxing power of the State of Oregon must be pledged to the payment of the principal, premium, if any, and interest on the general obligation bonds; however, the ad valorem taxing power of the State of Oregon may not be pledged to the payment of the bonds issued under this section.

(3) As used in this section, "public education building" means a building owned by the State Board of Higher Education, a school district, an education service district, a community college district or a community college service district. [Created through S.J.R. 21, 2001, and adopted by the people Nov. 5, 2002]

Section 2. Sources of repayment. The principal, premium, if any, interest and other amounts payable with respect to the general obligation bonds issued under section 1 of this Article must be repaid as determined by the Legislative Assembly from the following sources:

(1) Amounts appropriated for the purpose by the Legislative Assembly from the General Fund, including taxes, other than ad valorem property taxes, levied to pay the bonds;

(2) Amounts allocated for the purpose by the Legislative Assembly from the proceeds of the State Lottery or from the Master Settlement Agreement entered into on November 23, 1998, by the State of Oregon and leading United States tobacco product manufacturers; and

(3) Amounts appropriated or allocated for the purpose by the Legislative Assembly from other sources of revenue. [Created through S.J.R. 21, 2001, and adopted by the people Nov. 5, 2002]

Section 3. Refunding bonds. General obligation bonds issued under section 1 of this Article may be refunded with bonds of like obligation. [Created through S.J.R. 21, 2001, and adopted by the people Nov. 5, 2002]

Section 4. Legislation to effectuate Article. The Legislative Assembly may enact legislation to carry out the provisions of this Article. [Created through S.J.R. 21, 2001, and adopted by the people Nov. 5, 2002]

Section 5. Relationship to conflicting provisions of Constitution. This Article supersedes conflicting provisions of this Constitution. [Created through S.J.R. 21, 2001, and adopted by the people Nov. 5, 2002]

ARTICLE XI-N
SEISMIC REHABILITATION OF EMERGENCY SERVICES BUILDINGS

Note: RF8. Article XI-N was designated as "Article XI-L" by S.J.R. 22, 2001, and adopted by the people Nov. 5, 2002.

Section 1. State empowered to lend credit for seismic rehabilitation of emergency services buildings; bonds. (1) In the manner provided by law and notwithstanding the limitations contained in section 7, Article XI of this Constitution, the credit of the State of Oregon may be loaned and indebtedness incurred, in an aggregate outstanding principal amount not to exceed, at any one time, one-fifth of one percent of the real market value of all property in the state, to provide funds for the planning and implementation of seismic rehabilitation of emergency services buildings, including surveying and conducting engineering evaluations of the need for seismic rehabilitation.

(2) Any indebtedness incurred under this section must be in the form of general obligation bonds of the State of Oregon containing a direct promise on behalf of the State of Oregon to pay the principal, premium, if any, interest and other amounts payable with respect to the bonds, in an aggregate outstanding principal amount not to exceed the amount authorized in subsection (1) of this section. The bonds are the direct obligation of the State of Oregon and must be in a form, run for a period of time, have terms and bear rates of interest as may be provided by statute. The full faith and credit and taxing power of the State of Oregon must be pledged to the payment of the principal, premium, if any, and interest on the general obligation bonds; however, the ad valorem taxing power of the State of Oregon may not be pledged to the payment of the bonds issued under this section.

(3) As used in this section:

(a) "Acute inpatient care facility" means a licensed hospital with an organized medical staff, with permanent facilities that include inpatient beds, and with comprehensive medical services, including physician services and continuous nursing services under the supervision of registered nurses, to provide diagnosis and medical or surgical treatment primarily for but not limited to acutely ill patients and accident victims. "Acute inpatient care facility" includes the Oregon Health and Science University.

(b) "Emergency services building" means a public building used for fire protection services, a hospital building that contains an acute inpatient care facility, a police station, a sheriff's office or a similar facility used by a state, county, district or municipal law enforcement agency. [Created through S.J.R. 22, 2001, and adopted by the people Nov. 5, 2002]

Section 2. Sources of repayment. The principal, premium, if any, interest and other amounts payable with respect to the general obligation bonds issued under section 1 of this Article must be repaid as determined by the Legislative Assembly from the following sources:

(1) Amounts appropriated for the purpose by the Legislative Assembly from the General Fund, including

taxes, other than ad valorem property taxes, levied to pay the bonds;

(2) Amounts allocated for the purpose by the Legislative Assembly from the proceeds of the State Lottery or from the Master Settlement Agreement entered into on November 23, 1998, by the State of Oregon and leading United States tobacco product manufacturers; and

(3) Amounts appropriated or allocated for the purpose by the Legislative Assembly from other sources of revenue. [Created through S.J.R. 22, 2001, and adopted by the people Nov. 5, 2002]

Section 3. Refunding bonds. General obligation bonds issued under section 1 of this Article may be refunded with bonds of like obligation. [Created through S.J.R. 22, 2001, and adopted by the people Nov. 5, 2002]

Section 4. Legislation to effectuate Article. The Legislative Assembly may enact legislation to carry out the provisions of this Article. [Created through S.J.R. 22, 2001, and adopted by the people Nov. 5, 2002]

Section 5. Relationship to conflicting provisions of Constitution. This Article supersedes conflicting provisions of this Constitution. [Created through S.J.R. 22, 2001, and adopted by the people Nov. 5, 2002]

ARTICLE XI-O
PENSION LIABILITIES

Section 1. State empowered to lend credit for pension liabilities. (1) In the manner provided by law and notwithstanding the limitations contained in section 7, Article XI of this Constitution, the credit of the State of Oregon may be loaned and indebtedness incurred to finance the State of Oregon's pension liabilities. Indebtedness authorized by this section also may be used to pay costs of issuing or incurring indebtedness under this section.

(2) Indebtedness incurred under this section is a general obligation of the State of Oregon and must contain a direct promise on behalf of the State of Oregon to pay the principal, premium, if any, and interest on that indebtedness. The State of Oregon shall pledge its full faith and credit and taxing power to pay that indebtedness; however, the ad valorem taxing power of the State of Oregon may not be pledged to pay that indebtedness. The amount of indebtedness authorized by this section and outstanding at any time may not exceed one percent of the real market value of all property in the state. [Created through H.J.R. 18, 2003, and adopted by the people Sept. 16, 2003]

Section 2. Refunding obligations. Indebtedness incurred under section 1 of this Article may be refunded with like obligations. [Created through H.J.R. 18, 2003, and adopted by the people Sept. 16, 2003]

Section 3. Legislation to effectuate Article. The Legislative Assembly may enact legislation to carry out the provisions of this Article. [Created through H.J.R. 18, 2003, and adopted by the people Sept. 16, 2003]

Section 4. Relationship to conflicting provisions of Constitution. This Article supersedes all conflicting provisions of this Constitution. [Created through H.J.R. 18, 2003, and adopted by the people Sept. 16, 2003]

ARTICLE XI-P
SCHOOL DISTRICT CAPITAL COSTS

Section 1. State empowered to lend credit for grants or loans to school districts to finance capital costs; general obligation bond proceeds as matching funds. (1) In the manner provided by law and notwithstanding the limitations contained in section 7, Article XI of this Constitution, the State of Oregon may loan its credit and incur indebtedness, in an aggregate outstanding principal amount not to exceed, at any one time, one-half of one percent of the real market value of the real property in this state, to provide funds to be advanced by grant or loan to school districts to finance the capital costs of the school districts. Bonds issued under this section may not be paid from ad valorem property taxes.

(2) Indebtedness incurred under this section must be in the form of general obligation bonds of the State of Oregon containing a direct promise to pay the principal, interest and premium, if any, of the bonds in an aggregate outstanding principal amount not to exceed the amount authorized in subsection (1) of this section. The bonds are the direct obligation of the State of Oregon and must be in such form, run for such periods of time, have such terms and bear such rates of interest as may be provided by statute. The State of Oregon shall pledge its full faith and credit and taxing power to the payment of the principal, interest and premium, if any, of the bonds. However, the State of Oregon may not pledge its ad valorem taxing power to the payment of the bonds.

(3) The proceeds from bonds issued under this section may be used only to provide matching funds to finance the capital costs of school districts that have received voter approval for local general obligation bonds and to provide for the costs of issuing bonds and the payment of debt service.

(4) The proceeds from bonds issued under this section may not be used to finance the operating costs of school districts. [Created through H.J.R. 13, 2009, and adopted by the people May 18, 2010]

Section 2. Sources of repayment. The principal, interest and premium, if any, of the bonds issued under section 1 of this Article must be repaid as determined by the Legislative Assembly from the following sources:

(1) Amounts appropriated for repayment by the Legislative Assembly from the General Fund, including taxes levied to pay the bonds except ad valorem property taxes;

(2) Amounts appropriated or allocated for repayment by the Legislative Assembly from other sources of revenue; or

(3) Any other available moneys. [Created through H.J.R. 13, 2009, and adopted by the people May 18, 2010]

Section 3. Refunding bonds. Bonds issued under section 1 of this Article may be refunded with bonds of like obligation. [Created through H.J.R. 13, 2009, and adopted by the people May 18, 2010]

Section 4. School capital matching fund. (1) There is created a school capital matching fund. Moneys in the fund may be invested and the earnings shall be retained in the fund or expended as provided by the Legislative Assembly.

(2) The Legislative Assembly may by law appropriate, allocate or transfer moneys or revenue to the school capital matching fund.

(3) The Legislative Assembly may appropriate, allocate or transfer moneys in the school capital matching fund and earnings on moneys in the fund for the purposes of providing:

(a) State matching funds to school districts to finance capital costs; and

(b) Payment of debt service for general obligation bonds issued pursuant to this Article. [Created through H.J.R. 13, 2009, and adopted by the people May 18, 2010]

Section 5. "Capital costs" defined. As used in this Article, "capital costs" means costs of land and of other assets having a useful life of more than one year, including costs associated with acquisition, construction, improvement, remodeling, furnishing, equipping, maintenance or repair. [Created through H.J.R. 13, 2009, and adopted by the people May 18, 2010]

Section 6. Legislation to effectuate Article. The Legislative Assembly may enact legislation to carry out the provisions of this Article. [Created through H.J.R. 13, 2009, and adopted by the people May 18, 2010]

Section 7. Relationship to conflicting provision of Constitution. This Article supersedes any conflicting provision of this Constitution. [Created through H.J.R. 13, 2009, and adopted by the people May 18, 2010]

ARTICLE XI-Q
REAL OR PERSONAL PROPERTY OWNED OR OPERATED BY STATE

Note: RF8. Article XI-Q was designated as "Article XI-P" by S.J.R. 48, 2010, and adopted by the people Nov. 2, 2010.

Section 1. State empowered to lend credit for real or personal property to be owned or operated by state; refinancing authority. (1) In the manner provided by law and notwithstanding the limitations contained in section 7, Article XI of this Constitution, the credit of the State of Oregon may be loaned and indebtedness incurred to finance the costs of:

(a) Acquiring, constructing, remodeling, repairing, equipping or furnishing real or personal property that is or will be owned or operated by the State of Oregon, including, without limitation, facilities and systems;

(b) Infrastructure related to the real or personal property; or

(c) Indebtedness incurred under this subsection.

(2) In the manner provided by law and notwithstanding the limitations contained in section 7, Article XI of this Constitution, the credit of the State of Oregon may be loaned and indebtedness incurred to refinance:

(a) Indebtedness incurred under subsection (1) of this section.

(b) Borrowings issued before the effective date of this Article to finance or refinance costs described in subsection (1) of this section. [Created through S.J.R. 48, 2010, and adopted by the people Nov. 2, 2010]

Note: RF8. The effective date of Senate Joint Resolution 48, 2010, is Dec. 2, 2010.

Section 2. Limit on indebtedness; general obligation of state. (1) Indebtedness may not be incurred under section 1 of this Article if the indebtedness would cause the total principal amount of indebtedness incurred under section 1 of this Article and outstanding to exceed one percent of the real market value of the property in this state.

(2) Indebtedness incurred under section 1 of this Article is a general obligation of the State of Oregon and must contain a direct promise on behalf of the State of Oregon to pay the principal, premium, if any, and interest on the obligation. The full faith and credit and taxing power of the State of Oregon must be pledged to payment of the indebtedness. However, the State of Oregon may not pledge or levy an ad valorem tax to pay the indebtedness. [Created through S.J.R. 48, 2010, and adopted by the people Nov. 2, 2010]

Section 3. Legislation to effectuate Article. The Legislative Assembly may enact legislation to carry out the provisions of this Article. [Created through S.J.R. 48, 2010, and adopted by the people Nov. 2, 2010]

Section 4. Relationship to conflicting provisions of Constitution. This Article supersedes conflicting provisions of this Constitution. [Created through S.J.R. 48, 2010, and adopted by the people Nov. 2, 2010]

ARTICLE XII
STATE PRINTING

Section 1. State printing; State Printer. Laws may be enacted providing for the state printing and binding, and for the election or appointment of a state printer, who shall have had not less than ten years' experience in the art of printing. The state printer shall receive such compensation as may from time to time be provided by law. Until such laws shall be enacted the state printer shall be elected, and the printing done as heretofore provided by this constitution and the general laws. [Constitution of 1859; Amendment proposed by S.J.R. 1, 1901, and adopted by the people June 6, 1904; Amendment proposed by initiative petition filed Feb. 3, 1906, and adopted by the people June 4, 1906]

ARTICLE XIII
SALARIES

Section 1. Salaries or other compensation of state officers.:RF8. [Constitution of 1859; Repeal proposed by S.J.R. 12, 1955, and adopted by the people Nov. 6, 1956]

ARTICLE XIV
SEAT OF GOVERNMENT

Section 1. Seat of government.:RF8. [Constitution of 1859; Repeal proposed by S.J.R. 41, 1957, and adopted by the people Nov. 4, 1958 (present section 1 and former 1958 section 3 of this Article adopted in lieu of this section and former original section 3 of this Article)]

Section 1. Seat of government. The permanent seat of government for the state shall be Marion County.

[Created through S.J.R. 41, 1957, and adopted by the people Nov. 4, 1958 (this section and former 1958 section 3 of this Article adopted in lieu of former original sections 1 and 3 of this Article)]

Section 2. Erection of state house prior to 1865. No tax shall be levied, or money of the State expended, or debt contracted for the erection of a State House prior to the year eighteen hundred and sixty five. —

Section 3. Limitation on removal of seat of government; location of state institutions.:RF8. [Constitution of 1859; Amendment proposed by S.J.R. 1, 1907, and adopted by the people June 1, 1908; Repeal proposed by S.J.R. 41, 1957, and adopted by the people Nov. 4, 1958 (present section 1 and former 1958 section 3 of this Article adopted in lieu of this section and former section 1 of this Article)]

Section 3. Location and use of state institutions.:RF8. [Created through S.J.R. 41, 1957, and adopted by the people Nov. 4, 1958 (this section, designated as "Section 2" by S.J.R. 41, 1957, and present section 1 of this Article adopted in lieu of former original sections 1 and 3 of this Article); Repeal proposed by S.J.R. 9, 1971, and adopted by the people Nov. 7, 1972]

ARTICLE XV
MISCELLANEOUS

Section 1. Officers to hold office until successors elected; exceptions; effect on defeated incumbent. (1) All officers, except members of the Legislative Assembly and incumbents who seek reelection and are defeated, shall hold their offices until their successors are elected, and qualified.

(2) If an incumbent seeks reelection and is defeated, he shall hold office only until the end of his term; and if an election contest is pending in the courts regarding that office when the term of such an incumbent ends and a successor to the office has not been elected or if elected, has not qualified because of such election contest, the person appointed to fill the vacancy thus created shall serve only until the contest and any appeal is finally determined notwithstanding any other provision of this constitution. [Constitution of 1859; Amendment proposed by H.J.R. 51, 1969, and adopted by the people Nov. 3, 1970]

Section 2. Tenure of office; how fixed; maximum tenure. When the duration of any office is not provided for by this Constitution, it may be declared by law; and if not so declared, such office shall be held during the pleasure of the authority making the appointment. But the Legislative Assembly shall not create any office, the tenure of which shall be longer than four years.

Section 3. Oaths of office. Every person elected or appointed to any office under this Constitution, shall, before entering on the duties thereof, take an oath or affirmation to support the Constitution of the United States, and of this State, and also an oath of office. —

Note: RF8. The amendments to sections 4, 4a, 4b and 4c and the repeal of section 4d by Measure No. 76, 2010, as submitted to the people was preceded by a preamble that reads as follows:

PREAMBLE: The people of the State of Oregon find that renewing the current dedication in the Oregon Constitution of fifteen percent of lottery revenues to parks, water quality and fish and wildlife habitats will provide lasting social, economic, environmental and public health benefits.

The people of the State of Oregon also find that renewal of the Parks and Natural Resources Fund will support voluntary efforts to:

(1) Protect and restore water quality, watersheds and habitats for native fish and wildlife that provide a healthy environment for current and future generations of Oregonians;

(2) Maintain and expand public parks, natural areas and recreation areas to meet the diverse needs of a growing population and to provide opportunities for [sic] to experience nature and enjoy outdoor recreation activities close to home and in the many special places throughout Oregon;

(3) Provide jobs and economic opportunities improving the health of our forests, prairies, lakes, streams, wetlands, rivers, and parks, including efforts to halt the spread of invasive species;

(4) Strengthen the audit and reporting requirements, identify desired outcomes and specify allowable uses of the fund in order to provide more strategic, accountable and efficient uses of the Parks and Natural Resources Fund; and

(5) Enhance the ability of public land managers, private organizations, individuals and businesses to work together in local, regional and statewide partnerships to expand recreation opportunities, improve water quality and conserve fish and wildlife habitat. —

Section 4. Regulation of lotteries; state lottery; use of net proceeds from state lottery. (1) Except as provided in subsections (2), (3), (4), (8) and (9) of this section, lotteries and the sale of lottery tickets, for any purpose whatever, are prohibited, and the Legislative Assembly shall prevent the same by penal laws.

(2) The Legislative Assembly may provide for the establishment, operation, and regulation of raffles and the lottery commonly known as bingo or lotto by charitable, fraternal, or religious organizations. As used in this section, charitable, fraternal or religious organization means such organizations or foundations as defined by law because of their charitable, fraternal, or religious purposes. The regulations shall define eligible organizations or foundations, and may prescribe the frequency of raffles, bingo or lotto, set a maximum monetary limit for prizes and require a statement of the odds on winning a prize. The Legislative Assembly shall vest the regulatory authority in any appropriate state agency.

(3) There is hereby created the State Lottery Commission which shall establish and operate a State Lottery. All proceeds from the State Lottery, including interest, but excluding costs of administration and pay-

ment of prizes, shall be used for any of the following purposes: creating jobs, furthering economic development, financing public education in Oregon or restoring and protecting Oregon's parks, beaches, watersheds and native fish and wildlife.

(4)(a) The State Lottery Commission shall be comprised of five members appointed by the Governor and confirmed by the Senate who shall serve at the pleasure of the Governor. At least one of the Commissioners shall have a minimum of five years experience in law enforcement and at least one of the Commissioners shall be a certified public accountant. The Commission is empowered to promulgate rules related to the procedures of the Commission and the operation of the State Lottery. Such rules and any statutes enacted to further implement this article shall insure the integrity, security, honesty, and fairness of the Lottery. The Commission shall have such additional powers and duties as may be provided by law.

(b) The Governor shall appoint a Director subject to confirmation by the Senate who shall serve at the pleasure of the Governor. The Director shall be qualified by training and experience to direct the operations of a state-operated lottery. The Director shall be responsible for managing the affairs of the Commission. The Director may appoint and prescribe the duties of no more than four Assistant Directors as the Director deems necessary. One of the Assistant Directors shall be responsible for a security division to assure security, integrity, honesty, and fairness in the operations and administration of the State Lottery. To fulfill these responsibilities, the Assistant Director for security shall be qualified by training and experience, including at least five years of law enforcement experience, and knowledge and experience in computer security.

(c) The Director shall implement and operate a State Lottery pursuant to the rules, and under the guidance, of the Commission. The State Lottery may operate any game procedure authorized by the commission, except parimutuel racing, social games, and the games commonly known in Oregon as bingo or lotto, whereby prizes are distributed using any existing or future methods among adult persons who have paid for tickets or shares in that game; provided that, in lottery games utilizing computer terminals or other devices, no coins or currency shall ever be dispensed directly to players from such computer terminals or devices.

(d) There is hereby created within the General Fund the Oregon State Lottery Fund which is continuously appropriated for the purpose of administering and operating the Commission and the State Lottery. The State Lottery shall operate as a self-supporting revenue-raising agency of state government and no appropriations, loans, or other transfers of state funds shall be made to it. The State Lottery shall pay all prizes and all of its expenses out of the revenues it receives from the sale of tickets or shares to the public and turnover the net proceeds therefrom to a fund to be established by the Legislative Assembly from which the Legislative Assembly shall make appropriations for the benefit of any of the following public purposes: creating jobs, furthering economic development, financing public education in Oregon or restoring and protecting Oregon's parks, beaches, watersheds and native fish and wildlife. Effective July 1, 1997, 15% of the net proceeds from the State Lottery shall be deposited, from the fund created by the Legislative Assembly under this paragraph, in an education stability fund. Effective July 1, 2003, 18% of the net proceeds from the State Lottery shall be deposited, from the fund created by the Legislative Assembly under this paragraph, in an education stability fund. Earnings on moneys in the education stability fund shall be retained in the fund or expended for the public purpose of financing public education in Oregon as provided by law. Except as provided in subsection (6) of this section, moneys in the education stability fund shall be invested as provided by law and shall not be subject to the limitations of section 6, Article XI of this Constitution. The Legislative Assembly may appropriate other moneys or revenue to the education stability fund. The Legislative Assembly shall appropriate amounts sufficient to pay lottery bonds before appropriating the net proceeds from the State Lottery for any other purpose. At least 84% of the total annual revenues from the sale of all lottery tickets or shares shall be returned to the public in the form of prizes and net revenues benefiting the public purpose.

(5) Notwithstanding paragraph (d) of subsection (4) of this section, the amount in the education stability fund created under paragraph (d) of subsection (4) of this section may not exceed an amount that is equal to five percent of the amount that was accrued as revenues in the state's General Fund during the prior biennium. If the amount in the education stability fund exceeds five percent of the amount that was accrued as revenues in the state's General Fund during the prior biennium:

(a) Additional net proceeds from the State Lottery may not be deposited in the education stability fund until the amount in the education stability fund is reduced to less than five percent of the amount that was accrued as revenues in the state's General Fund during the prior biennium; and

(b) Fifteen percent of the net proceeds from the State Lottery shall be deposited into the school capital matching fund created under section 4, Article XI-P of this Constitution.

(6) The Legislative Assembly may by law appropriate, allocate or transfer any portion of the principal of the education stability fund created under paragraph (d) of subsection (4) of this section for expenditure on public education if:

(a) The proposed appropriation, allocation or transfer is approved by three-fifths of the members serving in each house of the Legislative Assembly and the Legislative Assembly finds one of the following:

(A) That the last quarterly economic and revenue forecast for a biennium indicates that moneys available to the state's General Fund for the next biennium will be at least three percent less than appropriations from the state's General Fund for the current biennium;

(B) That there has been a decline for two or more consecutive quarters in the last 12 months in seasonally adjusted nonfarm payroll employment; or

(C) That a quarterly economic and revenue forecast projects that revenues in the state's General Fund in the current biennium will be at least two percent below what the revenues were projected to be in the revenue forecast on which the legislatively adopted budget for the current biennium was based; or

(b) The proposed appropriation, allocation or transfer is approved by three-fifths of the members serving in each house of the Legislative Assembly and the Governor declares an emergency.

(7) The Legislative Assembly may by law prescribe the procedures to be used and identify the persons required to make the forecasts described in subsection (6) of this section.

(8) Effective July 1, 1999, 15% of the net proceeds from the State Lottery shall be deposited in a parks and natural resources fund created by the Legislative Assembly. Of the moneys in the parks and natural resources fund, 50% shall be deposited in a parks subaccount and distributed for the public purposes of financing the protection, repair, operation, and creation of state, regional and local public parks, ocean shore and public beach access areas, historic sites and recreation areas, and 50% shall be deposited in a natural resources subaccount and distributed for the public purposes of financing the restoration and protection of native fish and wildlife, watersheds and water quality in Oregon. The Legislative Assembly shall not limit expenditures from the parks and natural resources fund, or from the parks or natural resources subaccounts. The Legislative Assembly may appropriate other moneys or revenue to the parks and natural resources fund.

(9) Only one State Lottery operation shall be permitted in the State.

(10) The Legislative Assembly has no power to authorize, and shall prohibit, casinos from operation in the State of Oregon. [Constitution of 1859; Amendment proposed by H.J.R. 14, 1975, and adopted by the people Nov. 2, 1976; Amendment proposed by initiative petition filed April 3, 1984, and adopted by the people Nov. 6, 1984 (paragraph designations in subsection (4) were not included in the petition); Amendment proposed by H.J.R. 20, 1985, and adopted by the people Nov. 4, 1986; Amendment proposed by H.J.R. 15, 1995, and adopted by the people May 16, 1995; Amendment proposed by initiative petition filed March 11, 1998, and adopted by the people Nov. 3, 1998; Amendment proposed by H.J.R. 80, 2002 (3rd s.s.), and adopted by the people Sept. 17, 2002; Revision proposed by H.J.R. 13, 2009, and adopted by the people May 18, 2010; Amendment proposed by initiative petition filed Dec. 22, 2009, and adopted by the people Nov. 2, 2010]

Note: RF8. The amendments to section 4, as adopted by the people in Measure No. 66, 1998, incorrectly set forth the text of section 4 as it existed at the time the measure was submitted to the people. The text of the measure, as approved by the voters, was printed here.

Note: RF8. The amendments to section 4, as adopted by the people in Measure No. 76, 2010, at the Nov. 2010 general election did not set forth the text of section 4 as it was revised by the people in Measure No. 68, 2010 (H.J.R. 13, 2009), at the May 2010 primary election. The text of section 4, as revised by Measure No. 68, 2010, and amended by Measure No. 76, 2010, is printed here.

Section 4a. Use of net proceeds from state lottery for parks and recreation areas. (1) In each biennium the Legislative Assembly shall appropriate all of the moneys in the parks subaccount of the parks and natural resources fund established under section 4 of this Article for the uses allowed in subsection (2) of this section, and to achieve all of the following:

(a) Provide additional public parks, natural areas or outdoor recreational areas to meet the needs of current and future residents of the State of Oregon;

(b) Protect natural, cultural, historic and outdoor recreational resources of state or regional significance;

(c) Manage public parks, natural areas and outdoor recreation areas to ensure their long-term ecological health and provide for the enjoyment of current and future residents of the State of Oregon; and

(d) Provide diverse and equitable opportunities for residents of the State of Oregon to experience nature and participate in outdoor recreational activities in state, regional, local or neighborhood public parks and recreation areas.

(2) The moneys in the parks subaccount shall be used only to:

(a) Maintain, construct, improve, develop, manage and operate state parks, ocean shores, public beach access areas, historic sites, natural areas and outdoor and recreation areas;

(b) Acquire real property, or interests therein, that has significant natural, scenic, cultural, historic or recreational values, for the creation or operation of state parks, ocean shores, public beach access areas, outdoor recreation areas and historic sites; and

(c) Provide grants to regional or local government entities to acquire property for public parks, natural areas or outdoor recreation areas, or to develop or improve public parks, natural areas or outdoor recreation areas.

(3) In each biennium the Legislative Assembly shall appropriate no less than twelve percent of the moneys in the parks subaccount for local and regional grants as authorized under paragraph (c) of subsection (2) of this section. However, if in any biennium the amount of net proceeds deposited in the parks and natural resources fund created under section 4 of this Article increases by more than fifty percent above the amount deposited in the 2009–2011 biennium, the Legislative Assembly shall appropriate no less than twenty-five percent of the moneys in the parks subaccount for local and regional grants as authorized under paragraph (c) of subsection (2) of this section. The grants shall be administered by a single state agency. The costs of the state agency in administering the grants shall not be paid out of the portion of the moneys in the parks subaccount appropriated for local and regional grants. [Created through initiative petition filed March 11, 1998, and adopted by the people Nov. 3, 1998; Amendment proposed by initiative petition filed Dec. 22, 2009, and adopted by the people Nov. 2, 2010]

Section 4b. Use of net proceeds from state lottery for fish and wildlife, watershed and habitat protection. (1) In each biennium the Legislative Assembly shall appropriate all of the moneys in the natural resources subaccount of the parks and natural resources fund established under section 4 of this Article for the uses allowed in subsections (2) and (3) of this section, and to accomplish all of the following:

(a) Protect and improve water quality in Oregon's rivers, lakes, and streams by restoring natural watershed functions or stream flows;

(b) Secure long-term protection for lands and waters that provide significant habitats for native fish and wildlife;

(c) Restore and maintain habitats needed to sustain healthy and resilient populations of native fish and wildlife;

(d) Maintain the diversity of Oregon's plants, animals and ecosystems;

(e) Involve people in voluntary actions to protect, restore and maintain the ecological health of Oregon's lands and waters; and

(f) Remedy the conditions that limit the health of fish and wildlife, habitats and watershed functions in greatest need of conservation.

(2) In each biennium the Legislative Assembly shall appropriate no less than sixty-five percent of the moneys in the natural resources subaccount to one state agency, and that agency shall distribute those moneys as grants to entities other than state or federal agencies for projects that achieve the outcomes specified in subsection (1) of this section. However, if in any biennium the amount of net proceeds deposited in the parks and natural resources fund created under section 4 of this Article increases by more than fifty percent above the amount deposited in the 2009–2011 biennium, the Legislative Assembly shall appropriate no less than seventy percent of the moneys in the natural resources subaccount to one state agency, and that agency shall distribute those moneys as grants to entities other than state or federal agencies for projects that achieve the outcomes specified in subsection (1) of this section. In addition, these moneys shall be used only to:

(a) Acquire from willing owners interests in land or water that will protect or restore native fish or wildlife habitats, which interests may include but are not limited to fee interests, conservation easements or leases;

(b) Carry out projects to protect or restore native fish or wildlife habitats;

(c) Carry out projects to protect or restore natural watershed functions to improve water quality or stream flows; and

(d) Carry out resource assessment, planning, design and engineering, technical assistance, monitoring and outreach activities necessary for projects funded under paragraphs (a) through (c) of this subsection.

(3) In each biennium the Legislative Assembly shall appropriate that portion of the natural resources subaccount not appropriated under subsection (2) of this section to support all of the following activities:

(a) Develop, implement or update state conservation strategies or plans to protect or restore native fish or wildlife habitats or to protect or restore natural watershed functions to improve water quality or stream flows;

(b) Develop, implement or update regional or local strategies or plans that are consistent with the state strategies or plans described in paragraph (a) of this subsection;

(c) Develop, implement or update state strategies or plans to prevent, detect, control or eradicate invasive species that threaten native fish or wildlife habitats or that impair water quality;

(d) Support local delivery of programs or projects, including watershed education activities, that protect or restore native fish or wildlife habitats or watersheds;

(e) Pay the state agency costs of administering subsection (2) of this section, which costs shall not be paid out of the moneys available for grants under subsection (2) of this section; and

(f) Enforce fish and wildlife and habitat protection laws and regulations. [Created through initiative petition filed March 11, 1998, and adopted by the people Nov. 3, 1998; Amendment proposed by initiative petition filed Dec. 22, 2009, and adopted by the people Nov. 2, 2010]

Section 4c. Audit of agency receiving certain net proceeds from state lottery. The Secretary of State shall regularly audit any state agency that receives moneys from the parks and natural resources fund established under section 4 of this Article to address the financial integrity, compliance with applicable laws, efficiency and effectiveness of the use of the moneys. The costs of the audit shall be paid from the parks and natural resources fund. However, such costs may not be paid from the portions of such fund, or the subaccounts of the fund, that are dedicated to grants. The audit shall be submitted to the Legislative Assembly as part of a biennial report to the Legislative Assembly. In addition, each agency that receives moneys from the parks and natural resources fund shall submit a biennial performance report [sic] the Legislature [sic] Assembly that describes the measurable biennial and cumulative results of activities and programs financed by the fund. [Created through initiative petition filed March 11, 1998, and adopted by the people Nov. 3, 1998; Amendment proposed by initiative petition filed Dec. 22, 2009, and adopted by the people Nov. 2, 2010]

Note: RF8. Added as section 4c to the Constitution but not to any Article therein by initiative petition (Measure No. 66, 1998) adopted by the people Nov. 3, 1998.

Section 4d. Subsequent vote for reaffirmation of sections 4a, 4b and 4c and amendment to section 4.:RF8. [Created through initiative petition filed March 11, 1998, and adopted by the people Nov. 3, 1998; Repeal proposed by initiative petition filed Dec. 22, 2009, and adopted by the people Nov. 2, 2010]

Section 4e. Transfer of moneys in school capital matching subaccount to school capital matching fund created under section 4, Article XI-P.:RF8. [Created through H.J.R. 13, 2009, and adopted by the people May 18, 2010; Repealed Jan. 2, 2011, as specified in text of section adopted by the people May 18, 2010]

Section 5. Property of married women not subject to debts of husband; registration of separate property. The property and pecuniary rights of every married woman, at the time of marriage or afterwards, acquired by gift, devise, or inheritance shall not be subject to the debts, or contracts of the husband; and laws shall be passed providing for the registration of the wife's seperate [sic] property. —

Section 5a. Policy regarding marriage. It is the policy of Oregon, and its political subdivisions, that only a marriage between one man and one woman shall be valid or legally recognized as a marriage. [Created through initiative petition filed March 2, 2004, and adopted by the people Nov. 2, 2004]

Note: RF8. Added as unnumbered section to the Constitution but not to any Article therein by initiative petition (Measure No. 36, 2004) adopted by the people Nov. 2, 2004.

Section 6. Minimum area and population of counties. No county shall be reduced to an area of less than four hundred square miles; nor shall any new county be established in this State containing a less area, nor unless such new county shall contain a population of at least twelve hundred inhabitants. —

Section 7. Officers not to receive fees from or represent claimants against state. No State officers, or members of the Legislative Assembly, shall directly or indirectly receive a fee, or be engaged as counsel, agent, or Attorney in the prosecution of any claim against this State. —

Section 8. Certain persons not to hold real estate or mining claims; working mining claims.:RF8. [Constitution of 1859; Repeal proposed by S.J.R. 14, 1945, and adopted by the people Nov. 5, 1946]

Section 8. Persons eligible to serve in legislature. Notwithstanding the provisions of section 1 article III and section 10 article II of the Constitution of the State of

Constitution

Oregon, a person employed by the State Board of Higher Education, a member of any school board or employee thereof, shall be eligible to a seat in the Legislative Assembly and such membership in the Legislative Assembly shall not prevent such person from being employed by the State Board of Higher Education or from being a member or employee of a school board. [Created through initiative petition filed June 13, 1958, and adopted by the people Nov. 4, 1958]

Section 9. When elective office becomes vacant. The Legislative Assembly may provide that any elective public office becomes vacant, under such conditions or circumstances as the Legislative Assembly may specify, whenever a person holding the office is elected to another public office more than 90 days prior to the expiration of the term of the office he is holding. For the purposes of this section, a person elected is considered to be elected as of the date the election is held. [Created through S.J.R. 41, 1959, and adopted by the people Nov. 8, 1960]

Section 10. The Oregon Property Protection Act of 2000. (1) This section may be known and shall be cited as the "Oregon Property Protection Act of 2000."

(2) Statement of principles. The People, in the exercise of the power reserved to them under the Constitution of the State of Oregon, declare that:

(a) A basic tenet of a democratic society is that a person is presumed innocent and should not be punished until proven guilty;

(b) The property of a person generally should not be forfeited in a forfeiture proceeding by government unless and until that person is convicted of a crime involving the property;

(c) The value of property forfeited should be proportional to the specific conduct for which the owner of the property has been convicted; and

(d) Proceeds from forfeited property should be used for treatment of drug abuse unless otherwise specified by law for another purpose.

(3) Forfeitures prohibited without conviction. Except as provided in this section, a judgment of forfeiture of property in a civil forfeiture proceeding by the State or any of its political subdivisions may not be entered until and unless the person claiming the property is convicted of a crime in Oregon or another jurisdiction and the property:

(a) Constitutes proceeds of the crime for which the claimant has been convicted;

(b) Was instrumental in committing or facilitating the crime for which the claimant has been convicted;

(c) Constitutes proceeds of one or more other crimes similar to the crime for which the claimant was convicted; or

(d) Was instrumental in committing or facilitating one or more other crimes similar to the crime for which the claimant was convicted.

(4) Forfeiture based on similar crimes. Property may be forfeited under paragraph (c) or (d) of subsection (3) of this section only if the claimant is notified in writing of the other crime or crimes claimed to be similar to the crime for which the claimant was convicted. The notice must be given at the time the claimant is given notice of the seizure of the property for forfeiture, and the claimant must have an opportunity to challenge the seizure and forfeiture of the property.

(5) Forfeiture without conviction of claimant. The property of a claimant who has not been convicted of a crime may be forfeited in a civil forfeiture proceeding only if the claimant consents to the forfeiture of the property or the forfeiting agency proves the property constitutes proceeds or an instrumentality of crime committed by another person as described in subsection (3) of this section and:

(a) The claimant took the property with the intent to defeat forfeiture of the property;

(b) The claimant knew or should have known that the property constituted proceeds or an instrumentality of criminal conduct; or

(c) The claimant acquiesced in the criminal conduct. A person shall be considered to have acquiesced in criminal conduct if the person knew of the criminal conduct and failed to take reasonable action under the circumstances to terminate the criminal conduct or prevent use of the property to commit or facilitate the criminal conduct.

(6) Standard of proof.

(a) Except as provided in paragraph (b) of this subsection, if the property to be forfeited in a civil forfeiture action is personal property, the forfeiting agency must prove the elements specified in subsection (3) or (5) of this section by a preponderance of the evidence. If the property to be forfeited in a civil forfeiture action is real property, the forfeiting agency must prove the elements specified in subsection (3) or (5) of this section by clear and convincing evidence.

(b) If a forfeiting agency establishes in a forfeiture proceeding that cash, weapons or negotiable instruments were found in close proximity to controlled substances or to instrumentalities of criminal conduct, the burden is on any person claiming the cash, weapons or negotiable instruments to prove by a preponderance of the evidence that the cash, weapons or negotiable instruments are not proceeds of criminal conduct or an instrumentality of criminal conduct.

(7) Value of property forfeited. The value of the property forfeited under the provisions of this section may not be excessive and shall be substantially proportional to the specific conduct for which the owner of the property has been convicted. For purposes of this section, "property" means any interest in anything of value, including the whole of any lot or tract of land and tangible and intangible personal property, including currency, instruments or securities or any other kind of privilege, interest, claim or right whether due or to become due. Nothing in this section shall prohibit a person from voluntarily giving a judgment of forfeiture.

(8) Financial institutions. In a civil forfeiture proceeding, if a financial institution claiming an interest in the property demonstrates that it holds an interest, the financial institution's interest is not subject to forfeiture.

(9) Exception for unclaimed property and contraband. Notwithstanding the provisions of subsection (3) of this section, if, following notice to all persons known to have an interest or who may have an interest, no person claims an interest in the seized property or if the property is contraband, a judgment of forfeiture may be allowed and entered without a criminal conviction. For purposes of this subsection, "contraband" means personal property, articles or things, including but not limited to controlled substances or drug paraphernalia, that a person is prohibited by Oregon statute or local ordinance from producing, obtaining or possessing.

(10) Exception for forfeiture of animals. This section does not apply to the forfeiture of animals that have been abused, neglected or abandoned.

(11) Law enforcement seizures unaffected. Nothing in this section shall be construed to affect the temporary seizure of property for evidentiary, forfeiture, or protective purposes, or to alter the power of the Governor to remit fines or forfeitures under Article V, Section 14, of this Constitution.

(12) Disposition of property to drug treatment. Any sale of forfeited property shall be conducted in a commercially reasonable manner. Property forfeited in a civil forfeiture proceeding shall be distributed or applied in the following order:

(a) To the satisfaction of any foreclosed liens, security interests and contracts in the order of their priority;

(b) To the State or any of its political subdivisions for actual and reasonable expenses related to the costs of the forfeiture proceeding, including attorney fees, storage, maintenance, management, and disposition of the property incurred in connection with the sale of any forfeited property; and

(c) To the State or any of its political subdivisions to be used exclusively for drug treatment, unless another disposition is specially provided by law.

(13) Restrictions on State transfers. Neither the State of Oregon, its political subdivisions, nor any forfeiting agency shall transfer forfeiture proceedings to the federal government unless a state court has affirmatively found that:

(a) The activity giving rise to the forfeiture is interstate in nature and sufficiently complex to justify the transfer;

(b) The seized property may only be forfeited under federal law; or

(c) Pursuing forfeiture under state law would unduly burden the state forfeiting agencies.

(14) Penalty for violations. Any person acting under color of law, official title or position who takes any action intending to conceal, transfer, withhold, retain, divert or otherwise prevent any moneys, conveyances, real property, or any things of value forfeited under the law of this State or the United States from being applied, deposited or used in accordance with the requirements of this section shall be subject to a civil penalty in an amount treble the value of the forfeited property concealed, transferred, withheld, retained or diverted. Nothing in this subsection shall be construed to impair judicial immunity if otherwise applicable.

(15) Reporting requirement. All forfeiting agencies shall report the nature and disposition of all property seized for forfeiture or forfeited to a State asset forfeiture oversight committee that is independent of any forfeiting agency. The asset forfeiture oversight committee shall generate and make available to the public an annual report of the information collected. The asset forfeiture oversight committee shall also make recommendations to ensure that asset forfeiture proceedings are handled in a manner that is fair to innocent property owners and interest holders.

(16) Severability. If any part of this section or its application to any person or circumstance is held to be invalid for any reason, then the remaining parts or applications to any persons or circumstances shall not be affected but shall remain in full force and effect. [Created through initiative petition filed Jan. 5, 2000, and adopted by the people Nov. 7, 2000; Amendment proposed by S.J.R. 18, 2007, and adopted by the people May 20, 2008]

Note: RF8. The leadlines to section 10 and subsections (2), (3), (9) and (11) to (16) of section 10 were a part of the measure submitted by initiative petition (Measure No. 3, 2000) adopted by the people Nov. 7, 2000. The leadlines to subsections (4) to (8) and (10) of section 10 were a part of S.J.R. 18, 2007, which was adopted by the people May 20, 2008.

Note: RF8. The text of section 11 (sections 1 to 3, Measure No. 99, 2000) as submitted to the people was preceded by a preamble that reads as follows:

WHEREAS, thousands of Oregon seniors and persons with disabilities live independently in their own homes, which they prefer and is less costly than institutional care (i.e. nursing homes), because over 10,000 home care workers, (also known as client employed providers), paid by the State of Oregon provide in-home support services;

WHEREAS, home care workers provide services that range from housekeeping, shopping, meal preparation, money management and personal care to medical care and treatment, but receive little, if any, training in those areas resulting in a detrimental impact on quality of care;

WHEREAS, the quality of care provided to seniors and people with disabilities is diminished when there is a lack of stability in the workforce which is the result of home care workers receiving low wages, minimal training and benefits;

WHEREAS, both home care workers and clients receiving home care services would benefit from creating an entity which has the authority to provide, and is held accountable for the quality of services provided in Oregon's in-home system of long-term care.

Section 11. Home Care Commission. (1) Ensuring High Quality Home Care Services: Creation and Duties of the Quality Home Care Commission. (a) The Home Care Commission is created as an independent public commission consisting of nine members appointed by the Governor.

(b) The duties and functions of the Home Care Commission include, but are not limited to:

(A) Ensuring that high quality, comprehensive home care services are provided to the elderly and people with disabilities who receive personal care services in their homes by home care workers hired directly by the client and financed by payments from the State or by payments from a county or other public agency which receives money for that purpose from the State;

(B) Providing routine, emergency and respite referrals of qualified home care providers to the elderly and people with disabilities who receive personal care services by home care workers hired directly by the client and financed in whole or in part by the State, or by payment from a county or other public agency which receives money for that purpose from the State;

(C) Provide training opportunities for home care workers, seniors and people with disabilities as consumers of personal care services;

(D) Establish qualifications for home care workers;

(E) Establish and maintain a registry of qualified home care workers;

(F) Cooperate with area agencies on aging and disability services and other local agencies to provide the services described and set forth in this section.

(2) Home Care Commission Operation/Selection.

Constitution

(a) The Home Care Commission shall be comprised of nine members. Five members of the Commission shall be current or former consumers of home care services for the elderly or people with disabilities. One member shall be a representative of the Oregon Disabilities Commission, (or a successor entity, for as long as a comparable entity exists). One member shall be a representative of the Governor's Commission on Senior Services, (or a successor entity, for as long as a comparable entity exists). One member shall be a representative of the Oregon Association of Area Agencies on Aging and Disabilities, (or a successor entity, for as long as a comparable entity exists). One member shall be a representative of the Senior and Disabled Services Division, (or a successor entity, for as long as a comparable entity exists).

(b) The term of office of each member is three years, subject to confirmation by the Senate. If there is a vacancy for any cause, the Governor shall make an appointment to become immediately effective for the unexpired term. A member is eligible for reappointment and may serve no more than three consecutive terms. In making appointments to the Commission, the Governor may take into consideration any nominations or recommendations made by the representative groups or agencies.

(3) Other Provisions — Legal Duties and Responsibilities of the Commission.

(a) The Home Care Commission shall, in its own name, for the purpose of carrying into effect and promoting its functions, have authority to contract, lease, acquire, hold, own, encumber, insure, sell, replace, deal in and with and dispose of real and personal property.

(b) When conducting any activities in this Section or in subsection (1) of this section, and in making decisions relating to those activities, the Home Care Commission shall first consider the effect of its activities and its decisions on improving the quality of service delivery and ensuring adequate hours of service are provided to clients who are served by home care workers.

(c) Clients of home care services retain their right to select the providers of their choice, including family members.

(d) Employees of the Commission are not employees of the State of Oregon for any purpose.

(e) Notwithstanding the provisions in paragraph (d) of this subsection, the State of Oregon shall be held responsible for unemployment insurance payments for home care workers.

(f) For purposes of collective bargaining, the Commission shall be the employer of record of home care workers hired directly by the client and paid by the State, or by a county or other public agency which receives money for that purpose from the State. Home care workers have the right to form, join and participate in the activities of labor organizations of their own choosing for the purpose of representation and collective bargaining with the Commission on matters concerning employment relations. These rights shall be exercised in accordance with the rights granted to public employees with mediation and interest arbitration as the method of concluding the collective bargaining process. Home care workers shall not have the right to strike.

(g) The Commission may adopt rules to carry out its functions. [Created through initiative petition filed Nov. 10, 1999, and adopted by the people Nov. 7, 2000]

Note: RF8. The leadlines to subsections (1), (2) and (3) of section 11, except the periods in subsections (2) and (3), were a part of the measure submitted to the people by initiative petition (Measure No. 99, 2000) and adopted by the people Nov. 7, 2000.

Note: RF8. Section 11 was submitted to the voters as sections 1, 2 and 3 and added to the Constitution but not to any Article therein by Measure No. 99, 2000.

Note: RF8. In Measure No. 99, 2000, subsection (1)(a) and (b)(A) to (F) were designated as section 1 (A) and (B)(1) to (6); subsection (2)(a) and (b) as section 2 (A) and (B); and subsection (3)(a) to (g) as section 3 (A) to (G). The reference to subsection (1) of this section was a reference to Section 1 above, and the reference to paragraph (d) of this subsection was a reference to subsection (D) of this section.

Note: RF8. In Measure No. 99, 2000, the period in subsection (1)(b)(F) appeared as a semicolon, and there was no period in subsection (3)(e).

ARTICLE XVI
BOUNDARIES

Section 1. State boundaries. The State of Oregon shall be bounded as provided by section 1 of the Act of Congress of February 1859, admitting the State of Oregon into the Union of the United States, until:

(1) Such boundaries are modified by appropriate interstate compact or compacts heretofore or hereafter approved by the Congress of the United States; or

(2) The Legislative Assembly by law extends the boundaries or jurisdiction of this state an additional distance seaward under authority of a law heretofore or hereafter enacted by the Congress of the United States. [Constitution of 1859; Amendment proposed by S.J.R. 4, 1957, and adopted by the people Nov. 4, 1958; Amendment proposed by H.J.R. 24, 1967, and adopted by the people Nov. 5, 1968]

ARTICLE XVII
AMENDMENTS AND REVISIONS

Section 1. Method of amending Constitution. Any amendment or amendments to this Constitution may be proposed in either branch of the legislative assembly, and if the same shall be agreed to by a majority of all the members elected to each of the two houses, such proposed amendment or amendments shall, with the yeas and nays thereon, be entered in their journals and referred by the secretary of state to the people for their approval or rejection, at the next regular general election, except when the legislative assembly shall order a special election for that purpose. If a majority of the electors voting on any such amendment shall vote in favor thereof, it shall thereby become a part of this Constitution. The votes for and against such amendment, or amendments, severally, whether proposed by the legislative assembly or by initiative petition, shall be canvassed by the secretary of state in the presence of the governor, and if it shall appear to the governor that the majority of the votes cast at said election on said amendment, or amendments, severally, are cast in favor thereof, it shall be his duty forthwith after such canvass, by his proclamation, to declare the said amendment, or amendments, severally, having received said majority of votes to have been adopted by the people of Oregon as part of the Constitution thereof, and the same shall be in effect as a part of the Constitution from the date of such proclamation. When two or more amendments shall be submitted in the manner aforesaid to the voters of this state at the same election, they shall be so submitted that each amendment shall be voted on separately. No convention shall be called to amend or propose amendments to this Constitution, or to propose a new Constitution, unless the law providing for such convention shall first be approved by the people on a referendum vote at a regular general election. This article shall not be construed to impair the right of the people to amend this Constitution by vote upon an initiative petition therefor. [Created through initiative petition filed Feb. 3, 1906, and adopted by the people June 4, 1906]

Note: RF8. The above section replaces sections 1 and 2 of Article XVII of the original Constitution.

Section 2. Method of revising Constitution. (1) In addition to the power to amend this Constitution granted by section 1, Article IV, and section 1 of this Article, a revision of all or part of this Constitution may be proposed in either house of the Legislative Assembly and, if the proposed revision is agreed to by at least two-thirds of all the members of each house, the proposed revision shall, with the yeas and nays thereon, be entered in their journals and referred by the Secretary of State to the people for their approval or rejection, notwithstanding section 1, Article IV of this Constitution, at the next regular state-wide primary election, except when the Legislative Assembly orders a special election for that purpose. A proposed revision may deal with more than one subject and shall be voted upon as one question. The votes for and against the proposed revision shall be canvassed by the Secretary of State in the presence of the Governor and, if it appears to the Governor that the majority of the votes cast in the election on the proposed revision are in favor of the proposed revision, he shall, promptly following the canvass, declare, by his proclamation, that the proposed revision has received a majority of votes and has been adopted by the people as the Constitution of the State of Oregon or as a part of the Constitution of the State of Oregon, as the case may be. The revision shall be in effect as the Constitution or as a part of this Constitution from the date of such proclamation.

(2) Subject to subsection (3) of this section, an amendment proposed to the Constitution under section 1, Article IV, or under section 1 of this Article may be submitted to the people in the form of alternative provisions so that one provision will become a part of the Constitution if a proposed revision is adopted by the people and the other provision will become a part of the Constitution if a proposed revision is rejected by the people. A proposed amendment submitted in the form of alternative provisions as authorized by this subsection shall be voted upon as one question.

(3) Subsection (2) of this section applies only when:

(a) The Legislative Assembly proposes and refers to the people a revision under subsection (1) of this section; and

(b) An amendment is proposed under section 1, Article IV, or under section 1 of this Article; and

(c) The proposed amendment will be submitted to the people at an election held during the period between the adjournment of the legislative session at which the proposed revision is referred to the people and the next regular legislative session. [Created through H.J.R. 5, 1959, and adopted by the people Nov. 8, 1960]

ARTICLE XVIII
SCHEDULE

Section 1. Election to accept or reject Constitution. For the purpose of taking the vote of the electors of the State, for the acceptance or rejection of this Constitution, an election shall be held on the second Monday of November, in the year 1857, to be conducted according to existing laws regulating the election of Delegates in Congress, so far as applicable, except as herein otherwise provided.

Section 2. Questions submitted to voters. Each elector who offers to vote upon this Constitution, shall be asked by the judges of election this question:

Do you vote for the Constitution? Yes, or No.

And also this question:

Do you vote for Slavery in Oregon? Yes, or No.

And in the poll books shall be columns headed respectively.

"Constitution, Yes." "Constitution, No."

"Slavery, Yes." "Slavery, No."

And the names of the electors shall be entered in the poll books, together with their answers to the said questions, under their appropriate heads. The abstracts of the votes transmitted to the Secretary of the Territory, shall be publicly opened, and canvassed by the Governor and Secretary, or by either of them in the absence of the other; and the Governor, or in his absence the Secretary, shall forthwith issue his proclamation, and publish the same in the several newspapers printed in this State, declaring the result of the said election upon each of said questions. [Constitution of 1859; Amendment proposed by S.J.R. 7, 2001, and adopted by the people Nov. 5, 2002]

Section 3. Majority of votes required to accept or reject Constitution. If a majority of all the votes given for, and against the Constitution, shall be given for the Constitution, then this Constitution shall be deemed to be approved, and accepted by the electors of the State, and shall take effect accordingly; and if a majority of such votes shall be given against the Constitution, then this Constitution shall be deemed to be rejected by the electors of the State, and shall be void. —

Section 4. Vote on certain sections of Constitution. If this Constitution shall be accepted by the electors, and a majority of all the votes given for, and against slavery, shall be given for slavery, then the following section shall be added to the Bill of Rights, and shall be part of this Constitution:

"Sec. ___ "Persons lawfully held as slaves in any State, Territory, or District of the United States, under the laws thereof, may be brought into this State, and such Slaves, and their descendants may be held as slaves within this State, and shall not be emancipated without the consent of their owners."

And if a majority of such votes shall be given against slavery, then the foregoing section shall not, but the following sections shall be added to the Bill of Rights, and shall be a part of this Constitution.

"Sec. ___ There shall be neither slavery, nor involuntary servitude in the State, otherwise than as a punishment for crime, whereof the party shall have been duly convicted." [Constitution of 1859; Amendment proposed by S.J.R. 7, 2001, and adopted by the people Nov. 5, 2002]

Note: RF8. See sections 34 and 35 of Article I, Oregon Constitution.

Section 5. Apportionment of Senators and Representatives. Until an enumeration of the inhabitants of the State shall be made, and the senators and representatives apportioned as directed in the Constitution, the County of Marion shall have two senators, and four representatives.

Linn two senators, and four representatives.

Lane two senators, and three representatives.

Clackamas and Wasco, one senator jointly, and Clackamas three representatives, and Wasco one representative.

Yamhill one senator, and two representatives.

Polk one senator, and two representatives.

Benton one senator, and two representatives.

Multnomah, one senator, and two representatives.

Washington, Columbia, Clatsop, and Tillamook one senator jointly, and Washington one representative, and Washington and Columbia one representative jointly, and Clatsop and Tillamook one representative jointly.

Douglas, one senator, and two representatives.

Jackson one senator, and three representatives.

Josephine one senator, and one representative.

Umpqua, Coos and Curry, one senator jointly, and Umpqua one representative, and Coos and Curry one representative jointly. [Constitution of 1859; Amendment proposed by S.J.R. 7, 2001, and adopted by the people Nov. 5, 2002]

Section 6. Election under Constitution; organization of state. If this Constitution shall be ratified, an election shall be held on the first Monday of June 1858, for the election of members of the Legislative Assembly, a Representative in Congress, and State and County officers, and the Legislative Assembly shall convene at the Capital on the first Monday of July 1858, and proceed to elect two senators in Congress, and make such further provision as may be necessary to the complete organization of a State government. —

Section 7. Former laws continued in force. All laws in force in the Territory of Oregon when this Constitution takes effect, and consistent therewith, shall continue in force until altered, or repealed. —

Section 8. Officers to continue in office. All officers of the Territory of Oregon, or under its laws, when this Constitution takes effect, shall continue in office, until superseded by the State authorities. —

Section 9. Crimes against territory. Crimes and misdemeanors committed against the Territory of Oregon shall be punished by the State, as they might have been punished by the Territory, if the change of government had not been made. —

Section 10. Saving existing rights and liabilities. All property and rights of the Territory, and of the several counties, subdivisions, and political bodies corporate, of, or in the Territory, including fines, penalties, forfeitures, debts and claims, of whatsoever nature, and recognizances, obligations, and undertakings to, or for the use of the Territory, or any county, political corporation, office, or otherwise, to or for the public, shall inure to the State, or remain to the county, local division, corporation, officer, or public, as if the change of government had not been made. And private rights shall not be affected by such change. —

Section 11. Judicial districts. Until otherwise provided by law, the judicial districts of the State, shall be constituted as follows: The counties of Jackson, Josephine, and Douglas, shall constitute the first district. The counties of Umpqua, Coos, Curry, Lane, and Benton, shall constitute the second district. — The counties of Linn, Marion, Polk, Yamhill and Washington, shall constitute the third district. — The counties of Clackamas, Multnomah, Wasco, Columbia, Clatsop, and Tillamook, shall constitute the fourth district — and the County of Tillamook shall be attached to the county of Clatsop for judicial purposes. —

Index

World War I era soldiers guard the exterior of the 1935 Armory Building in Klamath Falls. The building is now the home of the Klamath County Museum—Oregon State Archives Scenic Photograph klaDA0110

Index

Alphabetization is word-by-word (e.g., "Labor unions" precedes "Laboratories").

A

B

Index

C

Index

D

E

Index

F

Index

G

H

I

J

K

L

Index

M

N

Index

O

P

R

S

Index

U

V

W

X

Y

Z